Biographical Sketches of Loyalists of the American Revolution; With an Historical Essay

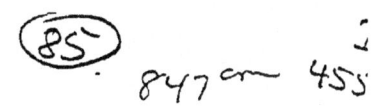

BIOGRAPHICAL SKETCHES

OF

LOYALISTS

OF THE

AMERICAN REVOLUTION,

WITH

AN HISTORICAL ESSAY.

BY

LORENZO SABINE.

IN TWO VOLUMES.
VOLUME I.

BOSTON:
LITTLE, BROWN AND COMPANY.
1864.

Entered according to Act of Congress, in the year 1864, by
LORENZO SABINE,
in the Clerk's Office of the District Court of the District of Massachusetts.

RIVERSIDE, CAMBRIDGE:
PRINTED BY H. O. HOUGHTON AND COMPANY.

PREFACE.

Of the reasons which influenced, of the hopes and fears which agitated, and of the miseries and rewards which awaited the Loyalists — or, as they were called in the politics of the time, the "Tories" — of the American Revolution, but little is known. The most intelligent, the best informed among us, confess the deficiency of their knowledge. The reason is obvious. Men who, like the Loyalists, separate themselves from their friends and kindred, who are driven from their homes, who surrender the hopes and expectations of life, and who become outlaws, wanderers, and exiles, — such men leave few memorials behind them. Their papers are scattered and lost, and their very names pass from human recollection.

Hence the most thorough and painstaking inquirers into their history have hardly been rewarded for the time and attention which they have bestowed. My own pretensions are extremely limited. Yet, as my home, for twenty-eight years, was on the eastern frontier of the Union, where the graves and the children of the Loyalists were around me in every direction; as I enjoyed free and continual intercourse with persons of Loyalist descent; as I have had the use of family papers, and of rare documents; as I have made journeys to confer with the living, and pilgrimages to graveyards; in order to complete the records of the dead;—I may venture to say, that the BIOGRAPHICAL NOTICES which are contained in these volumes, will add *something* to the stock of knowledge obtained by previous gleaners in this interesting branch of our Revolutionary Annals.

Still, I have to remark, that I have repeatedly been ready to abandon the pursuit in despair. For, to weave into correct and continuous narratives the occasional allusions of books and State Papers; to join together fragmentary events and incidents; to distinguish persons of the same surname or family name, when only that name is mentioned; and to reconcile the disagreements of various epistolary and verbal communications; has seemed, at times, utterly impossible. There are *some* who can fully appreciate these, and other difficulties, which beset the task, and who will readily understand why many of the NOTICES are meagre; and why, too, it is possible for others to be, in one or more particulars, inaccurate. Indeed, I may appeal to the closest students of our history, as my best witnesses, to prove that *entire* correctness and fulness of detail, in tracing the course, and in ascertaining the fate, of the adherents of the Crown, are not *now* within the power of the most careful and industrious.

Of several of the Loyalists who were high in office, of others who were men of talents and acquirements, and of still others who were of less consideration, I have been able, after long and extensive researches, to learn scarcely more than their names, or the single fact, that, for their political opinions or offences, they were proscribed and banished. But I have deemed it best to exclude no one, whether of exalted or humble station, of whose attachment to the cause of the mother country I have found satisfactory, or even reasonable, evidence. In following out this plan, repetition of the same facts, as applicable to different persons, has been unavoidable. That I have sometimes erred, by including among the "Tories" a few who finally became Whigs, is very probable. To change from one side to the other, both during the controversy which preceded the shedding of blood, and at various periods of the war, was not uncommon; and I have been struck, in the course of my investigations, with the absence of fixed principles, not only among people in the common walks of life, but in many of the prominent personages of the day.

The number of books from which information is to be obtained is limited. A few, however, have afforded me essential aid: among these, I gladly notice Force's American Archives; Onderdonk's Revolutionary Incidents of the counties of Queen's, Suffolk, and King's, New York; Brewster's Rambles about Portsmouth; Hall's History of Eastern Vermont; Holland's History of Western Massachusetts; McRee's Life and Correspondence of Iredell; O'Callaghan's Documentary History of New York; Pennsylvania Archives; Gentleman's Magazine; Sprague's Annals of the American Pulpit; Updike's Rhode Island Bar, and Narragansett Church; Wheeler's Historical Sketches of North Carolina; White's Historical Collections of

Georgia; Van Schaack's Life of Peter Van Schaack; Almon's Remembrancer; Shippen Papers; Journals of the Provincial Congress of the Thirteen States; Meade's Old Churches, Ministers, and Families of Virginia; Army and Navy Lists; Miss Caulkins's History of Norwich; Lee's War in the South; Burke's British Peerage; Sparks's Washington; McCall's History of Georgia; Curwen's Journal; Simcoe's Journal; Stone's Life of Brant; Simms's Life of Greene and of Marion; State Papers of the United States; American Quarterly Register; and Pamphlets and Tracts of the Revolutionary era, both British and American.

So, too, I gladly acknowledge my obligations to Winthrop Sargent, Henry Onderdonk, Jr., George Chandler, E. W. B. Moody, Porter C. Bliss, Edward D. Ingraham, Henry Pennington, William S. Leland, Robert H. Gardiner, J. B. Bright, John Watts De Peyster, and Edward D. Harris, for contributions of materials, or for personal researches in my behalf, or for the use of rare papers.

In conclusion, a word of grateful mention of Messrs. Little, Brown & Co., the publishers. Seventeen years ago, when the "Tories" had seemingly passed into utter and deserved oblivion, these gentlemen published the "American Loyalists," without the hope of gain, and with the probability, indeed, of actual loss; and they voluntarily take the risk of the present Work under circumstances adverse to adequate pecuniary profit. For them and for myself I may venture to add, that the principal reward is found in the belief that we have done *something* for the cause of human brotherhood, by lessening the rancor — even the hate — which long existed between the children of the winners, and the children of the expatriated losers, in the civil war which dismembered the British Empire.

ROXBURY, MASSACHUSETTS,
April, 1864.

CONTENTS

OF THE

HISTORICAL ESSAY.

CHAPTER I.

Taxation did but accelerate the Dismemberment of the British Empire. Several Causes of Disaffection on the part of the Colonists briefly stated. Acts of Parliament which inhibited Labor in the Colonies. Opposition to the Navigation Act and the Laws of Trade in the Time of the Stuarts. Renewed after the lapse of nearly a Century. Mobs and Collisions, Seizures and Rescues, in consequence. The Question of "Three Pence" the Pound on Tea discussed. The Barbarous Commercial Code of England. The Contraband Trade in Tea, Wine, Fruit, Sugar, and Molasses. The Measures of the Ministry to suppress it. One fourth part of the Signers of the Declaration of Independence Merchants or Shipmasters. Hancock prosecuted in the Admiralty Courts to recover nearly Half a Million of Dollars. The Loyalists great Smugglers after removing from the United States 1–14

CHAPTER II.

State of Political Parties in the New England Colonies . . 15–27

CHAPTER III.

State of Political Parties in the Middle Colonies 28–33

CHAPTER IV.

State of Political Parties in the Southern Colonies . . 34–48

CONTENTS.

CHAPTER V.

Newspapers in the Thirteen Colonies. Political Writers, Whig and Loyalist, North and South. Seminaries of Learning. Condition of the Press, &c., at the Revolutionary Era. Means for diffusing Knowledge limited 49–54

CHAPTER VI.

Political Divisions in Colonial Society. Most of those in Office adhered to the Crown. Charge of the Loyalists that the Whigs were mere needy Place-Hunters, answered. Loyalist Clergymen, Lawyers, and Physicians 55–61

CHAPTER VII.

The Reasons given for Adherence to the Crown. The Published Declarations of the Whigs that they wished for a Redress of Wrongs and the Restoration of Ancient Privileges, as found in "Novanglus." Rapid Statement of Colonial Disabilities, which the Whig Leaders hardly mentioned in the Controversy, and which appear embodied for the first time in the Declaration of Independence. Denials of Whig Leaders, North and South, that they designed at the Beginning of the Controversy to separate from England. Reasons of the Loyalists for the Course adopted by them, concluded 62–68

CHAPTER VIII.

Loyalists who entered the Military Service of the Crown . . 69–74

CHAPTER IX.

Whig Mobs before the Appeal to Arms, and tarring and feathering. Punishments of Loyalists during the War for overt Acts in favor of the Crown, and for speaking, writing, or acting against the Whigs. Proscription, Banishment, and Confiscation Acts of the State Governments. The Laws which divested the Loyalists of their Estates examined 75–87

CONTENTS.   xi

CHAPTER X.

The Course of the "Violent Whigs" towards the Loyalists, at the Peace, discussed and condemned 88–93

CHAPTER XI.

Discussions at Paris between the Commissioners for concluding Terms of Peace, on the Question of Compensation to the Loyalists for their Losses during the War, by Confiscation and otherwise. Reasons why Congress refused to make Recompense, stated and defended. The Provisions of the Treaty unsatisfactory in this particular. The Parties interested appeal to Parliament. Debates in the Lords and Commons. The Recommendation of Congress to the States to afford Relief in certain Cases, disregarded 94–103

CHAPTER XII.

The Loyalists apply to Parliament for Relief. The King, in his Speech, recommends Attention to their Claims. Commissioners appointed. Complaints of the Loyalists on various Grounds. Number of Claimants, and Schedules of their Losses. Delay of the Commissioners in adjusting Claims, and Distresses in consequence. Discussion in Parliament. Final Number of Claimants, Final Amount of Schedules, and Final Award. In the Appeals to their respective Governments, the Loyalists fared better than the Whigs 104–113

CHAPTER XIII

The Banished Loyalists and their Descendants. Progress of Whig Principles in the Canadas, in New Brunswick, and Nova Scotia. The whole System of Monopoly, on which the Colonial System was founded and maintained, surrendered. The Colonists now manufacture what they will, buy where they please, and sell where they can. England herself has pronounced the Vindication of the Whigs. The Heir to the British Throne at Mount Vernon and Bunker Hill The Colonists claim to hold the highest Places in the Government, in the Army, and in the Navy. Effects of the Change of Policy. The Children of the Whigs and of the Loyalists, reconciled 114–137

CHAPTER XIV.

Introductory Remarks. Principles of Unbelief prevalent. The Whigs lose sight of their Original Purposes, and propose Conquests. Decline of Public Spirit. Avarice, Rapacity, Traffic with the Enemy. Gambling, Speculation, Idleness, Dissipation, and Extravagance. Want of Patriotism. Excessive Issue of Paper might have been avoided. Recruits for the Army demand Enormous Bounty. Shameless Desertions and Immoralities. Commissions in the Army to men destitute of Principle. Court-martials frequent, and many Officers Cashiered. Resignations upon Discreditable Pretexts, and alarmingly prevalent. The Public Mind fickle, and Disastrous Changes in Congress 138–152

PRELIMINARY HISTORICAL ESSAY.

[In this Essay, I avail myself of such parts of my own contributions to the "North American Review" as are pertinent to my purpose.]

CHAPTER I.

Taxation did but accelerate the Dismemberment of the British Empire. Several Causes of Disaffection on the part of the Colonists briefly stated. Acts of Parliament which inhibited Labor in the Colonies. Opposition to the Navigation Act and the Laws of Trade in the Time of the Stuarts. Renewed after the lapse of nearly a Century. Mobs and Collisions, Seizures and Rescues, in consequence. The Question of " Three Pence " the Pound on Tea discussed. The Barbarous Commercial Code of England. The Contraband Trade in Tea, Wine, Fruit, Sugar, and Molasses. The Measures of the Ministry to suppress it. One fourth part of the Signers of the Declaration of Independence Merchants or Shipmasters. Hancock prosecuted in the Admiralty Courts to recover nearly Half a Million of Dollars. The Loyalists great Smugglers after removing from the United States.

THE thoughts and deductions which I shall present are essentially my own, and I shall address the reader directly and without reserve. Many things which are necessary to a right understanding of the revolutionary controversy have been, as I conceive, wholly omitted, or only partially and obscurely stated.

To me, the lives of the instruments of human progress run into one another, and become so interwoven as to appear but the continuation of a single life. It is so in the history of a country; and I am weary of reading that the stamp duty and the tea duty were the "causes" of the American Revolution. Colonies become nations as certainly as boys become men, and by a similar law. The "Declaration" of the fifty-six, at Philadelphia, was but the "Contract" signed by the forty-one sad and stricken ones in the waters of Provincetown, with the growth of one hundred and fifty-six years. The intermediate occurrences were sources of discipline, of development, and of preparation. At most, taxation and the kindred questions did but *accelerate* the dismemberment of the British Empire, just as a man whose lungs are half consumed hastens the crisis by suicide.

The writers who insist that the Whigs "went to war for a preamble," and who confine their views to the question of "taxation without representation," seem to forget that the conquest of Canada relieved the Colonies of all apprehension as related to the French, and was the beginning of a series of events, which, as we reason of cause and effect, led naturally and certainly to freedom. They forget, too, the discussions on the subject of introducing Episcopal bishops, and giving precedence to the Established Church; the misrepresentations in Parliament and elsewhere of the principal officers who served in the French war; the plan to consolidate British America, to take away the charters of Massachusetts, Rhode Island, and Connecticut; to reduce the whole Thirteen to a common system of government, with new boundaries to some, and with restrictions to all; the suggestion to create a colonial peerage; the practice of conferring legislative, executive, and judicial offices on the same person; the neglect of native talents in civil life, except when connected with officials of English birth, or with the "old colonial families;" and the denial of promotion to officers of distinguished military ability, as well as the studied insult of allowing a captain in the "regulars" to rank and to command a colonel in the "provincials."

And let us examine the POLITICAL questions which formed elements in the momentous struggle as they really were, and as we speak of passing events in which we ourselves participate. To me, the documentary history, the state-papers of the revolutionary era, teach nothing more clearly than this, namely, that almost every matter brought into discussion was *practical*, and in some form or other related to LABOR,— to some branch of COMMON INDUSTRY. Our fathers did indeed, in their appeals to the people, embody their opposition to the measures of the mother country, in one expressive term — "Taxation" — "Taxation without Representation." But whoever has examined the acts of Parliament which were resisted, has found that nearly all of them inhibited Labor. There were no less than twenty-nine laws, which restricted and bound down Colonial industry. Neither of these laws touched so much as the "southwest side of a hair" of an "abstraction," and hardly one of them, until the passage of the "Stamp Act," imposed a direct "Tax." They were aimed at the North, and England lost the affection of the mercantile and maritime classes of the northern Colonies full a generation before she alienated the South. They forbade the use of waterfalls, the erecting of machinery, of looms and spindles, and the working of wood and iron; they set the king's arrow upon trees that rotted in the forest; they shut out markets for boards and fish, and seized sugar and molasses, and the vessels in which these articles were carried; and they defined the limitless ocean as but a narrow pathway to such of the lands that it embosoms as wore the British flag. To me, then, the great object of the Revolution was to release LABOR from these restrictions. *Free-laborers* — inexcusable in this — began with sacking houses, overturning public offices, and emptying tar-barrels and pillow-cases upon the heads of those who were employed to enforce these oppressive acts of Parliament; and when the skill and high intellect which were enlisted in their cause, and which vainly strove to moderate their excess, failed to obtain a peaceable redress of the wrongs of which they complained, and were driven either to abandon the end in view, or to combine and wield their strength, men of all avocations rallied upon the field and embarked upon the sea, to retire from neither until the very framework of the Colonial system was torn away, and every branch of industry could be pursued without fines or imprisonment.

Such are the opinions, at least, that I have formed on the questions upon which, among the mass of the people, the contest hinged; which finally united persons of every employment in life in an endeavor to get rid of prohibitions that remonstrance could not repeal, or even humanize. For a higher or holier purpose than this, men have never expended their money, or poured out their lifeblood in battle!

The claims of the merchants and ship-owners have never, as it seems to me, been fully or fairly stated.

They were undoubtedly the first persons in America who set themselves in array against the measures of the ministry. The causes of their opposition have already incidentally appeared, but some farther notice should now be taken of their efforts to obtain the right of free navigation of the ocean. The Stamp Act, and other statutes of a kindred nature, have been made, I think, to occupy too prominent a place among the causes assigned for that event. The irritation which the duties on stamps excited in the planting Colonies subsided as soon as the law which imposed them was repealed; and I submit, that, but for the policy which oppressed the commerce and inhibited the use of the waterfalls of New England, the "dispute" between the mother and her children would have been "left," as Washington breathed a wish that it might be, "to posterity to determine."

While Cromwell lived, Colonial trade was free; but after his death, the maritime interests of America soon felt the difference between a Puritan and a Stuart. Measures were taken by Charles, with all possible speed, to restrain and regulate the intercourse of the Colonies with countries not in subjection to him, and even that with England herself. At the period when his designs were to be executed, Massachusetts, foremost in all marine enterprises, not only traversed the sea at will, but had her own plan of revenue, and a collector of her customs, and exacted fees of vessels arriving at her ports. The merchants of Boston had dealings with Spain, France, Portugal, Holland, the Canaries, and even with Guinea and Madagascar, and had accumulated considerable wealth. The trade of Connecticut, of Rhode Island,

and of the other Colonies, was small and limited. But as a commercial spirit existed everywhere, and as every Colony had some share in the traffic which was to be checked, or, if possible, to be entirely broken up, none were disposed to submit quietly to the measures which were meant to effect either of these purposes. When, then, the royal collectors of the customs came over from England to carry out the will of their sovereign, they were met with resistance from one end of the continent to the other. In truth, the difficulties with Randolph, in Massachusetts, and with Bacon, in Virginia; the strenuous opposition to the establishment of a custom-house in Maryland, and the killing of Rousby; the insurrection in North Carolina, and the imprisonment of Miller; the quarrels with Muschamp in South Carolina; the indictment of the Duke of York's collector in New York, and the conduct of juries in New Jersey, in prosecutions against smugglers, serve to show that the Colonists, when few, scattered, and weak, asserted their right to manage their affairs upon the ocean according to their own pleasure. In a word, the *first* effort to fasten upon American merchants and ship-owners the Navigation Act and Laws of Trade was a signal failure; and all serious endeavors to arrest the course or restrain the limits of their maritime enterprises were discontinued for nearly a century. Collectors of the customs were, however, continued at all the principal ports; but they seldom interfered to trouble those who embarked in unlawful adventures, and such adventures were finally undertaken without fear, and almost without hazard. In truth, the commerce of America was practically free. Some merchants "smuggled" whole cargoes outright; others paid the king's duty on a part, gave "hush-money" to the under-officers of the customs, and "run" the balance.

Suddenly, and without warning, there came a change. The year 1761 was filled with events of momentous consequence. We find the merchants of the ports of New England, and especially those of Boston and Salem, deeply exasperated by the attempts of the revenue officers, under fresh and peremptory orders, to exact strict observance of the laws of navigation and trade; and, by a pretension set up under these instructions, to enter and search places suspected of containing smuggled goods. To submit to this pretension, was to surrender the quiet of their homes and the order of their warehouses to the underlings of the government, and the property which they held to the rapacity of informers, whose gains would be in proportion to their wickedness. Those, therefore, of the two principal towns of Massachusetts, who were interested in continuing the business which they had long pursued without molestation, and under a sort of prescriptive right, and in preserving their property from the grasp of pimps and spies, determined to withstand the crown-officers, and to appeal to the tribunals for protection against their claims. James Otis threw up an honorable and profitable station to become their advocate, and, by his plea in their behalf, became also the first champion of the Revolution.

From this period until the commencement of hostilities, there was no season of quiet in either of the Colonies which depended upon maritime pursuits;

and in Massachusetts, the scenes of tumult and wild commotion which occurred, were the prelude of open war. The nine years which preceded the affray—absurdly called the "Boston Massacre"—were crowded with acts, which show to what extent the quarrels had spread, and what strength the popular wrath had attained. The revision of the "Sugar Act," and the exertions to carry out its new provisions, aided, as the revenue officers now were, by ships of war and an increase of their own corps, carried consternation to every fireside in the North.

Another step in the controversy, and we stand beside the "tea-ships." I have no space to discuss the question of the "three-pence the pound duty on tea," but I must enter my dissent from the common view of it. To me, it was not, as it has been regarded, a question of "*taxation*," but essentially, like all the others between the merchants and the crown, one of *commerce*. The statements of Hutchinson, the debates in Parliament, and the state-papers and the documents which I have examined, all go to prove that the object of the mother country was mainly to break up the contraband trade of the Colonial merchants with Holland and her possessions, and to give to her own East India Company the supply of the Colonial markets. The value of the tea consumed in America was estimated at £300,000 annually. Nearly the whole quantity was "smuggled." Pennsylvania, New York, and Massachusetts, were the great marts. The risk of seizure for many years was small; and it is said, that, at one period, not one chest in five hundred of that which was landed in Boston fell into the hands of the officers of the customs. Some of the merchants of that town had become rich in the traffic, and a considerable part of the large fortune which Hancock inherited from his uncle [1] was thus acquired.

In this condition of things the Company could not sell the qualities of tea which, year after year, they provided for the American market, and which were not wanted anywhere else; and the result finally was, the loss of millions of dollars, the suspension of dividends to shareholders, and inability to meet their large pecuniary engagements to the government. The embarrassments of the Company, in fine, gave a shock to commercial credit generally; bankruptcy was frequent; manufacturers stopped work; thousands of weavers roamed the streets in utter distress, and thousands more subsisted on charity. Under these circumstances, to break up the contraband trade was of vast moment; and the ministry were forced, as they reasoned, to assist the Company on grounds of interest and policy. The Dutch tea was inferior to the English, as was universally admitted, and the latter, if afforded to the consumer at as low a price, would, it was thought, expel the poorer, or the smuggled article at once. Opposition to the measure on the part of the Colonists, does not seem to have been apprehended for a moment. To *reduce* the duty from a *shilling* the pound, payable in England, to "three-pence," payable in the ports to which it should be exported from the Company's warehouses, allowed the article to be sold in America nine-pence the pound *cheaper* than it had been afforded under the *old* rate of duty;

---

[1] Thomas Hancock's plan of smuggling was to put his tea in molasses-hogheads, and thus " run " it, or import it without payment of duties.

while, by securing the market, it at the same time secured a revenue on whatever quantity might actually be entered at the Colonial custom-houses. Such is my understanding of the plan, its reasons, and its objects; and it is pertinent to remark, that, if the "tax" had really been its objectionable feature, it is singular that no clamor was raised while the duty was four times "three-pence" the pound. At *that* rate, Whig merchants, as well as others, had made small importations from England, in order " to cover" the larger and illicit importations from Holland and her dependencies. It is equally pertinent to observe, that the English merchants, who sent tea to parts of America where the contraband trade was less extensively pursued, were as hostile to a measure which threatened *them* with the loss of *their* customers, as were their commercial brethren in the Colonies, who were to be sufferers from the same cause.

The "tea" which came charged with "three-pence" duty, payable on being landed, was disposed of in various ways. As a punishment for the destruction of that sent to Boston, that port was shut up, and its commerce thus struck down at a blow. The cutting off the fisheries, which were then the very lifeblood of New England, soon followed the passage of the "Boston Port Bill," and was the crowning act of the policy which produced an appeal to arms. When the tidings that no vessels could now enter or leave the harbor of the capital of the North spread through the land, the cry that "Boston is suffering in the cause which henceforth interests all America," rose spontaneously. Public meetings were held in all parts of the country. People met in the open air, in churches, and court-houses, to express their horror of the oppressors, and their sympathy with the oppressed. I have examined the proceedings of no less than sixty-seven of these meetings, of which twenty-seven were held in Virginia, and all but one in places south of New England. The day that the Port Bill went into operation was one of gloom and sadness everywhere; and the predictions, on both sides of the Atlantic, that it would produce a general confederation, and end in a general revolt, were of rapid fulfilment.

In their opposition to the Navigation Act and Laws of Trade, the merchants and ship-owners were entirely right. Obedience to humane laws is due from every member of the community. But the barbarous code of commercial law, which disgraced the statute book of England for the exact century which intervened between the introduction and expulsion of her Colonial collectors and other officers of the customs, was entitled to no respect whatever.

The commercial code was so stern and cruel, that an American merchant was compelled to evade a law of the realm, in order to give a sick neighbor an orange or cordial of European origin, or else obtain them legally, loaded with the time, risk, and expense of a voyage from the place of growth or manufacture to England, and thence to his own warehouse. An American ship-owner or ship-master, when wrecked on the coast of Ireland, was not allowed to unlade his cargo on the shore where his vessel was stranded, but was required to send his merchandise to England, when, if originally destined for, or wanted in, the Irish market, an English vessel might carry it thither. At the North, a market for *all* the dried fish which were caught was indispensable to the prosecution of the fisheries. But the policy of the mother country provided penalties, and the confiscation of vessel and cargo, for a sale of such proportion of the annual "catch" as was unfit for her own ports, or was not wanted in her own possessions in the Caribean Sea, if carried to the islands which owned subjection to France or Spain. These were *some* of the features of the odious system which prevailed, and which was never abolished, until American vessels went out upon the ocean under a new flag.

Nine tenths, probably, of all the tea, wine, fruit, sugar, and molasses, consumed in the Colonies, were smuggled. To put an end to this illicit traffic was the determined purpose of the ministry. The commanders of the ships of war on the American station were accordingly commissioned as officers of the customs; and, to quicken their zeal, they were to share in the proceeds of confiscations; the courts to decide upon the lawfulness of seizures, were to be composed of a single judge, without a jury, whose emoluments were to be derived from his own condemnations; the governors of the Colonies and the military officers were to be rewarded for their activity by sharing, also, either in the property condemned, or in the penalties annexed to the interdicted trade. Boston was the great offender; and soon twelve ships of war, mounting no less than two hundred and sixty guns, were assembled in the harbor of that port, for revenue service on the Atlantic coast. The merchants of the sea-ports were roused to preserve their business; and when the controversy came to blows, lawyers who had espoused their cause in the mere course of professional duty, were among the efficient advocates for liberty. One quarter part of the signers of the Declaration of Independence were bred to trade, or to the command of ships,[1] and more than one of them was branded with the epithet of "smuggler." It was fit, then, that Hancock, who, at the shedding of blood at Lexington, was respondent in the Admiralty Court, in suits of the Crown, to recover nearly half a million of dollars as penalties alleged to have been incurred for violations of the statute-book: it was fit that *he* should be the first to affix his name to an instrument which, if made good, would save him from ruin, and give his countrymen free commerce with all the world.

In conclusion, a single word more. The Loyalists who, at the peace, removed to the present British Colonies, and their children after them, smuggled almost every article of foreign origin from the frontier ports of the United States, for more than half a century, and until England relaxed her odious commercial policy. The merchant in whose counting-house I myself was bred, sold the "old Tories" and their descendants large quantities of tea, wine, spices, silks, crapes, and other articles, as a part of his regular business. I have not room to relate the plans devised by sellers and buyers to elude the officers of the Crown, or the perils incurred by the latter, at times, while crossing the Bay of Fundy on their pas-

---

[1] John Hancock, John Langdon, Samuel Adams, William Whipple, George Clymer, Stephen Hopkins, Francis Lewis, Philip Livingston, Elbridge Gerry, Joseph Hewes, George Taylor, Roger Sherman, Button Gwinnett, and Robert Morris.

sage homeward. But I cannot forbear the remark, that, as the finding of a single box of contraband tea caused the confiscation of vessel and cargo, the smugglers kept vigilant watch with glasses, and committed the fatal herb to the sea, the instant a revenue cutter or ship of war hove in sight in a quarter to render capture probable. When a spectator of the scene, as I often was, how could I but say to myself, — "The destruction of tea in Boston, December, 1773, in principle, how like!"

CHAPTER II.

State of Political Parties in the New England Colonies.

LEAVING here this course of general remark, I propose to take a view of the revolutionary controversy, and of the state of parties, in each Colony separately and in course. And first in Massachusetts' Colony of Maine. Of the immense domains, embracing almost the half of our continent, which, in 1620, King James conferred upon those gentlemen of his court who, in popular language, are known as the "Council of Plymouth," Maine formed a part. Among the most distinguished members of this Council was Sir Ferdinando Gorges; to whom, and to John Mason, the Council, two years after the date of their own patent, conveyed all the lands and "fishings" between the rivers Merrimack and Sagadahoc. Subsequently, and rapidly, other grants covered the same soil, and angry and endless contentions followed. But Gorges, bent on leaving his name in our annals, obtained of Charles the First a grant for himself, individually, of the territory between the Piscataqua and Sagadahoc, and thence from the sea one hundred and twenty miles northward. These were the ancient limits of the "Province of Maine." Having now a sort of double title, Gorges might reasonably hope that his rights were perfect, and that he might pursue his plans without interruption. But Massachusetts, on the one hand, insisted that her boundaries were narrowed by the grants to Mason and himself; while the Council, on the other, with inexcusable carelessness or dishonesty, continued to alienate the very soil which he held, both from themselves and their common master. Thus he was harassed his life long, and went to his grave old and worn out with perplexities and the political sufferings and losses of a most troubled period. He was a soldier, and a tried friend of the Stuarts in their times of need, of which their reigns were full, and was plundered and imprisoned in their wars.

Thus, then, Maine was not founded by a Puritan. But after the death of Gorges, his son deemed his possessions in America of little or no worth, and took no pains to retain them, or to carry out his designs; and his grandson, to whom his rights descended, gave to Massachusetts a full assignment and release for the insignificant consideration of twelve hundred and fifty pounds sterling; a sum less than one sixteenth of the amount which had been actually expended. By this purchase, however, Massachusetts acquired only a part of Maine as now constituted. France made pretensions to all that part lying east of the Penobscot, and the Duke of York to the part between the Penobscot and the Kennebec; nor was it until the reign of William and Mary, that disputes about boundaries were merged, and the St. Croix and Piscataqua became the acknowledged charter frontiers.

Soon after the bargain was made with Gorges's heir, Massachusetts lost her own charter; and it was not among the least of the causes of Charles's anger against her, that she had thwarted his design of procuring Maine for his natural son, the Duke of Monmouth. The newly acquired province was thought valuable only for its forests of pine, and for the fisheries of its coasts. But Massachusetts had objects beyond cutting down trees and casting fishing-lines. Her "presumption" in crossing the path of royalty has often been condemned. But the citizens of Maine cannot too often commend the indomitable spirit which she evinced in her struggle to root out Gorges and the Cavaliers or Monarchists of his planting, and to put in their place the humbler but purer Roundheads or Puritans of her own kindred. Had she faltered, when dukes and lords signed parchments that conveyed away soil which she claimed; had she not sought to push her sovereignty over men and territories not originally her own; had she not broken down French seigniories and English feoffdoms, Maine, east of Gorges's eastern boundary, might have continued a part of the British empire to this hour. This opinion is given considerately, and not to round out a period. And whoever will consult the diplomacy of 1783, will learn that, *even as it was*, the British Commissioners contended that the Kennebec should divide the thirteen States from the Colonies which had remained true to the crown.

Yet fishing and lumbering continued to be the two great branches of industry in Maine, until the Revolution. The new charter, procured of William and Mary, confirmed Massachusetts in her acquisitions east of the Piscataqua; but it contained several restrictions which bore hard upon both of these interests. The most prominent I shall briefly notice, because they had a direct influence in the formation of political parties. And, first, that instrument provided, that all pine-trees, of the diameter of twenty-four inches at more than a foot from the ground, on lands not granted to private persons, should be reserved for masts for the royal navy; and that, for cutting down any such tree without special leave, the offender should forfeit one hundred pounds sterling. This stipulation was the source of ceaseless disquiet, and it introduced, to guard the forests from depredation, an officer called the " Surveyor-General of the King's Woods." Between this functionary, who enjoyed a high salary, considerable perquisites, and great power, and the lumberers, there was no love. The officials of the day, who were now of royal appointment, and not, as under the *first* charter, elected by the people, generally ranged themselves on the side of the surveyors, their deputies and menials; while the House of Representatives, as commonly, opposed their doings, and countenanced the popular clamors against them. Nor were the controversies, caused by the efforts of the surveyors to preserve spars for the royal navy, confined to the halls of legislation in Massachusetts. For, beside these, and the frequent quarrels in the woods and at the saw-mills, the disputes between the parties were carried to the Board of Trade in England. There seemed, indeed, in the judgment of several of the colonial governors, no way for them to please their royal master more, than by discoursing about the care which should be exercised over the "mast-trees," and about the severity with which the statute-book should provide against " trespassers." In a word, prerogative and the popular sentiment never agreed.

Discussions about the forests of Maine again and again ended in wrangles. Friendships were broken up, and enmities created for life. This is emphatically true of Shute's administration, when Cooke, the Counsellor of Sagadahoc, and the champion of the "fierce democracy" — as his father had been before him — involved the whole government of Massachusetts in disputes, which, in the end, drove the Governor home to England. And so, subsequently, a forged letter, probably written by "trespassers" or their friends to Sir Charles Wager, first lord of the Admiralty, charging Governor Belcher with conniving with depredators, though seemingly aiding the king's surveyor, — that "Irish dog of a Dunbar," — did its intended work. Shirley, Belcher's successor, when he pressed upon the House the necessity of further enactments to protect the masts and spars for the royal navy, and to punish those who obstructed or annoyed the royal agents, was tartly told in substance, by that body: "Our laws are sufficient; *we* have done our duty in passing them; let the crown officers do *their* duty in enforcing them." Hutchinson, for a like call upon the House, was in like manner reminded, in terms hardly more civil, that there were already charter and statute penalties for "trespassers," a surveyor-general and deputies, and courts of law; and that, provided with these, he must look to the pines "twenty-four inches in diameter, upwards of twelve inches from the ground," for himself. The means for dealing with offenders, it must be confessed, were ample: the crown could try them in the Court of Admiralty, where there was no jury; upon conviction for a *common* trespass, a fine of £100 could be imposed; and for the additional misdeed of plundering the interdicted trees under a painted or disguised face, twenty lashes could be laid on the culprit's back; while, more than all, convictions could be had on *probable* guilt, unless the accused would, on oath, declare his innocence.

But there was no such thing as executing these laws, when it was the popular impression that the woods were "the gifts as well as the growth of nature;" and that the king's right to them was merely "nominal," at the most. The provision of the charter was both unwise and unjust. To reserve to the crown a thousand times as many trees as it could ever require, and to allow all to decay that were not actually used, was absurd. Men of the most limited capacity saw and felt this; and to wean them from a power which insisted, in spite of all remonstrance, in enforcing the absurdity, was an easy task. And we can readily imagine, what indeed is true, that the woodmen of Maine, when rid, by the Revolution, of the presence of surveyor-generals and their deputies, exulted as heartily as did the peasants of France, when the outbreak there abolished forest laws somewhat dissimilar, but equally obnoxious.

Again. The action of Parliament with regard to taxing lumber, admitting it free, or even encouraging its exportation, by bounties, was eagerly watched. The mother country pursued all of these courses at different times, and gave dissatisfaction, or created discontent, among the getters and dealers in the article, as changes occurred in her policy; just as she does now, with those Colonial possessions which yet remain to her. The "mast-ships" at the North, like the "tobacco-ships" at the South, were the common, and oftentimes the only, means for crossing the ocean; and royal governors and other high personages were occasionally compelled to embark in them. In these clumsy, ill-shapen vessels, also went ladies and lovers to visit friends in that distant land, which some Americans yet call "home." Merchandise, fashions, and the last novel had a slow voyage back; but men and maidens were models of patience, and the arrival of the eleven weeks "mast-er" gave as much joy when all was safe, as does the eleven days steamer now. In port, while loading, the "mast-ships" were objects of interest, and their decks and cabins the scenes of hilarity and mirth. We read of illuminations and firings of cannon, of frolics and feasts.

The mast-trade was confined to England; and the transportation of spars thither, and of the sawed and shaved woods required by the planter, to islands in the West Indies possessed by the British crown, was about the only *lawful* modes of exporting lumber for a long period. By the statute-book, the "king's mark" was as much to be dreaded by the mariner and the owner of the vessel, as by the "logger" and the "mill-man." But the revenue officers caused less fear than the surveyors of the woods, until fleets and armies were employed to aid them; when the interdicted trade with the French and Spanish islands, which had been carried on by a sort of prescriptive right, was nearly, if not entirely, broken up. No enactments of the mother country operated to keep down Northern industry so effectually, poorly as they were obeyed, as the navigation and trade laws; and on none did they bear more severely than on that portion of the people, whose position or necessities left them no choice of employments. There were some, nor were they few, who were obliged to plunder the forests, and to work up trees into marketable shapes, or starve. Included with these inhabitants of Maine, were those who lived upon the coasts — the mariners and the fishermen. The interests of all these classes were identical; and to them the maritime policy of the government of England was cruel in the extreme; since it robbed unremitting toil of half its reward. Lumber and fish were inseparable companions in every adventure to the islands in the Caribbean sea. Enterprises to get either were hazardous, at the best; and, as practical men can readily perceive, all who engaged in obtaining them, were obliged then, as they are now, to seek *different* markets; so that to shut *some* marts, when access to *all* would barely remunerate the adventurers, was, in effect, to close the whole. These employments were, as they still are, among the most difficult and severe in the whole round of human pursuits; and attempts to alleviate the burdens of parliamentary legislation upon both were made in Massachusetts, long before a whisper of discontent was elsewhere uttered in America. The discussions in that Colony, in behalf of her citizens at home and of those in Maine who were engaged in getting and transporting the products of the forest and of the sea, though commenced without reference to separation from the mother country, took fast hold of the public mind. When, then, Otis at length spoke out, thousands who never heard or read his reasonings, and might not have felt their force if they had, were ready, at the first call, to clear the woods, and docks, and warehouses, and decks of vessels of the "swarms of officers" who "harassed" them, and " eat out their substance."

The troubles which I have now enumerated, the disputes which grew out of the question, whether, as the territories purchased of Gorges had never reverted to the crown, the surveyor-general's duty did, in fact, require him to mark and protect the mast-trees within their limits, and especially the charter inhibition of grants east of the Kennebec without the king's consent, kept out settlers, held titles in suspense, and were sufficient not only to alienate the affections of the people from the British crown, but to confine them to a narrow belt of country.

As may be supposed, the body of the people were Whigs. Still, Maine had a considerable number of Loyalists or Tories. To afford them a place of refuge and protection was the principal object, as I have been led to conclude, of establishing a military post at the mouth of the Penobscot. The descendants of Loyalists who found shelter in the garrison at Castine, represent that it was thronged with adherents of the crown and their families; and, after the discomfiture of Saltonstall and Lovell, they were left in undisturbed quiet during the remainder of the war. The names of all the Tories of Maine who were proscribed and banished under the act of Massachusetts, as well as many others, will be found in their proper connections.

In passing from Maine to New Hampshire, we shall find the general state of things very similar. The occupations of the people of the two Colonies were much alike. New Hampshire, though not an appendage of Massachusetts in 1775, had been twice annexed to the mother of New England, and had thus acquired much of her spirit. Collisions between the revenue officers and the mariners and ship-owners of Portsmouth, and between the guardians of the "king's woods" and the lumberers of the interior, had been frequent. Indeed the "loggers" and "sawyers" had whipped the deputies of the surveyor-general so often and so severely, that the term "*swamp-law*" was quite as significant a phrase as that of "*lynch-law*" in our own time. Yet, as will appear, the Whigs had many and powerful opponents in the Colony planted by Mason, the associate patentee of Gorges.

With regard to Massachusetts, it seems to have been taken as granted, that, because here the Revolution had its origin; because the old Bay State furnished a large part of the men and the means to carry it forward to a successful issue; and because, in a word, she fairly exhausted herself in the struggle, the people embraced the popular side, almost in a mass. A more mistaken opinion than this has seldom prevailed.

The second charter, or that granted by William and Mary, had several obnoxious provisions besides those which had peculiar reference to Maine, and its acceptance was violently opposed. And Phips, the Earl of Bellamont, Shute, Burnet, Belcher, Shirley, and Pownall, the several governors who were appointed by the crown under one of these provisions, encountered embarrassments and difficulties, and some of them were actually driven from the executive chair by the force of party heats. In fact, the "old-charter," or "liberty-men," arrayed on the one side, and the "new-charter," or "prerogative-men," on the other, kept up a continual warfare. When, then, in the quarrel, which was commenced with Bernard, which was continued with Hutchinson and Gage, his successors, and which finally spread over the continent and severed the British empire, the terms "Whig" and "Tory" were employed, they were not used to distinguish *new* parties, but were simply epithets borrowed from the politics of the mother country, and did but take the place of the party names which had previously existed, and under which political leaders had long moved and trained their followers. As the Revolutionary controversy darkened, individuals of note did indeed change sides; but, though some of our writers have hardly mentioned that such a state of things preceded the momentous conflict, the general truth was as I have stated.

As some further details of the state of parties in Massachusetts will be given in another connection, a brief notice of the Loyalists who abandoned their homes and the country will serve my present purpose. Of this description, upwards of eleven hundred retired in a body with the royal army at the evacuation of Boston. This number includes, of course, women and children. Among the men, however, were many persons of distinguished rank and consideration. Of members of the council, commissioners, officers of the customs and other officials, there were one hundred and two; of clergymen, eighteen; of inhabitants of country towns, one hundred and five; of merchants and other persons who resided in Boston, two hundred and thirteen; of farmers, mechanics, and traders, three hundred and eighty-two.

Other emigrations preceded and succeeded this; but they consisted principally of individuals, or small parties of intimate friends, or families and their immediate connections. But the whole number who embarked at different ports of Massachusetts, pending the controversy and during the war, were, as I am inclined to believe, two thousand, at the lowest computation. The names and the fate of a considerable proportion of them will be found in these pages. Most of them took passage for Halifax, Nova Scotia, where they endured great privations. Many, however, subsequently went to England, and there passed the remainder of their lives.

Rhode Island and Connecticut may be considered together. There is but little to detain us in either. Both were governed by charters like Massachusetts, and both were "pure democracies," since, says Chalmers, "the freemen exercised without restraint every power, deliberate and executive. Like Ragusa and San Marino, in the Old World, they offered an example to the New, of two little republics embosomed within a great empire." In 1704, Montpesson, the Chief Justice of New York, wrote to Lord Nottingham, that when he "was at Rhode Island, they did in all things as if they were out of the dominions of the crown." Of Connecticut, at the same period, Chalmers remarks, that, "being inhabited by a people of the same principles though of a different religion, they acted the same political part as those of Rhode Island;" and he quotes from a dispatch of Lord Cornbury to the Board of Trade, the pithy saying, that the inhabitants of these Colonies "hate everybody that owns any subjection to the Queen" [Anne].

The Revolution, which so essentially affected the governments of most of the Colonies, produced no very perceptible alteration in those of either Rhode Island or Connecticut. After Wanton, the governor of the first, was deposed, the Whigs succeeded to power without turmoil, and in the ordinary course of legislative action. Trumbull, the governor of the latter, was a sound Whig, and occupied the executive chair from 1769 to 1783. The charters of both Colonies were admirably adapted to their wants and condition, whether regarded as dependencies or as free States; and while Connecticut continued without any other fundamental law until the year 1818, Rhode Island has but lately recovered from the disquiets and animosities occasioned by the adoption of a Constitution.

Yet, though less restrained by charter provisions than Massachusetts, and though in theory "pure democracies," and bearing "hate" towards all who, in Queen Anne's time, acknowledged her authority, there was no greater unanimity of sentiment on the questions which agitated the country in 1775, than elsewhere in New England. Indeed, I feel assured that, in Connecticut, the number of adherents of the crown was greater, in proportion to the population, than in Maine, Massachusetts, or New Hampshire. This impression is warranted by documentary evidence, and is fully sustained by facts, which have been communicated to me by descendants of Loyalists of that Colony.

CHAPTER III.

State of Political Parties in the Middle Colonies.

IN passing from New England, we are to speak of American Colonists of different origin, and who lived under different forms of government. Thus, New York had no charter, but was governed by royal instructions, orders in council, and similar authority, communicated to the governors by the ministers "at home." The governor and council were appointed by the king, but vacancies at the council board were filled by the governor. The people elected the popular branch, which consisted of twenty-seven members. To say that the political institutions of New York formed a *feudal aristocracy*, is to define them with tolerable accuracy. The soil was held by a few. The masses were mere retainers or tenants, as in the monarchies of Europe. Nor has this condition of society been entirely changed, since the "anti-rent" dissensions of our own time arose from the vestige which remains.

Such a state of things was calculated to give the king many adherents. The fact agreed with the theory. Details may be spared. One circumstance will prove the preponderance of the royal party beyond all doubt; namely, that soon after the close of the Revolution, a bill passed the House of Assembly, which prohibited persons who had been in opposition from holding any office under the State. This bill, on being sent to the other branch of the legislature, was rejected, and on the ground principally, that if allowed to become a law, no elections could be held in some parts of the State, inasmuch as there were not a sufficient number of Whigs, in certain sections, to preside at or conduct the election meetings.

While so large a proportion of the people of New York preferred to continue their connection with the mother country, very many of them entered the military service of the crown, and fought in defence of their principles. Whole battalions, and even regiments, were raised by the great landholders, and continued organized and in pay throughout the struggle. In fine, New York was undeniably the Loyalists' stronghold, and contained more of them than any other colony in all America. I will not say that she devoted her resources of men and of money to the cause of the enemy; but I *do* say, that she withheld many of the one, and much of the other, from the cause of the right. Massachusetts furnished 67,907 Whig soldiers between the years 1775 and 1783; while New York supplied but 17,781. In adjusting the war balances, after the peace, Massachusetts, as was then ascertained, had overpaid her share in the sum of 1,248,801 dollars of silver money; but New York was deficient in the large amount of 2,074,846 dollars. New Hampshire, though almost a wilderness, furnished 12,496 troops for the continental ranks, or quite three quarters of the number enlisted in the "Empire State."

These facts show the state of parties in this Colony

in a strong light. One other incident, which presents the wavering, time-serving course that prevailed, even after Washington had been appointed to the command of the army, and when, of course, the whole country was committed to sustain him, will suffice. On the 25th of June, 1775, a letter was received by the New York Provincial Congress, which communicated intelligence that the Commander-in-chief was on his way to headquarters at Cambridge, and would cross the Hudson and visit the city. "News came at the same time," says Mr. Sparks, "that Governor Tryon was in the harbor, just arrived from England, and would land that day. The Congress were a good deal embarrassed to determine how to act on this occasion; for though they had thrown off all allegiance to the authority of their governor, they yet professed to maintain loyalty to his person. They finally ordered a colonel so to dispose of his militia companies, that they might be in a condition to receive '*either the General, or Governor Tryon, whichever should first arrive, and wait on both as well as circumstances would allow.*' Events proved less perplexing than had been apprehended, as General Washington arrived several hours previous to the landing of Governor Tryon." That a Congress of *Whigs* should have been so irresolute and timid, after the blood of their brethren had been poured out at Lexington and on Breed's Hill, is unaccountable. If such was *their* conduct, what must have been the state of feeling among the Tories, what the courage and confidence which animated them?

New Jersey, says Chalmers, was " a scion from New York, and either prospered or withered, during every season, as the stock flourished or declined." Again he says, that "planted by Independents from New England, by Covenanters from Scotland, by conspirators from England, such scenes of turbulence were exhibited, ... age after age, as acquired ..... the characteristic appellation of 'The Revolutions.'" Chalmers was fond of strong and pointed expressions, and some of his statements are to be received, therefore, with allowance. He saw — as the students of our history well know — designs to throw off allegiance, to "set up for independency," and to effect "Revolutions," in the common quarrels between the Colonial Assemblies and the Governors, and in the ordinary petitions to the mother country, for redress of real or supposed wrongs.

New Jersey was indeed politically annexed to New York, and the connection was dissolved and renewed several times prior to 1738. So, too, that part of it which was originally known as "East Jersey," at one period was assigned to William Penn; while both "East and West Jersey" were subsequently added to the jurisdiction of New England. In 1702, the "Jersies" were united under one government, and received the present name; and from 1738 to the Revolution, New Jersey had a separate Colonial government. The losses of New Jersey, in proportion to her population and wealth, were greater, probably, than those of any other member of the Confederacy. Her soldiers, who entered the service of Congress, gained enviable renown; and within her borders are some of the most memorable battle-grounds of the Revolution. It was in New Jersey, that Washington made his best military movements, and displayed his highest qualities of character; it was there that he encountered his greatest distresses and difficulties, and earned his most enduring laurels.

We come now to the "proprietary government" of Pennsylvania; and a proprietary government in America was a monarchy in miniature.

The proprietary governors were not, generally, bad men, but the rapacity of some of them was unbounded. Chalmers quotes the remark as a shrewd saying, that "a dignitary of this description had two masters: one who gave him his commission, and one who gave him his pay; and that he was, therefore, on his good behavior to both."[1] Several, I suspect, cared very little for either of their two masters; and he who said, that they had *three* things to attend to, "First, to fleece the people for the king, then for *themselves*, and lastly, for the proprietaries, their employers," told more truth, and had more wit, than the person cited by our well-informed but much prejudiced annalist.

It is perhaps true, that as a body, the party of which Franklin was a member in these dissensions, was the Whig party of the Revolution. Yet, there were exceptions; and some of his warmest personal and political friends were found among the adherents of the crown; while old opponents ranged themselves by his side, and did good service during the trying scenes which preceded deeds of hostility. For a time, the course of Pennsylvania was extremely doubtful. Besides the differences which existed else-

---

[1] The reader will find some further particulars of the nature of the political institutions of Pennsylvania, in the biographical notice of John Penn.

where, the religious faith of the people was opposed to the adoption of forcible means to dissolve their connection with the mother country. Hence, as in New York, timidity and indecision were evinced among the most prominent Whigs. To me, the line of conduct pursued by John Dickinson is a perfect riddle. His various, eloquent, and able tracts and essays, and the important papers and addresses which came from his pen, between the "Stamp-act Congress" in 1765 and the close of the first Continental Congress in 1774, gave him a wide and just fame. But in the Congress of 1776, he opposed the passage of the Declaration of Independence with great zeal; and, as John Adams was its "great pillar and support," and "its ablest advocate and champion," so he, of all others, was the uncompromising antagonist of the lion-hearted patriot of the North.

Unless Galloway — a name often to appear in this work — was mistaken, the Loyalists of the Middle Colonies were ready to enter the military service of the crown in large numbers. His statement is, that had Sir William Howe issued a Proclamation when in Philadelphia, 3,500 men would have repaired to his standard; that, in that city, in New Jersey, and in New York, he could have embodied quite 5,000; that upwards of fifty gentlemen went to his camp to offer their services in disarming the disaffected, but, failing to obtain even an interview, retired in disgust; and that, under Sir William's successor, 5,000 actually appeared in arms for the defence of the city of New York.

CHAPTER IV.

State of Political Parties in the Southern Colonies.

I have been able to ascertain so little of a definite character of the political condition of Delaware and Maryland, at the period to which these remarks relate, that I shall detain the reader in neither; and pass to the "Old Dominion." Virginia, like New York, was a feudal aristocracy. But *there* a large proportion of the landholders, *unlike* those of New York, were Whigs, and, of course, favored the revolutionary movement. Yet, it does not appear, that, *upon the questions of dissolving her relations with the mother country*, she was as ready as, from her early and firm opposition to the Stamp Act, might be expected. Indeed, there is the highest possible evidence for believing that Virginia broke her Colonial bonds with hesitation. Early in March, 1776, Colonel Joseph Reed, of Pennsylvania, in a letter to Washington, observed, that there was "a strange reluctance in the minds of many to cut the knot which ties us to Great Britain, particularly *in this Colony and to the southward*." In writing again on the 15th of the same month, he was more explicit. "It is said," — are his words, — "*the Virginians are so alarmed with the idea of independence, that they have sent Mr. Braxton on purpose to turn the vote of that Colony, if any question on that subject should come before Congress.*" Washington, in his reply to the letter of the 15th, admits that the people of Virginia, "*from their form of government, and steady attachment heretofore to royalty, will come reluctantly into the idea of independence;*" but says, that "*time* and persecution bring many wonderful things to pass," and that, by private letters which he had lately received, he found Paine's celebrated essay, called "Common Sense," (which recommended separation,) was "working a powerful change in the minds of many men."

This correspondence, as will be seen, occurred but a little more than three months previous to the time when Congress actually declared the Thirteen Colonies to be free and independent States; and the opinions of persons so well informed, so intimate in friendship, and occupying so responsible public stations, are to be regarded as decisive.

Yet Washington, Henry, the Lees, Jefferson, and Bland, were, undoubtedly, the true exponents of her principles.

The institutions of North Carolina were decidedly monarchical from the first. Political or social disorder seems to have prevailed, to some extent, throughout her colonial existence. Martin, the last royal governor, stated, in 1775, that literature was hardly known, and that there were but two schools in the whole Colony. After the final overthrow of the Stuarts, many of the adherents of the last of that name who sought the British throne, fled for refuge to America, and settled within her borders. And it was singular that most of them were Loyalists; that men who had become exiles for the part which they had taken *against* the House of Brunswick should here, and in another civil war, espouse its cause, and, a second time the losers, go a second time into banishment. Equally remarkable in the politics of this Colony was the course of those who, in 1771, rose in insurrection, and were known as "Regulators." These men complained of various oppressions, but especially of those which attended the practice of law; they appeared in arms, and were determined to prostrate the government. Governor Tryon totally defeated them, and left three hundred of their number dead on the field. They were the earliest revolutionists in America — as far as hostile deeds were concerned — and, it might be reasonably concluded, became Whigs. But disappointing expectation, like the followers of the Pretender above mentioned, a large majority joined the royal party, and enlisted under the king's banner.

North Carolina, then, originally monarchical, and adding to her native Loyalists the survivors of the large emigration from Scotland, was nearly divided. Some of her leading Whigs, as well as their descendants, have endeavored to prove that the popular party was much in the majority. Facts, as it seems to me, hardly sustain them.

How was it with a *portion* of the Whigs? There is proof that many were as unstable as the wind. If the sky was bright, and a Whig victory had been obtained somewhere, and if, above all, no king's troops were near, why, *then* these changing men were steadfast for the right; but if news of reverses reached them, or the royal army came among or near them, then they "supported," and, by their own account, "always had supported, their lawful sovereign, his most gracious Majesty."

I would willingly do the Whigs of North Carolina no injustice; on the other hand, I would relieve them from all imputations which cannot be sustained by ample and the most unobjectionable testimony. It is in this spirit that I dissent from some of the declarations of Mr. Jefferson. That distinguished man, in a written statement made a few years before his decease, distinctly alleges, that William Hooper, one of the delegates in Congress from that State in 1776, was a rank and out and out Tory. Mr. Hooper was born in Massachusetts, and was educated at Harvard University. His father, and nearly all of his relatives, were, indeed, Loyalists: but he was a student of James Otis, and imbibed *his* political sentiments; nor did he leave New England until after parties were formed and the "Stamp-Act" difficulties had passed away. I have read several of his confidential letters to his friends, while he was in Congress; letters in which, if he possessed the political sympathies attributed to him by Mr. Jefferson, the inclinations of his mind would have been shown. That he was a timid man, like Morton of Pennsylvania, is very probable. Yet, I submit that no defence is necessary. Hooper signed the Declaration of Independence; and of all documents to which a " *Tory* " would have affixed his name, *that*, certainly, was among the very last

It is grateful, now, to turn to the brighter side, and to bestow words of praise. The original Whig party of North Carolina embraced a large proportion of the wealth, virtue, and intelligence of the State. In the county of Bute, especially, the king had no friends, except a few Scotch merchants and vagrant pedlers; while the number of wavering Whigs was so small, that the county was nearly unanimous in favor of the change which the leaders advocated, and put their fortunes and lives at hazard to obtain. Nor should it be forgotten that, in the county of Mecklenburgh, a Declaration of Independence was passed more than a year before the more celebrated instrument of the same name was adopted by the Continental Congress at Philadelphia. As late as the year 1819, Mr. Jefferson made a labored argument to prove that no such document exists. But that such a paper *was* written, considered, signed, and promulgated, is *now* as well established as is any event in our history. It is known, moreover, that Colonel Thomas Polk originated the measure, and that the Declaration itself was from the pen of Dr. Ephraim Brevard.

I pass to speak of the political condition of South Carolina. The statements in the first edition of this work exposed me to much reproach as a gentleman, and to sharp criticisms as a student of history. On the discovery of a single but grave error,[1] — which I took pains in my correspondence North and South to

---

[1] I said . . . "it is hardly an exaggeration to add, that more Whigs of New England were sent to her aid, and now lie buried in her soil, than she sent from it to every scene of strife from Lexington to Yorktown." The fact, however, is, that no troops belonging to New England went to South Carolina, nor, as far as I know, south of the country about the James River, in Virginia. The common opinion is otherwise. Even Mr. Webster, in his reception-speech at *Charleston*, remarked that, "New England blood has moistened the soil where we now stand, shed as readily as at Lexington, or Concord, or Bunker Hill." Again, at *Savannah*, "The blood of New England, in her turn, was freely poured out upon Southern soil, and her sons stood shoulder to shoulder with those of Georgia in the common cause." Still again, the Hon. B. F. Hunt, in addressing Mr. Webster, at *Charleston*, said, "*Every battle-field of our State contains beneath its sod the bones of New England men, who fell in defence of the South.*" Webster's Works, vol. 2, pp. 377, 380, 403.

HISTORICAL ESSAY. 39

correct, — and in 1848, soon after the attack of the "Southern Quarterly Review," I examined my principal authorities anew; and I performed the same duty in 1856, immediately after reading the speech of Mr. Keitt in the House of Representatives, and the speeches of Messrs. Evans and Butler in the Senate of the United States.[1] I did not try to make out a case against South Carolina; nor do I believe that candid readers have ever pronounced my strictures upon *her* delinquencies more severe than those which I uttered against the several — though quite different — faults and crimes of Massachusetts herself. I did, indeed, detest the heresy of "Nullification" with all my heart, and as I now abhor the damnable doctrine of "Secession;" but still felt to do as exact justice to the State of Laurens, — father and son, — of Gadsen, of Sumter, of Moultrie, and Pickens and Marion, and other noble Whigs, — as exact justice to South Carolina as to my own native New Hampshire. And besides, I remembered in 1847, as I shall still endeavor to bear in mind, that the command, "Thou shalt not bear false witness against thy neighbor," is obligatory at all times and under all circumstances.

All honor to South Carolina, for the band of Whigs who favored the dismemberment of the British empire at an early day; all honor, for being the first of the Thirteen States to frame an independent constitution; all honor, for the payment of $1,205,978 more than her proportion of the expenses of the war;

---

[1] See *Southern Quarterly Review*, July and October numbers, 1848, and the Speeches, *Congressional Globe*, 1st Session, 34th Congress, pp 625, 702, 833.

and all honor, for her mercy, at the close of the struggle, to the unhappy, the ruined adherents to the crown.

And now I reaffirm, that South Carolina, at first, and for about half a century, was a proprietary government, and, like Pennsylvania, was a sort of monarchy in miniature; that, in 1719, the people abolished this form, took from the proprietors the power of appointing the governor, and erected a temporary republic; that, two years after, a regal government was established which continued until the Revolution. I again say, that, in all the essential features, the British constitution was the model, and that, of consequence, the institutions of South Carolina were thoroughly monarchical.

The public men of that State, of the present generation, claim that her patriotic devotion in the Revolution was inferior to none, and superior to most, of the States of the confederacy; and I again aver that, as I have examined the evidence, it was not so. The great body of the people were emigrants from Switzerland, Germany, France, Great Britain, and the Northern Colonies of America, and their descendants; and were opposed to a separation from the mother country. I renew the accusation, that she failed to meet the requisitions of Congress for troops to the extent of her ability; and repeat, that her remissness compares sadly, sadly enough, with the enlistments elsewhere, especially in New England.

Charleston was the great mart of the South, and, as Boston still is, the centre of the export and import trade of a large population. In grandeur, in splendor of buildings, in decorations, in equipages, in shipping, and in commerce, that city was equal to any in America. I reaffirm, that, with troops from other States to aid her, South Carolina could not, or would not, save her own capital; that, so general was the defection after the capitulation by Lincoln, persons who had refused to enlist under the Whig banner, flocked to the royal standard by hundreds; that those who had enjoyed Lincoln's confidence and participated in his councils, bowed their necks anew to the yoke of colonial vassalage; that Sir Henry Clinton considered the triumph complete, and informed the ministry that the whole State had submitted to the royal arms, and had become again a part of the empire; that, to the women of South Carolina, and to Marion, Sumter, and Pickens, — who kept the field without the promise of men, money, or supplies, — it was owing that Sir Henry's declaration proved untrue, and that the spirit and name of liberty did not become utterly extinct.

I reaffirm, that the Whigs and their opponents did not always meet in open and fair fight, nor give and take the courtesies, and observe the rules, of civilized warfare; but that, on the contrary, they murdered one another! General Greene and Chief-Justice Marshall are my authorities. "The animosities between the Whigs and Tories," wrote the first, "render their situation truly deplorable. The Whigs seem determined to extirpate the Tories, and the Tories the Whigs. Some thousands have fallen in this way in this quarter, and the evil rages with more violence than ever. If a stop cannot be put to these massacres, the country will be depopulated in a few months, as neither Whig nor Tory can live." "The people of the South," remarks the eminent jurist, in his Life of Washington, "felt all the miseries which are inflicted by war in its most savage form. Being almost equally divided between the two contending parties, reciprocal injuries had gradually sharpened their resentments against each other, and had armed neighbor against neighbor, until it had become a war of extermination. As the parties alternately triumphed, opportunities were alternately given for the exercise of their vindictive passions." And I state here, as in the first edition, that it were a hard task to determine, by an examination of the accounts of the time, which party perpetrated the greatest barbarities; and that, whatever the guilt of the Tories, the Whigs disgraced the cause and the American name.

And while I thus retain the substance of the original averments against South Carolina, — the grave error once mentioned excepted, — and while, too, I insert the obnoxious Table[1] of the "Continentals" furnished by the several States, in a new form but without alteration as relates to results, I add, that though the battles of Fort Moultrie, of Stono, of the Siege of Charleston, of Camden, of Hanging Rock, of Musgrove's Mill, of Blackstock's, of Georgetown, of Black Wings, of Cowpens, of Fish-Dam Ford, of Ninety-Six, of Fort Galpin, of Fort Watson, of Fort Mott, of Hobkirk's Hill, of Granby, of Cedar Spring, of Hammond's Store, of Quimby, of Eutaw, of Rocky

---

[1] CONTINENTAL ARMY.

In 1790, General Henry Knox, Secretary of War, communicated to Congress a Report of "Troops, including Militia, furnished by the several States, during the War of the Revolution," from which I have compiled the following Table. As relates to the "Regulars," he remarks, that the numbers are "stated from the official returns deposited in the War Office,

HISTORICAL ESSAY.

Mount, of Port Royal, of Tulafinny, of Coosahatchie, of Waxhaw, of Cloud's Creek, of Hay's Station, of and "may be depended upon." The army of the Northern Department was discharged November 5th, 1783, and of the Southern States, just ten days later.

State.	Number of Troops Furnished.	
	Year 1775.	Year 1776.
New Hampshire	2,824	3,019
Massachusetts	16,444	13,372
Rhode Island	1,193	798
Connecticut	4,507	6,390
New York	2,075	3,629
New Jersey		3,193
Pennsylvania	400	5,519
Delaware		609
Maryland		637
Virginia		6,181
North Carolina		1,134
South Carolina		2,069
Georgia		351
	27,443	46,901

In September, 1776, quotas were fixed by Congress for three years, or during the war.

State.	Quota Required.	Troops Furnished.	Strength of the Regular or Continental Army.	
			Year.	Troops.
New Hampshire	10,194	6,653	1775	27,443
Massachusetts	52,728	38,091	1776	46,901
Rhode Island	5,694	3,917	1777	34,820
Connecticut	28,336	21,142	1778	32,899
New York	15,734	12,077	1779	27,694
New Jersey	11,396	7,534	1780	21,015
Pennsylvania	40,416	19,689	1781	13,292
Delaware	3,974	1,778	1782	14,256
Maryland	26,608	13,275	1783	13,476
Virginia	48,522	20,491		
North Carolina	23,994	6,129		
South Carolina	16,932	4,348		
Georgia	3,974	2,328		
	288,502	157,452		
Add Continental Troops for year 1775		27,443		
Add Continental Troops for year 1776		46,901		
		231,796		231,796

It thus appears that the number of Continental troops from New England, was 118,350; from the Middle States, 54,116, and from the South-

Kettle Creek, and of Huck's Defeat, — I add, that though these battles, thirty in all, were fought within the limits of South Carolina, the Tories were not subjugated; but, on the other hand, after the fall of Charleston and until the peace were in the ascendant.

A word, finally, respecting the alleged attempt of South Carolina " to secede " when Charleston was invested by the British general, Prevost. The explanation of late years is, that the proposition was a mere artifice to gain time. If the fact is so, how strange that Henry Lee, a Virginian, an officer in service, and an intelligent observer and chronicler of military events, — how strange that *he* did not know it? He records, in his "History of the War in the South," that, after a day's negotiation to adjust terms of surrender, " the correspondence closed with the proposal, on our part, of neutrality to the town and State during the war,— the peace to fix its ultimate condition." Again, in commenting upon Prevost's rejection of this *chivalrous* overture to desert the Confederacy : " No British force would have been retained

---

ern States, 59,330. So, too, it appears that Massachusetts furnished 67,907, and 13,791 more than the aggregate from New York, New Jersey, and Pennsylvania, and 8,577 more than the aggregate from Delaware, Maryland, Virginia, North and South Carolina, and Georgia. The accuracy of this Table has been disputed. Some inquirers suppose that 231,796 *different individuals* enlisted, forgetting that the army, when the strongest, consisted of only 46,901 men, and that, as is well known, the same soldier reenlisted once, twice, and in some cases, thrice, and in the aggregate of 231,796, is counted accordingly. Again, other persons are sceptical as to the existence of General Knox's Report; such are referred to the *History of Congress*, where it is recorded that it was submitted to that body, May 11, 1790, and to the 12th vol. p. 14, of the *American State Papers*, folio edition, where it is inserted entire. I respectfully request those who have questioned my figures, to examine for themselves.

from the field to preserve the neutral State; and the sweets of peace, with the allurements of British commerce, would probably have woven a connection with Great Britain, fatal in its consequences to the independence of the Southern States." Thus early, if we may believe Lee, was the germ of "Secession," — thus early the germ of the war which is now waged against a government so gentle, so motherly even, as never to have roughly, unjustly touched the hair of a cotton-planter's head.

Georgia, the remaining Colony, was in its infancy, and Oglethorpe, its founder, lived until after it became an independent State. The designs of himself and his associates in its settlement, were highly benevolent and generous; and the public purse contributed a considerable sum to aid their undertaking. By their charter, the king was to model the government at the end of twenty-one years; and accordingly, in 1752, at the expiration of this period, a royal government was established similar to that in the Carolinas, which existed until the Revolution. Georgia sent no delegates to the first Continental Congress; and that she was represented in the second, was owing, I am led to conclude, principally to the zeal and exertions of Lyman Hall, a native of Connecticut, who, having graduated at Yale College and fitted himself for the practice of medicine, removed to Sunbury. His ardor in the Whig cause exposed him to the indignation of his opponents, and after the royal army penetrated Georgia, his property was seized and confiscated. The Rev. Dr. Zubly, another of the delegates, proved himself unworthy of confidence, and lost his estate at the hands of his former friends and associates. To form a party of "liberty-men" within the borders of Georgia, to organize this party and commit it in favor of the "rebellion," which was fast hastening to "treason" and Revolution in other parts of the continent, was attended with difficulty, and required time and labor. But such a party finally existed and acted; and the AMERICAN CONFEDERACY was thus completed.

Though overrun by the king's troops, and governed by military law during a considerable part of the war, Georgia overpaid her quota of money in a small sum, and furnished 2,679 men for the Continental service. If, then, it be considered, that her population was small, her resources limited; that Sir James Wright, the last royal governor, was an able and popular man, and rallied a considerable body of Loyalists; and that, in the course of events, the Whigs were compelled to flee into the neighboring States for safety, — her efforts and sacrifices are entitled to commendation.[1]

From this rapid survey of the Thirteen Colonies, it has appeared that the adherents of the crown were

---

[1] Georgia was, however, regarded as highly loyal. One of the ablest and best informed of the Loyalists, thus speaks. "Georgia had not only been recovered out of the hands of the insurgents, in 1779, but the province was put at the peace of the king by his Majesty's Commissioners, and the king's civil government restored, and all the loyal inhabitants required by proclamation to return to their settlements, and an Assembly called, and actually subsisting, and all the civil officers in the exercise of their functions, when orders came in 1782, to evacuate the country, and deliver it up to the rebels, which was done accordingly, without any stipulation in favor of the attainted Loyalists, or their confiscated properties, although the rebel force in that country was so inconsiderable, that the *Loyalists offered to the king's general to preserve the province for his Majesty, if he would leave them a single regiment of foot, and the ' Georgia Rangers,' to assist them.*"

more numerous at the South, and in Pennsylvania and New York, than in New England. Neither in the regulations of the crown, nor in the enactments of parliament, had there been much either to offend the feelings or check the industry of the planters and agriculturists. Towards the Colonies that sold raw produce, the policy of the mother country had been mild, perhaps liberal. They were the Round-heads, and not the Cavaliers, who met her upon the ocean and in the workshop; hence, it was to them that she showed the most odious features of the Colonial system. But taunted, for a century and a half, with the heresy of their faith, and impeded in all their enterprises ever after the death of Cromwell, the people of the North were driven to invoke the sympathy of their Colonial brethren whose religion and pursuits had been the more favored objects of her regard; and when their joint appeals to her justice and magnanimity failed to shake her purposes, then, by the union of counsel, arms, and effort, all the Colonies together broke from her dominion. If, therefore, the war of the Revolution had its origin in a long course of aggression upon the rights of the North, its successful issue was due in some measure to the more meritorious, because more disinterested, exertions of the South. If, too, this course of aggression gradually diffused a spirit of resistance throughout the country, so that Episcopal and monarchical Virginia at last furnished a commander for the Puritan and Republican soldiers of Massachusetts, the conclusion becomes irresistible, that the wrongs which united men of so different characters and pursuits, were far too deep and grave to be excused or extenuated.

The examination, now completed, of the political condition of the Colonies, and of the state of parties, leads to the conclusion that the number of our countrymen who wished to continue their connection with the mother country was very large. In nearly every Loyalist letter or other paper which I have examined, and in which the subject is mentioned, it is either assumed or stated in terms, that the *loyal were the majority;* and this opinion, I am satisfied, was very generally entertained by those who professed to have a knowledge of public sentiment. That the adherents of the crown were mistaken, in this particular, is certain.

CHAPTER V.

Newspapers in the Thirteen Colonies. Political Writers, Whig and Loyalist, North and South. Seminaries of Learning. Condition of the Press, &c., at the Revolutionary Era. Means for diffusing Knowledge limited.

OF the thirty-seven newspapers which were published in the Colonies, in April, 1775, if the result of my inquiries be correct, seven or eight were in the interest of the crown, and twenty-three were devoted to the service of the Whigs. Of these thirty-seven, however, one on each side had little or no part in discussing the great questions at issue, as they were established only in the preceding month of January; and of those which did participate in these discussions and maintain the right, no less than five went over to the Loyalists in the course of the war. Of the number first named, two were printed in German, and one in German and English; and, as another of the thirty-seven was commenced in April, there were, in fact, but thirty-one newspapers in the vernacular tongue at the close of 1774. Up to the beginning of the strife, printing had been confined to the capitals or principal towns; but hostile deeds, interfering with all employments, caused the removal of some of the public journals to places more remote, and were the means of interrupting or wholly discontinuing the publication of others. Those that existed at the period of which we are speaking, were very unequally distributed; thus Maryland, Virginia, the two Carolinas, and Georgia, taken together, had but one more than Pennsylvania, and but three more than Massachusetts. In New Hampshire, the "Gazette" was alone; while Rhode Island had both a "Gazette" and a "Mercury." Of the editors and proprietors who originally opposed the right, or became converts to the wrong, several sought refuge in Nova Scotia and New Brunswick, where they established newspapers, which were the first published in these Colonies.

From what has now been said, it is evident that a very considerable proportion of the professional and editorial intelligence and talents of the Thirteen Colonies was arrayed against the popular movement. This volume contains notices of more than two hundred persons who were educated at Harvard College, or some other American or foreign institution of learning; and could the whole number of Loyalists who received college honors be ascertained, it would be found, probably, that the list is far from being complete. It was alleged, however, by a distinguished adherent of the crown in New Jersey, that "most of the colleges had been the grand nurseries of the rebellion;" and, in a plan which he submitted for the government of the Colonies after the suppression of the revolt, he proposed to check their pernicious influence by introducing several reforms. But if, in connection with the facts above named, it be considered that, in 1761, there were but six colleges in America, and only nine at the commencement of hostilities, we shall hardly find reason to believe that the loyal had cause to complain of them. It is said, on what appears to be good authority, that, as late as 1746, there were but fifteen liberally educated persons in the whole Colony of New York. The increase between that period and the Revolution could not have been very considerable; and, of the number named, several were alive in 1776, and belonged to the ministerial party. But whatever was the relative strength of the two parties in the single particular of graduates of colleges, the Whigs far exceeded their opponents in effective writers. Among the newspaper essayists in Massachusetts, on the royal side, were Joseph Green, a wag and a wit; Samuel Waterhouse, an officer of the customs, who was stigmatized as the "most notorious scribbler and libeller" of the time; Lieutenant-Governor Oliver; Jonathan Sewall; and Daniel Leonard. The last wrote a series of papers entitled "Massachusettensis," and had John Adams for his antagonist, over the signature of "Nov-Anglus." Mr. Adams attributed these papers to his friend Sewall; but the fact that Leonard was the author is now well established. None of these "government-men" were so effective, as popular writers, as Samuel Adams, and his single pen was probably a match for them all. Hutchinson was so annoyed by his peculiar tact, and his power to agitate and move the public mind, as to declare that, of all persons known to him, he was the most successful " in robbing men of their characters." But, besides the two Adamses, James Otis was the author of four political tracts, and Oxenbridge Thacher, Chauncy, and Cooper were continually transmitting their thoughts in popular forms; while Josiah Quincy, junior, often gave his countrymen the effusions of his rich, pure, and classical mind, and his "Observations on the Boston Port Bill" is to be regarded not only as a clear and cogent political essay, but as a finished specimen of the literature of the period.

Among the Loyalists of New York who contributed to the press, were the Rev. Samuel Chandler, the Rev. John Vardill, and Isaac Wilkins. The opponent of the latter was the youthful Hamilton.[1] In the South, I am disposed to conclude that the crown commanded no writer of ability except Daniel Dulany, the attorney-general of Maryland, who was in the field against Charles Carroll. I know of no ministerial writer in Virginia. Those on the Whig side were, it is believed, limited to three; namely, Jefferson, Richard Bland, and Arthur Lee. Some of the popular leaders in the planting Colonies conducted an extensive correspondence, but others seem to have been almost silent. It is somewhat remarkable, that the only editor and best biographer of Washington found, or has preserved, but three letters in which the disputes that agitated the country are incidentally mentioned; and but three others in which the subjects in controversy are fully and explicitly discussed. At the North it was essentially different, and the letters of Massachusetts-Whigs contain full and valuable materials for history.

In concluding the topic, it may be remarked; that, while the number of the highest seminaries of learning was small, the other means of disseminating

---

[1] Hamilton's own sympathies were at first on the royal side, as he himself admits in his reply to Wilkins; and his biographer relates that a visit to Boston changed the current of his thoughts; I may add,—the whole course of his life

knowledge were extremely limited. It suited the views of the mother country to keep the Colonial press shackled; and it seems hardly credible that the accomplished Addison, when a minister of state, should have directed the governors in America to allow of no publications and of no printing, without license. For a considerable period the most rigid censorship prevailed in the Colonies, and even almanacs were subject to examination.[1] The result of this state of things was, that, prior to the Revolution, most of the books were imported from England. As in

[1] In 1719 it was deemed necessary to obtain a license from Governor Shute, to publish a pamphlet upon the very harmless subject of providing Boston with market-houses, of which the town was then destitute The pulpit was, however, free, and Dr. Colman preached a sermon the same year on " the reasons for a market in Boston." Censorship of the newspapers, at this period, continued to be enforced so rigidly that, four years after, matter intended for publication in them was required to be examined by the Colonial Secretary. Though no particular officer may have been charged with the duty of supervision later than the year 1730, a publisher was sent to prison in 1754, upon suspicion of having printed remarks derogatory to some members of the Colonial government.

It may not be without interest to show what was thought of the freedom of the newspaper press fifty years ago. In February, 1812, the attorney-general and solicitor-general of Massachusetts state, in an official report to Governor Gerry, that, in their judgment, there had appeared in the Boston papers, since the preceding first of June, no less *than two hundred and fifty-three libellous articles,* to wit: in *The Scourge,* ninety-nine ; *The Centinel,* fifty-one ; *The Repertory,* thirty-four ; *The Gazette,* thirty-eight ; *The Palladium,* eighteen ; *The Messenger,* one ; *The Chronicle,* eight; and *The Patriot,* nine ; while in *The Yankee* there had been none. The report gives the dates of the papers, and divides the libellous matter into two kinds: that in which the truth *could* be, and that in which it *could not* be, given in evidence to justify the party accused These law-officers state, moreover, that their examinations had not embraced complete files of all these prints; and that they had not included in their list calumnious publications against foreign governments or distinguished foreigners, nor libels of the editorial brethren against each other. It appears that the inquiry was instituted at his Excellency's request.

other respects, however, the statute-book was sometimes disobeyed while this system was in force, and works were published which bore the English imprint, and which closely resembled the English copies used in the publication. Besides, provision for educating the people was seldom made, and reading and writing in some sections of the country were " rare accomplishments." The system of free-schools in New England, of schools to be ordained and continually maintained by law, was established at an early period; but in Virginia, it is believed education was never a subject of legislation, during the whole course of her Colonial existence.

CHAPTER VI.

Political Divisions in Colonial Society. Most of those in Office adhered to the Crown. Charge of the Loyalists that the Whigs were mere needy Place-Hunters, answered. Loyalist Clergymen, Lawyers, and Physicians.

WE enter now upon a brief inquiry to show the divisions in the different classes and avocations of Colonial society. And first, those who held office. Nearly all the officials of all grades adhered to the crown. This was to have been expected. Men who lived in ease, who enjoyed all the consideration and deference which rank and station invariably confer, especially in monarchies, and who, therefore, had nothing to gain, but much to lose, by a change, viewed the dissensions that arose between themselves and the people, in a light which allowed their self-love and their self-interest to have full play. "They were appointed and sworn to execute the laws, and, in obeying the instructions of the ministry at home to enforce the statutes of the realm, they did but perform common acts of duty." These were the arguments, and they were neither the first nor the last persons in office who have reasoned in the same manner, and who have kept their places at the expense of their patriotism. Besides, they affected to believe that the Whig leaders were mere needy office-hunters, and that the contests between them were in some measure personal. The descendants of Loyalists, whose homes are across our northeastern border, in conversations with citizens of the republic continue to repeat the tale. They have been answered, that, were the charge true, *our* fathers were still the more patriotic of the two; since, upon this issue, it would seem that *theirs*, who were the fat and sleek possessors, would not give up the much-coveted stations to the lean and hungry expectants and claimants, even to preserve the British empire from dismemberment. It has been said, too, that if it be admitted that the younger Otis actually did vow he would set Massachusetts in flames, though he should perish in the fire, because his father was not appointed to a vacant and promised judgeship; that, as has been alleged, John Adams was at a loss which side to take, and became a "rebel" because he was refused a commission in the peace; that Samuel Adams was a defaulting collector of taxes, and paid up his arrears of money in abuse of honest men; that, as his enemies say, Hancock possessed neither stability nor principle, and that wounded vanity caused his opposition to the king's servants; that Joseph Warren was a broken man, and sought, amid the turmoils of civic strife, to better his condition; that Washington was soured because he was not retained in the British army, in reward for his services in the French war; that the Lees were all unsound men, and that Richard Henry was disappointed in not receiving the office of stamp distributor, which he solicited; that Franklin was vexed at the opposition to his great land-projects and plans for settlements on the Ohio; and that a large majority of the prominent Whigs of every Colony were young men who had their fortunes to make, and distinction to win,—that, if all this be admitted, what then? The argument is as two-edged as the first, and, though it be granted that one side of the blade wounds the Whigs, the other still cuts deep the Tories. For, upon this ground it may be asked, what claim to perpetuity had the institutions which denied to a man like John Adams the humble place of a justice of the peace; and to George Washington, an opportunity to display *his* qualities of character on the great field which the Being who made him intended for him? And if the thought ever obtruded itself upon John Marshall, that, by living and dying a Colonist, he should live and die undistinguished and without leaving his name in his country's annals, I know not that the emotion was blamable. The destiny marked out for *him*, was to found the jurisprudence of a NATION; and has the world been the loser because he fulfilled it?

The children of the Loyalists, though thus met, complain because the offices, at the close of the conflict, passed from the "old families" into the hands of "upstarts." It has been replied to this, that, revolution or no revolution, it was high time the persons stigmatized as "upstarts" had a share of the royal patronage: first, to break up the practice of bestowing upon the son, however unworthy or incompetent, the place held by the father; and, secondly, to introduce faithfulness and responsibility, and to dismiss arrogant and disobliging incumbents.

The allegations thus noticed are proved, as those who make them sagely imagine, by the fact that the Whigs, at the peace, received the executive chairs of the several States, the judgeships, the collectorships, the great law-offices, and other public situations, previously held by their opponents. This argument is sufficient to disturb the gravity of a man who never smiled in his life; and yet it is sometimes soberly urged by the intelligent and well informed, and enforced in strong and impassioned tones.

But, it is time to inquire, what became of the office-holders whom the Revolution expelled? Did they, did the adherents of the crown, generally, evince an unconquerable aversion to public employment, after their retirement or banishment from the United States? The answer to these questions will be found in these pages. It will be seen, that they not only filled all the principal offices in the present British Colonies, but that their places descended to their sons, connections, and relatives. In no point of view, then, are the Loyalists entitled to become the accusers of the Whigs; since it is the innocent only who can properly cast stones at the offending or the faulty. Nor is it to be overlooked, that offices under the British crown are, in many respects, of the nature of life-estates or life-annuities; since the practice which prevailed in the "old thirteen," of perpetuating official distinctions in families, still continues to a very great extent, and since, too, while places are not thus lost and won at every turn of the political wheel as with us, the salaries, fees, and emoluments are much greater than are paid either under our state or national governments. Instead, therefore, of our being compelled to defend the Whigs against the charge of undue or of improper love of office, the Loyalists, and those of their descendants who repeat their fathers' accusations, are to be turned upon in quiet good nature, and *to be put upon their own defence.*

Our attention, now, will be directed to the professional classes. It has often been asserted that nearly all the clergy were Whigs. The truth of this may admit of a doubt; since most of those of the Episcopal faith not only espoused the adverse side, but abandoned their flocks and the country. I need not say, that, at the period of the Revolution, the clergy possessed vast influence. In the early settlement of the country, as is well known, the duty of the ministers was not confined to instructions in things spiritual, but embraced matters of temporal concern; and, on questions of pressing public exigency, their counsel and advice were eagerly sought and implicitly followed. This deference to their office and to their real or supposed wisdom, though less general than at former periods, had not ceased; and clergymen, both Whigs and Tories, often made a recruiting house of the sanctuary. Some of those of both parties disregarded the obligations of Christian charity, and sacrificed their kindly affections as men, in their earnest appeals from the pulpit. Generally, the minister and his people were of the same party; but there were still some memorable divisions and quarrels, separations, and dismissions.

We pass to members of the bar. I incline to believe that a majority of the lawyers were Whigs, and for several reasons. First, because in the course of my researches I have found but comparatively few who adhered to the crown; secondly, because of the well-known fact, that a large part of the speakers and advocates on the popular side were educated to the law; and, thirdly, because one of the objects of the "Stamp Act" was to drive from the profession those members of it who annoyed the royal governors and other officials, and who, as a member of the House of Commons said, were mere "pettifoggers." Besides, many gentlemen of the bar, on being retained by the merchants, became impressed with the enormities of the commercial code, and, in advocating the cause of clients who claimed to continue their contraband trade on the ground of usage and prescription, they were impelled to follow the example of Otis, and to take the lofty stand that commerce should be, and, on principles of justice, really was, as open and as free to British subjects in the New World, as it was to those in the Old.

Still, the ministry had their partisans among the barristers-at-law, and some of them were persons of great professional eminence. In fact, the "giants of the law" in the Colonies were nearly all Loyalists. As in the case of the clergy, many of them were driven into exile. Several entered the military service of the crown, and raised and commanded companies, battalions, and even regiments. At the peace, a few returned to their former abodes and pursuits; but the greater number passed the remainder of their lives either in England, or in her present possessions in America. The anti-revolutionary bar of Massachusetts and New York furnished the admiralty and common-law courts of New Brunswick, Nova Scotia, Canada, and the Bermudas, with many of their most distinguished judges.

The physicians who adhered to the crown were numerous, and the proportion of Whigs in the profession of medicine was less, probably, than in either that of law or theology. But, unlike persons of the latter callings, most of the physicians remained in the country, and quietly pursued their business. There seems to have been an understanding that, though pulpits should be closed, and litigation be suspended, the sick should not be deprived of their regular and freely chosen medical attendants. I have been surprised to find, from verbal communications and from various other sources, that, while the "Tory doctors" were as zealous and as fearless in the expression of their sentiments as "Tory ministers" and "Tory barristers," their persons and property were generally respected in the towns and villages, where little or no regard was paid to the bodies and estates of gentlemen of the robe and the surplice.[1] Some, however, were less fortunate, and the dealings of the "sons of liberty" were occasionally harsh and exceedingly vexatious. A few of the Loyalist physicians were banished; others, and those chiefly who became surgeons in the army or provincial corps, settled in New Brunswick or Nova Scotia, where they resumed practice.

[1] Since writing this passage, I have met more than once with the suggestion, that the physicians owed their safety to "the exigencies of the ladies."

CHAPTER VII.

The Reasons given for Adherence to the Crown. The Published Declarations of the Whigs that they wished for a Redress of Wrongs and the Restoration of Ancient Privileges, as found in "Noyanglus." Rapid Statement of Colonial Disabilities, which the Whig Leaders hardly mentioned in the Controversy, and which appear embodied for the first time in the Declaration of Independence. Denials of Whig Leaders, North and South, that they designed at the Beginning of the Controversy to separate from England. Reasons of the Loyalists for the Course adopted by them, Concluded.

The concluding number of "Novanglus," by John Adams, was sent to press only two days before the shedding of blood at Lexington, and we are to consider it as an authorized exposition of the avowed sentiments of the Whig leaders. But yet, its aim is limited to a degree that has often caused me to muse, and to ask, — Why were discussions on the subject of Colonial inabilities so carefully avoided?

The private and the professional life of Mr. Adams afford us a fair illustration of these disabilities; and why did he not once mention them?

If his horse flung a shoe, the stinging, insulting declaration of Pitt, that an American could not, of right, make so much as the nails required to set it, rung in his ears. If he entered the Court of Admiralty to defend the "smugglers," or illicit traders, who were prosecuted by the Crown officers, he was reminded that his countrymen were forbidden by statute to make a voyage to Asia or Africa, to South America, to all the foreign islands in the Caribbean Sea, to nearly all continental Europe, or even to Ireland, on pain of confiscation of ship and cargo. If he bought a hat, the legislation against Colonial, and in favor of British, hatters, occurred to him. If, in journeying to the courts of Massachusetts and Maine, he passed waterfalls running to waste, he mused upon the acts of Parliament which secured the Colonial market in monopoly to the manufacturers of Manchester. If he entered a public office, he met the pampered functionaries who, "English born," or members of the "old families," held their places by life tenures, and by descent from father to son. If he walked the streets, the chariots of the high officers of the customs, sent over to revive obsolete, and to enforce new, laws of trade, rolled in grandeur by him. If he had traffic with his neighbor, he was compelled to remember that, while the mother-country drained all America of coin, the Board of Trade — a curse to the New England Colonies from beginning to end — had suggested, and Parliament had enacted, not amendments in the manner of emitting and redeeming a paper currency, as bound to do, but its suppression. Nor, if he read the speeches of British Whigs, did his keen eye see more in behalf of his country than an opposition to particular measures, and to the party in power; for there stood out in characters of fire, the bold, unqualified statement of Burke, that the sole purpose of Colonies was to be "serviceable" to the parent State. In a word, with him, and everywhere around him, were the humiliating evidences that an American was, politically, socially, and commercially, the inferior of an Englishman.

If neither the author of "Novanglus" nor any other Whig addressed the American people on these momentous wrongs and denials, which, for generations had palsied the arm of New England and had rankled in the universal American heart, and which, in less than fifteen months, were embodied — in stirring array — in the Declaration of Separation, the Loyalists are to be excused for acting in conformity with the grievances stated by their opponents.

The denial that independence was the final object, was constant and general. To obtain concessions and to preserve the connection with England, was affirmed everywhere; and John Adams, years after the peace, went farther than this, for he said: — "*There was not a moment during the Revolution, when I would not have given everything I possessed for a restoration to the state of things before the contest began, provided we could have had a sufficient security for its continuance.*" If Mr. Adams be regarded as expressing the sentiments of the Whigs, *they* were willing to remain Colonists, provided they could have had their rights secured to them; while the Tories were contented thus to continue, *without* such security. Such, as it appears to me, was the only difference between the two parties *prior* to hostilities; and many Whigs, like Mr. Adams, would have been willing to rescind the Declaration of Independence, and to forget the past, upon proper guarantees for the future. This mode of stating the question, and of defining the difference between the two parties — down to a certain period, at least — cannot be objected to, unless the sincerity and truthfulness of some of the most eminent men in our history are directly impeached; and, if any are prepared to dispute their veracity, it may still be asked, whether *the Tories ought not to be excused for believing* them. Franklin's testimony, a *few days before* the affair at Lexington, was, that he had "more than once travelled almost from one end of the continent to the other, and kept a variety of company, eating, drinking, and conversing with them freely, [and] *never had heard in any conversation from any person, drunk or sober, the least expression of a wish for a separation, or a hint that such a thing would be advantageous to America.*" Mr. Jay is quite as explicit. "During the course of my life," said he, "and until the second petition of Congress in 1775, *I never did hear an American of any class, or of any description, express a wish for the independence of the Colonies.*" "It has always been, and still is, my opinion and belief, that our country was prompted and impelled to independence by *necessity*, and not by *choice.*" Mr. Jefferson affirmed, "What, eastward of New York, might have been the dispositions towards England before the commencement of hostilities, I know not; but *before that* I never heard a whisper of a disposition to separate from Great Britain; *and after that, its possibility was contemplated with affliction by all.*" Washington, in 1774, fully sustains these declarations, and, in the "Fairfax County Resolves," it was complained, that "*malevolent falsehoods*" were propagated by the ministry to prejudice the mind of the king: "*particularly that there is an intention in the American Colonies to set up for independent States.*" Mr. Madison was not in public life until May, 1776, but he says, "It has always been my impression, that a *reëstablishment of* *the Colonial relations to the parent country, as they were previous to the controversy,* was the *real* object of *every* class of the people, till the despair of obtaining it,"* &c.[1]

I have to repeat, that the only way to dispose of testimony like this, is to impeach the persons who have given it. I am of Whig descent, and am proud of my lineage. With the principles of men who, when it was ascertained that a redress of grievances could *not* be obtained, preferred to remain British subjects, I have neither communion nor sympathy; and I may be pardoned for adding that I have watched the operations and tendencies of the Colonial system of government too long and too narrowly, modified as it now is, not to entertain for it the heartiest dislike. Yet I would do the men who were born under it, and were reconciled to it, justice — simple justice; and if, as Mr. Jefferson says, a "*possibility*" of the necessity of a separation of the two countries, "was contemplated with *affliction by all,*" and if the statements made by Franklin, Adams, Jay, Madison, and Washington, are to be considered as true and as decisive, I renewedly ask, what other line of difference existed between the Whigs and Tories, than the *terms on which the connection of the Colonies with England should be continued.*

My object in the attention bestowed on this point has been to remove the erroneous impression which seems to prevail, that the Whigs *proposed,* and the Tories *opposed* independence, at the very beginning of the controversy. Instead of this, we have seen,

[1] See Sparks' *Washington,* Vol II. pp. 498, 500, 501. The italics are my own, except in the extract from the "Fairfax County Resolves"

that quite fourteen years elapsed before the question was made a party issue, and that, even then, "necessity," and not "choice," caused a dismemberment of the empire. Since it has appeared, therefore, from the highest sources, that the Whigs resolved finally upon revolution because they were denied the rights of Englishmen, and not because they disliked monarchical institutions, the Tories may be relieved from the imputation of being the only "monarchy-men" of the time.

Again, and to conclude : Intelligent loyalists, when asked why they adhered to the Crown, have said, that those who received the name of "Tories" were at first, indeed for some years, striving to preserve order and an observance of the rights of persons and property; that many, who took sides at the outset as mere conservators of the peace, were denounced by those whose purposes they thwarted, and were finally compelled, in pure self-defence, to accept of royal protection, and thus to become identified with the royal party ever after. Again, it has been stated, that, had the naked question of independence been discussed before, minor, and in many cases, local, events had shaped their course, many, who were driven forth to live and die as aliens and outcasts, would have terminated their career far differently; that many were opposed to war on grounds purely religious; that some thought the people enjoyed privileges enough; that others were influenced by their official connections or aspirations; that another class, who seldom mingled in the affairs of active life, loved retirement, and would, had the Whigs allowed them, have remained neutrals; that some were timid men, some were old men; and that tenants and dependents went with the landholders without inquiry, and as a thing of course. All of these reasons, and numerous others, have been assigned at different times, and by different persons. But another cause, quite as potent as any of these, operated, it would seem, upon thousands; namely, a dread of the strength and resources of England, and the belief that successful resistance to her power was impossible; that the Colonies had neither the men nor the means to carry on war, and would be humbled and reduced to submission with hardly an effort.

That motives and considerations, hopes and fears, like these, had an influence in the formation of the *last* Colonial parties, cannot be disputed, and the unprejudiced minds of this generation should be frank enough to admit it.

CHAPTER VIII.

Loyalists who entered the Military Service of the Crown.

As I have preferred connection of subject to mere chronological order, some of the details belonging to this branch of our inquiry have been given, in order to complete the questions already discussed.

We are now to speak of the Loyalists who opposed the Whigs in the field. Upon this topic, our writers of history have been almost silent; and it is not impossible that some persons have read books devoted exclusively to an account of the Revolution, without so much as imagining that a part, and a considerable part, of the force employed to suppress the "rebellion" was composed of our own countrymen. The two wars between England and France, which immediately preceded the revolt of the Colonies, were caused principally by disputes about rights of fishing, and by unsettled questions of maritime and territorial jurisdiction in America; and in these wars the American people had taken a distinguished part. In fact, in aiding to put down French pretensions, our fathers acquired the skill necessary to the successful assertion of their own.

The age was decidedly military. Office in the militia was even a qualification for civil employments. The number of colonels, majors, and captains that appear as members of the colonial assemblies, and, subsequently, of provincial congresses, startles us. The quarrels about rank in the Congress of the continent disgust us.

And of what account the newspaper essays and letters of Samuel Adams and others? the eloquent appeals in Fanueil Hall, and in the House of Burgesses of Virginia? What of the success of the revolutionary movement everywhere, but for the military skill and experience acquired in the seven-years' war with France? The Colonies furnished in that war quite twenty-eight thousand men in more than one of the campaigns, and every year to the extent of their ability.

In fine, it is literally true that, for years together, more troops, in proportion to population, were raised in America than in England; while, on the ocean, full twelve thousand seamen were enlisted in the royal navy and in the Colonial privateers. Without the aid of the survivors of these, resistance, or the thought of it, would have been downright madness. And the unanimity and alacrity with which those who had fought at Ticonderoga, Crown Point, du Quesne, Niagara, and Quebec, espoused the popular cause at first, and rallied under the Whig banner in the last resort, was one of the most honorable incidents of the era.

But, on the other hand, several officers of merit, and some of very considerable military talents, adhered to the royal side.

It may not be possible to ascertain the number of the Loyalists who took up arms, but, from the best evidence which I have been able to obtain, I conclude there were twenty-five thousand at the lowest computation; and, unless their killed and wounded in the different battles and affrays in which they were engaged were unusually large, I have put their aggregate force far too low. Thus, in the fight at Bennington, or, more properly, Hoosick; in the enterprise of Sullivan at Staten Island; in the adventure of Nelson at New Jersey; in the affray of Pickens with a band of Tories who were on their way to the British camp in Georgia; in the battle of King's Mountain; in four actions of Colonel Washington, Marion, Lee, and Sumter, the aggregate of slain, wounded, and prisoners, was upwards of twenty-three hundred, or nearly a tenth part of my estimate. That, in the various conflicts of the illustrious commander-in-chief; in those of Greene, Lincoln, and Gates, in the South; in the rencounters of Marion, Lee, and Sumter, not mentioned above; in the losses of Tryon, Simcoe, De Lancey, Johnson, and Arnold; in their various actions with the Whig forces or hastily assembled neighborhoods; in the strifes between Whigs and Tories, hand to hand, and in cases where neither had authorized or commissioned leaders, another tenth part of twenty-five thousand met with a similar fate is nearly certain. At the time of Cornwallis's surrender, a portion of his army was composed of native Americans, and his Lordship evinced great anxiety for their protection. Failing to obtain special terms for them in the articles of capitulation, he availed himself of the conceded privilege of sending an armed ship northerly, without molestation, to convey away the most obnoxious among them. Burgoyne had been spared this trouble; for, as his difficulties had increased and his dangers thickened, the Loyalists had abandoned him to his fate.

And yet again : In an address of the Loyalists who were in London in 1779, presented to the king, it is said that their countrymen, then in his Majesty's army, "*exceeded in number the troops enlisted* [by. Congress] *to oppose them*," exclusive of those who were "in service in private ships of war." In a similar document, dated in 1782, and which was addressed to the king and both houses of Parliament, the same declaration is repeated, though in stronger terms, since the language is, that "there are *many* more men in his Majesty's provincial regiments than there are in the continental service." These last addresses declare, moreover, that "the zeal" of the Loyalists must be greater than that of the "rebels;" for "the desultory manner in which the war has been carried on by first taking possession of Boston, Rhode Island, Philadelphia, Portsmouth, and Norfolk in Virginia, and Wilmington in North Carolina, and then evacuating them;" had ruined thousands, and involved others in the greatest wretchedness, and had rendered enlistments tardy under "such" discouragements and "very unequal circumstances." The descendants of Loyalist officers who entered the military service early in the struggle, and continued in commission until its close, entertain the general views expressed in these extracts; and the opinion that Americans in the pay of the crown were *quite* as numerous as those who entered the army of Congress, is very commonly held by persons with whom I have conversed. Still, I doubt whether either the written or verbal statements are to be relied on implicitly, and for the reason, that, in the former, I am sure there are exaggerations on other subjects, and the latter rest on the assertions of men who were equally ready to attribute the success of the Whigs and their own ruin to the inefficiency and bad management of Sir William Howe and other royal generals. The names of these various corps,[1] and the names of hundreds of officers who were attached to them, will be found in these volumes. The impression that the revolutionary con-

[1] The King's Rangers; the Royal Fencible Americans; the Queen's Rangers; the New York Volunteers; the King's American Regiment; the Prince of Wales's American Volunteers; the Maryland Loyalists; De Lancey's Battalions; the Second American Regiment; the King's Rangers Carolina; the South Carolina Royalists; the North Carolina Highland Regiment; the King's American Dragoons; the Loyal American Regiment; the American Legion; the New Jersey Volunteers; the British Legion; the Loyal Foresters; the Orange Rangers; the Pennsylvania Loyalists; the Guides and Pioneers; the North Carolina Volunteers; the Georgia Loyalists; the West Chester Volunteers. These corps were all commanded by colonels or lieutenant-colonels; and, as De Lancey's Battalions and the New Jersey Volunteers consisted each of three battalions, here were twenty-eight. To these, the Loyal New Englanders, the Associated Loyalists, and Wentworth's Volunteers, remain to be added. Still further, Col. Archibald Hamilton, of New York, commanded at one period seventeen companies of loyal militia.

Again, at different periods, several battalions were in the field at the South. The officers of twenty-one corps were considered entitled to half-pay, as will be seen by the proceedings in the House of Commons, June 27, 1783.

"The order of the day for going into a Committee of Supply being moved and carried, —

"Lord North rose to move that it be an instruction to the said Committee to receive and take into their consideration a proportion of half-pay to the officers of certain American corps, raised to serve in America during the late war. His Lordship said, that the half-pay for the whole of the officers of the twenty-one corps would amount to £31,783. 5s. 10d., but that he would, in the Committee, move only for £15,000 towards, and on account of, half-pay to these corps.

"The question was carried without a division. The House then went into the Committee of Supply, and voted the half-pay without any debate."

test should have terminated differently was very common, and in many it was very strong. That they — "the loyal, the true" — should have been the losers in the strife, and "the false and the rebellious" the winners; and that the former should have been driven from the country in which they were born, to commence life anew in unbroken forests, were circumstances over which they continually brooded, and to which they were never reconciled. They insisted, and those who have inherited their names and possessions, and many of their prejudices and opinions, still insist, that either Sir William Howe, or Sir Henry Clinton, his successor, could and should have quelled "the rebellion," and that the former, especially, is wholly inexcusable. If, by their course of reasoning, Sir William had occupied Dorchester Heights and the highlands of Charlestown, as a sagacious general would have done, and as his force and park of artillery allowed him to do, all the disasters to the royal arms which followed would have been prevented.

CHAPTER IX.

Whig Mobs before the Appeal to Arms, and tarring and feathering. Punishments of Loyalists during the War for overt Acts in favor of the Crown, and for speaking, writing, or acting against the Whigs Proscription, Banishment, and Confiscation Acts of the State Governments. The Laws which divested the Loyalists of their Estates examined.

WE pass to take a rapid view of the measures which were adopted by the Whigs to awe and to punish their adversaries. I find some things to condemn. And first, the "mobs," a large part of which were in Massachusetts. That a cause as righteous as men were ever engaged in lost many friends by the fearful outbreaks of popular indignation, is not to be doubted. The wise man of Israel said, " A brother offended is harder to be won than a strong city." Those who took upon themselves the sacred name of "Sons of Liberty," needlessly, and sometimes in their very wantonness, "offended," beyond all hope of recall, persons who hesitated and doubted, and who, for the moment, claimed to occupy the position of "neutrals." The practice of "tarring and feathering," however reprehensible, had, perhaps, but little influence in determining the final choice of parties. This form of punishment, though so frequent as to qualify the saying of the ancient, that man is a two-legged animal *without* feathers, was borrowed from the Old World, where it has existed since the Crusades;

and was confined principally to the obnoxious customhouse officers, pimps, and informers against smuggled goods, who adhered to the Crown.

But what " brother," upon whose vision the breaking up of the Colonial system and the sovereignty of America had not dawned, and who saw — as even the Whigs themselves saw — with the eyes only of a British subject, was won over to the right by the arguments of mobbing, burning, and smoking? Did the cause of America and of human freedom gain strength by the deeds of the five hundred who mobbed Sheriff Tyng, or by the speed of the one hundred and sixty on horseback who pursued Commissioner Hallowell? Were the shouts of an excited multitude, and the crash of broken glass and demolished furniture, fit requiems for the dying Ropes? Were Whig interests promoted because one thousand men shut up the Courts of Law in Berkshire, and five thousand did the same in Worcester, and mobs drove away the judges at Springfield, Taunton, and Plymouth? — because, in one place, a judge was stopped, insulted, and threatened; in another, the whole bench were hissed and hooted; and, in a third, were required to do penance, hat in hand, in a procession of attorneys and sheriffs? Did the driving of Ingersoll from his estate, of Edson from his house, and the assault upon the home of Gilbert, and the shivering of Sewall's windows, serve to wean them, or their friends and connections, from their royal master? Did Ruggles, when subsequent events threw his countrymen into his power, forget that the creatures which grazed his pastures had been painted, shorn, maimed, and poisoned; that he had been pursued on the highway by day and night; that his dwelling had been broken open, and he and his family driven from it? What Tory turned Whig because Saltonstall was mobbed, and Oliver plundered, and Leonard shot at in his own house?[1] Was the kingly arm actually weakened or strengthened for harm, because thousands surrounded the mansions of high functionaries, and forced them into resignation; or because sheriffs were told that they would perform their duties at the hazard of their lives? Which party gained by waylaying and insulting, at every corner, the " Rescinders," the " Protesters," and the "Addressers?" — which, by the burning of the mills of Putnam? Had widows and orphans no additional griefs, because the Probate Courts were closed by the multitude, and their officers were driven under cover of British guns? Did it serve a good end to endeavor to hinder Tories from getting tenants, or to prevent persons who owed them from paying honest debts? On whose cheek should have been the blush of shame, when the habitation of the aged and feeble Foster was sacked, and he had no shelter but the woods? — when Williams, as infirm as he, was seized at night, dragged away for miles, and smoked in a room with fastened doors and a closed chimney-top? What father, who doubted, wavered, and doubted still, whether to join or fly, determined to abide the issue in the land of his birth, because foul words were

[1] Many Loyalists *were* confined in private houses, some were sent to jails, and others to "Simsbury Mines." But the prisons were hardly proper places for the confinement of such people; and it is believed that a large proportion of the persons whom it was deemed proper to arrest preferred banishment to the loss of liberty, even though they were sure to be comfortably quartered in the families or houses of Whigs.

spoken to his daughters, or because they were pelted when riding, or moving in the innocent dance? Is there cause for wonder that some who still live should say, of their own or of their fathers' treatment, that "persecution made half of the king's friends?" The good men of the period mourned these and similar proceedings, and they may be lamented now. The warfare waged against persons at their own homes and about their lawful avocations is not to be justified; and the "mobs" of the Revolution are to be as severely and as unconditionally condemned as the "mobs" of the present day.

The acts of legislative bodies for the punishment of the adherents of the Crown were numerous. In Rhode Island, death and confiscation of estate were the penalties provided by law for any person who communicated with the ministry or their agents, or who afforded supplies to the forces, or piloted the armed ships of the king.

In Connecticut, the offences of supplying the royal army or navy, of giving them information, of enlisting or procuring others to enlist in them, and of piloting or assisting naval vessels, were punished more mildly, and involved only the loss of estate, and of personal liberty for a term not exceeding three years. To speak or write or act against the doings of Congress, or the Assembly of Connecticut, was punishable by disqualification for office, imprisonment, and the disarming of the offender.

In Massachusetts, a person suspected of enmity to the Whig cause could be arrested under a magistrate's warrant, and banished, unless he would swear fealty to the friends of liberty; and the selectmen of towns could prefer charges of political treachery in town-meeting, and the individual thus accused, if convicted by a jury, could be sent into the enemy's jurisdiction. Massachusetts also designated by name, and generally by occupation and residence, three hundred and eight of her people, of whom seventeen had been inhabitants of Maine, who had fled from their homes, and denounced against any one of them who should return, apprehension, imprisonment, and transportation to a place possessed by the British; and, for a second voluntary return, without leave, death, without benefit of clergy.

New Hampshire passed acts similar to these, under which seventy-six of her former citizens were prohibited from coming within her borders, and the estates of the most obnoxious were declared to be forfeited.

Virginia passed a resolution to the effect that persons of a given description should be deemed and treated as aliens, and that their property should be sold, and the proceeds go into the public treasury for future disposal; and also a law prohibiting the migration of certain persons to that Commonwealth, and providing penalties for the violation of its provisions.

In New York, the county committees were authorized to apprehend, and decide upon the guilt of such inhabitants as were supposed to hold correspondence with the enemy, or had committed some other specified act; and they might punish those whom they adjudged to be guilty with imprisonment for three months, or banishment. There, too, persons opposed to liberty and independence were prohibited from practising law in the courts; and the effects of fifty-nine persons, of whom three were women, and their rights of remainder and reversion, were to pass, by confiscation, from them to the "people."

In New Jersey, one act was passed to punish traitors and disaffected persons; another, for taking charge of and leasing the real estates, and for forfeiting the personal estates, of certain fugitives and offenders; a third, for forfeiting to and vesting in the State the real property of the persons designated in the second statute; and a fourth, supplemental to the act first mentioned.

In Pennsylvania, the number of persons who were attainted of treason to the State by special acts, or by proclamations of the President and Council, was nearly five hundred.

The act of Delaware provided that the property, both real and personal, of certain persons who were named, and who were forty-six in number, should be forfeited to the State, "subject nevertheless to the payment of the said offenders' just debts," unless, as in Pennsylvania, they gave themselves up to trial for the crime of treason in adhering to the royal cause.

Maryland seized, confiscated, and appropriated all property of persons in allegiance to the British crown, and appointed commissioners to carry out the terms of three statutes which were passed to effect these purposes.

In North Carolina, the confiscation act embraced sixty-five specified individuals and four mercantile firms; and, by its terms, not only included the "lands" of these persons and commercial houses, but their "negroes and other personal property."

The law of Georgia, which was enacted very near the close of the struggle, declared certain persons to have been guilty of treason against that State, and their estates to be forfeited for their offences.

South Carolina surpassed all other members of the Confederacy, Pennsylvania and Massachusetts excepted. The Loyalists, whose rights, persons, and property were affected by legislation, were divided into four classes. The persons who had offended the least, — who were forty-five in number, — were allowed to retain their estates, but were amerced twelve per cent. of their value. Soon after the fall of Charleston, and when disaffection to the Whig cause was so general, two hundred and ten persons, who styled themselves the "principal inhabitants" of the city, signed an address to Sir Henry Clinton, in which they state that they have every inducement to return to their allegiance, and ardently hope to be readmitted to the character and condition of British subjects. These "Addressers" formed another class. Of these two hundred and ten, sixty-three were banished, and lost their property by forfeiture, either for this offence or the graver one of affixing their names to a petition to the royal general, to be armed on the royal side. Eighty persons, composing another class, were also banished and divested of their estates, for the crime of holding civil or military commissions under the Crown, after the conquest of South Carolina. And the same penalties were inflicted upon thirteen others, who, on the success of Lord Cornwallis at Camden, presented his Lordship with their congratulations; and still fourteen others were banished, and deprived of their estates, because they were obnoxious.

In discussing the expediency and justice of the laws which drove or kept the Loyalists in exile, as well as those which alienated their estates, two points present themselves; namely, whether the Whigs were right in opposing the pretensions of England, and whether they did more than others have done in civil wars, — wars which are always the most bitter and unrelenting, — always the most obstinate and difficult to terminate. The question suggested by the first query is no longer open to dispute; for the mother-country has herself admitted that she was wrong in her treatment of the thirteen Colonies.

If, now, the Whigs were in the right, *they might do everything necessary to insure success;* and we are thus brought to the second point of inquiry. The question of the banishment of the Loyalists addresses itself to me in two forms: that of the *temporary* and that of the *permanent* exile of the men who suffered it. Among these men were many persons of great private worth, who, in adhering to the Crown, were governed by conscience and a stern regard to duty; and the offences of others consisted merely in a nominal attachment to the mother-country, or in a disinclination to witness or participate in the horrors of a civil war. Yet they *were* Loyalists; and it so happened that the *best* men of that party were, of all others, those who could do the Whigs the greatest mischief; since, if they remained at liberty, their character and moderation rendered their counsel and advice of vast service to their own, and of vast harm to the opposite party, amidst the doubts and fears which prevailed, and had a direct tendency to prolong and embitter the contest. It became *necessary*, therefore, to secure them either by imprisonment or by exile. The first course, while requiring a considerable force to guard them, which the Whigs could not spare, would have been far less *merciful* than the other, and banishment, consequently, was best for both parties. Again, a considerable proportion of those who were proscribed, voluntarily abandoned the country, and were absent from it at the passage of the banishment acts; and this was especially the case in Massachusetts. To prevent the return of these persons was as *necessary* to accomplish the objects of the struggle, as it was to secure those who remained at or in the neighborhood of their homes.

Still it may be wished that greater discrimination had been exercised in selecting those who were deemed fit objects of severity. Persons whose crimes against the country and against humanity deserved death, escaped the banishment acts of the States to which they belonged; while, on the other hand, these acts embraced persons who, from the circumstances of their condition, were utterly powerless, who had done, and could do, no evil. It may be wished, also, that those who were deemed fit objects of severity had been allowed the forms of trial. Courts of Admiralty were established for condemning prizes, and men might reasonably claim that, while their property was dealt with according to the established rules of society, their persons should not be more summarily disposed of. Means for the trial of Loyalists were abundant. It is our boast, indeed, that, unlike the usual course of things in civil war, civil government was maintained throughout the whole period of our Revolution, with hardly an interruption anywhere. This is a fact as honorable as it is remarkable. " I will maintain as long as I live," said Dupin, the great French advocate, " that the condemnation of Marshal Ney was not just, for his defence was not free." Perhaps posterity will entertain something of the same sentiment with regard to the course pursued by our fathers in not allowing their opponents an opportunity to appeal to the tribunals. In this particular, Pennsylvania and Delaware, as it will be remembered, adopted a mode less objectionable than that of some other States, inasmuch as they " summoned " the persons against whom they proceeded, to appear and " surrender themselves for trial." Besides, it was common, during the war, for the military commanders to order courts-martial to take cognizance of the offences, and to fix the punishment of Tories; and a future generation may possibly ask, why, when the sword was suspended amid the turmoils of the camp, to hear the defence of the accused, that weapon was so wielded in the hands of civilians as to " transform them into persecutors, and into martyrs those whom it smote."

The laws which divested the Loyalists of their estates demand a moment's examination. Keeping in view that the Whigs were *right* in resisting the pretensions of the mother-country, and that, therefore, they might very properly use *every necessary means to insure success*, we shall find no difficulty in admitting that the property of their opponents could be rightfully appropriated to aid in the prosecution of the war. They devoted their own fortunes, they importuned several of the powers of Europe for loans, and they entailed upon their posterity a large debt; and it would indeed be strange, if they could not have made forced levies upon the estates of those who not only refused to help them, but were actually in arms, or otherwise employed against them. To emancipate the American continent was a great work: the Whigs felt and knew, what is now everywhere conceded, that the work was both necessary and righteous; and requiring, as its speedy accomplishment did, the labor of every hand and contributions from every purse, the throwing into the treasury the jewels of women and the holiday allowances of children, they are to stand justified for a resort to the sequestration of the possessions of those who assisted in the vain endeavor to subdue them, and to renew the bonds which had bound them. The property of those who held commissions in the king's army and in the Loyalist corps was the property of enemies, and, as such, could be converted to public uses; while that of others, who made their election to accept of service in civil capacities, is to be regarded in the same light. The "Absentees," or those who retired from the country and lived abroad in privacy, were a different class; and it may be doubted whether the same rule was applicable to them, and whether fines or amercements were not the more proper modes of procedure against the estates which they abandoned in quitting the country. The Whigs assumed, however, that "every government hath a right to command the *personal* services of its own members, whenever the exigencies of the State shall require, especially in times of impending or actual invasion;"

and that "no member thereof can then withdraw himself from the jurisdiction of the government, without justly incurring the forfeiture of his property, rights, and liberties, holden under and derived from that constitution of government, to the support of which he hath refused his aid and assistance."

It is to be further urged in defence of the *principle* of confiscation, that in civil conflicts the right of one party to levy upon the other has been generally admitted; that the practice has frequently accorded with the theory; and, what is still more to the purpose, that the royal party and king's generals exercised that right during the struggle. Thus, then, the seizure and confiscation of property in the Revolution was not the act of one side merely, but of both.

But, as has been remarked, there was not with us, as there commonly has been in similar outbreaks, a *transition* period between the throwing off of one government and the establishment of another; and the regret that was expressed with regard to the indiscriminate banishment of persons, is equally applicable to the disposal of their estates; and I cannot but feel, that, inasmuch as the Whigs when compared with other revolutionists, "were without spot or wrinkle, or any such thing," so they will be held to a stricter accountability by those who shall hereafter speak of them; and that we shall be asked to show for them, why, with tribunals established and open for the trial of prizes made upon the sea, the fundamental rule of civilized society, that no person shall be deprived of "property but by the judgment of his peers," was violated; and why, without being "confronted by witnesses," and without the verdict of a "jury" and decrees of a court, any man in America was divested of his lands.

CHAPTER X.

The Course of the " Violent Whigs" towards the Loyalists, at the Peace, discussed and condemned.

AT the peace, *a majority* of the Whigs of several of the States committed a great crime. Instead of repealing the proscription and banishment acts, as justice and good policy required, they manifested a spirit to place the humbled and unhappy Loyalists beyond the pale of human sympathy. Discrimination between the conscientious and pure, and the unprincipled and corrupt, was not perhaps possible during the struggle; but, hostilities at an end, *mere loyalty should have been forgiven.* When, in the civil war between the Puritans and the Stuarts, the former gained the ascendency, and when, at a later period, the Commonwealth was established, Cromwell and his party wisely determined not to banish nor inflict disabilities on their opponents; and so, too, at the restoration of the monarchy, so general was the amnesty act in its provisions, that it was termed an act of oblivion to the *friends* of Charles, and of grateful remembrance to his *foes*.[1] The happy consequences which resulted from the conduct of *both* parties and in both cases, were before the men of their own

[1] At the restoration of Charles the Second, so general was the adhesion to that monarch, that historians pause to express wonder, and to inquire what had become of the Cromwell or Commonwealth men who had overturned the monarchy.

political and religious sympathies, the Puritans of the North, and the Cavaliers of the South, in America.

All honor to Theodore Sedgwick for staking his popularity in behalf of his countrymen who adhered to the Crown; to Nathaniel Greene, for the sentiment "that it would be the excess of intolerance to persecute men for opinions which, but twenty years before, had been the universal belief of every class of society;" to Alexander Hamilton, for his earnest and continued efforts to induce the Whigs to forget and forgive; to John Jay, for the letter in which he said that he "had no desire to conceal the opinion, that, to involve the Tories in indiscriminate punishment and ruin, would be an instance of unnecessary rigor and unmanly revenge without a parallel, except in the annals of religious rage in times of bigotry and blindness;" to James Iredell, for the "hearty wish that the termination of the war could have been followed with an oblivion of its offences;" to Christopher Gadsen and Francis Marion, who, with every personal reason to be inexorable, bravely contended for the restoration of the rights of their fallen, expatriated countrymen.

In North and South Carolina, the Whigs and Tories waged a war of extermination. Seldom enough did either party meet in open and fair fight, and give and take the courtesies and observe the rules of civilized warfare. But these States, at the peace, exceeded all the rest in moderation and mercy. On the other hand, Massachusetts, Virginia, and New York adopted measures of inexcusable severity. In the latter State, such was the violence manifested, that, in August, 1783, Sir Guy Carleton wrote to the

President of Congress that the Loyalists "conceive the safety of their lives depends on my removing them;" that, "as the daily gazettes and publications furnish repeated proofs, not only of a disregard to the articles of peace, but barbarous menaces from committees formed in various towns, cities, and districts, and even at Philadelphia, — the very place which the Congress had chosen for their residence,— I should show an indifference to the feelings of humanity, as well as to the honor and interest of the nation whom I serve, to leave any that are desirous to quit the country, a prey to the violence they conceive they have so much cause to apprehend."

From another source, it appears that, when the news of peace was known, the city of New York presented a scene of distress not easily described; that adherents to the Crown, who were in the army, tore the lappels from their coats and stamped them under their feet, and exclaimed that they were ruined; that others cried out they had sacrificed everything to prove their loyalty, and were now left to shift for themselves, without the friendship of their king or their country. Previous to the evacuation, and in September, upwards of twelve thousand men, women, and children embarked at the city, at Long and Staten Islands, for Nova Scotia and the Bahamas. Some of these victims to civil war tried to make merry at their doom, by saying that they were "bound to a lovely country, where there are nine months winter and three months cold weather every year;" while others, in their desperation, tore down their houses, and, had they not been prevented, would have carried off the bricks of which they were built.

Those who came North landed at Port Roseway (now Shelburne) and St. John, where many, utterly destitute, were supplied with food at the public charge, and were obliged to live in huts built of bark and rough boards.

These volumes contain the names of most who embarked in the "September fleet" for Nova Scotia, and of many who went to that province and to Canada subsequently.

Among the banished ones thus doomed to misery were persons whose hearts and hopes had been as true as Washington's own; for, in the divisions of families which everywhere occurred, and which formed one of the most distressing circumstances of the conflict, there were wives and daughters, who, although bound to Loyalists by the holiest ties, had given their sympathies to the right from the beginning; and who now, in the triumph of the cause which had had their prayers, went meekly — as woman ever meets a sorrowful lot — into hopeless, interminable exile.

I have stood at the graves of some of these wives and daughters, and have listened to the accounts of the living, in shame and anger. If, as Jefferson said, separation from England was "*contemplated with affliction by all;*" if, as John Adams testified, Whigs like himself " would have given everything they possessed for a restoration to the state of things before the contest began, provided they could have had a sufficient security for its continuance;" and on the ground of policy alone, — how ill-judged the measures that caused the settlement of the hitherto neglected possessions of England in this hemisphere, —

Nova Scotia. By causing the expatriation of many thousands of our countrymen, among whom were the well-educated, the ambitious, and the versed in politics, we became the founders of two agricultural and commercial Colonies; for it is to be remembered, that New Brunswick formed a part of Nova Scotia until 1784, and that the necessity of the division then made was of our own creation. In like manner we became the founders of Upper Canada. The Loyalists were the first settlers of the territory thus denominated by the act of 1791;[1] and the principal object of the line of division of Canada, as established by Mr. Pitt, was to place them as a body by themselves, and to allow them to be governed by laws more congenial than those which were deemed requisite for the government of the French on the St. Lawrence. For twenty years the country bordering on the great lakes was decidedly American.

Dearly enough have the people of the United States paid for the crime of the "violent Whigs" of the Revolution; for, to the Loyalists who were driven away and to their descendants, we owe almost entirely the long and bitter controversy relative to our northeastern boundary, and the dispute about our right to the fisheries in the Colonial seas.

The mischief all done, — thousands ruined and banished, new British colonies founded, animosities to continue for generations made certain, — the "violent

---

[1] It was in a debate on this bill that Fox and Burke severed the ties of friendship which had existed between them for a long period. The scene was one of the most interesting that had ever occurred in the House of Commons. Fox, overcome by his emotions, wept aloud. Burke's previous course with regard to the French Revolution had rendered a rupture at some time probable, perhaps certain.

Whigs" of Massachusetts, New York, and Virginia, were satisfied; all this accomplished, and the statute-book was divested of its most objectionable enactments, and a few of the Loyalists returned to their old homes: but by far the greater part died in banishment.

CHAPTER XI.

Discussions at Paris between the Commissioners for concluding Terms of Peace, on the Question of Compensation to the Loyalists for their Losses during the War, by Confiscation and otherwise. Reasons why Congress refused to make Recompense, stated and defended. The Provisions of the Treaty unsatisfactory in this Particular. The Parties interested appeal to Parliament. Debates in the Lords and Commons. The Recommendation of Congress to the States to afford Relief in certain Cases, disregarded.

The subject of restitution and compensation to the Loyalists, was a source of great difficulty during the negotiations for peace. The course of the matter may be learned better from the negotiators themselves, than from any words of mine; and I therefore make some extracts from the Journal of Mr. Adams,[1] who was one of them: —

[1] The full conversations occupy several pages of Mr. Adams's Journal. In making these Extracts, I have always given the substance of what was said; but I have sometimes compressed a passage, or changed a word.

The Articles of the Treaty which relate to the Loyalists are the fourth, fifth, and sixth: —

Art. 4. "It is agreed, That Creditors on either side shall meet with no lawful impediment to the recovery of the full value in sterling money of all *bonâ fide* debts heretofore contracted."

Art. 5. "It is agreed, That the Congress shall earnestly recommend it to the Legislatures of the respective States, to provide for the Restitution of all Estates, Rights, and Properties which have been confiscated, belonging to real British subjects; and also of the Estates, Rights and Properties of those Persons, residents in Districts in Possession of his Majesty's Arms, and who have not borne arms against the said United States;. and that Persons of any other description shall have free liberty to go to any part or parts of any of the Thirteen United States, and

November 3d, 1782. "Dr. Franklin, on Tuesday last, told me of Mr. Oswald's demand of payment of debts, and compensation to the Tories; he said his answer had been, we had not the power, nor had Congress. I told him I had no notion of cheating anybody. The question of paying debts, and compensating, were two. I had made the same observation that forenoon to Mr. Oswald and Mr. Strachey."

November 10. [Mr. Adams waited on Count Vergennes.] "The Count asked me how we went on with the English. I told him we divided on the Tories and the Penobscot. The Count remarked that the English wanted the country there 'for masts.' I told him I thought there were few masts there; but that I fancied it was not masts, but Tories, that again made the difficulty. Some of them claimed lands in the territory, and others hoped for grants there."

November 11. "Mr. Whiteford, the secretary of Mr.

therein to remain Twelve Months unmolested in their endeavors to obtain the Restitution of such of their Estates, Rights, and Properties, as may have been confiscated; and that Congress shall also earnestly recommend to the several States, a Reconsideration and Revision of all Acts or Laws regarding the Premises, so as to render the said Laws or Acts perfectly consistent, not only with Justice and Equity, but with that spirit of Conciliation, which, on the return of the blessings of Peace, should universally prevail. And that the Congress shall also earnestly recommend to the several States, that the Estates, Rights, and Properties of such last-mentioned Persons shall be restored to them, they refunding to any Persons who may be now in possession, the *bonâ fide* price (where any has been given) which such Persons may have paid on purchasing any of the said Lands, Rights, or Properties, since the Confiscation. And it is agreed, That all Persons who have any Interests in Confiscated Lands, either by Debts, Marriage Settlements, or otherwise, shall meet with no lawful impediment in prosecution of their just Rights"

ART. 6. "That there shall be no future Confiscations made, nor any Prosecutions commenced against any Person or Persons for or by reason of the Part which he or they may have taken in the present War; and that no Person shall on that account suffer any future Loss or Damage, either in his Person, Liberty, or Property; and that those who may be in confinement on such charges at the Time of the Ratification of the Treaty in America, shall be immediately set at liberty, and the Prosecutions so commenced be discontinued."

Oswald, came. We soon fell into politics. [Mr. Adams said] Suppose a French minister foresees that the presence of the Tories in America will keep up perpetually two parties, — a French party and an English party." " The French minister at Philadelphia has made some representations to Congress in favor of compensation to the Royalists. We are instructed against it, or rather have no authority to do it; and if Congress should refer the matter to the several States, every one of them, after a delay, probably of eighteen months, will determine against it."

November 15. "Mr. Oswald came to visit me. He said, if he were a member of Congress, he would say to the refugees, Take your property; we scorn to make any use of it in building up our system. I replied, that we had no power, and Congress no power; that if we sent the proposition of compensation to Congress, they would refer it to the States; and that, meantime, you must carry on the war six or nine months, certainly, for this compensation, and consequently spend, in the prosecution of it, six or nine times the sum necessary to make the compensation; for I presume this war costs, every month, to Great Britain, a larger sum than would be necessary to pay for the forfeited estates."

November 17. " Mr. Vaughan came to me; he said Mr. Fitzherbert had received a letter from Mr. Townshend, that the compensation would be insisted on."

November 18. " Returned Mr. Oswald's visit. We went over the old ground concerning the Tories. He began to use arguments with me to relax. I told him he must not think of that, but must bend all his thoughts to convince and persuade his court to give it up; that if the terms now before his court were not accepted, the whole negotiation would be broken off."

November 25. " Dr. Franklin, Mr. Jay, and myself, met at Mr. Oswald's lodgings. Mr. Strachey told us he had been to London, and waited personally on every one of the king's cabinet council, and had communicated the last propositions to them. They, every one of them, unanimously condemned that respecting the Tories; so that that unhappy affair stuck, as he foresaw and foretold it would."

November 26. [Dr. Franklin, Mr. Jay, and Mr. Adams] " in consultation upon the propositions made us yesterday by Mr. Oswald. We agreed unanimously to answer him, that we could not consent to the article respecting the refugees, as it now stands. The rest of the day was spent in endless discussions about the Tories. Dr. Franklin is very staunch against them; more decided, a great deal, on this point, than Mr. Jay or myself."

November 27. " Mr. Benjamin Vaughan came in, returned from London, where he had seen Lord Shelburne. He says, he finds the ministry much embarrassed with the Tories, and exceedingly desirous of saving their honor and reputation in this point; that it is reputation, more than money," &c.

November 29. " Met Mr. Fitzherbert, Mr. Oswald, Dr. Franklin, Mr. Jay, Mr. Laurens, and Mr. Strachey, and spent the whole day in discussions about the fishery and the Tories. Mr. Fitzherbert, Mr. Oswald, and Mr. Strachey retired for some time; and, returning, Mr. Fitzherbert said, that Mr. Strachey and himself had determined to advise Mr. Oswald to strike with us according to the terms proposed as our *ultimatum*, respecting the fishery and the Loyalists. We agreed to meet to-morrow, to sign and seal the treaties."

Besides the want of power in Congress to make the demanded recompense to the Loyalists, as stated in these extracts, there were other objections, and some quite as serious. First, many of them, by their falsehoods, misrepresentations, and bad counsels to the ministry, had undoubtedly done much to bring on and protract the war; so that, in a good measure at least, it was just to charge them with being the authors of their own sufferings. In the second place, those of them who had borne arms, and assisted to ravage and burn the towns on different parts of the coast, or had plundered the defenceless families of the interior settlements, should have *made*, rather than *received*, compensation. Thirdly; to restore the identical property of any had become nearly impossible, as it had been sold, and, in many cases, divided among purchasers, and could only be wrested by plenary means from the present possessors. Fourthly, the country was in no condition to pay those who had toiled and bled for its emancipation, or even to make good a tithe of the losses which they had suffered in consequence of the war; much less was there the ability to adjust the accounts of enemies, whether domestic or foreign. The Loyalists, as a body, looked upon the subjugation of the Whigs as almost certain, to the last; and their delegates in New York even went so far as to entertain a plan for the government of the Colonies, whenever their day of triumph should come. If that day had arrived, how would the Whigs have fared at *their* hands? Would the claims of thousands who expended their estates in the cause of liberty, and who had no shelter for their heads, have been allowed?

Grounds somewhat similar to those which I have assumed, induced Congress, very probably, to instruct their commissioners to enter into no engagements respecting the Americans who adhered to the Crown, unless Great Britain would stipulate, on her part, to make compensation for the property which had been destroyed by persons in her service. With this injunction the commissioners found it impracticable to comply, inasmuch as they deemed it necessary to admit into the treaty a provision to the effect, that Congress should *recommend* to the several States to provide for the restitution of certain of the confiscated estates; that certain persons should be allowed a year to endeavor to recover their estates; that persons having rights in confiscated lands should have the privilege of pursuing all lawful means to regain them; and that Congress should use its recommendatory power to cause the States to revoke or reconsider their confiscation laws. Congress unanimously assented to this arrangement, and unanimously issued the recommendation to the States, which the treaty contemplated.

These terms were very unsatisfactory, and loud clamors arose in Parliament and elsewhere. In the House of Commons, Mr. Wilberforce said, that "when he considered the case of the Loyalists, he confessed he there felt himself conquered; there he saw his country humiliated; he saw her at the feet of America: still he was induced to believe, that Congress would religiously comply with the article, and that the Loyalists would obtain redress from America." Lord North said, that "never were the honor, the principles, the policy of a nation, so grossly abused as in the desertion of those men, who are now exposed to every punishment that desertion and poverty can inflict, because they were not rebels." Lord Mulgrave declared, that " the article respecting the Loyalists he could never regard but as a lasting monument of national disgrace." Mr. Burke said, that "a vast number of the Loyalists had been deluded by England, and had risked everything, and that, to such men, the nation owed protection, and its honor was pledged for their security at all hazards." Mr. Sheridan "execrated the treatment of those unfortunate men, who, without the least notice taken of their civil and religious rights, were handed over as subjects to a power that would not fail to take vengeance on them for their zeal and attachment to the religion and government of the mother-country;" and he denounced as a "crime," the cession of the Americans who had adhered to the Crown, "into the hands of their enemies, and delivering them over to confiscation, tyranny, resentment, and oppression." Mr. Norton said, that "he could not give his assent to the treaty on account of the article which related to the Loyalists." Sir Peter Burrell considered, that "the fate of these unhappy subjects claimed the compassion of every human breast; for they had been abandoned by the ministers, and were left at the mercy of a Congress highly irritated against them." Sir Wilbraham Bootle's "heart bled for the Loyalists; they had fought and had run every hazard for England, and, at a moment when they had a claim to the greatest protection, they had been deserted." Mr. Macdonald "forbore to dwell upon the case of these men, as an assembly of human beings could scarcely trust their judgments, when so powerful an attack was made upon their feelings."

In the House of Lords, the opposition was quite as violent. Lord Walsingham said, that "he could neither think nor speak of the dishonor of leaving these deserving people to their fate, with patience." Lord Viscount Townshend considered, that, "to desert men who had constantly adhered to loyalty and attachment, was a circumstance of such cruelty as had never before been heard of." Lord Stormont said, that "Britain was bound in justice and honor, gratitude and affection, and every tie, to provide for and protect them." Lord Sackville regarded "the abandonment of the Loyalists as a thing of so atrocious a kind, that, if it had not been already painted in all its horrid colors, he should have attempted the ungracious task, but never should have been able to describe the cruelty in language as strong and expressive as were his feelings;" and again, that "a peace founded on the sacrifice of these unhappy subjects, must be accursed in the sight of God and man." Lord Loughborough said, "that the fifth article of the treaty had excited a general and just indignation;" and that neither "in ancient nor modern history had there been so shameful a desertion of men who had sacrificed all to their duty, and to their reliance upon British faith."

Such attacks as these did not, of course, pass without replies in both Houses. The nature of the defence of the friends of the ministry will sufficiently appear, by the remarks of the minister himself. Lord Shelburne frankly admitted, that the Loyalists were left without better provision being made for them, "from the unhappy *necessity* of public affairs, which induced the extremity of submitting the fate of their property to the discretion of their enemies." And he continued, "I have but one answer to give the House; it is the answer I gave my own bleeding heart. A *part* must be wounded, that the *whole* of the empire may not perish. If better terms could be had, think you, my Lord, that I would not have embraced them? *I had but the alternative either to accept the terms proposed, or continue the war.*" The Lord Chancellor parried the assaults of the opposition with other weapons. He declared, that the stipulations of the treaty are "specific," and, said he, "my own conscious honor will not allow me to doubt the good faith of others, and my good wishes to the Loyalists will not let me indiscreetly doubt the dispositions of Congress," since the understanding is, that "all these unhappy men shall be provided for;" yet, if it were not so, "Parliament could take cognizance of their case, and impart to each suffering individual that relief which reason, perhaps policy, certainly virtue and religion, required."

It was not expected, probably, by the British government, that the "recommendation" of Congress to the States would produce any effect. In 1778, and after the evacuation of Philadelphia, the urgent request of Congress to repeal the severe enactments against the adherents of the Crown and to restore their confiscated property, had been disregarded; and a similar desire at the conclusion of hostilities, though made for different reasons, it could not have been supposed would be more successful. Indeed, the idea that the States would *refuse* compliance, and that Parliament would be required to make the Loyalists some compensation for their losses, seems to have been entertained from the first. Lord Shelburne, in the speech from which I have just quoted, remarked, that, "*without one drop of blood spill, and without one fifth of the expense of one year's campaign, happiness and ease can be given to them in as ample a manner as these blessings were ever in their enjoyment.*" He could have meant nothing less by this language than that, by putting an end to the war, the empire saved both life and treasure, even though the amount of money required to place the Loyalists in "happiness and ease," should amount to some millions; and the Lord Chancellor, it may be observed, hinted at compensation as the remedy, provided the "recommendation" of Congress should not result favorably. Besides, during the negotiation of the treaty, it appears to have been considered by the commissioners on both sides, that each party to the contest must bear its own losses and provide for its own sufferers. But, whatever were the expectations at Paris or in London, all uncertainty was soon at an end. A number of Loyalists who were in England, came to the United States to claim restitution of their estates, but their applications were unheeded, and some of them were imprisoned, and afterwards banished.

CHAPTER XII.

The Loyalists apply to Parliament for Relief. The King in his Speech recommends Attention to their Claims. Commissioners appointed. Complaints of the Loyalists on various Grounds. Number of Claimants, and Schedules of their Losses. Delay of the Commissioners in adjusting Claims, and Distresses in Consequence. Discussion in Parliament. Final Number of Claimants, Final Amount of Schedules, and Final Award In the Appeals to their Respective Governments, the Loyalists fared better than the Whigs.

THE claimants now applied to the government which they had ruined themselves to serve; and many of them, who had hitherto been "Refugees" in different parts of America, went to England to state, and to recover payment for, their losses. They organized an agency, and appointed a committee, composed of one delegate or agent from each of the thirteen States, to enlighten the British public, and adopt measures of procedure in securing the attention and action of the ministry in their behalf. In a tract,[1] printed by order of these agents, it is maintained, that "it is an established rule, that all sacrifices made by individuals for the benefit or accommodation of others, shall be equally sustained by all those who partake of it;" and numerous cases are cited from Puffendorf, Burlamaqui, and Vattel, to show that the "sacrifices" of the Loyalists were embraced in this principle. As a further ground of claim, it is stated,

[1] "The Case and Claim of the American Loyalists, impartially stated and considered," published in 1783

that, in the case of territory alienated or ceded away by one sovereign power to another, the rule is still applicable; for that, in treatises of international law, it is held, "the State ought to indemnify the subject for the loss he has sustained beyond his own proportion." The conclusion arrived at from the precedents found in history and diplomacy, and in the statute-book of the realm, is, that, as the Loyalists were as "perfectly subjects of the British State as any man in London or Middlesex," they were entitled to the same protection and relief. The claimants, said the writers of the tract, had been " called on by their sovereign, when surrounded by tumult and rebellion, to defend the supreme rights of the nation, and to assist in suppressing a rebellion which aimed at their destruction. They have received from the highest authority the most solemn assurances of protection, and even reward for their meritorious services;" and that "his Majesty and the two Houses of Parliament having thought it necessary, as the *price of peace*, or to the interest and safety of the empire, or from some other motive of public convenience, to ratify the independence of America, without *securing any restitution whatever* to the Loyalists, they conceive that the nation is bound, as well by the fundamental laws of society as by the invariable and eternal principles of natural justice, to make them a compensation."

At the opening of Parliament, the king, in his speech from the throne, alluded to the "American sufferers" who, from "motives of loyalty to him, or attachment to the mother-country, had relinquished their properties or professions," and trusted, he said, that "generous attention would be shown to them." Both parties assented to the suggestion; and a motion was made early in the session for leave to bring in a bill, "*For appointing* Commissioners to inquire into the Circumstances and former Fortunes of such Persons as are reduced to Distress by the late unhappy Dissensions in America." Leave was given; but in fixing the details of the bill, there was some difficulty and considerable debate. The measure was finally made agreeable to all, and was adopted without opposition. The act, as passed, created a Board of Commissioners, who were empowered to examine all persons presenting claims under oath, to send for books, papers, and records; and who were directed to report all such as fraudulently claimed a greater amount than they had lost, in order that they should be deprived of all compensation whatever.

The first thing to be ascertained by the commissioners was the "loyalty and conduct of the claimants." In their first report, they divided them into six classes,[1] and very properly placed the apostates from the Whigs in the last; but no difference was finally made on account of the time or circumstances of adhering to the cause of the Crown, and all, without reference to differences in merit, who were able to establish losses, shared alike.

---

[1] *First Class.* Those who had rendered services to Great Britain.
  Second Class. Those who had borne arms for Great Britain.
  Third Class. Uniform Loyalists.
  Fourth Class. Loyal British subjects resident in Great Britain.
  Fifth Class. Loyalists who had taken oaths to the American States, but afterwards joined the British.
  Sixth Class. Loyalists who had borne arms for the American States, but afterwards joined the British navy or army.

The claimants were required to state in proper form every species of loss which they had suffered, and for which *they* thought they had a right to receive compensation. In making up their schedules agreeably to this rule, some sufferers claimed for losses which others did not; and, in adjusting the claims, the disproportion between the sum asked and the sum allowed was often very large. A few received their whole demands, without the deduction of a shilling, while others received pounds only where they had demanded hundreds; and a third class obtained nothing, having been excluded by inability to prove their losses, or deprived of the sum which they could prove, by attempts to obtain allowance for claims which the commissioners reported upon as fraudulent, in accordance with the provisions of the act. The rigid rules enforced, which it would seem applied to all claimants, created much murmuring. The mode pursued of examining the claimant and the witnesses in his behalf, separately and apart, was branded with severe epithets, and the commission was called an "Inquisition." With all the caution which it was possible for the commissioners to exercise, men who did not really lose a single penny, who were entirely destitute of property when the war began, and to whom hostilities were actually beneficial by affording pay and employment, were placed in comfortable circumstances; and stories which show the plans and schemes that were devised to baffle the rigid scrutiny of the board are still repeated.

The 26th of March, 1784, was the latest period for presenting claims which was allowed; and on or before that day, the number of claimants was two thousand and sixty-three, and the property alleged to have been lost was, according to their schedules, the alarming sum of £7,046,278, besides debts to the amount of £2,354,135. The second report, which was made in December of the same year, shows that one hundred and twenty-eight additional cases had been disposed of, and that for £693,257 claimed, the total allowance was only £150,935. Much the same difference is to be seen in the succeeding one hundred and twenty-two cases, which were disposed of in May and July of 1785, and in which £253,613 were allowed for £898,196 claimed. In April, 1786, the fifth report announced that one hundred and forty-two other claims, to the amount of £733,311, had been liquidated at £250,506. The commissioners proceeded with their investigations during the years 1786 and 1787. Meantime, South Carolina had restored the estates of several of her Loyalists, and caused the withdrawal of the claims of their owners, except that, in instances of alleged strip and waste, amercement, and similar losses, inquiries were instituted to ascertain the value of what was taken, compared with that which was returned.

On the 5th of April, 1788, the commissioners in England had heard and determined one thousand six hundred and eighty claims (besides those withdrawn), and had liquidated the same at £1,887,548. Perhaps no greater despatch was possible, but the delay caused great complaint. The king, his ministers, and Parliament were addressed and petitioned, either on the general course pursued by the commissioners, or on some subject connected with the Loyalist claims. Letters and communications appeared in the newspapers, and the public attention was again awakened by the publication of essays and tracts which renewed the statements made in 1783 of the losses, services, and sacrifices of the claimants. Two years previously (1786), the agents of the Loyalists had invoked Parliament to hasten the final action upon the claims of their constituents in a petition drawn up with care and ability. "It is impossible to describe," are words which occur in this document, " the poignant distress under which many of these persons now labor, and which must daily increase, should the justice of Parliament be delayed until all the claims are liquidated and reported; .... ten years have elapsed since many of them have been deprived of their fortunes, and, with their helpless families, reduced from independent affluence to poverty and want; some of them now languishing in British jails, others indebted to their creditors, who have lent them money barely to support their existence, and who, unless speedily relieved, must sink more than the value of their claims when received, and be in a worse condition than if they had never made them; others have already sunk under the pressure and severity of their misfortunes; and others must, in all probability, soon meet the same melancholy fate, should the justice due to them be longer postponed. But that, on the contrary, should provision be now made for payment of those whose claims have been settled and reported, it will not only relieve them from their distress, but give a credit to the others whose claims remain to be considered, and enable all of them to provide for their wretched families, and become again useful members of society." This vivid picture of the condition of those who waited the tardy progress made in the final adjustment of their losses is possibly highly colored. Mr. Pitt had introduced and carried through, in 1785, a bill for the distribution of £150,000 among the claimants; but as that sum, it was held, was to be applied to a distinct class, — namely, to those who had lost "property," and to neither those who had lost "life-estate" in property, nor to those who had lost "income," — it is not improbable that many of these classes were at this time greatly in want of the relief which their agents so earnestly implored the government to afford.

A tract[1] printed in 1788, which was attributed to Galloway, a Loyalist of Pennsylvania, presses the claims and merits of the sufferers with much point and vigor, and rebukes the injustice of neglecting and deferring payment of the compensation conceded on all hands to be due them, with singular spirit and boldness, and states their situation in the following forcible language: "It is well known," says the writer, "that this delay of justice has produced the most melancholy and shocking events. A number of the sufferers have been driven by it into insanity, and become their own destroyers, leaving behind them their helpless widows and orphans to subsist upon the cold charity of strangers. Others have been sent to cultivate a wilderness for their subsistence, without having the means, and compelled through want to throw themselves on the mercy of the American States and the charity of their former friends, to support the life which might have been

---

[1] "The Claim of the American Loyalist reviewed and maintained upon incontrovertible Principles of Law and Justice."

made comfortable by the money long since due from the British Government; and many others, with their families, are barely subsisting upon a temporary allowance from government,— a mere pittance when compared with the sum due to them."

The commissioners submitted their *eleventh* Report in April of the year in which this statement was made; and Mr. Pitt, in the month following, gave way to the pressing importunities of the claimants, to allow their grievances to be discussed in Parliament. Twelve years had elapsed since the property of most of them had been alienated under the confiscation acts, and five, since their title to recompense had been recognized by the law under which their claims had been presented.

The minister, meantime, by frequent conferences with the commissioners, had made himself familiar with all the points involved and requiring consideration, and, in expressing his views, raised three questions: first, whether there should be any deduction made from the value put upon the estates to be paid for; secondly, if any, what the deduction should be; and, thirdly, what compensation should be made to the Loyalists who had lost their incomes by losing their offices and professions. In his speech, Mr. Pitt laid down as the basis of his plan, that, however strong might be the claims of either class, neither should regard the relief to be extended as due on principles " of right and strict justice." In proceeding with his remarks, he proposed to pay all of six designated classes, who consisted of thirteen hundred and sixty-four persons, whose liquidated losses did not exceed ten thousand pounds each, the full amount reported by the commissioners; while, increasing the rate of discount with the increase of losses, he proposed a deduction of ten per cent. on the losses (of persons of these six classes) between ten and thirty-five thousand pounds, and of fifteen per cent. on those between thirty-five and fifty thousand, and of twenty per cent. on those exceeding fifty thousand; casting, however, these several rates of deduction only on the differences between ten thousand pounds and the amounts lost as reported by the commissioners.[1] With regard to persons of another description, whose losses had been caused principally, if not entirely, by deprivation of official or professional income, he submitted a plan of *pensions*.[2]

After this adjustment, several additional claims were presented, examined, and allowed; and, upon the settlement of the whole matter, it appeared that the number of claimants in England, Nova Scotia, New Brunswick, and Canada, was five thousand and seventy-two, of whom nine hundred and fifty-four withdrew or failed to prosecute their claims; that the amount of losses, according to the schedules rendered, was £8,026,045, of which the sum of £3,292,452 was allowed.[3] The Loyalists, then, were well cared for.

[1] This plan was objected to by the Loyalists, and their reasons were transmitted to Mr. Pitt, in a document of some length.

[2] The number of these persons was two hundred and four; amount of income lost, £80,000; pensions granted, £25,785.

[3] The principal facts with regard to the compensation of the Loyalists are derived from a "Historical View of the Commission," &c., by John Eardley Wilmot, Esq., one of the commissioners. In the aggregate amount *claimed*, there seems some discrepancy. According to the summary of Mr. Wilmot, made in March, 1790, "the claims preferred" were £10,358,413; whereas, in a table from which I take the statistics above, the amount is stated at £8,026,045. Again, in March, 1790, it is said by Mr. Wilmot,

Whatever were the miseries to individuals occasioned by delay; whatever the injury sustained by those who were unable to procure sufficient evidence of their losses; and whatever were the wrongs inflicted upon others by the errors in judgment on the part of the commissioners, the Americans who took the royal side, as a body, fared infinitely better than the great body of the Whigs, whose services and sacrifices were quite as great; for, besides the allowance of fifteen and a half millions of dollars in money, numbers received considerable annuities, half-pay as military officers, large grants of land, and shared with other subjects in the patronage of the Crown.

that the number of "claims preferred in England and Nova Scotia was three thousand two hundred and twenty-five, of which were examined two thousand two hundred and ninety-one, disallowed three hundred and forty-two, withdrawn thirty-eight, not prosecuted five hundred and fifty-three;" that the amount of claims allowed was £3,033,091; whereas, in the table which I have followed as giving a later and *final* view, the claims *examined* are stated at four thousand one hundred and eighteen, and the amount allowed at the sum in the text; from which it follows, that one thousand eight hundred and twenty-seven persons recovered only the difference between £3,292,455 and £3,033,91, or the small sum of £259,364.

CHAPTER XIII.

The Banished Loyalists and their Descendants. Progress of Whig Principles in the Canadas, in New Brunswick, and Nova Scotia. The whole System of Monopoly on which the Colonial System was founded and maintained, surrendered. The Colonists now manufacture what they will, buy where they please, and sell where they can. England herself has pronounced the Vindication of the Whigs. The Heir to the British Throne at Mount Vernon and Bunker Hill. The Colonists claim to hold the highest Places in the Government, in the Army, and in the Navy. Effects of the Change of Policy. The Children of the Whigs and of the Loyalists, reconciled.

WE are now to discuss the political changes in the Colonies to which the banishment and confiscation acts during the war, and the hostile feeling at the peace, compelled large bodies of Loyalists to retire. When, in 1821, in ignorance and poverty, I went to the eastern frontier, I saw in wonder that, across the border, natives of Massachusetts and graduates of her ancient university, with exiles from other States, had reëstablished the Colonial system of government with hardly a modification; and, young as I was, well did I mark the administration of affairs. Indeed, as I read and inquired, I almost imagined that I was actually living in ante-revolutionary times. For some years, no political changes of moment occurred: but, in the course of events, important concessions were demanded; and, finally, the whole system of monopoly on which the system is founded, was abandoned, as I purpose to relate so fully as my limits will allow.

HISTORICAL ESSAY.   115

In 1783, the French at Quebec and Montreal, and the English at Halifax, were few in numbers, and generally poor and ignorant; while the countries now called Canada West and New Brunswick, were almost unbroken forests.

Canada claims our first attention. As was predicted by wise statesmen in 1763, the French possessions then acquired have caused England great disquiet and immense expenditures. After the conquest, and before the cession by treaty, an exciting discussion arose, whether, as the ministry had the option between Canada and Guadaloupe, they should not restore to France the former, and retain the latter. The fear was, that, if Canada were kept, the thirteen Colonies, rid of all apprehensions from the French, would increase too rapidly, and, in the end, throw off their dependence on the mother country. This view was supported in a tract supposed to be from the pen of one of the Burkes; and was answered by Franklin, in his happiest and ablest manner. The ministry, having resolved to keep Canada, organized a military government; and the king, by proclamation, announced his intention of granting, as soon as circumstances would permit, a legislative assembly. That this promise was not redeemed for twenty-eight years was an error in policy, and a breach of royal faith. For a time, officers of the army were both governors and judges. Abuses, at last, became so serious as to attract the notice of the Crown. The change which followed gave much offence to the Whigs of the thirteen Colonies, and is mentioned in the Declaration of Independence.

In 1791, Mr. Pitt, in opposition to Fox and other

British Whigs, carried through Parliament a bill which divided Canada into two provinces, and which provided for a better administration of affairs than had ever existed. It was in the debate on this measure, that Burke and Fox severed the ties which had bound them together for a long period.

Tolerable harmony prevailed in Canada for a number of years. The first dispute of consequence immediately preceded the war of 1812; when the Assembly demanded that the judges should vacate their seats as legislators, and confine themselves to their judicial duties. A sharp contest followed. The Governor dissolved the Assembly; but his conduct was not approved in England, and he was removed. The appointment of the popular Sir George Prevost, and the war with the United States, hushed for awhile the clamors of the discontented. At the peace, however, when Prevost relinquished the executive chair to Sir George Gordon Drummond, a second quarrel arose between the judges and a new House of Assembly; and two occupants of the bench were impeached. Drummond was succeeded by the excellent Sir John C. Sherbroke, under whose rule there was a period of quiet. On his retirement, his successor, the Duke of Richmond, abandoned the practice of submitting to the Assembly an estimate in detail of the sums of money required for each branch of the public service; and thus added *another* element of discord. The Assembly refused to comply with the Duke's wishes, and a long and angry controversy followed. His Grace died of hydrophobia; and the dispute was renewed by the Earl of Dalhousie, who was appointed governor-general in his place.

This rapid narrative brings us to the year 1820, and to the first organized party in opposition to the established order of things. The Assembly, moderate in their earliest demands, — and for three or four years, — merely contested the right of the servants of the Crown to designate the manner of expending certain of the Colonial revenues; and, in justification, complained of previous misapplication of the public money. In 1825, during the temporary absence of Lord Dalhousie, Sir Francis Burton, who administered the government in the exigency, made such large concessions as to induce the Assembly to assume a bolder position, and to claim the control of the *whole* of the Colonial revenues, as well as to designate the objects to which they should be applied. This masterly movement for the entire fiscal power excited an interest in Canadian politics never before manifested, and afforded cause of serious alarm in England. The Assembly persisted; and, after a discussion of two years, the ministry proposed to surrender the management of the revenues on the condition, that what is termed the "Civil List" should be paid out of them. And the matter would have been adjusted on this basis, probably, but for the act of Lord Dalhousie, in disapproving and setting aside the election of Mr. Papineau to the Speaker's chair of the Assembly. The popularity of that gentleman in his own party was almost unbounded. The "Liberals," as his friends were called — the Liberals, enraged beyond what such a circumstance warranted, gave vent to their feelings in the most exciting appeals to the people; and Dalhousie's administration closed amid denunciations and imprecations.

Sir James Kempt undertook the difficult duty of hushing the storm in 1828; and, to this end, he invited Papineau and another leader of the Liberals to take seats in his cabinet; and he gave assurances that the *graver* differences should be disposed of at the meeting of Parliament. This promise, in consequence of the death of George the Fourth, was not fulfilled. But Lord Aylmar, on succeeding to Sir James's place, renewed the pledge; and, as the Liberals affirmed, without conditions. However this may be, when he came to make known the precise concessions of the ministry, the quarrel which apparently had come to a termination, was opened anew and with increased violence. The Assembly, strong now in popular favor, assumed the most determined attitude and refused every overture. At last, in 1831, the ministry yielded the essential points in dispute, and the considerate among the Colonists hoped for a cessation of strife. But, though the home government conceded much, Lord Aylmar was still instructed to ask for *special* appropriations of money. This produced new difficulties. The result was, that the breach between the Assembly and the servants of the Crown became as wide as ever before. Encouraged by the advantages they had obtained in this long and wearisome dispute about the revenues, the Liberals now commenced an attack upon the Legislative Council. This body, in its powers, is much like the senate with us; but its members held their places at the royal pleasure, and for life. Several of the incumbents, for reasons which I have not time to state, had become extremely obnoxious. The Assembly demanded, not the removal of the offensive members, but the abolition of the Council itself, and its reconstruction on an elective basis. To this demand, the ministry gave a flat refusal. As monarchists reason, well they might refuse; since, to have surrendered the Council to the popular party, was to lose all check upon it, and to reduce the power and authority of the Crown to a mere shadow.

The Assembly, on this rebuff, seemed to lose all sense of official propriety. In hot haste, the Liberals prepared a long list of new and enormous wrongs; they declared many old ones to be insufferable; they rejected the bill granting money to support the government; they severely censured Lord Aylmar, and insisted upon his removal; and, in the most determined tone, renewed the demand for an elective Council. Among the people the excitement was intense. Affairs, indeed, had come to a crisis. In nine sessions of the Canadian Parliament, immediately preceding, the deeply-hated Legislative Council had rejected no less than one hundred and twenty-two of the bills passed by the Assembly, and had so amended forty-seven others, that the latter body had refused concurrence. In a word, legislation was at an end. The reconstruction of the Council was the fixed purpose on one side; the Council, without change, was the determined resolution on the other.

Such was the general condition of things in Canada, when, on a change of administration in England, Sir Robert Peel became Prime Minister in place of Lord Melbourne. To redress every *real* wrong, to send over a commissioner with ample powers to examine and decide upon the complaints which had been so pertinaciously urged, year after year, was the prompt resolve of Sir Robert; but, before he could execute his plan, another change occurred which restored Lord Melbourne to power. And yet, Lord Aylmar was recalled, and Lord Gosford was appointed both governor and commissioner. This mission was an utter failure. The year 1836 is memorable in Canadian politics. Lord Gosford was disgraced. The Assembly manifested desire for an appeal to arms, as the only remaining means to accomplish their long-cherished schemes. For the first time, the *two* great parties in England were brought to consider that the interposition of the Imperial Parliament was indispensable to the peace and integrity of the British empire; for, at this time, disaffection had spread, as we shall see, to other Colonies.

It is to be borne in mind, that Lower and Upper Canada were not, as now, united, and that my remarks, thus far, relate entirely to the former. We pass to speak of the course of events in the latter, which, since the union, is known as Canada West. On the election of a new Assembly in 1834, the Liberals achieved a triumph over the Conservatives; and, elated with their success, they assumed, as it were in a moment, the extreme pretensions which had been slowly matured, in the dissensions of fifteen years, in the sister Colony.

There was no department of the government which they did not assail; no public servant whom they did not accuse. Their wish to secede from England was hardly denied or concealed under a decent veil. In fine, to pass from a state of ordinary quiet to loud murmurs and open rebellion, was scarcely the work of a single year. In the hope of allaying the excitement, the ministry recalled Sir John Colburn, and appointed Sir Francis Bond Head governor in his stead. Never, in politics, was there a greater blunder. Sir Francis, whatever his merits as a writer or a soldier, was a mere child among politicians. He himself thought so; and others said that his appointment was a ministerial joke. The juncture required the wisdom of the *wisest* of England's many wise statesmen; and her ministers were inexcusably remiss in refusing to see that it was so. Indications that the royal authority would soon be disputed in the field, were too manifest to be mistaken. Yet the military force of the Crown was tardily increased. At last, but too late, the ministry appealed to Parliament, irrespective of party distinctions, for the calm judgment and the united ability of that body. The death of King William quickly followed. To involve the Illustrious Lady who now occupies the throne, in a conflict with her subjects, at the beginning of her reign, was a measure which ministers and nobles and commoners might well wish to avoid; and, in the irresolution of the moment, the Canadas defied her, and met her troops in deadly combat. The last months of 1837, and the opening of 1838, were crowded with deeds of violence and blood. I recall, in sadness, the attempt to seize upon Toronto, the capital of Upper Canada, the battles of St. Denis, of St. Charles, and of Bois Blanc. These, and other hostile affairs, exposed the weakness of the Liberals as a revolutionary party; disclosed that they had no hold on the hearts of the masses; disclosed that they had ventured into open war with a mighty empire without resources; disclosed how miserably deficient they were in military talents, and how slight was the confidence of their leaders in one another. And so, too, I recall in horror the butcheries at St. Eustache, as affording melancholy proof of what, indeed, human history is full of — that, when brother fights brother, no outrage, no wickedness, is too great; since there, men were needlessly maimed and slain; weeping, famishing women were driven out to perish, and were plundered and murdered; since there, the dead were mangled, and suffered to lie unburied, and to be eaten by dogs. These, and other deeds as awful as these, but of which I shall make no mention, shocked the civilization of the age.

The subsequent efforts of the leaders of the Liberals to form a provisional government at Navy Island, where they concentrated their scattered followers, drew down upon them universal contempt. They strove to inspire the deceived, shivering, and starving creatures around them with the belief that citizens of the United States would flock to their standard, and enable them to retrieve their fortunes. But, deluded from first to last; incessantly quarrelling among themselves; and showing to the world, in the columns of the newspapers, the meanness of their personal disputes; the movement, which, in their infatuation they designed for a revolution, and for an imposing page in American annals, terminated in a disgraceful insurrection. In their appeals to the popular ear, previous to the outbreak, they had likened their situation, and the objects for which they contended, to those of our fathers, — the Whigs of 1776; but they were answered, and truly, that several of the graver disabilities which restrained and oppressed the thirteen Colonies, had been removed. So, too, they had adopted the general sentiments of our Declaration of Independence, and incorporated a large portion of it into their Manifesto of Wrongs.

For reasons which will appear anon, I was a calm and interested observer; and the opinion which I then formed, I repeat after the lapse of twenty years. I need not to be told, that of the fallen, we should always speak in pity, and of the guilty, in mercy. But, we are not to repress our indignation, when, as in the case before us, men of talents and education, of political knowledge and experience, skulk away, and leave their dupes to die on the scaffold, or to pine and perish in prison. Such men, — the men who slip the halter for themselves, but fasten it round the necks of the ignorant and the lowly, — should stand accursed.

At the suppression of the insurrection, Canada was in a deplorable condition, as the imagination can well picture. It often happens in human affairs, that the mischief all done, and the mischief all exposed, a remedy is thought of and applied. It was so then. Civil war produced, with all its miseries, needy or second and third rate knights, and baronets and barons were no longer sent to govern, or rather to mis-govern, the people of Canada. Lord Durham, a statesman of acknowledged wisdom, moderation, and ability, was solicited to undertake the task of healing the disorders which other persons of rank had helped to increase, and which, had *he* been employed at the outset, could, and would have been prevented. His powers as ambassador were as great as were ever conferred on a British subject. The Colonial gentlemen with whom I constantly mingled, hailed his coming, much as they would have done the advent of an angel. His keen vision surveyed all Canada at a glance. Plans for bold and comprehensive reforms, were formed with the rapidity of intuition. His heart was in the work, and he labored incessantly. As Washington had been the saviour of the thirteen Colonies, so he proudly thought to become the saviour of the domains which England conquered from France, and which, strangely enough, are all the continental possessions that remain to her in this hemisphere.

Alas, that Lord Durham should have been arrested in his glorious career. But in politics, the idol of to-day is the martyr of the morrow, if he recognize the doctrines of human brotherhood rather than the dictations of his party.

His Lordship found the prisons full of persons charged with participation in the insurrection, and with crimes against persons and property. The clamors for the life of the leaders were awful. But there had been enough of death,— he nobly said,— enough of widowhood and orphanage; and so, true to his nature, he resolved to save and to spare. In the intense excitement which prevailed, he feared that justice would not be done by juries, and, in pure mercy to the ruined and the fallen, he banished to the Bermudas several of the insurgents who made written confession of guilt, as the best means of allaying animosities, and of preventing further communication between the leading spirits who had been arrested, and those who were still at large. Unfortunately for himself, his course was technically wrong, for the Bermudas were not within his jurisdiction; and, according to the letter of criminal law, a British subject cannot be deprived of his liberty, without the finding of a jury and the sentence of a judge. The decree of banishment was accordingly disapproved; and Lord Durham abandoned his mission at once, and returned to England without leave of the queen or her ministers.

He was proud and sensitive; and the proud and sensitive will not brook dishonorable imputation. That he erred, may be admitted. With some of his peers, his high character, his motives in this particular case, were of no avail. In a word, his foes pursued him much as the famished wolf follows a lone, lost child in the forest — to lap blood, drop by drop. The vulgar of our race murder with the knife and with the club; the gentlemen, to gain in politics, destroy with the tongue, with the pen, and with the press.

Lord Durham did not long survive his disgrace. He lived long enough, however, to complete for posterity an elaborate report of what he did, of what he intended to do, and of what should be done, in British America. This document, in the passion of the hour, was reviewed in Parliament and elsewhere with merciless severity. I quote a single instance. In 1839, the "London Quarterly," in a notice of it, said, in concluding some very pungent remarks: "*We can venture to answer, that every uncontradicted assertion of that volume will be made the excuse of future rebellions, — every unquestioned principle will be hereafter perverted into a gospel of treason; and that, if that rank and infectious Report does not receive the high, marked, and energetic discountenance and indignation of the imperial crown and parliament, British America is lost.*"

But this Report, so filled with treasons, so sure to dismember the British empire a second time, in the apprehension of those who denounced it, is already considered a masterly State paper; and, curious to add, *its recommendations have been adopted in almost every essential particular.*

The insurrection in Canada involved the United States. That some of our citizens were concerned in it, is beyond question; the burning of the American steamer Caroline by officers of the Crown; the seizure and trial of McLeod, the principal actor in the affair; the avowal of the British ministry that they justified him, with their demand on the Federal government for his release; these, and other circumstances, formed a complication of difficulties, which caused the wisest to ponder. At this juncture, the peace of the country depended on the grand and massive man who now rests at Marshfield. It was easy for party men who were secure in their homes to call upon him, for party purposes, to quit the Department of State; but we,[1] who lived upon the border, who daily saw the elements of strife gaining strength, and who were exposed to the marauder's bludgeon and the marauder's torch; we watched his movements with intense interest, and when we found that he would not be driven from his post, we blessed him.

It is not necessary to trace the course of events in Canada further. Lord Durham's mission, in its results, terminated the strifes.

We pass to New Brunswick. The original popu-

---

[1] My home was still at Eastport, Maine.

lation of this Colony was composed almost entirely of the Loyalists of the Revolution. It was set off from Nova Scotia in 1784, without pressing necessity, except to provide for these unhappy victims to civil war. The judges of the Supreme Court first appointed were natives of Massachusetts, and graduates of Harvard University. The secretary of the province was an Episcopal minister of New Jersey, who was in communication with Arnold while he was plotting treason. The judges of the inferior courts, the sheriffs, collectors of the customs, and other functionaries, were also our banished countrymen; and most of them were born in New England and the Middle States. Thus the offices were given to Loyalist families, and descended from father to son.

The first political agitation of moment in New Brunswick was, I think, in 1837, when Sir Archibald Campbell,—who had served his king as a soldier in almost every part of the world,—was compelled to retire, upon address of the House of Assembly for his removal from the executive chair. Sir John Harvey was his successor. He, too, was a military officer of much merit. He had warm friends and bitter foes. His career was even more stormy than that of his predecessor; but he cared little for angry newspapers and angry politicians. The American people on the eastern frontier have reason to remember his course when the controversy relative to the North-Eastern Boundary had reached a point to threaten hostilities. Congress had conditionally placed millions of money and a large army at the disposal of the President; and Maine, to defend the territory in dispute, had authorized a loan, raised troops and established garrisons. The roads in one section of the State were filled miles together with sleds loaded with soldiers and the munitions of war. British regulars were moving in every direction, and a British frigate, with a regiment detached from Bermuda, lay anchored within a mile of my own home. All was dread, confusion, alarm. Worship was disturbed on the Sabbath, and business was neglected on week-days. In this condition of things, General Scott was ordered to Maine, to consult with the governor and the members of the legislature, to negotiate with Sir John Harvey, and, if possible, to prevent extremities. The two warriors, to the displeasure of demagogues, but to the satisfaction of the country generally, agreed upon terms which prevented bloodshed at the lone military posts on the upper waters of the St. John ; and thus saved, probably, England and the United States from the calamities of war.

Sir William Colebrooke, another officer in the British army, followed Sir John Harvey, and, for a time, was very popular. The appointment, however, of his son-in-law to an office next in rank to his own, gave much offence, and caused an organized opposition to his administration. In the end, the dispute broke up Sir William's cabinet, and produced a memorial from the Assembly to the queen.

Lord Stanley, (who now is the Earl of Derby, and lately Prime Minister of England,) who was then Secretary for the Colonies, so far approved of the course of the opposition, as to disallow the appointment, and to direct the return of the members of the Council who had retired.

The Liberals claimed to have gained a point never before conceded, namely, that, *in filling Colonial offices, persons born in England were to be excluded.* In fact, it was so; for when a similar question arose in Canada, subsequently, the governor-general affirmed *that* view of Lord Stanley's despatch. Let the reader mark the change: the Whigs of the Revolution made no demand like this; they asked merely for a recognition of Colonial talents and a *share* of the patronage of the Crown;—it remained for the children of Loyalists to ask for and obtain the *monopoly* of public office.

The principal leader of the Liberals at this time, was the Hon. Lemuel A. Wilmot, who, of Loyalist descent, is a grandson of Daniel Bliss, a native of Concord, Massachusetts, and a graduate of Harvard University. Mr. Wilmot possesses brilliant powers, and is an eloquent and effective speaker. It happened that I made his acquaintance when his fortunes were considered desperate; when some of his most ardent personal friends said he was a madman; and when his adversaries told him to his face that he was a traitor. He accepted, finally, the office of attorney-general, and at the present moment is a judge of the Supreme Court.

Sir William Colebrooke was transferred to the government of British Guiana in 1848, and was succeeded by Sir Edmund Head, late governor-general of British America.

Unlike most who have administered Colonial affairs, Sir Edmund is a civilian. His life in New Brunswick was not without vexations; but he kept opposing politicians in tolerable humor, and departed for

Canada, with the hearty good wishes of most of the people.

Nothing which need detain us has occurred within ten or twelve years, and we hasten to Nova Scotia.

In that Colony, the first difficulty of consequence with the servants of the Crown was in 1836, when the government was administered by Sir Colin Campbell, an old soldier, with many scars. Unskilled in *wordy* strife, and used only to move men by the tap of the drum and the sound of the bugle, he made sad work of it among politicians and newspaper editors, and was soon involved with both. At this time there was not an incorporated city in Nova Scotia. The magistrates who held commissions from the Crown, and who were entirely independent of the people, controlled everything in their respective parishes and counties. "Neglect, mismanagement, and corruption, were perceptible everywhere." In the government of the Province, the legislative, executive, and judicial powers were strangely blended; for the same individual — such was the exact fact — was called upon in one capacity to make laws; in another, to advise the governor as to their execution; and, in a third, to administer them as a judge[1] on the bench. Nay, more; the Episcopal bishop of the Province was a member of the Council; five other members of that body were of two family connections, and five more were copartners in one mercantile firm; while the sessions were with closed doors, and the incumbents held office for life. To add that the Council was composed of only twelve members,

[1] Even the chief justice of the Province performed these threefold and incompatible duties.

and was not responsible, because it could not be reached; to add this, and the reader has the outlines of the political institutions of Nova Scotia, and in several important particulars, of all British America, hardly more than thirty years ago.

In this condition of affairs, the Hon. Joseph Howe, who is now known as a statesman, was elected to the House of Assembly. Like other leaders of the Liberals of whom I have spoken, he is of Loyalist descent. His father was John Howe, of Boston, who embarked for Halifax with the British army at the evacuation, and became postmaster-general of the Province. Mr. Howe himself was bred a printer. Prosecuted for an article which appeared in his paper, arraigning the magistrates of Halifax for gross corruption and neglect of duty, and acquitted by the jury, to the great joy of those who wished for reform, he was adopted at once as their champion. With a temerity that amazed his own friends, he assailed the Council and the abuses of the existing system of government generally, in twelve carefully drawn resolutions. In the Canadas, as we have seen, the Reformers, or Liberals, were fast hurrying matters to a bloody issue; and these resolutions, embracing as they did radical changes in every department, were opposed in a temper that would have silenced forever any common man. But they passed the Assembly finally, and were transmitted to England. Such was the beginning.

Sir Colin Campbell resisted Mr. Howe, and the party of which he was the recognized head, for about three years, when the ministry wisely transferred him to another Colony.

Lord Falkland, who succeeded, married a daughter of King William the Fourth. His Lordship endeavored to put an end to the animosities which Sir Colin had bequeathed him; and his first important measure was, the formation of a coalition cabinet, in which Mr. Howe accepted a place. So diverse, however, were its members in opinion and in social rank, that the "Coalition" — as sure to fail there as everywhere else — lasted hardly a year and a half. He next dissolved the Assembly, and met a new one, only to encounter increased difficulties. In truth, the Liberals were determined upon extensive reforms, and would not listen to overtures of compromise. In 1844, such had become the tone of the press and the people that favored and insisted upon change, that political discussions took the place of all others. In the Assembly there was a debate on fourteen successive days, in a temper that was not even decent. The relations between Lord Falkland and Mr. Howe had become personally hostile, and remarks were made by the latter which are not to be approved.

It had ordinarily happened, that on the adjournment of the Assembly, the people gradually became quiet and pursued their avocations, in forgetfulness of politics. It was not so then.

To hear the fishermen and the wood-choppers speculate upon the wonders to be accomplished by "Reform," one would have thought that "Jo Howe," as they called him, once in power, fish and fuel would advance in price in Boston market full one quarter part. In 1845, Mr. Howe traversed Nova Scotia, and increased the popular excitement. He addressed throngs in all the principal places, and often spoke three, and even four hours at a time.

It was "Jo Howe," by day and by night. The Yankee pedler who is immortalized in Sam Slick, drove good bargains in "Jo Howe" clocks. In the coal mine, in the plaster quarry, in the ship-yard, and in the forest, and on board the fishing-pogy, the jigger, and the pinkey, it was still "Jo Howe." Ships and babies were named "Jo Howe." The topers of the shops and taverns swore great oaths about "Jo Howe." The young men and maidens flirted and courted in "Jo Howe" badges, and played and sang "Jo Howe" glees. It was "Jo Howe" everywhere.

In the Assembly, the same year, Mr. Howe's speeches were frequent and personal. His invectives against Lord Falkland were bitter beyond example, and he declared, on one occasion, that it might become necessary "to hire a black fellow to horsewhip his Lordship through the streets of Halifax."

Meantime the Liberals made steady progress, and effected changes which, at the outset, they themselves did not deem possible.

Sir John Harvey, already mentioned as governor of New Brunswick, was ordered to assume the direction of affairs in 1846, and specially instructed to adopt conciliatory measures, and to calm the public mind. He attempted to form a cabinet, as Lord Falkland had done, of Liberals and Conservatives, but giving the latter party a majority of one. He failed, because the Liberals claimed to be in the ascendant, and because some of that party were averse to a second "Coalition." Sir John promptly referred the contest to the people, by dissolving the Assembly and ordering a general election. The Conservatives were defeated.

The new Assembly met early in 1848, when the existing Council retired. The Liberals filled the vacant seats with their own leaders, and disposed of the great law-offices of the Crown at pleasure. Mr. Howe became a member of the cabinet, and received, besides, the lucrative post of provincial secretary, which, as Colonists fix rank, is inferior only to the office of governor. Thus, in twelve years, the political millennium was ushered in; but sooth to say, the Boston price-current continued to quote fish and wood and grindstones, according to the old commercial law of supply and demand, to the utter astonishment of many a simple "Bluenose" who had neglected his business, year after year, to make "Jo Howe" a great man.

Men's motives are generally mingled, and it may be admitted that Mr. Howe desired, in this long struggle, to win personal distinction; but it is due to him to say that he declined office more than once, and that by his labors and sacrifices he achieved great and permanent good for his native Colony. His speeches and political papers have been published in Boston in two octavo volumes, and show that he well deserves the name of statesman.[1]

Such are the outlines of the political agitations in the British possessions, north and east of us.

It remains to consider the *results* of these agitations, — to speak of the *concessions* of the mother-

[1] See the notice of John Howe

country. Upon this subject, details are unnecessary.

The whole system of monopoly, on which the Colonial form of government was founded, has been swept away. The disabilities, as relates to commerce and manufactures, which existed in our fathers' time, have disappeared. There is not an imperial custom-house, or an imperial revenue-officer, in all British America. Colonial ships voyage to all parts of the world. The substance of a long despatch from Earl Grey to Lord Elgin, in 1846, was, that *the Colonists may* MAKE *what they will; may* BUY *where they please; may* SELL *where they can.* Had this State paper been framed seventy years earlier, and in 1776, the public debt of England would have been five hundred millions of dollars less than it is, and one hundred thousand Anglo-Saxon men and women would not have perished in battle, in storm, and in prison.

Mark the progress in civilization and in political freedom. "*Make* what you will; *buy* where you please; *sell* where you can!" In the annunciation of these words, England herself pronounced the vindication of the "upstart barristers," — John Adams, John Jay, and John Marshall, — the vindication of the "upstart tobacco planter" of Mount Vernon, and of their associates; and in the face of the civilized world she abandoned the accusation that the Whigs of the Revolution "were but successful rebels and traitors." In the old thirteen Colonies, she endeavored to maintain, by arms, the monopoly of ships and workshops and places of honor, for natives of the British Isles; and humanity weeps over smouldering ruins and divided and expatriated families, to save the Colonial system of government, which, without an element of human brotherhood, was transmitted by heathen Carthage and Rome, and which, all now agree, should never have been fastened upon the Colonists of any Christian nation. Mark the change! Fourteen years after the promulgation of Earl Gray's despatch, the heir to the British throne, and his suite of nobles, mused at the spot where Washington is buried, and on the battle-ground where Warren died![1]

Again, England no longer excludes Colonial talents from places of honor or emolument. The governor-general and the governors of the separate Colonies are still appointed by the Crown, but the subordinate posts are open to Colonists, in accordance with the popular will. Nay, more. Mr. Howe, in several elaborate letters to Lord John Russell, claims that natives of the Colonies shall be eligible to the highest places in the church, in the army and navy; shall be allowed to represent England at foreign courts, and to occupy the position of cabinet ministers at home.

In view of *these* pretensions, recall that a governor of Massachusetts once refused to appoint John Adams a justice of the peace; that Washington was denied the commission of colonel in the army, and that John Marshall, who lived to found the jurisprudence of a nation, was doomed, as a Colonist,

---

[1] The Prince of Wales visited Mount Vernon, October 5, and Bunker Hill, October 19, 1860. Among the distinguished personages who accompanied him on his visit to the Colonies and to the United States, were the Duke of Newcastle, the Earl of St. Germans, Viscount Hincherbroke, and Honorable Major-General Robert Bruce.

to plead before English-born judges, in the county courts of Virginia. A single word more.

A few years ago the most intense hate was cherished by Colonists towards people of the United States. *Their* fathers were the losers, *ours* were the winners, in the war of the Revolution. Nor was kind feeling entertained among us. It was thought disloyal in a Colonist, and to evince a want of patriotism in a citizen of the republic, to seek to promote sentiments of love on either side, and to unite kinsmen who, two generations ago, were severed in the dismemberment of the British empire. But the change is wonderful; and some persons who commenced the work of reconciliation live to witness the consummation of their highest hopes. The children of the Whigs and the children of the Tories have become reconciled.[1] God be praised that it is so! The controversy relative to our rights in the fisheries in the British colonial seas, which for awhile, on the American side of the frontier, was conducted by my single pen, opened, as I venture to record, the way for the adjustment of all the questions of difference. The Treaty of Reciprocity, concluded in 1854, was the crowning measure of peace and good-will; since, if revised — as it should be — it will be lasting.

[1] This chapter was written before the breaking out of the present unhallowed rebellion, but I make no change in the text, in consequence of the feeling towards the North by a *part* of the politicians and of the newspapers in British America; for what is said and written is not worthy of thought, much less does it represent the great Colonial heart.

CHAPTER XIV.

Introductory Remarks. Principles of Unbelief prevalent. The Whigs lose sight of their Original Purposes, and propose Conquests. Decline of Public Spirit. Avarice, Rapacity, Traffic with the Enemy. Gambling, Speculation, Idleness, Dissipation, and Extravagance. Want of Patriotism. Excessive Issue of Paper might have been avoided. Recruits for the Army demand Enormous Bounty. Shameless Desertions and Immoralities Commissions in the Army to men destitute of Principle Court-martials frequent, and many Officers Cashiered. Resignations upon Discreditable Pretexts, and alarmingly prevalent. The Public Mind fickle, and Disastrous Changes in Congress. The Whigs of England.

It has been my constant endeavor to speak of those who opposed the Whigs, in the momentous conflict which made us an independent people, calmly and mildly. For—

>"Mercy to him that shows it is the rule
>And righteous limitation of its act,
>By which Heaven moves in pardoning guilty man;
>And he that shows none, being *ripe in years*,
>*And conscious of the outrage he commits*,
>Shall seek it, and not find it, in his turn."

Virtuous men, whatever their errors and mistakes, are to be respected; and with regard to others, it is well to remember the beautiful sentiment of Goldsmith, that "we should never strike an unnecessary blow at a victim over whom Providence holds the scourge of its resentment."

While intending to be just, I have felt that I might also be generous.

> " Can he be strenuous in his country's cause
> Who slights the charities for whose dear sake
> That country, if at all, must be beloved ? "

A word now of the winners in the strife. I premise that I am of Whig descent. My father's father received his death-wound under Washington, at Trenton; my mother's father fought under Stark, at Bennington. There are those who are still ready to do battle for *every* " Whig," and to denounce *every* " Tory ;" who still believe that all who were known by the former name were disinterested and virtuous, and that all to whom the latter epithet was applied, were selfish and vicious, and deserving of reproach. To these, I address the concluding chapter of this Essay.

I do not care, of all things, to be thought to want appreciation of those of my countrymen who broke the yoke of Colonial vassalage ; nor, on the other hand, do I care to imitate the writers of a late school, and treat the great and the *successful* actors in the world's affairs as little short of divinities, and as exempt from criticism. In speaking of men who have left their impress upon their age, something, I own, is due to the dignity of history ; but something, too, is due to the dignity of truth. The bandaged eyes and the even scales, I apprehend, are as fit emblems for the student as for the judge ; and so, upon the evidence, and upon the law of progress, I say that we are not to look for as great intellectual development, or for as high civilization, among bound or even emancipated British Colonists, as, after the lapse of two generations, exist around us, and in Anglo-Saxon countries everywhere.

We have now the off-hand limnings of John Adams and of others, of the men and manners of the second half of the last century; and those who are well informed as to the leading personages and events of that period will not doubt the general accuracy of the pictures. These sketches of the principal characters in Boston, New York, Philadelphia, and in Congress, as well as the mention of the sectional jealousies that prevailed, — of the personal quarrels and alienations that existed among the Whigs of high position in the civil and military line at home, and among those who were employed abroad on embassies of the last importance to the Whig cause, — show clearly that the prominent men of the Revolutionary era were great and good, little and bad, mingled; just as elsewhere in the annals of our race. The Whigs of lofty virtue, like William III. of England, were compelled by the necessities of their condition to employ as instruments persons whom they knew or believed to be mere mercenaries, who would fall off and join the royal side the moment that interest or a case for individual safety should appear to require; and, like William, they seemed oblivious of this fact, simply because, under the circumstances, it was sound policy to be blind, forgetful, and ignorant.

Nay, this general statement will not serve my purpose. Justice demands as severe a judgment of the Whigs as of their opponents; and I shall here record the result of long and patient study. At the Revolutionary period, the principles of unbelief were diffused to a considerable extent throughout the Colonies. It is certain that several of the most conspicuous personages of those days were either avowed disbelievers in Christianity, or cared so little about it, that they were commonly regarded as disciples of the English or French schools of sceptical philosophy. Again, the Whigs were by no means exempt from the lust of dominion. Several of them were among the most noted land speculators of their time. As I have elsewhere said, in the progress of the war, and in a manner hardly to be defended, we find them sequestering and appropriating to themselves the vast estates of those who opposed them. So we find that while the issue of the contest was yet doubtful, they lost sight of its original purposes, and in their endeavors to procure the alliance of France, they proposed that she should join them in an enterprise to conquer her own former Colonial possessions in America; and the Saxon thirst for boundless sway may be seen in their calm and thoughtful proposition, to keep nearly all the soil and fishing-grounds to be acquired for their own use and aggrandizement. Still again, avarice and rapacity were seemingly as common then as now. Indeed, the stock-jobbing, the extortion, the forestalling, the low arts and devices to amass wealth, that were practised during the struggle, are almost incredible. Washington mourned the want of virtue as early as 1775, and averred that he "trembled at the prospect." Soldiers were stripped of their miserable pittance, that contractors for the army might become rich in a single campaign. Many of the sellers of merchandise monopolized articles of the first necessity, and would not part with them to their suffering countrymen, and to the wives and children of those who were absent in the field, unless at enormous profits. The traffic carried on with the royal troops was immense. Men of all descriptions finally engaged in it, and those who at the beginning of the war would have shuddered at the idea of any connection with the enemy, pursued it with avidity. The public securities were often counterfeited; official signatures were forged; and plunder and robbery openly indulged. Appeals to the guilty from the pulpit, the press, and the halls of legislation, were alike unheeded. The decline of public spirit; the love of gain of those in office; the plotting of disaffected persons; and the malevolence of faction became widely spread, and in parts of the country were uncontrollable. The useful occupations of life, and the legitimate pursuits of commerce, were abandoned by thousands. The basest of men enriched themselves; and many of the most estimable sunk into obscurity and indigence. There were those who would neither pay their debts nor their taxes. The finances of the State, and the fortunes of individuals were to an alarming extent at the mercy of gamblers and speculators. The indignation of Washington was freely expressed. "It gives me very sincere pleasure," he said, in a letter to Joseph Reed, "to find the Assembly [of Pennsylvania] is so well disposed to second your endeavors in bringing those murderers of our cause, the monopolizers, forestallers, and engrossers, to condign punishment. It is much to be lamented, that each State long ere this has not hunted them down as pests to society, and the greatest enemies we have to the happiness of America. No punishment, in my opinion, is too great for the man who can build his greatness upon his country's ruin." In a letter to another, he drew this picture, which he solemnly declared to be a true one: "From what I have seen, heard, and in part know," said he, "I should in one word say, that idleness, dissipation, and extravagance, seem to have laid fast hold of most; that speculation, peculation, and an insatiable thirst for riches, seem to have got the better of every other consideration and almost every order of men; and that party disputes and personal quarrels are the great business of the day." In other letters he laments the laxity of public morals, the "distressed, ruinous, and deplorable condition of affairs;" the "many melancholy proofs of the decay of private virtue;" and asks if "the paltry consideration of a little pelf to individuals is to be placed in competition with the essential rights and liberties of the present generation, and of millions yet unborn." And scattered through his correspondence are passages which show "the increasing rapacity of the times;" the "declining zeal of the people;" and in which he rejoices over the "virtuous few," who were struggling against the corruptions and "stock-jobbing of the multitude."

I pass next to discuss the question of patriotism. In the first place, then, it should be remembered that the war was undertaken for the holiest cause which ever arrayed men in battle; that the Whigs were a minority in some of the States, barely equalled their opponents in others, and in the whole country composed but an inconsiderable majority; and that of consequence, there was every incentive to exertion, to action, to union, and to sacrifice for the common good. But what is the truth? To say nothing of the Whigs of Vermont, who at one period were declared by Washington to be "a dead weight upon the cause;" some examination of the resources of the thirteen Federal States has served to convince me, that, had the advice and plans of the illustrious Commander-in-Chief, of Franklin, and other judicious and patriotic persons been adopted; and had there been system and common prudence and integrity in the management of affairs, the army might have been well fed, clothed, and paid throughout the struggle. The prevalent impression is that America was poor. In my judgment it was not so. The people who, before the Revolution, bought tea to the amount of two and a half millions of dollars annually, and who, in the most distressing periods of the contest, imported useless articles of luxury, were not poor, but able to maintain those who served in the field. Particular States, and thousands of individuals, exhausted their means to aid in achieving the independence of their country; but I am satisfied that the want of patriotism in other States, and in other individual Whigs, produced the appalling calamities of the war, and compelled the resort to the seizure of private property, and other objectionable expedients. The issuing of bills of credit was, perhaps, unavoidable; but their excessive depreciation might and should have been prevented. The exports of the Colonies prior to 1775 were large; and with a liberal allowance for diminished production during hostilities, there were still provisions at all times to feed the people, and both the Whig and the Royal forces. In fact, the prizes taken by the numerous privateers were very valuable, and increased the ability of the country, probably, nearly as much as it was lessened by the partial interruption of agriculture. The King's troops were well supplied; for his generals paid "hard money," and not the "continental stuff." "I am amazed," said Washington to Colonel Stewart, "at the report you make of the quantity of provision that goes daily into Philadelphia[1] from the County of Bucks;"—and mark that this was written in January of that memorable winter which the American army passed in nakedness and starvation at Valley Forge. So, too, there were men enough who in name were Whigs, to meet the strongest force that was ever employed to suppress the popular movement. There was always an army—on paper; but the votes of Congress were seldom executed by the States. At the close of one campaign there was not a sufficient number of troops in camp to man the lines; and at the opening of another, when the Commander-in-Chief was expected to take the field, "scarce any State in the Union," as he himself said, had "an eighth part of its quota" in service. The bounty finally paid to soldiers was enormous. Omitting details, the general fact will be indicated by stating that the price for a single recruit was as high sometimes as seven hundred and fifty, and one thousand dollars, on enlistment for the war, besides the bounty and emoluments given by Congress; and that one hundred and fifty dollars "in specie" was exacted and paid for a term of duty of only five months. Such were the extraordinary inducements

[1] Then occupied by the British Army.

necessary to tempt some men to serve their country, when their dearest interests were at issue. Still, large numbers of Whigs demanded that Washington should face and fight their enemies, without troops, without stores, and at times, without even their own confidence and sympathy. If we allow that much of the reluctance to enter the army arose from the knowledge of the privations and sufferings to be endured in camp, and from aversion to receive payment for service in a depreciated currency, we shall palliate the conduct of the class expected to be soldiers only to censure by implication another class, who possessed, but kept back, the means of supporting those who fought their battles.

Making every allowance for the effects of hunger and want, for the claims of families at home, and for other circumstances equally imperative; desertion, mutiny, robbery, and murder, are still high crimes. There were soldiers of the Revolution who deserted in parties of twenty and thirty at a time, and several hundred of those who thus abandoned the cause, fled to Vermont, and were among the early settlers of that State. A thousand men, the date of whose enlistment had been misplaced, perjured themselves in a body, as fast as they could be sworn, in order to quit the ranks which they had voluntarily entered. In smaller parties, hundreds of others demanded dismission from camp under false pretexts, and with lies upon their lips. Some, also added treason to desertion, and joined the various corps of Loyalists in the capacity of spies upon their former friends, or of guides and pioneers. Many more enlisted, deserted, and reënlisted under new recruiting officers, for the purpose of receiving double bounty; while others, who placed their names upon the rolls, were paid the money to which they were entitled, but refused to join the army; and others still, who were sent to the hospitals, returned home without leave after their recovery, and were sheltered and secreted by friends and neighbors, whose sense of right was as weak as their own. Another class sold their clothing, provisions, and arms, to obtain means for revelling, and to indulge their propensity for drunkenness; while some prowled about the country, to rob and kill the unoffending and defenceless. A guard was placed over the grave of a foreigner of rank, who died in Washington's own quarters, and who was buried in full dress, with diamond rings and buckles; "lest the soldiers should be tempted to dig for hidden treasures." In a word, I fear that whippings, drummings from the service, and even military executions, were more frequent in the Revolution than at any subsequent period of our history.

If we turn our attention to the officers, we shall find that many had but doubtful claims to respect for purity of private character; and that some were addicted to grave vices. It is certain that appointments were conferred upon unworthy persons throughout the war. Knox wrote to Gerry, that there were men in commission "who wished to have their power perpetuated at the expense of the liberties of the people;" and who "had been rewarded with rank without having the least pretensions to it, except cabal and intrigue." There were officers who were destitute alike of honor and patriotism, who unjustly clamored for their pay, while they drew large sums of public money under pretext of paying their men, but applied them to the support of their own extravagance; who went home on furlough, and never returned; and who, regardless of their word as gentlemen, violated their paroles, and were threatened by Washington with exposure in every newspaper in the land, as men who had disgraced themselves and were heedless of their associates in captivity, whose restraints were increased by their misconduct. At times, courts-martial were continually sitting; and so numerous were the convictions that the names of those who were cashiered were sent to Congress in lists. "Many of the surgeons," — are the words of Washington — "are very great rascals, countenancing the men to sham complaints to exempt them from duty, and often receiving bribes to certify indispositions, with a view to procure discharges or furloughs;" and still further, they drew for the public "medicines and stores in the most profuse and extravagant manner, for private purposes." In a letter to the governor of a State, he affirmed that the officers who had been sent him therefrom were "generally of the lowest class of the people;" that they "led their soldiers to plunder the inhabitants, and into every kind of mischief." To his brother, John Augustine Washington, he declared that the different States were nominating such officers as were "not fit to be shoeblacks." Resignations occurred upon discreditable pretexts, and became alarmingly prevalent. Some resigned at critical moments, and others combined together in considerable numbers for purposes of intimidation, and threatened to retire from the service at a specified time, unless certain terms were complied with. For a single instance, to show the extent of the evil, I again quote from the Commander-in-Chief, who wrote to a member of Congress, in 1778, that "the spirit of resigning commissions has been long at an alarming height, and increases daily. The Virginia line has sustained a violent shock. Not less than ninety have already resigned to me. The same conduct has prevailed among the officers from other States, though not yet in so considerable degree; and there are but too just grounds to fear that it will shake the very existence of the army, unless a remedy is soon, very soon, applied." The spirit did not abate; since, two years after, he informed the President of Congress, that he had "scarcely a sufficient number [of officers] left to take care even of the fragments of corps which remained." I would not be understood to assert that there were not proper and imperative causes to justify the retirement of many; but the illustrious man whose words I have so often quoted, and who was obliged to bear the disheartening consequences of these frequent resignations, was a competent judge of the motives and reasons which influenced those with whom he was associated; and as we have his assertion that he was often *deserted*, I have not hesitated to class the numerous throwing up of commissions with other evidences of a want of principle.

The complaints of wives and children at home; the inattention of Congress and of the State legislatures, to whom the officers had a right, both legal and moral, to look for sympathy and support in the poverty to which some were reduced, are to be taken into the account in forming, and should do much to soften, our judgment; but with the proofs before me, obtained entirely from the writings of distinguished Whigs, I am compelled to believe that many of those who abandoned Washington were guilty of a crime, which, when committed by private soldiers, is called desertion, and punished with death. Eighteen of the generals retired during the struggle: one for drunkenness; one to avoid disgrace for receiving double pay; some from declining health; others from the weight of advanced years; others to accept civil employments; but several from private resentments, and real or imaginary wrongs inflicted by Congress or associates in the service. The example of the latter class was pernicious; since, when heads of divisions or brigades quit their commands for reasons chiefly or entirely personal, it was to be expected that regiments, battalions, and companies would be left in like manner, without officers. Abundant testimony can be adduced to show that individuals of all ranks entered the army from interested motives, and abandoned it from similar reasons. John Adams wrote, in 1777:—"I am wearied to death with the wrangles between military officers, high and low. They quarrel like cats and dogs. They worry one another like mastiffs, scrambling for rank and pay like apes for nuts." Washington, more guarded to Congress, uses language almost as pointed in his letters to private friends.

Again, the public mind was as fickle in the Revolution as at present. McKean, of Delaware, was the only member of Congress who served eight successive years; and Jefferson, Gerry, and Ellery were the only signers of the Declaration of Independence who were in service when the definitive treaty of peace was ratified. The attendance of members, too, was at times irregular, and public affairs often suffered by their absence. There were periods when several of the States were without representation; and others, when the requisite number for the transaction of business, were not in their places. The entire control of matters, executive and legislative, of measures to be taken to procure loans in Europe, and to raise money at home to provide for the army, and for every other branch of the public service, devolved frequently upon as few as thirty delegates; and some of the most momentous questions were determined by twenty. Those who steadily attended to their duties were worn down with care and excessive labor. John Adams, one of them, was in Congress three years and three months, during which time he was a member of ninety committees, and chairman of twenty-five. In the course of the war, persons of small claims to notice or regard obtained seats in Congress, and by their want of capacity and principle, prolonged the contest, and needlessly increased its burdens and expenses. By the force of party discipline, as was bitterly remarked by a leading Whig, men were brought into the management of affairs "who might have lived till the millennium in silent obscurity, had they depended on their mental qualifications."

Such, rapidly told, is the dark side of the story of the Revolution, as concerns the *winners*. I relate it here for several reasons. First, because it is due to the *losers* in the strife. Second, to show, what many persons are slow to believe, that there were wicked

"Whigs" as well as wicked "Tories." Third, to do something to correct the exaggerated and gloomy views which are often taken of the degenerate spirit of the present times, founded on erroneous, because on a partial, estimate of the virtues of a by-gone age.

AMERICAN LOYALISTS.

ABBOTT, BENJAMIN. Minister of the Methodist Episcopal Church. He was born on Long Island, N. Y., in 1732. His youth was passed in dissipation. Before the Revolution he became religiously inclined, and after due spiritual preparation, entered the ministry. The prevalent impression was, that few preachers of his denomination favored the popular movement, and in common with most of them, " he was suspected of Toryism." But he persisted in addressing the people, as he had opportunity, though sometimes " at the peril of his life." Once, while preaching " in a private house, a mob of soldiers came rushing in with guns and fixed bayonets, one of whom approached him, and presented his gun as though he would run him through, while his associates in the adventure were standing around the door." Mr. Abbott, heedless of the interruption, finished his discourse; and his assailants, awed by his intrepidity, retired without injuring him. On another occasion, a hundred armed men assembled at the place of meeting, but, instead of violence, they listened as orderly as others. Thus far, and indeed until 1789, he labored according to his own pleasure. After he placed himself under the direction of the Conference, he was stationed on several circuits in the State of New York, on one in New Jersey, and on one in Maryland. He died at Salem, N. J., in 1796, aged sixty-four, and in the twenty-third year of his ministry.

ACKERLY, OBADIAH. Of New York. In 1783 he abandoned his home and property, and settled in New Brunswick. He died at St. John in 1843, aged eighty-seven. Catharine, his wife, died at the same city in 1830, at the age of seventy-two.

ADAMS, DOCTOR ——. Of the State of New York. In 1774, or early in 1775, he was hoisted up and exposed upon "Landlord Fay's sign-post, where was fixed a dead catamount." The party who inflicted this punishment regretted that they had not tied him and given him instead five hundred lashes. His residence was at Arlington.

ADDISON, REV. H. Of Maryland. Episcopal minister. He was attainted and lost his estate. In 1783, he was at New York, a petitioner for lands in Nova Scotia. In a Loyalist tract published at London in 1784, I find it said, that he was a gentleman of large property, and that on his arrival in England, Lord North allowed him a pension of £150 per annum, to support himself and son, which was less than he had formerly given his coachman and footman. And, adds the writer, Mr. Addison, disgusted at so small a consideration, resigned his pension and returned to New York, where he endeavored to make terms with the Whigs, and to effect the restoration of his estate which he valued at £30,000, but that he failed to obtain leave even to reside in Maryland.

ADDISON, DANIEL DELANY. Of Maryland. He entered the Maryland Loyalists in 1776; was a captain in 1782, and a major at the peace. He went to England, and received half-pay. He died suddenly at the age of fifty, in Charlotte Street, Fitzroy Square, London, 1808.

AGNEW, JOHN. He was rector of the Established Church, parish of Suffolk, Virginia. On the 24th of March, 1775, the Whig Committee of Nansemond County called him to an account for the loyalty of his pulpit performances.

I have before me a copy of Lord Dunmore's Proclamation, dated November 7, 1776, on board the ship *William*, of Norfolk, which Mr. Agnew was ordered to read in church, and the indorsement on the back is, "which was done accordingly." He soon after quitted that part of the country, and became chaplain of the Queen's Rangers. He finally settled in New Brunswick, and died near Fredericton, in 1812, aged eighty-five. He was taken prisoner with Stair Agnew and others, during the Revolution, and carried to France. On the passage out, the ship encountered a severe gale, and lay a wreck for twenty-four hours.

AGNEW, STAIR. Believed to have been a son of the Rev. John Agnew. He was certainly from Virginia, and a captain in the Queen's Rangers, and settled at Fredericton, where he resided until his death, in 1821, at the age of sixty-three. He enjoyed half-pay. While attached to the Rangers he was taken prisoner and carried to France, and was not exchanged until near the close of the war. It seems that at the battle of the Brandywine he was severely wounded, and while on his passage to Virginia, for recovery, was captured by the French squadron. Franklin, Minister to France, was appealed to, to effect his release and that of others made prisoners at the same time. Captain Agnew's letter from the Castle of St. Maloes, February 26, 1782, details the circumstances of his captivity, and contains some feeling allusions to his "aged and beloved mother." He closes: " O, God! who knows, perhaps she at this moment, from an independent affluence, is reduced by the vicissitudes of the times to penury. My heart, afflicted with the misfortunes of our family, can no more ———." He was a member of the House of Assembly of New Brunswick for thirty years, and a magistrate of York County for a considerable period. His wife, Sophia Winifred, died in that county in 1820, at the age of fifty-two.

AIKMAN, ALEXANDER. Of South Carolina. He was born in Scotland in 1755, and at the age of sixteen he emigrated to Charleston, and became the apprentice of Robert Wells, a bookseller and printer of that city. He left the country in consequence of the Revolution, and after some wanderings, fixed his residence in Jamaica, where, in 1778, he established a newspaper called the "Jamaica Mercury," which title was changed to that of the "Royal Gazette," on his obtaining the patronage of the government of the Colony. For many years he was a member of the House of Assembly, and printer to that body and to the King. In 1795 he visited Great Britain, but was captured on the passage, and compelled to ransom his property. He visited his native land three times subsequently, but remained at home after the year 1814. He bore the character of an honorable, worthy, and charitable man. His estates in the parish of St. George's were known as Birnam Wood and Wallenford. He died at Prospect Pen, St. Andrew's, July, 1838, at the age of eighty-three. His wife was Louisa Susanna, second daughter of Robert Wells, his former master. This lady was four years his fellow-*clerk* in her father's office at Charleston, and joined him from England after no little peril, since she was taken once by the French, and kept in France three months, and was detained a second time by a British cruiser, because she took passage in a slave ship. She died at West Cowes in 1831, aged seventy-six. Her mother was a Ruthven, and of the lineage of the Earls of Gowrie. Mr. Aikman's children were ten, of whom there were two survivors at the time of his decease, namely, Mary, the wife of James Smith, of Jamaica; and Ann Hunter, the widow of John Enright, surgeon in the Royal Navy. Of his sons, Alexander, who succeeded to his business, died in 1831, leaving a large family.

AKERLY, ———. In 1782, in command of a small party of Loyalists in New York. Among his prisoners was one Strong, who was hung.

ALDEN, ABIATHER. Of Maine. Physician. One of the two Loyalists of Saco and Biddeford. An armed party took him, placed him on his knees upon a large cask, and with their guns presented to his body, told him to recant his opinions, or suffer instant death. He signed the required confession, and was released. Subsequently he removed to Scarborough, in the same State. He was distinguished in metaphysics.

ALLAIRE, ANTHONY. In 1782 he was a lieutenant in the Loyal American Regiment, and at the peace a captain in the same corps. He settled in New Brunswick, and received half-pay. He was one of the grantees of the city of St. John, but, removing to the country, died in the parish of Douglas, in 1838, at the age of eighty-four.

ALLEN, WILLIAM. Chief Justice of Pennsylvania. He accepted and held that office at the request of distinguished men in the Province; its emoluments were appropriated to charities. On the approach of the Revolution he went to England, and died September, 1780. He was distinguished for his love of literature and the arts; was a friend to Benjamin West when he needed a patron, and assisted Franklin to establish a college at Philadelphia. His father was an eminent merchant, and died in 1725. No person in Pennsylvania, probably, was richer than Judge Allen, or possessed greater influence. A wag of the time said, he joined the royal side "because the Continental Congress *presumed* to declare the American States free and independent without first asking the consent, and obtaining the approbation, of himself and *wise* family." It is stated, that in 1761, he was one of the three persons in Philadelphia who kept a coach. His own was drawn by four horses, and his coachman, who was imported from England, was "a great whip."

ALLEN, WILLIAM. Of Pennsylvania, and son of Chief Justice Allen. He was a Whig, and accepted the commission of lieutenant-colonel in the Continental service, and served under St. Clair. But in 1776 he abandoned the cause of his country, and joined General Howe, with his brothers. In Continental Congress, when he asked to resign his commission — " Resolved that leave be granted." In 1778 he raised a corps called the Pennsylvania Loyalists, and, with the rank of lieutenant-colonel, was the commanding officer. From the influence of his family, and from his own personal standing, he expected to make rapid enlistments, but was disappointed. At the siege of Pensacola, one of this corps attempted to desert, was seized, whipped to the extent of five hundred lashes, drummed out of camp, with his hands tied behind, with a large label pinned to his breast stating his crime, escorted close to the enemy's line, and left to his fate. The day following, a shell was thrown into the door of the magazine, as the men were receiving powder, and forty-five of this regiment were killed, and a number wounded. In 1782, and near the close of the contest, though still in service, the Pennsylvania Loyalists were of but little consequence in point of numbers. Colonel Allen was noted for wit, for good-humor, and for affable and gentlemanly manners. The names of all the officers under his command at the period last mentioned will be found in this work. He was attainted of treason and lost his estate under the confiscation acts. I find his name last, in 1783, as a grantee of St. John, New Brunswick.

ALLEN, ANDREW. Of Pennsylvania, son of Chief Justice Allen, and himself the successor of Judge Chew, who succeeded his father. He, at first, was found among the leading Whigs, and was a member of Congress, and of the Committee of Safety. In 1776 he put himself under protection of General Howe, at Trenton, and during the war went to England. He was attainted, and lost his estate under the confiscation acts. In 1779 he was directed to testify before Parliament on the inquiry into the conduct of Sir William Howe and General Burgoyne, while in America, but was not examined. He died in London in 1825, at the age of eighty-five. His son Andrew, a very accomplished gentleman, was many years, prior to the war of 1812, British Consul at Boston.

ALLEN, JOHN. Of Pennsylvania, a son of Chief Justice Allen. In 1776 he joined the British under General Howe, at Trenton. Unlike his brother, he was an avowed Loyalist from the first. He was attainted of treason, but died at Philadelphia, February, 1778, in his thirty-ninth year, before the day on which he was ordered to surrender himself for trial.

ALLEN, JAMES. Of Philadelphia; the remaining son of Chief Justice Allen, and the only one of them who did not join the Royal Army. He remained at home wholly inactive, though his sympathies were supposed to be loyal. He was in declining health in 1776, and died before the close of the following year. His children were James; Anne Penn, who married James Greenleaf; Margaret, who married Chief

Justice Tilghman; and Mary, who married Harry Walter Livingston, of Livingston's Manor, New York. The last-named daughter was living in 1855. Mrs. Allen, who died in the year 1800, was the only daughter of John Lawrence, and cousin of Margaret Shippen, second wife of Benedict Arnold.

ALLEN, ISAAC. A lawyer of Trenton, New Jersey. He entered the military service of the Crown, and in 1782 was lieutenant-colonel of the second battalion of New Jersey Volunteers. He had property in Pennsylvania, and the executive council of that State ordered, that, unless he should surrender himself and take his trial for treason within a specified time, he should stand attainted. He went to St. John, New Brunswick, at the peace, and was one of the grantees of that city. He rose to distinction in that Province, and among other offices held a seat in the Council, and was a judge of the Supreme Court. His residence was at Fredericton, and he died there in 1806, aged sixty-five. His sister Sarah died at the same place in 1835, aged ninety-one.

ALLEN, ADAM. He was an officer in the Queen's Rangers, and, it is believed, a lieutenant. He went to St. John, New Brunswick, at the peace, and was one of the grantees of that city. He received half-pay. In 1798 he was in command of a post at Grand Falls, on the River St. John, and wrote a piece in verse descriptive of these Falls, which his son, Jacob Allen, of Portland, New Brunswick, sent to the press in 1845. He died in York County, New Brunswick, in 1823, aged sixty-six.

ALLEN, JOLLEY. Of Boston. In an account of his sufferings and losses, he relates that, "sometime, I think in the month of October, 1772, I bought two chests of tea of Governor Hutchinson's two sons, Thomas and Elisha, about eleven o'clock in the forenoon." This purchase was the prime cause of all his subsequent misfortunes. He sold goods "cheap for cash;" he boarded many of the British officers; and he kept "horses and chaises to let." In a word, Jolley was a shrewd, dashing, thriving man. A Loyalist, body and soul, he left Boston with the Royal Army, at the evacuation in March, 1776. The man who engaged to convey his family and property to Halifax, was a knave, and unskilful in the management of a vessel. Soon parting with the fleet, they arrived, not in Nova Scotia, but at Cape Cod; where his goods were seized and confiscated, and where all on board were imprisoned. His brother Lewis petitioned for leave to take his seven children; and the Assembly, in granting the request, stipulated that Lewis should receive £36.8 from Jolley's effects; that he should give bonds to support the children, and should maintain Jolley himself; while a committee were to take possession of all the property, to deliver to Lewis "the children's four feather beds and bedding, and the wearing apparel of the children and of the late wife of Jolley," and his own clothing. In September, 1776, our unhappy Loyalist was allowed to make sale of a part of his goods at Cape Cod, in order to pay the debts contracted there by himself and family; while the selectmen of Provincetown were directed to deliver the remainder to a committee of the Court, to be disposed of on public account. I find him next in 1779, when he was in London, and one of the Loyalists who addressed the king. He died in England in 1782. Sir William Pepperell and George Erving were his executors; and he directed that, after the troubles were over, his remains should be removed to the family vault under King's Chapel, Boston.

ALLISON, EDWARD. Of Long Island, New York. He acknowledged allegiance in 1776, and was subsequently a captain in De Lancey's Third Battalion. At the peace he settled in New Brunswick, and received half-pay. He died in that Province.

ALTHOUSE, JOHN. Of New York. In 1782 he was a captain in the New York Volunteers. At the peace he went to St. John, New Brunswick, and was one of the grantees of the city. He died in that Province.

AMBROSE, MICHAEL. In 1782 he was a lieutenant in the Prince of Wales' American Volunteers. He went to New

Brunswick at the peace, and received half-pay. He died in the parish of St. Martin in that Province.

AMORY, THOMAS. Of Boston. He was born in Boston in 1722, and graduated at Harvard University in 1741. He studied divinity, but never took orders. In 1765 he married Elizabeth, daughter of William Coffin, and purchased the house built by Governor Belcher, at the corner of Harvard and Washington Streets, which was his principal residence for the rest of his life. He took very little part in the controversies which preceded the Revolution, except that he was one of the Addressers of Gage. He was, however, on terms of friendship with many of the British officers stationed in Boston; and, it is related that, while several were dining with him, a mob attacked his house, and broke some of the windows. Mr. Amory spoke to them from the porch, and commanded them to disperse; meanwhile, the officers made their escape through the garden. He remained in Boston during the siege, and at the evacuation in March, 1776, accompanied by his younger brother Jonathan, he went to Washington, at the instance of the selectmen, to request that the British might be permitted to retire without molestation, on condition that they embarked without injury to the town. This proposition had the sanction of Sir William Howe; and, though no positive arrangement was concluded, an understanding to this effect was respected on both sides. His wife's family — the Coffins — were mostly refugee Loyalists. Of her nephews, two were distinguished: namely, Isaac, who became an Admiral in the Royal Navy; and John, who rose to the rank of Lieutenant-General in the British Army. Suspected of sympathy with the enemy, Mr. Amory removed to Watertown, where he lived some years. He died in 1784; his widow survived until 1823. He left nine children, seven of whom were married, and resided in Boston.

The mingling of the blood of the loyal and of the disloyal, at the present time, causes one to muse on the political asperities of the past. On the memorable 17th of June, 1775, Linzee, of the King's ship-of-war *Falcon*, cannonaded the works which Prescott, the "rebel," defended; but the granddaughter of the first was the wife of Prescott the historian, who was a grandson of the last; and this lady is a daughter of Thomas C., the eldest son of the subject of this notice. Jonathan, the second son of our Loyalist, married Hettie, daughter of James Sullivan, Governor of Massachusetts; while the wife of John Amory, another son, was near of kin to Henry Gardner, the "rebel," who succeeded Harrison Gray, the last royal treasurer of the same State. Again, Nathaniel, still another son, married a niece of *our* Commodore Preble, and her sister was the wife of Admiral Wormley of the *Royal* Navy. Once more: William, a fifth son of the Loyalist, was an officer in the navy of *both* countries, and under our own flag distinguished himself in several engagements. But "loyalty," as understood in olden time, is still represented in the family, by the union of Mr. Amory's grandson Charles, with Martha Greene; and of his grandson James Sullivan, with Mary Greene, nieces of the late Lord Lyndhurst. We leave this pleasant record of oblivion of the differences of another age, to add that Mr. Amory's grandson, Thomas C., married Esther Sargent; and that William, of the same degree of consanguinity, is the husband of Anna, daughter of David Sears, of Boston. Of the *sons* here mentioned, Thomas C. was a successful merchant, and died in 1812; Jonathan, also a merchant, died in 1828. Thomas C. Amory, Jr., also a descendant, is the author of the "Life of Governor Sullivan;" (his grandfather on his mother's side,) in two vols., 8vo.

AMORY, JOHN. Of Boston. Brother of the preceding. He was born in Boston in 1728, and married Catherine, daughter of Rufus Greene, by whom he was the father of nine children, who grew up and settled in his native town. He built the house opposite the Stone Chapel, corner of Tremont and Bowdoin Streets, and lived there, and in Washington Street on the site of Amory Hall. He engaged extensively in commerce with his younger brother. The letters of his business house from 1760, during the Stamp Act excitement and the Tea war, give many interesting particulars of that stirring period. These letters moreover, predicted, long before the war broke out, a sanguinary contest, and the actual separation of the Colonies from the mother-country, if the government persisted in its measures of coercion. Parts of this correspondence were published in the English papers, and to one letter a member of Parliament ascribed influence in the repeal of the Stamp Act. At the beginning of hostilities, his house owed their English creditors £23,000 sterling; and while those who owed *them*, from inability, or taking advantage of the times, paid, if at all, in a depreciated currency, they remitted their whole debt without delay. In 1774 it became important that one of the partners should go to England. The subject of this notice went, taking his wife. Her protracted illness, which terminated in her death in 1778, prevented his return; and, considered a "refugee," his property was put in sequestration. His brother wrote that, should the result be confiscation, he would share what he had with him. His sympathies, it is said, were with his countrymen in the struggle in which they were engaged for their liberties;. and he left England and lived on the Continent. He embarked for America shortly before the peace; but landing at New York, then held by the British, was forced to take the oath of allegiance to the Crown, not being permitted to live in Boston in consequence of the " Banishment Act." He went, however, to Providence, where he remained until 1784, when, on his petition to the Legislature of Massachusetts, he was restored to the rights of citizenship. He died in 1805, leaving a large estate. One of his daughters married John Lowell, widely known as a political writer; and another was the wife of John McLean, who liberally endowed the Massachusetts General Hospital.

ANDERSON, SAMUEL. Of New York. At the beginning of the Revolution he went to Canada. He soon entered the service of the Crown, and was a captain under Sir John Johnson. In 1783 he settled near Cornwall, Upper Canada, and received half-pay. He held several civil offices: those of magistrate, judge of a district court, and associate justice of the Court of King's Bench, were among them. He continued to reside upon his estate near Cornwall, until his decease in 1836, at the age of one hundred and one. His property in New York was abandoned and lost.

ANDERSON, WILLIAM. Of West Chester County, New York. Was a Protester against the Whigs at White Plains in 1775. At the peace, accompanied by his family of four persons, and by one servant, he went from New York to Shelburne, Nova Scotia, where the Crown granted him fifty acres of land, one town and one water-lot. His losses in consequence of his loyalty were estimated at £300. He removed from Shelburne to St. John, New Brunswick, and was a grantee of that city.

ANDERSON, PETER. In 1782 a Loyalist Associator at New York, to settle at Shelburne, Nova Scotia, the following year. He went to St. John, New Brunswick, and was a grantee of that city. He died at Fredericton, in that Province, in 1828, at the age of ninety-five.

ANDERSON, JOSEPH. Lieutenant in the King's Regiment, New York. At the peace he retired to Canada. He died near Cornwall, Canada West, in 1853, aged ninety. He drew half-pay for a period of about seventy years. "One of the last survivors of the United Empire Loyalists."

ANDERSON, JAMES. Of Boston, Massachusetts. Was an Addresser of Hutchinson in 1774, and of Gage in 1775. December, 1775 : — " I am credibly informed," wrote Washington to the president of Congress, " that James Anderson, the consignee and part-owner of the ship *Concord* and cargo, is not only unfriendly to American liberty, but actually in arms against us, being captain of the Scotch company at Boston." In 1778 he was proscribed and banished. He was at New York in July, 1783, and one of the fifty-five who petitioned for lands in Nova Scotia.

ANDERSON, CULBERT. Of South Carolina. Died prior to 1785. Estate confiscated ; but two plantations in the neighborhood of Ninety-Six, restored to Mary his widow and her children, by act of the General Assembly.

ANDREWS, JOHN, D. D. Provost of the University of Pennsylvania. He was born in Maryland in 1746, and educated at Philadelphia. In 1767 he was ordained in London as an Episcopal clergyman, and became a missionary; and subsequently a rector of Queen Ann's County, Maryland. "Not partaking of the patriotic spirit of the times," he removed from Maryland, and was absent several years. In 1785 he was appointed to the charge of an Episcopal academy at Philadelphia, and four years after received the professorship of moral philosophy in the college of that city. In 1810 he succeeded Doctor McDowell as provost. He died in 1813, aged sixty-seven. "In stature he was tall and portly, and his personal appearance and carriage commanded respect. . . . . . He was a fine specimen of the old school gentleman of a former generation." His wife deceased in 1798. He was the father of ten children, the eldest of whom, Robert, graduated at Philadelphia in 1790.

ANDREWS, SAMUEL. An Episcopal clergyman of Connecticut. His principles separated him from his flock, and he became the first rector of the church of his communion at St. Andrew, New Brunswick. After a ministry of fifty-eight years, he died at that place, September 26, 1818, aged eighty-two. His wife Hannah died at St. Andrew, January 1, 1816, at the age of seventy-five.

ANDREWS, SAMUEL. Of North Carolina. Major in the Loyal Militia. At the beginning of the Revolution he left his seat at Newbern, and took refuge on board a ship-of-war at Wilmington. Early in 1776 he received a commission as lieutenant, served under General McDonald, and was taken prisoner. In 1781 he raised a company, and joined Lord Cornwallis. He was engaged in the capture of Governor Burke, and when Fanning was wounded, he assumed command, and conducted the prisoners to the British lines. Promotion followed. At the evacuation of Charleston, he retired with his family to Florida. Obnoxious to the Whigs by his course during the war, he was one of the three whom they refused to pardon, in the act of oblivion. I have a copy of his memorial claiming compensation for his services and losses, in his own handwriting, by which it appears that he lost by confiscation, a farm, dwelling-house, two stores, a grist-mill, with a stone house, two negroes, fifty head of cattle, several horses and sheep, furniture, &c. He was at Shelburne, Nova Scotia, in July, 1785, for the purpose of pressing his claim upon the commissioners, "under very disagreeable circumstances." Unsuccessful, he subsequently employed David McPherson, London.

ANSLEY, OZIAS. In 1782 he was an ensign in the first battalion of New Jersey Volunteers, and adjutant of the corps. At the peace he settled in New Brunswick, and received half-pay. He was a magistrate and a judge of the Common Pleas for several years. He died at Staten Island, New York, in 1828, aged eighty-five. His son, the Rev. Thomas Ansley, an Episcopalian clergyman of Nova Scotia, died at St. Andrew, New Brunswick, in 1831, aged about sixty-five. His grandson, Daniel Ansley, Esq., (1847,) resides at St. John. His daughter Charity, wife of Nathaniel Brittain, died in 1848, in her seventieth year.

ARDEN, DOCTOR CHARLES. Of Jamaica, New York. In 1775 he was a signer of a declaration against the Whigs. In 1776 he was accused of further defection; and one of his offences consisted in persuading other adherents of the Crown to have no concern with a congress or with committees. Several witnesses were examined. He went to England before the peace.

ARMSTRONG, WILLIAM. He was a captain in a Loyalist corps. At the peace he retired on half-pay, and, as is believed, settled in New York. In 1806 he joined the celebrated Miranda in his expedition to effect the independence of the province of Caraccas, and, in due time, of all Spanish America. Captain Armstrong was known to possess considerable military knowledge, method, industry, and vigilance, and received a commission as colonel, and the command of the First Regiment of Riflemen in the Columbian Army; and, as he had become familiar with the duties of the quartermaster's department, in the Revolution, he was created, also, quartermaster-general, with two assistants. Under Miranda, Colonel Armstrong was extremely unpopular, and was accused of "obsequiousness to his superiors, and of superciliousness and tyranny in his treatment of those in his power." He seems to have been involved in many quarrels. While the *Leander* was in the harbor of Jacquemel, (February, 1806,) he and Captain Lewis, the ship's commander, had a warm controversy regarding their rank and rights while associated on shipboard. The steward's slovenly habits displeased the former, and he gave the delinquent a "hearty rope's ending," which enraged Lewis, and drew from him the declaration, that every person in his vessel was subject to his authority, and should be punished by no other. Armstrong insisted, on the other hand, that he would chastise whomsoever he pleased. Both resorted to great bitterness of speech in the war of words which ensued. Miranda took the side of the Colonel, and behaved worse than even Lewis or Armstrong, and, "before the storm was over, appeared to be more fit for bedlam than for the command of an army." Not long after this occurrence, the *Bee*, another of the vessels attached to the expedition, ran foul of the flag-ship, and caused considerable damage; when Armstrong, seizing a trumpet, called to the master of that vessel, and bade him never to approach so near the *Leander* in future. Lewis, angry at the interference of the quarermaster-general, rebuked him severely for the act, and the quarrel between them was renewed. In this instance, Miranda decided in favor of Lewis. The dislike between the two officers, who took so opposite views of their right to supremacy, became settled and irreconcilable, and a third quarrel soon occurred, in which the chief sustained Armstrong; and Lewis, in the violence of his passion, resolved to resign, and ordered his servant to collect his baggage and prepare to leave the ship. A mediator was, however, found, and the dispute apparently settled. At a subsequent time, Miranda and the Captain became involved in a controversy, and Armstrong endeavored to produce a reconciliation between them; but he not only failed in this, but drew upon himself the resentment of both. Lewis renewed his threat to resign, and now actually threw up his commission. Besides these quarrels, the Colonel had several others. The moment the *Leander* cast anchor at Grenada, Lieutenant Dwyer quitted the ship. During the passage, he had been in continual collision with Armstrong, either on his own account, or in defence of his officers and men, whom the lordly personage assailed with words or violence. The notions of the Quartermaster-General of the Columbian Army appear to have been not a little tyrannical and arbitrary. It is related, that he kept three officers (on very slight provocation), confined to the ship's forecastle upwards of two weeks, and during this time refused them the liberty of walking on the quarter-deck and of entering the cabin.

Miranda required of his officers subscription to the following oath: " I swear to be true and faithful to the free people of South America, independent of Spain, and to serve them honestly and faithfully against all their enemies or opposers whatsoever, and to observe and obey the orders of the supreme government of that country legally appointed; and the orders of the general and officers set over me by them." Some objection was made to the form of this oath, which the General obviated by assurances to the gentlemen who were citizens of the United States, that they might annex to their signatures the condition that they did not intend to cancel their allegiance to their own country. After this difficulty was settled, Armstrong read and explained the Articles of War of the United States, and the alterations in *form*, not in substance or spirit, which had been made to adapt them to the service in which they were engaged. " Notice, gentlemen," said the Colonel, " the object of the change is to suit the wording of the Articles to the local names and situations of the country where they are to take effect. Thus, for the Army of the United States, will be substituted the Army of South America; and for the President, or Congress of the United States, will be used, the Supreme Authority of the free people of South America, or something of this kind."

The Americans who had connected themselves with this enterprise were generally persons of some ability, but it is understood that most, if not all of them, were in straitened circumstances, and that some were extremely needy. Armstrong's half-pay as a Loyalist officer might have prevented him from being in a situation of destitution. His pay under Miranda was fixed at ten dollars per day, to commence Jan. 1, 1806, which was the date of his commission of colonel.

The common men, sailors and soldiers were an ignorant and undisciplined mob, and the quartermaster-general had enough to do to keep them quiet. As in his intercourse with the officers, his disputes with them were continual, hardly a day passed without some one or more of them being taken to task for misconduct, or placed in arrest and confinement.

The failure of Miranda to pay his officers was a new source of difficulty and contention, and was a principal cause of bringing matters to a crisis. John Orford, a lieutenant of engineers, was especially importunate, and in answer to his second communication on the subject of arrearages due to him, received the following letter: —

"PORT OF SPAIN, December 2d, 1806.

"SIR, — By order of General Miranda, I have to inform you, that he received yours of the twenty-ninth ult., the purport of which he conceives to be highly improper, and contrary to every military principle; that in duty to himself, and for the good of the service, he thinks it proper that you should be dismissed from it, and you are hereby dismissed from it, and no longer to be considered as an officer under his command."

Other officers connected with this ill-starred attempt to revolutionize South America, *applied* for dismissals, and the defection became general. Armstrong, however, retired without notice or leave, and his chief accused him of *desertion*. Departing in the sloop-of-war *Hawk*, for Dominica, the quartermaster-general of the Columbian army took passage at that island for London. Inferior officers, induced to believe that the desertion of one so near Miranda's person gave them full liberty to abandon him in the same informal manner, retired from his service without writing letters of resignation, though some of them did observe that form in taking their leave of him and his fortunes. Of Armstrong's career after his arrival in England I have obtained no information.

ARMSTRONG, RICHARD. Major in the Queen's Rangers. Entered the corps as a captain. He was one of the most efficient partisan officers in service on the side of the Crown. In 1783, he and Captain Saunders were deputed to write Colonel Simcoe a parting address.

APTHORP, EAST. An Episcopal clergyman of Massachusetts. He was born in 1733, and was educated in England. In 1761 he was appointed a missionary at Cambridge, by the Society for the Propagation of the Gospel in Foreign Parts; and during his labors there, was engaged in a warm theological controversy with Doctor Mayhew. Retiring to England, he died there in 1816, aged eighty-three years. His wife was a niece of Governor Hutchinson, and a daughter of Judge Foster Hutchinson. His only son was a clergyman. One daughter married Doctor Cary; one, Doctor Butler; and a third, a son of Doctor Poley; — the husbands of the two first were heads of colleges. Mr. Apthorp was a distinguished writer. In 1790 he lost his sight.

APTHORP, THOMAS AND WILLIAM. Of Boston, Massachusetts. Both merchants; were proscribed and banished in 1778. The year after, William came from New York to Boston to solicit the mercy of his countrymen, and occupied for awhile a private room in the deputy jailer's house; but letters were received to his disadvantage, and he was committed to close prison by order of the Council.

APTHORP, CHARLES WARD. Of New York. He was appointed a member of the Council of that Colony in 1763, and served until 1783. He had lands in Maine, and property in Brookline and Roxbury, Massachusetts, which were confiscated. He died at his seat, Bloomingdale, in 1797.

ARNOLD, MARGARET. Daughter of Edward Shippen, Chief Justice of Pennsylvania, and second wife of General Benedict Arnold. Born in 1760, or in the year following; — died in London in 1804, in her forty-fourth year. She was very beautiful, and, it would seem, very ambitious. By her father, her relatives, and her circle of friends, she was dearly loved. She appeared with her knight at the gorgeous fete, or *mischianza*,[1] in honor of Sir William Howe, on his return to England. British and American officers admired her. The ill-fated André visited her often while he was stationed in Philadelphia, and was a correspondent after the Royal Army retired to New York. By some she was thought frivolous, vain, and artful; but I have no means of ascertaining the truth. To the additional fault charged — "extravagance" — she may be held amenable, since her father wrote in December, 1778, that, "the style of life his fashionable daughters had introduced into his family," and "their dress," were obstacles to his remaining in Philadelphia. Margaret was the youngest. Though her marriage followed in less than four months, her hand, I conclude, was not promised; for it said in the same letter that, while she was "much solicited by a certain general," the consummation of the proposed union "depended upon circumstances." As a maiden, she was happy. As a wife, she bore great trials and many sorrows. Her name appears here, because the third Vice-President of the United

---

[1] Much has been *inferred* against Mrs. Arnold because of her acquaintance with André before her marriage, and because he — honoring her above all others — was her knight at this the great fête of the Royal Army of the Revolution. Fortunately, there is conclusive evidence that on this occasion he gave his attentions to another lady I have a copy of a long and minute account of the "*mischianza*," written by André himself. Lord Cathcart appeared in honor of Miss Auchmuty. The knights were of two Orders. the "Blended Rose," and the "Burning Mountain." André was the third of the former. These are his own words, — "*Captain André, in honor of Miss P. Chew* — Squire, Lieut. André; Device, two game-cocks; Motto, *No rival.*"

The knight of Margaret Shippen, the subject of this notice, was Lieutenant Sloper, of the "Blended Rose" The knights of the two other Misses Shippen, were Lieutenants Underwood and Winyard.

States accused that she instigated one of the startling crimes in history.

The first husband uttered of the first wife — " The woman, whom thou gavest to be with me, she gave me of the tree, and I did eat." So, if we are to believe Aaron Burr, the principal miscreant of the American Revolution could have said, " Margaret my wife, she gave me of the tree of treason, and I did eat."

A gentleman may, if he will, pass lightly over the sins of a lady, because of his sympathy for the innocent of her lineage; but, I purpose to examine the accusation against this unfortunate wife with care, and to determine the case upon the probabilities and the evidence. There is no testimony, as far as I know, except her own alleged confession, in the presence of two persons. According to Davis, she told Mrs. Prevost that " she was heartily sick of the theatricals she was exhibiting;" that " she was disgusted with the American cause, and those who had the management of public affairs; and that, through great persuasion and unceasing perseverance, she had ultimately brought the General into an arrangement to surrender West Point to the British." Parton, the latest biographer of Burr, is more particular. He relates, that one evening while Burr was at Mrs. Prevost's, a lady veiled and attired in a riding-habit, burst into the room, and, after assurance of her safety, exclaimed — " Thank God! I've been playing the hypocrite, and I'm tired of it." He relates further, that Mrs. Arnold gave an account of the way she had deceived Washington, Hamilton, and others at West Point, who believed her innocent of the treason; that she avowed participation in the negotiations with the enemy, and " induced her husband to do what he had done;" and that, while at Mrs. Prevost's, she took " care to resume her acting of the outraged and frantic woman, whenever strangers were present." — Such are the material points.

The falsehood of Burr's story is apparent at once. For to believe it, is also to believe that a woman, who, not nineteen years old when her husband opened the correspondence with Sir Henry Clinton, was able and wise enough to herself conceive and to assist in executing a great, possibly to the Whig cause, a decisive, military crime; and was yet such an utter fool, as, while the country was ringing with the cry of "Treason! Treason!" to needlessly, boastingly confess her guilt in the presence of a Whig officer, who, in the performance of a common duty, would have arrested her at the instant. How absurd; surpassing intellectual strength and pitiable mental weakness in the same character! Burr told too much; and his lie drops apart by the very weight of its contradictions.

She had "deceived" Washington and Hamilton. Did Burr, in his malignity, mean to strike at the sagacity of both? He disliked the first; and thus early did he hate the man he afterwards slew. And, what was the deception? "Arnold, a moment before the setting out," wrote Hamilton to Colonel Laurens, went to the apartment of his wife, "and informed her that some transactions had just come to light which must forever banish him from his country. She fell into a swoon at this declaration, and he left her in it to consult his own safety, till the servants, alarmed by her cries, came to her relief. She remained frantic all day, accusing every one who approached her with an intention to murder her child (an infant in her arms); and exhibiting every other mark of the most genuine and agonizing distress. Exhausted by the fatigue and tumult of her spirits, her frenzy subsided towards evening, and she sank into all the sadness of affliction. It was impossible not to have been touched with her situation. Everything affecting in female tears, or in the misfortunes of beauty; everything pathetic in the wounded tenderness of a wife, or in the apprehensive fondness of a mother; and, I will add, till I have reason to change the opinion, everything amiable in the sufferings of innocence; conspired to make her an object of sympathy to all who were present. She experienced the most delicate attention, and every friendly office, till her departure for Philadelphia."

Again, in a letter to his future wife, Hamilton said, that

Mrs. Arnold, "for a considerable time, entirely lost herself. The General (Washington) went up to see her, and she upbraided him with being in a plot to murder her child. One moment she raved, another she melted into tears. Sometimes she pressed her infant to her bosom, and lamented its fate, ... in a manner that would have pierced insensibility itself. All the sweetness of beauty, all the loveliness of innocence, all the tenderness of a wife, and all the fondness of a mother, showed themselves in her appearance and conduct. We have every reason to believe that she was entirely unacquainted with the plan; and that the first knowledge of it was when Arnold went to tell her he must banish himself from his country and from her forever. She instantly fell into a convulsion, and he left her in that situation."

Parton, in commenting upon the letter to Laurens, remarks, that the Aid of the Commander-in-Chief gave "the romantic falsehood of the affair," and, in "love," was full of tenderness to woman; and that "it fell to Burr's lot to become acquainted with the repulsive truth." The reply is, that, *Washington was not in "love;"* nor, as Parton says of Hamilton, was he "*a young gentleman of rhetorical turn;*" and it is quite probable that some of "the other American officers," who were also "deceived," were married, and of mature years. Besides, — as will be seen in the course of this inquiry, — Mrs. Arnold's physical organization was somewhat peculiar; and, at times, she lost entire control of her lips, just as she did on the distressing occasion under consideration. A German dramatist has the beautiful sentiment that, "a mother with an infant in her arms, has nature's passport through the world." If this deserted wife, in her agony, felt and uttered that *her* child was without this "passport," and was to fall a victim to its father's wickedness, — constituted as she was — who can wonder? The very idea of "playing the hypocrite," at such a moment, is monstrous. "Theatricals," in a mother, when her husband disgraces and abandons her!

Mrs. Arnold was bred a gentlewoman; and, so young, was she so fallen, so fertile in the resources of sin; was she so destitute of the feelings of her sex, as to act a part? With the grave, penetrating eye of Washington upon her, did she dare to play the "hypocrite" *so* far as to upbraid him, and to declare that he was "in a plot to murder her child?" Impossible! "Theatricals" — in the presence of the illustrious man who only six months before had written his congratulations[1] on the birth of Edward Shippen Arnold — this very babe! Would Burr have us believe that the daughter of Chief Justice Shippen had less affection for *her* young, than is manifested by the bird and the beast, for the fledgling and the lamb?

Again, Arnold himself acquitted her of all complicity in his crime. "The mistaken vengeance of my countrymen," he said in a letter to Washington after the treason, "ought to fall only on me. She is as good and innocent as an angel, and is incapable of doing wrong." The declaration of a criminal is not evidence, I well know, unless corroborated. Major Franks, who *is* a competent witness, confirms the statement. He was an Aid; and, because he was charged with the particular duty of attending her, was laughingly called — "the nurse." When asked by a lady to express his opinion concerning her knowledge of her husband's plans, he replied, — "Madam, she knew nothing of them — nothing! She was ignorant of them as a babe." And further, Arnold could not venture to trust her, because, "she was subject to occasional paroxysms of physical indisposition, attended by nervous debility, during which she would give utterance to anything and everything in her mind;" and this "was a fact well known amongst us of the General's family, so much so as to cause us to be scrupulous of what was told her or said within her hearing." I submit with confidence, that Major Franks, in these few words, explains Mrs. Arnold's mental condition, as stated by Hamilton; for any proud, well-bred,

---

[1] Arnold had announced the birth; and the Commander-in-Chief, at the close of a letter dated at Morristown, March 28, 1780, said in reply, — "Let me congratulate you on the late happy event. Mrs. Washington joins me in presenting her wishes for Mrs Arnold on the occasion."

sensitive woman, with a constitutional tendency to "paroxysms" and "nervous debility," would do much, if not precisely as she did, when informed of her own ruined hopes in life, and that the author of her woes must fly to save his life.

Again: as soon as the traitor was safe on board of the *Vulture*, he addressed a letter to Washington, in which he asserts his wife's innocence, and uses these significant words: " I beg she may be permitted to return to her friends in Philadelphia, or to come to me, as she may choose." Mark the order of thought. If she was the partner, nay, the *author* of his crime, he would not have suggested the possibility of a separation; but doubt was predominant in his mind, and he expressed himself accordingly. This is of moment, since nature and observation teach that, husband and wife, when guilty of the same sin, cling to one another as by a new vow, and as closely as did the pair who were expelled from Eden. Mrs. Arnold's decision was free; and, if principal or accomplice, the laws of her being would have impelled her to renew the relations which legally existed between herself and the father of her child. But the bond was broken; and, under an escort of horse, with the protection of a flag, she departed from West Point for the parental roof.

I conclude here the circumstantial part of her case. The allegation of the third Vice-President of the United States concerns common girlhood, common wifehood, and universal motherhood; hence the time bestowed upon it. In my judgment, the subject of this notice should be acquitted. The *probabilities* are all in her favor, and there is no *evidence* against her. Indeed, more; dates and facts prove her entire innocence.

Her husband began to complain of the "ingratitude" of his country as early as February, 1777, *before he ever saw her, and more than two years before he married her;* and, from that time down to the discovery of his crime, in September, 1780, he was continually quarrelling with individuals, or State authorities, or members of Congress, or officers in the army. In a word, before his second marriage, (April 8, 1779,) his clamor about his "wrongs," his importunities for "redress," his questionable business and pecuniary transactions, together with his arrogance, had disgusted his enemies, and exhausted the patience of those who labored earnestly and sincerely to relieve his embarrassments, to appease his anger, and to do him more than justice. Benedict Arnold, mentally, morally, betrayed his country, while his wife was a maiden. The Loyalists seem to have known his true character far better than the Whigs; and to have supposed that he favored them long previous to his overt treason. There is proof of this in the private correspondence of Galloway, the leading Loyalist of Pennsylvania. Thus Charles Stewart wrote, December 17, 1778: "General Arnold is in Philadelphia. It is said that he will be discharged, *being thought a pert Tory*. Certain it is, that he *associates mostly with these people*, and is to be married to Miss Shippen," &c. David Sproat, in a letter dated January 11, 1779, remarked — "You will hear that General Arnold, commandant in Philadelphia, has *behaved with lenity to the Tories*, and that he is on the eve of marriage to one of Edward Shippen's daughters."

I pass to the distinct question of Burr's veracity. There are so many victims to prejudice, to persecution in our history, that, when I began to trace *his* strange career, I was prepared to find him one of them. But I incline to the opinion now, that his life was a long, an unbroken lie; for I own my inability to determine, when, and under what circumstance, I can put faith in a man who averred, as he did, that he never so much as wished harm to any human being; that he never did, said, or wrote anything to throw a cloud over any woman's name; and that no woman could lay her ruin to him. In the eighty-three years which have elapsed since the alleged eager, imprudent boasting of Mrs. Arnold at Mrs. Prevost's, hundreds of volumes of biography and correspondence of the Revolutionary era have been published; but, as far as my knowledge extends, not one of them contains a syllable to corroborate Burr's story, or in any way to implicate the subject of this notice. Nor is this all. When I mingled with

Loyalist families in the British Colonies, Arnold himself, the beauty, character, and fate of his wife, were among the favorite topics of conversation. Gentlemen of the lineage of the Colonel, who went up the Hudson in the *Vulture* with André and other well-informed persons, never once suggested that by tradition, even, Mrs. Arnold was involved in the treason.

My purpose is accomplished. I have attempted the vindication of the second wife of Benedict Arnold, simply as a duty to her and to her sex. The stain of descent from *him*, from a man, who, in trade was a vulgar, dishonest horse-jockey and cattle-dealer, and who, as a military officer, was false to his duty; this, this, her children's children must bear.

I hasten to complete this article, which is already too long for the limits of this work. When she stopped at Mrs. Prevost's, she was on her way from West Point to Philadelphia. She never meant to see her husband again. On her arrival at her father's house she was treated with the utmost kindness, nor were the endeavors to soothe her anguish by affectionate attentions, entirely lost; but new sorrows awaited her. On the 27th of October, 1780, the Executive Council of Pennsylvania issued an order commanding her to depart the State within fourteen days from that date, and not to return during the war. Her father and others sought to avert this decree of exile. The representation that she had resolved to separate from the man who had destroyed her happiness; the pledge of her word that she would hold no correspondence with him; the promise of every security for her good conduct, were disregarded; and on the 9th of November she obeyed the edict of banishment. At the peace, she again thought of leaving her husband; but concluded, finally, to follow him to New Brunswick. The Loyalists who went to that Province in 1783, lived, at first, in log or rough-board huts. The country was an unbroken wilderness; and bears sometimes came to the very doors of these rude dwellings. Arnold was among those who soon built frame-houses, and secured many of the comforts of civilized life. Within the traitor's home there, within his home in England, was a sad, a stricken woman. "Her heart was broken." She came once to her native land. Her visit is mentioned in a letter dated at Philadelphia, in January, 1790. The writer remarks, that she had been there six months, and intended to stay the remainder of the winter; that "she is handsome, and a woman;" that out of respect to her family, many warm Whigs had been to see her, though the common opinion was, that, as her presence placed her friends in a painful position, she would have shown more feeling by staying away. I learn from another source, that she was treated with so much coldness and neglect, even by those who had most encouraged her ill-starred marriage, that her feelings were continually wounded. — " She never could come again."

Her portrait by Sir Thomas Lawrence, is (1855) in the possession of the Misses McIlvaine, Philadelphia. That she was very beautiful, is said by all who speak of her. Accounts differ as to the time and place of her decease; the English and correct record is, that she died in 1804, in Bryanstone Street, Portman Square, London, in her forty-fourth year. Her sisters would have brought her younger children to America, — wisely enough was the offer declined. The story of Margaret Shippen has a moral for maidens; she married against the wish, the *judgment*, of a fond, of a devoted father.

Mrs. Arnold was the mother of four sons and one daughter: namely, Edward Shippen, who was a lieutenant in the Bengal Cavalry, and paymaster of Mattra, and who died in India, in 1813; James Robertson, of whom presently; George, who was a lieutenant-colonel in the Bengal Cavalry, and who died in India in 1828; William Fitch, who, a magistrate in the County of Bucks, England, and late a captain in the Lancers, married the only daughter of Captain Ruddach, of the Royal Navy; and who, the father of six children, was living in 1855; and Sophia Matilda, the wife of Colonel Pownall Phipps, of the East India Company Service, who was also living eight years ago, and the mother of one son and two daughters.

A word in conclusion, of the most distinguished son. James Robertson Arnold entered the corps of Royal Engineers in

1798. He served two years at Bermuda, and from 1818 to 1823, commanded the Engineers in Nova Scotia and New Brunswick. After the accession of William IV. he was one of his Majesty's aids. While in the Provinces just named, he visited his father's house, — King Street, St. John, — and, as I have often been told, "threw himself into a chair, and wept like a child." He expressed a wish to see his mother's family in the United States; but added, — "I suppose I should be insulted on account of my father," &c. A gentleman who was in service with him, and an intimate acquaintance, speaks of him in terms of high commendation; and relates that he was a small man, with eyes of remarkable sharpness, and in features thought to resemble his father. His wife was Virginia, daughter of Bartlett Goodrich, of the Isle of Wight. In 1841, he was transferred from the Engineers, and appointed a Major-General, and a Knight of the Hanoverian Guelphic Order. He died in London, December, 1852.

ARNOLD, BENEDICT. Of Connecticut. Major-General in the Continental Army. Nothing need be said in these volumes of a man whose life and infamy are so universally known. A word, however, of his private character, in further vindication of Margaret, his second wife. He was descended from the Arnolds of Rhode Island, an honorable family, who for a long period figured in the public affairs of that Colony. He was bred an apothecary, and from 1763 to 1767 was settled at New Haven, as a druggist and bookseller. I am inclined to believe that he was a finished scoundrel from early manhood to his grave. Nor do I believe that he had any real and true hearted attachment to the Whig cause. He fought as a mere adventurer, and took sides from a calculation of personal gain, and chances of plunder and advancement.

No honorable man would have formed a copartnership with others for purchasing goods within the enemy's lines as he did, and to the enormous amount of one hundred and forty thousand dollars. And no honest man would have lived, could have lived as he did, while at Philadelphia. His play, his balls, his concerts, his banquets, were enough to have impaired the fortune of an European noble. His house was the best in the city, and had been the mansion of Penn, the last royal governor of Pennsylvania, and the descendant of the illustrious founder of the Colony. This dwelling he furnished magnificently, kept his coach-and-four, and a numerous retinue of servants, and indulged in every kind of luxury, and ostentatious and vain profusion and display.

But Arnold should have the benefit of every circumstance which, in the judgment of any, can lessen or palliate his guilt. Beyond all doubt, then, Congress treated him unjustly. If his case had never been submitted to that body, or if it had been examined and disposed of by Washington, it is certainly *possible* that his career might have terminated far less dishonorably.

He was made a brigadier-general in the British service, and received a large amount of gold to cover his alleged losses in deserting the standard of his country. After he went to England, Mr. Van Schaack, a New York Loyalist, who was also there, paid a visit to Westminster Abbey. "His musings were interrupted by the entrance of a gentleman accompanied by a lady. It was General Arnold, and the lady was doubtless Mrs. Arnold. They passed to the cenotaph of Major André, where they stood and conversed together. What a spectacle! The traitor Arnold in Westminster Abbey, at the tomb of André, deliberately perusing the monumental inscription which will transmit to future ages the tale of his own infamy. The scene, with the associations which naturally crowded upon the mind, was calculated to excite various emotions in an American bosom; and Mr. Van Schaack turned from it with disgust."

From the conclusion of the war till his death, Arnold resided chiefly in England; but for a while he was engaged in trade and navigation at St. John, New Brunswick. He was disliked, was unpopular, and even hated at St. John. [See Elias Hardy and Alpheus Pine, in this work, for illustration.] Persons of that city still relate instances of his perfidy and meanness. George Gilbert, Esquire, (a son of Bradford

Gilbert, who was a Massachusetts Loyalist,) has now (August, 1846,) twelve chairs which are called the "Traitor's Chairs," and which were carried from England to St. John by Arnold. When he removed from New Brunswick he sold them to the first Judge Chipman, who, after keeping them some years, sold them to their present possessor. They are of a French pattern, are large, and covered with blue-figured damask; the wood-work is white, highly polished or enamelled, and striped with gold.

The *Lord Sheffield*, the first ship built in New Brunswick, came over the falls of the River St. John, in June, 1786. The current story in that Province is, that the builder was unable to purchase the necessary sails and rigging, and that Arnold became the owner — by fraud.

He died in London, June 14, 1801. The following brief notice appeared in the "Gentleman's Magazine:" — "At his house in Gloucester Place, Brigadier-General Arnold. His remains were interred on the 21st, at Brompton. Seven mourning-coaches and four state-coaches formed the cavalcade."

His first wife bore him, — Benedict, who was an officer of artillery in the British Army, who, it is believed, was compelled to quit the service, and who died young in the West Indies; and Richard and Henry, of whom presently. The names of five other children appear in the preceding notice.

"We" (the English nation), said the 'London Times,' in 1850, "are actually this moment supporting, out of the public funds, the descendants of Arnold the American traitor."

It may be added that General Arnold's mother had six children, of whom he and his sister Hannah alone lived to the years of maturity. This sister adhered to her brother Benedict throughout his eventful and guilty career, and was true to him in the darkest periods of his history. She died at Montague in Upper Canada in 1803, and was, as is uniformly stated, a lady of excellent character. She was accomplished; pleasing in person, witty and affable. She loved, but at the bidding of her brother, broke off the engagement. She never married.

In 1852 the newspapers announced the decease at Norwich, Connecticut, of Elizabeth Arnold, cousin of the TRAITOR, and the last of his kindred in that vicinity. Her age was ninety-two. She was carried to the poor-house at her own request, and died there.

ARNOLD, HENRY. A son of General Arnold by his first marriage. He entered the king's service after his father's defection, and was a lieutenant of cavalry in the American Legion. He accompanied his father to St. John, and was employed in his business. He slept in the warehouse near Lower Cove in that city, and lodged there the night the building was burned. He lived afterwards at Troy, New York, with his aunt Hannah, and was engaged in mercantile pursuits. At a subsequent period, he removed to Canada, where, in 1829, he was a man of property. He received half-pay, and a grant of lands from the British government.

ARNOLD, RICHARD. Brother of Henry. In 1782 he was also a lieutenant of cavalry in the American Legion, commanded by his father. In every particular his history, down to the year 1829, is identical with that of his brother Henry, and need not, therefore, be repeated. Persons are still living at St. John, who resided there when General Arnold's store was burned. The impression was, at the moment, and still is, that the fire was caused by design, and for the purpose of defrauding a company in England, that had underwritten upon the merchandise which it contained, to an amount far exceeding its worth.[1] These persons differ as to the fact, whether Arnold himself was at St. John, or absent in England, at the time of the fire; and hence, the degree of blame which should be attached to the two sons may be uncertain.

---

[1] The story as first told was as follows — "We learn from Nova Scotia, that the highest suspicion prevails there, that the infamous traitor, Benedict Arnold, set fire to his own house, (store,) having previously effected an insurance in London upon it, to a much larger amount than the real value of his property."—*Newport Herald* of September 11, 1788.

That both Henry and Richard slept in the store on the night of the conflagration, and that neither could give a satisfactory account of its cause, seems, however, to be certain.

ARNOLD, OLIVER. Of Connecticut. He was born in that State, and graduated at Yale College, in 1776. He went to St. John at the peace, and was one of the grantees of that city. Having labored some years as an Episcopal missionary, he was inducted into office as Rector of Sussex, New Brunswick, and finished his course in that capacity in 1834, at the age of seventy-nine. He was ardently attached to the Episcopal Church, and was regarded as an excellent man. In domestic life he was peculiarly kind and affectionate.

ASBY, JAMES. Of Boston. An Addresser of Hutchinson in 1774, and a Protester against the Whigs the same year. A Boston Whig wrote to a friend at New York as follows: "The Addressers of Mr. Hutchinson, and the Protesters against our public measures, lead a devil of a life. In the country the people will not grind their corn, and in the town they refuse to purchase from, and sell to, them."

ASHLEY, JONATHAN. Minister of Westfield, and subsequently of Deerfield, Massachusetts. He graduated at Yale College in 1730. He was a warm Loyalist, and difficulties occurred between him and his people in consequence. An Ecclesiastical Council, convened in May, 1780, by mutual consent, to arrange the difference, dispersed after a session of eleven days without arriving at any conclusion. He expressed his particular sentiments freely and boldly. His flock was so nearly divided, that sometimes one party had the ascendency, sometimes the other. "When the Whigs were in the majority, they refused to vote him his firewood." Among the anecdotes which show his zeal in the royal cause, I select two: "When the provincial Congress of Massachusetts issued the proclamation for the Annual Day of Thanksgiving, they substituted the ejaculation, 'God save the people,' instead of the former one, 'God save the king.' He read the proclamation from the pulpit, but when he had come to the close, he raised himself above his ordinary height, and, with great vehemence, subjoined, 'And God save the king,' I say, 'or we are an undone people.' "

The other relates to an exchange with the Rev. Mr. Newton of Greenfield, who also was a Loyalist. The Deerfield minister was told by his Greenfield brother that he might avail of the occasion to speak of the Revolution, "by way of caution to his people." I find the result stated thus: "Mr. Ashley somewhat enlarged upon the liberty granted him, and seriously offended the congregation. During the intermission of service at noon, the friends of the patriot cause assembled, and talked the matter over. They finally resolved themselves into a meeting, and chose a committee to take measures in relation to the afternoon preaching, which they did by fastening up the meeting-house. When Mr. Ashley came to commence the afternoon service, he was met at the door by one of his Deerfield parishioners, who gave him a significant nudge with his elbow. After repeating this form of salutation, Mr. Ashley asked him the reason of the attack, and admonished him that he "should not rebuke an elder." "An elder?—an elder?" replied his tormentor, "if you had not said you was an elder, I should have thought you was a poison sumach." Mr. Ashley had to retire without entering the church. But this was not the last of the reverend gentleman's troubles. Returning to his own parish, at Deerfield, he soon after preached a sermon in which he spoke against the patriot cause, and gave his opinion that those Americans who fell at Lexington had met with a fearful doom in the next world. On the following Sabbath, he undertook to enter his pulpit, but found it spiked up. After ineffectual attempts to enter, he turned to one of his deacons, and requested him to go and get his hammer, and force for him an entrance. The deacon was a blacksmith, but informed his pastor that he did not work on the Sabbath. At last, an axe was procured and the pulpit entered."

He was a man of strong mind, and an earnest preacher. He died in 1780, aged sixty-seven. Several of his sermons were published.

"During the forty-eight years of his ministry at Deerfield, he officiated in 249 marriages and 1009 baptisms, and admitted 392 members to his church."

ASHLEY, JOSEPH, JR. Of Sunderland, Massachusetts. He went to Halifax in 1776, and was proscribed and banished in 1778. He died in New York before the peace. The Hon. Chester Ashley, Senator in Congress, from Arkansas, who died at Washington in 1848, at the age of fifty-seven, was of the same family.

ASPDEN, MATTHIAS. Of Philadelphia. Son of Matthias Aspden and Rebecca, daughter of Philip Packer. He was born in that city about the year 1756; and at the beginning of the Revolution was a merchant, the owner of a house, wharf, and warehouses, and transacting business which gave him a profit of £2000 annually. At first, he inclined to the Whigs, and joined a company of volunteers; but his confidence in the invincible power of the Crown, and the fate of his friends Hunt and Kearsley, caused a change of sentiment. In 1776 he abandoned the country. He intended to embark in one of his own vessels, but at the moment he was ready, "the carting" of the two gentlemen just mentioned, occurred, and he resolved to remain rather than be thought remiss in their trials. Yet, he soon obtained leave of the Whigs to sail from New York in the packet *Swallow*, and was disappointed a second time, in consequence of difficulties with Governor Tryon. At last, he took passage in the schooner *Bertham*, bound to Corunna, Spain, and arrived in London before the close of the year.

By a proclamation of the Council of Pennsylvania in 1780, he was required to appear and be tried for treason, before April 1, 1781, on pain of being attainted and losing his estate by confiscation. He failed; and his house, wharf, and warehouses in Philadelphia (which, after the peace, according to his statement, rented for £1000 per annum), were given to the University.

In 1785 he returned to America, but finding his life in peril, hastened back to England. However, he petitioned for and received a full pardon from the State in April, 1786; and thenceforward seems to have passed a life undisturbed by aught save his own self-caused vexations and his incessant clamors for pecuniary compensation from all the governments with which he had ever been connected. The Legislature of Pennsylvania, the House of Commons, the Board of Commissioners on Loyalist Claims, the High Chancellor, the Privy Council, the Lords of the Treasury, all turned a deaf ear to his complaints; whereon he published them in the " London Morning Post." Like the bat in the fable, he sought to find gain from both parties, and obtained it from neither. He was in France, under the Alien Bill, in 1802; at New York, under a passport, in 1815; and in July, 1817, departed Philadelphia for England, by way of Canada. He was addressed by the South Sea Company on the election of officers in 1823, as the *Right Honorable Matthias Aspden, at Messrs. Hoare & Co., Bankers, Fleet Street;* a title which he claimed, because, as he said, his grandfather, Thomas Aspden, married Elizabeth Scroop, " a descendant of the ancient and noble family of that name." He died at London, August 9, 1824.

His will gave rise to the most extraordinary suit that ever occurred under the confiscation acts of the Revolution. The documents which pertain to the case were printed in 1837, and make upwards of three hundred pages: the eye seldom rests on so curious a medley of transactions in business, of every-day gossip, of personal complaints, and general mention of human vicissitudes — joy, sorrow, affliction, death. Some of his own letters and other papers are strange enough. Travelling in Italy, in 1804, he seems to have been convinced that now and then he met relatives of persons (particularly servants of foreign extraction), whom he had once known. " At this place (Avignon) saw a good many Philadelphia-looking faces, and relations, I am sure, of Anna, that many years ago lived with my Aunt Bailey; . . . . am inclined to think I also met in Italy old Conrad, that lived with her about the same time, and used to carry me to school on a pillow before him, — or a cousin of his — at Naples;

. . . . and at this place, relations of my neighbor, the razor-grinder's wife, who passed for Germans." But perhaps the queerest of these is a letter from London, on business, to the president, for the time being, of the United States Bank, in 1808; in which he complains bitterly of being annoyed by spirits, and calls for the application of the laws against sorcery: "For my own part, I had no idea of anything of this kind untill the winter of 1798, in Ormond Street, when for the first time in my life I slept with a light in my chamber, and forced to the resource of it all the winter thro'. Going to Richmond in the summer, I had there frequent and repeated proofs of there being spirits and dæmons, from hearing and seeing, if the latter are not also spirits. And now, and for several years past, nothing more clear, notorious, and common; for I seldom go out to a coffee-house that I am not dog'd or bitched all the way; and while there, to my great annoyance and others present, and back, by voices out of the air that I mostly know, and to the great reproach and scandal of the police of this city, or the bench of bishops, at whichever door the laying of evil spirits may lay. As early as the age of four or five, I was taught to believe there was no such things as spirits, and was not afraid to go anywhere alone, or to sleep in a strange house in a chamber alone, with a window looking into a churchyard; and which the commands of the Lord in the Bible to the Jews, to destroy the witches and wizards out of the land, had tended to strengthen and confirm. And this by one that was a spirit or dæmon herself or itself, if I am not much mistaken, and which accident led me to discover, in looking for lodgings a few years agoe, at a lodging-house in my present neighborhood, where I met the original, and was struck with it; who, very soon after I came into the room, went out with a person like a clergyman with her; she was something bigger than the counterfeit; when she returned home in the year 1762, sent the counterfeit abroad; excellent hands for a motherless babe to fall into. But as I am alive and tolerably well, except some remains of the gout in my feet, I may say from this, and many other things, that I am truly sensible that there is a Providence over all."

To return to Mr. Aspden's will. The suit to determine the rightful heirs to his property was brought in 1824, in the United States Circuit Court, and decided, finally, in 1848. He devised his estate, real and personal, " to the person who should be his heir-at-law," and in another part of the instrument, " to the person who should be his lawful heir." The claimants were upwards of two hundred, and were divided into three classes: 1. The heirs of Mary Harrison, sister of the half-blood on the father's side, and the heirs of Roger Hartley, half brother on the mother's side. 2. The Packers — cousins of the whole blood, a very large and constantly increasing class of claimants, one of whom originally instituted the proceedings, the suit standing — Packer *vs.* Nixon, Executor of Matthias Aspden. 3. The English Aspdens — relations of the whole blood of the father, and who would have been heirs at common law.

The opinion of Judge Grier was in substance as follows: The testator left neither wife nor lineal descendant; but there were the issue of the half-blood descendants of Mary Harrison and Roger Hartley. The issue on the father's side, the first cousins, (the Packers,) are dismissed; they have no claim on any possible construction of this will. The only question is between the heir at common law and the half-blood.

The 11th section of the act of 1794, gives the estate of an intestate who dies, leaving no child or issue of such child, to the brother or sister of the half-blood, unless where the estate is acquired by descent, gift of devise from the parents, in which case, all who are not of the blood of the parent from whom the estate was derived, shall be excluded. It is evident, therefore, that the issue of the half-blood is in this case substituted to the heir at common law.

" The Court are, therefore, of opinion that the issue of the brother and sister of the half-blood are the lawful heirs, and the persons entitled."

The decision was therefore in favor of the American heirs, of the issue of Mary Harrison and Roger Hartley; to whom the decree gave property valued at more than $500,000.

The English claimants appealed. The Supreme Court affirmed the opinion of Judge Grier, and the estate was divided accordingly.

I conclude this singular story with a paragraph which appeared in a Philadelphia paper, March, 1853: —

"ROMANCE IN REAL LIFE. — John Aspden, whose sudden death on Monday was noticed in our columns, is to be buried this afternoon. Mr. Aspden was one of the English claimants of the immense estate left by Matthias Aspden. Before the case was decided by the Supreme Court in favor of the American heirs, the latter proposed to the deceased to compromise the matter, and offered to pay him the sum of $200,000 to relinquish his claim; this he refused to do, and the decision of the Court cut him off without a farthing. On Monday morning the estate was divided between the heirs-at-law, and almost at the same moment John Aspden fell dead, at a tavern in Carter's Alley, of disease of the heart, supposed to have been induced by disappointment and mortification. At the time of his death his pocket contained a solitary cent — his entire fortune! To day the man who might have been the possessor of a quarter of a million of dollars, will be borne to his grave from an obscure part of the District of Southwark."

ATHERTON, JOSHUA. Of Amherst, New Hampshire. He was born at Harvard, Massachusetts, in 1737, and graduated at Harvard University in 1762. He was the law-student of Abel Willard, of Lancaster, and of James Putnam, of Worcester, and opened an office at Petersham. He removed to Litchfield, and, in 1773, — when he was appointed Register of Probate of the County of Hillsborough — to Amherst, where he soon acquired property and reputation in his profession.

An open and firm Loyalist, in the events that followed, he was a sufferer in person and estate. He was entreated by his Whig friends to change his course, while other friends who adhered to the Crown, urged him to fly to England or Nova Scotia; but he refused to adopt the counsels of either. His house was often surrounded by his political foes, who marched him off to a tavern and drank freely of flip, punch, and toddy at his expense. He bore the indignities to which he was exposed so meekly, and "treated" so geneiously, as to win the good nature of his tormentors, and to cause them to toss their hats, to hurrah for the Tory, and to express their regrets, that he "was not one of the sons of liberty." Minor annoyances I must pass without mention. In 1777 he was sent prisoner to Exeter by order of the Committee of Safety, where he remained nearly or quite a year. Though released on entering into recognizance with sureties in a large sum, he was still confined to the limits of the county until late in 1778, when, upon his petition, and his acknowledgment of the authority of the Whigs, his liberty was restored by proclamation. He took the oath of allegiance to the United States, and the oath of an attorney, in 1779, and was admitted to practice in the Superior Court. His pecuniary affairs at this time were in a deplorable condition. "He lay like some thrifty tree uprooted by the late gale, prostrate, divested of its foliage, its limbs broken and scattered. His family was much increased, and increasing. His and their sufferings will hardly bear relation." In a few years, however, his business became extensive, and he was often the leading counsel in the trial of important cases. So, too, his loyalty was forgotten, and marks of respect and confidence were frequent, and grateful to his feelings. He was a member of the Convention for the adoption of the Federal Constitution, and led the party that opposed it. His principal objections to that instrument, personally, were the provisions relative to slaves and slavery. Subsequently, he was elected to the House and Senate of New Hampshire, and, in 1793, was appointed Attorney-General of that State. Taking part with the Federalists in the discords here occasioned by the French Revolution, he lost his popularity; and when, in 1798, he accepted the office of Commissioner under the Act to levy a Direct Tax in the United States, "he had the honor to be hung in effigy in the town of Deering." Two years later, shattered mentally and physically, he retired to private life. His disease — an organic affection of the heart — terminated in death, April, 1809, in his seventy-third year. "He was remarkable for his social qualities. His courtesy and urbanity will ever be remembered by those who were familiar with him. His hospitality was unbounded. The clergy, the gentlemen of the bar, the judges, officers of the Revolution, and every stranger of distinction within the reach of his invitations, were his welcome guests." He was a good scholar, and possessed one of the best libraries in the State. Abigail, daughter of the Rev. Thomas Goss, of Bolton, Massachusetts, became his wife in 1765, and died in 1801. At the time of her marriage she was hardly more than sixteen years of age; — "in the joyous day of her nuptials, little did this young girl know or think of the trials, hardships, and mortifications of her future life." She proved an "angel wife and mother." Charles Humphrey Atherton, who graduated at Harvard University in 1794, who was at the head of the Hillsborough County bar for several years; who was a representative in Congress, and who died at Amherst in 1853, was his son. He was the father of six daughters: namely, Frances, Abigail, Rebecca Wentworth, Nancy Holland, Catharine, and Elizabeth Willard; some of whom (1852), survive, and all of whom, the fourth excepted, married. The late Hon. Charles G. Atherton, Representative and Senator in Congress from New Hampshire, who died in 1853, was a grandson of our Loyalist.

ATKINS, GIBBS. Of Boston. He went to Halifax in 1776, and was proscribed and banished in 1778. He returned to the United States, and died in Boston in 1806, aged sixty-six.

ATKINS, CHARLES. Of Charleston, South Carolina. In 1774 he was appointed a member of the Committee of Correspondence of that city. In 1780 he was an Addresser of Sir Henry Clinton, and a Petitioner to be armed on the side of the Crown. He received a military commission, and in 1782 was an officer in the Volunteers. He was banished, and his property was confiscated. He went to England. In 1794, in a memorial dated at London, he stated to the British Government, that large debts due to him in America at the time of his banishment remained unpaid, and he desired relief.

ATKINSON, THEODORE. Of Portsmouth, New Hampshire. He graduated at Harvard University in 1718, and in afterlife rose to much distinction. He held, at various times, the offices of Representative in the Assembly, Naval Officer, Sheriff, Clerk of the Court of Common Pleas, Colonel of the Militia, Collector of the Customs, Secretary of the Colony, and Chief Judge of the Superior Court; and had a seat in the Council. In 1775 a committee of the Provincial Congress requested him to deliver up all the records and papers in the Secretary's office, which he refused, as "against his oath and honor." On a second visit the committee, without heeding his objections, took possession of the documents of his office, except the volumes which contained the charter grants of lands, which were then in the hands of Governor Wentworth. The missing books, Congress, by resolution of July 7, 1775, voted that Mr. Atkinson should be held accountable for to the people. He died in 1779, at the advanced age of eighty-two. He bequeathed £200 sterling to the Episcopal Church of Portsmouth, the interest of which he directed to be expended in bread, and distributed on Sundays to the poor of the parish, which, as I understand, has been dealt out under the provision of his will, until the present time, (1859,) a period of eighty years. "His coach was the coach of the town." He was a man of wealth, and owned more silver plate, probably, than any other person in New Hampshire. The town of Atkinson perpetuates his name.

ATKINSON, THEODORE, JR. Of New Hampshire, and son of the preceding. He graduated at Harvard University in 1757. Entering upon political life, he became a member of the Council and Secretary of the Colony. He died at Portsmouth, on Saturday, October 28, 1769, at the early age of thirty-three, and his remains were deposited in the family tomb, Queen's Chapel, with great pomp and circumstance. On Saturday, November 11th — *just two weeks after* — his widow, whose maiden name was Frances Deering

Wentworth, was married in the same chapel by the Rev. Arthur Browne, to Governor John, afterwards Sir John Wentworth. She was a Boston lady, very accomplished and gay; and, as Lady Wentworth, had a diversified career. She was a cousin of both husbands, and her earliest attachment was for Wentworth; but while he was absent in England she married Atkinson. There was much gossip at Portsmouth about the three cousins at the Revolutionary era, founded on the facts here stated. And within a few years, a story relating to the parties appeared in one of the magazines, which, extracted by the newspaper press, went the rounds. The leading incidents of the tale were both ridiculous and untrue. The towns of Francestown, Deering, and Wentworth, in New Hampshire, perpetuate the wife's name.

AUCHMUTY, REV. SAMUEL, D. D. Of New York. Rector of Trinity Church. Son of Robert, Judge of Vice-Admiralty. Graduated at Harvard University in 1742. I lose sight of him until 1754, when he was employed by the Society for the Propagation of the Gospel in Foreign Parts, as Catechist to the negroes in New York, at a salary of £50; and where, he wrote the Society, that in six months he had baptized twenty-three children and two adults, and was preparing three others. He succeeded the Rev. Dr. Barclay as Rector, in 1764, with the Rev. Mr. Inglis and the Rev. Mr. Ogilvie, as assistants. Oxford, England, conferred the degree of S. T. D. in 1766, and King's College, New York, the year following. In 1771, I find his name first on an Address to the Episcopalians of Virginia, urging the necessity of an "American Episcopate," or, the residence of bishops in the Colonies. Trumbull calls him a "high-church clergyman," and makes him the subject of remark in McFingal. In April, 1775, Dr. Auchmuty wrote from New York to Captain Montresor, chief engineer of General Gage's army at Boston, that "we have lately been plagued with a rascally Whig mob here, but they have effected nothing, only Sears, the king, was rescued at the jail-door." . . . . "Our magistrates have not the spirit of a louse," &c.

In September, 1776, nearly one thousand buildings were burned in the western part of the city, and among them Trinity Church, the Rector's house, and the Charity School; St. Paul's Chapel and King's College barely escaped. The Vestry of Trinity reported the loss by this fire to the Church to be — Trinity Church and organ, £17,500; two Charity School-houses and fences, £2000; Library, £200; Rector's house, £2500; total, £22,200; besides the annual rent of two hundred and forty-six lots of ground, — the tenant buildings being all consumed. After the fire, Dr. Auchmuty searched the ruins of his church and of his large and elegant mansion, but found no articles of value, except the church plate and his own. His personal losses by the conflagration, he estimated at upwards of $12,000. He died in 1777. His wife was a daughter of Richard Nichols, Governor of New York. Notices of his two sons follow. His daughter Jane was the second wife of Richard Tylden, of the family of Tylden, Milsted, County of Kent, England; one of her sons is the present Sir John Maxwell Tylden, who was in the army twenty years; and another, William Burton Tylden, is a major in the Royal Engineers. Of Dr. Auchmuty's two other daughters, I have no account, save that they were married.

AUCHMUTY, SIR SAMUEL. Of New York. Lieutenant-General in the British Army. Eldest son of the Rev. Dr. Auchmuty. At the beginning of the Revolution he was a student at King's College, and was intended by his father for the ministry. But his own inclinations were military from his boyhood.

Soon after he graduated, and in 1776, he joined the Royal Army under Sir William Howe, as an ensign in the 45th Regiment, and was present in most of the actions in that and the following year. In 1783 he commanded a company in the 75th Regiment, in the East Indies, and was with Lord Cornwallis in the first siege of Seringapatam. In 1801 he joined the expedition to Egypt, and held the post of adjutant-general. He returned to England in 1803, and three years after was ordered to South America, where, as brigadier-general, he assumed command of the troops; and, in 1807, assaulted and reduced — after a most determined resistance — the city and fortress of Monte Video. In 1809 he was transferred to India. Subsequently, he succeeded Sir D. Baird, as chief of the staff in Ireland. He was knighted in 1812; his nephew, Sir John Maxwell Tylden, lieutenant-colonel of the 52d Regiment, being his proxy. He twice received the thanks of Parliament, and was presented with a service of plate by that body, and by the East India Company. His seat, — Syndale House, — was in Kent, near Feversham. He died in Ireland, suddenly, in 1822, at the age of sixty-four.

AUCHMUTY, ROBERT NICHOLS. Of New York. Son of Rev. Dr. Samuel Auchmuty. He was a graduate of King's College, New York; and, in the Revolution, served as a volunteer in the British Army. He died at Newport, Rhode Island, in 1813. His wife was Henrietta, daughter of Henry John Overing. His daughter Maria M., widow of Colonel E. D. Wainwright, of the United States Marines, died at Washington, D. C., January, 1861, aged seventy-one.

AUCHMUTY, RICHARD HARRISON. Of New York. Surgeon in the British Army. Taken prisoner in the storming of Stoney Point. With Cornwallis at Yorktown; — and died soon after the surrender, while on parole.

AUCHMUTY, ROBERT. Of Boston. In 1767 he was appointed Judge of Vice-Admiralty of Massachusetts and New Hampshire, in place of Chambers Russell, deceased. John Adams, with whom he was associated in the defence of Captain Preston, for the affair in King Street, March 5, 1770, called the "Boston Massacre," describes his arguments at the bar thus: — "Volubility, voluble repetitions and repeated volubility; fluent reiterations and reiterating fluency; such nauseous eloquence always puts my patience to the torture."

His letters to persons in England were sent to America, with those of Governor Hutchinson, by Franklin, in 1773, and created much commotion. He went to England in 1776, and at one period was in very distressed circumstances. He never returned to the United States. His estate was confiscated. His mansion in Roxbury became the property of Governor Increase Sumner, and was occupied by him at the time of his decease. Mr. Auchmuty died in 1788

Walker & Son, booksellers, London, have on their Catalogue of 1856, among their rare American tracts, the following:—
"AUCHMUTY (Robert, *an Absentee*,) Certificate of the Commonwealth of Massachusetts of the Sale of R. Auchmuty's Library, at Public Auction, according to Law, *Signed and Sealed* 12th Feb. 1784, with Autograph Certificate of John Browne, Chairman of the Committee of Sequestration, Signed and Dated 10th Feb. 1784, Boston; Statement of the Manner in which Mrs. Brinley and Mrs. Breynton Executed the Directions of the Will of R. Auchmuty, Esq., with his Will annexed, &c., showing every thing that was done for those purposes, 20 pages, 4to."

AUCHMUTY, JAMES. Of New York. Son of Robert. "I send you," wrote General Scott to the Provincial Congress, July 5, 1776, "James Auchmuty, storekeeper in the Engineer Department, and brother to Dr. Auchmuty, with his wife and child." He himself wrote Mr. Jay, in October of the same year, that, while others held as prisoners of war were paid the regular allowance, not a shilling had been given him. Soon after, he gave his parole to depart to Danbury, Connecticut, and to remain neutral until exchanged or discharged. At the peace he removed to Nova Scotia, where he became eminent as a lawyer, and was appointed judge. He had a son in the British Army, who was killed in battle in the West Indies.

AVERY, EPHRAIM. Of Pomfret, Connecticut. Episcopal minister. He received the degree of A. B. from Yale College, and that of A. M. from King's College, New York. In 1765 he succeeded Mr. Punderson as minister of Rye, and continued his pastoral relations until the Revolution, "when he became so obnoxious to the Whigs," that his farm animals were driven off and his other property plundered. He died

November, 1776. General Israel Putnam was one of the husbands of his mother. She died in the Highlands in 1777, and was deposited in Beverly Robinson's tomb.

AXTELL, WILLIAM. Of New York. Member of the Council of that Colony. He was descended from David Axtell, a colonel in Cromwell's army, who was beheaded at the restoration of the Stuarts. When examined by the Whig Committee, in 1776, he stated that the bulk of his property was in Great Britain and the West Indies. In reporting his case to the Provincial Congress, the Committee remarked that they believed him to be "a gentleman of high honor and integrity." He had a country-seat at Flatbush, was the first man in wealth and importance there, and invited Whig prisoners to sup with him. Miss Shipton, a relative and an inmate of his house, married Colonel Giles, of the Continental Army. In 1778 Mr. Axtell was commissioned by Sir William Howe, colonel of a corps of Loyalists. In 1783 the colors of the regiment of Waldeck were consecrated in front of his mansion at Flatbush. The troops formed in a circle, and officers and men took a solemn oath to support the new standards; a splendid dinner and a ball followed; and the ladies presented the officers who bore the colors, with a knot of blue and yellow ribbons. In November of the last mentioned year, Colonel Axtell's furniture was sold by auction at his town-house, Broadway, New York. His estate was confiscated. He went to England, received a considerable sum for his losses, and was allowed the half-pay of a colonel. He died at Beaumont Cottage, Surrey, in 1795, aged seventy-five. His wife died before his departure from America. He left no issue.

AYMAR, FRANCIS. Descended from a family that fled to the United States during the religious persecutions in France. Was born in the city of New York in 1759, and died at St. Andrew, New Brunswick, October, 1843, aged eighty-four years. He was one of the grantees of, and settled at St. John, New Brunswick, in the autumn of 1783, and continued his residence there until 1807, when he returned to the United

States, and lived alternately at Eastport, Maine; New York; and St. Andrew, up to the time of his decease. He was the father of fifteen children, of whom the following survived him: Daniel, William, John, Francis, Nancy, Mary, Betsey, Eleanor, Sarah, and Phebe.

BABBIT, DANIEL. He died at Gagetown, New Brunswick, 1830, at the age of eighty-seven.

BABCOCK, REV. LUKE. An Episcopal minister. He was the youngest son of Chief Justice Babcock, of Rhode Island, was born in 1738, and graduated at Yale College in 1755. Having been ordained by the Bishop of London, he was appointed to the mission of Philipsburgh, New York. In 1774, King's College conferred the degree of A. M. Soon after the breaking out of the Revolution his papers were examined, and he was personally interrogated touching his allegiance to the Crown. The result was, that in October, 1776, he was ordered to Hartford, where he remained until the following February, when his health failed, and he was directed to remove within the lines of the Royal Army. "He got home in a raging fever, and delirious," and died, February 18, 1777. Mr. Seabury said, — "I know not a more excellent man, and I fear his loss, especially in that mission, will scarcely be made up." His remains were deposited in the family vault of the Van Cortlands.

In 1780 the parsonage was broken into by a band of "cowboys," with disguised persons and blackened faces, and the ladies robbed of their valuables. The leader, in parting, made a profound bow, and thus addressed Mrs. Babcock: —

"Fare you well, and fare you better,
And when I die, I'll send you a letter."

Mr. Babcock's brother Henry, a graduate of Yale College, was a lawyer, a colonel in the Whig service, in command at Newport, Rhode Island, and "a man of fine person, accomplished manners, and winning eloquence."

BACHE, THEOPHYLACT. Of New York. He came to America, probably, in 1755. He was a merchant, and his business was principally with the West Indies and Newfoundland. He was also agent of the packets which plied between Falmouth, England, and New York. In 1773 he was elected President of the Chamber of Commerce. He was a determined Loyalist. His brother Richard married Sarah, daughter of Doctor Franklin, and was a Whig. The political sympathies of Theophylact were, possibly, the same as Richard's at the outset, since he was associated with Jay and Lewis on the Committee of Correspondence.

July 1, 1776, in a letter to Philip Livingston, he denied that he was inimical to American rights, and said, that the distressed state of his wife and numerous family, required all his attention, and would, he hoped, be a sufficient apology for not appearing before Congress, as required to do by that body. At one period of the war his place of residence was at Flatbush, Long Island. Obnoxious to some of the Whigs, in the course of events, a daring attempt to carry him off was made in 1778, by a Captain Marriner, an eccentric, witty, and ingenious partisan, which resulted successfully. Marriner's plan embraced three other Loyalists of rank and consequence; but Bache and Major Moncrieffe, with four slaves, were those whom he actually captured, and they were placed in a boat and conveyed to New Jersey. The marauders struck Mrs. Bache several times for entreating them not to deal harshly with her husband, and they plundered the house of plate, wounded a female servant, and dragged off Mr. Bache himself without giving him time to put on his clothes. Such is the account.

Mr. Bache was kind to Colonel Graydon, a Whig; gave him frequent invitations to tea, and to partake of his Madeira, and offered his purse to relieve his supposed necessities. "He is remembered as a fine specimen of a gentleman, — courteous, hospitable, with a touch of the sportsman, loving his gun and his dog, and everywhere acceptable as a polished and agreeable companion." He died in New York, in 1807, aged seventy-eight. His wife was a Miss Barclay.

BACON, JOHN. Of New Jersey. Leader of a band of

marauders in the counties of Burlington and Monmouth. In the fight at Cedar Bridge, he was accused of killing one Cook, and the State offered a reward for his capture, dead or alive. In April, 1782, a brother of Cook, John Stewart, and four others, all heavily armed, surprised him on a very dark night, in a tavern, when he surrendered and was disarmed. But Cook thrust his bayonet into his body, and, on his attempt to escape, Stewart shot him dead.

BADGELY, ——. June 20, 1782, he was condemned to death for treason in New Jersey, and the day of execution appointed. His case caused a spirited letter from Sir Guy Carleton to Washington. The papers show that Badgely "joined the enemy long after the passing of the treason act."

BADGER, MOSES. An Episcopal minister. He graduated at Harvard University in 1761. His wife was a daughter of Judge Saltonstall of Massachusetts, and sister of Colonel Richard and Leverett, the two Loyalist sons of that gentleman. Mr. Badger went to Halifax in 1776, but was at New York at or about the time of the death of Leverett, and wrote to the family on the subject. At one period he was chaplain to De Lancey's second battalion. After the Revolution, Mr. Badger was Rector of King's Chapel, Providence, and died in that city in 1792. It appears, that some years prior to the war he was an Episcopal missionary in New Hampshire, authorized to labor throughout that Colony.

BAILEY, JACOB. He graduated at Harvard University in 1755. Principally through the instrumentality of the Plymouth proprietors in Maine, an Episcopal Church was erected at Pownalborough, now Dresden, in that State, and for several years Mr. Bailey was the officiating clergyman, as a missionary of the Society for the Propagation of the Gospel. Few around him agreed with him in political sentiment.

For the single offence of continuing divine service, he relates, he was threatened, insulted, condemned, laid under heavy bonds, and doomed to transportation. His family consisted of a wife, a young infant, and two girls of about eleven years. Informed of a design against his life, he resolved to leave them, destitute of money, and of provisions except a few garden roots; and escape, as he best could do. He accomplished his purpose, but returned. Again molested, and told that if he attempted to officiate in public or in private, immediate confinement in prison would follow, he determined to abandon the country, and in the summer of 1779 he went to Halifax, N. S. I give an account of his appearance when he landed in that city, in nearly his own words. His feet were adorned with shoes which sustained the marks of rebellion and independence. His legs were covered with a thick pair of blue woollen stockings, which had been so often mended and darned by the fingers of frugality, that scarce an atom of the original remained. His breeches, which just concealed the shame of his nakedness, had been formerly black, but the color being worn out by age, nothing remained but a rusty gray, bespattered with lint, and bedaubed with pitch. Over a coarse tow and linen shirt, manufactured in the looms of sedition, he wore a coat and waistcoat of the same dandy gray russet; and, to secrete from public inspection the innumerable rents, holes, and deformities, which time and misfortunes had wrought in these ragged and weather-beaten garments, he was furnished with a blue surtout, fritted at the elbows, worn at the button-holes, and stained with a variety of tints. To complete the whole, a jaundice-colored wig, devoid of curls, was shaded with the remnants of a rusty beaver, its monstrous brim replete with notches and furrows, and grown limpsy by the alternate inflictions of storm and sunshine, lopped over his shoulders, and obscured a face meagre with famine and wrinkled with solicitude. His wife's dress was no better. She was arrayed in a ragged baize night-gown, tied round the middle with a woollen string; her petticoats were jagged at the bottom, were ragged above, and drabbled in mud. He became Rector of St. Luke's Church, Annapolis, Nova Scotia, and died in that relation in 1808, at the age of sixty-seven. During the last twenty-six years of his life he was absent from his church only one Sunday.

His wife, Sally, daughter of Dr. John Weeks, of Hampton, N. H.; three sons and three daughters, survived him. Charles Percey, the oldest son, who was remarkable for personal beauty, was a captain in the British Army, and was killed at the battle of Chippewa, in the war of 1812. Rebecca Lavinia died at Annapolis. Charlotte Maria is (1853) still living. Thomas Henry was an officer in the militia, and died young, leaving a wife and three children. William Gilbert was a lawyer of extensive practice, died young, also, and left a family. Elizabeth Anna married Mr. James Whitman. Mrs. Bailey died at Annapolis in 1818, at the age of seventy. Mr. Bailey was poor throughout his life. " Though oppressed himself by want and debt, his hospitality never ceased to flow, and by the kindness of his nature he always retained the personal regard of all who knew him."

The Life of Mr. Bailey, by the Rev. William S. Bartlet, late Rector of St. Luke's Church, Chelsea, Mass., is instructive and interesting, and has afforded materials for several notices in these pages.

BAILEY, WILLIAM. In 1782 was captain-lieutenant of the Loyal American Regiment; he settled after the war in New Brunswick, and received half-pay. He died on the River St. John, near Fredericton, in 1832, at the advanced age of ninety-seven.

BAILEY, ZACHARIAH. Died at Fredericton, New Brunswick, in 1823, aged seventy-two.

BAILIE, GEORGE. Of Georgia. In 1777 the Committee of Safety for the parish of St. John, gave him and two others permission to ship rice to Surinam, under bond and security that it should not be landed in a British port. He had purchased goods to a considerable amount of William Parton, (a Loyalist mentioned in these volumes,) and that gentleman, by an arrangement with the Governor of Florida, changed the destination of the vessels, and the bond was forfeited. The result was that Bailie was included in the Banishment and Confiscation Act.

BAINBRIDGE, ABSALOM. Of Princeton, New Jersey. Physician. He was descended from Sir Arthur Bainbridge, of Durham County, England, and his American ancestor was one of the founders of New Jersey. At the Revolutionary era the family was of great respectability. Soon after the beginning of the war, he retired to New York. In 1778 he was a surgeon in the New Jersey Volunteers; and at Flatbush that year, offered two guineas reward for a runaway negro boy, Priam, — " hair light-colored and of the woolly kind." His wife was a daughter of John Taylor, of Monmouth County, N. J. He died at New York in 1807, aged sixty.

His son William, born at Princeton, N. J., in 1774, entered the United States Navy during the aggressions of France, as a lieutenant; was commissioned post-captain in 1800, before he was twenty-six; and, December 29, 1812, in command of the frigate *Constitution*, he captured the British frigate *Java*. He died in 1833, in his sixtieth year. Another son, Joseph, was also a captain in the United States Navy.

BAIRD, WILLIAM and ARCHIBALD. The first went to St. John, New Brunswick, at the peace, and was a grantee of that city. Archibald was collector of the customs at Georgetown, S. C.; and, expelled for refusing to swear allegiance to the Whigs, he went to Europe, and died previous to August, 1777.

BALDWIN, JOHN. Of Philadelphia. Accused, in 1776, of refusing to receive " Continental money," he was summoned before the Council of Safety, and when informed of the complaint against him, acknowledged its truth. The Council urged the pernicious influence of his conduct, and gave him several days for reflection, in the hope that he would change his purpose. Persisting, at a second hearing, he was proclaimed " an enemy to his country, and precluded from all trade and intercourse with the inhabitants of these States;" and he was ordered to jail, there to remain without bail or mainprise until he shall be released by order of the Council, or some other power lawfully authorized so to do."

There died at St. George, N. B., in 1840, at the age of ninety-one years, a Loyalist of the name of John Baldween, who served the Crown nearly the whole of the Revolution, who was distinguished for bravery, and who, I suppose, was the subject of this notice.

BALL, ———. Captain of a militia company in the town of Berne, New York. His command consisted of eighty-five men; of whom sixty-three joined him in going over to the king at the commencement of hostilities. His ensign, Peter Deitz, and the remainder of his men, were Whigs. Deitz was commissioned captain, and his brother, William Deitz, lieutenant. Peter was killed in 1777, and William succeeded him in command, and by his activity incurred the hate of the Tories, when with his family they made him their prisoner, and tied him to his gate-post to witness the death of his father and mother, his wife and children, who were successively brought out and murdered before his eyes. The unhappy Deitz himself was carried to Niagara, where he ultimately became a victim of Tory cruelty.

BALLINGALL, ROBERT. Of South Carolina. He was in commission under the Crown after the surrender of Charleston in 1780, and his estate was confiscated.

When Sir Henry Clinton issued his proclamation ordering all prisoners taken at the capitulation to return to that city, Ballingall waited upon the ill-fated Colonel Isaac Hayne, and communicated the orders he had received on the subject. Hayne asserted that he was not bound to obey, and plead that his children were all ill with the small-pox, that one child had died, and that his wife was on the eve of dissolution; and finally declared, that no human force should remove him from the side of his dying wife. A discussion followed, and, at last, Hayne consented to give Ballingall a written stipulation to "demean himself as a British subject, so long as that country should be covered by the British Army."

BALMAINE, WILLIAM. He settled at Grand Lake, New Brunswick. While at St. John, in 1809, he fell from a window and was killed. His age was seventy-two.

BANNISTER, JOHN. A "young man of family, property, and convivial habits," who went to England during the war, and was on intimate terms with Count Rumford. He died previous to 1813.

BANYAR, GOLDSBROW. Of New York. He was born in London in 1724, and came to America at the age of fourteen. In 1746 he was sworn in as Deputy Secretary of the Colony, Deputy Clerk of the Council, and Deputy Clerk of the Supreme Court; and, six years later, was appointed Register of the Court of Chancery; and in 1753, Judge of Probate. His public employments ceased with the termination of the Royal Government. When the Whigs assumed the direction of affairs, he retired to Rhinebeck, New York. At the peace he removed to Albany, "where he always took a great interest in the internal improvements of the State, and contributed to all a liberal support." His wife was the widow of John Appy, Judge-Advocate of the forces in America. Blind in the last years of his life, he was led about the streets by a colored servant. He died at Albany in 1815, at the age of ninety-one; "leaving to his descendants a large fortune, and a more enduring inheritance, — the recollection of his many virtues and the example of a life devoted to duty." His son Goldsbrow died in New York in 1806.

BARBARIE, JOHN. Captain in the New Jersey Volunteers. Taken prisoner at Staten Island in 1777, and sent to Trenton. In garrison during the siege of Ninety-Six, South Carolina, and wounded. In the battle of Eutaw Springs, again wounded. He went to St. John, New Brunswick, at the peace, and was a grantee of that city. He received half-pay. He was a colonel of the militia, and a magistrate of the County of York. He died at Sussex Vale in 1818, at the age of sixty-seven. His son, Andrew Barbarie, Esq., was a member of the House of Assembly.

BARBARIE, OLIVER. In 1782 he was a lieutenant in the Loyal American Regiment. He settled at St. John in 1783, and was the grantee of a city lot. He died at Sussex Vale, New Brunswick.

"Euphemia, relict of Oliver Barbarie, late of the Barrack Department," died at Holyhead, England, at the house of her brother, Captain Skinner, in 1830, aged sixty-four.

BARCLAY, THOMAS. Was the son of Henry Barclay, D. D., Rector of Trinity Church, New York, and was born in that city, October 12, 1753. He was a graduate of Columbia College, and a student of law of John Jay. At the beginning of the Revolution he entered the British Army under Sir William Howe, as a captain in the Loyal American Regiment, and was promoted to a major by Sir Henry Clinton in 1777. He continued in active service until the peace. His estate in New York was confiscated, and at the close of the contest he fled with his family to Nova Scotia. Of the House of Assembly of that Province he was for some time Speaker; and of the militia, Adjutant-General. From 1796 till 1828 he was employed in civil stations, under the British crown, of great trust and honor. He was successively a commissioner under Jay's Treaty, the Consul-General for the Northern and Eastern States, and Commissary for the care and exchange of prisoners. At the conclusion of the war of 1812, between the United States and Great Britain, he was appointed Commissioner under the fourth and fifth Articles of the Treaty of Ghent, which post he continued to hold until within two years of his decease.

In an autograph letter in my possession, dated at Annapolis in 1799, he said to a fellow-exile: — " I find that those who were termed Royalists or Loyalists, in addition to their attachment to their king and country, preserve their principles of honor and integrity, of openness and sincerity, which marked the Americans previous to the year 1773; while those who have sold their king for a Republican Government, have adopted all the frivolity, intrigue, and insincerity of the French, and in relinquishing their allegiance, resigned at the same time, almost universally, religion and morality."

In private life he was estimable. He was a sincere and devout Christian of the communion of the Church of England. A prominent trait in his character was kindness and charity to the poor. His official conduct was the subject of frequent and marked approbation of the sovereigns whom he served, and at the close of his services he was rewarded with a pension of £1200 per annum. His habits of industry and application were extraordinary; and he was never in bed at sunrise for forty years. He died at New York in April, 1830, aged seventy-seven years. His son, Colonel Delancey Barclay, an aide-de-camp to George the Fourth, died in 1826; he had repeatedly distinguished himself, particularly at Waterloo.

BARD, SAMUEL. Of New York. Physician, L.L. D. He was born in Philadelphia in 1742, and graduated at King's College, N. Y. In 1762 he went to Edinburgh to complete his medical education, and was absent five years. Soon after his return, he helped to organize a medical school, of which he became a professor. In 1772 his father, Dr. John Bard, retired to the country, when he succeeded him in practice, and became eminent. Averse to war, unwilling to break off connection with England, and to mingle in the turmoils of the time, he joined his father at Hyde Park, in 1775. Other removals followed; but he finally settled in New Jersey. He returned to New York after the Royal Army took possession, and found himself an object of suspicion, and of utter neglect. Reduced to his last guinea, he accidentally met the mayor, (Matthews) who treated him kindly, and who, by his good offices subsequently, was the means of restoring him to the confidence of his former friends. The leaders of the Royal party became at last his frequent guests. At the peace he was urged to leave the country on account of his known associations and political sentiments; but he declined. After the Federal Government was organized, he was Washington's family physician. He died in 1821, in his eightieth year; his wife departed just one day before him, and a common grave received their remains. The universal testimony is, that he possessed almost every virtue which adorns manhood.

BARDAN, JOHN. Arrested by Lieutenant Nowell, he was asked what he intended to do with the Rebels, and answered: — "Kill them, as fast as I can." Nowell released him on payment of seven dollars in paper currency, and was tried by a court-martial, and "dismissed from the army with infamy."

BARFIELD, ———. Captain of a company of Tories. In an affair with the Whig partisan Melton, he was successful. Gabriel Marion, a nephew of the General, fell into his hands, and as soon as recognized, was put to death. "His name was fatal to him."

BARKER, WILLIAM. Of Maine. Born in England in 1734; emigrated to Massachusetts about the year 1774; removed to the Kennebec River in 1775. "Opposed to the Revolution at heart," but did not often publicly avow his opinions. In the course of the war he lived a year or two in Dresden. The Whigs annoyed him in various ways, but he did not leave the country. He died at Gardiner, in 1822. Dorothy, his wife, died in 1814. One daughter, Nancy, married Peter Grant; another, Elizabeth, was the wife of Joshua Lord.

BARKER, JOSHUA. He entered the British Army during the French war, and served with distinction in the West Indies. After he attained the rank of captain, he retired on half-pay. In the Revolution, he "was as little obnoxious as perhaps any man in his situation could be; always wishing for the blessings of peace, and the good of his country." In his address he was courteous and graceful; in his temper, calm; in his counsels, clear and determined. He bore a long indisposition with fortitude and resignation. He died at Hingham, Massachusetts, in 1785, aged seventy-three.

BARNARD, JOHN. Of Massachusetts. He was born in 1745, and graduated at Harvard University in 1762. He went to St. John, New Brunswick, and was a merchant. He died in 1785, aged forty.

BARNARD, THOMAS. Of Salem, Massachusetts. Settled in Nova Scotia, and died at Yarmouth, about the year 1833.

BARNES, HENRY. Merchant of Marlborough, Massachusetts. He was a magistrate and a man of some note. The records of the town, however, as examined by a friend, show hardly more than that he distilled a liquor from cider, which he exported, and which he petitioned the selectmen for leave to sell there at retail.

Towards the close of February, 1775, General Gage ordered Captain Brown and Ensign D'Bernicre, to go through the Counties of Suffolk and Worcester, and to sketch the roads as they went, for his information, "as he expected to have occasion to march troops through that country the ensuing spring." The two officers set out from Boston, disguised like countrymen in brown clothes and reddish handkerchiefs round their necks. Their adventures until their arrival at Marlborough, do not belong to this sketch. Recommended to Mr. Barnes "as a friend to government," they found his house in a snow-storm, discovered themselves, and were told by him, that they need not be at "the pains of telling him, he knew their situation." That "the town was very violent," that "they could be safe nowhere but in his house," and that "they had been expected the night before," &c., &c. The people were suspicious, and began to assemble in groups in all parts of the village. Messages were sent to Barnes, and other circumstances occurred, which, after the lapse of twenty minutes, compelled him to declare to his guests that they would be attacked, and that he could not protect them. He accordingly took them out of his house by the stables, and directed them to a by-road. They made their escape to the tavern of Jones, the Tory landlord of Weston; "it snowed and blew," relates one of them, "as much as I ever see it in my life."

In the House of Representatives, November, 1775, the "Petition of Henry Knox[1] humbly showeth: That your petitioner having been obliged to leave all his goods and house furniture in Boston, which he has no prospect of ever getting possession of again, nor any equivalent for the same, therefore begs the Honorable Court, if they in their wisdom see fit, to permit him to exchange house furniture with Henry Barnes, late of Marlborough, which he now has it in his power to do." The prayer was refused; but the Whig was allowed

[1] Subsequently, Chief of Artillery in the Continental Army, and Secretary at War under Washington.

to *use* the Loyalist's household goods, on giving receipt to account for them to the proper authorities.

In December, 1775, Catharine Goldthwait prayed the interposition of the General Court, stating in a petition that she was the niece and adopted heir of Barnes; that she had resided with him about seventeen years; that at his departure from town, she was left with a part of his family in possession, and that the committee of Marlborough had entered upon his estate, sold a part, and proposed to dispossess her entirely. Barnes went to England. In 1777 he was at Bristol with his wife and niece, and in September, thirteen of his fellow Loyalists were his guests; and, later still the same year, he dined with several of the Massachusetts exiles at Mr. Lechmere's, when the conversation was much about the political condition of their native land.

In 1778, Mr. Barnes was proscribed and banished. In 1781 he supped with one of his countrymen, who told him that the people of the Old Bay State complained of Congress and of their French allies, without restraint. He died at London in 1808, at the age of eighty-four.

BARNES, JOSHUA. A captain in DeLancey's corps. In 1778, the Whig Major Leavenworth, of Massachusetts, hearing that Barnes was out on a plundering expedition, formed the plan of capturing him; and, leading him into an ambuscade, took him with his full company of sixty-four, prisoners.

BARNES, JOHN. Of New Jersey. Sheriff of the County of Hunterdon. After the Declaration of Independence, he refused to act under the Whigs; and, when summoned before the State Convention, said he was willing to be superseded. In 1778, he was a major in the New Jersey Volunteers.

BARRELL, WALTER. Of Boston. Inspector-General of the Customs. In his religious sentiments he was, with his family of five persons, a follower of Robert Sandeman; he embarked at Boston with the British Army in 1776, for Halifax, and arrived in England in the summer of the same year. In 1779 he was a member of the Loyalist Association formed in London; his second daughter, Polly, died in London in 1810.

BARRELL, COLBURN. Of Boston. At the Boston Latin School in 1744. With his wife and daughter, the guest of John Adams in 1771. An Addresser of Hutchinson and a Protestor against the Whigs in 1774. He was at New York in 1783, and one of the fifty-five petitioners for lands in Nova Scotia. [See *Abijah Willard.*] He was a Sandemanian.

BARRETT, CHARLES. Of Ipswich, New Hampshire. He was born in Concord. At the beginning of the war, he was a man of property and influence, and in command of a company of militia. He was fearless in his utterance against the measures of the Whigs; was often involved in difficulty, and suffered many indignities. At one time, by vote of the town, he was confined to the limits of his own farm. He gave his adhesion to the new State government at the peace, and was a delegate to the Convention to consider the Federal Constitution, when, it would seem, he was an ultra Democrat. He opposed the adoption of the Constitution with warmth; and, as relates to the Executive, said that " The Presidents will be four-year old Kings, and soon Kings for life." He died in 1808.

BARRON, WILLIAM. Of Petersham, Massachusetts. Prior to the Revolution, he held a commission in the British Army. In the struggle, his sympathies were entirely with the Crown; but he was not active. He was a gentleman of refined manners, and a brave soldier. He died at Petersham in 1784, greatly lamented. Two of his sons graduated at Harvard University; William Amherst, who was a tutor there in Mathematics and Natural Philosophy, and who died unmarried, in 1825; and Thomas, who studied law, was some time in England, and died, probably, in Ohio, in 1830, or the next year. John Quincy Adams was a classmate of William Amherst.

BARRY, ROBERT. At the close of the Revolution he embarked at New York for Shelburne, Nova Scotia. He became an eminent merchant, established branch-houses in various parts of the Province, and his name is connected with the largest of the early commercial enterprises of Nova Scotia.

He was distinguished for qualities which adorn the Christian character, and throughout life was highly esteemed. His death occurred at Liverpool, Nova Scotia, September, 1843, in the eighty-fourth year of his age.

BARRY, W. Lieutenant in the Royal Foresters. He died of a fever in October, 1781, near Hellgate, New York, and was buried at Hallet's Cove, with the honors of war.

BARTON, THOMAS. An Episcopal minister. He graduated at Trinity College, Dublin, and in 1754, was sent by the Society for the Propagation of the Gospel to the new Mission in the Counties of York and Cumberland, Pennsylvania. His post was on the frontier, and his duties particularly onerous. "He had to ride one hundred and forty-eight miles every six weeks, to attend his three congregations, and, often at the head of his people, went to oppose the savages." In 1758, he was chaplain to the expedition against Fort Duquesne, and formed the acquaintance of several distinguished persons. In 1770 he received the degree of A. M. from King's College, New York. Adhering to the Royal cause, subsequently, he was first confined to the limits of his county, and finally to his house. In November, 1776, he wrote: "I have been obliged to shut up my churches, to avoid the fury of the populace, who would not suffer the Liturgy to be used, unless the Collects and Prayers for the King and Royal Family were omitted, which neither my conscience nor the declaration I made and subscribed when ordained, would allow me to comply with; and, although I used every prudent step to give no offence even to those who usurped authority and rule . . . . yet, my life and property have been threatened, upon mere suspicion of being unfriendly to what is called the American cause."

After a restraint of two years, and in November, 1778, he withdrew to New York. His loss of liberty occasioned a disease, of which he died May 25, 1780. The Memoirs of Rittenhouse were written by his son William Barton. Another son, Benjamin Smith Barton, doctor of medicine, was a distinguished professor in the University of Pennsylvania, and succeeded the celebrated Rush. Professor Barton was the first American who published an elementary work on botany.

BARTON, THOMAS. Colonel, and in command of a body of Loyalists. Three incidents occur in 1777: First, that he attempted to cut off a party of Whig militia, and was defeated. Second, that he was successful against a detachment of Whigs at Paramus. Third, that he was captured on Staten Island, with about forty of his men, and sent to New Jersey. At the peace he retired to Nova Scotia, and received a large grant of land at Digby. He died about the year 1790. His family returned to the United States.

BARTRAM, JOHN. Of Pennsylvania. An eminent botanist. He was born in Chester County, Pennsylvania, in 1701. His taste was for botany, from his youth, and in this department he became so eminent as to be appointed American botanist to George the Third. The first botanic garden in this country was founded by him on the Schuylkill, about four miles below Philadelphia. He was so earnest in pursuit of knowledge that he hardly allowed himself time to eat. He was a proficient in the learned languages, in medicine and surgery, and in natural history. Linnaeus pronounced that he was "the greatest natural botanist in the world." Besides these accomplishments, he was an ingenious mechanic; built his own stone house, and made most of his own farming tools and other articles required on his estate. He was gentle in manners, amiable in disposition, modest, and charitable. He died in 1777, aged seventy-five.

His son, William, who was elected Professor of Botany in the University of Pennsylvania, in 1782, but declined on account of ill health, deceased in 1823, at the age of eighty-four. His youngest son, John, who succeeded him in the botanic garden above mentioned, died in 1812.

BASS, REV. EDWARD, D. D. First Bishop of Massachusetts. He was born in Dorchester in 1726, and graduated at Harvard University in 1744. He fitted for the ministry as a Congregationalist. Ordained in England in 1752; he was

Rector of St. Paul's Church, Newburyport, fifty-one years. Elected Bishop of Massachusetts in 1797, his jurisdiction was subsequently extended over the Episcopalian churches in Rhode Island and New Hampshire. His course in the Revolution is in dispute; but of his loyalty I entertain no doubt. He died at Newburyport in 1803, after two days illness, aged seventy-seven. A marble monument has been erected to his memory. "He was a sound divine, a critical scholar, an accomplished gentleman, and an exemplary Christian."

BATES, WALTER. Of Stamford, Connecticut. In the spring of 1783 he arrived at St. John, New Brunswick, in the ship *Union*. He settled in King's County, and for many years was its sheriff. He died at Kingston in that county in 1842, aged eighty-two.

BATWELL, REV. DANIEL. Of Pennsylvania. Episcopal minister in York and Cumberland Counties. He received a grant of land from the Proprietaries of the Colony near Carlisle. Soon after the Declaration of Independence he became an active Loyalist, was apprehended and committed to York jail. Congress gave him leave to dispose of his personal estate, and to remove with his family to the city of New York. In 1782 he was chaplain of the third battalion of the New Jersey Volunteers. He went to England, and died there.

BAUM, JEREMIAH. Of Maine. He was tried by a court-martial, and executed in Maine in 1780, by General Wadsworth, who commanded the Eastern department between the Piscataqua and the St. Croix. This act of severity gave the General himself great pain, and was condemned by many Whigs; but it appears to have been necessary, and to have checked the treacherous intercourse of the eastern Tories with their British friends who held Castine.

Eaton, in his history of Warren, thus relates the transaction: —

"General Wadsworth 'issued a proclamation denouncing death upon any one convicted of aiding or secreting the enemy. Subsequent to the proclamation, a man by the name of Jeremiah Baum, residing back of Damariscotta, was taken up, charged with piloting a party of the British through the back country for the purpose of pillaging. He was tried on the twenty-third and twenty-fourth of August, by a court-martial at Wadsworth's head-quarters, condemned and sentenced to be hung." Many efforts were made to procure his pardon, but Gen. W. remained inflexible.

"On the day after the sentence, a gallows was erected on Limestone Hill, and the miserable man was conducted to it in a cart, fainting at the sight, and rendered insensible from fear. Mr. Coombs, who was standing near, was asked to lend his handkerchief to tie over the prisoner's eyes. Supposing it a farce, he complied; and the prisoner, to appearance already dead, was swung off, to the astonishment of the spectators. The General was greatly moved, and was observed walking his room in apparent agitation the most of the following day. Many friends of the Revolution regretted that such an example of severity, however necessary, should fall on such a victim."

BAXTER, SIMON. Of New Hampshire. Was proscribed and banished, and lost his estate under the Confiscation Act. He fell into the hands of a party of Whigs during the war, and was condemned to die. When brought out for execution, he broke and fled with the rope about his neck, and succeeded in reaching Burgoyne's army. He went to New Brunswick at the peace, and died at Norton, King's County, in 1804, aged seventy-four. His widow, Prudence, died the same year, at the age of seventy-three.

BAXTER, STEPHEN. Of Bedford, New York. He made humble confession at Stamford, Connecticut, December 1775, that he "had opposed the liberties of America by horrid cursing and profane swearing," and he asked the forgiveness of those whom he had abused personally, and of the Whigs generally. But a "Recanter" was still a Tory; and in 1783 he went to Nova Scotia.

BAXTER, JOSEPH. Settled in New Brunswick and died there. Joanna, his widow, died in that Province in 1842, aged eighty-six.

BAXTER, ELIJAH. Died at Norton, King's County, New Brunswick, in 1852.

BAYARD, SAMUEL VETCH. Of New York. In 1777 Governor Tryon appointed him to succeed Colden as Surveyor and Searcher of the Customs, and said to Lord George Germain: "From the steady loyalty of his father, and the depredations made on his estate, and in consideration that his two sons are now in the Provincial service, I rest in absolute confidence that his Majesty will confirm my appointment in opposition to all solicitations whatever."

I find the death of a Samuel Vetch Bayard, at Wilmot, Nova Scotia, in 1832, aged seventy-five. Possibly, one of the "sons" mentioned by Tryon, as it is said "he served under the Crown, and was a military officer."

BAYARD, SAMUEL. Of New York. In 1774 he was engaged in a controversy with other proprietors of lands in New York, and in behalf of himself and associates, submitted a memorial to the British Government, praying to be put in quiet possession of a part of the tract called the Westenhook Patent. After General Lee took command in the city in 1776, Mr. Bayard was made prisoner, and placed under guard at the house of Nicholas Bayard. He entered the service of the Crown, and in 1782 was major of the King's Orange Rangers.

BAYARD, WILLIAM. Of New York. Head of the mercantile house of William Bayard & Co. He was associated with Jay, Lewis, and others, as a member of the Committee of Fifty, and he appears to have been of Whig sympathies at the beginning of the controversy. In 1773, Mr. Quincy, of Massachusetts, on his return from the South, passed through New York, and recorded in his journal, under the date of May 12th, — "Spent the morning in writing and roving, and dined with Colonel William Bayard at his seat on the North River." In 1775 the Massachusetts delegates to the Continental Congress were his guests also. In 1776 he was an Addresser of Lord and Sir William Howe. He went to England, and his property was confiscated. Governor Franklin recommended him to Lord George Germain, for relief. He died very aged, in 1804, at his seat, Greenwich House, Southampton, England.

BAYLEY, RICHARD. Of New York. An eminent physician. He was born in Connecticut in 1745, and in 1769 and 1770 attended lectures and hospitals in London. In 1772 he began practice in New York, and his attention was early attracted to the croup, which professional men had treated as putrid sore throat. His experiments resulted in the adoption of active treatment, and in an entire change of remedies for that formidable disease. In 1776 he was in 'the British Army under Howe, as a surgeon, but incapable of enduring separation from his wife, he resigned just before her decease in 1777. For the remainder of his life he was engaged in duties of a professional kind. He occupied the chairs of anatomy and surgery in Columbia College, and published letters and essays on medical subjects. He died in 1801, aged fifty-six. He is represented as a man of high temper, strong in his attachments, invincible in his dislikes, and of honorable, chivalrous character.

BAYLEY, PHILIP. Of Portsmouth, New Hampshire. In 1775 he signed and published a Submission, or Recantation, in which he asked forgiveness for the past, and promised that his future conduct should convince the public that he would risk his life and interest in defence of the liberties of the country. In his case, as in several others, the written recantation was probably extorted from an unwilling mind to avert some impending blow. Many recanters went into exile. Bayley, in 1778, was proscribed and banished. The captain-lieutenant of the Royal Fencible Americans in 1782 was Philip Bailey, and, possibly, the subject of this notice.

BEACH, REV. ABRAHAM, D. D. Episcopal minister. He was born in Cheshire, Connecticut, in 1740, and graduated at Yale College in 1757. He went to England for ordination in 1767, and was appointed missionary at New Brunswick, and Piscataqua, New Jersey. In July, 1776, he was told that unless he omitted prayers for the King and Royal Family, he must discontinue service on the Sabbath. As he would not consent to this condition, he shut the churches in which he officiated. In a few months, however, worship was resumed in one of them. Early in 1777 he said: "My present condition is truly distressing, being situated about a quarter of a mile beyond the picket-guard of the King's troops. Parties of Washington's army are every day skulking about me. A few days ago, they drove off my cattle, horses and sheep; and since I sat down to write this letter, about fifty of them surrounded my house, and fired from thence on the out-sentry of the Hessians," &c. Until the peace, he continued in his perilous position, but, " dispensing spiritual consolation alike to Whigs and Tories." In 1783 he was appointed temporary missionary at Amboy; and in 1784, assistant minister of Trinity Church, New York. After twenty-nine years' duty, and in 1813, he resigned; when the Vestry, " in consideration of his very long and faithful services in the church, as one of its most faithful pastors, granted him an annuity of £1500 for life, secured by bond, under seal of the Corporation." He retired to his farm on the Raritan River, where he passed the remainder of his life. He died in 1828, at the age of eighty-eight. His wife Ann, daughter and sole heiress of Evart Van Winkle, one of the original Dutch settlers of New Jersey, died in 1808. "In his intercourse with society, no man could be more frank or more free from all guile. . . . . While his dignified person, expressive countenance, and lively feelings, commanded the respect and affection of all who knew him."

BEACH, REV. JOHN. He graduated at Yale College in 1721, and for several years was a Congregational minister in Connecticut; but finally became an Episcopalian. In 1732 he went to England for ordination, and on his return, was employed as an Episcopalian missionary in Reading and Newtown, Connecticut. After the Declaration of Independence, he continued to pray for the King, and to give other evidence of his loyalty. His course gave great displeasure to the Whigs, and he suffered at their hands. He died in March, 1782. During his life, he was engaged in one or more religious controversies. Several of his compositions of this description, and a number of sermons, were published. The following extracts from two of his letters to the Society for the Propagation of the Gospel, whose missionary he was, contain interesting information. The last, as will be seen, was dated only a few months before his death.

"Newtown, May 5, 1772.

"As it is now forty years since I have had the advantage of being the venerable Society's missionary in this place, I suppose it will not be improper to give a brief account how I have spent my time, and improved their charity. Every Sunday I have performed divine service, and preached twice, at Newtown and Reading alternately. And in these forty years I have lost only two Sundays through sickness; although in all that time I have been afflicted with a constant colic, which has not allowed me one day's ease or freedom from pain. The distance between the churches at Newtown and Reading is between eight and nine miles, and no very good road, yet have I never failed one time to attend each place according to custom, through the badness of the weather, but have rode it in the severest rains and snow-storms, even when there has been no track, and my horse near miring down in the snow-banks, which has had this good effect on my parishioners, that they are ashamed to stay from church on account of bad weather, so that they are remarkably forward to attend the public worship. As to my labors without my parish, I have formerly performed divine service in many towns where the Common-prayer had never been heard, nor the Scriptures read in public; and where now are flourishing congregations of the Church of England, and in some places where there never had been any public worship at all, or any sermon preached by any preacher of any denomination.

"In my travelling to preach the Gospel, once was my life remarkably preserved in passing a deep and rapid river. The retrospect on my fatigues, as lying on straw, &c., gives me pleasure, while I flatter myself that my labor has not been quite in vain, for the Church of England people are increased much more than twenty to one ; and what is infinitely more pleasing, many of them are remarkable for piety and virtue; and the Independents here are more knowing in matters of religion than they who live at a great distance from our church. We live in harmony and peace with each other, and the rising generation of the Independents seem to be entirely free from every pique and prejudice against the church, &c., &c.

" John Beach."

"Newtown, October 31, 1781

" It is a long time since I have done my duty in writing to the venerable Society, not owing to my carelessness, but to the impossibility of conveyance from here, and now do it sparingly. A narrative of my troubles I dare not now give. My two congregations are growing; that of Reading being commonly about three hundred, and at Newtown about six hundred. I baptize about one hundred and thirty children in one year, and lately two adults. Newtown, and the Church of England part of Reading are, (I believe,) the only parts of New England that have refused to comply with the doings of the Congress, and for that reason have been the butt of general hatred ; but God has delivered us from entire destruction. I am now in the eighty-second year of my age, yet do constantly alternately perform and preach at Newtown and Reading. I have been sixty years a public preacher, and, after conviction, in the Church of England fifty years ; but had I been sensible of my insufficiency, I should not have undertaken it. But now I rejoice in that I think I have done more good towards men's eternal happiness than I should have done in any other calling. I do most heartily thank the venerable Society for their liberal support, and beg that they will accept of this, which is, I believe, my last bill, £325, which, according to former custom, is due.

" At this age I cannot well hope for it, but I pray God I may have an opportunity to explain myself with safety; but must conclude now with Job's expression — ' Have pity upon me, have pity upon me, O ye my friends.' "

BEAMAN, THOMAS. Of Petersham, Massachusetts. Captain. In 1770, he claimed that a school-house in town was on his land, and to prevent the obnoxious Whig school-master from entering it, [see *Ensign Man*,] he locked it. How and Man broke in, and Beaman commenced a suit for trespass; the case was in the courts for some time; the costs were considerable, and finally paid by the defendants. April, 1775, Beaman acted as a guide to the British troops on their march to Lexington and Concord. He fled to Nova Scotia. In 1778 he was proscribed and banished.

BEAN, THOMAS. He went from New York to St. John, New Brunswick, in 1783, and of the latter city was a grantee. He and Dowling were contractors for the building of Trinity Church, St. John. He died at Portland, New Brunswick, in 1823, aged seventy-nine.

BEARD, ———. Of North Carolina. Captain of Tories. After a bloody affray in the house of a Whig, whose daughter had refused his hand, he was captured, tried by a court-martial, and hung.

BEARDSLEY, REV. JOHN. Of Poughkeepsie, New York. Episcopal minister. He was born in Stratford, Connecticut, in 1732. He entered Yale College, but did not graduate; King's (now Columbia) College, New York, however, conferred the degrees of A. B. and A. M. He went to England for ordination, and returned early in 1762. In addition to the performance of his parochial duties at Poughkeepsie, he officiated a part of the time at Fishkill. At the beginning of the war he refused to take the oath of allegiance to Congress, and suffered indignities in consequence. In the end, his property was seized, and poor and even destitute, he and his family took refuge in New York. In 1778, he was appointed chaplain in the Loyal American Regiment, commanded by Beverley Robinson, who had been a chief supporter of the Episcopal Church at Fishkill. At the peace, Mr. Beardsley accompanied his regiment to New Brunswick. After many deprivations and sufferings, he was settled over the parish in Maugerville, on the river St. John, and remained there more than seventeen years. His pastoral relations were dissolved in consequence of his infirmities. He retired to Kingston in that Province, on the half-pay of a chaplain, and died there in 1810. He had four daughters. The eldest married a German officer who, some years after the peace of 1783, returned with his wife and children to his native land. His son John died at Woodstock, New Brunswick, in 1852. His youngest son, Hon. Bartholomew Crannel Beardsley, who died in Canada West, in 1855, was Chief Judge of the Court of Common Pleas, and a member of the House of Assembly of New Brunswick. His grandson, H. H. Beardsley, of Woodstock, is (1852) a counsellor at law, and a member of the Assembly.

BEARMORE, ———. Major in a Loyalist corps, New York. In 1778, he attacked a Whig force of about forty, quartered in a dwelling-house and barns. He was taken prisoner the next year, much to the joy of the people who called him " a troublesome officer."

BECKWITH, NEHEMIAH. He settled at St. John, New Brunswick, but removed to Fredericton, where he died in 1815.

BECRAFT, ———. A Tory leader, cruel, and noted for deeds of blood. He boasted to his associates of having assisted to massacre the family of a Mr. Vrooman, in Schoharie, New York. The family, he said, were soon despatched, except a boy of fourteen, who ran from the house, when he started in pursuit, overtook him, and cut his throat, took his scalp, and hung his body across the fence. After the peace, he had the hardihood to return to Schoharie. He was seized, stripped naked and bound to a tree, and whipped nearly to death by ten men, some of whom had been his prisoners, and had heard him recount this exploit. Thus beaten, he was dismissed with a charge never to show himself in that country again; an injunction which he carefully kept.

BEDLE, JOHN. Of Staten Island, New York. Born in 1757. In the Revolution, private secretary to Colonel Billop. Went to St. John, New Brunswick, at the peace, and was employed a year or two in surveying that city. Removed to Woodstock about the year 1794, where he was a magistrate for forty years; and after the division of York County, was a magistrate, a Judge of Common Pleas, and Register of Wills and Deeds for the County of Carlton; he died in 1838, aged eighty-three. He married Margaret Dibble, now (1852) living at the age of eighty-six. His children were ten: William Jarvis and Paul M., magistrates; John, a Judge of the Court of Common Pleas; George A., Register of Deeds; Joseph, Tyler, Walter Dibble, and three daughters.

BELL, ANDREW. Of New Jersey. Secretary to Sir Henry Clinton. A diary kept by him during the march of the British Army, prior to the battle of Monmouth, is preserved in the Proceedings of the New Jersey Historical Society. In 1783 he was a petitioner for lands in Nova Scotia. [See *Abijah Willard*.] A correspondent who knew him well, says, he "esteemed him highly for his probity, intelligence, and urbanity." His wife was Susannah, daughter of Daniel O'Brien, of Perth Amboy. Governor Paterson, of New Jersey, married his sister. He died without children in 1843.

BELL, JOSEPH. Of New York. He was born in England, and emigrated to America just before the Revolution. He settled on a farm near Troy, but removed to the city of New York. At the peace, having suffered much for his loyalty, he went to Shelburne, Nova Scotia, in command of a company of exiled Loyalists, accompanied by his family of three and a servant. In 1792 he removed to Yarmouth, Nova Scotia, where he died in 1829, aged eighty-nine. His wife died in 1809; but two children survived him. One, a daughter, married Joseph Bond, M. D., who arrived at New York in a privateer, who volunteered to serve in the army, was present at the capture of Cornwallis, was an officer of the customs and sheriff in Nova Scotia after the war, and who died in 1830, aged seventy-two, leaving ten children.

BENEDICT, ELI. Of Danbury, Connecticut. Guide to the British troops to his native town. In 1782 an ensign in the Guides and Pioneers. At the peace he returned to Danbury with the intention of living there. Threatened with a ride on the *wooden-horse*, he fled. In 1799, administration on the estate of a person of this name, in the Province of New Brunswick.

BENNERMAN, JOHN. Of Portsmouth, Virginia. A captain. He went to England, and was one of " his Majesty's Band of Gentleman Pensioners." In 1781 he married a Miss Rolt of Lincolnshire. He died in England in 1785.

BERNARD, SIR THOMAS, Baronet. He was the third son of Sir Francis Bernard, Baronet, Governor of Massachusetts, and graduated at Harvard University in 1767. He went to England, where he married a lady of fortune. On the death of his brother, Sir John Bernard — who was a Whig — he succeeded to the title. His time was much devoted to institutions of benevolence in London; and he wrote several essays with a design to mitigate the sorrows, and improve the condition of the humbler classes of English society. The University of Edinburgh conferred on him the degree of Doctor of Laws. He died in England in 1818. Lady Bernard died in 1813, while preparing to go to church.

BERNARD, SIR JOHN, Baronet. The brother of Sir Thomas — above mentioned — remained in America; and, as remarked, was a Whig. To preserve the following incidents, then, is the reason for this notice. Soon after the Revolution he was in abject poverty, and the misfortunes of himself and his family seem to have unsettled his mind. When, in 1769, Sir Francis was recalled from the government of Massachusetts, he possessed a considerable landed estate in Maine, of which the large island of Mount Desert, Moose Island, (now Eastport,) and some territory on the main, formed a part. John, at or about the time of his father's departure. had an agency for the settlement of these and other lands; and, probably, until the confiscation of the property of Sir Francis, in 1778, was in comfortable circumstances. His place of residence during the war appears to have been at Bath, though he was sometimes at Machias.

Not long after the peace, he lived at Pleasant Point, a few miles from Eastport, in a small hut built by himself, and with no companion but a dog. An unbroken wilderness was around him. The only inhabitants at the head of the tide-waters of the St. Croix were a few workmen, preparing to erect a saw-mill. Robbinston and Perry were uninhabited. Eastport contained a single family. Yet, at the spot now occupied by the remnant of the tribe of the Passamaquoddy's, he attempted to make a farm. He had been bred in ease, had hardly done a day's work in his life; and yet he believed that he could earn a competence by labor. He told those who saw him, that "other young men went into the woods, and made themselves farms, and got a good living, and he saw no reason why he could not." But he cut down a few trees, became discouraged, and departed. His abject condition in mind and estate rendered him an object of deep commiseration; and his conduct during hostilities having entitled him to consideration, the Legislature of Massachusetts restored to him one half of the island of Mount Desert. Of his subsequent history, while he continued in the United States, but little is known to me. He came to Maine occasionally, and was much about Boston. Later in life he held offices under the British crown at Barbadoes and St. Vincent; and was known as Sir John Bernard, Baronet. He died in the West Indies in 1809, in his sixty-fifth year, without issue, and was succeeded by his brother Thomas.

BERGUYN, ———. Of North Carolina. Was in England, June, 1778, and about to return to America, on news that the Assembly of that State had voted to admit all Loyalists who might apply. In 1786 the Commissioner for the district of Wilmington, instead of selling his whole property as allowed by law, consented to the sale of a part of it, in a manner to test the legality of the Confiscation Act itself. The next year he was party to a suit, in which the question of his right to sue was decided in his favor, and a lawyer wrote — "We may be sure" that the attempt to forfeit his estate "will end in smoke."

BERTON, PETER. Of Long Island, New York. He went to New Brunswick in 1783, and was a Judge of the Court of Common Pleas. His youngest son, James D., a native of Long Island, died at Fredericton in 1848, aged seventy.

BETHUNE, JOHN. Of North Carolina. Chaplain in the Loyal Militia. Taken prisoner in the battle at Cross Creek, 1776, confined in Halifax jail, but ordered, finally, to Philadelphia. After his release, his continued loyalty reduced him to great distress. He was appointed chaplain to the 84th Regiment, and restored to comfort. At the peace he settled in Upper Canada, and died at Williamstown in that Colony in 1815, in his sixty-fifth year.

BETHUNE, GEORGE. Of Boston. He graduated at Harvard University in 1740. In 1774 he was an Addresser of Hutchinson in May, and one of the Protesters against the proceedings of the town meeting in June of that year. The next year he had retired to Jamaica, New York, where he was suspected of carrying on a correspondence with the British forces, and was summoned to appear before the Committee with his papers. He died in 1785, at Cambridge, aged sixty-four. Mary, his widow, daughter of Benjamin Faneuil, died at the same place in 1797, aged sixty-three.

BETTS, AZOR. Of New York. Physician. In January, 1776, he was arraigned before the Committee of Safety, for denouncing Congresses and Committees, both Continental and Provincial, and for uttering that they were " a set of damned rascals, and acted only to feather their own nests, and not to serve their country," &c. Ordered to close confinement in Ulster County jail. In April the Committee of Safety voted his discharge, on condition of acknowledging penitence, paying expenses of confinement, and taking an oath to be of good behavior; or, dispensing with the oath, executing a bond with sureties in £200. He settled in Nova Scotia, and died at Digby in that Province in 1809. His widow, Gloriannah, died at St. John, New Brunswick, soon after, aged sixty-nine.

BETTYS, JOSEPH. A noted Tory. " Joe Bettys " was

known as a shrewd, intelligent, daring, and bad man. It is said, that pity and mercy were emotions which he never felt, and that to all the gentler impulses he was thoroughly insensible. At the breaking out of the Revolution he lived at Ballston, New York, and was a Whig. Entering the Whig service he performed feats of extraordinary valor in Arnold's battle with Carleton on Lake Champlain, where he was taken prisoner and carried to Canada. While a captive, he was unfortunately seduced to attach himself to the interests of the Crown, and to accept the commission of ensign. Admirably fitted to act as a messenger and spy, he undertook to perform the duties of one or both as occasion should require, but was captured by his former friends, tried, and condemned to the gallows. Washington, however, spared his life on his promise of reformation, on the entreaties of his aged parents and the solicitations of influential Whigs. But Bettys returned directly to the ranks of the enemy, and his subsequent career was marked by almost every enormity that can disgrace a human being. His very name struck terror, and a record of his enterprises and crimes would fill a book. He burned the dwellings of persons whom he hated, or took them off by murder. Fatigue, distance, or danger, were no obstacles in the accomplishment of his designs. He knew that he carried his life in his hand. He scorned disguise or concealment. He fell upon his victims at noon as well as at midnight. Many plans were laid, many efforts made to seize him. At last, in 1782, the Whigs were successful, and detected him with a despatch to the commander of the British forces in New York. He was taken to Albany and executed as a spy and traitor. His death was deemed an event of no small consequence, both because it put an end to his own misdeeds, and because his fate was calculated to awe others who were engaged in the same perilous employments.

BIDDLE, JOHN. Of Bucks County, Pennsylvania. Was collector of excise, and a deputy-quartermaster of the Whig Army. He changed sides, and in 1779 his estate was confiscated. His office of collector of excise was worth, in 1775, but £15. In a Loyalist tract published at London in 1784, he is called " a creature of John Potts, and once a rebel commissary."

BIGG, JOHN. He died in New Brunswick in 1836, aged seventy-eight.

BILLOPP, CHRISTOPHER. Of Staten Island, New York. Prior to the Revolution, " the eldest son of Thomas Farmar married the daughter of Captain Christopher Billopp, an officer in the British Navy, who had succeeded in obtaining a patent for a large tract of land on Staten Island, containing one or two thousand acres. Young Farmar, upon his wife's inheriting this estate, adopted her father's name, and became a very noted character." He commanded a corps of Loyalists, or of loyal militia, raised in the vicinity of New York city, and was actively employed in military duty. He was taken prisoner by the Whigs, and confined in the jail at Burlington, New Jersey. Mr. Boudinot, the commissary of prisoners, in the warrant of commitment, directed that irons should be put on his hands and feet, that he should be chained to the floor of a close room, and that he should be fed on bread and water, in retaliation for the cruel treatment of Leshier and Randal, two Whig officers who had fallen into the hands of the Royal troops. In 1782 Colonel Billopp was Superintendent of Police of Staten Island. His property, which was large, was confiscated under the Act of New York. At the old Billopp House, which he erected, Lord Howe, as a commissioner of the mother-country, met Franklin, John Adams, and Edward Rutledge, a Committee of Congress, in the hope of adjusting difficulties, and of inducing the Colonies to return to their allegiance. During the war, Lord Howe, General Kniphausen, Colonel Simcoe, and other officers of rank in the Royal service, were frequent guests of Colonel Billopp, at this house. In 1783 he was one of the fifty-five petitioners for lands in Nova Scotia. [See *Abijah Willard.*] He went to New Brunswick soon after, and for many years bore a prominent part in the administration of its affairs. He was a member of the House of Assembly, and of the Council, and on the death of Governor Smythe, in 1823, he claimed the Presidency of the Government, and issued his proclamation accordingly; but the Honorable Ward Chipman was a competitor for the station, and was sworn into office. Colonel Billopp died at St. John in 1827, aged ninety. His wife Jane died at that city in 1802, aged forty-eight. His daughter Louisa married John Wallace, Esq., Surveyor of the Customs. His daughter Mary, the wife of the Reverend Archdeacon Willis, of Nova Scotia, died at Halifax in 1834, at the age of forty-three. His daughter Jane, wife of the Honorable William Black, of St. John, died in 1836. His two sons settled in the city of New York, and were merchants. They were partners, and in business at the time of the yellow fever; — the one married, the other single. The unmarried brother said to the other, "It is unnecessary that both should stay here. You have a family, and your life is of more consequence than mine; go into the country until the sickness subsides." The married brother retired from the city accordingly, while the other remained and was a victim of the fever. The survivor, whose name was Thomas, failed in business some time after; joined the expedition of the celebrated Miranda, and was appointed a captain; was taken prisoner by the Spaniards and executed.

BIRDSILL, BENJAMIN. Of New York. Went to New Brunswick in 1783, and settled in Queen's County. He died at Gagetown in that county in 1834, at the age of ninety-one. Descendants to the number of two hundred and two survived him. Rachel, his widow, died at Gagetown in 1843, aged ninety-seven.

BISSETT, REV. GEORGE. Of Newport, Rhode Island. Episcopal minister. Employed as assistant and school-master in 1767; he succeeded Mr. Browne, as Rector of Trinity Church, four years later, and continued in office until the evacuation of the town by the Royal Army, in 1779. Leaving his wife and child "in the most destitute circumstances," he followed the British troops to New York. His furniture was seized; but, on petition of Mrs. Bissett, the General

Assembly restored it, and gave her permission to join her husband. Soon after his departure, the church was entered, and the altar-piece — ornamented with emblems of royalty — was torn down and spoiled. I lose sight of him until 1786, when he was in England, about to embark for America. He resumed his professional duties in St. John, New Brunswick, and died there in 1788. His wife was Penelope, daughter of James Honyman, Judge of the Court of Vice-Admiralty, Rhode Island.

The Rev. Dr. Peters said of Mr. Bissett, — "He is a very sensible man, a good scholar and compiler of sermons, although too bashful to appear in company, or in the pulpit."

BLAIR, JAMES. Died at Halifax, Nova Scotia, where he was Barrack-master, in 1833, aged seventy-five.

BLAIR, JOHN. Was tried as a spy in 1778, and executed at Hartford, Connecticut. A large amount of counterfeit money was found in his possession.

BLAIR, CAPTAIN ———. Of Virginia. Joined Lord Dunmore. Taken prisoner and perished, as supposed, on the passage to France.

BLAKE, WILLIAM. Of South Carolina. In 1782 his estate was amerced twelve per cent. In an English work, I find that there "died in Great Cumberland Place, in 1803, in his sixty-fifth year, William Blake, Esq., of South Carolina." His remains were interred at Hanway with great funeral pomp: twelve outriders, four mourning-coaches, and nearly fifty other coaches, forming the procession. He left property valued at half a million of dollars.

BLAKSLEE, ABRAHAM. Of Connecticut. Commanded a company in the second regiment of the militia, and the House of Assembly appointed a Committee, in 1775, to inquire into charges against him of disaffection and contemptuous speaking.

BLAKSLEE, ASA. Removed to St. John, New Brunswick, in 1783, and died in that city in 1843, aged eighty-seven.

BLANCHARD, JOTHAM. Of Dunstable, New Hampshire. Served in a Loyalist corps. At the peace he settled in Nova

Scotia; received a grant of lands; carried on an extensive business in lumber; was active in exploring the country and in obtaining grants for fellow-exiles, and was a colonel in the militia. He died about the year 1800.

BLANVELT, TUNIS. Of New Jersey. In the war an active "bush-ranger." Lost considerable property in consequence of his loyalty. At the peace, went to Shelburne, Nova Scotia, with a family of six and three servants. Settled finally in Tusket, Nova Scotia, where he kept a boarding-house. Died in 1830, leaving several sons, of whom two are now (1861) shipmasters. His second wife was Hannah, daughter of Gabriel Van Nordan.

BLEAU, WALDRON. Of New York. In 1776 an Addresser of Lord and Sir William Howe; in 1782 a Captain in the third battalion New Jersey Volunteers. Went to St. John, New Brunswick, in 1783, and died five days after landing there. His house and land in the city of New York confiscated, but restored to his widow and daughter.

BLEAU, URIAH. Was an Ensign in the third battalion of New Jersey Volunteers in 1782. Taken prisoner in the battle of Eutaw Springs.

BLISS, DANIEL. Of Concord, Massachusetts. Was a son of Rev. Samuel Bliss, of that town. He was born in 1740, graduated at Harvard University in 1760, and died at Lincoln, near Fredericton, in the Province of New Brunswick, in 1806, aged sixty-six years. He was one of the barristers and attorneys who were Addressers of Hutchinson in 1774; and was proscribed under the Act of 1778; and joining the British Army, was appointed Commissary. After the Revolution, he settled in New Brunswick, and became a member of the Council, and Chief Justice of the Court of Common Pleas. His widow died in 1807, at the age of sixty.

BLISS, JOHN MURRAY. Son of Daniel Bliss. He was a native of Massachusetts, whence he removed at the beginning of hostilities. He did not settle in New Brunswick until 1786. Having practised law for several years, and filled several offices connected with his profession, and having represented the County of York in the House of Assembly, he was, in 1816, elevated to the bench and to a seat in his Majesty's Council. In 1824, on the decease of the Honorable Ward Chipman, who was President and Commander-in-Chief of the Colony, Judge Bliss succeeded to the administration of the government, and continued in office until the arrival of Sir Howard Douglas, — a period of nearly a year. At his death, he was senior Justice of the Supreme Court. He commanded universal confidence and esteem. His manners were dignified, and his conduct open, frank, and independent. He died at St. John, August, 1834, aged sixty-three years. His daughter Jane died at Halifax in 1826, and his daughter Sophia Isabella died at St. John the same year.

BLISS, JONATHAN. Of Springfield, Massachusetts. Graduated at Harvard University in 1763, and died at Fredericton, New Brunswick, in 1822, at the age of eighty years. His wife and the wife of Fisher Ames were sisters. He was a member of the General Court of Massachusetts in 1768, and one of the seventeen Rescinders; and was proscribed under the Act of 1778. In New Brunswick, he was a personage of distinguished consideration, and attained, finally, to the rank of Chief Justice, and to the Presidency of the Council.

BLISS, SAMUEL. Of Massachusetts. Was a brother of the Honorable Daniel Bliss. He died at St. George, New Brunswick, in 1803.

BLOOMER, JOSHUA. Episcopal clergyman of Jamaica, New York. He graduated at King's College, New York, in 1761, and went to England for ordination in 1765. In 1769 he settled at Jamaica, where he continued until his death, in 1790. Before taking orders, he was an officer in the Provincial service, and a merchant in New York. While at Jamaica, he officiated, occasionally, at Newtown and Flushing, and Domine Rubell, an itinerant Dutch minister, whose loyalty induced him to pray heartily for the royal family, occupied his pulpit.

BLOWERS, SAMPSON SALTER. Of Boston. Proscribed and banished. He graduated at Harvard University in 1763.

The class of that year is celebrated for the numbers of Loyalists and Judges of Courts. Mr. Blowers entered upon the study of law with Hutchinson, then Judge of Probate and Lieutenant-Governor. In 1770 he was associated with Messrs. Adams and Quincy in behalf of the British soldiers who were tried for their agency in the Boston Massacre, so termed, in that year. In 1774 he went to England, and returning, in 1778, found his name in the Proscription Act. He was imprisoned, but being soon released, went to Halifax, Nova Scotia, and in that Colony was long a distinguished character. I find the following in a Halifax newspaper of January 26, 1784: —

"*Extract from General Orders, Head-quarters.*

"That the outstanding Accounts against Government, for contingent Expenses incurred within this District, may be properly considered and liquidated; all Applications for Monies due on such Accounts are to be presented before the 1st May next; after which no Memorial for Payment will be received.

"*Published by Order of Major-General Campbell.*
"S. S. BLOWERS, Secretary."

In 1785 he was appointed Attorney-General, and Speaker of the House of Assembly, and in 1797 was created Chief Justice of the Supreme Court; having had for some years previous to his judicial elevation a seat in his Majesty's Council. He retired from public life in 1833. When ex-President Adams was in Nova Scotia, in 1840, he paid Judge Blowers a visit. The Judge himself, it is believed, never set foot on the land of his nativity, after he was driven from it. Sarah, his widow, died at Halifax, July, 1845, in the eighty-eighth year of her age. She, I think, was a daughter of Benjamin Kent, of Massachusetts, who, at first a Whig, became a Loyalist and a refugee. Judge Blowers died in 1842. He "never wore an overcoat in his life," says the Hon. Joseph Howe, in a speech which is published.

BOARDMAN, REV. RICHARD. Minister of the Methodist Episcopal Church. He was born in England in 1738, and in 1763 was received by Wesley as an itinerant preacher. In 1769, he arrived at Philadelphia and began his labors as a missionary, confining his services principally to that city, to New York, and the adjacent country. In the spring of 1772, however, he made a visit to the North, and preached at various places on his way. At Boston he formed a society. Thus, as it appears, he introduced "Methodism in New England one year before the first Conference was held in America, and eleven years before Jesse Lee, who has been styled 'the Apostle of Methodism in New England,' entered the travelling connection." At the approach of the Revolution, Mr. Boardman, unwilling to renounce his allegiance to the Crown, returned to his native land. He died at Cork, Ireland, in 1783.

BOGGS, JAMES. Of Pennsylvania. He entered the service of the Crown, and was attached to the medical staff of the Royal Army. In 1783 he went to Nova Scotia, and for many years was surgeon of the forces at Halifax. He died in that city in 1832, at the age of ninety-one. His daughter Elizabeth, widow of John Stuart, died at Halifax in 1852, in her eighty-fifth year.

BOND, PHINEAS. Of Philadelphia. Physician. He received the principal part of his medical education in Europe, and enjoyed a high professional reputation. He was one of the founders of the University of Pennsylvania, and a professor in that institution. In 1777 he signed a parole, but notified the Council that he did not consider himself bound by it, because his liberty was restrained contrary to the promise made to him when the paper was presented. In 1786 he was appointed British Consul for the Middle States, and the question of recognizing him as such, was discussed in Congress the following year. Mr. Jay reported in favor. Mr. Madison was opposed on public grounds. Mr. Varnum objected because of Mr. Bond's "obnoxious character." Mr. Bond was also Commissary for Commercial Affairs, which

Mr. Jay thought was designed to confer some of the powers of a Minister to the United States, and recommended that in that capacity he should not be recognized. He was finally received as Consul, and continued in office many years. A correspondent remarks, that when a little boy he heard the "Rogue's March" played before Dr. Bond's door, on the occasion of the attack on the *Chesapeake*. He died in England in 1816.

BOND, THOMAS. Physician. Of Philadelphia. About 1754, he published medical memoirs on professional topics, which were reprinted in London. He always rode in a small phæton.

Chief Justice Shippen wrote to his father, at Lancaster, from Philadelphia, January 8, 1758: — "Our Assembly have taken up William Moore and the Provost, and put them into custody for writing a libel against the former Assembly. Thomas Bond and Phineas (Bond), were on the point of being committed on the same account. The latter was actually in the custody of the Sergeant-at-Arms, but afterwards discharged. How the matter will end is yet uncertain." Dr. Bond died in 1784.

BONNELL, ISAAC. Of New Jersey. Sheriff of Middlesex County under Governor William Franklin, of whom he was an intimate friend and correspondent. In 1776 he was apprehended by order of Washington, and directed by the Provincial Congress to remain at Trenton on parole; but leave was given, finally, to live elsewhere. Subsequently, he retired to the British lines, and became Barrack-master on Staten Island. At the peace, he went to Digby, Nova Scotia, where, for fifty guineas, he bought a log-hut, with windows of greased paper, and a lot of land. His property in New Jersey was confiscated. In Nova Scotia he was a merchant, and a Judge of the Court of Common Pleas. He died in 1806, aged sixty-nine. His only son bore the name of William Franklin, as does a grandson, who is now (1861) Postmaster of Gagetown, New Brunswick.

BONNETT, ISAAC. He was born in New Rochelle, New

York. He abandoned his property at the close of the war, and removed to Annapolis Royal, Nova Scotia, where he passed the remainder of his life. He died in 1838, aged eighty-six, leaving a widow and five children.

BONSALL, RICHARD. He was a native of Wales, and a brother of Sir Thomas Bonsall. He commenced the study of medicine, but abandoned it. In consequence of a disagreement with Sir Thomas, he emigrated to New York some years prior to the Revolution, where he remained until the close of hostilities. In 1783 he went to St. John, and was a grantee of that city. He died at that city in 1814, aged seventy-two. His wife was a lady of the name of Smith, of Long Island, New York. Six children survived him; only one is now (1846) living.

BORLAND, JOHN. Of Boston. Son of Francis and Jane Borland. He owned and occupied the mansion in Cambridge built by Rev. Dr. Apthorp, first Rector of Christ Church in that town. In 1774 he was an Addresser of Hutchinson. He died in 1775, aged forty-six, in consequence of "injuries received by a misstep in descending stairs, after his removal to Boston," and his remains were deposited in the family tomb, in Granary burying-ground. His widow, Anna Vassall, married William Knight of Portsmouth, New Hampshire, and died a widow at Boston, in 1823. Mr. Borland was the father of twelve children, namely: Phebe, who married George Spooner, of Boston; John Lindall, of whom presently; Francis, who graduated at Harvard University in 1774, became a physician, and died in 1826; Jane, who was the wife of Jonathan Simpson; Leonard Vassall, who died on shipboard on a voyage from Batavia, in 1801; James, who entered the University just mentioned, but did not graduate, and who deceased soon after the year 1783; Samuel, who graduated at Harvard University in 1786, and died at Hudson, New York; and five others, who did not survive childhood.

BORLAND, JOHN LINDALL. Of Cambridge, Massachusetts. Son of John Borland. Graduated at Harvard University in 1772, entered the British Army and became lieutenant-colonel. He died in England, November, 1825.

BOSTWICK, REV. GIDEON. Of Massachusetts. Episcopal minister. He was born at New Milford in 1742, and was bred a Congregationalist. He graduated at Yale College in 1762. Went to England for ordination; and in 1770 became Rector of St. James' Church, Great Barrington. He had charge also of St. Luke's Church, Lanesborough; and late in life officiated a part of the time at Hudson, New York. He died in his native town in 1793, while on a visit, aged fifty. His remains, after a temporary burial, were removed to Great Barrington, "which had so long been the place of his residence and the scene of his labors." His wife, who died in 1787, was Gessie, daughter of John Burghardt. One of his daughters married Dr. Benajah Tucker, surgeon in the United States Navy. Two sons, John and Henry, settled in Canada, and, in the war of 1812, were colonels in the militia.

BOTSFORD, AMOS. Of Newtown, Connecticut. He graduated at Yale College in 1763. In 1775, in a document remarkable for its guarded form of expression, though drawn up in opposition to a paper which disapproved of the proceedings of the Continental Congress, he made known his determination to be compliant with the measures of that body. But, subsequently, adhering to the side of the Crown, he removed to New Brunswick after the conclusion of hostilities, and devoted himself to the profession of the law. In 1784 he was elected a member of the House of Assembly, and was uniformly returned from the County of Westmoreland at every election during his life. He was Speaker of the House of Assembly as early as 1792. He died at St. John in 1812, at the age of sixty-nine; and was the senior barrister at law in the Colony. His wife was Sarah, daughter of Joshua Chandler. His two daughters married brothers: Sarah, Stephen Milledge, Sheriff of Westmoreland County; and Ann, the Rev. John Milledge of the Episcopal Church. His son, the Honorable William Botsford, was appointed Judge of Vice-Admiralty of New Brunswick in 1803, and for a long period subsequently was a member of the Council, and a Judge of the Supreme Court. I record the following despatch to show the liberal course of the British Government to aged functionaries on retiring from office:—

"DOWNING STREET, 19th January, 1847.

"SIR,—I have read with very lively concern the letter to myself from Mr. Botsford, of the 11th December, 1846, accompanying your despatch of the 23d of that month, (No. 117.) Lord Stanley obviously accepted Mr. Botsford's resignation under the conviction that the claims of that gentleman to a retired allowance, at his advanced period of life, and after so long a course of honorable public service in so high and eminent a station, would be favorably received by the Legislature of New Brunswick; nor do I doubt that if his Lordship had regarded their concurrence in such a grant as questionable, he would have directed that the resignation should not be actually made until that question had been set at rest. To have taken such a precaution might indeed have appeared to imply some unbecoming distrust of the justice and liberality of the Assembly; and for that reason, as I presume, Lord Stanley omitted to take it. The omission is now irreparable, except by a reconsideration on the part of the Local Legislature, of their refusal of the proposed grant. Her Majesty has, by the Civil List arrangement, been entirely divested of all resources for satisfying any such demands on the justice or liberality of the Crown. To the Assembly, therefore, the case must be again referred, with as strong a recommendation of the claim to their favorable notice, as it may be possible to address to them. I am convinced that if the case had been understood by that House, as it is now represented by Mr. Botsford and by yourself, they would not have declined to accede to his request. A repetition of their refusal, would, in any future case, render impossible the voluntary resignation of any Judge, however much age or infirmity might have disqualified him for his judicial duties. The saving of a charge of £300 per annum to the Local Treasury, or even the habitual saving of any such charges, would be a very inadequate compensation for the injury which the public at large would sustain from the continuance on the Bench of men who had survived the power of discharging aright that most important and arduous trust.

"I have, &c.,
"(Signed,) GREY.
"Lieut.-Governor SIR WILLIAM COLEBROOKE."

BOUCHER, JONATHAN. Episcopal clergyman of Virginia. He was Rector, first of Hanover, and then of St. Mary. Governor Eden gave him also the rectory of St. Anne, Annapolis, and of Queen Anne. His home was in Maryland, several years, and he owned an estate there which was confiscated. He was an unshaken and uncompromising Loyalist. In 1775, resolving to quit the country, he preached a farewell sermon, in which he declared that as long as he lived, he would say with Zadok, the priest, and Nathan, the prophet, "God save the king." Arriving in England, he was appointed Vicar of Epsom, and there he spent the remainder of his life. He died in 1804, aged sixty-seven. He was regarded as one of the best preachers of his time. While in Virginia, the son of Mrs. Washington, by her first marriage, was his pupil. During the last fourteen years of his life, Boucher was employed in making a glossary of provincial and archæological words, and in 1831 his manuscripts were purchased of his family by the proprietors of "Webster's Dictionary." In 1799 were published fifteen discourses preached in America, between the years 1763 and 1775, on the causes and consequences of the American Revolution, which were dedicated to his old friend, Washington.

His wife, Eleanor, of the name and family of Addison, died at Paddington, in 1784. She bore without a murmur, the loss of country, friends, fortune, and preferment, consequent upon her husband's loyalty; and "was a woman of great merit, possessing the esteem and friendship of all who knew her." His third daughter, Jane, died in London, in 1810, of inflammation of the lungs, after a few days' illness, in the sixteenth year of her age. In the "Gentleman's Magazine" it is said: "An elegant form, and a countenance of engaging sweetness, were among the least attractions of this amiable girl, whose mild and placid temper, whose affectionate disposition, whose solid understanding beyond her years, whose compassionate feeling for the distresses of others, had justly endeared her to her family, and rendered her a child of uncommon promise."

BOURA, PETER. An early settler at St. John, New Brunswick. In 1795 he was a member of the Loyal Artillery of that city. He died in 1804, while on a homeward passage from Jamaica, at the age of forty-nine. He was a shipmaster.

BOURK, WILLIAM. Of North Carolina. In March, 1776, he was charged with being inimical to the liberties of America; and on a hearing before the Council, John Strange, a witness against him, swore, in the course of his testimony, that Bourk said " General Gage deserved to be d——d, because he had not let the guards out at Bunker Hill; and it would have settled the dispute at that time." This, and other particulars, Bourk acknowledged; when it was resolved to commit him to close jail until further orders.

BOURN, EDWARD, ELISHA, LEMUEL, and WILLIAM. Of Sandwich, Massachusetts. Were proscribed and banished. Lemuel joined the Royal forces at Rhode Island. Citizenship restored to Edward and Elisha, by Act of the Legislature, 1788.

BOURNE, SHEARJASHUB. Of Scituate, Massachusetts. He graduated at Harvard University in 1743. In 1774 he was among the barristers and attornies-at-law who were Addressers of Governor Hutchinson on his departure. He died at Bristol, Rhode Island, in 1781.

BOUTINEAU, JAMES. Of Boston. Attorney-at-law. Was appointed Mandamus Counsellor in 1774, and was one of the ten who took the oath of office. He was included in the Conspiracy Act of 1779, and his estate was confiscated under its provisions. In 1772 his son-in-law, John Robinson, a commissioner of the customs, was found guilty of a most violent assault on James Otis, for which the jury assessed two thousand pounds sterling damages. Boutineau appeared as attorney for Robinson, and in his name signed a submission, asking the pardon of Otis, who, thereupon, executed a free release for the two thousand pounds. Otis never recovered from the effect of this assault, and, shattered in health and reason, soon retired from public life.

Mr. Boutineau went to England, and died there. I have been allowed to copy three letters, from which I make such extracts as serve to show the course of affairs among the Loyalists in exile. The first is dated at Bristol, England, April 6, 1778, and is addressed to Mrs. Mary Ann, wife of Edward Jones, merchant, Boston, and sister of Mrs. Boutineau. Both ladies, it may be remarked, were sisters of Peter Faneuil; and Mrs. Jones was then at Halifax, Nova Scotia. Mr. Boutineau speaks of an attack of the gout which had compelled him to keep house for some time, and then discourses upon matters which are not without interest at the present time. Thus, he says, that "Mr. and Mrs. Faneuil, who lodge in the same house with us, make it agreeable;" and that "there are one or two other genteel gentlemen and ladies, so that during the winter we drank tea with each other four days in the week." Of other fellow-Loyalists, he writes, that "Lodgings have been taken for Mr. Sewell, of Cambridge, and family, — they are expected here this day. Colonel Murray's family are gone to Wales, as well as Judge Brown and Apthorp's. All the New England people here, are Barnes and family, Captain Fenton and daughter, besides those in the house." In a postcript, he adds: "I desire you to inform me (if you can) who lives in my house in Boston."

The first letter of Mrs. Boutineau is addressed to her nephew, Edward Jones, merchant, Boston, and is dated at Bristol, February 20, 1784. It relates principally to affairs of business. "I had determined," she says, "to send a power-of-attorney to you and another gentleman to settle with [Mr. Bethune] and likewise to dispose of all my property in America; but upon reflection I have deferred it, until the acts of your Assembly's that are inimical to persons of my description are repealed, for which reason I have asked the favor of Judge Lee to let my brother Faneuil's bond remain in his hands. This, I say, is my present idea; perhaps some occurrence may take place which may alter it; in the meantime, I beg the favor of you to send me a blank power-of-attorney drawn in as full and ample a manner as possible, to sell real estates, &c. My addition must be, Susanna Boutineau, widow, and sole executor of James Boutineau, Esq. If you have no objection, I should be glad it might be got from Mr. James Hughes, to whom you will please to present my compliments, and thank him in my name for the letter I received from him. I should be glad to be informed at the same time, if it is necessary to send an authenticated copy of my late husband's will from Doctor's Commons, which will be expensive, but if necessary, it must be done. About two years since, Mr. Bethune made me (through Mr. Prince) an offer of £500 sterling for my third of sister Phillips's estate, which you may be sure I refused. Mr. Prince is to pay me in a few days, by Mr. Bethune's order, £100 sterling, I suppose on account of rents," &c. &c.

The second letter of Mrs. Boutineau is also addressed to her sister, Mrs. Mary Ann Jones, who, at its date, April 1, 1785, had returned to Boston. Like the first, it is devoted to matters of unsettled business, and especially to her share of her sister Phillips's estate. It would seem that this letter was delivered by Mr. James Hughes, to whom, with Mr. Nathaniel Bethune, she had sent a power-of-attorney to effect a final adjustment of her interest in the estate just mentioned. She concludes with the remark, that her health is "very indifferent," that "Mr. Fanueil had a letter lately from Mr. Jones, who is going soon to be very well married," &c. &c.

BOWDEN, THOMAS. Of New York. Entered the military service, and in 1782 was Major in De Lancey's Second Battalion. At the peace he went to England.

BOWDEN, REV. JOHN, D. D. Of New York. Was born in Ireland in 1751. Graduated at King's (Columbia) College in 1772. Was ordained in 1774, and the same year was settled as Assistant Rector of Trinity Church, New York. Soon after the beginning of hostilities he retired to Norwalk, Connecticut, but returned to New York when the British obtained possession of the city. Informed that harm was intended him, he fled to Long Island at night, where he occasionally assisted the Rector of the Episcopal Church of Jamaica. In 1784 he accepted the Rectorship of the Church at Norwalk. In 1789 he took charge of a small parish in the West Indies. In 1801 he was elected Professor of Moral Philosophy, Belles-lettres and Logic in Columbia College. He died at Ballston Spa in 1817, aged sixty-five. His wife — whose maiden name was Mary Jervis — bore him three sons, one of whom, James J., graduated at Columbia College in 1813, was Rector of St. Mary's Parish, St. Mary's County, Maryland, and died at the age of twenty-six.

BOWES, WILLIAM. Merchant of Boston. An Addresser of Hutchinson in 1774, and of Gage in 1775. He went to Halifax in 1776, accompanied by his family of four persons. In 1778 he was proscribed and banished. He died in England in 1805.

BOWERS, JERATHMIEL. Of Swansey, Massachusetts. In 1777, by a resolve of the General Court, he was disqualified from holding any post of honor or profit in Massachusetts. In 1783 he was elected a member of that body, and petitions for his exclusion therefrom, setting out that "he had not shown himself friendly in the late struggle with Great Britain," were sent by the Selectmen of Rehoboth, and sundry inhabitants of his own town. The House held that the resolve above mentioned, was still in force, and that therefore Mr. Bowers was not entitled to membership. He vacated his seat accordingly.

BOWIE, REV. JOHN, D. D. Of Maryland. Episcopal minister. He was a native of Prince George's County, Maryland, and was admitted to Holy Orders in England. About the year 1771 he became a Curate in Montgomery County. In 1774 he was Rector of a parish in Worcester County. He was a violent Loyalist, and, in consequence, was imprisoned at Annapolis two years. On being released he settled in Talbot County, where he taught school, and was Rector of the parish in which he lived. In 1785 he was in charge of another parish; and in 1790 of still another. He died in 1801, leaving three sons and a daughter. He was a man of great talents, "a complete classical scholar, and of unblemished morals."

BOWLES, WILLIAM AGUSTUS. Of Maryland. In 1791 he was among the Creeks, with whom he possessed great influence, and styled himself General William Augustus Bowles. On the 18th of May, 1792, James Seagrove, Esquire, our Commissioner of Indian Affairs, in "a talk" with the kings, chiefs, headmen and warriors of the Creek nation, said of him: "This Bowles is an American of low, mean extraction, born in Maryland; he was obliged, on account of his villany, to fly from home and follow the British Army, where he was despised and treated as a bad man and a coward. Finding he could not live there, he returned to America; but being too lazy to work at his trade for a living, he renewed his bad acts, for which he was compelled to fly from his native country, or be hanged." Bowles had assumed to act among the Indians under authority of the British Government; but on inquiry by the President, the ministry promptly and explicitly denied that they had afforded him countenance, assistance, or protection. At the time of Seagrove's "talk," it would appear that Bowles had absented himself from the Creek country; but in 1801 he was again in mischief there, or in its vicinity, and means were taken by our Government to counteract his plans and plots. A gentleman connected with Indian Affairs, saw a portrait of this creature suspended in the house of a chief, under which was written, "General Bowles, Commander-in-Chief of the Creek and Cherokee nations." He saw also a number of engraved dinner-cards, which Bowles had received while in England, styling him "Commander-in-Chief of the Creek nation."

He was undoubtedly a bold and wicked man. At one time the Spanish Government offered a reward of six thousand dollars for his apprehension, on account of his pernicious influence over the Florida Indians. He was accordingly seized, and sent prisoner to Madrid, and thence to Manilla. Obtaining leave to go to Europe, he repaired to the Creek country, where he commenced his mischievous course anew. In 1804 he fell into Spanish hands a second time, and was sent to the Moro Castle, Havana. Deprived of light and air, fed on bread and water, and losing, finally, all hope of release, he refused sustenance, and died in December, 1805, of starvation. His wife was a Creek woman.

BOYD, ———. Of Carolina. Colonel, and in command of a corps of Tories, who were robbers rather than soldiers. What they could not consume or carry off, they burned. Boyd himself was bold, enterprising, and famed for his dishonesty. He had a conference with Sir Henry Clinton at New York, and planned an insurrection in the back part of South Carolina, to be executed as soon as the Royal Army should obtain possession of Savannah.

In 1779, at the head of eight hundred men, he passed through the district of Ninety-Six on his way to Georgia, and destroyed life and property by sword and fire, along his whole route. In a skirmish with a party of Whigs, under Anderson, of Pickens's corps, he acknowledged a loss of one eighth of his command in killed, wounded, and missing. He endeavored to avoid Pickens himself, but, overtaken by that officer, when unapprehensive of danger, was surprised and defeated. He received three wounds, which proved mortal. After the battle he was visited by Pickens, who recommended preparation for death, and tendered services suited to the occasion. Boyd expressed thanks; said the Whigs owed their success to his fall; desired that two men might remain with him to give him water, and to bury his body after he died; and asked that his wife should be informed of his fate by letter, and that some articles about his person should be sent to her. Neighbor had fought against neighbor; and in the exasperation of the moment, the Whigs doomed seventy of their prisoners to death; but they executed only five. About three hundred escaped, and formed the intended junction with the British troops in Georgia.

Boyd, George. Of Portsmouth, New Hampshire. A member of the Council under the Royal Government of that Province. On approach of the troubles of the Revolution, he abandoned the country, and was included in the Proscription Act of New Hampshire of 1778. While abroad he acquired wealth. In 1787, he adjusted his affairs, and embarked for his native land, full of hope. Riding was among his enjoyments; and he procured a handsome coach and an English coachman. He died at sea, two days before the ship arrived at Portsmouth, and his remains were interred from his elegant mansion.

His wife was Jane, daughter of Joseph Brewster. She bore him five sons and five daughters. *Submit*, the youngest of the latter, born in 1774, was thus named, as is said, to indicate his opinion of the duty of the Colonies in the existing controversy with the mother country.

Boyle, Robert. Went to New Brunswick in 1783, and died at Portland, in that Province, in 1848.

Boylston, Ward Nicholas. Of Boston. He was born in that town in 1749. His father was Benjamin Hallowell, one of the Commissioners of the Customs. I have before me the original license, bearing the signature of George the Third, by which he was authorized to change his name; it recites — that " Nicholas Boylston, his uncle by his mother's side, has conceived a very great affection for him, the petitioner, and has promised to leave him, at his death, certain estates, which are very considerable," &c., &c. In 1773 Mr. Boylston went to Newfoundland, thence to Italy, Turkey, Syria, Palestine, Egypt, and along the coast of Barbary; and arrived in England in 1775, through France and Flanders. He dined at Governor Hutchinson's, London, with some fellow-Loyalists, July 29, 1775, and entertained the company with an account of his travels; and, at subsequent periods, he exhibited the curiosities which he brought from the Holy Land, Egypt, and other countries, to the unhappy exiles from his native State. In the autumn of the next year, he was in lodgings at Shepton Mallet. He was a member of the Loyalist Association, formed in London in 1779. He returned to Boston in the year 1800. In 1810 he presented Harvard University with a valuable collection of medical and anatomical works and engravings. He died at his seat, Roxbury, in 1828, aged seventy-eight. His son, John Lane Boylston, died at Princeton in 1847, aged fifty-eight.

BOYLSTON, THOMAS. Of Boston. John Adams said of him in 1766, — "Tom is a firebrand. Tom is a perfect viper, a Jew, a devil, but is orthodox in politics, however." He was among the citizens of Boston who were detained by General Gage, in consequence of the imprisonment of Jones and Hicks in the jail at Concord; and was released by exchange, August, 1775. He fell off. In 1777 he was — as is said — the hero of the following incident, which is related by Mrs. Adams: —

"It was rumored," she wrote her husband, "that an eminent, wealthy, stingy merchant, (who is a bachelor,) had a a hogshead of coffee in his store, which he refused to sell to the Committee under six shillings per pound. A number of females, some say a hundred, some say more, assembled with a cart and trucks, marched down to the warehouse, and demanded the keys, which he refused to deliver. Upon which one of them seized him by the neck and tossed him into the cart. Upon his finding no quarter he delivered the keys, when they tipped up the cart and discharged him; then opened the warehouse, hoisted out the coffee themselves, put it into the truck, and drove off. . . . A large concourse of men stood amazed, silent spectators of the whole transaction."

He went to England, invested his fortune in commerce, and was utterly ruined. Said Aspden, a fellow-Loyalist, in 1793, "I called to see, in Newgate, Mr. Thomas Boylston, of Boston, whom they want to bring in as a sleeping partner in the house of Lane, Son & Frazer, lately failed; or, if this won't do, to milk him for lending them money at usurious interest. So much for being a stranger and friendless." He died in London in 1798, of a broken heart. The simple record is — " Aged 77, Thomas Boylston, late a very eminent merchant of Boston, and relative of the President of the United States."

BOYLSTON, JOHN. Of Boston. Merchant. Went to England in 1776, and was at Bristol in August of that year. Remained abroad, and died at Bath, England, in 1795, aged eighty-six.

BRADFORD, WILLIAM. Of Massachusetts. Graduated at Harvard University in 1760. He removed from the country, and held an office under the Crown at the Bahamas. He died in 1801.

BRADISH, EBENEZER. A lawyer of Worcester, Massachusetts. He graduated at Harvard University in 1769. In 1774 he was one of the barristers and attorneys who were Addressers of Hutchinson. He died in 1818.

BRADSHAW, ELEAZER. Of Waltham, Massachusetts. Said he would sell " tea," and do as he thought fit, in spite of Whig committees, and that he would be the death of any person who should molest him. The committees of Waltham, Newton, Watertown, Weston, and Sudbury, examined the case, and resolved that he had proved himself inimical to his country, and cautioned all persons against dealing with him until he should repent.

BRANNAN, CHARLES. He was in the King's service during the war, and at its close went to St. John, New Brunswick. He removed from that city to Fredericton in 1785, and continued there until his decease in 1828, at the age of eighty-one.

BRANTLEY, ———. Of Georgia. Captain of a Tory band. The captor of three Whigs, who, doomed to die, were stripped to the shirt, and placed in a position to be shot. Two were killed, the other escaped. The survivor, David Emanuel, lived to become President of the Senate, and to fill the Executive-chair of Georgia.

BRATEN, THOMAS. Of Charlotte County, New York. He was a constable; and in 1775 some Whigs declared that " they would have him, if he could be found above ground."

BRATTLE, THOMAS. Of Massachusetts. He was born at Cambridge in 1742, and graduated at Harvard University in 1760, and received the degree of A. M. at Yale and at Nassau. His family connections were among the most respectable of New England. In 1775 he went to England, and was included in the Proscription and Banishment Act of 1778. While abroad, he travelled over various parts of Great Britain, and made a tour through Holland and France; and was noticed by personages of distinction. Returning to London, he zealously and successfully labored to ameliorate the condition of his countrymen, who had been captured, and were in prison. In 1779 he came to America, and landed at Rhode Island. In 1784 the enactments against him in Massachusetts were repealed, and he took possession of his patrimony. He was a gentleman of liberality, humanity, and science; of public spirit, and of large and noble views of men and things. He died in February, 1801.

The late Governor James Sullivan, who knew him well, thus wrote: " Major Brattle exercised a deep reverence to the principles of Government, and was a cheerful subject of the laws. He respected men of science as the richest ornament of their country. If he had ambition, it was to excel in acts of hospitality, benevolence, and charity. The dazzling splendor of heroes, and the achievements of political intrigues, passed unnoticed before him; but the character of the man of benevolence filled his heart with emotions of sympathy." . . . . " In his death, the sick, the poor, and the distressed, have lost a liberal benefactor; politeness an ornament; and philanthropy one of its most discreet and generous supporters."

BRATTLE, WILLIAM. Of Massachusetts. A man of more eminent talents and of greater eccentricities has seldom lived. He graduated at Harvard University in 1722; and, subsequently, was representative from Cambridge, and for many years a member of the Council. He seems to have been of every profession, and to have been eminent in all. As a clergyman, his preaching was acceptable; as a physician, he was celebrated, and had an extensive practice; as a lawyer, he had an abundance of clients; while his military aptitudes secured the rank of major-general of the militia, an office in his time of very considerable importance and high honor. He loved good living. He possessed the happy faculty of pleasing the officers of Government and the people. An Addresser of Gage, and approving of his plans, he at length forfeited the good will of the Whigs, and went into exile. Accompanying the British troops at the evacuation of Boston, he went to Halifax, and died there in 1776, a few months after his arrival. His father was Reverend William Brattle of Cambridge. His first wife was a daughter of Governor Saltonstall. His son, Thomas Brattle of Cambridge, died in 1801.

BRATTLE, JAMES. Servant to Governor Tryon, and subsequently to James Duane, a member of Congress. He was in the habit of stealing the papers of the latter, and of transmitting them, with other information, to the former. He was detected, and sent to England by Tryon.

BREMNER, JOHN. Of Queen's County, New York. In 1776 he signed a profession of loyalty and allegiance. A person of this name died at Halifax, Nova Scotia, in 1807, aged fifty-four.

BRENTON, JAHLEEL. Of Rhode Island. Rear-Admiral in the Royal Navy. The Brentons emigrated to Massachusetts in the reign of Charles the First. The first Jahleel was a civil officer of some note in Boston, and, removing to Rhode Island, died Governor of that Colony near the end of the reign of Charles the Second. The second Jahleel, who was son of the first, was Collector of the Customs in New England, in the reign of William and Mary. The third Jahleel was a large land-owner, and married a daughter of Samuel Cranston, Governor of Rhode Island; this Jahleel was the father of five sons, of whom notices follow; of three other sons, and of seven daughters.

The fourth Jahleel is the subject of this notice. He was born in 1729, entered the navy in his youth; and, a lieutenant at the beginning of the Revolution, was living quietly on his patrimonial estate. It is stated that he was a gentleman of high character and respectable talents, that he had many warm friends among the Whig leaders who endeavored to enlist his sympathies on the popular side, and who offered him the highest rank in the naval service of Congress. Unyielding in his loyalty, a system of annoyance and persecution was commenced against him, which compelled him to leave his wife and younger children, and to seek shelter on board of an armed ship of the Crown on the coast. Two of his elder sons accompanied him. He went to England, and was put on active duty. Before the peace he was a post-captain. His estate in Rhode Island was confiscated. During the latter years of his life, he received " the comfortable appointment of Regulating Captain at Edinburgh," which situation he held until his death in 1802. His wife was Henrietta Crowley, and was the mother of a large family. She joined him in England in 1780, with the children, who remained with her at his flight. Of Jahleel, the oldest, presently. Edward Pelham, the second son, who died a post-captain, in London, in 1839, and whose widow, Margaretta Diana, died in the same city in 1843, wrote the "Naval History of Great Britain from 1783 to 1822," and a Biography of Admiral Earl St. Vincent, and was the founder of the Children's Friend Society. James, the third son, lost his life in 1799, while performing a daring exploit in the Mediterranean, under Nelson. His widow, Henrietta, died in 1820, in her seventy-seventh year. Mary, his second daughter, died at Bath, England, in 1845, aged seventy-six.

BRENTON, SIR JAHLEEL, Baronet. Of Rhode Island. Rear-Admiral of the Blue, K. C. B. and K. S. F. The *fifth* Jahleel, and son of the fourth. He was born in Rhode Island in 1770; entered the navy as a midshipman in 1781, and served first in the *Queen*, commanded by his father. At the peace he was placed in the Naval School, Chelsea, where he remained two years. From 1787 to 1789, he was an officer of the *Dido*, Captain Sandys, employed in surveying the coast of Nova Scotia. Until the peace of Ameins, in 1802, he was constantly afloat, and performed much hard duty. The captains under whom he served during this period, uniformly commended his conduct. Among the distinguished naval officers who were his warm friends in after life, were Saumarez, St. Vincent, Collingwood, and Nelson. After several years' service in the renewed warfare against Napoleon, and in 1812, he was appointed to the command of the *Stirling Castle* 74, but resigned that ship the same year; was created a Baronet, and commissioned Resident-Commissioner of the Balearic Islands. In 1815 he was transferred to the Cape of Good Hope, as Commissioner of the Dock-yard, and remained in office until 1821. He returned to England in 1822, and the year after was appointed a Colonel of Marines. In 1829 he was in command of the ship *Donegal*, at Sheerness. Subsequently, he was created Vice-Admiral and Lieutenant-Governor of Greenwich Hospital. He retired from duty in 1840, and received the pension "dropped" by the decease of his old companion, Sir Sidney Smith. He established his residence in Westmoreland, thence removed to a cottage in Staffordshire. He died at Elford, April, 1844, in his seventy-fourth year.

His first wife, who died at the Cape of Good Hope in 1817, was Isabella, daughter of Anthony Stewart, a Loyalist of Maryland. Sir Jahleel met her at Halifax, (to which place her father had fled during the Revolution) in 1787, when a midshipman on the Nova Scotia station; and though a mutual attachment arose, they were separated eleven years without seeing each other once. They met in England, and were married in the year 1802. His second wife (whom he married in 1822) was his cousin Harriet, daughter of James Brenton, of Halifax.

BRENTON, BENJAMIN. Of Rhode Island. Brother of the fourth Jahleel. In the Revolution, a "contractor" for the Royal forces. Estate confiscated. Died in 1830. His wife was Rachel, daughter of Silas Cooke.

BRENTON, SAMUEL. Of Rhode Island. Brother of the fourth Jahleel. I glean simply, that he died in 1797; and that his wife was Susan Cooke, sister of the wife of his brother Benjamin.

BRENTON, JAMES. Of Rhode Island. Brother of the fourth Jahleel. He went to Nova Scotia, and was a notary-public as early as September, 1775, at Halifax. He was afterward a Judge of the Supreme Court, and a member of the Council. In the year 1800 he was appointed Judge of Vice-Admiralty. He died at Halifax in 1806, or early the year following.

His first wife was Rebecca Scott; his second, a Miss Russell, of Halifax. Edward, the only son of the first marriage, was bred to the law, and in 1835 was a Judge in Newfoundland. Another son, John, was secretary to Admiral Provost on the East India station, and a captain in the British Navy. Harriet, a daughter, married her cousin, (the fifth Jahleel), Admiral Sir Jahleel Brenton.

BRENTON, WILLIAM. Of Rhode Island. Brother of the fourth Jahleel. Born in 1749. In exile during the Revolution, he was allowed, by a law of 1783, to visit and remain with his friends one week; then required to depart and not to return. His wife was Frances Wickham. In 1835 two of his sons were in the British Navy.

BREWERTON, GEORGE. Of New York. In the French war he was in command of a regiment of that Colony. In June, 1776, he was charged with dangerous designs and treasonable conspiracies against the Whig cause; and, at the instance of Livingston, Morris, and Jay, a warrant was issued by General Greene for his apprehension and the seizure of his papers. Brewerton surrendered himself to the General, who sent him to his accusers. In his examination he stated that "instead of aiding the Ministerial armies, he had advised and persuaded men to enlist in the Continental service." But he was held to good behavior to the Whigs in a bond for £500, with Jacob Brewerton as surety. Subsequently, he entered the service of the Crown, and commanded the second battalion of De Lancey's brigade. He died in 1779. His widow, three sons, and two daughters, arrived at New York, from London, September, 1786.

BRICE, RIGDEN. Of Georgia. In the effort to reëstablish the Royal Government, in 1779, he was appointed Marshal of the Court of Admiralty. In 1782 he was Muster-master-General of the Loyalist forces in the South. He went to England and died there in 1796.

BRIGDEN, EDWARD. Of North Carolina. An estate, confiscated during the war, was restored to him by Act of November, 1785; I find it said, at the express recommendation of Dr. Franklin.

BRIGG, STEPHEN. In December, 1783, warrant issued on petition of the Selectmen of Stanford, Connecticut, ordering him to depart that town forthwith, and never return.

BRIDGHAM, EBENEZER. Merchant of Boston. Was proscribed and banished in 1778. He went to Halifax in 1776, with his family of four persons. In 1782 he was Deputy Inspector-General of the Loyalist forces. In 1783 he went to St. John, New Brunswick, and was a grantee of that city.

BRIDGMAN, ———. An "American Loyalist," whose daughter married Sir John Hatten, Baronet, of Long Stanton, Cambridgeshire, in 1798. Sir John died in 1811, and was succeeded by his brother, Thomas Dingley Hatten, the present Baronet.

BRIDGEWATER, JOHN. In 1782 he was a captain in the Prince of Wales American Volunteers. He went to England, and died there in 1803, in his seventieth year.

BRILL, DAVID. Went to New Brunswick in 1783. Died in Queen's County in 1848, aged eighty-seven.

BRINLEY, THOMAS. Merchant of Boston. Graduated at Harvard University in 1744. His name appears among the one hundred and twenty-four merchants and others, who addressed Hutchinson at Boston, in 1774; and among the ninety-seven gentlemen and principal inhabitants of that town, who addressed Gage in October of the following year. He went to Halifax in 1776, and to England the same year. In 1778 he was proscribed and banished. He died in 1784. Elizabeth, his widow, died in England in 1793.

BRINLEY, GEORGE. Merchant of Boston. An Addresser

of Hutchinson in 1774, and of Gage in 1775; was proscribed and banished in 1778. He was in England in 1783, at which time he was Deputy Commissary-General. In 1799 he was appointed Commissary-General of his Majesty's forces in British America. He died at Halifax, Nova Scotia, in 1809; and Mary, his widow, died at the same place in 1819. His son Thomas, Lieutenant-Colonel in the army, and Quartermaster-General of the British troops in the West Indies, died in 1805 on one of the islands of his station. I find the death of William Birch Brinley, at Halifax, 1812, aged forty.

BRINLEY, NATHANIEL. Of Framingham, Massachusetts, and son of Colonel Francis Brinley. About the year 1760, he leased the "Brinley Farm" of Oliver DeLancey, agent of the owner, Admiral Sir Peter Warren of the Royal Navy, and, as is said, employed fifteen or twenty negroes, (slaves, probably,) in its cultivation. It is related, too, that Daniel Shays, the leader of the insurrection in 1786, was in the service of Mr. Brinley on this farm. In 1775, our Loyalist was an Addresser of Gage, and was ordered, in consequence, to confine himself to his own leasehold. He soon fled to the Royal Army in Boston. After the evacuation of that town, he was sent to Framingham by sentence of a Court of Inquiry, ordered to give bond in £600, with two sureties, to remain there four months and to be of good behavior. In September, 1776, Ebenezer Marshall, in behalf of the Committee of Correspondence, Inspection and Safety, represented that the "people take him for a very villian," as he had declared that "Parliament had an undoubted right to make void the charter in part or in whole;" that "ten thousand troops, with an artillery, would go through the Continent, and subdue it at pleasure;" that he had conveyed "his best furniture to Roxbury, and moved his family and goods into Boston," and had himself remained there "as long as he could have the protection of the British troops;" that "he approved of General Gage's conduct in the highest terms;" that "his most intimate connections were some of our worst enemies and traitors;" and that, while he had been under their inspection, they had seen nothing "either in his conduct or disposition, that discovers the least contrition, but otherwise."

To some of these allegations, Mrs. Brinley replied in two memorials to the General Court. She averred that, by the conditions of the recognizance, her husband was entitled to the freedom of the whole of the town of Framingham; that he was in custody on the sole charge of addressing Gage; and that, instead of being a refugee in Boston, he was shut up in that town while accidentally there, &c. She complained that at one time, he had been compelled to work on John Fisk's farm, without liberty to go more than twenty rods from the house, unless in Fisk's presence; and that he was denied the free use of pen, ink and paper. Again, she said that Mr. Brinley, after his transfer to the care of Benjamin Eaton, was restricted to the house, and was fearful that his departure from it would occasion the loss of his life; and that no person, even herself, was allowed to converse with him, unless in the hearing of some member of Eaton's family. And she prayed that he might be removed to some other inland town, and be treated in accordance with his sentence. Mr. Brinley's defence of himself seems to have been the simple remark: "I am a gentleman, and have done nothing to forfeit that character."

I am able to trace this unhappy "Government-man" only a step farther. On the 17th September, 1776, the General Court, by resolve, committed him to the care of his father, on security in £600 for his appearance; and, in October of the same year, the Committee of Framingham reported to the Council that they had disposed of his farm-stock, farm-utensils, and household furniture. Possibly, Nathaniel Brinley, who died at Tyngsborough in 1814, aged eighty-one, was the subject of this notice.

BRITTAIN, JAMES. Of New Jersey. He wished to take no part in the Revolutionary controversy, but having become obnoxious, his house was surrounded by a party of about thirty, who robbed and plundered him at pleasure. He escaped to the woods, where his wife fed him for nearly a month. Emerging from his hiding place, he joined Skinner with seventy men, whom he had engaged to bear arms against the rebels. He was in a number of battles. In one, he was taken prisoner, and doomed to suffer death. The day before that appointed for his execution, he broke from prison, swam the Delaware, and joined his corps. In 1782 he was an ensign in the first battalion of New Jersey Volunteers, and at the peace, a lieutenant. In 1783 he went to St. John, New Brunswick, in the ship *Duke of Richmond*, and was the grantee of a city lot. He received half-pay. He was a colonel of New Brunswick militia, and, at his decease, the oldest magistrate in King's County. He died at Greenwich in that county in 1838, at the age of eighty-seven. Ten children survived him. His widow, Eleanor, died at Greenwich in 1846, aged ninety-four. His daughter Eleanor married Walker Tisdale, Esquire, of St. John.

BRITTAIN, JOSEPH. Of New Jersey. Brother of James. He was an ensign in the New Jersey Volunteers, and was taken prisoner with James, doomed to the same fate, and made his escape at the same time. He went to St. John in the ship *Duke of Richmond* in 1780, and died in 1830, at the age of seventy-two, in King's County. He received half-pay.

BRITTAIN, WILLIAM. Of New Jersey. Brother of James and Joseph. He was in the King's service, but not in commission. He shared in the captivity, and in the escape of James and Joseph. He went to St. John, New Brunswick, at the peace, and was a grantee of that city. He died in New Brunswick about the year 1811.

BRITTENNY, JOHN. In 1783 he removed to New Brunswick, and settled in King's County, where he continued to reside until his decease, a period of upwards of sixty-three years. He died at Greenwich in 1846, in the ninety-fifth year of his age.

BROKENBOROUGH, AUSTIN. Of Virginia. He was son of Colonel William Brokenborough, and served with Washington under Braddock. "Like some of the old clergy, he thought he was perpetually bound by his oath of allegiance to the king." He wished to remain here, however, on account of his family, friends, and property; and petitioned the Assembly to be allowed the position of a neutral — to obey the laws, but to keep clear of the "rebellion." His request was not only refused, but five companies of men proceeded to his house to inflict signal punishment for his contumacy. He escaped and went to England. While abroad, he lived principally in London, with several other Loyalists of the South, who, by his account, "had a merry time of it, dining and supping at various inns," visiting theatres and other places of amusement. He "speaks of taking two dinners at different taverns . . . the same day, and of two suppers the same night, and of being quite drunk, with all the rest of the company," on another occasion. Again, he mentions an evening at Vauxhall with ladies, and says that all, except the young ones, "drank too freely, and were vociferous." But he went to church, and was a frequent listener to the debates in Parliament. It was his fortune to hear Chatham's last speech, when, as all recollect, his Lordship fainted and was carried home.

Mr. Brokenborough was absent seven years. Time, finally, passed heavily. His father and youngest son were dead; his estate was mismanaged, wasting away, and liable to confiscation. He resolved to return, and arrived in Virginia in 1782, but, by advice of his brother, did not venture home. For awhile, he was in Charleston, S. C.; but, at last, resumed his abode in the Old Dominion.

Brooks, James. It was reported that letters written by him, by Dr. Kearsley, and others, were in possession of a woman who concealed them in a pocket sewed to the lower part of her inner garment, and who was on ship-board, bound to London; and the letters having been secured, and found abusive of the Whigs and of their cause, he was committed to prison in Philadelphia, thence transferred to the jail of Lancaster. The Committee of Safety of Pennsylvania resolved that he was an enemy to the liberties of America.

He was kept in confinement two years, lacking a single day. His own account is, that the windows next to the street were blocked up; that thirty-five barrels of gunpowder were stored on the floor above his head,—and tons more in the next room, defended from the common misfortune of fire by a shingled roof merely; that a guard of fourteen men beat their drums for the sake of persecution; that he was denied the sight and speech of mankind, and the use of pen, ink and paper.; and that he "had the use of his legs taken from him by day, and was brought to by warm water at night."

BROOKS, CAPTAIN ———. Commanded a party of plunderers. On one occasion, early in 1783, while on an expedition in the Delaware, a Methodist preacher fell into his hands, and was required to preach or to be whipped to death. The minister declining to give a sermon to such hearers, was tied up and received nearly one hundred lashes. On his promise never to serve the rebels more, he was allowed to depart, much exhausted and lacerated.

BROWNE, THOMAS. Of Augusta, Georgia. Was an early victim of a mob, and was tarred and feathered, soon after the division and array of parties in the Southern Colonies. He entered the Royal service, and commanded, as lieutenant-colonel, a corps called the King's Rangers, Carolina. At the peace, he retired, it is believed, to Florida, and thence to the Bahamas. He was known during hostilities as a sanguinary and active officer, and his conduct is open to severe censure.

Such the text, such the meagre account of this partisan leader, in the first edition. The notice of him now is as full as the reader can desire, and is the result of more labor than I care to state.

Mr. Simms, in the Advertisement to "*Mellichampe*," says that Barsfield's story, as related in the thirty-seventh chapter of that work, "bears a close resemblance to the recorded history of the notorious Colonel Browne, of Augusta, one of the most malignant and vindictive among the Southern Loyalists, and one who is said to have become so solely from the illegal and unjustifiable means employed by the Patriots to make him otherwise." And, adds Mr. Simms, with truth, "The whole history is one of curious interest, and, if studied, of great public value. It shows strikingly the evils to a whole nation, and through successive years, of a single act of popular injustice."

Whoever would know the nature of the warfare between the Whigs and Tories at the South, should carefully read "Mellichampe," and the other tales of the distinguished author, of the same era. He vouches for their general historical accuracy, and no well-informed person will question the faithfulness of his pen. The perusal of the tale in question, excited my own curiosity, I confess, and led me to examine every book and document within reach, which seemed likely to afford me information of the original of "Barsfield."

I find Browne at Augusta in 1775, expressing his enmity to the Whigs, and ridiculing them in toasts at dinner. Warned of danger, he fled. By order of the "Committee," he was pursued to New Richmond, South Carolina, brought back, tried, and sentenced to be tarred and feathered; to be publicly exposed in a cart; to be drawn three miles, or until he should confess his error, and swear fealty to the popular cause. He refused to make any concession, was punished as doomed, and published as "no gentleman." To conceal his disgrace as well as he could, he kept his hair short, and wore a handkerchief around his head. He soon retreated to Florida. In 1776 he was in command of a corps, and made fearful incursions on the banks of the Savannah; but his force was small. In 1778, when he was joined by about three hundred Tories from the interior of Georgia and South Carolina, his regiment was completed, and put in uniform. A year later, at the head of four hundred mounted men, he made a forced march to Augusta; and, after being wounded, and twice defeated by Whigs under Twiggs and Few, he reached that place, and established a military post. Reinforced by detachments from other corps, of undoubted skill and bravery, exact in discipline, among the very people who had treated him with the greatest indignity, and relentless in his mode of warfare, the "Rebels" had everything to fear from his disposition and his operations. As soon as the condition of the Whigs would allow, and in 1780, Colonel Clarke appeared with a force, sufficient, as was thought, to compel him to submit to terms of capitulation. Browne's conduct during the siege illustrates the best and the worst qualities of his character. The accounts are conflicting. But it seems certain that, as the town did not afford an eligible position for defence, Browne marched out with his troops and some Indians, assailed Clarke on an eminence, and dislodged him, after a sanguinary fight. It appears, also, that the Loyalist leader was subsequently driven, with the men under his personal command, into a sort of garrison house, from which he maintained a desperate resistance; that he himself was shot through both thighs; that while tortured with the pain of dangerous wounds and swollen legs, he still directed every movement; that the besiegers cut off the supply of water, for which, in the fertility of his resources, he found a remedy, in saving and dealing out urine, of which he was the first to drink; that his wounded died for the want of surgical aid and hospital stores; that he was repeatedly summoned to surrender; and that he held out four days, and until relieved by Cruger. All this, in a military man, is admirable; what followed is unconditionally infamous. Clarke, in his retreat, left a part of his wounded, of whom thirteen were hung in the stair-way, and four in other parts of the garrison-house, and several others were turned over to the Indians and burned alive. The thirteen, it is said, were executed in Browne's presence, "that he might have the satisfaction of seeing the victims of his vengeance expire." So, too, in 1780, he ordered five persons to be hung, and when nearly dead, they were cut down and delivered to the Indians, who scalped and and otherwise mutilated one of them. One of these was a youth of seventeen, and the son of a widow.

He kept Augusta until June, 1781, when, after a siege of nearly three months, in which he displayed his usual courage, activity, and patience under sufferings, he surrendered the post to Pickens and Lee. The accusation against him at this time is, that he placed an aged prisoner in a bastion, where he was exposed to death from the hands of his own son, who commanded a Whig battery. By the terms of capitulation, Colonel Browne was allowed to go to Savannah; and he was so generally hated that, had he not been specially and strongly guarded, while on the way thither, it is probable he would have been torn limb from limb. He passed among the inhabitants whose houses he had burned and whose relatives and friends he had executed. The mother of one whom he had put to death said to him: "In the late day of your prosperity, I visited your camp, and on my knees supplicated for the life of my son, but you were deaf to my entreaties. You hanged him, though a beardless youth, before my face. These eyes saw him scalped by the savages under your immediate command. . . . When you resume the sword, I will go five hundred miles to demand satisfaction at the point of it."

This woman met Browne and his escort, as is said, armed with a knife, for the purpose of killing him, but was not allowed to speak to him until she promised to forbear; and she was accompanied by a son who went with the same intention. Though he escaped assassination, the adherents of the Crown seem to have expected that he would be publicly executed. After the fall of Charleston, the firm Whigs who refused to swear allegiance were sent to Florida, and the officer in command at St. Augustine threatened to hang six of them if Browne was not treated as a prisoner of war. After he was exchanged, he served at Savannah. In May, 1782, he marched out of the garrison at the head of a considerable force, with the apparent intention of attacking the Whigs; but Wayne, by a bold movement, got between him and the town, assailed him at midnight, and routed his whole command.

In October, 1782, the Rangers were sent from Charleston to relieve the troops at St. Augustine. At the peace, when they were disbanded, a part remained in Florida, and a part attempted to settle at a place in Nova Scotia, called St. Mary's. Colonel Browne had estates in Georgia and South Carolina, which were confiscated; and, attainted of treason in both States, he retreated to the Bahamas. From these islands, and in 1786, he wrote an elaborate reply to Ramsay's comments on his conduct during the war, addressed to the historian himself. The paper is not without ability.

He relates the unjustifiable course of the Whigs, and dwells with emphasis on special cases; he insists that in the instances which are cited to show his own barbarity, he did but execute retributive justice on offenders who were identified, and who confessed their crimes. He refers to the tarring and feathering twelve years previously, in these words: " Could violations of humanity be justified by example, the cruelties exercised on my person by a lawless committee . . . . might have justified the severest vengeance; but, esteeming it more honorable to forgive than to revenge an injury to those men who had treated me with the most merciless cruelty, I granted protection and safeguards to such as desired them." He avers that all the allegations against him which touch his reputation as an officer and as a man, are false; and thus, — " In the discharge of the duties of my profession, I can say with truth, I never deviated from the line of conduct the laws of war and humanity prescribed." And again: " The criminal excesses of individuals were never warranted by authority, nor ever obtained the sanction of my approbation." He speaks of Lee, as a gentleman of the most honorable and liberal sentiments; but of Pickens, as permitting murder of prisoners under his own eye.

In 1809, Colonel Browne was in England, and petitioned for a grant of Crown lands in the West Indies. The government gave him six thousand acres in the island of St. Vincent. I find it stated that, by some mistake, a part of the tract had been previously granted to persons who could not be dispossessed without great injury; and that the munificent sum of £80,000 was allowed him in money as an equivalent. It is said, too, that the Colonel was subsequently implicated in matters connected with this very domain; and that, in 1812, he was convicted in London of forgery. The story seems to me improbable. There was hardly a Loyalist in the thirteen Colonies who, for his individual losses, received so large a sum as — in whole numbers — one hundred and fifty thousand dollars; and, at the period in question, a man adjudged guilty of forgery, in England, would have been executed, especially if the crime, — as alleged in this case, — was a fabrication of the signatures of high officers of the Government.

Colonel Browne died in St. Vincent in 1825. His wife died there in 1807. Of his own decease there appeared the following notice: — "At an advanced age, Colonel Thomas Browne. During the American war he distinguished himself as a gallant and enterprising officer, and among other repeated marks of his Sovereign's approbation, was promoted to the rank of Colonel-Commandant of his Majesty's late regiment of South Carolina, or Queen's Rangers, and made also Superintendent-General of Indian Affairs, in the Southern districts of North America."

BROWNE, WILLIAM. Of Salem, Massachusetts. Was a grandson of Governor Burnet, a great-grandson of Bishop Burnet, and a connection of Winthrop, the first resident Governor of Massachusetts; and graduated at Harvard University in 1755. A member of the General Court in 1768, he was one of the seventeen Rescinders. He was a Colonel of the Essex County militia; one of the ten Mandamus Counsellors who were sworn in, and a Judge of the Supreme Court.

In 1774, John Adams[1] said: "I had a real respect for the Judges. Trowbridge, Cushing, and Browne, I could call my friends." That very year, the Essex County Convention voted, "That a Committee be raised to wait on the Honorable William Browne, Esquire, of Salem, and acquaint him, that with grief this County has viewed his exertions for carrying into execution the Acts of Parliament, calculated to enslave and ruin his native land," &c., &c.

This Committee consisted of Jeremiah Lee, Samuel Holton, and Elbridge Gerry. They waited upon Mr. Browne in Boston, on the 19th of September, who returned a written

[1] A classmate of Judge Browne, at Harvard.

answer, in which he says that he "cannot consent to defeat his Majesty's intentions and disappoint his expectations, by abandoning a post to which he has been graciously pleased to appoint him," &c., and that, "as a Judge, and in every other capacity," he "intended to act with honor and integrity," &c., &c.

He was an Addresser of Gage, was included in the Banishment Act of 1778, and in the Conspiracy Act of the year following. He was the owner of immense landed estates, which were confiscated. Prior to the Revolutionary troubles, he enjoyed great popularity, and strong inducements were held out to him to join the Whigs. He was in London as early as May 4, 1776, and gave his fellow-exiles some particulars relative to the evacuation of Boston. His wife, who complained of her treatment at Salem and Boston, after his departure, does not appear to have joined him in England, until the spring of 1778. In 1781, he was appointed Governor of the Bermudas, and administered the affairs of these islands in a manner to secure the confidence and respect of the people. He died in England, February, 1802, aged sixty-five.

BROWNE, ARTHUR. Of Portsmouth, New Hampshire. An Episcopal clergyman. Was educated at Trinity College, Dublin. He was ordained by the Bishop of London, and assumed the charge of a society at Providence, Rhode Island. In 1736 he removed to Portsmouth, and became the first minister of the Episcopal Church of that town, and continued his connection until his decease. He died at Cambridge, Massachusetts, in 1773, aged seventy-three. His remains were carried to Portsmouth and deposited in the Wentworth tomb.

In the Episcopal Church, he was considered a man of most noble and benevolent disposition, of sound doctrines, and a good preacher. He married Governor *Benning* Wentworth to his servant girl. The story, as told by Brewster is, that "the Governor invited a dinner party, and with many other guests, in his cocked hat, comes the beloved Rev. Arthur Browne. The dinner is served up in a style becoming the Governor's table, the wine is of good quality, &c. In due time, as previously arranged, Martha Hilton, the Governor's maid-servant, 'a damsel of twenty summers,' appears before the company. The Governor, bleached by the frosts of sixty winters, rises: ' Mr. Browne, I wish you to marry me.' ' To whom,' asked the Rector, in wondering surprise. ' To this lady,' was the reply. The Rector stood confounded. The Governor became imperative. '*As the Governor of New Hampshire I command you to marry me.*' The ceremony was performed, and Martha Hilton became Lady Wentworth."

On the day Mr. Browne married Governor *John* Wentworth to Atkinson's widow, and soon after he had performed the ceremony, he fell over a number of stone steps and broke his arm.

He was missionary of the Society for the Propagation of the Gospel in Foreign Parts. His salary in 1754 was £60, and £15 additional for officiating at Kittery. Until the appointment of his son as assistant missionary, he was the only Episcopal clergyman in New Hampshire.

In honor of the consort of George the Second, his church was called "Queen's Chapel." Dr. Franklin was one of the benefactors and a proprietor. There was a pew which, prior to the Revolution, was fitted up in state, and known as the "Governor's." It contained two chairs, which were the gift of the Queen, for the use of the Governor and his secretary. The decorations were taken down after the war; but the pew and the chairs remained, and were occupied by Washington and *his* secretary in 1789, when they attended service in Portsmouth.

Mr. Browne's children were four sons and five daughters, namely: Thomas, who died young; Marmaduke, of whom presently; Arthur, who, after a long service in the British Army, sold his commission and was Governor of Kinsale; and Peter, who entered the army at the age of fourteen, and rose to the rank of major. The daughters were all married:

Lucy, to Colonel Smith, of the British Army; Jane, to Samuel Livermore, Chief Justice of New Hampshire and Senator in Congress from that State; Mary, to the Rev. Winwood Serjeant; Anne, to Captain George St. Loe, of the British Navy, from whom she was divorced, and, the widow of a second husband, a third time to one Kelly, who, "of reckless character, treated her with the utmost neglect;" and, last, Elizabeth, who was the wife of the noted Major Robert Rogers, and, after his decease, of Captain John Roche, of Concord, New Hampshire.

BROWNE, REV. MARMADUKE. Son of Arthur. He was born in Providence, Rhode Island, in 1731, and graduated at Trinity College, Dublin, in 1754. On taking orders, he was first employed as an itinerant missionary in New Hampshire. In 1760, he became Rector of Trinity Church, Newport, R. I., and died there in 1771. His wife deceased in 1767, and his own death was "doubtless hastened by the severity of that affliction." His son Arthur, who was Doctor of Laws, and King's Professor of Greek in Trinity College, Dublin, who erected a marble tablet to his memory on the wall of Trinity Church, Newport, in 1795, and who was a very eminent man, died in 1805.

BROWNE, WILLIAM. Of Salem, Massachusetts. Son of Judge William Browne. An officer in the British Army, and at the siege of Gibraltar. He was in England in 1784.

BROWN, THOMAS. Of Boston. Embarked with his family of five persons for Halifax, in 1776. Went into business, and failed soon after the year 1779, and established a school. Rev. Jacob Bailey wrote in 1781: "This poor gentleman is still detained under complaint of his unmerciful creditors." Mr. Brown was in Halifax as late as 1792. I find the death of a Thomas Brown, at Salem, Massachusetts, in 1809, at the age of eighty-six.

BROWN, REV. THOMAS. Episcopal minister. He came to America in the French war, as supposed, with the 27th Regiment, of which he was chaplain, and which he accompanied on the expedition to Martinico, in 1762. He returned to England; and, in 1764, was appointed a missionary to America. He was in charge of St. Peter's Church, Albany, for three or four years; and in 1772, was appointed Rector of Dorchester, Maryland. He died in 1784, aged forty-nine. His wife, whose maiden name was Martina Hogan, and who belonged to Albany, and seven children, survived him.

BROWN, ELISHA. Of Northampton, New York. "Cowboy." Killed by a fellow "cow-boy" named Norton, in an affray, in 1783.

BROWN, DANIEL. Of Maine. Emigrated in early youth from Scotland to Castine, and in the Revolution took an active part in the Royal cause. At the peace he removed to New Brunswick, where he passed the remainder of his days. He died at St. Stephen, March, 1835, aged ninety-one, and left upwards of two hundred descendants. His memory was good, and the events of his life were impressed upon its tablets to the last. His daughter Catharine died a few days after him, aged fifty-five.

BROWN, ZACHARIAH. Residence unknown. A lieutenant in De Lancey's Third Battalion, retired to New Brunswick, received half-pay, and died in the county of Sunbury, in 1817, aged seventy-eight.

BROWN, HENRY B. Settled in New Brunswick. Was Registrar of Deeds and Wills for the county of Charlotte, and died there.

BROWNELL, JOSHUA, and JEREMIAH. Went to St. John, New Brunswick, at the peace. The first was a grantee of that city; the other died in Westmoreland County, in that Province, in 1835, aged eighty-eight.

BROTHERS, JOSEPH. He died at Carleton, New Brunswick, in 1836, aged seventy-two.

BRUCE, JAMES. Of Boston. Was proscribed and banished. This gentleman, I conclude, commanded the ship *Eleanor;* and if so, he, like Hall, of the *Dartmouth,* and Coffin, of the *Beaver,* is connected with the celebrated tea controversy. The *Eleanor,* Captain James Bruce, arrived in Boston, December

1, 1773, with a part of the tea sent over by the East India Company, which, after several days of fruitless negotiation, was thrown into the harbor, at Griffin's Wharf. There was a Loyalist of this name at Shelburne, Nova Scotia, about the year 1805.

BRUNSKILL, REV. JOHN. Of Virginia. Episcopal minister. About the beginning of the Revolution, on an occasion when his church was full, two or three Whigs entered in regimentals. He rose and rebuked them, said they were rebels, and that he should immediately inform the King of their misdeeds. Nearly every person left the house; some, as they departed, warning him that on a repetition of such language, he would be insulted and treated harshly. He never preached again; but lived uncomfortable and secluded at the glebe until his death. He never married; and for years, "it is believed, he was a dead weight upon the church."

BRUSH, CREAN. Of Cumberland County, "New Hampshire Grants." Born in Dublin, Ireland, about the year 1725, and bred to the law; he emigrated to America, probably in 1762. In New York, he was admitted to practice, and had employment in the office of the Provincial Secretary. In 1771, he removed to the "*Grants*," and was soon appointed Clerk and Surrogate of Cumberland County. In the troubles which existed on the "*Grants*," as Vermont was then called, he took the side of New York; and, elected to the Assembly of that Colony, he became a man of considerable note and influence. In 1775, he delivered a set-speech against electing delegates to the second Continental Congress, which the Whig leaders, Clinton, Schuyler, and Woodhull, answered. Trumbull, in McFingal, refers to him thus: —

"Had I the poet's brazen lungs,
As sound-board to his hundred tongues,
I could not half the scribblers muster
That swarmed round Rivington in cluster;
Assemblies, councilmen, forsooth:
Brush, Cooper, Wilkins, Chandler, Booth:
Yet all their arguments and sap'ence
You did not value at three half-pence."

At Boston, January, 1776, he proposed to Sir William Howe to raise a body of volunteers, not less than three hundred, on the same terms, as to pay and gratuity, as the Royal Fencible Americans, a corps just organized. The result is to be inferred from the fact, that on the 10th of March, he was ordered by Sir William to take possession of the goods of certain described persons, and put them on board of the ship *Minerva*, or the brigantine *Elizabeth*. Under this commission, Brush, at the head of parties of Tories, broke open stores and dwelling-houses, stripped them, and conveyed his plunder to the ships. Lawless bands of men from the fleet and army, followed his example; and Boston, for the last few days of the siege, was given to violence and pillage. As for Brush, he was captured after the evacuation, on board of the brigantine above mentioned.

The property on board the *Elizabeth* was worth quite one hundred thousand dollars; difficulties arose between the claimants and the captors, which were expensive and vexatious, but which I have no room to relate. The robber, Brush, was rightly enough put in close jail in Boston, and denied privileges, which, to an educated man, are invaluable; but he endeavored to lesson his woes by intemperance. Early in 1777 he was joined by his wife. The term of his imprisonment was more than nineteen months. Later in the autumn of the year last mentioned, Mrs. Brush provided him with money and a horse, preparatory to his escape; and on the night of the 5th of November, he passed the turnkey, disguised in her garments, and fled to New York. We hear of the miscreant next in Vermont, where he went to look after his lands. But his career was nearly at an end. The Whigs sequestered his estate; and the British Commander-in-Chief, to whom he applied to redress his personal wrongs and compensate his losses, not only refused, but told him that his "conduct merited them, and more." His cup was full. "Goaded by the scorpion whip of remorse, too proud to strive to redeem the errors of his past life by an honorable future," in May, 1778, he put a pistol to his head, and was found dead, "his brains besmearing the walls of the apartment." Such, rapidly traced, was the life of Crean Brush. He was ambitious to be a man of consideration, to be proprietor of a vast domain. He became an outcast; and, of nearly fifty thousand acres of the soil of New York, and the "New Hampshire Grants," which he owned, his heirs recovered possession of a small part only. His step-daughter, Frances, was wife of no less a character than Ethan Allen. She was a widow, dashing, and imperious; and though fascinating and accomplished, sometimes spoke in tones as rough and unseemly as the summoner of Ticonderoga himself. His only child, Elizabeth Martha, married Thomas Norman, of Ireland. Of her it is said that she was a lady of refined manners, of dignified deportment, and in every other respect an ornament to her sex.

BRYAN, SAMUEL. Of North Carolina. Authorized by Governor Martin, January, 1776, to erect the King's standard, to enlist and array in arms the loyal subjects of Rowan County, and "to oppose all rebels and traitors." In 1780, with a corps of eight hundred Loyalists, who abandoned their homes to avoid prison and death, after Moore's defeat by Rutherford, he marched towards South Carolina, and arrived unmolested at Cheraw Hill, where he joined the detachment of British under McArthur. Many had not seen their families for months, but had lived in the woods to avoid the parties of Whigs that were in constant pursuit at this period. Three of his companies were nearly annihilated by the Whig Major Davie, near Hanging Rock. Soon afterward, Sumter fell upon the remainder of his troops, and put them to flight; they "dispersed as soon as pressed." But, reassembled, Bryan's corps was in the rear division under the orders of Lord Rawdon, at the battle of Camden. The estate of Colonel Bryan was confiscated in 1779. The excitement against him was intense. Our Loyalist was indeed an unfortunate man, since it seems that his conduct gave serious offence to his own party, as well as to the Whigs. In a letter to Sir James Wright, dated in London, March, 1783,

Lord Cornwallis states, that "the premature rising at Ramsour's, Colonel Bryan's junction with us in South Carolina, both directly contrary to my recommendation," with the defeat of Ferguson on King's Mountain, "occasioned the ruin of many families, and furnished pretexts to exercise cruelties on individuals, to a degree neither believed nor conceived in " England.

BRYMER, ALEXANDER. Merchant of Boston. An Addresser of Gage in 1775. Was proscribed and banished in 1778. In 1782 a gentleman of this name, and supposed to be the same, was sworn in as a member of his Majesty's Council of Nova Scotia. The *Councillor* died at Ramsgate, England, in 1822, aged seventy-five.

BUCHANAN, JOHN. Of Maryland. Went to England, and established himself as a merchant in London. His widow died at Bromley, Kent, in 1784.

BUDD, ELISHA. Of New York. Ensign in the King's American Regiment. He was born at White Plains, and settled in Rye. His father, James Budd, was shot at his own door by a party of "cow-boys." He was at the siege of Savannah, and in several engagements at the South. His property was confiscated; and at the peace he went to Digby, Nova Scotia, where he became a merchant and a Justice of the Common Pleas. He died at Liverpool, England, in 1813, aged fifty-one. His widow, a daughter of Isaac Bonnell, died in 1850, at the age of eighty-two, leaving five children, of whom three now (1861) reside at Digby.

BULL, WILLIAM. Lieutenant-Governor of South Carolina. His father, who died in 1755, at the age of seventy-two, had the same Christian name, and held the same office. He was a pupil of Boerhaave. Returning to this country, after completing his studies, he rose to distinction in literature, medical science, and politics. In 1751 he was a member of the Council; in 1763 Speaker of the House of Delegates; and in 1764 Lieutenant-Governor. In the last office he continued many years, and was Commander-in-Chief of the Colony. He accompanied the British troops to England in 1782, and continuing there, died in London, July 4, 1791, aged eighty-one.

BULL, GEORGE. He was born in the city of New York. In 1782 he was a lieutenant of cavalry in the American Legion under Arnold. He retired on half-pay at the peace, and settled in New Brunswick. He died at Woodstock, in 1838, at the age of eighty-six.

BULL, CAPTAIN ———, Of New York. He was in the service of the Crown, and his name appears in the interview between the celebrated Mohawk, Brant, and the Whig General Herkimer, at Unadilla, New York, in 1777. When the Indian chief met the Whig, he was accompanied by Bull, a son of Sir William Johnson by Brandt's sister, Mary, or Molly, and about forty warriors. During the meeting, Herkimer demanded the surrender of several Tories, which Brant peremptorily refused. This was the last conference held with the hostile Mohawks.

BULLMAN, REV. JOHN. Of Charleston, South Carolina. Episcopal minister. In 1774 he preached a sermon which gave great offence. I extract a single passage: " Every idle projector who cannot, perhaps, govern his own household, or pay the debts of his own contracting, presumes he is qualified to dictate how the State should be governed, and to point out the means of paying the debts of a nation." Again: " Every silly clown and illiterate mechanic will take upon him to censure the conduct of his Prince or Governor, and contribute, as much as in him lies, to create and foment those misunderstandings . . . . which come at last to . . . . sedition and rebellion," &c.

A meeting of his parishioners was called, when it was found that, exclusive of the vestry and church-wardens, forty-two disapproved, and thirty-three approved, of his conduct in the pulpit. Attempts at reconciliation followed, but without success; and in March, 1775, Mr. Bullman sailed for England.

BULYEA, JOHN, and ABRAHAM. The first, in 1795, was a member of the Loyal Artillery of St. John, New Brunswick. Sarah, his widow, died in King's County, in that

Province, in 1843, aged ninety-nine, leaving six children, fifty-five grandchildren, and fifty-seven great-grandchildren. Abraham settled in New Brunswick in 1783, and died in King's County in that Colony, in 1833, aged seventy-seven.

BUNHILL, SOLOMON. Of Lanesborough, Massachusetts. In the battle of Bennington he shot two of his neighbors through the head, as was alleged, and was sent to Northampton jail. An agent was appointed to procure the evidence against him, and to attend his trial. His property was confiscated, and in 1784 advertised for sale by a Committee of the Commonwealth.

BUNTING, ROLAND. He died at Loch Lomond, New Brunswick, in 1839, at the great age of one hundred years.

BURCH, WILLIAM. Commissioner of the Customs, Boston. Was proscribed and banished in 1778, and included in the Conspiracy Act of 1779. He went to England, where, I conclude, he took no part in affairs. Charles Paxton, one of his fellow-commissioners, died at his seat; and this is the only instance that I find his name so much as mentioned.

BURNET, JOHN. Of Georgia. To cover his dark deeds, he pretended to be a Whig. When, in 1781, Browne surrendered Augusta, the goods and stores which were found in Fort Cornwallis, and which were allotted to the Georgia troops, were placed in his possession for safe keeping until a division could be safely made of them. His party had previously secreted about sixty negroes, who, he averred, had been taken from the enemy, and who he promised to add to the other property at the time of distribution. The officers, not suspecting him, were duped. He proceeded towards the mountains on pretence of seeking a place of safety, passed through Kentucky to the Ohio River, procured boats and descended to Natchez, where he and his companions appropriated the fruits of their knavery.

BURNET, MATHIAS. Of Jamaica, New York. He was born in New Jersey, and graduated at Princeton College in 1769. He was settled at Jamaica in 1775, and continued with his people during the war. After the peace, and in

1785, he was compelled, by the force of party spirit, to dissolve the connection. It is said that he was the only Presbyterian minister of Queen's County who was reputed to be a friend to Government. His wife was an Episcopalian, and, removing to Norwalk, Connecticut, he took charge of a church of that communion. He died at Norwalk in 1806.

BURNS, WILLIAM and MICHAEL. Of Connecticut. Brothers. The first was a forage-master in the Royal Army, who settled on Digby Neck, Nova Scotia, at the peace, and died in 1797. Michael settled at the same place, and died in 1817. Phebe, daughter of William, married Edmund Fanning, and has two daughters now (1861) living in England.

BURRIS, SAMUEL. A Whig soldier. In 1778 he was tried on a charge of attempting to desert to the Royal side. He confessed his guilt, and was sentenced to receive one hundred lashes.

BURTIS, WILLIAM. Of West Chester County, New York. In 1779 he was sent prisoner from White Plains by Burr, who wrote Malcolm that Burtis wished to secure the favor of the Whigs by giving them information. In 1780 he was confined at West Point, under sentence of death, for communication with the British General Mathews. At the peace he went to New Brunswick, and died at St. John in 1835, aged seventy-five.

BURTON, NAPIER CHRISTIE. General in the British Army. "An American by birth," who entered the military service in August, 1775, as an ensign. He was in several actions in New Jersey, and accompanied his regiment to Virginia, and to South Carolina. He was engaged in the affairs of the Catawba and Yadkin, in the battles of Guilford and Cross Creek, and was taken prisoner in the siege of Yorktown. In 1789 he attained the rank of Lieutenant-Colonel, and subsequently served in Flanders. In 1799 he was appointed Lieutenant-Governor of Upper Canada. His commission of Lieutenant-General, bears date January 1, 1805, and of General, June 4, 1814. From 1796 to 1806, he was a member of Parliament for Beverley. For several years previous to his decease, he was an invalid. He died in England, in January, 1835, in his seventy-seventh year.

BURWELL, JAMES. Of New Jersey. Born at Rockaway, January 18, 1754. His father, Samuel Burwell, was eldest son of John Burwell, who removed from Jamestown, Virginia, in the year 1721, a relative of the extensive family of Burwells, in this country, formerly from Bedford and Northampton, England, the first of whom was buried at York River, Gloucester County, 1652. One of his ancestors was of the Virginia deputation in the year 1646, to invite the fallen monarch, Charles the First, to come to America for protection against the rebellious Puritan subjects. Our Loyalist enlisted in his Majesty's service in the year 1776, at the age of twenty-two, and served seven years, and was present at the battle of Yorktown, when Lord Cornwallis surrendered, and was there slightly wounded. After the war he moved to Nova Scotia, where he remained four years; he then returned to New Jersey, to take care of his aged mother; married, and removed to Pennsylvania, and from thence came to Upper Canada in the year 1796, too late to obtain the king's bounty of family land, but was placed on the Upper Canada list, and received two hundred acres for himself and each of his children. He removed to the Talbot settlement in the year 1810. He died in the county of Elgin, Canada, July, 1853, aged ninety-nine years and five months.

BUSKIRK, ———. Lieutenant-Colonel of a Loyalist corps. In 1777, he attempted to cut off a party of Whig militia stationed at Paramus; but the commander had notice of the design, and escaped by moving to another post. In 1779, with a considerable part of the garrison of Powle's Hook, and some other troops, he proceeded up the North River for the purpose of falling in with a detachment of Whigs, supposed to be out foraging upon the Tories. He met a larger force than he expected, and retreated. The illustrious John Marshall states the facts in detail, from his personal observation.

In 1780, with one hundred dragoons and upwards of three hundred infantry, he crossed from Staten Island to Elizabethtown, at midnight, took several prisoners, burnt the church and town-house, plundered some of the inhabitants, and retired without loss. He was with Arnold in the expedition to New London, and in command of a regiment or battalion.

BUSKIRK, ———. Son of Lieutenant-Colonel Buskirk, and lieutenant in the New Jersey Volunteers, or, "Skinner's Greens." In the attack by General Dickinson, November, 1777, he was made prisoner. I suppose the Captain Buskirk wounded in the battle of Eutaw Springs, 1781, was the same.

BUSKIRK, HENRY. Of New York. He removed to Nova Scotia in 1783, and was many years a magistrate of King's County. He died at Aylesford, Nova Scotia, in 1841.

BUSTIN, THOMAS. Of Virginia. He joined the Royal Army at New York after the commencement of hostilities; and at the peace removed to St. John, New Brunswick, where he lived until his decease, at the age of ninety. Seven children survived him. Mary, his widow, died in the same city, in 1848, at the age of ninety-two.

BUTLER, JOHN. Of Tryon, now Montgomery, County, New York. Before the war, Colonel Butler was in close official connection with Sir William, Sir John, and Colonel Guy Johnson, and followed their political fortunes. At the breaking out of hostilities, he commanded a regiment of New York militia, and entered at once into the military service of the Crown. During the war his wife was taken prisoner, and exchanged for the wife of the Whig Colonel Campbell. The deeds of rapine, of murder, of hellish hue, which were perpetrated by Butler's corps, cannot be related here. It is sufficient, for the purpose of these Notes, to say, that he commanded the sixteen hundred incarnate fiends who desolated Wyoming. I feel quite willing to allow, that history has recorded barbarities which were not committed. But though Butler did not permit or directly authorize women to be driven into the forest, where they became mothers, and where their infants were eaten by wild beasts, and though captive officers may not have been held upon fires with pitchforks until they were burned to death, sufficient remains undoubted, to stamp his conduct with the deepest, darkest, most damning guilt. The human mind can hardly frame an argument which shall clear the fame of Butler from obloquy and reproach. To admit even as a solved question, that the Loyalists were in the right, and that they were bound by the clearest rules of duty to bear arms in defence of lawful and existing institutions, and to put down the rebellion, will do Butler no good. For, whatever the force of such a plea in the minds of those who urge it, *he was still bound to observe the laws of civilized warfare.*

That he, and he alone, will be regarded by posterity as the real and responsible actor in the business and slaughter at Wyoming, may be considered, perhaps, as certain. The chieftain Brant was, for a time, held accountable, but the better information of later years transfers the guilt from the savage to the man of Saxon blood. There was nothing for which the Mohawk's family labored more earnestly than to show that their renowned head was not implicated in this bloody tragedy, and that the accounts of historians, and the enormities recounted in Campbell's verse, as far as they relate to him, are untrue. It has been said very commonly, that the Colonel Butler who was of the Whig force at Wyoming, and Colonel John, were kinsmen; but this, too, has been contradicted. The late Edward D. Griffin, — a youth, a writer, and a poet of rare promise, — and a grandson of the former, denied the relationship.

Colonel John Butler was richly rewarded for his services. Succeeding, in part, to the agency of Indian Affairs — long held by the Johnsons — he enjoyed, about the year 1796, a salary of £500 sterling per annum, and a pension as a military officer of £200 more. Previously, he had received a grant of five hundred acres of land, and a similar provision for his children. His home, after the war, was in Upper Canada. He was attainted during the contest, by the Act of New York, and his property confiscated. He lived before the Revolution in the present town of Mohawk. His dwelling was of one story, with two windows in front, and a door in the centre.

It was standing in 1842, and was then owned and occupied by Mr. Wilson. The site is pleasant and commanding, and overlooks the valley of the Mohawk.

BUTLER, WALTER N. Son of Colonel John Butler. Entered the British service, and became a major. His name is connected with some of the most infamous transactions of the Revolution. While a lieutenant under St. Leger, he was taken prisoner at the house of a Loyalist who lived near Fort Dayton, and was put upon his trial as a spy, convicted, and received sentence of death. But at the intercession of several American officers who had known him while a student at law in Albany, his life was spared by a reprieve. The friends of the Butler family, in consequence of his alleged ill health, induced his removal from rigorous confinement to a private house under guard, and he soon escaped, and joined his father. It is believed that he took mortal offence at his treatment while a prisoner of the Whigs, and that he reëntered the service of the Crown, burning with resentment and thirsting for revenge. His subsequent career was short, bold, cruel, and bloody. He was killed in battle in 1781, and his remains were left to decay without even the rudest rites of sepulture. It is represented that his disposition was so vindictive and his passions so strong, that British officers of rank and humanity viewed him with horror. The late Doctor Dwight — a careful writer — relates, that at Cherry Valley he ordered a woman and child to be slain in bed, and that the more merciful Brant interposed and said: " What! kill a woman and child! No! That child is not an enemy to the King, nor a friend to the Congress. Long before he will be big enough to do any mischief, the dispute will be settled."

BUTLER, JAMES. Of Georgia. Went to England, and died there in 1817, aged seventy-nine. " An American Loyalist," says the record.

BUTLER, BENJAMIN. Of Norwich, Connecticut. He was a gentleman of respectability and talents, and continued loyal throughout the contest. Arrested and imprisoned, in 1776, for defaming the Continental Congress, he was tried by the Superior Court, and sentenced to be deprived of the liberty of wearing arms, and of being incapable of holding office. He died of a lingering disease in 1787. While in health, he selected a small tree to be used at his decease to enclose his remains; but the sapling grew slowly, and his coffin was constructed of other wood, and kept in his chamber for years, to remind him of his end. The expressive motto on his gravestone — " ALAS, POOR HUMAN NATURE! " — was placed there by his own direction. " His wife, Diadema, and his daughters, Rosamond and Minerva, repose by his side " in the Norwich burial-ground. The survivors of his family removed to Oxford, New York. The wife of Commodore John Rogers, United States Navy, was a granddaughter.

BUTLER, JOSIAH. He died at St. John, New Brunswick, in 1812, aged fifty.

BUTLER, CAPTAIN ———. He was a Tory leader, whose crimes and ferocity were well known in the region of the Pedee. During a period of Whig ascendency in that part of South Carolina, he went into General Marion's camp at Birch's Mills, and submitting himself, claimed the protection which the Whig officer had granted to some other Loyalists who had preceded him. Against this some of Marion's officers, whose friends had suffered at Butler's hands, protested. But Marion took the humbled Butler to his own tent, and declared that he would protect him at the hazard of his own life. The officers, still determined to gratify their hate, sent their commander an offensive message, to the effect that " Butler should be dragged to death from his tent," and that, " to defend such a wretch was an insult to humanity." Marion was not to be intimidated; and though the meeting among his followers threatened to be formidable, he succeeded in conveying Butler under a strong guard to a place of safety.

BUTLER, ELEAZER. Of Pennsylvania. On the Royal side in the slaughter at Wyoming. Went to Nova Scotia, and is now (1854) living at Yarmouth.

BYLES, MATHER, D. D. Of Boston. He was born in Boston in 1706, graduated at Harvard University in 1725, and was ordained the first pastor of the Hollis Street Church in 1733. On his mother's side, he was descended from Richard Mather and John Cotton. He continued to live happily with his parish until 1776, when the connection was dissolved, and never renewed. In 1777 he was denounced in town-meeting, and having been by a subsequent trial pronounced guilty of attachment to the Royal cause, was sentenced to confinement, and to be sent with his family to England. This doom of banishment was never enforced, and he was permitted to remain in Boston. He died in 1788, aged eighty-two years. He was a scholar; and Pope, Lansdowne, and Watts were his correspondents. His witticisms would fill many pages; some of his finest sayings having been preserved. In his pulpit he avoided politics, and on being asked the reason, replied: "I have thrown up four breastworks, behind which I have entrenched myself, neither of which can be enforced. In the first place, I do not understand politics; in the second place, you all do, every man and mother's son of you; in the third place, you have politics all the week, pray let one day in seven be devoted to religion; in the fourth place, I am engaged in work of infinitely greater importance; give me any subject to preach on of more consequence than the truth I bring to you, and I will preach on it the next Sabbath." On another occasion, when under sentence of the Whigs to remain in his own house, under guard, he persuaded the sentinel to go on an errand for him, promising to perform sentinel's duty himself; and to the great amusement of all gravely marched before his own door with a musket on his shoulder, until his keeper returned. This was after his trial; and alluding to the circumstances that he had been kept prisoner, that his guard had been removed, and replaced again, he said, that "*he had been guarded, re-guarded, and disregarded.*" Near his house, in wet weather, was a very bad slough. It happened that two of the selectmen who had the care of the streets, driving in a chaise, stuck fast in this hole, and were obliged to get out in the mud to extricate their vehicle. Doctor Byles came out, and making them a respectful bow, said: "Gentlemen, I have often complained to you of this nuisance, without any attention being paid to it, and I am very glad to see you *stirring* in this matter now." On the celebrated Dark-day in 1780, a lady who lived near the Doctor, sent her young son with her compliments, to know if he could account for the uncommon appearance. His answer was: "My dear, you will give my compliments to your mamma, and tell her that I am as much in the *dark* as she is." He paid his addresses unsuccessfully to a lady, who afterwards married a gentleman of the name of Quincy; the Doctor, on meeting her, said: "So, madam, it appears that you prefer a Quincy to Byles." "Yes, for if there had been anything worse than *biles*, God would have afflicted Job with them."

Doctor Byles's wit created many a laugh, and many an enemy. In person he was tall and commanding. His voice was strong and harmonious, and his delivery graceful. His first wife was a niece of Governor Belcher, the second, a daughter of Lieutenant-Governor Tailer. His two daughters lived and died in the old family house at the corner of Nassau and Tremont streets. One of them deceased in 1835, the other in 1837. They were stout, unchanging Loyalists to the last hour of their existence. Their thread of life was spun out more than half a century after the Royal government had ceased in these States; yet they retained their love of, and strict adherence to, monarch and monarchies, and refused to acknowledge that the Revolution had transferred their allegiance to new rulers. They were repeatedly offered a great price for their dwelling, but would not sell it, nor would they permit improvements or alterations. They possessed old-fashioned silver plate, which they never used, and would not dispose of. They worshipped in Trinity Church — under which their bodies now lie — and wore on Sunday dresses almost as old as themselves. Among their furniture was a pair of bellows two centuries old; a table on which Franklin drank tea on his last visit to Boston; a chair which more than a hundred years before the Government of

England had sent as a present to their grandfather, Lieutenant-Governor Tailer. They showed to visiters commissions to their grandfather, signed by Queen Anne, and three of the Georges; and the envelope of a letter from Pope to their father. They had moss, gathered from the birthplace of the unfortunate Lady Jane Grey. They talked of their walks, arm-in-arm, on Boston Common, with General Howe and Lord Percy, while the British Army occupied Boston. They told of his Lordship's ordering his band to play under their windows for their gratification.

In the progress of the improvements in Boston, a part of their dwelling was removed. This had a fatal influence upon the elder sister; she mourned over the sacrilege, and, it is thought, died its victim. "That," said the survivor, "that is one of the consequences of living in a Republic. Had we been living under a king, he would have cared nothing about our little property, and we could have enjoyed it in our own way as long as we lived. But," continued she, "there is one comfort, that not a creature in the States will be any better for what we shall leave behind us." She was true to her promise, for the Byles's estate passed to relatives in the Colonies. One of these ladies, of a by-gone age, wrote to William the Fourth, on his accession to the throne. They had known the "sailor-king" during the Revolution, and now assured him that the family of Doctor Byles always had been, and would continue to be, loyal to their rightful sovereign of England.

BYLES, MATHER, JR., D. D. Of Boston. An Episcopal clergyman. Son of Mather Byles, D. D. He graduated at Harvard University in 1751. In 1757, at about the age of twenty-three, he was ordained at New London; his father preached the sermon. Eleven years after, his ministry came to an abrupt termination. Without previous intimation, he called a meeting of his church, and requested dismission, that he might accept an invitation to become Rector of the North Episcopal, or Christ Church, Salem street, Boston.

Among the reasons he gave in the course of the discussions

that ensued, were, that "another minister would do much better for them than he had done or could do, for his health was infirm, and the position of the church very bleak, the hill wearisome, ... he was not made for a country minister, and his home and friends were all in Boston," &c., &c. He also complained bitterly of the persecutions he had suffered from the Quakers, and the negligence of the authorities in executing the laws against them.

The debate was long and warm, and produced total alienation. April 12, 1768, the record is, "The Rev. Mr. Byles dismissed *himself* from the church and congregation." He hastened to depart with the rapidity of a criminal escaping for crime. His change to Episcopacy was soon a matter of discussion all over New England. In New London his conversion was ridiculed. The song — "The Proselyte," set to the tune of the "Thief and Cordelier," which embraced the facts of the case, was sung about the country. Before the close of 1768, he was inducted into the desired rectorship; and of Christ Church, was the third in succession. He continued to discharge his ministerial duties until 1775, when the force of events compelled him to abandon his flock. In 1776, accompanied by his family of four persons, he went to Halifax. In 1778 he was proscribed and banished. He settled at St. John, New Brunswick, after the war, and was Rector of the city, and Chaplain of the Province. He died at St. John in 1814. His daughter Anna married Thomas Deisbrisay, Lieutenant-Colonel of Artillery in the British Army, in 1799. His daughter Elizabeth married William Scovil, Esquire, of St. John, and died in 1808, at the age of forty-one. His son Belcher died in England in 1815, aged thirty-five. His daughter Rebecca, born in New London, 1762, married W. J. Almon, M. D., and died at Halifax, Nova Scotia, 1853. His son Mather died at Grenada, in 1803, aged thirty-nine.

BYRNE, BENEDICT. Of Maryland or Virginia. He entered a Loyalist corps and was taken prisoner, but made his escape to New York, where he was employed as a pilot. At the peace, accompanied by his family of three persons, and by two servants, he removed to Shelburne, Nova Scotia, where the Crown granted him fifty acres of land, one town and one water lot. His losses in consequences of his loyalty were estimated at £300. He went to England soon afterwards to obtain compensation for his services and sufferings, but was unsuccessful. He died at Digby, Nova Scotia, in 1830, aged eighty-six. His first wife was Hannah Carroll, of Virginia, who died in Nova Scotia in 1786; his second, Mrs. Wilson, a widow, of Shelburne. His daughter Margaret married William Whipple, of Boston.

CALDWELL, CAPTAIN ———. Was killed in Pennsylvania in 1780, by a Whig captain, McMahon, whom he and an Indian had taken prisoner. Possibly William Caldwell, of Chester County, Pennsylvania, who was attainted of treason by proclamation, and whose property was confiscated.

CALEF, JOHN. Of Ipswich, Massachusetts. Physician. Son of Robert Calef, and Margaret, daughter of Deacon John Staniford. He was born in Ipswich, 1725, and represented that town in the General Court several years. Driven into exile by the Revolution, he became surgeon of one of the regiments stationed at Castine, Maine, and a part of the time officiated as chaplain. At the peace he settled at St. Andrew, New Brunswick, and died there in 1812, aged eighty-seven. His wife was a daughter of Rev. Jedediah Jewett, of Rowley, Massachusetts.

CALEF, ROBERT. Son of John Calef. Died at Norfolk, Virginia, in 1801, at the age of forty-one.

CALLAHAN, CHARLES. Mariner, of Pownalborough, now Wiscasset, Maine; was proscribed and banished in 1778. Though a Loyalist in principle, he was not disposed to be active on the side of the Crown, or to abandon the country. But, "drafted" repeatedly to serve in the Whig corps, he fled to Halifax, Nova Scotia. Made a King's pilot, and subsequently, in command of the *Gage*, an armed vessel of twelve guns, he became a terror to the "Rebels." Wrecked, finally, and failing to obtain another ship, he was still retained in service and paid the wages of a pilot. He perished, with one hundred and sixty-four others, on board the *North* ship-of-war, near Halifax, in 1779. His widow received a pension of £40 annually; she returned to Pownalborough about the year 1790, and died there in 1816. The estate of her husband was confiscated, but his farm and buildings came into her possession.

CALP, PHILIP. Of Pennsylvania. In 1778, he was tried for attempting to carry flour to a post occupied by the Royal forces, and was sentenced to receive fifty lashes, and to be employed on the public works during the time the British remained in Pennsylvania, unless he would enter the Whig service for the war. The lashes were disapproved by the Commander-in-Chief, and were not inflicted.

CAMERON, ALEXANDER. Deputy Indian Agent of the Cherokees. Connected with the first settlement of East Tennessee. In 1768, a few adventurers from the neighborhood of Raleigh, North Carolina, crossed the mountains in search of a new home. Cameron soon ordered them to remove. They refused, received accessions, organized a sort of government, and continued prosperous. When it was apparent that the controversy would end in general war, Cameron changed his course, and by flattering promises of protection, if they would remain loyal, endeavored to seduce them to the side of the Crown. They could send five hundred riflemen to the field, at the least, and their adhesion was worth the effort. They were a lone people, in the midst of savages, and yet they declined his offers unanimously and peremptorily. His Majesty's official then formed a design to destroy them with a force of Cherokees, by falling upon them suddenly, and in all quarters at the same moment. The plan was discovered. Most of the hapless Whigs fled to the several places of their nativity. A few established and maintained a garrison until succored. In 1775, the Council of Safety proposed to him to join the popular side, and offered him a salary equal to that which he received from the British Government, and compensation for any losses he might sustain;

he declined the overture, and, to ensure his personal safety, retired to the Cherokees. In 1776, he was in arms at the head of Tories and Indians, and was in several skirmishes; but he abandoned them, and fled to St. Augustine, in the belief that the Whigs would subdue them.

Among the papers taken with Moses Kirkland on his way to Boston to confer with Gage, was a " talk " between Cameron and Indian chiefs, in which the latter expressed their readiness to aid in the massacre of the people in the back settlements of Georgia and South Carolina. Cameron owned two large plantations near the Savannah river, on which he had placed a number of negroes, horses and cattle, and from the produce of which he promised himself a fortune in a few years.

CAMERON, MEDERICH. Of New York. His son Mederich, who was a Whig, fled from school, and joined the army as a drummer. The father followed the youth to camp, and succeeded in obtaining his release. At the peace, Mr. Cameron went to Shelburne, Nova Scotia. He owned three houses in the city of New York, two of which he demolished at leaving, and transported the bricks of which they were built to Shelburne, to serve in the construction of a new dwelling there. He died at Liverpool, Nova Scotia, during the war of 1812, at the age of ninety-eight. Two children survived him. The son above mentioned went to Nova Scotia with his father, but returned to New York.

CAMPBELL, LORD WILLIAM. Last Royal Governor of South Carolina. He was the youngest son of the fourth Duke of Argyle. Entered the navy, and became a captain in 1762. The year after, he married Sarah, daughter of Ralph Izard, of Charleston, South Carolina, and in 1764 was a member of the British House of Commons. In 1766, he was appointed Governor of Nova Scotia, and remained there until 1773. He assumed the Executive Chair of South Carolina in 1775, while the first Provincial Congress was in session, and refused to acknowledge that body. He was zealous in opposing the popular movement, and, distrustful, finally, " of his personal safety, retired to the *Tamor* sloop-of-war." In the attack on Charleston, in 1776, he served on board of one of the British ships, and received a wound which in the end was mortal. He died September, 1778.

While Governor of Nova Scotia, he granted to Captain William Owen, father of the late Admiral Owen, the island of Campo Bello, opposite Eastport and Lubec, Maine. " Lord William and the Captain," remarked the Admiral to the writer, "were both poor at the time of the grant."

CAMPBELL, FARQUARD. Of North Carolina. Was a gentleman of wealth, education, and influence, and regarded as a "flaming Whig." Was elected a member of the Provincial Congress, took his seat, and evinced much zeal in the popular cause. When, however, Governor Martin abandoned his palace and retreated, first to Fort Johnston, and thence to an armed ship of the Crown, it was ascertained that he visited Campbell at his residence. And this circumstance gave rise to a suspicion of his fidelity. Soon after, the Governor asked Congress to give his coach and horses safe conduct to Campbell's house in the county of Cumberland. The President of Congress submitted the request to that body, when Mr. Campbell rose in his place, and expressed his surprise that such a proposal should have been made without his knowledge and consent, and implored that his Excellency's property might not thus be disposed of. On this positive disclaimer, a resolution was passed, which not only acquitted him of all improper connection with the Governor, but asserted his devotion to the Whig interests. But his character never recovered from the shock, and the belief that he continued a secret correspondence with the retreating representative of Royalty, was commonly entertained by his associates. Yet his votes, his services on committees, and his course in debate, remained unchanged. After the Declaration of Independence, his part became too difficult to act, and his double-dealing could no longer be concealed. In the fall of 1776 he was seized at his own house, while entertaining a party of Loyalists, and borne off for trial. His name next appears in the Revolutionary annals of North Carolina, in the Banishment and Confiscation Act. But several years after the Revolution, he was a member of the Senate of North Carolina.

CAMPBELL, ALEXANDER. Of Falmouth, Virginia. Merchant. Emigrated from Scotland some years before the war, adhered to the Crown, and returned, probably, in 1776. Thomas Campbell, the poet, was his youngest son. Another son married a daughter of Patrick Henry. His brother Archibald, an Episcopal minister, was a Whig, and Washington and the Lees were among his parishioners. This array of great names may be completed by adding, that Patrick Henry "was descended on his mother's side from the stock of Robertson, the historian, and in that way a relative of Lord Brougham."

CAMPBELL, PETER. Of Trenton, New Jersey. He entered the military service of the Crown, and at the peace was a captain in the New Jersey Volunteers. He had property in Pennsylvania, and was directed by the Executive Council of that State to surrender himself for trial within a specified time, or stand attainted of treason. He settled in New Brunswick, and received half-pay. He died at Maugerville, in that Colony, in 1822, and was buried at Fredricton.

CAMPBELL, COLIN. Was an ensign in De Lancey's Second Battalion, quartermaster of the corps, and subsequently a lieutenant. His son, Colin Campbell, was Sheriff of Charlotte County, New Brunswick. Died at St. Andrew, in that Province, in 1843.

CAMPBELL, WILLIAM. Of Worcester, Massachusetts. In 1775 the Committee of that town appointed to watch and deal with the disaffected, resolved to send him to the Provincial Congress at Watertown, to be disposed of as that body, or the Commander-in-Chief at Cambridge, should think proper; "it being judged highly improper that he should tarry any longer" at Worcester. He was at Boston in 1776, and embarked with the Royal Army at the evacuation. In 1783 he was at New York, and one of the fifty petitioners for lands in Nova Scotia. [See *Abijah Willard.*] He went to Halifax in the last mentioned year, where he remained in 1786, when he removed to St. John, New Brunswick. He was Mayor of St. John twenty years, and died in that city in 1823, aged eighty-two. Elizabeth, his widow, died in 1824, at the age of eighty-four. Agnes, his only daughter, died at St. John in 1840, aged seventy-eight.

CAMPBELL, WILLIAM. Major in the South Carolina Royalists. Killed in the affair at Stono Ferry, South Carolina, June, 1779.

CAMPBELL, JOHN. Of North Carolina. Captain in the Loyal Militia. Killed in the battle of Cross Creek, 1776.

CAMP, ABIATHAR, ABIATHAR JR., and ELDAD. Loyalists of Connecticut. Settled at St. John, New Brunswick, in 1783, and received grants of city lots. Abiathar was one of the fifty-five petitioners for lands in Nova Scotia. He died in New Brunswick, in 1841, aged eighty-four. He appears to have been a Recanter, but, like most of this class, finally became an exile. October 2, 1775, he wrote and subscribed the following: —

"I, Abiathar Camp, of New Haven, in the County of New Haven, in the Colony of Connecticut, although I well knew that it was the opinion of a number of the inhabitants of said town, that vessels ought not to clear out under the *Restraining Act*, which opinion they had, for my satisfaction, expressed by a vote when I was present; and although I had assured that I would not clear out my vessel under said *Restraining Act*, did, nevertheless, cause my vessel to be cleared out agreeable to said *Restraining Act;* and did, after I knew that the Committee of Inspection had given it as their opinion, that it was most advisable that vessels should not clear out under said *Restraining Act*, send my vessel off to sea with such clearance, for which I am heartily sorry; and now publicly ask the forgiveness of all the friends of America, and hope that they will restore me to charity. And I do now most solemnly assure the public, though I own that I have by my said conduct given them too much reason to question my veracity, that I will strictly comply with the directions, and fully lend my utmost assistance to carry into execution all such measures as the Continental Congress have or may advise to.   ABIATHAR CAMP."

CANBY, JOSEPH, and THOMAS. Of Pennsylvania. Were attainted of treason and lost their property by confiscation. Joseph went to St. John, New Brunswick, at the peace, and was a grantee of that city. He commenced business as a merchant. In 1795 he was a member of the company of Loyal Artillery. He was killed by falling from a wharf in 1814, at the age of fifty-seven.

CANE, BARNEY. He boasted of having killed upon Diamond Island, Lake George, a gentleman named Hopkins, who was there with a number of others on an excursion of pleasure. "Several were killed by our party," said Cane, "among whom was one woman who had a suckling child, which was not hurt. This we put to the breast of its dead mother, and so we left it. Hopkins was only wounded, but, with the butt of my gun, and the third blow, I laid him dead."

CANER, HENRY, D. D. He graduated at Yale College in 1724, and in 1727 went to England for ordination. For some years, subsequently, his ministry was confined to Norwalk and Fairfield, Connecticut; but in 1747 he was inducted into office as Rector of the First Episcopal Church, (King's Chapel) Boston. The troubles of the Revolution drove him from his flock in 1776. He said, the evacuation of Boston was so sudden, that he was prevented from saving his books, furniture, or anything else, except bedding, wearing apparel, and a few stores for his small family during the passage. May 10, 1776, he wrote at Halifax, that he was without means of support, and was dependent on the charity of the Rev. Dr. Breynton. He took away the King's Chapel church registers and plate, and a part of the vestry records. After the lapse of more than twenty-five years, the registers were obtained of his heirs. He went from Halifax to England; but returned and officiated at Bristol, Rhode Island. He was proscribed and banished, under the statute of Massachusetts, in 1778. His talents were good, his manners agreeable, and he was highly esteemed by his people. A fellow-Loyalist wrote, in 1785: "By letters from London, I am informed that Dr. Caner had retired with his young wife to Cardiff, in Wales."

His estate, which was confiscated, was next to the Chapel burying-ground, and is now owned by the Massachusetts Historical Society. He died at Long Ashton, England, in 1792, aged ninety-three.

CANFIELD, ———. Of Northampton, Massachusetts. He was a Whig, and a soldier in the 1st New Hampshire Regiment, but deserted and joined the Rangers. While on a plundering excursion in 1782 he was captured, tried for his life, and sentenced to be executed at Saratoga on the 6th of June of that year.

CAPEN, HOPESTILL. Of Boston. An Addresser of Hutchinson in 1774, and a Protestor against the Whigs, the same year. He was a Sandemanian.

In 1776, the Council ordered his arrest, and he was committed to the jail in Boston; and in October of that year, his wife petitioned for his release, urging, among other reasons, that both herself and children had suffered great distress in consequence of his long confinement. More than eighty citizens of Boston joined Mrs. Capen, and said in his behalf, that he was an honest and peaceable man, and, that while the Royal Army occupied the town, he had exerted himself to save the property of absentees. In December, Mr. Capen himself addressed a paper to Joseph Greenleaf, the sheriff, in which he complains of his treatment in severe terms, and from which it appears that he had been a close prisoner for one hundred and forty-seven days. As the sheriff was personally accused, he laid the communication before the House, and begged to be protected from Mr. Capen's insults. Before me, also, is a long document which this unfortunate Loyalist prepared to read to a Court of Inquiry, expected by him to take cognizance of his case, and which, though of some ability, bears evidence of a mind disordered by fanaticism. He was in Boston in 1795, and lived near the Market. Before the Revolution, he was a merchant, and the celebrated Count Rumford was, at one time, his clerk.

CAPERS, GABRIEL. Of South Carolina. An officer under the Crown after the surrender of Charleston. Estate confiscated. Probably a Whig at first; as in 1775 he was a member of the Provincial Congress, and was placed upon an important standing committee of that body. His wife, and his daughter Catherine, (wife of Hugh Patterson), died at Charleston in 1808.

CARBERY, ———. A captain in the Whig service, and apparently in Colonel Moyland's Regiment. In June, 1783, he fled to London with Lieutenant John Sullivan, in whose plot he was implicated. Sullivan says of him: "This young gentleman served with *eclat* in the army, and spent a pretty fortune in the service of his country."

CARDEN, JOHN. Major in the Prince of Wales's American Regiment. In 1780 he was in command of the post at Hanging Rock, when, assaulted by Sumter, he exposed himself to censure and disgrace, by resigning to Captain Rouslet of the Infantry of the Legion, in the heat of the battle. He died in April, 1783.

CAREW, SIR BENJAMIN HALLOWELL. Of Massachusetts. Admiral of the Blue in the British Navy, G. C. B., K. St. F M. He was the son of Benjamin Hallowell, one of the Commissioners of the Customs at Boston, and entered the service at an early age. His commission as Lieutenant, bears date August, 1781; as Captain, in 1793; as Rear-Admiral, in 1811; as Vice-Admiral, in 1819. He was made a Knight Commander of the Bath in 1819, and was promoted to the rank of Grand Cross in 1831. His employments at sea were various and arduous. He was with Rodney in the memorable battle with de Grasse; in the siege of Bastia; and in command of a ship-of-the-line under Hotham, in the encounter with the French off the Hieres Islands. He served as a volunteer on board the *Victory*, in the battle of Cape St.

Vincent. In the battle of the Nile, he commanded the *Swiftsure*, of seventy-four guns, and contributed essentially to the success of the day. From a part of the mainmast of *L'Orient*, which was picked up by the *Swiftsure*, Hallowell directed his carpenter to make a coffin, which was sent to Nelson with the following letter : —

"Sir, I have taken the liberty of presenting you a coffin made from the mainmast of *L'Orient*, that when you have finished your military career in this world, you may be buried in one of your trophies. But that that period may be far distant is the earnest wish of your sincere friend,

BENJAMIN HALLOWELL."

Southey, in his "Life of Nelson," remarks: "An offering so strange, and yet so suited to the occasion, was received in the spirit in which it was sent. And, as if he felt it good for him, now that he was at the summit of his wishes, to have death before his eyes, he ordered the coffin to be placed upright in his cabin. . . . . An old favorite servant entreated him so earnestly to let it be removed, that at length he consented to have the coffin carried below; but he gave strict orders that it should be safely stowed, and reserved for the purpose for which its brave and worthy donor had designed it."

After the battle, Nelson said, that had it not been for Trowbridge, Ball, Hood, and Hallowell, he should have sunk under the fatigue of refitting the squadron. "All," he stated, "had done well ; but these officers were his supporters."

In 1799, Sir Benjamin was engaged in the attacks on the castles of St. Elmo and Capua, and was honored with the Neapolitan Order of St. Ferdinand and Merit. Two years later, he fell in with the French squadron, and surrendered his ship — the *Swiftsure* — after a sharp contest. During the peace of Amiens, he was stationed on the coast of Africa. He was with Hood in the reduction of St. Lucia and Tobago; with Nelson in the West Indies ; in command of the convoy of the second expedition to Egypt ; with Martin, off the mouth of the Rhone, where he assisted in driving on shore several French ships-of-war; and in the Mediterranean. His last duty seems to have been performed on the Irish station, and at the Nore.

Sir Benjamin succeeded to the estates of the Carews, of Beddington, and assumed the name and arms, pursuant to the will of his cousin, Mrs. Anne Paston Gee, who died in 1828. These estates are entailed on his sons in succession, and their male issue. He died at Beddington Park, in 1834, at the age of seventy-three. His wife was a daughter of Commissioner Inglefield, of Gibraltar Dock-yard. His son and heir, Charles Hallowell Carew, who, at the time of his decease, had attained the rank of captain in the Royal Navy, and who married Mary, daughter of the late Sir Murray Maxwell, C. B., died at the Park, in 1848. In 1851, his fifth son, Robert Hallowell Carew, late captain in the 36th Regiment, married Ann Rycroft, widow of Walter Tyson Smythes.

CARLETON, JOHN. Of Woolwich, Maine. A man, says Rev. Jacob Bailey, "of the highest integrity, the most undaunted fortitude, and inflexible loyalty." Met in a forest by near two hundred men, and required to sign a certain paper, or consent to be buried alive, he chose the latter, and assisted in digging his own grave. Swearing that he was a brave fellow, the Sons of Liberty allowed him to depart. Afterwards plundered, he escaped to the British post at the mouth of the Penobscot, and was there early in 1781. At that time, he had a wife and ten children.

CARLISLE, ABRAHAM. Of Philadelphia. When the Royal troops took possession of that city, he received a commission from Sir William Howe, to watch and guard its entrances, and to grant passports. For this offence he was tried for his life in 1778, and having been found guilty of an overt act of aiding and assisting the enemy, was executed. Thomas McKean, a signer of the Declaration of Independence, and at that time Chief Justice of Pennsylvania, presided at the trial. In 1779, and after his death, the estate of Carlisle was confiscated; but a part was restored to his son Abraham, in 1792. By some, the execution of Carlisle was denounced as judicial murder. Great efforts were made to save him.

CARLO, JOHN, and MARTIN. Of Maine. Brothers. Set out to travel to Halifax by land, in 1778, and, after enlisting with the "Rebels" to avoid detection, and various other adventures, they arrived in Nova Scotia. The year following, Martin was at Lunenburg, in that Colony, and John at the British post at the mouth of the Penobscot. In 1782 Martin had "gone to live at home in peace."

CARMAN, RICHARD. Of New York. Went to St. John, New Brunswick, at the peace, and was a grantee of that city. Sarah, his widow, died in the county of York, New Brunswick, in 1835, aged seventy-one. Several persons of the name of Carman, of Queen's County, New York, acknowledged allegiance to Lord Richard and Sir William Howe in 1776.

CARNEY, ANDREW. Of Georgia. Captain in the first battalion of the Continental line raised in that State. He lived between the Altamaha and St. Mary's Rivers, and owned a large herd of cattle, which he secretly sold to the British. After his own stock was exhausted, he began to steal from his neighbors. Alarmed, finally, for his personal safety, he purposely exposed himself to capture, and, with his son, became active on the side of the Crown. His name was stricken from the rolls of the Whig Army, not only as a deserter, but a traitor, and his property was confiscated.

CARPENTER, WILLET. Settled in New Brunswick in 1783, and died at St. John in 1833, aged seventy-seven.

CARSON, MOSES. Captain in the Continental Army. He deserted to the Royal Army in 1777. In 1779 he was caught, and tried by a court-martial, and sentenced to be drummed through the army in the vicinity of West Point, with a halter round his neck, and a label fastened to his back, bearing these words: "Moses Carson, late Captain in the American Army: — this I suffer for deserting to the enemies of the United States of North America." This punishment inflicted, he was sentenced, further, to be confined during the remainder of the war; and the Commander-in-Chief approved the finding of the Court.

CASTILLES, WILLIAM. Of Albany, New York. In 1780, a lieutenant in Cuyler's corps, and stationed on Long Island. At the peace, accompanied by his family and by six servants, he went from New York to Shelburne, Nova Scotia, where the Crown granted him fifty acres of land, one town and one water-lot. His losses, in consequence of his loyalty, were estimated at £500.

CAYFORD, RICHARD. Of New Jersey. Convicted of enmity to his country, of "cursing and ill-treating all Congresses and Committees," by the Committee of Cumberland County; and, January, 1776, ordered by the Committee of Safety to be disarmed, to pay the expenses of proceedings against him, to be kept in close prison until he should manifest contrition for his offences, and give security for his future good behavior. He entered the service of the Crown, and in 1777 was a captain in the New Jersey Volunteers.

CAZNEAU, ANDREW. Of Boston. His name is found among the Addressers of Hutchinson in 1774, and among those of Gage in 1775, and in the Banishment and Proscription Act of 1778. He was educated to the bar; was a barrister-of-law and a Judge of Admiralty; and a gentleman of character, talents, and virtue. In 1775 he went to England; but not remaining long there, took up his residence in Bermuda, where he held an honorable post under the Crown. He returned to Boston in 1788, and died at Roxbury, in 1792. His wife was Hannah, daughter of John Hammock, merchant, of Boston. The only daughter who survived him married Thomas Brewer, a merchant of the same town, who, as is supposed, perished about the year 1812, on a voyage from the Cape of Good Hope to Sumatra. The property of Mr. Cazneau escaped the Confiscation Act, and was inherited by Mrs. Brewer. That lady, a venerable relic of the "old school" of manners, respected and beloved, died at Eastport, Maine, September, 1851, aged eighty.

CAZNEAU, EDWARD. Of Boston. He was the foreman in the druggist store of Dr. Sylvester Gardiner, and in 1776 went to Halifax. At the peace he returned to the United

States, and settled as a physician at Charleston, South Carolina. He died in Boston, unmarried.

CECIL, LEONARD. Of Maryland. Went to England. In July, 1779, he was in London, and met with other Loyalists at the Crown and Anchor Tavern.

CHALMERS, GEORGE. Of Maryland. Was a native of Scotland, and was born in 1742. After receiving an education at King's College, Aberdeen, and after studying law at Edinburgh, he emigrated to Maryland, and entered upon the practice of his profession. The revolutionary troubles caused his return to England, where he was soon appointed to office. For many years he filled the station of chief clerk of the Committee of the Privy Council. He died in England in 1825, aged eighty-two. In person, he was tall, stout, and manly, and so nearly resembled Lord Melville, that they were often taken for each other.

He possessed rare opportunities for the examination of State papers, which he diligently improved. As a writer he was able, honest, and labor-loving, but strongly prejudiced. He was never so happy, I will venture to say, as when delving among State papers. He had official concern with those of England, for nearly half a century. His historical works were numerous, are highly esteemed, and generally cited by annalists. His style is concise and vigorous, but is deficient in simplicity, clearness, and finish. He designed to inform political men about political events, rather than to amuse and please the general reader. He was fond of short and pithy expressions; but what he thus meant for maxims, is not always beautiful or sound. His "Political Annals of the United Colonies" appeared in 1780; his "Estimate of the Strength of Great Britain," in 1782; his Opinions on Subjects of Law and Policy, arising from American Independence," in 1784; his "Opinions of Lawyers and English Jurisprudence," in 1814. His "Life of Mary, Queen of Scots," published in 1822, shows the ardor and zeal which he could bring to bear upon a favorite subject; it is the plea of an advocate, to prove from official documents, that this unfortunate daughter of the Stuarts was innocent of the murder of her second husband; and most manfully and earnestly did he perform the task.

In 1845, his "Introduction to the History of the Revolt of the British Colonies" was issued at Boston. Its publication was commenced in England during the Revolution, but was abandoned, and the part printed suppressed. As Mr. Chalmers had access to the highest sources of information, as he possessed remarkable industry, the "Introduction" is valuable to students of history. It embraces a political view of all the Colonies, and of the whole period between the early settlements in Virginia and the close of the reign of George the Second. But the author's dislike to New England was unconquerable, and is sometimes manifested at the expense of truth and propriety. It was meant to serve a particular end, and implicit faith, therefore, is not due to his statements or conclusions; for, as already remarked, his antipathies were strong, and sometimes disturbed his judgment. But he often laments and severely rebukes the inattention, weakness, and ignorance which prevailed in the councils of England with regard to her American Colonies; and few who administered her affairs during the period of which he speaks, escape his censures. Still, the leading principle or doctrine of the work is, that British subjects in America were allowed far too much freedom, and that their final independence was the natural result of continued and ill-advised indulgence. In other words, he thought that carelessness and kindness, and not extreme watchfulness and undue severity, were the causes of their "Revolt." His opening passage is singular, and thus: "Whether the famous achievements of Columbus introduced the greatest good or evil by discovering a New World to the Old, has in every succeeding age offered a subject for disputation." Perhaps, were he now alive, he might so far yield his prejudices as to admit that the "good of the achievement" greatly predominates over the "evil." He was a stout, and it is readily conceded, an honest Loyalist. But since he would have kept the New World in a state of vassalage to the

Old, and would have had our country to remain as it was when he wrote of it, there need be no better refutation of his political errors than can be found in contrasting his own account of our condition as Colonies with our present wealth and power.

CHALMERS, JAMES. Of Maryland. He was a gentleman of consideration in his neighborhood, and raised and commanded a corps called the Maryland Loyalists, with the rank of Lieutenant-Colonel. Though more successful than Colonel Clifton, he does not appear to have completed his quota of recruits. His corps was in service in 1782, but was very deficient in numbers. He himself went to England; but, in September, 1783, the Maryland Loyalists embarked at New York for St. John, New Brunswick; were wrecked near Cape Sable, and more than half their number perished.

CHALONER, NIAYON. Settled in New Brunswick, and was Register of Deeds and Wills for King's County. He died at Kingston in 1835.

CHALONER, WALTER. Of Rhode Island, and sheriff of the county of Newport. He was at New York in 1782, a deputy commissary of prisoners. In 1783 he was one of the fifty-five petitioners for lands in Nova Scotia. [See *Abijah Willard*.] He went to St. John, New Brunswick, at the close of the contest, and was a grantee of that city. He died at St. John in 1792. Ann, his widow, died in 1803. Elizabeth, his daughter, in 1814, and John, his son, in 1827.

CHALONER, WILLIAM. Of Newport, Rhode Island. Went to Nova Scotia, and died there in 1792.

CHAMPNEY, EBENEZER. Of New Ipswich, New Hampshire. He was born at Cambridge, Massachusetts, and graduated at Harvard University in 1762. He designed to enter the ministry, and actually officiated for some time; but, relinquishing theology for the law, entered the office of Samuel Livermore, and was admitted to the bar in 1768. He was "a moderate Tory," deprecating war, and wishing to preserve his loyalty. During hostilities, he was very unpopular. After the war, however, he gave his adhesion to the new Government; and, in 1795, was appointed Judge of Probate for Hillsborough County. He died in 1810, aged sixty-seven.

CHANDLER, REV. THOMAS B., D. D. Of Elizabethtown, New Jersey. Episcopal minister. He was born in Woodstock, Connecticut, and graduated at Yale College in 1745. Bred a Congregationalist, he embraced Episcopacy in 1748; and, three years later, went to England for ordination. On his return, he became Rector of St. John's Church, and long maintained a high character for erudition and talents. He was an early and an uncompromising Loyalist. He had a contest with William Livingston on the subject of Episcopacy, before the Revolution; and he is among the persons to whom was ascribed the famous pamphlets, "A Friendly Address to all Reasonable Americans," and "What think ye of Congress now?" He advocated the appointment of Bishops for the Colonies, in an Address to the Episcopalians of Virginia. In 1776, he, with others, petitioned the King for a grant of 100,000 acres of land in Canada, in consideration of their eminent services to the Crown, &c. His flock diminished in consequence of his political views and the manner of expressing them; but he was not molested, or treated with personal indignity. He was elected first Bishop of Nova Scotia, but declined on account of failing health. He lingered under a painful disease for ten years, and died in 1790, aged sixty-four. Jane, his widow, died in 1801, at the age of sixty-eight. General Maxwell, in a communication to the Legislature, in 1779, said of this lady: "There is not a Tory that passes in or out of New Jersey . . . . but waits on Mrs. Chandler, and mostly all the British officers going in or out on parole or exchange, wait on her; in short, the Governor, the whole of the Tories, and many of the Whigs. I think she would be much better off in New York, and to take her baggage with her, that she might have nothing to come back for."

One of his daughters, who died in 1806, was the wife of General E. B. Dayton; another, who died in 1847, of Bishop

Hobart; and the youngest, who was living in 1857, of William Dayton. Dr. Chandler was an able man. He "was large and portly, of fine personal appearance, of a countenance expressive of high intelligence, though considerably marred by the small pox, of an uncommonly fine blue eye, of a strong, commanding voice, and a great lover of music."

CHANDLER, WILLIAM. Of New Jersey. Son of Rev. Dr. Thomas B. Chandler. He graduated at King's (Columbia) College, in 1774. He fled in January, 1776, on account of his loyalty and parentage, but returned in December, and remained until the evacuation of Elizabethtown by the Royal troops, January, 1777. He states these facts in a memorial to Lord George Germain, in 1779, and adds, that General Skinner gave him a warrant to be captain in the New Jersey Volunteers, April, 1777, but that he had received no pay for two years; and he prays his Lordship's recommendation to Sir Henry Clinton, for a commission. He died in England in 1784, at the age of twenty-eight.

CHANDLER, JOHN. Of Worcester, Massachusetts. "The honest Refugee." He was born in New London, Connecticut, in 1720. When at the age of eleven years, his father removed to Worcester, where he held the principal county offices. To these, the subject of this notice, succeeded. He was a Colonel in the militia, and was in service in the French war; and he was Sheriff, Judge of Probate, and County Treasurer. In 1774, he was driven from his family, and took refuge in Boston. In 1776, he accompanied the Royal Army to Halifax; and, two years after, was proscribed and banished. His estate, which was appraised at £36,190 1s., was confiscated. I am assured that, while he was at Boston, he was supported for a considerable time by the sale of silver plate sent him by his family; and that, when he left home, he had no intention of quitting the country. I am assured, also, that when the Whig Commissioners took an inventory of his household furniture, the females were plundered of their very clothing. His adherence to the Crown, and his departure for England, seem to have been his only offences; yet he was treated as harshly as though he had borne arms in the field. The late President Dwight spoke of Colonel Chandler and his family, as distinguished for talents and virtue. He represented to the Commissioners of Loyalist Claims, that his losses of real and personal estate were £11,067 sterling, and of business, offices, &c., about £6,000 sterling more. His statement was so moderate in comparison with many others of the same nature, that he was allowed the full amount; and was afterwards known in England as "the honest Refugee." Here, he is spoken of as having been "cheerful in temperament, engaging in manner, hospitable as a citizen, friendly and kind as a neighbor, industrious and enterprising as a merchant, and successful as a man of business." He died in 1800, aged eighty, in London. In 1741, he marmaried Dorothy, daughter of Colonel Nathaniel Paine, who bore him four children, and died in 1745. His second wife was Mary, daughter of Colonel Church, of Bristol, Rhode Island, a descendant of the warrior who fought King Philip,— who was the mother of thirteen children, and who died at Worcester in 1783. The notices of her decease speak of her as an excellent woman. Colonel Chandler was buried at Islington; an iron fence and a slab mark the spot where he rests. His portrait, in oil, is preserved in the rooms of the American Antiquarian Society, Worcester. George Bancroft, the distinguished historian, and the widow of the late Governor John Davis, of Massachusetts, are Colonel Chandler's grandchildren.

CHANDLER, CLARK. Of Worcester, Massachusetts. Son of Colonel John. He was born in that town in 1743. At first a clerk in the office of the Register of Probate, he became joint Register with Timothy Paine. In 1774 he entered upon the town Records a remonstrance of the Loyalists, to the great anger of the Whigs, who, in town meeting, voted that he should then and there "obliterate, erase, or otherwise deface, the said recorded protest, and the names thereunto subscribed, so that it may become illegible and unintelligible." A vote of admonition followed, which is too long to insert in this work. Mr. Chandler, as required, in open town meeting, blotted out the obnoxious record, and the work of the pen not being satisfactory, his fingers were dipped in ink and drawn over the page.

He left home in June, 1775, and went to Halifax, Nova Scotia, and thence to Canada. He returned in September of the same year, and surrendered himself a prisoner to the common jail. Confinement impaired his health, and he was removed to his mother's house. Finally, he was allowed to go to Lancaster, on giving security that he would not depart from that town. He returned to Worcester, subsequently, and engaged in trade. His person was small. He wore bright red small-clothes, was odd and singular, and often provoked the jeers of those with whom he mingled; but, apt at reply, "he paid the jokers in their own coin." He was never married. He died in Worcester in 1804.

CHANDLER, RUFUS. Of Worcester, Massachusetts. Fifth child of Colonel John, by Mary Church, his second wife. He was born in that town in 1747, and graduated at Harvard University in 1766. He studied law with his uncle, James Putnam, and opened an office in Worcester, and continued in practice there until September, 1774, when the courts were closed by popular tumult. He was one of the barristers and attornies who addressed Hutchinson, in the last-mentioned year. He went to Halifax in 1776, and in 1778 was proscribed and banished. His mother used a part of his estate for the support of his daughter; but the remainder, appraised at £820 9s. was confiscated. He died in London in 1823, at the age of seventy-six, and was buried at Islington, by the side of his father. His wife was Elizabeth Putnam; his only child, who bore her mother's name, married Solomon Vose, of Augusta, Maine.

CHANDLER, GARDNER. Of Hardwich, Massachusetts. Son of Colonel John. He was born in 1749, and was a merchant in that town. His property was confiscated. He made acknowledgments satisfactory to his townsmen, who voted, that, as he had said he was sorry for his past conduct, they " would treat him as a friend and neighbor as long as he should behave well." He removed to Brattleboro', Vermont, and again to Hinsdale, New Hampshire. He died in the last-named town. His wife was Elizabeth, daughter of Brigadier Timothy Ruggles.

CHANDLER, NATHANIEL. Of Worcester, Massachusetts. Son of Colonel John. He was born in that town in 1750; graduated at Harvard University in 1768; and commenced the practice of the law in Petersham. He was one of the eighteen country gentlemen who addressed Gage on his departure, in 1775. In 1776 he went to Halifax. In 1778 he was proscribed and banished. Entering the British service, he led a corps of Volunteers. He returned to Petersham in 1784, and engaged in trade, but relinquished business on account of ill health, and returned to Worcester. Citizenship was restored in 1789, by Act of the Legislature of Massachusetts. He was a very pleasant companion, and a favorite singer of songs in social parties. In early life he was a pupil of John Adams. His brother-in-law, the Rev. Dr. Bancroft, wrote that " he possessed personal manliness and beauty," that " he was endowed with a good mind and a lively imagination," that " in disposition he was cheerful," but that " his course of life drew him from those pursuits which might have rendered him a distinguished character." He never married. He died at Worcester in 1801.

CHANDLER, WILLIAM. Of Worcester, Massachusetts. Eighth child of Colonel John. He was born in that town in 1752, and graduated at Harvard University in 1772. At that time, the students in that institution were ranked according to " dignity of family;" and William was placed in the highest class. He was one of the eighteen country gentlemen who were driven from their homes to Boston, and who addressed Gage on his departure, in 1775. In 1776 he went to Halifax. He was proscribed under the Act of 1778, but returned to Massachusetts after the close of the Revolution. He died in Worcester in 1793. Seven pairs of silk hose, at fourteen shillings; plated shoe-buckless, six shillings; and two pairs of velvet breeches, are among the articles in the inventory of his estate.

CHANDLER, THOMAS. Of Cumberland County, "New Hampshire Grants." Son of John, of Woodstock, Connecticut, and uncle of John, "the honest Refugee." He was born in Woodstock in 1709. He was a lieutenant-colonel in the expedition to Cape Breton, in 1745; and about the year 1762, went to Walpole, New Hampshire, intending to settle there. In 1764, he removed to the "Grants," and two years after obtained for himself and others a patent of the township of Chester. As the grant was from the Governor of New York, he was held to be a "Tory," on that account alone. He, and his sons John and Thomas, were allowed their choice of five hundred acres each, as the first three settlers. In 1775, when the difficulties occurred between the Whigs and Loyalists at Westminster, [see *W. Patterson*,] he was Chief Justice of the County Court, and was induced by Judge Sabin, an associate, to favor the New York or Tory side of the controversy. The Whigs put him in jail, as being of the "Court party." Towards the close of his life he became poor, and was imprisoned for debt. He died in Westminster jail, in 1785. One account is, that he was buried within its limits; another, that his remains were disposed of "without the ceremony of a funeral." His wife was Elizabeth Eliot, of the lineage of John, the "Apostle of the Indians."

CHANDLER, GARDINER. Of Worcester, Massachusetts. Brother of Colonel John. He was born in Woodstock, Connecticut, in 1723. In the French war he was a major, and was in service at the surrender of Fort William Henry. He was Treasurer of Worcester County eight years, and succeeded his brother John, as sheriff, in 1762. He presented Gage an Address in behalf of the Judges of the Court of Common Pleas, in 1774; and was compelled by a Convention of the Committees of Correspondence to sign a "Recantation." In time, he regained the confidence of the community, and was suffered to live undisturbed. He died in Worcester, in 1782. His first wife was Hannah Greene, of Providence,

Rhode Island; his second, Ann Leonard, of Norton, Massachusetts.

CHANDLER, JOSHUA. Of New Haven, Connecticut. Barrister-at-law. He was born in Woodstock, in that State, in 1728, and graduated at Yale College in 1747. He was a member of the General Assembly in 1775. In an Address to Governor Franklin, August 10, 1782, he said: "After placing the most unlimited confidence in the Royal assurances we have at different times received, and after our sacrifice and loss of property, we should feel ourselves but ill requited, were we to be abandoned and dismembered from the empire; but our misery and distress must be complete should we become subjected finally to a Republican system."

His property in and near New Haven, which he valued at £30,000, was confiscated. In 1783 he went to Annapolis, Nova Scotia, and thence to England, to obtain compensation for his losses. In March, 1787, he crossed the Bay of Fundy, to meet the Commissioners on Loyalist Claims at St. John, New Brunswick, and, in a violent snow-storm, missing the entrance of the harbor, was wrecked on Musquash Point, about nine miles from the city. He himself perished by a fall from a precipice; his daughter Elizabeth, and the widow of Major Alexander Grant, died of cold and exhaustion. The Hon. Charles W. Upham, of Salem, Massachusetts, is a grandson. Mr. Chandler's son Samuel died in Nova Scotia about the year 1840, aged eighty; and his son Charles died in the same Province in 1853, at the age of eighty-five. His daughter Sarah married Hon. Amos Botsford.

CHANDLER, WILLIAM. Of New Haven, Connecticut. Son of Joshua. He graduated at Yale College in 1773. He conducted the Royal forces to that town, in 1779, and was a captain in a Loyalist corps. At the peace he retired to Nova Scotia. He was with his father [see *Joshua Chandler*] in the fatal voyage across the Bay of Fundy, in 1787, and was crushed to death between the vessel and the rocks. The ill-fated Nathan Hale was a class-mate.

CHANDLER, THOMAS. Of Connecticut. Son of Joshua.

An officer in a Loyalist corps. Assisted his brother William in guiding the Royal forces to New Haven in 1779. Went with others of the family to Nova Scotia, in 1783. Married a daughter of Major Alexander Grant, whose widow perished with the father of the subject of this notice, in 1787.

CHANDLER, JOHN. Of Connecticut. Son of Joshua. Went to Nova Scotia in 1783; but returned to his native State, and died at New Haven.

CHAPMAN, SAMUEL. Of Pennsylvania. He joined the British Army, as was averred, in 1776, and accepted a commission. He was captured by a vessel-of-war, and carried to Massachusetts. In 1780, the President of the Council wrote to ask that, having been attainted of treason in Pennsylvania, and particularly obnoxious as an officer of a corps employed to harass the inhabitants, in stealing horses and similar offences, he might not be exchanged in the ordinary way, but be kept in custody until an opportunity occurred to send him home to "be dealt with according to his demerits." He was tried in 1781, and much to the disappointment of the "violent Whigs," acquitted.

CHAPMAN, JOHN. Was a magistrate in New Brunswick, and died at Dorchester, in that Colony, in 1833, aged seventy-two.

CHASE, SHADRACH. Of Massachusetts. Was proscribed and banished in 1778. In 1782 he was an ensign in De Lancey's Third Battalion. He went to St. John, New Brunswick, at the peace, and was one of the grantees of that city. He received half-pay. His death occurred in New Brunswick about the year 1829.

CHAUNCEY, JOSIAH, and ISAAC. Of Amherst, Massachusetts. The first was charged with disaffection to the popular cause, examined in 1775, and required to surrender his firearms, and to burn all the commissions he had ever held under the Crown. He gave up the arms, which, however, the Whigs soon voted to return to him. He was a great-grandson of Charles Chauncey, President of Harvard University. Isaac was advertised by the Committee of that town, August,

1776, as convicted of being notoriously inimical to the American States, and as having disregarded the limits which they had assigned to him.

CHESNEY, ALEXANDER. Of South Carolina. A gentleman of family and fortune, who settled in that Colony about the year 1758. In the Revolution he bore arms on the side of the Crown. He left several children, of whom were Major-General Chesney, the Oriental explorer, and Captain Charles Chesney, who died of his wounds in India. Four sons of the latter have been distinguished in the military schools of England; and a daughter, Mrs. Pullan, lives (1859) in New York.

CHEW, BENJAMIN. Of Pennsylvania. Was Recorder of Philadelphia, Register of Wills, and Attorney-General, and, finally, Chief Justice. His course was doubtful in the early part of the controversy, and he was claimed by both parties. In 1774, Washington dined with him. The same year, John Adams records: "Dined with Mr. Chew, Chief Justice of the Province. . . . . We were shown into a grand entry and staircase, and into an elegant and magnificent chamber, until dinner. About four o'clock we were called down. . . . . The furniture was all rich. Turtle, flummery, jellies, sweetmeats of twenty sorts, trifles, ... and then a desert of raisins, almonds, pears, peaches. Wines most excellent and admirable. I drank Madeira at a great rate, and found no inconvenience in it."

In 1776 his opposition to the Whigs was fixed, and he retired to private life. After the Revolution, and in 1790, he was appointed President of the High Court of Errors and Appeals, and held the office until the tribunal was abolished in 1806. He died in 1810, aged eighty-seven. His father, the Hon. Samuel Chew, was of the religion of the Friends, and a judge and physician. William Tilghman, who became Chief Justice of Pennsylvania, read law in his office, as did Francis Hopkinson, a signer of the Declaration of Independence. Judge Chew's daughter Sophia married Henry Philips, of the family of Philips of Bank Hall, county of Lancaster, England; his daughter Henrietta died at Philadelphia in 1848, aged eighty-one. The wife of James M. Mason, late Senator in Congress from Virginia, is a granddaughter.

CHEW, WILLIAM. He was a lieutenant in a corps of Loyalists. He settled in New Brunswick at the close of the war, and received half-pay. He died at Fredericton in 1812, aged sixty-four.

CHILD, JOSEPH. Of the New York Artillery. In 1776 he was tried by a court-martial for defrauding Christopher Stetson of a dollar; for drinking damnation to all Whigs and Sons of Liberty; and for profane cursing and swearing. He was found guilty, and sentenced to be drummed out of the army.

CHIPMAN, WARD. Of Massachusetts. He was born in 1754, and graduated at Harvard University in 1770. In 1775 he was driven from his habitation to Boston, and was one of the eighteen country gentlemen who that year were Addressers of Gage. He left Boston at the evacuation in 1776, and went to Halifax, and thence to England, where he was allowed a pension. Relinquishing his stipend in less than a year, he returned to his native country, and joined the King's troops at New York. During the remainder of the war he was employed in the military department and Court of Admiralty. In 1782 he held the office of Deputy Mustermaster-General of the Loyalist forces. In 1783 he was one of the fifty-five who petitioned for extensive grants of lands in Nova Scotia. [See *Abijah Willard.*] Removing to New Brunswick, he attained the highest honors. He was a member of the House of Assembly, Advocate-General, Solicitor-General, Justice of the Supreme Court, Member of the Council, and President and Commander-in-Chief of the Colony. He died at Fredericton, the capital, in 1824. His remains were taken to St. John, where a tablet recites his public services. The wife of the Hon. William Gray, of Boston, was his sister. Elizabeth, his widow, died at St. John in 1852, in her eighty-sixth year. Ward, his only child, graduated at Harvard University in 1805, held many places of trust, was finally Chief Justice of New Brunswick, and died at St. John in 1851, in his sixty-fifth year. While the Prince of Wales was in that city, August, 1860, he occupied the Chipman mansion.

CHRISTIE, JAMES, JR. Merchant, of Baltimore. In July, 1775, the Committee of that city published him "as an enemy to his country," for sentiments contained in a letter written by him to Lieutenant-Colonel Gabriel Christie of the British Army, which letter had been intercepted and laid before them. Regarding "his crime of a dangerous and atrocious nature," the Committee determined to consult their delegates at the Continental Congress, and meantime to keep a guard at his house to prevent his escape; he to pay the expense thereof, "each man five shillings for each twenty-four hours, and the officers seven shillings and sixpence." This Committee was large, and on this occasion thirty-four members were present; the vote against Christie was unanimous. He had recently lost his wife, and was at this time sick and confined to his bed. Near the close of July, however, the guard was dismissed by a vote of twenty-one to fourteen, on his parole not to quit the Province without leave of the Whig authorities, and to abide whatever sentence should be pronounced against him, with six gentlemen as sureties, to be bound to submit, in case of his escape, "to the same punishment as would have been inflicted on him if he had not departed."

In August, his case was taken up in the Maryland Convention, when, after reading his memorial, it was resolved that "he ought to be considered as an enemy to America;" and that he make a deposit of £500 sterling on account of his proportion of the expense incurred for the defence of the country; "the overplus, if any, to be returned, after a reconciliation shall happily be effected with Great Britain."

CHRISTIE, CN. Of Maryland. He adhered to the Royal Army, and his estate was confiscated. But the Act did not apply to his debts; since, after the Revolution, he recovered of Colonel Richard Graves of that State, upwards of £1200 sterling, for a debt due him before the war.

Chubb, John. Of Philadelphia. Went to St. John, New Brunswick, at the peace, and was a grantee of that city. In 1795 he was a member of the Loyal Artillery Company. He died in 1822, aged sixty-nine. His son, the late Henry Chubb, was proprietor of the "St. John Courier" many years.

Church, Doctor Benjamin. Of Massachusetts. Proscribed and banished. He was equally distinguished as a scholar, physician, poet, and politician, and among the Whigs he stood as prominent, and was as active and as popular, as either Warren, Hancock, or Samuel Adams. He graduated at Harvard University in 1754. About 1768 he built an elegant house at Raynham, which occasioned pecuniary embarrassments, and it has been conjectured that his difficulties from this source caused his defection to the Whig cause. However this may be, he was regarded as a traitor, having been suspected of communicating intelligence to Governor Gage, and of receiving a reward in money therefor. His crime was subsequently proved, Washington presiding, when he was convicted of holding a criminal correspondence with the enemy. After his trial by a court-martial, he was examined before the Provincial Congress, of which body he was a member, and though he made an ingenious and able defence, was expelled. Allowed to leave the country, finally, he embarked for the West Indies, and was never heard of afterward. Sarah, his widow, died in England in 1788.

Chypher, Jacob. See [*Jacob Sypher.*]

Clark, James. Of Rhode Island. Went to St. John, New Brunswick, at the peace, and was one of the grantees of that city. He died at St. John in 1820, aged ninety. His son James died at the same place in 1803, at the age of forty-one.

Clark, John. Of Rhode Island. At the peace he settled at St. John, New Brunswick. He arrived at that city on the 29th of June, 1783, at which time only two log huts had been erected on its site. He received, the same year, the grant of land. The Government gave him, and every other grantee, five hundred feet of very ordinary boards towards covering their buildings. City lots sold in 1783 from two to twenty dollars. He bought one for the price of executing the deed of conveyance, and "a treat." Mr. Clark was clerk of Trinity Church nearly fifty years. He died at St. John, in 1853, in his ninety-fourth year, leaving numerous descendants.

CLARK, JOSEPH. A physician, of Stratford, Connecticut. In 1776 he fled to the British Army. His wife and children, whom he left at home, were sent to New York, where he joined them. He went to New Brunswick, accompanied by his family, consisting of nine persons, in 1783, and resumed the practice of medicine. He settled at Maugerville, on the river St. John, and was a Judge of the Court of Common Pleas for the county of Sunbury. In 1799 he visited his friends in the United States. He was a physician, in business, for quite half a century. He died at Maugerville in 1813, aged seventy-nine; and his widow, Isabella Elizabeth, died the same year, at the age of seventy-one.

CLARK, JOSEPH. Of Stratford, Connecticut. Son of Dr. Joseph Clark. He accompanied the family to New Brunswick, and became a resident of the Colony. He died in New York, while on a visit to some friends, in 1828, at the age of sixty-five.

CLARK, JOHN. Of New Jersey. Went to New Brunswick in 1783. Died in Wickham, in that Province, in 1848.

CLARK, NEHEMIAH. During the Revolution he was a surgeon in the King's service. He went to St. John, New Brunswick, at the peace, and was one of the grantees of that city. He received half-pay. He died at Douglas, in that Province, in 1825, aged eighty-six.

CLARK, SAMUEL. Of New Jersey. In 1780 he was detected in conducting an illicit trade with the Royal forces, and committed to prison. A Loyalist of this name was the grantee of a lot in the city of St. John, in 1783, and died in 1804.

CLARKE, REV. WILLIAM. Of Dedham, Massachusetts. Episcopal minister. He was son of Rev. Peter Clarke of Danvers, Massachusetts, and graduated at Harvard University in 1759. After ordination in England, he became Rector of St. Paul's Church. He lived in peace in Dedham until the spring of 1777, when he was sentenced to be confined on board a ship, because he refused " to acknowledge the Independency of America," which, he adds, " was contrary to the sentiments I had of my duty to my king, my country, and my God." Released, and permitted to depart, he went to Rhode Island, thence to New York, thence to Ireland, thence to England. In 1786, he was at Halifax, Nova Scotia, and soon after removed to Digby. He returned to the United States, finally, and died in Quincy, Massachusetts, in 1815. His wife was Mrs. Dunbar, a widow. The Rev. Mr. Bailey wrote, at the time of the marriage, she is "a little, pretty, delicate, chattering woman, about twenty-eight, as unable to rough it as himself."

CLARKE, JAMES. Of Rhode Island. Secretary of the Association of Loyal Refugees, formed at Newport, March, 1779. The object appears in a paper signed by himself, namely, to " retaliate upon and make reprisal against the inhabitants of the several Provinces in America, in actual rebellion against their Sovereign." The Association was formed under the sanction of the British Commander-in-Chief in Rhode Island, who gave commissions to the officers.

To execute the purpose above indicated, they conceived " themselves warranted, by the laws of God and man, to wage war upon their inhuman persecutors," the Rebels, "and to use every means in their power, to obtain redress and compensation for the indignities and losses they had suffered." The document concludes with an invitation to all who had preserved their loyalty, as well as those who had grown weary of Congressional tyranny and paper money, and who hated French frippery, French politics, French religion and alliances, to join with them in their endeavors to recover for their country its ancient form of government. He wrote Governor Franklin twice the same year, giving an account of the proceedings and success of the Association. In 1783, Mr. Clarke was a petitioner for lands in Nova Scotia. [See *Abijah Willard.*] He was at Halifax in 1797, and his wife, Mary, died there that year.

CLARKE, RICHARD. Of Boston. Merchant. Graduated at Harvard University in 1729. He and his sons were consignees of a part of the tea destroyed in Boston by the celebrated " Tea-Party," December, 1773. A great number of rioters assembled in front of his house, attempted to force an entrance, broke the windows, and otherwise damaged it. His family removed. One of the consignees, however, fired upon the mob, soon after, when they dispersed. His name is found among the Addressers of Gage. The Whigs treated him with much severity, and his son Isaac, while at Plymouth for the collection of some debts, was assaulted, and fled at midnight. He arrived in London, December 24, 1775, after a passage of " only " twenty-one days from Boston. The Loyalist Club, for a weekly dinner, was formed early in the next year, and he was one of the original members. He lived with his son-in-law, Copley, the painter, Leicester Square. He died in England in 1795. The late Lord Lyndhurst was a grandson.

CLARKE, RICHARD SAMUEL. The tablet, which covers his remains, records that he was minister of New Milford, Connecticut, nineteen years; of Gagetown, New Brunswick, twenty-five years; and of St. Stephen, New Brunswick, thirteen years: in all, an Episcopal clergyman for fifty-seven years. He was the first Rector of the Church at St. Stephen, and the oldest missionary in the present British Colonies. He was much beloved by the people of his charge, and his memory is still cherished. He died at St. Stephen, October 6, 1824, aged eighty-seven. His wife Rebecca died at the same place, May 7, 1816, aged sixty-nine. His only surviving daughter, Mary Ann, who was born in Connecticut before his removal, and who was never married, died at Gagetown, New Brunswick, February, 1844, at the age of seventy-three, highly and deservedly lamented.

CLARKE, WILLIAM. He was born at North Kingston, Rhode Island. He entered the service of the Crown, and was a captain in Colonel Whiteman's Regiment of Loyal New Englanders. He settled in New Brunswick in 1783, and was an alderman of St. John. He died in that city in 1804.

CLARKE, REV. RICHARD. Of Charleston, South Carolina. Rector of St. Philip's Church. Went to England, and was Rector of Hartley, Kent. Died suddenly in England, in 1802, in his eighty-third year.

CLARKE, ISAAC WINSLOW. Of Boston. He became Commissary-General of Lower Canada, and died in that Colony in 1822, after he had embarked for England. His daughter Susan married Charles Richard Ogden, Esq., Solicitor-General of Lower Canada, in 1829.

CLARKE, JONATHAN. Of Boston. Son of Richard Clarke. Went to England; was a member of the Loyalist Club, London, 1776; had lodgings in Brompton Row the next year. In 1778, proscribed and banished. After the Revolution he was in Canada.

CLARKE, GEORGE. Secretary of the Colony of New York. Went to England and died there in 1777. He was of the family of Clarke of Hyde Hall, Cheshire, England.

CLARKE, ALEXANDER. Died at Waterborough, New Brunswick, in 1825, aged eighty-two. For several years he was Master Armorer in the Ordnance Department at St. John.

CLARKE, WILLIAM. Of New Jersey. A noted horse-thief. It was computed that, between 1776 and June, 1782, he stole upwards of one hundred valuable horses from New Jersey, which he sold to the Royal Army. It was known that he came very frequently within the American lines, but no effort of scouts and sentries to seize him proved successful. He was finally written to as by accomplices, as is said, to the effect that two fine horses were at a certain place, which he could carry off. He came, as suggested, in June, 1782, and was shot down dead in the vicinity of Woodbridge, New Jersey, by the party who devised the stratagem.

CLARKE, JOHN. Died at Windsor, Nova Scotia, in 1825, aged eighty-four.

CLAUS, DANIEL. He married a daughter of Sir William Johnson, and served for a considerable time in the Indian Department of Canada, under his brother-in-law, Colonel Guy Johnson. Brant, the celebrated Mohawk chief, entertained towards him sentiments of decided personal hostility. His wife died in Canada in 1801. William Claus, Deputy Superintendent-General of Indian Affairs, was his son; and Brant, in the name of the Five Nations, made a speech of condolence on the death of Mrs. Claus, on the 24th of February of that year. William, deeply affected at the loss of his mother, was not able to reply, although he met the chiefs in council; but he afterwards transmitted a written answer.

CLAYTON, FRANCIS. Of Wilmington, North Carolina. At first a Whig, he was a member of the Committee of Safety in 1774, and a Representative in the House of Assembly; but, in the course of the war, he adhered to the Crown, and abandoned the State. He returned to Wilmington in a flag of truce, in 1782, and determined to hazard a trial for his political offences. He was owner of Clayton Hall, a very fertile plantation.

CLEGHORN, ROBERT. Of New York. At the peace, accompanied by his family of three persons, he went from New York to Shelburne, Nova Scotia, where the Crown granted him one town lot.

CLEMENTSON, SAMUEL. Of Boston. Merchant. Died at Windsor, England, in 1782, aged forty-nine.

CLEMENT, CAPTAIN JOSEPH. Of Boston. He held a commission in the Royal service during the war, and at the peace settled in New Brunswick. His wife, Mary, died at St. John in 1812.

CLEMENTS, PETER. He entered the service of the Crown, and at the close of the war was a captain in the King's American Regiment. In 1783 he went to St. John, New Brunswick, and was a grantee of that city. He received half-pay. He removed to the county of York, and was a magistrate.

He died at his residence on the river St. John, near Fredericton, in 1833, at the age of ninety-four. His daughter Clarissa died in 1814, aged thirty-two. His daughter Abigail Julia married Charles R. Hatheway, Esq., of St. Andrew, New Brunswick.

CLINCH, PETER. In 1782 he was a lieutenant in the Royal Fensible Americans, and adjutant of the corps. He settled in New Brunswick, and received half-pay. He died in the county of Charlotte, in that Province.

CLOPPER, JAMES. He was a lieutenant in a corps of Loyalists, and at the close of the contest settled in New Brunswick, enjoyed half-pay, and was a magistrate of the county of York. He died at Fredericton, in 1823, aged sixty-seven.

CLOPPER, GARRETT. In 1782 he was an ensign in the New York Volunteers, and quartermaster of the corps. He went to St. John, New Brunswick, in 1783, and was the grantee of a city lot. He received half-pay, was sergeant-at-arms of the House of Assembly, and a magistrate of York County. He died in that Province.

CLOSSEY, SAMUEL. Of New York. Physician. He was a native of Ireland. Previous to his emigration to America he had attained eminence in his profession, not only by successful practice but by the publication of a work entitled "Observations on some of the Diseases of the Human Body, chiefly taken from the Dissections of Morbid Bodies." While at New York, he was chosen to the Anatomical Chair, and to the Professorship of Natural Philosophy in King's (Columbia) College; and, upon the organization of a Medical School, was placed at the head of the Department of Anatomy. He returned to his native country in consequence of the Revolution, and died there soon after his arrival.

CLOWES. There were several Loyalists of this name in New York. Gerardus Clowes was a captain, and Samuel and John were lieutenants in De Lancey's Third Battalion, and, with Timothy, went to St. John, New Brunswick, at the peace, and were grantees of that city. The three who were officers received half-pay. Samuel, John, and Timothy lived for some time in New Brunswick, but their fate has not been ascertained. Gerardus, who was a major of militia and a magistrate, and resided in the county of Sunbury, was killed in 1798 by a fall from his horse. In 1781 a person of the name of Samuel Clowes, who had been an Addresser of Governor Robertson, was appointed Clerk and Surrogate of Queen's County, New York, and died at Hempstead in the year 1800, aged seventy-six. This Samuel, says my informant, " was in office a large part of his life."

COCHRAN, CAPTAIN JOHN. Of Portsmouth, New Hampshire. Son of James Cochran, and a native of Londonderry. Was proscribed and banished. The "Portsmouth Journal," from which paper I derive the following, states that the account is published on the authority of his daughter, who (November, 1845), is still living in that town. Captain Cochran led a seafaring life in his younger days, and sailed out of Portsmouth a number of years, as a ship-master, with brilliant success. A short period before the war of the Revolution broke out, he was appointed to the command of the fort in Portsmouth harbor. The day after the battle of Lexington, he and his family were made prisoners of war by a company of volunteers under the command of John Sullivan, afterwards the distinguished Major-General Sullivan of the Revolution, President of New Hampshire, &c. Captain Cochran and his family were generously liberated on parole of honor.

Not far from this time, Governor Wentworth took refuge in the fort, and Captain Cochran attended him to Boston. In his absence, the only occupants of the fort were Mrs. Cochran, a man and a maid-servant, and four children. At this time all vessels passing out of the harbor had to show their pass at the fort. An English man-of-war one day came down the river, bound out. Mrs. Cochran directed the man to hail the ship. No respect was paid to him. Mrs. Cochran then directed him to discharge one of the cannon. The terrified man said: " Ma'am, I have but one eye, and can't see the touch-hole." Taking the match, the heroic lady applied it herself; the frigate immediately hove to, and showing that all was right, was permitted to proceed. For this discharge of duty to his Majesty's Government, she received a handsome reward.

It was thought by some of the enemies of Governor Wentworth that he was still secreted at the fort, after he had left for Boston. A party one day entered the house in the fort, (the same house recently occupied by Captain Dimmick), and asked permission of Mrs. Cochran to search the rooms for the Governor. After looking up stairs in vain, they asked for a light to examine the cellar. "O yes," said a little daughter of Mrs. Cochran, "I will light you." She held the candle until they were in a part of the cellar from which she well knew they could not retreat without striking their heads against low beams, when the roguish girl blew the light out. As she anticipated, they began to bruise themselves, and they swore pretty roundly. The miss from the stairs, in an elevated tone, cried out, "Have you got him?" This arch inquiry only served to divide their curses between the impediments to their progress and the "little Tory."

Captain John Cochran, (who was a cousin, and not the father, as has been stated, of Lord Admiral Cochran) immediately joined the British in Boston, and, as it was believed, being influenced by the double motive of gratitude towards a government that had generously noticed and promoted him to offices of honor, trust, and emolument, and for the sake of retaining a valuable stipend from the Crown, remained with the British Army during the war. At the peace, he returned to St. John, New Brunswick, lived in the style of a gentleman the remainder of his days, and died at the age of fifty-five.

Among the papers of the Cochran family, we find the following letter, written from England, by Governor Wentworth, at the close of the war, to Captain John Cochran. It held out no very strong inducements for Loyalists to take refuge in England: —

"HAMMERSMITH, May 6, 1783

"MY DEAR SIR, — I received your kind letter by Captain Dawson, and render you many thanks; be assured there is scarce any object so near to me as your welfare, which I should rejoice to promote. As to my advice, at this distance from the scene of action, it can only be conjectural. However, as you ask it, I can only say, that you will find it expedient to remove to and settle in Nova Scotia. The Commander-in-Chief will most certainly cause your pay to be issued there; nor do I conceive there is any probability of its being reduced, especially as Captain Fenton's is suppressed here, among other reasons, as it is said, because you were paid in America and resident there. As to your coming here, or any other Loyalist, that can get clams and potatoes in America, they most certainly would regret making bad worse. It would be needless for me to enter into reasons; the fact is so, and you will do well to avoid it. It is the advice all our friends will be wise to follow; hard as it is, they that are fools enough to try, will find it harder here. I hope this will find you and your family in good health. We are all well. Charles is grown a stout boy; we are obliged for your kind inquiries about him. My destination is quite uncertain; like an old flapped hat, thrown off the top of an house, I am tumbling over and over in the air, and God only knows where I shall finally alight and settle to rest. It would give me great pleasure if it so happens as to afford me any means to add to the comfort of those I esteem and regard. Be assured, my dear Sir, in that description you would have my early attention. Pray present Mrs. W.'s and my compliments to your family; old Mrs. W. also begs to joins us. Benning has been nearly four years a captain, and not being able to establish his rank as he expected, has sold out, and is now in the country; so that we are all seeking something to do.

"Adieu, my dear friend, and always believe me to be, with great regard, your faithful and obedient servant,

"J. Wentworth."

Cochran, James. Of New Hampshire. His father in his youth, and about the year 1730, lived in the vicinity of the present town of Belfast, Maine. His family subsequently removed to Londonderry, New Hampshire. He went to St.

John, New Brunswick, where he closed his life in 1794, aged eighty-four years.

COCK, CLARK. Of Long Island, New York. Professed himself a loyal subject in 1776. Subsequently, his house was robbed of a considerable amount in money, and of goods to the value of £400, in 1779. Others of the name were quite as unfortunate. Thus, a party of Rebels from Connecticut plundered the dwelling of William Cock of goods to the amount of £140, in 1778; and Abraham Cock, master of the schooner *Five Brothers*, was captured early in 1779.

CODDINGTON, ASHER. Of New Jersey. Went to St. John, New Brunswick, at the evacuation of New York. Was a grantee of the former city, and of a lot at Long Beach, near General Coffin's land. Removed to Maugerville, New Brunswick, and died there, well in years, about 1828. A son was living on the island of Grand Menan in 1848.

CODNER, JAMES. In 1782 he was an ensign in the Second American Regiment. He went to St. John, New Brunswick, in 1783, and was a grantee of that city, and a magistrate of the county. He died at St. John in 1821, aged sixty-seven.

COFFIELD, THOMAS. At the termination of the war he was a lieutenant in the North Carolina Regiment. As he was preparing to leave New York, the following advertisement appeared in Rivington's paper of September 10, 1783: —

"Whereas Martha, wife of Thomas Coffield, lieutenant in the North Carolina Regiment, is concealed from him, (supposed by her mother, Melissa Carman of Hempstead,) to keep her from going with her loving husband to Nova Scotia, or St. Augustine, the public are cautioned," &c.

The "loving" and bereaved lieutenant arrived at St. John, New Brunswick, before the close of 1783, and received the grant of a city lot.

COFFIN, NATHANIEL. Of Boston. Last Receiver-General and Cashier of his Majesty's Customs at that port. An Addresser of Hutchinson, 1774, and of Gage, 1775. With his family of three persons he accompanied the Royal Army to Halifax in 1776, and in July of that year embarked for England in the ship *Aston Hall*. He died at New York in 1780. His wife was Elizabeth, daughter of Henry Barnes, merchant of Boston. Notices of several of his sons follow. I do not include Admiral Sir Isaac Coffin, Baronet, who died at Chettenham, England, in 1840, at the age of eighty; because he entered the British Navy, May, 1773, or *before* the Revolution.

COFFIN, JOHN. Of Boston. He was a son of the preceding. A warm and decided Loyalist, he volunteered to accompany the Royal Army in the battle of Breed's or Bunker's Hill, and soon after obtained a commission. He rose to the rank of captain in the Orange Rangers in a short time, and effecting an exchange into the New York Volunteers, went with that corps to Georgia, in 1778. At the battle of Savannah, at that of Hobkerk's Hill, and in the action of Cross Creek, near Charleston, and on various other occasions, his conduct won the admiration of his superiors. At the battle of Eutaw Springs, which he opened on the part of the King's troops, he was a brevet major, and his gallantry and good judgment attracted the notice and remark of General Greene, who commanded the Whig forces. He retired to New Brunswick at the close of the contest, with the rank of major, and received half-pay. He was appointed a Colonel in the British Army in 1797; a Major-General in 1803; Lieutenant-General in 1809; and General in 1819.

In the war of 1812, he raised and commanded a regiment, which was disbanded in 1815. He served in several civil offices; was a member of the House of Assembly, chief magistrate of King's County, and a member of the Council. Of the latter dignity he was deprived, in 1828, in consequence of his not having attended the sessions of the Council for several previous years. Had his place not been thus vacated, the government of the Colony would have devolved upon him as senior Councillor, during the absence of Sir Howard Douglas. Though sensitive, the personal controversies of General Coffin were not numerous. But he fought a duel with Colonel Campbell in 1783, and was wounded in his groin; and after he went to New Brunswick, he had a public controversy with a high functionary of that Province, which was long and bitter.

His estate was large and valuable, as will be seen by his own description of it in 1811, when he offered it for sale: "The Manor of Alwington, in the Parish of Westfield, King's County, situated twelve miles from the City of St. John; containing 6000 acres, well covered with Pine and Spruce Spars, great quantities of the finest Ship Timber and other Hard-Wood as yet unculled, possessing several convenient places for Ship-Building; an excellent Salmon and Herring Fishery; a large Grist and Saw-Mill, that are doing extensive business; four well settled Farms, each having extensive meadows, with high and low intervale sufficient to maintain a large stock, together with the Farming Utensils of each. The greater part of the enclosures are under Cedar fence, with a navigable River running through the centre of the estate. The well known local advantage of this property and its commanding prospects render any further description unnecessary. — Terms of Payment will be made easy to the purchaser."

In his dealings he was exact; yet to the poor he dispensed liberally in charity, and for persons in his neighborhood devised useful and profitable employment. His own habits were extremely active and industrious. He was fond of talking with citizens of the United States of the Revolution, and of the prominent Whigs of his native State. "Samuel Adams used to tell me," said he, "'Coffin, you must not leave us; we shall have warm work, and want you.'" The battle of Breed's Hill was regarded by General Coffin as the event which controlled everything that followed. "You could not have succeeded without it," he frequently said to his American friends, "for *something* was indispensable in the then state of parties, to fix men *somewhere*, and to show the planters at the South, that Northern people were really in earnest, and could and would — fight. That, *that* did the business for you." While the British claimed and held Eastport, General Coffin seldom visited it. He would sail round Moose Island

— as he ever continued to call that town — in his sloop *Liberty*, examine the movements on shore through his spy-glass, and, after gratifying his curiosity, return to St. John. After the surrender to the United States, in 1818, he came to Moose Island frequently. Notwithstanding his choice of sides in the Revolution, he never lost his interest in the " Old Thirteen," and he remembered that he was " Boston-born," from first to last. " I would give more for one pork-barrel made in Massachusetts," was one of his many sayings, " than for all that have been made in New Brunswick since its settlement. Why, sir, I have now some of the former which are thirty years old, but I can hardly make the Province barrels last through one season." In his person, General Coffin was tall and spare. Until well advanced in years, he was remarkably erect. His countenance indicated a quick and sensitive nature. His manners were easy, social, and polite. His conversation was animated and interesting, frank, and without reserve. He died at his seat, King's County, in 1838, aged eighty-seven. Anne, his widow, and daughter of William Mathews, of South Carolina, died at Bath, England, in 1839, aged seventy-four. His children were seven, namely: Guy Carleton, who (1838) is a major in the Royal Artillery; Nathaniel, who died young; John Townsend, (1850) a post-captain; and William Henry, an officer in the Royal Navy; Caroline; Elizabeth, who married Captain Kirkland; and Anne, who married Captain Pearson.

COFFIN, NATHANIEL, JR. Of Boston. Son of Nathaniel, the Cashier. Was an Addresser of Hutchinson in 1774, and a Protester against the Whigs the same year. He was at New York in 1783, and one of the fifty-five petitioners for lands in Nova Scotia. [See *Abijah Willard.*] At a subsequent period he was appointed Collector of the Customs at the island of St. Kitt's, and filled that station for thirty-four years. He died in London in 1831, aged eighty-three.

COFFIN, WILLIAM. Of Boston. Son of Nathaniel, the Cashier. An Addresser of Hutchinson in 1774; went to Halifax, 1776; proscribed and banished, 1778. The last-mentioned year, the Rev. Jacob Bailey, in recording a visit at Mr. Inman's, remarks: "We were joined at supper by Mrs. Coffin and her daughter Polley. Both the mother and dughter appeared very modest, sensible, and engaging. . . . I quickly perceived that Mrs. Coffin had her husband (Mr. William Coffin) and two or three sons in the British service," &c. After the peace, he was at St. John, New Brunswick, and a merchant.

COFFIN, WILLIAM. Of Boston. Died in that town in 1775. Sir Thomas Aston Coffin was a grandson.

COFFIN, WILLIAM, JR. Of Boston. Son of William. He was an Addresser of Gage in 1775, and accompanied the Royal Army to Halifax the next year.

COFFIN, SIR THOMAS ASTON, Baronet. Of Boston. Son of William, Jr. He graduated at Harvard University in 1772. At one period of the Revolution he was Private Secretary to Sir Guy Carleton. In 1804 he was Secretary and Comptroller of Accounts of Lower Canada. At another part of his life, he was Commissary-General in the British Army. He died in London in 1810, at the age of fifty-six.

COFFIN, EBENEZER. Of Boston. Son of William, Jr. He settled in South Carolina, and was a merchant. He was living in 1804, married, and a father.

COFFIN, NATHANIEL. Of Boston. After the Revolution he settled in Upper Canada. In the war of 1812 he served against the United States. For a number of years he was Adjutant-General of the Militia of Upper Canada. He died at Toronto in 1846, aged eighty.

COFFIN, JOHN. Of Boston. Was Assistant Commissary-General in the British Army, and died at Quebec in 1837, aged seventy-eight.

COGGESWELL, JAMES. Of Rhode Island. In 1782 he was an officer in the Superintendent Department established at New York. Went to St. John, New Brunswick; was an officer of the Customs; died there in 1786.

COIL, ———. Of North Carolina. Notorious miscreant Taken and hung.

COKE, WILLIAM. Of New Jersey. Stamp-master of the Colony. He applied for the office; but, alarmed by the popular manifestations, refused to execute his duties, and even to take charge of the stamps. After his resignation, Governor Franklin asked General Gage if he could have the aid of military force, and was answered in the affirmative.

COLDEN, CADWALLADER. Of New York. He was born in Scotland, and came to America in 1708, and was a successful practitioner of medicine for some years. In 1718, Governor Hunter having become his friend, he settled in the city of New York, and was the first Surveyor-General of the Colony. Besides this office, he filled that of Master in Chancery; and, on the arrival of Governor Burnet, in 1720, he was made a member of the King's Council. Succeeding to the Presidency of the Council, he administered the government in 1760. Having previous to the last-mentioned time purchased a tract of land in the vicinity of Newburgh, on the Hudson, he retired there with his family about the year 1755. In 1761 he was appointed Lieutenant-Governor of New York, and held the commission during the remainder of his life, and was repeatedly at the head of affairs in consequence of the death or absence of several of the Governors. While administering the government, the stamped paper came out, and was placed under his care. A multitude of several thousand persons, under leaders, assembled, and determined that he should give up the paper to be destroyed. Unless he complied with their wishes, the massacre of himself and adherents was threatened; but he exhibited great firmness, and prevented them from accomplishing their design. Yet the mob burned his effigy, and destroyed his carriages in his sight. Governor Tryon relieved him from active political duty in 1775, and he retired to Long Island, where he had a seat, and where he died the following year, at the age of eighty-eight. He was hospitable and social, and gave his friends a cordial welcome. The political troubles of his country caused him pain and anguish. These troubles he long predicted. In science Mr. Colden was highly distinguished. Botany and astronomy were favorite pursuits. As his death occurred previous to the passage of the Confiscation Act, his estate was inherited by his children.

COLDEN, DAVID. Of New York. Son of the Lieutenant-Governor. The farm at Spring Hill, Flushing, Long Island, which was devised to him by his father, is now (1847) the property of the Hon. Benjamin W. Strong. Mr. Colden went to England at the close of the war, and died there July 10, 1784. His estate, of two hundred and forty acres, was sold by the Commissioners of Confiscation, the year of his decease. He was fond of retirement, was much devoted to scientific pursuits, and maintained a correspondence with the learned of his time, both in Europe and in America. Ann, his widow, daughter of John Willet, of Flushing, died in August, 1785. Four daughters and one son survived him. The son, Cadwallader D. Colden, of New York, (a lad in the Revolution,) was a lawyer of great eminence, and one of the earliest and most efficient promoters, in connection with De Witt Clinton, of the Erie Canal, and other works of extensive improvement. He died at Jersey City, February 7th, 1834, universally lamented.

COLDEN, ALEXANDER. Of New York. Son of Lieutenant-Governor Colden. He was Postmaster, and successor of his father in the office of Surveyor-General. He died in 1774, aged fifty-eight. His eldest daughter, Alice, married Colonel Archibald Hamilton; the second, Major John Antill, of Skinner's Brigade of New Jersey Volunteers; his third, Captain Anthony Farrington, of London.

COLDEN, RICHARD NICHOLLS. Of New York. Son of Alexander Colden. He was an ensign in the Royal Highlanders, in 1766; but left the army prior to the Revolution, and was appointed Surveyor and Searcher of the Customs in the city of New York. He died in 1777. His sons were Alexander and Cadwallader.

COLDEN, CADWALLADER. Of New York. When, in June, 1776, he was examined and committed to jail in Ulster County, the Committee reported that he said, "he should ever oppose independency with all his might, and wished to the Lord that his name might be entered on record as opposed to that matter, and be handed down to latest posterity." I find, next, that on petition of Whigs, in 1784, he was permitted by law to return to the State.

COLE, EDWARD. Of Rhode Island. He commanded a regiment under Wolfe, at the seige of Quebec, in 1759; and at Havanna, subsequently. Adhering to the Crown in the Revolution, he was insulted, and his furniture and pictures were much mutilated. He fled to the British lines, and was commissioned as Colonel. He settled in Nova Scotia. His pension was £150 per annum. He died well in years. His brother John was a Whig, and was appointed Advocate-General of the Court of Vice-Admiralty when the government of Rhode Island passed to the popular party.

COLLINS, DAVIS. An early settler of St. David, New Brunswick. Died at Tower Hill, August, 1837. His death was caused by the falling of a tree.

COMBS, CAPTAIN ———. Probably of Maine. At Halifax, Nova Scotia, December, 1779. The Rev. Jacob Bailey wrote to Thomas Brown: "You may regard him as a person of real worth and unshaken integrity, who has resisted all the efforts of his countrymen to seduce and subdue him, with amazing fortitude, and his honest attachment to the British Government is nearly without example."

COMELY, ROBERT. Of Pennsylvania. Arrived at St. John. New Brunswick, in the spring of 1783, in the ship *Union*. He died at Lancaster, in that Province, in 1838, aged eighty-three.

COMPTON, WILLIAM. Went to St. John, New Brunswick, and was a grantee of that city. He died at St. Martin's in that Province, in 1804.

CONKLIN, ———. Captain in DeLancey's First Battalion. Killed in Georgia, in 1780, on an enterprise to disperse the Whigs in the vicinity of the Ogechee.

CONNEL, JOHN. Of Chester County, Pennsylvania. Schoolmaster. Joined the Royal Army in Philadelphia, and accompanied it to New York. In 1779, he was captured on board of the British privateer *Intrepid*, and put in prison.

CONNER, CONSTANT. In 1782 he was a lieutenant in the Royal Fencible Americans. He went to Nova Scotia after the war, where he fought a duel and killed his antagonist. He died at Halifax.

CONOLLY, JOHN. He was born in Lancaster County, Pennsylvania, and was bred a physician. Before the Revolution he lived at or near Pittsburg, and was in correspondence with Washington on matters of business. In 1770 Washington, on his tour to Ohio, invited Doctor Conolly to dine with him, and said he was "a very sensible, intelligent man." His difficulties with the authorities of Pennsylvania, in 1774, occupy considerable space in the records of the Council of that Colony. In the course of these difficulties, and while he was at the head of an armed party, he was seized and imprisoned. It appears that he claimed lands under Virginia, at the falls of the Ohio, which, it was contended by Pennsylvania, Lord Dunmore, the Governor of the former Colony, had no right to grant. But he and John Campbell advertised their intention of laying out a town there, and invited settlers. They set forth the beauties and advantages of the location in glowing terms, and said, that "we may with certainty affirm, that it (the proposed town) will, in a short time, be equalled by few inland places on the American continent."

As the controversy ripened to war, Conolly became active on the side of the Crown, and in 1775 was employed by Lord Dunmore, who authorized him to raise and command a regiment of Loyalists and Indians, to be enlisted in the Western country and Canada, and to be called the Loyal Forresters. While on his way to execute this design, he was taken prisoner. His papers having been sent to Congress, it was determined to retain his person. He wrote to Washington several times, but the Commander-in-Chief declined to interfere, and he remained a captive till near the close of the contest. The Loyal Forresters were in service in 1782, and probably later.

Always, as it would seem, moving in some doubtful enterprise, we hear of Colonel Conolly soon after the peace, and about the year 1788, at Detroit. At this time he and other disaffected persons held conferences with some of the prominent citizens of the West as to the seizure of New Orleans, and the control of the navigation of the Mississippi by force. The precise plan, and the degree of support which it received, are not, perhaps, known. But the attention of Washington was attracted to the subject, and measures were taken to detect and counteract the plot.

COPLEY, JOHN SINGLETON. Of Boston. An eminent painter. His father, "Richard Copley, of the county of Limerick, who emigrated to America, and became of Boston, in the United States, married Sarah, younger daughter of John Singleton." The subject of this notice was born in 1738, and achieved distinction early. John Adams wrote: "Copley is the greatest master that was ever in America. His portraits far exceed West's." He himself said that he had as many commissions in Boston as he could execute. His price for a half-length was fourteen guineas.

In 1774 he was an Addresser of Hutchinson; and, the same year, he deposited several pictures with his mother, arranged his affairs generally, and sailed for Italy by way of England, with the design of three years' residence abroad. In 1776 he was in London, and a member of the Loyalist Club, for weekly conversation and a dinner. He subsequently resumed his profession, and increased his fame. "The Death of Chatham;" "King Charles ordering the Arrest of the Five Members of Parliament;" and "The Death of Major Peirson," are among his celebrated works. His last pictures, it is believed, are "The Resurrection," and the portrait of his son. He died in England, September, 1815, aged seventy-eight. His wife, who deceased in 1836, was a daughter of Richard Clarke, one of the Boston consignees of the tea. One son and three daughters survived him.

His son, John Singleton Copley, rose to eminence as a jurist and a statesman. He was a native of Boston; and the tradition is, that, born a few weeks after the Hon. Josiah Quincy, Senior, "the monthly nurse went directly from Mrs. Quincy to attend Mrs. Copley." Mr. Copley was admitted to the bar in 1804, was made Sergeant-at-law in 1813, and became a Judge in 1818. Later, he was Solicitor and Attorney-General, and Master of the Rolls. In 1827, on the retirement of Lord Eldon, he was appointed Lord Chancellor; and the same year was elevated to the peerage as Baron Lyndhurst. He was Lord Chief Baron of the Exchequer, subsequently; and held the office of Lord Chancellor a second and third time.

Lord Lyndhurst died October, 1863, in his ninety-second year. By his first wife, Sarah Geray, daughter of Charles Brunsden, and widow of Lieutenant-Colonel Thomas, who fell at Waterloo, he was the father of Sarah Elizabeth, Susan Penelope, and Sophia Clarence. His second wife, Georgiana, daughter of Lewis Goldsmith, bore him a single child, Georgiana Susan. His Lordship's sister, widow of the late Gardner Greene, of Boston, and several other relatives in Massachusetts, survive.

Cook, Abiel. Of Little Compton, Rhode Island. He was denounced as "an enemy to his country, and the liberties of America," in 1775, for selling sheep to go on board of the *Swan*, British ship-of-war, at Newport. The Whigs took the sheep at Forkland Ferry, and voted to send them as a present to the army at Cambridge. Cook confessed the sale, and avowed his intention of repeating the act every opportunity.

Cooke, Rev. Samuel, D. D. Of Shrewsbury, New Jersey. Episcopal minister. He was educated at Cambridge, England, and came to America as missionary of the Society for the Propagation of the Gospel in Foreign Parts, as early, probably, as 1749. In 1765 he had the care of the churches in Shrewsbury, Freehold, and Middletown. The Revolution divided and dispersed his flock, and he became Chaplain to the Guards. In 1785 he settled at Fredericton, the capital of New Brunswick, as the first Rector of the Church there. In 1791 he was Commissary to the

Bishop of Nova Scotia. He was drowned in crossing the river St. John, in a birch canoe, in 1795. His son, who attempted to save his life, perished with him. His wife was Miss Kearney, of Amboy, New Jersey. Lydia, his fifth daughter, died at Fredericton in 1846, aged seventy-six; and Isabella, the last survivor of his family, and widow of Colonel Harris William Hales, died at the same city in 1848.

COOMBE, REV. THOMAS, D. D. Of Philadelphia. He was a native of that city, and graduated at the College there in 1766. He was chosen Assistant Rector of the Churches of Christ and St. Peter's in 1772. Five years later, he was confined for disaffection to the Whig cause, and finally ordered to be sent prisoner to Virginia. In 1778 he resigned his Rectorship and went to England. He lived some time in Ireland, as Chaplain to Lord Carlisle; was in charge of a parish; a Prebendary of Canterbury, and a Chaplain to the King. The degree of D. D. was conferred by Trinity College, Dublin.

COOMBS, MICHAEL. Of Marblehead, Massachusetts. Merchant. Went to England during the war, returned at the peace; died at Marblehead in 1806, aged seventy-three.

COOMBS, JOHN. Lieutenant in the Second Batallion of New Jersey Volunteers. Settled in New Brunswick in 1783, and died in that Province in 1827, at the age of seventy-four.

COOPER, REV. ROBERT. Of Charleston, South Carolina. Episcopal minister. Rector of St. Michael's; previously, however, Rector of Prince William's Parish, and Assistant Rector of St. Philip's. The Church of St. Michael's, with the bells, clock, and organ, cost about forty thousand dollars; which, if we consider the value of labor and materials, a century ago, was a large sum; it was opened for worship early in 1761. Mr. Cooper officiated until the Revolution. The Vestry, having official information that he declined to take an oath prescribed by law, met on the morning of Sunday, June 30th, 1776, and resolved to omit service on that day, and to appoint a meeting of parishioners on Tuesday, July 2d.

He refused to confer with his flock, on the ground that he considered himself already dismissed; and the pulpit was accordingly declared vacant. He soon went to England, and after having been employed as a joint curate and lecturer, became a rector. The Government gave him a pension of £100 per annum, as a Loyalist. He died in 1812, or the year following, at the age of more than eighty.

COOPER, MYLES, D. D. He was educated at Oxford, England, and coming to America in 1762, was elected President of King's College, New York, the year following. In 1771, he advocated the appointment of Bishops for the Colonies, in an Address to the Episcopalians of Virginia. His political opinions rendered his resignation of that office necessary as the Revolutionary storm darkened, and in 1775 he retired to England. He died at Edinburgh in 1785, aged about fifty, having previously lived there, and officiated as an Episcopal clergyman. He was a gentleman of literary distinction, and published several works. Four lines of an epitaph written by himself are: —

> "Here lies a priest of English blood,
> Who, living, liked whate'er was good:
> Good company, good wine, good name;
> Yet never hunted after fame."

The son of Mrs. Washington was a pupil of Doctor Cooper at King's College; and Washington, after Mr. Custis left the institution, late in 1773, expressed the conviction, that he had been under the care of "a gentleman capable of instructing him in every branch of knowledge." Young Custis, it appears, abandoned his studies, and married against Washington's wish, though with the approbation of his mother and most of the family friends.

CORNELL, SAMUEL. Of Newbern. A member of the Council of North Carolina. In 1775 he was present in council, and concurred in the opinion that Whig meetings were objects of the highest detestation, and gave his advice to Governor Martin to issue his proclamation to inhibit and forbid them. Before the Declaration of Independence he went to Europe, but left his family at Newbern. During the war he returned to New York, and went to Newbern in a flag of truce, but was forbidden to land, unless he would take an oath of allegiance to the State under its Whig rulers. This he refused to do. While on board of the vessel in the harbor, he conveyed his estate to his children by several deeds of gift, and duly proved and registered the conveyances. Having thus arranged his affairs, he removed his family, by permission of the Executive of the State, to New York. Subsequently this property was confiscated and sold. A Mr. Singleton became the purchaser of a part of it, and the portion which Mr. Cornell had given to one of his daughters. This lady claimed to hold under her father's deed, and instituted a suit to eject Singleton; but, on a hearing and trial, the Confiscation Act was held to be valid, and judgment was given against her. This case, of course, determined that all the deeds of gift were void. The conveyances were made, it will be recollected, *prior* to the passage of the Confiscation Act of North Carolina. His daughter Hannah married Herman Le Roy, of New York, in 1786.

CORBIN, JOHN TAYLOE. Of Virginia. Ordered to be confined to a certain part of the county of Caroline, by the Virginia Convention, May, 1776, and to give bond with security, in the sum of £10,000, not to depart the territory assigned to him.

CORRIE, REV. ———. Of Delaware. Episcopal minister. Rector of St. David's Church. Came from England in 1770. Resigned, because of the opposition to his praying for the King.

CORRIE, JOHN. Of Charleston, South Carolina. Died at Dumfries, Scotland, in 1791.

CORSA, COLONEL ISAAC. Of Long Island, New York. An officer in the French war, of distinguished merit. In 1776 he was arrested by order of Washington, and sent prisoner to Middletown, Connecticut; but was released on parole. He died at Flushing, in 1805, by one account, in 1807, by another, in his eightieth year, " beloved as a man and a Christian." "He was small in stature, and juvenile in appearance." Maria Franklin, his only child, married John I. Staples, and (1852) is still living.

COSKEL, THOMAS. A Whig soldier. In 1778 he was tried on a charge of attempting to desert to the Royal side; and, confessing his guilt, was sentenced to receive one hundred lashes.

COSSTELL, CHARLES M. Of South Carolina. Was an Assistant Judge of the Supreme Court of the Colony. He went to England.

COTHAM, THOMAS. Of the State of New York. Went to Shelburne, Nova Scotia, and taught school there nearly fifty years. He died in 1830.

COTTEN, JAMES. Of North Carolina. Lieutenant-Colonel in the Militia. A "friend of Government," and in confidential communication with Governor Martin after he had taken refuge on board a ship-of-war. He was summoned before the Provincial Congress, subsequently, and made a solemn recantation. In 1776 he was on the Royal side at Moore's Creek Bridge, but "fled," it is said, "at the first fire." In 1779 he was attainted, and his estate was confiscated.

COTTON, JOHN. Of Boston. John Cotton, the celebrated pastor of the First Church in that town, was his great-grandfather. His father, Thomas Cotton, lived first in Brookline, Massachusetts, and subsequently in Pomfret, Connecticut. The subject of this notice graduated at Harvard University in 1747; and was, I suppose, the last Royal Deputy Secretary of Massachusetts. He died at Boston in 1776. His wife was Mary, daughter of William Dudley.

COUGLE, JAMES. Of Pennsylvania. Was a captain in the First Battalion of New Jersey Volunteers. He went to New Brunswick at the close of the contest, and died at Sussex Vale in 1819, aged seventy-three.

COULBOURNE, CHARLES. Of Norfolk, Virginia. Was a lieutenant in the Loyal-American Regiment, and quartermaster of the corps. At the peace he settled at Digby, Nova Scotia, and was a ship-master; but returned finally to his native State, and died there. His wife was the widow of James Budd, who was shot by a party of "cow-boys" at Rye.

COULSON, THOMAS. Merchant and ship-owner, of Falmouth, now Portland, Maine. "Captain Coulson," wrote the good Parson Smith in his Journal, April 12, 1775, " is very troublesome." On the 10th of May following, Coulson's house, which was on King Street, was rifled by the Whigs, under Colonel Thompson. The difficulties with him caused the burning of that town by Mowatt. It appears that, contrary to the agreement of the Association as to importation of merchandise, a vessel arrived at Falmouth with the sails and rigging for a ship which he was fitting for sea. These articles, it was determined by the Whigs, should be returned to England, together with some goods brought in the same vessel. Coulson resolved otherwise. A quarrel ensued, which continued for several weeks. The *Canseau* sloop-of-war arrived for the protection of himself and property, and mobs and tumults and conflagration were the final results.

Coulson returned to England, and his wife, Dorcas, daughter of the elder Dr. Nathaniel Coffin, of Falmouth, soon followed him. Both died in England; Mrs. Coulson about the year 1800.

COURTNEY, THOMAS, RICHARD, and JAMES. Of Boston. The first was an Addresser of Gage in 1775, went to Halifax in 1776, was proscribed and banished in 1778, and lost £2000 in consequence of his loyalty. The three removed to Shelburne, Nova Scotia, from New York, at the peace; Thomas, with a family of four, and four servants. They built largely at their new home; but Shelburne soon declined, and Richard went to Charleston, South Carolina, and James to Wilmington, North Carolina.

COVERT, ABRAHAM. He died at Maugerville, New Brunswick, in 1824, aged seventy-nine. His widow, Phebe, died at the same place in 1838, at the age of eighty-seven.

COWDEN, THOMAS. Of Fitchburg, Mass. He was known as disaffected to the popular cause, but made a written confession, and applied for a commission in the army. Washington and Greene communicated his application to the Assembly of Massachusetts, and the case was referred to a Committee of both Houses, who reported adversely; yet said, that as he had given ",some" evidence of reformation, he might safely and properly be released from confinement, and allowed to return to his family and estate.

COWLING, JOHN. Of Virginia. At the peace, accompanied by his family of three persons, and by one servant, he went from New York to Shelburne, Nova Scotia, where the Crown granted him one town and one water lot. His losses in consequence of his loyalty were estimated at £5000, and in 1783 he was poor. He opened a school, and was assisted by his wife Phebe, who, after his death, kept a small shop.

Cox, DANIEL. Of New Jersey. Was a member of his Majesty's Council of that Colony. In January, 1777, his elegant house at Trenton Ferry was burned, not by Whigs, but by persons in the Royal Army, who, in their progress through New Jersey, committed almost every imaginable crime. Through his agency, principally, it is believed that the Board of Refugees, consisting of delegates from the Loyalists of the Colonies, was established at New York in 1779. Of this Board, he was a president; and Christopher Sower, an highly influential Loyalist of Pennsylvania, in a letter of December 5th, 1779, wrote as follows: "The Deputies of the Refugees from the different Provinces meet once a week. Daniel Cox, Esquire, was appointed to the chair, to deprive him of the opportunity of speaking, as he has the gift of saying little with many words." In the year last mentioned, he addressed a memorial to Lord George Germain, to which Governor Franklin called his Lordship's attention. He went to England, and was followed by his wife and children, in 1785. Mrs. Cox was daughter of the distinguished Dr. John Redman. At her departure her parents were well-nigh inconsolable. When, by the death of her sister, in 1806, she became the only surviving child, she came across the ocean to soothe her afflicted father, and to minister to the wants of her dying mother. Mr. Cox's property in New Jersey and Pennsylvania was confiscated. Sarah, his widow, died at Brighton, England, in 1843, aged ninety-one.

Cox, Lemuel. Of Boston, Massachusetts. Near the close of the year 1775, he was in prison at Ipswich for his attachment to the cause of the Crown. Mr. Felt, in his very interesting work, the "Annals of Salem," supposes this Lemuel Cox to have been the chief architect of Essex Bridge in 1788, and who, subsequently, constructed bridges in England and Ireland. "In 1796," says Mr. Felt, "he had a grant of 1000 acres of land in Maine from our Legislature, for being the first inventor of a machine to cut card-wire, the first projector of a powder-mill in Massachusetts, the first suggestor of employing prisoners on Castle Island, to make nails, and for various other discoveries in mechanical arts."

Cox, Francis. Of Salem, Massachusetts. Was a lieutenant in the regiment commanded by Colonel Mansfield, and deserted from the camp at Cambridge, in June, 1775, and left the service. General Ward submitted to the Provincial Congress the propriety of making him a public example, for, besides his own desertion, he incited his men to follow his example.

Cox, John. Of Falmouth, Maine. Was the son of John Cox, of that town, and married Sarah Proctor in 1739, who died in 1761. He married again at Falmouth; and, molested for his political opinions, removed with the family by his second wife, to Cornwallis, Nova Scotia, about the year 1783. The Crown made him a grant of land, now, (1848,) as I understand, occupied by his descendants, and known as *Coxtown*. He married a third time; his children were twenty in number.

Cox, James. Of Virginia. Some time in the war, he was at Newtown, New York. At the peace, accompanied by his family of four persons, and by four servants, he went from New York to Shelburne, Nova Scotia, where the Crown granted him one town lot. His losses in consequence of his loyalty were estimated at £3000. He died at New York.

Coxe, Tench. Of Pennsylvania. Son of William Coxe, of New Jersey. His loyalty is disputed, as I understand, on two grounds. First, because, after he was attainted of treason, he surrendered himself, and was discharged; second, because, after the organization of the Federal Government, he was employed by Washington and Hamilton. These facts prove nothing either way. The accusation against him was that, on the approach of the Royal Army, he went from Philadelphia to join it, and marched into the city under its banners. Of this, he was *legally* acquitted; but, unless I am misinformed, his sympathies were on the side of the Crown. As relates to the other point, I cite a single incident to show the degree of confidence reposed in him.

In February, 1795, it became necessary to provide for the temporary performance of the duties of Comptroller, and the President consulted Hamilton, who, in reply, objected to Coxe (then Commissioner of the Revenue) because his appointment " could not fail, for strong reasons, to be unpleasant to Mr. Wolcott," (Secretary of the Treasury) " and because there is real danger that Mr. Coxe would first perplex and embarrass, and afterwards misrepresent and calumniate."

He published an " Address on American Manufactures ; " an " Inquiry on the Principles of a Commercial System for the United States ; " an " Examination of Lord Sheffield's Observations ; " a " View of the United States ; " " Thoughts on Naval Power, and the Encouragement of Commerce and Manufactures ; " " Memoir on the Cultivation, Trade, and Manufacture of Cotton ; " " Memoir on a Navigation Act ; " and " Statement of the Arts and Manufactures of the United States." He died at Philadelphia, in 1824, at the age of sixty-eight. Rebecca, his wife, died in the same city in 1806.

Coyle, Francis. Of New York. Went to Shelburne, Nova Scotia, at the peace, and in the excitement of the time, paid a guinea a foot for a house-lot. A few years after, he could hardly have sold his property at one tenth of its cost. He died at Shelburne, leaving a family.

Coy, Amasa. Of Connecticut. He went to New Brunswick in 1783. He died at Fredericton in 1838, aged eighty-one.

COZENS, DANIEL. Captain in the New Jersey Volunteers. Killed in 1779, during the siege of Savannah.

CRANE, JONATHAN. Settled in Nova Scotia, and was a magistrate, a colonel in the militia, and a member of the Assembly. Coming out of the Government-House one day, John Howe asked him — " What is going on ? " " Oh," replied Crane, " 't is all a game of whist; the honors are divided, and nothing is to be got except by *tricks*." His son William, who died rich, was a member of the Assembly, Speaker of that body, and a delegate of the Province to England. His widow, Rebecca, died in Horton, in that Province, in 1841, aged eighty-eight.

CRANNELL, BARTHOLOMEW. Of New York. He was a public notary in the city, in 1782. The year following he announced his intention of removing to Nova Scotia, and was one of the fifty-five petitioners for lands in that Colony. He arrived at St. John, New Brunswick, before the close of 1783, and received the grant of a city lot. He commenced business as a merchant. In 1785 he was Clerk of the Common Council.

CREIGHTON, JAMES, and ALEXANDER. The first, Secretary of the Police Department of Long Island, New York, in 1782; the other, of Georgia, and attainted of treason, in 1778. A person named James Creighton died at Halifax, Nova Scotia, in 1813, aged eighty-one.

CROCKER, JOSIAH. Of Barnstable, Massachusetts. Son of Cornelius Crocker. He graduated at Harvard University in 1765. He taught school in Barnstable a short time; " but, on account of his feeble health and Tory proclivities," took but little part in public affairs. He died of consumption in 1780, in his thirty-sixth year. His wife was Deborah, daughter of Hon. Daniel Davis. His five children were Robert, Uriel, Josiah, Deborah and Mehitable.

CROFT, FREDERICK. Of North Carolina. In the battle at Cross Creek, 1776, he " shot Captain Dent in cold blood."

He was made prisoner, confined in Halifax jail, and sent, finally, to Maryland.

CROMWELL, JOSIAH. He died at Portland, New Brunswick, in 1803.

CROSS, WILLIAM. He went from New York to Nova Scotia, at the close of the war, and died at Annapolis Royal, in 1834, aged eighty-three.

CROSSING, WILLIAM. Of Newport, Rhode Island. A noted marauder and robber. He was employed at first as a pilot of the Royal troops, but, in 1778, seems to have belonged to Wightman's motley regiment. The account of him is, that he plundered women of their jewelry and fancy articles of dress; that he robbed and burned houses; and that he carried off Whigs in mere wantonness. He was taken prisoner in the year above mentioned, and confined at Providence.

CROW, CHARLES. Of Boston. In September, 1777, he was seized in that town, fastened to a cart and carried to Roxbury, where another party conveyed him to Dedham. The object was to "cart him" through every town to the Rhode Island line, and compel him to join the British.

CROW, JONATHAN. Of Massachusetts. Was buried in Trinity Church-yard, New York, in October, 1780.

CROWELL, JOSEPH. Was a captain in the First Battalion of New Jersey Volunteers. He settled in New Brunswick, received half-pay, and died at Carleton in that Colony. His son Thomas died at Shelburne, Nova Scotia, in 1845, aged eighty. His only daughter married Luther Wetmore.

CRUGER, JOHN HARRIS. Of New York. Lieutenant-Colonel Commandant of DeLancey's First Battalion. He succeeded his father, Henry Cruger, as member of the Council of the Colony; and at the beginning of the Revolution, held, beside, the office of Chamberlain of the City. He entered the military service in 1777, and from 1779 to the peace, few Loyalist officers performed more responsible or arduous duty. We hear of him in the last-mentioned year, as made prisoner at a dinner-party in Georgia, on the King's birthday, but as soon exchanged; as in command of the garrison at Sunbury, but ordered to evacuate the post and repair to Savannah, with all possible haste. In July, 1780, he was at Ninety-Six, when, in the condition of affairs, he was directed to send a part of his force to Camden. In August, Lord Cornwallis wrote to him to execute all in his district who had borne arms on the side of the Crown, and who afterwards fought with the Whigs; and that he obeyed appears from his own letter to Major Ferguson, in which he said that he had fallen in with the Rebels, taken most of their plunder, killed a great number, had hung several others, and designed to hang many more. In September, he made a forced march to Augusta, to relieve Colonel Browne, and arrived just in time to save him. In 1781, Lord Rawdon was sorely pressed in South Carolina, and sent repeated expresses to Cruger to abandon Ninety-Six, to join Browne, assume command of the whole force, and act at his discretion. But not one of the messengers reached him, and he was left in ignorance of his Lordship's situation. While completing the defences by throwing up a bank of earth, building block-houses, and the like, General Greene encamped in a wood within cannon shot of the village, and summoned him to surrender. Cruger replied that he should maintain the post to the last. The Whig attempted to burn the barracks by shooting African arrows; the Loyalist defeated the plan by directing all the buildings to be unroofed, which exposed officers and men to the night air and to rains the remainder of the siege. Greene made an assault, which, after a terrible conflict, failed. The besieged suffered much for water; the negroes went out naked at night, that they might not be distinguished from the trees, and brought in a scanty supply. During these trying scenes, Cruger's courage, skill, and fertility of resource, drew commendation even from his foes. Without relief, he knew that he must submit at last; when almost in despair, an American lady who had lately married one of his officers, (and who, it is related, was bribed by a considerable sum of money,) arrived with a letter assuring him that Rawdon was near with a reinforcement.

Mrs. Cruger was with her husband during the perils of his command at Ninety-Six. When General Greene approached that post, he found her and the wife of Major Green in a farm-house, and not only allowed them to remain, but placed a guard to protect them. Indeed, among the last acts of the General, though defeated and worn with care, was a leave-taking of these ladies, and measures to ensure their continued safety. At his departure, he left the guard; and Cruger, as generous as his antagonist, sent it with his passport, to rejoin the Whig Army on the retreat. Nay, more; Mrs. Cruger pointed out the route of the retiring " Rebels " to a returning scouting party, that, absent some days, were unconscious of the condition of things, and so were on their way to the supposed Whig camp; and they, too, reached their companions.

The dreadful civil war, which desolated South Carolina, "began at Ninety-Six," and many who had incurred the hate of the Whigs were in garrison when besieged by Greene, and fought in fear of the halter. Rawdon decided to evacuate the post, and moving himself toward the Congaree, ordered Cruger to protect the Loyalists and to escort such as wished to remove to a place of safety. Most, apprehending a general slaughter, determined to abandon their homes. "Melancholy was the spectacle that followed; trooping slowly and gloomily in the van and rear of the British Army, went the families of this unhappy faction. For days the roads from Ninety-Six were crowded with the wretched cavalcade; men, women, children, and slaves, with cattle and wagons" — all journeying to the seaboard.

In the battle of Eutaw Springs, Colonel Cruger occupied the centre of the British line, and was distinguished. On leaving Charleston, July 1782, the inhabitants presented him an Address. In June, 1783, his furniture was sold at auction at his house, Hanover Square, New York; and soon after he embarked for England. His estate was confiscated, and he remained in exile. He died in London, in 1807, aged sixty-nine. Mrs. Cruger, who died at Chelsea, England, in 1822.

at the age of seventy-eight, was a daughter of the senior Oliver DeLancey, and was at her father's house in 1777, when it was burned at night by a party of Whigs. It was in the counting-house of Colonel Cruger's "brother Nicholas, at St. Croix, that Alexander Hamilton commenced his mercantile clerkship." His brother, Henry Cruger, who died in New York in 1827, aged eighty-eight, was a member of Parliament for Bristol, and a colleague of Burke. His sister Mary married Jacob Walton; his sister Elizabeth married Peter Van Schaack.

CRUGER, JOHN. Of New York. In 1775 he was Speaker of the House of Assembly, and during the recess that year, with thirteen other members of the Ministerial party, addressed a letter to General Gage on the alarming state of public affairs. This communication is dated May 5th, on which day two members of the Council of New York sailed for England. When, in 1769, he was elected to the Assembly, the success of his party was deemed a victory of the Episcopalians over the Presbyterians.

CUMBERLAND, ———. Of North Carolina. Captain. Killed in 1780, in the battle of Ramsour's Mill.

CUNARD, ROBERT. Of Philadelphia County, Pennsylvania. He was attainted of treason and lost his estate by confiscation. He died at Portland, New Brunswick, in 1818, aged sixty-nine. His son Abraham settled in Halifax, became a merchant, and died in that city. The Brothers Cunard, so widely known as the projectors of the Royal Mail Steamship Line, are sons of Abraham.

CUNNABEL, EDWARD G. He died at Union Point, New Brunswick, in 1838, aged seventy-six.

CUNNINGHAM, ROBERT. Of South Carolina. One of the most prominent Loyalists of the whole South. In 1769, he settled in the district of Ninety-Six, and was soon commissioned a Judge. He incurred the displeasure of the Whigs in 1775, when he disapproved of their proceedings in sustaining the cause of Massachusetts, and in the adoption of the Non-Importation Act. In the course of that year he was seized and imprisoned at Charleston. His brother Patrick assembled a body of friends in order to effect his release. The Whigs despatched Major Williamson with a force to prevent the accomplishment of this object, but Cunningham's party being superior, he was compelled to retreat. A truce or treaty was finally arranged, and both Whigs and Loyalists dispersed. In July of 1776, Robert Cunningham was allowed his freedom without conditions, and removed to Charleston. Colonel Williamson wrote to William Henry Drayton, the same month he appeared in camp, and "declared himself our fast friend, and that he came to stand and fall with us." "I have no doubt," adds Williamson, "of his proving true to his declaration, but at present it would be improper to confer any public trust on him." In 1780 he was created a Brigadier-General, and placed in command of a garrison in South Carolina; but in 1781 was at the head of a force in the field, and encountered Sumter. His estate was confiscated in 1782. After the peace, he petitioned to be allowed to continue in South Carolina. His request was refused, and he removed to Nassau, New Providence. The British Government made him a liberal allowance for his losses, and gave him an annuity. He died in 1813, aged seventy-four years.

CUNNINGHAM, PATRICK. Of South Carolina. Brother of General Robert. In 1769 he was appointed Deputy Surveyor-General of the Colony. He was connected with the earliest military movements at the South. In 1775, at the head of one hundred and fifty Loyalists, he intercepted a party of Whigs that were conveying ammunition; and the same year assembled a force of fifteen hundred men to oppose Major Williamson, who was compelled to retire. After attempting to effect the release of his brother Robert in 1776, and the temporary accommodation of affairs that year, Patrick removed to Charleston, where he was committed to prison by order of the Provincial Congress.

In 1780 he received the commission of Colonel, and the command of a regiment. His estate was confiscated in 1782. At the conclusion of the contest, he joined Robert in a request to be allowed to remain in the State. The application was not successful, and he went to Florida. In 1785, a second petition to be restored to his rights in South Carolina was more favorably received; and the Legislature, amercing his estate twelve per cent., and imposing some personal disabilities for a term of years, annulled the previous act of banishment and confiscation. He was elected a member of the Legislature, but his position was an unpleasant one, and, after serving for a short time, he retired. He died in 1794.

CUNNINGHAM, DAVID. Brother of General Robert. Before the Revolution, he was Deputy Surveyor of the District of Ninety-Six. During the war, he accepted the place of Commissary of the Royal Army at Charleston. He was allowed to continue in the State at the peace, and became a planter in Ninety-Six.

CUNNINGHAM, JOHN. Of South Carolina. Was also a brother of General Robert. He was a planter; but in the course of the war, removing with his brothers to Charleston, was a Commissary in the British Army. In 1782 his property was confiscated. He was permitted to reside in the State at the conclusion of hostilities; and, embarking in commercial pursuits, accumulated a large fortune.

CUNNINGHAM, WILLIAM. Of South Carolina. Was known as "Bloody Bill;" and there is no little evidence to show that he well deserved the appellation. At the beginning of the controversy he was inclined to be a Whig, and indeed accepted a military commission, and served in the campaign of 1776. Changing sides, he became an officer and a major in the service of the Crown, and was engaged in many desperate exploits, and hand-to-hand fights. About the close of the year 1781, when the Royal Army was confined to the vicinity of Charleston, this monster adopted the infernal scheme of taking his last revenge, by carrying fire and sword into the settlements of the Whig militia. At the head of a band of Tories, he reached the back country without discovery, and began to plunder, to burn, and to murder. To show the nature of the man and the kind of warfare which he waged, two cases will suffice. First, a party of twenty under Captain Turner, armed in self-defence, took post in a house, and fought until their ammunition was nearly expended, when they surrendered on condition of being treated as prisoners of war. But Cunningham put every one of them to instant death. Second, a number of Whigs, in the District of Ninety-Six, commanded by Colonel Joseph Hayes, took shelter in a building which was set on fire, and, on promise of protection, yielded, rather than be burned alive. Hayes, and Captain Daniel Williams were immediately hung on a pole, which broke, and both fell; thereupon, Cunningham "cut them into pieces with his own sword." This done, he turned upon his other prisoners, and hacked, and maimed, and killed, until his strength was exhausted. Not yet glutted with blood, he called upon his comrades to complete the dreadful work, and to slay whoever of the survivors they pleased. The end was the slaughter of twelve more, or of fourteen in all. Thus, "Bloody Bill," murdered thirty-five persons in these two instances. In 1782, his property was confiscated, and, at the peace, he retreated to Florida.

CUNNINGHAM, ARCHIBALD. Of Boston. Merchant. Member of the North Church, and high in office among the Free Masons. Went to New York in 1776, and was proscribed and banished in 1778.

At the peace, accompanied by his family of six persons, and by one servant, he went from New York to Shelburne, Nova Scotia. His losses in consequence of his loyalty were estimated at £1100. In Nova Scotia he was Clerk of the Peace, and Register of Probate. He was a man of reading and observation, and left valuable papers. He died in 1820.

CUNNINGHAM, ANDREW. Of the District of Ninety-Six, South Carolina. He held a commission under the Crown, and lost his estate under the Confiscation Act. But the General Assembly, by special Act, subsequently, gave Margaret, his widow, and her children, an estate on Rexburns Creek, which had not been sold by the Commissioners of Forfeited Estates, and which seems to have been the homestead.

CUNNINGHAM, WILLIAM. Of New York. Provost Marshal. To receive as authentic the "Confession" which appeared in the newspapers about the time of his death, we have the following facts, namely: that his father was a trumpeter in the Dragoons, and that he was born in the barracks at Dublin; that he arrived at New York in 1774, with some indented servants, kidnapped by him in Ireland; that his first employment here was the breaking of horses and the teaching of young gentlemen and ladies to ride; that his course in the Revolutionary controversy rendered him obnoxious to the Whigs of New York; that he fled to Boston, where, continuing his opposition to the popular movement, he attracted the attention of General Gage, who, as the quarrel came to blows, appointed him Provost Marshal to the Royal Army, which gave him an opportunity to wreak his vengeance on the Americans. The details of his crimes are horrible. Of the prisoners under his care, two thousand were starved to death, and more than two hundred and fifty were privately hung without ceremony. To reject this paper, there is quite enough in the documents of the time to show that he was an incarnate devil. At the peace he went to England, and settled in Wales. Persuaded to go to London, he became dissipated; and, to relieve his embarrassments, mortgaged his half-pay, and subsequently forged a draft. Convicted of forgery, he was executed in London in 1791.

CUNNINGHAM, JAMES. Pilot to the fleet under the command of Lord Howe. He went to England, and died there in 1783.

CURWEN, SAMUEL. Of Massachusetts. Graduated at Harvard University in 1735. He was in the commission of the peace for thirty years, and at the breaking out of the Revolution, a Judge of Admiralty. He went to England in 1775, remained there until 1784, when he returned to Salem, where he passed the remainder of his days, dying in 1802, at the age of eighty-six years. While in exile, he kept a journal, which has been published, and is an interesting book; its editor, George A. Ward, Esq., of New York, has enriched it with several notices of his relative's fellow-Loyalists, and thus added greatly to is value. No work extant contains so much information of the unhappy exiles while abroad.

A rapid synopsis of the journal follows: " Visited Westminster Hall. Went to Vauxhall Gardens. Dined with a fellow-refugee. Saw the Lord Mayor in his court. Dined with Governor Hutchinson, in company with several Massachusetts refugees. Walked to Hyde Park. A whole army of sufferers in the cause of loyalty are here, lamenting their own and their country's unhappy fate. 'The fires are not to be compared to our large American ones of oak and walnut, nor near so comfortable; would that I were away!' Saw many curiosities brought from Egypt and the Holy Land. Visited Hampton Court; saw there chairs of state with rich canopies; pictures of the reigning beauties of the times of Charles the Second; pictures of monks, friars, nuns; pictures of former kings and queens. Went to Windsor. Heard news from America. Went to Governor Hutchinson's; he was alone, reading a new pamphlet, entitled ' An Enquiry whether Great Britain or America is most in Fault.' Dined with eleven New Englanders. Went to meeting of Disputation Club. Bought Dr. Price on ' Civil Liberty and the American War.' Visited Governor Hutchinson, who was again alone. Went to Herald's office. Went to New England Coffee-house. New England refugees form a Club. Went to Chapel Royal, and saw the King and Queen; Bishop of London preached. Heard Dr. Price preach. Dinner, tea, and evening with several refugees. Attended funeral of fellow-refugee; many have died. At the New England Club dinner, twenty-five members present. News of Banishment and Confiscation Acts. Saw procession of peers for trial of Duchess of Kingston. Went to St. Paul's; Dr. Porteus preached; several high church dignitaries present. Saw Lord Mansfield in Court, his train borne by a gentleman. Went to Bunyan's tomb. Heard Dr. Peters, a Connecticut Loyalist, preach. News from America. Strive hard for some petty clerkship; application was unsuccessful;

such offices openly bought and sold. Hopes and fears excited by accounts from native land. Visited ancient ruins, supposed to be either of Roman or Danish origin. Witnessed election of a member of Parliament. Discuss probability of war's closing. Sigh to return to America. Fear to be reduced to want; lament distressed and forlorn condition. Visited noblemen's estates and castles. Heard of death of Washington. Letter from a friend in America. Visited different colleges and public gardens. Fears about losing pension, and horror of utter poverty. Attended sessions of Parliament; heard Fox, Burke, and other great orators. Heard that Washington and his army were captured. Heard Wesley preach to an immense throng in the open air. Visited a fishing-town, and reminded of fishing-towns in Massachusetts. Heard that Washington is declared Dictator, like Cromwell. King implored to drive Lord North from his service, and take Chatham, and men of his sentiments, instead. Witnessed equipment of fleets and armies to subdue America. Angry and mortified to hear Englishmen talk of Americans as a sort of serfs. Wearied of sights. Sick at heart, and tired of a sojourn among a people, who, after all, are but foreigners. New refugees arrived to recount their losses and sufferings. Fear of alliance with France. Great excitement in England among the opposers of the war. Continued and frequent deaths among the refugee Loyalists. Pensions of several friends reduced. Fish dinner at the Coffee-house. O for a return to New England! Anxious as to the result of the war. News of surrender of Cornwallis, and admission on all hands, that England can do no more. All the Loyalists abroad deeply agitated as to their future fate. Failure of British Commissioners to procure in the treaty of peace any positive conditions for the Americans in exile Long to be away, but dare not go. Some refugees venture directly to return to their homes; others embark for Nova Scotia and Canada, there to suffer anew. Know of forty-five refugees from Massachusetts who have died in England; among them, Hutchinson, the Governor, and Flucker, the Secretary."

Such were some of the things which Curwen saw and heard, such the hopes and fears which agitated him during his exile, and the course of life of hundreds of others, we may very properly conclude, was not dissimilar. Would that all the opposers of the Revolution had passed their time as innocently! Some of those who remained in the country, did in fact do so; since they were nominal Loyalists only, and lived quietly upon their estates, or pursued their ordinary employments at their usual homes, in the towns occupied by the Royal forces.

CURRY, JOHN. He settled in New Brunswick after the war, and as early as 1792 was senior Justice of the Court of Common Pleas for the County of Charlotte. He died in that county. His son, Cadwallader Curry, was for some years a merchant at Eastport, Maine, and subsequently at Campo Bello, New Brunswick.

CURRY, ROSS. Of Philadelphia. A Whig at first, and a lieutenant in the army. Attainted of treason, and property confiscated. Was a lieutenant in the Pennsylvania Loyalists, and adjutant of the corps. He settled in New Brunswick, received half-pay, and devoted himself to the profession of the law. He died in that Province.

CURTIS, CHARLES. Of Scituate, Massachusetts. Graduated at Harvard University in 1765. He was one of the eighteen country gentlemen who were driven into Boston, and who were Addressers of Gage on his departure, in October, 1775. He was proscribed under the Act of 1778. His death occurred at New York previous to 1832.

CUTLER. Two persons of the name of Thomas Cutler were proscribed and banished in 1778; one by the Act of New Hampshire, the other by that of Massachusetts. The Thomas of the latter belonged to Hatfield. There died at Gaysborough, Nova Scotia, in 1838, Thomas Cutler, Esq., at the age of eighty-five, who was a Loyalist, and who was, undoubtedly, one of them.

CUTLER, EBENEZER. Of Northborough, Massachusetts. In May, 1775, the Northborough Committee of Correspondence made charges against him, and sent him, with the evidence of his misconduct, to General Ward at Cambridge. His case was submitted to Congress, when it appeared that he had spoken " many things disrespectful of the Continental and Provincial Congresses," that he had " acted against their resolves," had said that " he would assist Gage," had called such as signed the town-covenant or non-consumption agreement, " damned fools," &c., &c. A resolve to commit him to prison was refused a passage, and a resolve that he be allowed to join the British troops at Boston, was also lost. But subsequently he was allowed to go into that town " without his effects." Cutler had formerly lived at Groton. In 1776 he accompanied the British Army to Halifax. In 1778 he was proscribed and banished. He settled in Nova Scotia, and was protonotary of the county of Annapolis. He was a zealous Episcopalian ; and, it is related that, seeing his cow drinking from a stream which passed under a Methodist meeting-house, " he beat her severely for her apostacy from the true faith." He died at Annapolis Royal, in 1831, quite aged. Mary, his widow, died at the same place in 1839.

CUTTING, LEONARD. An Episcopal clergyman, of New York. He graduated at Cambridge, England, in 1747, and shortly after was appointed a tutor and a professor in King's College, New York. In 1766 he was settled as minister of St. George's Church, Hempstead, New York. In 1776 he signed an acknowledgment of allegiance, and professed himself a loyal and well-affected subject. While at Hempstead, he preached occasionally at Huntington and Oyster Bay. He also taught a classical school of high repute, and educated several young men who became eminent. In 1784 his pastoral relations at Hempstead were dissolved, and he accepted the Rectorship of the Episcopal Church at Snow Hill, Maryland. Subsequently, he was called to Christ Church, Newbern, North Carolina ; and, after officiating there about eight years, he returned to New York. He died in 1794, in his seventieth year. His wife survived until 1803. One of his sons was the father of Francis B. Cutting, an eminent lawyer of the city of New York. He was small and of slender frame; and was "beloved, equally by his pupils, his parishioners, and his friends."

Cutter, Samuel. Of Edenton, North Carolina. Physician. Born in Brookfield, Massachusetts, in 1741; graduated at Harvard University, 1765. After travelling in Europe, he settled at Edenton, and enjoyed the respect of several leading Whigs. At one period of the war, he was in practice at Newtown, New York. His fortunes subsequently were various. In 1785 he was at Hartford, Connecticut, where he formed business relations with an English gentleman, by which, he said, he hoped to live comfortably the remainder of his days. Though treated with every civility, his situation was disagreeable; because he was among people whose genius and manners were totally different from those with whom he had mingled for twenty years, and because he was entirely separated from old friends to whom he was most tenderly attached. In December of the same year he was at New London, where — he wrote — his employment called him up before the sun, kept him on foot the whole day, and often still later. I find him next in 1795, when he was in Vermont. His two sons were with him, but his wife was at Hartford. His circumstances were easy, but there was no society around him, and he lived almost in solitude. He had relinquished practice, but acted occasionally in consultations. He was a trader, farmer, miller, and distiller. He had been a member of the Legislature; and had he not been loyal in the Revolution, would have enjoyed popular favor. He died at Walpole, New Hampshire, in 1821, in his eightieth year.

Cutter, Zacheus. Of Amherst, New Hampshire. Abandoned the country. Commissioners appointed to examine claims against his estate, June, 1781. For a time during the war, he was at Newtown, New York. Prior to the peace, he sailed for London for the purchase of goods, intending to establish himself in New York, and perished at sea on the return passage. Dr. Samuel Cutter was a kinsman.

Cuyler, Abraham C. Of Albany, New York. Mayor

of that city. Confined at Hartford, he applied to the New York State Convention, (August, 1776,) for permission to visit his wife, who, he said, was sick and unable to take care of his children and large family; and, in the mean time, to settle some of his private affairs.

Released after some delay, he was authorized by the British Commander-in-Chief to raise a battalion of six hundred men for the Royal service, and in November, 1779, was recruiting loyal refugees at Bett's tavern, Jamaica, New York. He was attainted, and his property confiscated. In 1781 he went to England. He returned to Albany, and lived where the North Dutch Church now stands; but his course in the Revolution rendered his situation uncomfortable, and he removed to Canada, and died there in 1810, aged sixty-eight. "He was a man of dignified and gentlemanly deportment." His son, Cornelius, a major in the British Army, died at Montreal in 1807.

CUYLER, HENRY. Colonel in the British Army. He entered the service in 1782, as an ensign; was commissioned a Major in 1797, a Lieutenant-Colonel in 1800, and Colonel in 1810. He died in England in 1841, aged seventy-two.

CUYLER, SIR CORNELIUS, Baronet. Of Albany, New York. General in the British Army. He was born at Albany, and entered the service young. Besides the honors above mentioned, he was Governor of Kinsale, and Colonel of the 69th Foot. He died at St. John's Lodge, Herts, England, in 1819, and was succeeded by his son Charles, the present (1857) Baronet. Lady Cuyler, who died in 1815, was Anne, daughter of Major Richard Grant. George, a son, Colonel of the 11th Foot, and K. C. B., died at Portsmouth, England, in 1818, immediately after his return from Gibraltar.

DABNEY, NATHANIEL. Of Salem, Massachusetts. Physician. An Addresser of Hutchinson in 1774, but one of the "Recanters." He went to England in 1777, and died before the peace. In 1781, his estate was advertised for sale by the Whig authorities.

DALGLISH, ANDREW. Of Salem, Massachusetts. An Addresser of Gage in 1774. He went to England. Was at Glasgow, November, 1781.

DANA, SAMUEL. Of Massachusetts. He was born in that part of Cambridge which is now Brighton, in 1739, and graduated at Harvard University in 1755. Six years later, the town of Groton voted unanimously to invite him to become their minister, with a settlement of £200, a salary of £80, and fire-wood, not to exceed thirty cords per annum. He was ordained June, 1761. In the crisis of 1775, he believed that resistance would lead to greater evils than were then endured, and used his influence on the side of non-resistance. In March, "he preached a sermon which gave great offence to the people, who were generally inclined to unwavering resistance. He was not allowed to enter the meeting-house on the next Sabbath, and his dismission by the town soon followed." . . . . "It is a matter of tradition, that the inhabitants were so enraged, that they shot bullets into Mr. Dana's house, to the great danger of his life and the lives of his family." That he was an excellent man, cannot be doubted. In May, he made a written confession, which, at the moment, was satisfactory. He had warm Whig friends. In the hope that all trouble might terminate, the Whig Committee of Groton, (of whom Colonel Prescott, who shortly after commanded the American force at Breed's Hill, was one,) published a card, to the effect that Mr. Dana had fully atoned for his offences. The good will of his parishioners was, however, alienated, and separation was the consequence. After his dismission at Groton, he continued in that town for some years, but finally removed to Amherst, New Hampshire, when he read law, and was appointed Judge of Probate for the County of Hillsborough. He died at Amherst in 1798, and was buried with Masonic honors. His son Luther was an enterprising ship-master, and father of Samuel L. Dana, physician and chemist, of Lowell, Massachusetts. His second son, Hon. Samuel Dana, who died in 1835, was bred to the law, was distinguished in his profession, and became President of the Senate of Massachusetts, and Chief Justice of the Circuit Court of Common Pleas; the Hon. James Dana, late Mayor of Charlestown, is his youngest son.

DANFORTH, SAMUEL. Of Massachusetts. Son of Rev. John Danforth of Dorchester, and was educated at Harvard University. For several years he was President of the Council, a Judge, and in 1774, a Mandamus Councillor. After the last appointment, the Middlesex County Convention — "Resolved, That whereas the Hon. Samuel Danforth, and Joseph Lee, Esquires, two of the Judges of the Inferior Court of Common Pleas for the County, have accepted commissions under the new Act, by being sworn members of his Majesty's Council, appointed by said Act, we therefore look upon them as utterly incapable of holding any office whatever." He died in 1777, aged eighty-one. He was distinguished for his love of natural philosophy and chemistry.

DANFORTH, SAMUEL. Physician. Of Boston. Son of the preceding. He was born in Massachusetts in 1740, and graduated at Harvard University in 1758. He pursued his medical studies with Doctor Rand, and commenced practice at Newport; but finally settled in Boston. The Revolutionary troubles disturbed his professional pursuits, and distressed his family. His wife and three children took refuge with her father; his brother went to England and never returned; while he himself continued in Boston during the siege. At the evacuation, he was treated harshly. But, as Whigs could not do without physicians better than others, he was soon in full practice, and the confidence of his patients was nearly unlimited, and their attachment almost without bounds. From 1795 to 1798 he was President of the Medical Society. He excelled in medicine, but not in surgery. He continued in full practice until he was nearly fourscore years. After about four years' confinement to his house, he died at Boston in 1827, aged eighty-seven. The family from which he was descended occupy a distinguished place in the annals of New England.

DANFORTH, THOMAS. Counsellor-at-law, Charlestown,

Massachusetts. Brother of the second Samuel. He was a graduate of Harvard University; an Addresser of Hutchinson; and was proscribed and banished. He was the only lawyer at Charlestown, and the only inhabitant of that town who sought protection from the parent country at the beginning of serious opposition. He went to Halifax in 1776. He died in London in 1825.

Daniel, Joseph. In December, 1783, warrant issued on petition of the Selectmen of Stamford, Connecticut, ordering him to depart that town forthwith, and never return.

Daniel, Timothy. Settled in New Brunswick in 1783, and died at Hampton in that Province, in 1847, aged one hundred years.

Darington, John. He emigrated to New Brunswick at the peace, and died there. Joanna, his widow, died in Portland, in that Province, in 1840, at the age of ninety-five.

Davenport, Captain ———. He was a Whig, and held a military commission under Congress, but "was found wholly destitute of honor and principle." His connections were respectable, and he possessed the air and manners of a man of the world. He remained at New York after the retreat of Washington from Long Island, and until the city was occupied by the British troops; and thus became a voluntary captive, if not a deserter.

Davenport, Joseph. Of Virginia. Went to England, and died there in 1783.

Davidson, Hamilton. He died in York County, New Brunswick, in 1841, aged ninety-two.

Davis, Benjamin. Merchant of Boston. Was an Addresser of Hutchinson in 1774, and of Gage in 1775. He left that town with his family, determined, he declared, to settle in some part of his Majesty's dominions. He went first to Halifax, Nova Scotia; and in his passage from that city to New York, in the ship *Peggy*, was captured and carried to Marblehead, and thence to Boston, and imprisoned. In a letter to James Bowdoin, dated in jail, October 10, 1776, he said he was denied pen, ink and paper, was required to keep in an apartment by himself, and was allowed to converse with others only in the presence of the jailer. When he left Boston he had goods in his store of the value of £1000 sterling, which he lost; and when taken at sea he lost £1500 sterling more. In addition, a large amount was due him which was never recovered. In 1778 he was proscribed and banished. He was in New York, July, 1783, and a petitioner for lands in Nova Scotia. In his religious faith Mr. Davis was a Sandemanian.

DAVIS, JOHN. Of Charleston, South Carolina. Was an Addresser of Sir Henry Clinton in 1780, and also a Petitioner to be armed on the side of the Crown. He was banished in 1782, and his property was confiscated. He probably went to England. John Davis, an attainted Loyalist, was in London in 1794, and represented to the British Government that he had been unable to recover several large debts due to him at the time of his banishment. It may be remarked here, that though the sums of money, due to Loyalists proscribed, were now included in the Confiscation Acts, the courts of some of the States were slow to coerce the debtors.

DAVIS, SOLOMON. Of Setauket, New York. Shipmaster in the London trade. His house was assailed, in 1779, by a band of marauders, who fired several balls through it. He was armed, and told them that he was used to the flying of balls around him. Neighbors were alarmed, and the gang went off without entering. In 1783, while returning home from the city of New York, he was met by two men, who shot him dead on the spot.

DAWKINS, GEORGE. Of South Carolina. In 1782 he was a captain of cavalry in the South Carolina Royalists. His estate was confiscated. Wounded, 1781, in the battle of Hobkirk's Hill.

DAWKINS, HENRY. Of New York. Taken on Long Island and sent to prison. In his despair, he stated to the Committee of Safety, that he was " weary of such a miserable life as his misconduct hath thrown him into," and prayed that honorable body to appoint the manner of terminating his sorrows by death.

DAWSON, DAVID. Of Chester County, Pennsylvania. Attainted of treason and property confiscated. Subsequently joined the Royal Army in Philadelphia, and went with it to New York, and was employed in passing counterfeit Continental money. He was detected in 1780, and executed.

DAWSON, JAMES. Of Pennsylvania. Deserted from the State galleys, and joined the British at Philadelphia. Captured at sea. In 1779, in jail and to be tried for treason.

DEALEY, JAMES. Of Charleston, South Carolina. He and Locklan Martin were tarred and feathered, and driven in a cart through the streets of that city in June, 1775; and Dealey was, besides, compelled to leave the country, and go to England. The Secret Committee of Charleston, at that time, was composed of distinguished men, one of whom was subsequently in nomination for the highest honors, and there is evidence that they countenanced, if they did not actually direct, the procedure.

DEAN, JACOB. Of New York. Was a loyal Declarator in 1775. He became an inhabitant of New Brunswick, and died at St. John in 1818, aged eighty.

DEANE, SILAS. Of Connecticut. Graduated at Yale College in 1758. He played a distinguished part among the Whigs in the early part of the contest, but his political sun went down in gloom, sorrow, and destitution. He may have been wronged. A member of the first Continental Congress in 1774, and the first diplomatic agent to France, a brilliant career was before him. But while abroad, his engagements and contracts embarrassed Congress, and he was recalled. Required to account for his pecuniary transactions, he did not dispel suspicion of having misapplied the public funds intrusted to his care. The delegates of Connecticut in Congress appear to have distrusted his integrity from the first. In turn, he accused Arthur and William Lee, who were abroad in public trusts, as well as their brothers in Congress, of conducting a secret correspondence with England. In 1784 he attempted to retrieve his fame, by an address to the country, but failed. He now went to England. Mr. Jay, who was in

Europe, had been his friend, and wished to aid him, and would have done so, had he been able to remove the accusations that had blighted his hopes and injured his character. But Mr. Jay had heard that he was on terms of familiarity with Arnold, and " every American who gives his hand to that man," he wrote to Deane, "in my opinion pollutes it." I have said that he may have been wronged. He may have been careless in his accounts, but not dishonest; he may have been incapable, not corrupt. In 1842 his long-disputed claims were adjusted by Congress, and a large sum was found to be due to his heirs, under the principles recognized by the Government, and applicable to all claimants; hence the doubt, whether he received entire justice at the hands of his associates. A man driven to despair is to be judged mercifully. He died on board the *Boston Packet*, in the Downs, in 1789, in his fifty-third year, after four hours' illness. His wife was " the rich widow Webb."

DEBLOIS, GILBERT. Merchant, of Boston. An Addresser of Hutchinson in 1774, and of Gage in 1775. He went to Halifax in 1776. In 1778 he was proscribed and banished. In 1779 he was in London, and addressed the King. He died in England in 1791, aged sixty-three.

DEBLOIS, GEORGE. Of Salem, Massachusetts. An Addresser of Gage in 1774. He went to England. In 1784, George Deblois, Jr., was a merchant at Halifax, Nova Scotia. The widow of *a* George Deblois, died at the same city, December, 1827, aged seventy-four.

DEBLOIS, ISAAC. He was in the service of the King, and a lieutenant. In 1784 a lot in the city of St. John, New Brunswick, was granted him by the Crown.

DEBLOIS, LEWIS. Merchant, of Boston. He was an Addresser of Gage in 1775, and in 1776 was at Halifax. In 1778 he was proscribed and banished. He was in London in 1779. He died very suddenly in England, (after being out all day,) in 1779, aged seventy-one.

DEBLOIS, LEWIS. Of Massachusetts. After the peace, a merchant in St. John, New Brunswick, and in 1795 a member of the company of Loyal Artillery. He died in that city in 1802. His daughter, Elizabeth Cranston, is the wife of James White, Esq., late (1847) sheriff of the county of St. John.

DEBOW, JAMES. Served in the Queen's Rangers; settled in New Brunswick in 1783, and died there. His widow, Huldah, died in that Province in 1847, aged ninety-four.

DE LANCEY, OLIVER. Of New York. In command of a Loyalist brigade. He was the eldest son of Stephen De Lancey and of his wife, Ann Van Cortlandt, and was born in the city of New York in 1717. He served with credit in two campaigns of the French war, at the head of a regiment. In 1759 he was elected to the House of Assembly, and the next year appointed a member of the Council. His father, who was a French refugee, was a gentleman of wealth, and of the first rank. His career for some years may be considered in connection with that of his brother James, who was Chief Justice and Lieutenant-Governor of that Colony. James was a man of talents, of learning, of great vivacity, and of popular manners; but, if the writers of the time are to be followed, he was also an unprincipled demagogue, who opposed the governors whom he could not rule, and who, for unworthy purposes of his own, kept the public mind in continual agitation. He was at the head of affairs and administered the government after the removal of Clinton and the death of Osborn, and a second time as the successor of Hardy. He died in 1760. The party opposed to his advancement, in denouncing his ambitious projects, did not spare Oliver, the subject of this notice. On some occasions, Oliver seems to have promoted his brother's designs, at the expense of propriety and decorum. But yet Oliver De Lancey, at the period of the French war, occupied a commanding position, and perhaps he did not overrate his personal influence when he said, that if in the expedition against Crown Point, he "should accept the command of the New York Regiment, he could in ten days raise the whole" quota of troops allotted to that Colony. This standing he maintained after his brother's death, and until the

Revolution. At the beginning of the controversy he may not have been a zealous adherent of the Crown. Some of the Whigs insisted, indeed, that he heartily approved of the course of the Ministry, and a letter appeared in a newspaper in England, in 1775, which, if genuine, authorized the opinion. But this letter he publicly averred to be an infamous and a malicious forgery. Nor did he stop there, for he submitted, as he declared upon his honor, the whole of his correspondence with his friends in England, from the earlist moment of the dispute, to Mr. Jay, who, finding nothing objectionable, so stated in a card which was published. But whatever was his course before the question of separation from the mother country was discussed, he opposed the dismemberment of the empire, and put his life and property at stake to prevent it. In 1776 he was appointed a brigadier-general in the Royal service. Skinner, of New Jersey; Brown, a former governor of the Bahamas; Arnold, the apostate; and Cunningham, of South Carolina, were of the same grade, but their commissions were of later dates. General De Lancey was, therefore, the senior Loyalist officer in commission during the contest. His command consisted of three battalions, known as De Lancey's Battalions. In his orders for enlistments, he promised to any well-recommended characters, who should engage a company of seventy men, the disposal of the commissions of captain, lieutenant, and ensign. The common soldiers, he said, would be " in British pay." * Yet his success in filling his battalions was not flattering. Of the fifteen hundred men required, only five hundred and ninety-seven were embodied in the spring of 1777, and but seven hundred and seven a year later.

It is stated, that, while he was raising his brigade on Long Island, Colonel Henry R. Livingston made a " little excursion " there, and carried off more than three thousand sheep and about four hundred horned cattle, and that £500 was

* Copies of several of his orders, which disclosed his plans for raising recruits and obtaining provisions, were sent to Washington, and transmitted by him to Congress, October, 1776.

offered for the "Rebel" officer's head. In November of the last-mentioned year, a small party of the Whig "advanced water-guard," passed the British ships in the night, burned his mansion at Bloomingdale, and rudely treated the inmates, who were ladies and servants of the family. Mrs. De Lancey, who was very deaf, hid herself in a dog-kennel, and came near being burned there. Her daughter Charlotte, (of whom presently,) and Elizabeth, daughter of Richard Floyd, (who married John Peter De Lancey, and was the mother of the wife of Cooper, the great American novelist,) wandered about in the woods, for hours, barefooted, and in their night clothes. The Council of Safety promptly disapproved of the act; not so much, however, because of its barbarity, but because of the apprehension that the British would retaliate.

In 1780, General Robertson, who had succeeded Tryon as Royal Governor of New York, wrote Lord George Germain: "Brigadier-General De Lancey is extremely desirous I should mention his name to your Lordship by this very occasion. I can't do this without saying that he is a man of consequence in this country, and has suffered much by the Rebellion, the authors of which he is earnest to punish."

The Whig Government of New York, which was organized in 1777, attainted him of treason and confiscated his estate. He went to England at the peace, but did not long survive. He died at Beverley in 1785, at the age of sixty-eight. In the "Life of Van Schaack," his decease is mentioned thus by a fellow-Loyalist: "Our old friend has at last taken his departure from Beverley, which he said should hold his bones; he went off without pain or struggle, his body wasted to a skeleton, his mind the same. The family, most of them, collected in town [London.] There will scarcely be a village in England without some American dust in it, I believe, by the time we are all at rest."

"The Gentleman's Magazine" announces simply the place of his death, his name, military rank, and "late of New York, who lost a large estate by his loyalty." His mother and the mother of Cortlandt Skinner were sisters. He married Phelia

Franks, of Philadelphia, who died in Smith Street, Chelsea, England, in 1811, in her eighty-ninth year. One of his daughters, Susan, was the wife of the celebrated Lieutenant-General Sir William Draper, Knight of the Bath; another, Charlotte, married Field-Marshal Sir David Dundas, Bart, who at one time was Commander-in-Chief of the British Army; a third married Lieutenant-Colonel John Harris Cruger.

DE LANCEY, OLIVER, JR. Of New York. Son of Brigadier-General Oliver De Lancey. General in the British Army. He was educated in Europe. At the beginning of the Revolution he was a captain. In 1776 he became a major; was a lieutenant-colonel as early as 1779, and succeeded André as adjutant-general of the army in America. His treatment of General Nathaniel Woodhull, an estimable Whig of New York, who became his prisoner in 1776, should never be forgotten. There seems no room to doubt, that when that unfortunate gentleman surrendered his sword to De Lancey, he stipulated for, and was promised, protection; but that his Loyalist countryman basely struck him, and permitted his men to cut and hack him at pleasure. And it is no less certain that the General, maimed and wounded, was denied proper care, attention, and accommodation, and that he perished in consequence of the barbarities of his captors.

I find De Lancey called Barrack-Master-General and Major-General in 1794; and, some years later, Lieutenant-General, and General. He went to England and died unmarried, nearly at the head of the British Army List. He was the father of a natural son and daughter who bore his name, and who were openly acknowledged. The latter was living in 1844. Possibly, the former was the Colonel Oliver De Lancey, who died at St. Sebastian in 1837, at the age of thirty-four, in consequence of wounds received in battle. It seems this officer had left the British Army, in which he was a captain in the 60th Rifles, and had espoused the cause of the Queen of Spain in the war with the Carlists.

The accuracy of the text as relates to General De Lancey's

conduct to General Woodhull, as it stood in the first edition of this work, and as it stands above, was questioned by Mr. Cooper, the novelist, over his own signature, in an article published in the "Home Journal," New York, February 12, 1848. A discussion ensued between us in that paper, in which Henry C. Van Schaack, Henry Onderdonk, Jr., and the writer, "Vindex," participated. A review of it is not necessary here, since the question between us was one of evidence, and to be determined by the opinion formed of the credibility of writers; except the following passage in Mr. Cooper's communication of May 6th, which, as it contains the denial of the party accused, I insert with great cheerfulness. Mrs. Cooper was a daughter of John Peter De Lancey, and her husband, after stating this fact, remarked that he well remembered a conversation with her father, who said: "They endeavored to put the death of General Woodhull on my cousin, General De Lancey. Colonel Troup made an affidavit, which Gouveneur Morris published. Troup and Morris [both were then alive] are respectable men, certainly — *but Oliver always indignantly denied it!*" The italics are Mr. Cooper's.

Robert Troup, in after life, was the personal friend and political associate of Jay and Hamilton, and of stainless honor. At the time of Woodhull's death, he was a lieutenant in Colonel Lasher's Battalion of New York Militia; and, a fellow-prisoner with the General, seems to have listened to his latest statement of his treatment. The curious reader who wishes to examine the case for himself, will find full details in "Onderdonk's Revolutionary Incidents of Queen's County." In 1775, the Committee of Safety of New York described General De Lancey as "a lusty, fat, ruddy young fellow, between twenty and thirty years of age." He died at Edinburgh in 1820.

DE LANCEY, JAMES. Of the city of New York. Son of Lieutenant-Governor James De Lancey. He was educated at Eton, and at Cambridge, England. He obtained a commission in the British Army, and in the campaign against Ticonderoga, during the French war, was an Aid of General Abercrombie. Soon after the decease of his father, he sold his commission. He inherited the principal family estates; and, at the Revolutionary era was one of the richest men in the country. From 1769 to 1775, he was a member of the House of Assembly, and his election was regarded as a triumph of the Episcopalians over the Presbyterians. In the last-named year, he went to England, and some time after was followed by his wife and children. Attainted of treason, and his property confiscated, he never returned. At the formation of the Loyalist Commission for the prosecution of claims, he was appointed Agent for New York, and became Vice-President of the Board. His own losses were large and difficult of adjustment, and occupied the attention of the Commissioners for some days. Excepting Sir William Pepperell, Colonel De Lancey appears to have been the most active member of the agency; and two papers on the subject of the Loyalists' claims which bear his signature contain much information. These papers produced no effect, except as is stated in the preliminary remarks to this work; no discrimination was finally made between Loyalists of different degrees of loyalty, merit, and grades of service. In this respect all were treated alike; but the Commissioners were not required to revise their proceedings, as was asked for in the Address to Parliament; nor was Mr. Pitt induced to change his purpose of making certain rates of reduction on the sums reported to be due to claimants by the Commissioners, as was solicited in the communication to him.

Indeed, the claimants appear to have acquiesced in the decision of the Minister; and the Board of Agents, after Mr. Pitt's plan was confirmed by an Act of Parliament, presented an Adress to the King. De Lancey affixed his signature to this Address, and with his associates had an audience of his Majesty, and "had the honor to kiss his Majesty's hand."

The time and place of his decease have not been ascertained. His wife was Margaret, daughter of Chief Justice Allen, of Pennsylvania. Five children grew up, namely: Charles, who entered the Navy, and died unmarried; James, who in 1851 was Lieutenant-Colonel of the First Dragoon Guards, and the only male survivor of the family; Anne and Susan, who were unmarried and living in 1848; and Margaret, who, the wife of Sir Juckes Granville Clifton, Baronet, died childless.

DE LANCEY, JAMES. Of West Chester County, New York. Lieutenant-Colonel Commandant of a battalion of his uncle, the senior Oliver De Lancey. He was the son of Peter De Lancey and Elizabeth Colden. For a considerable time he was sheriff of West Chester, in which, owing to his intimate acquaintance with the county, he was stationed during several years of the Revolution. "His corps made free with the cattle of that part of the country, and got the *soubriquet* of 'Cow-Boys,' in revenge for their knowledge of beef." In 1777 according to Governor Tryon, he raised and commanded a troop of light-horse, the "*elite*" of the Colony. The same year, one of Putnam's scouting parties surrounded the house in which he lodged, to take him prisoner. In the alarm, he jumped out of bed and hid himself under it. Discovered in the search, he was dragged out, and carried to camp. While in jail at Hartford, he received the following letter from Mr. Jay, who was an old friend:—

"SIR,—Notwithstanding the opposition of our sentiments and conduct relative to the present contest, the friendship which subsisted between us is not forgotten; nor will the good offices formerly done by yourself and family cease to excite my gratitude. How far your situation may be comfortable and easy, I know not; it is my wish, and it shall be my endeavor, that it be as much so as may be consistent with the interest of the great cause to which I have devoted everything I hold dear in this world. I have taken the liberty of requesting Mr. Samuel Broome immediately to advance you one hundred dollars on my account. Your not having heard from me sooner was unavoidable. A line by the first opportunity will oblige me. Be explicit, and avail yourself without hesitation of the friendship which was entertained as well as professed for you by

"Your obedient and humble servant,
"JOHN JAY."

"Poughkeepsie, January 2d, 1778"

In July, 1781, Colonel De Lancey was at Morrisania, and a plan was formed to capture or destroy his unpopular, nay, odious, corps. Washington ordered the Duke de Lauzun to proceed in advance, and directed General Lincoln to coöperate; while he himself put the army in motion, "in order," as he records in his *Diary*, "to cover the detached troops and improve the advantages which might be gained by them." Owing to circumstances which I have not room to state, the expedition failed. At the peace, the commander of the "Cow-Boys" retired to Nova Scotia.

Mr. Macdonald, in a paper read before the New York Historical Society, in 1861, gave an interesting account of Colonel De Lancey's final departure from West Chester. I make brief extracts: "The Outlaw of the Bronx," he said, "with a heavy heart mounted his horse, and riding to the dwellings of his neighbors, bade them each farewell." Again: "His paternal fields and every object presented to his view were associated with the joyful recollections of early life. The consciousness that he beheld them all for the last time, and the uncertainties to be encountered in the strange country to which banishment was consigning him, conspired to awaken emotions, such as the sternest bosom is sometimes compelled to entertain. It was in vain that he struggled to suppress feelings which shook his iron heart. Nature soon obtained the mastery, and he burst into tears. After weeping with uncontrollable bitterness for a few moments, he shook his ancient friend by the hand, ejaculated with difficulty the words of benediction — 'God bless you, Theophilus!' and spurring forward, turned his back forever upon his native valley."

Colonel De Lancey was appointed a member of the Council of Nova Scotia in 1794. He died at Annapolis in that Province in the year 1800. Martha, his widow, died at the same place in 1827, aged seventy-three.

DE LANCEY, JAMES. Of New York. He was an officer in Oliver De Lancey's Second Battalion. James De Lancey, Esq., Collector of his Majesty's Customs, died at Crooked Island, New Providence, in 1808, and was perhaps the same.

DE LANCEY, JOHN. Of New York. Son of Peter De Lancey, of West Chester County. Succeeded his father in the House of Assembly. In 1775, elected a member of the Provincial Congress. In 1776, an Addresser of Lord and Sir William Howe.

DE LANCEY, JOHN PETER. Of New York. He was born in that city in 1753. He was educated in England by his brother James. He entered the British Army, and was a captain. He participated in the battles of Brandywine and Monmouth, and was in service at the South. In 1789 he resigned his commission, and returned with his wife to his native State. The remainder of his life was passed in West Chester County, and he died there in 1828. Elizabeth, his wife, died in 1820.

DE LANCEY, STEPHEN. Of New York. Lieutenant-Colonel Commandant of the First Battalion of New Jersey Volunteers. The fragmentary accounts of this gentleman are conflicting. He was son of Peter, or of the senior Oliver, and in 1765 was appointed clerk of the city and county of Albany. The King's birthday, in 1776, " was ushered in with firing of guns, and other rejoicings, not agreeable to the inhabitants, and in the evening a party assembled to do honor to the day, with Abraham C. Cuyler, the Mayor, at their head, and were found carousing, and singing ' God save the King.' The citizens became exasperated, rushed in, and seized Stephen De Lancey and others, and carried them off to jail, whence they were shortly after removed to Hartford, Connecticut." Some time after his release by Governor Trumbull on parole, I find him in command, as above mentioned. At the close of the war, he went to Nova Scotia, and in 1786 was appointed member of the Council.

Omitting several discrepancies in facts and dates, which I cannot reconcile, I insert next the following notice which appeared in an English periodical in 1799: — " Died, at Portsmouth, in America, on board the brig *Nancies*, Captain Tibbets, from Tobago, Stephen De Lancey, Esq., who, for several years was Chief Justice of the Bahama Islands, and continued to hold that office in 1797, since when (we believe) he was appointed Governor of Tobago. His remains were attended by a numerous procession of friends and strangers, and deposited in the tomb of the late Governor Wentworth." He may have married twice. In one place his wife is called Esther Rynderts; in another, a daughter of the Rev. Henry Barclay, Rector of Trinity Church, New York. In 1817, it is recorded: " Died at Colchester, England, Mrs. Cornelia De Lancey, relict of S. De Lancey, Esq., formerly Governor of Tobago, and mother of Colonel Sir W. F. De Lancey, H. C. B., who fell at the battle of Waterloo." Sir William was Quartermaster-General of Wellington's army; and Susan De Lancey, his daughter, married Sir Hudson Lowe, who was Napoleon's *keeper* — I must use that offensive word — at St. Helena.

DE LANCEY, WARREN. Of New York. At the engagement on Chatterton's Hill, West Chester County, in 1776, De Lancey was a youth of fifteen years. " While the British were advancing up the hill, a shot struck one of the standard-bearers dead." Warren " instantly seized the colors, and, rushing forward, was one of the first to gain the summit, where he planted them in the ground." For this act of bravery, he afterwards received a cornet's commission from Sir William Howe, in the 17th Dragoons, commanded by Oliver De Lancey the younger. He left the army before the peace, and died in the State of New York, " near me," says the late J. Fenimore Cooper, (in a letter dated March 11, 1848) "a year or two since," leaving issue.

DE PEYSTER, ABRAHAM. Of New York. The De Peysters are of noble descent. Johannes de Peijster, (Peister, or Pester) the ancestor of this family in this country, was driven from his native land in the time of Charles the 9th, during that monarch's persecutions of his Protestant subjects. He settled in New York, and became an eminent merchant. " Portions of the costly articles of furniture, the elegant and massive family silver plate, and pictures, perfect gems of art . . . . which he brought out from Holland, are still in the possession of his descendants."

The subject of this notice was born in 1753. Two of his uncles, and one of his great-uncles, were members of the Council; another uncle was Chief-Justice of the Colony; and a brother-in-law was in command of a regiment of Royal Artillery. It is easy, therefore, to account for the loyalty of one so young and thus connected. He entered the King's service, and was a captain in the New York Volunteers. He was second in command at the battle of King's Mountain, in 1780, and, after the fall of Ferguson, hoisted a flag as a signal of surrender. The firing immediately ceased, and the Royal troops laying down their arms, the most of which were loaded, submitted to the conquerors at discretion. It seems not to be generally understood, that nearly the whole of Ferguson's force was composed of Loyalists; but such is the fact. He went into action with eleven hundred and twenty-five men, of whom only one hundred and sixty-two were Regulars. Of the Loyalists, no less than two hundred and six were killed, one hundred and twenty-eight wounded, and six hundred and twenty-nine taken prisoners. The loss of Regulars was eighteen slain and one hundred and three wounded and captured. Captain De Peyster was paid off the morning of the battle. Among the coin which he received was a doubloon, which he put in a pocket of his vest. While on the field, a bullet struck the gold and stopped, and his life was thus saved. Sims, in his "Life of Marion," relates that Major Postell, "who was stationed to guard the lower part of the Pedee, succeeded in capturing Captain De Peyster, with twenty-nine grenadiers." "De Peyster," he continues, "had taken post in the dwelling-house of Postell's father. The latter had with him but twenty-eight militia, but he knew the ground, and gaining possession of the kitchen, fired it, and was preparing to burn the house also, when" the Loyalist captain submitted. A gentleman of De Peyster's lineage informs me that Sims is inaccurate; that, in the court of inquiry which followed the surrender, it was proved that the Whig force was about one hundred, and entirely surrounded his kinsman's band of "twenty-nine." Captain

De Peyster went to St. John, New Brunswick, at the peace, and was one of the grantees of that city. He received half-pay. He was treasurer of that Province, and a colonel in the militia. He died previous to 1799, as, in that year, leave was given to sell a part of his estate in the hands of his administrator. His wife (whom he married in 1783) was Catharine, second daughter of John Livingston. The De Peysters of the Revolutionary era were allied by blood or marriage to several of the oldest and richest families in New York, and were themselves persons of great respectability.

DE PEYSTER, FREDERICK. Of New York. Brother of the preceding. While a minor, he was in command of a company raised for the protection of his uncle, Hon. William Axtell, a member of the Council, who lived in Flushing, Long Island. Subsequently, he was a captain in the New York Volunteers. In swimming a river on horseback, a rifle bullet passed through both his legs, and killed his horse. At the storming of Fort Montgomery in 1777, a detachment of his regiment, which was a part of the Royal force, was the first to enter the works. In 1784 Captain De Peyster was at St. John, New Brunswick, and received the grant of a city lot. In 1792 he was a magistrate in the county of York. He returned to the United States. His first wife was daughter of Commissary-General Hake; his second wife, daughter of Gerard G. Beekman, and granddaughter of Lieutenant-Governor Van Cortlandt.

DE PEYSTER, JAMES. Of New York. Brother of the preceding. He was captain-lieutenant in the King's American Regiment under Fanning, and entered the service when he was only nineteen years of age. His superior officers gave him high " testimonials of courage, ability, and conduct," after he closed his military life as a Loyalist. In 1786, he was commissioned as first lieutenant in the Royal Artillery, commanded by his brother-in-law, Colonel James. De Peyster is said to have been one of the handsomest men in the British Army.

I am indebted to one of his kinsmen in the State of New

York — who has contributed several curious and interesting works to the literature of the country — for an account of his fate. I extract as freely as my limits will allow. The date is 1793; the scene, the siege of Valenciennes: "This siege was remarkable, in that a greater portion than usual of the operations were subterranean. Mines and counter-mines innumerable were formed and sprung by both besiegers and besieged. On the 25th July, the English sprung two large ones under the glacis and horn-work, whose immediate result was to enable them to establish themselves in the covered way. Among the foremost, as usual, our hero was buried by one of these explosions, and reported among the 'missing.' After a search of more than an hour, he was discovered in a state of partial stupefaction. Thus he may have been said to have been restored to his regiment after having been buried alive.

"Three days afterwards, Valenciennes surrendered. A large share in this success was accorded to the British Artillery. The British now advanced and occupied a camp in the neighborhood of Menin, a fortified town of West Flanders, on the Lys." "Again," says my informant, "on the 18th August, three battalions of the English Guards, and detachments of the Royal Artillery, advanced to attack the French position. The enemy occupied a redoubt of uncommon size and strength upon a height adjoining to the high-road, in front of the village of Lincelles. The road itself was defended by other works strongly palisadoed; woods and ditches covered their flanks. The battalions were instantly formed, and advanced under a heavy fire, with an order and intrepidity for which no praise can be too high.

"To overcome such difficulties demanded great sacrifices and greater exertions, yet the fall of two gallant officers, and the brave men who have suffered on this occasion, must be a matter of regret. In the fore front of this glorious attack, and among the first who fell, was the subject of this article."

Still again: "Many years after, my grandfather, Frederick

De Peyster, was dining with his second cousin, Frederick C. White, General in the British Army, when the conversation turned upon the latter's military service in Holland, and particularly the combat of Menin, or, more properly speaking, of Lincelles. 'While advancing at the head of my corps,' said the General, 'on the 18th of August, 1793, I noticed a remarkably fine-looking dead officer, with his cocked hat slouched over his face, whom his men had raised up and fixed in an erect position, by taking advantage of the support afforded by the crotch of a tree. Not being able to recognize him, — for his chin had sunk down upon his chest, and his chapeau had been drawn down almost so as to cover his eyes, to keep it from falling off, — I turned aside, and, lifting his head, removed the hat, discovering thereby, to my grief and horror, that it was your beloved brother and my gallant cousin, James, who had been shot directly through the forehead.'" Finally: "Under contract of marriage to a lady of fortune, won by his physical and mental advantages, he postponed his union until the close of the campaign, and passed from the transient endearments of love to the lasting embrace of death. . . . . His portrait in New York attracts universal attention, and bears ample testimony to his advantages of person."

DE ROSSET, LEWIS H. A member of the Council of North Carolina. He was present April 2, 1775, and gave his assent to the issuing of a proclamation to forbid the meeting of a Whig Convention at Newbern on the following day. This Convention was for the purpose of electing delegates to the Continental Congress. He was in communication with Governor Martin after the Royal authority had ceased, and his Excellency had abandoned the palace. In the war against the "Regulators," he was called Lieutenant-General. A Whig, who knew him well, said he was "a cultivated and elegant gentleman." He was expelled from North Carolina.

DESCHAMP, ———. Committed suicide at Shelburne, Nova Scotia, about the year 1805.

DEVEAUX, ANDREW, JR. Of South Carolina. Lieutenant-Colonel in the Loyal Militia. In April, 1783, he commanded a successful expedition against the Bahamas. His own account of the affair follows : — " I have the honor to inform you," he wrote, " that, on the night of the 14th instant, we arrived at the Salt Key with our fleet, four miles distant from the Eastern Fort, which consisted of thirteen pieces of cannon. I landed about a mile from it, a little after daylight, with my formidable body of about one hundred and sixty men, and proceeded against it with all possible expedition, determined to storm immediately ; but there being a plain for some distance round their fortifications, gave the enemy an opportunity of discovering us, when they, in great confusion, abandoned the fort, and drew up in a field near a wood. As soon as I came up with them, they fired upon us. My young troops charged them, made two prisoners, and drove their main body, in great irregularity, into town. We sustained no loss on our side. Captains Wheeler and Dow detached about seventy men in boats, to board three formidable gallies that lay abreast of the Eastern Fort, which was effected about the time of my skirmish with the enemy. On my going to take possession of the fort, I smelt a match on fire, which circumstance, together with their abandoning their works so readily, gave me reason to suspect their intentions. I immediately had the two prisoners confined in the fort, and halted my troops at some distance from it; but, self-preservation being so natural a reflection, they soon discovered the match that was on fire, which, in half an hour, would have been communicated to the magazine and two mines that were laid for the purpose. About two hours after I had taken possession of the fort, his Excellency Governor Claraco sent out a flag, giving some trifling information of a peace. I supposed his information entirely for the purpose of putting off time and amusing me; I, therefore, shortly after the return of his flag, demanded the surrender of the garrison at discretion, in fifteen minutes. In answer to which his Excellency waved the surrender, and requested a conference with me personally, when he made offers which I thought prudent to accept, and to establish a truce between us for some days; but fortunately his Excellency was discovered to be carrying on his works, and not adhering so strictly to the terms of the truce as he ought; this gave me an opportunity of commencing hostilities once more with him. I immediately landed eight pieces of heavy cannon from the captured vessels, viz., one brig and two sloops, with twenty-four and twelve-pounders, with which I stole a march in the night of the 17th instant, and sunk my cannon in the solid rock on Society-hill, which is about four hundred yards from the grand fortress, consisting of twenty-one pieces of cannon, and two small flanking batteries of three guns each. On an adjacent hill I erected a work with one twelve and four four-pounders, which was not three hundred yards distance from them, commanded by Captain M'Kenzie; a third work of two nine-pounders was not complete. The enemy kept up a heavy fire, and throwing of shells during the night, which had no bad effect. On the morning of the 18th, having two batteries ready to open on them, and a third, which, though not complete, could have annoyed them greatly, besides two gallies, with twenty four-pounders, I gave his Excellency once more an opportunity of saving the lives of his men from the horrid consequences attending a work being carried by storm; upon which his Excellency surrendered the garrison." New Providence received quite an accession to its population from Loyalists who fled from the Southern States.

DE VEBER, GABRIEL. Of New York. He entered the military service of the Crown, and in 1782 was lieutenant-colonel of the Prince of Wales's American Volunteers. He settled in New Brunswick at the close of the war, and was a grantee of the city of St. John. He received half-pay. In 1792 he was sheriff of the county of Sunbury, and colonel in the militia. He died in that county. Margaret, his wife, third daughter of Doctor Nathaniel Hubbard, of Stamford, Connecticut, died in King's County in 1813.

DE VEBER, GABRIEL, JR. Of New York. Son of Gabriel. In 1782 he was a lieutenant in De Lancey's Third

Battalion. He went to St. John, New Brunswick, at the peace, was a grantee of that city, and received half-pay. He died in that Province.

DEVOE, FREDERICK. Of West Chester County, New York. Went to St. John, New Brunswick, and was a grantee of that city. His farm of three hundred acres, at New Rochelle, was confiscated, and given to Thomas Paine, by the Legislature of New York.

DEVOE, JAMES. Of the State of New York. A grantee of St. John, New Brunswick, in 1783. He died at Hampton, in that Province, in 1833, aged seventy-nine.

DIBBLEE, JOSEPH. Of Danbury, Connecticut. Known to be a Tory and to shelter Tories; he suffered, at the hands of the Whigs, for his principles and his deeds. He and his father entertained Tryon at Danbury, when that ruthless officer was on the expedition of devastation to Connecticut. Dibblee was once taken out of bed at night, by men in disguise, carried to a stream, and ducked until he expected to perish. At the peace he continued in his native town. "Time softened the asperities of feeling" against him; and, when visited by Lossing a few years ago, he was in his hundredth year, and had "lived among his old neighbors and their descendants, a worthy and respected citizen." He was never married.

DIBBLEE, FREDERICK. He was born at Stamford, Connecticut, and graduated at King's College, New York. He was a missionary of the Society for Propagating the Gospel in Foreign Parts, with a salary of £50. In December, 1783, a warrant was issued upon petition of the Selectmen of Stamford, ordering him and his family to depart that town forthwith, and never return. He settled in New Brunswick, and became Rector of the Episcopal Church at Woodstock. He died at that place in 1826, aged seventy-three. Nancy, his widow, died at the same place in 1838, at the age of eighty-three.

DIBBLEE, FYLER. Attorney-at-law, Stamford, Connecticut. In 1775 he was captain of the first military company of that town, and a person of consideration. He early incurred the displeasure of the Whigs, and the Assembly of Connecticut appointed commissioners to inquire into his conduct. In 1778, he and sixteen other Loyalists were taken prisoners on Long Island, New York, by a party of Whigs, who landed there from boats.. His property in Connecticut was confiscated. In 1783 he was a deputy agent for the transportation of Loyalists from New York to Nova Scotia, and, in April of that year, sailed from Huntington Bay in the ship *Union*, for St. John, New Brunswick, and arrived in May. He was accompanied by his wife, five children, and two servants. In 1784 he received the grant of two city lots. Some years after he committed suicide. Various reasons have been assigned for the melancholy termination of his life.

DIBBLEE, RALPH. Died at Kingston, New Brunswick, in 1799.

DIBBLEE, WALTER. Of Stamford, Connecticut. He arrived at St. John, New Brunswick, in the ship *Union*, in 1783. The Crown granted him a city lot in 1784. He died at Sussex Vale, in that Province, in 1817, aged fifty-three.

DICK, JOHN. Of New York. At the peace, accompanied by his family, he went from New York to Shelburne, Nova Scotia, where the Crown granted him one town lot. He died at St. George, New Brunswick, in 1839, aged ninety-five years.

DICKE, WALDO. Of Warren, Maine. His mother was daughter of a Scotch laird, and unacquainted with any kind of domestic labor. He was the first child born to the emigrants on the "Waldo Patent," after their arrival, and was named for the proprietor, who "promised to give him a lot of land as soon as he should get large enough to wear breeches; but, the General dying, the promise was never fulfilled."

During the Revolution, he was too active on the side of the Crown to be forgiven by the people of Warren; and at the peace went to St. Andrew, New Brunswick, where he was employed as a ship-master. About the year 1794, he was confined in irons at New London for some offence committed on ship-board, and succeeded in releasing himself from prison; but, attempting to escape by swimming, was drowned. Warren was the first town incorporated in Maine, after the Whigs of Massachusetts assumed the government; and was named in honor of the distinguished victim of June 17th, 1775.

DICKSON, ROBERT. Settled in Nova Scotia. Was a member of the House of Assembly, and magistrate of the District of Colchester. He died in 1835.

DICKSON, W. Of New York. He commanded a company in the New York Volunteers. In 1780 he was drowned at Long Island, while bathing. His body was found and interred.

DINGEE, SOLOMON. He died at Gagetown, New Brunswick, in 1836, aged eighty.

DINGEY, CHARLES. Of Pennsylvania. Imprisoned in 1778, on the charge of acknowledging himself to be still a subject of George the Third; of refusing to take the oath prescribed by the Whig Government; of declining to give his parole to do the popular cause no injury; and of attempting to go into Philadelphia while in possession of the Royal Army. Released, on furnishing three sureties, in £1000 each, to appear at Lancaster within ten days, to answer.

DINGWELL, ARTHUR. He went to St. John, New Brunswick, at the peace, and was one of the grantees of that city. In 1795 he was a member of the Loyal Artillery of St. John. In 1801, advertised that he was about to leave the Province.

DITMARS, JOHN J. Of Long Island, New York. Went to Nova Scotia, and died there in 1829, aged ninety-seven.

DIXON, CHARLES. He became an inhabitant of New Brunswick at the peace, or perhaps a little earlier, and continued a resident of the Province until his death, in 1817, at the age of eighty-nine.

DIXON, JOSEPH. He died at Hampton, King's County, New Brunswick, in 1842, aged ninety-two.

DOANE. Of Bucks County, Pennsylvania. Five brothers, namely: Moses, Joseph, Israel, Abraham, Mahlon. They were men of fine figure and address, elegant horsemen, great runners and leapers, and excellent at stratagems and escapes. Their father was respectable, and possessed a good estate. The sons themselves, prior to the war, were men of reputation, and proposed to remain neutral. But, harrassed personally, their property sold by the Whigs because they would not submit to the exactions of the time, the above-mentioned determined to wage a predatory warfare upon their persecutors, and to live in the open air, as they best could do. This plan they executed, to the terror of the country around; acting as spies to the Royal Army, and robbing and plundering continually; yet they spared the weak, the poor, and the peaceful. They aimed at public property and at public men. Generally, their expeditions were on horseback. Sometimes the five went together; at others, separately, with accomplices. Whoever of them was apprehended, broke jail; whoever of them was assailed, escaped. In a word, such was their course, that a reward of £300 was offered for the head of each.

Ultimately, three were slain; Moses, after a desperate fight, was shot by his captor; Abraham and Mahlon were hung at Philadelphia.

Joseph, before the Revolution, taught school. During the war, while on a marauding expedition, he was shot through the cheeks, fell from his horse, and was taken prisoner. He was committed to jail, but while waiting his trial, escaped to New Jersey. A reward of $800 was offered for his apprehension, without success. He resumed his former employment in New Jersey, and lived there under an assumed name, nearly a year; but finally fled to Canada. Several years after the peace, he returned to Pennsylvania, — "a poor, degraded, broken-down old man," — to claim a legacy of about £40, which he was allowed to recover, and to depart. In his youth he was distinguished for great physical activity.

The only separate mention of Israel is, that in February, 1783, he was in jail; that he appealed to the Council of Pennsylvania to be released, on account of his own sufferings and the destitute condition of his family, and that his petition was dismissed.

Beside these five brothers, there were three others: Joseph, their father, who was in Bedford County jail, September, 1783; Aaron, who was under sentence of death at Philadelphia, October, 1784, but was pardoned by the Council, March,

1785; and a second Aaron, who was in prison in 1785, and was reprieved under the gallows, at Newark, New Jersey, in July, 1788.

Dobbie, George. He died at the beginning of the Revolution, and the greater part of his property was lost to his family. His son, William Hugh Dobbie, captain in the British Navy, died in England in 1830, aged fifty-eight.

Dodd, Robert. Of Pennsylvania. Deserted from the State galleys. Joined the British in Philadelphia. Captured at sea. In jail in 1779, and to be tried for treason.

Dodd, ———. Was in the military service of the Crown, and engaged in the battles of White Plains and Monmouth, and in the siege of Yorktown. At the peace, he went to New Brunswick, and died there. His widow, Elizabeth, died at St. Stephen in that Province, in 1849, aged one hundred and eleven years. She was born on board of a British ship-of-the-line, in the Bay of Biscay. She accompanied her husband in the Revolution, and endured all the deprivations and hardships of life in the camp.

Doggit, John. Of Middleborough, Massachusetts. He went to New Brunswick, and died on the Island of Grand Menan, Bay of Fundy, in 1830, aged seventy.

Doharty, Edmund. Of Pownalborough, Maine. At Halifax, Nova Scotia, November, 1779, and employed by the Government. Implicated in concealing deserters from two ships-of-war, was dismissed. "How he will support his family," said the Rev. Jacob Bailey, "I know not, as his reputation is greatly blasted by his foolish conduct." He went subsequently to the British post at the mouth of the Penobscot; and one who knew him there, wrote in 1782, "Doharty has gone out on a cruise."

Doherty, Michael. Sergeant in the Delaware Regiment. Taken prisoner and confined. A British recruiting sergeant, "up to all manner of cajolery," — such is Michael's story, — "by dint of perpetual blarney, gained my good will, slipped the King's money into my hand, which I pocketed, and entered a volunteer in the 17th Regiment." Michael's corps was at Stony Point when stormed by "Mad Anthony," and our wag fell wounded into Whig hands, greatly to his amazement, for "he thought himself snugly out of harm's way." His wound cured, and "whitewashed of his sins," his old comrades received him with kindness. In the battle of Camden — "bad luck to the day!" — the Delaware Blues were "cut up root and branch," and poor Michael made prisoner. He put his wits at work, and concluded that a prison-ship was no better than a jail; and so 'listed under Tarleton. "Oh, botheration, what a mistake!" The battle of the Cowpens soon followed. "Howard and Old Kirkwood gave us the bayonet so handsomely, that we were taken one and all;" and a dragoon "added a scratch or two to the account already scored on my unfortunate carcass. As to all the miseries that I have since endured, afflicted with a scarcity of everything but appetite and musquitoes, I say nothing about them." No wonder his tale ends in these words: "I feel some qualms at the thought of battle, since, take whatever side I will, I am always sure to find it the wrong one."

DOMETTE, JOSEPH. Of Boston. Imprisoned there. He went to England, and for a time received a pension of £80 per annum from the Government. He became an Episcopal minister, and, probably, settled in Ireland or Wales. He passed "through many scenes of disappointment."

DONALDSON, SAMUEL. Of Virginia. He was at New York in July, 1783, and was one of the fifty-five who petitioned for grants of lands in Nova Scotia. [See *Abijah Willard.*]

In a Loyalist tract, published at London in 1784, I find it said that he was a Rebel committee man, then a spy at New York, and that, at the peace, he returned to his estate in Virginia, and took the oath of allegiance to the Whig Government.

DONGAN, ROBERT. Lieutenant-Colonel Commandant of the Garrison Battalion. He was continued in service at the peace, and, 1794, was commissioned a Major-General.

DONGAN, EDWARD VAUGHAN. Lieutenant-Colonel Commandant of the Third Battalion of New Jersey Volunteers. He was the youngest son of Walter Dongan, of Staten Island, and was bred to the law. He was killed in his twenty-ninth year, August, 1777, in a skirmish on Staten Island. He left a widow; but his only child died the very day of his own death.

Doud, ———. Of North Carolina. Captain in the Loyal Militia. Killed in 1781, in the attack of McNiel on Hillsborough, when Governor Burke, his Council, and other persons of distinction, were taken prisoners, and carried to Wilmington.

Dougherty, Edward. In 1776 he embarked at Boston for Halifax. A Loyalist of this name died in extreme poverty on the river St. John, New Brunswick, where he had lived many years, about the year 1808.

Doughty, ———. A captain in De Lancey's Brigade; perished in 1783, on his passage to Nova Scotia, in the wreck of the transport ship *Martha*. [See *James Henley*.]

Doughty, Rev. John. An Episcopal minister. He graduated at King's College, New York, in 1770. He was ordained in England for the Church at Peekskill, but was soon transferred to Schenectady.

In 1775 political troubles put an end to divine service, and he suffered much at the hands of the popular party. In 1777 he obtained leave to depart to Canada, (after having been twice a prisoner) where he became chaplain of the "King's Royal Regiment," of New York.

In 1781 he went to England; but returned to Canada in 1784, and officiated as missionary at Sorel. He resigned his connection with the Society for the Propagation of the Gospel in Foreign Parts, in 1803.

Dove, Abraham. Of New York. Went to Shelburne, Nova Scotia, kept a hotel, and died there in 1803.

Dove, James. Went to Shelburne, Nova Scotia; was a merchant and magistrate, and died there in 1824, leaving three sons.

Dowdney, Nathaniel. Of New Jersey. Convicted of

"cursing all Congresses and Committees," and of enmity to his country; and, January, 1776, ordered by the Committee of Safety to be disarmed, and to be kept in close prison until he should manifest contrition for his offences, pay the cost of proceedings against him, and give security for his future good behavior.

DOXSTADER, JOHN. A Tory leader. On an incursion to Currietown, he and his Indian associates took nine prisoners, who, in an affair at a place called Ourlagh, New York, the day succeeding their capture, were bound to standing trees, tomahawked, and scalped. The bodies of these unfortunate men were hastily buried by friends. But one of them, Jacob Diefendorff, was alive, and was afterwards found on the outside of his own grave; he recovered and lived to relate the story. In 1780, on one of his incursions in New York, Doxstader carried away a horse belonging to a Whig; but coming to the same region, from Canada, after the war, he was arrested by the owner, and compelled to pay the value of the animal.

DRAKE, JEREMIAH. Residence unknown. Settled in New Brunswick in 1783, and died at St. John in 1846, aged eighty.

DRAKE, FRANCIS. Died at Queensbury, New Brunswick; in 1836, aged eighty-one. He was in the service of the Crown for some years.

DRAKE, JOHN. Innkeeper, of Newcastle, Delaware. Was required in 1778 to surrender himself, or to submit to the forfeiture of his property.

DRAKE, URIAH. Of New York. Went to St. John, New Brunswick, at the peace, and was a grantee of that city. He died at Carleton, in that Province, in 1832, at the age of seventy.

DRAPER, RICHARD. Printer and proprietor of the "Massachusetts Gazette and Boston News Letter." He was the apprentice, silent partner, and successor of his father, John Draper. He was early appointed printer to the Governor and Council, which employment he retained during life. His paper was devoted to the Government, and, in the controversy between Great Britain and the Colonies, gave strong support to the Royal cause, and had some able contributors. He was a man of feeble health, and was remarkable for the delicacy of his mind and gentleness of his manners. No stain rested upon his character. He was attentive to his affairs, and was esteemed the best compiler of news of his day. He died June 6th, 1774, aged forty-seven years, without children.

DRAPER, MARGARET. Wife of Richard Draper, of Boston. With the aid of John Howe, continued the publication of the "Massachusetts Gazette and Boston News Letter" from the time of her husband's death, in 1774, until the evacuation of Boston, in 1776; and her paper was the only one that was published during the siege of that town. She accompanied the British Army to Halifax, and proceeding to England, lived there for the remainder of her days. She died about the year 1800. The British Government allowed her a pension. Trumbull, in his "McFingal," calls her "Mother Draper."

DREDDEN, W. Of New York. An officer in a band of marauders.

DREW, JOSEPH. A grantee of the city of St. John, New Brunswick; he died there in 1808.

DRUMMOND, ROBERT. Major in the Second Battalion of New Jersey Volunteers. Of this battalion, upwards of two hundred, who were his neighbors, enlisted under his influence and persuasion. A very large proportion of them fell victims to the climate of South Carolina, Georgia, and Florida, or perished in battle. Major Drummond himself went to England at the peace, and died at Chelsea, in 1789.

DRUMMOND, GEORGE. Of Pennsylvania. Physician. In 1777, confined to a small and inconvenient house, and deprived, he said, of his practice, of his means of support, and of his health, he appealed to the Council for such enlargement as they should think reasonable.

DRUMMOND, REV. WILLIAM. Of Connecticut. Died at Jamaica, Long Island, in 1778.

DRURY, WAKE. Of Burlington, New Jersey. One of

the "King's Justices of the Peace." It was charged that "he behaved scandlessly." He owned that he said the Whigs had no right to draft men; that the drafted men were fools if they went; and that, if they would come to him, he would protect them for not going. The County Committee sent him, under guard of ten persons, to the Provincial Congress. In conducting him to the city wharf, the order of procession was, as the record has it, " Ensign Smith; Fifer Haight; Four Guards; *Justice Wake;* Four Guards." His Majesty's formidable magistrate was soon back, however, to Burlington from Trenton, on his way to Salem, to be put in jail until further orders. Of the order and number of "guards," when he departed, history is silent.

DRY, WILLIAM. Of North Carolina. He was Collector of Customs, and a member of the Council. When Mr. Quincy, of Massachusetts, was on his Southern tour in 1773, he was his guest, and recorded in his journal, that "Colonel Dry's mansion is justly called the house of universal hospitality." At this time, it is probable, from circumstances related by Mr. Quincy, that Mr. Dry was inclined to the popular side. But, by the records of the Council, it appears that, April 12, 1775, he "took *again* the oath appointed to be taken by Privy Counsellors." The Board at this meeting dismissed from a commission of the peace Colonel John Harvey, one of the most zealous Whigs in North Carolina, and with the consent of all the members present. Yet I find that, after the adoption of the Constitution in 1776, Colonel Dry was elected a member of the new, or Whig Council. But a man who changed so often was not a Whig.

DUCHÉ, JACOB, D. D. An Episcopal minister of Philadelphia. He was born in that city, and graduated at the college there in 1757. He entered the ministry, and after the first Continental Congress assembled, in 1774, officiated as chaplain on the 7th of September, and was thanked by a vote of that body, "for the excellent prayer which he composed and delivered" on the occasion. At this time he was Assistant Rector of two churches; but on the death of Rev.

Doctor Richard Peters, an Episcopal minister of Philadelphia, in 1775, was appointed his successor. In 1776 he was elected chaplain to Congress, with a salary. The following is the form of prayer which he made use of after Independence was declared: —

"O Lord, our heavenly Father, high and mighty, King of kings, and Lord of lords, who dost from thy throne behold all the dwellers on earth, and reignest with power supreme and uncontrolled over all kingdoms, empires, and governments, look down in mercy, we beseech thee, on these our American States, who have fled to thee from the rod of the oppressor, and thrown themselves on thy gracious protection, desiring to be henceforth dependent only on thee; to thee have they appealed for the righteousness of their cause; to thee do they now look up for that countenance and support, which thou alone canst give: take them, therefore, heavenly Father, under thy nurturing care; give them wisdom in council, and valor in the field; defeat the malicious designs of our cruel adversaries; convince them of the unrighteousness of their cause, and if they still persist in their sanguinary purposes, oh! let the voice of thine own unerring justice, sounding in their hearts, constrain them to drop the weapons of war from their unnerved hands in the day of battle. Be thou present, O God of wisdom, and direct the councils of this honorable assembly; enable them to settle things on the best and surest foundation, that the scene of blood may be speedily closed, that order, harmony and peace may be effectually restored, and truth and justice, religion and piety, prevail and flourish amongst thy people; preserve the health of their bodies and the vigor of their minds; shower down on them, and the millions they represent, such temporal blessings as thou seest expedient for them in this world, and crown them with everlasting glory in the world to come. All this we ask in the name, and through the merits of Jesus Christ, thy Son and our Saviour. Amen."

He officiated as chaplain about three months, when he abandoned the Whigs, and resigned. In October, 1777, he wrote an extraordinary letter to Washington, which was delivered by Mrs. Ferguson, and which the Commander-in-Chief transmitted to Congress. The objects of this communication were, to cast a general odium on the Whig cause, to induce Washington to apostatize and resign his command of the army, or, at the head of it, to force Congress immediately to desist from hostilities, and to rescind the Declaration of Independence. If this is not done, said Duché, "you have an infallible resource still left; *negotiate for America at the head of your army.*" In the course of this letter he represents Congress in a most despicable view, as consisting of weak, obscure persons, not fit associates for Washington; and he speaks of the members from New England, especially, with great indelicacy. The army, in his estimation, both officers and men, were possessed neither of courage nor principle, and were taken from the lowest of the people.

Various motives were assigned for his apostasy; some believed that it was occasioned by the gloomy aspect of affairs; others supposed that it arose from a change in his sentiments respecting the justice of the Whig cause. But whatever was the reason, the aspersions contained in his letter admit of no excuse. After quitting Philadelphia, Doctor Duché went to England, and became chaplain to an asylum for orphans. He was a man of brilliant talents, an impressive orator, had a fine poetical taste, and figured as a preacher even in London. He was banished, and his estate was confiscated. His house was bought by Thomas McKean, a signer of the Declaration of Independence.

In April, 1783, he solicited Washington's influence to effect a repeal of the Act that kept him in banishment from his native country, "from the arms of a dear aged father, and the embraces of a numerous circle of valuable and long-loved friends." Washington replied that his feelings as an individual were favorable, but that his case must continue to rest with the authorities of Pennsylvania. In 1790 the laws of that State having allowed the refugee Loyalists to return, Dr. Duché came back to Philadelphia in shattered health.

He died in 1798, aged about sixty years. One account states that his decease occurred in 1794; another, in 1796. His wife, a sister of Francis Hopkinson, was killed at Philadelphia in 1797, by the falling of a sand-bag on her head, while opening a window. His daughter Sophia married John Henry, a person whose real or supposed connection with our politics, about the time of the war of 1812, caused considerable sensation. Dr. Duché published several sermons before his defection, and two volumes in London, in 1780.

DUCKINFIELD, SIR NATHANIEL, Baronet. Of North Carolina. He was a member of the Council of North Carolina, and owned large tracts of land in that Colony. He " was gay, good-humored, and popular." . . . . In 1772 he went to England, when his friends prevailed on him to purchase a commission in the British Army. When the war broke out he could not be induced to serve against America, and when his regiment was sent out, he contrived to remain behind. In 1779 his estate was confiscated. James Iredell, who, after the organization of the Federal Government was a Judge of the Supreme Court, and the Baronet, were on very intimate terms. They became rivals in love; " but the contest was so generously conducted, and the deportment of each so marked by magnanimity, that, so far from their friendship being shaken, their mutual esteem was increased."

The Baronet's " proposal met with a courteous but prompt refusal. . . . . . His disappointment so affected him, that he deserted the Province, to which he never returned; subsequently, when his estate was forfeited, 'most ably and eloquently did Mr. Iredell plead his cause.' They regularly corresponded until the close of 1791." Mr. Iredell records in his journal, Saturday, December 19th, 1772: "I have this morning had the happiness to receive a most pleasing friendly letter from Sir N. D., wherein he discovers a most noble soul, generously extolling in terms of the highest admiration a conduct severely killing his hopes, and congratulating me on a happiness raised on the ruin of his. Excellent young man! may your lot be a happy one; though indeed it will be very difficult to fix your affections on one so likely to insure it," &c. On the 20th of January, 1773, the Baronet wrote his rival: "I don't know any couple so deserving of each other as yourselves, and as it was not my good fortune to be the happy possessor of Miss Hannah Johnston's affections, I rejoice exceedingly that such felicity was destined for you. Happy may you long continue to be together. I, perhaps, may never be an eye-witness of it. My intentions of settling in America are now at an end, and I am in hopes some time or other to acquaint you with the fulfilling of your wish that I may select some lady *here* for my own. . . . . If I should again visit Carolina, I pledge you my assurance that the increase of happiness to yourself shall not in the least abate the ardor of my friendship for you and your partner. . . . . At present I think to amuse myself a little while in the army, and have a promise from Major-General Burgoyne of the next vacancy which shall happen in his Light Dragoons, if I shall not satisfy myself sooner," &c. Again, in a letter five days later, he said: "I wish you would acquaint me whether my addressing Miss Johnston was publicly known in North Carolina, and what she thought of my persisting to write to her." March 10th, of the same year, he wrote: "I have now the same reason to induce me to stay in England that I had to remain in Carolina, and which will, perhaps, be crowned with success. I am determined to marry as soon as I can meet with a lady whose person and fortune will be suitable, and who shall think me suitable for her," &c.

On the 14th of May: "I am now entirely free from the last tincture of that unhappy situation of being in love, but how long the warmth of my constitution will permit me to be thus cool, I will not venture to promise. I am, however, destined to a cold part of the island, to join the Queen's (or 7th) Regiment of Dragoons, now quartered at Edinburgh, in which I have purchased a cornetcy." On the 9th of August, 1773: "My passions are violent, and I cannot govern them. Since my last to you, in which I told you of one disappointment which I had met with, I have had another with a young lady who, 'tis supposed, will be a fortune of near £100,000, and though I was much distressed at first, I got the better of it in a short time. I saw Captain Messenger at Liverpool; he told me of my 'penchant' for Miss Hannah, and I think said my mother mentioned it to him. I did not expect that it could be kept a secret." Again, in the same letter: "I am quite out of conceit with matrimony at present, but can't promise how long it will continue. There are some very pretty girls in this neighborhood." In 1783 he wrote that he had been in command of a troop of dragoons three years; that he was then aide-de-camp to General Warde, with "nothing to do," and in a few days was to marry the General's niece, whose constitution would not allow her to cross the sea. A year later, he said he had made an exchange with an officer in a regiment of foot, and should retire on half-pay. "I am most perfectly happy," he continued, "and much fonder of my wife than when I married. She is not at all handsome, but what you may call *a devilish good one.*" Again, in 1784, he mentioned that he was the father of a boy who was a charming fellow, and attempted to talk and to scold; that Lady Duckinfield was soon to present him with another child; and closed with the remark: "You will not be surprised at my being desirous that the plantation should be sold, and the money secured for my use after my mother's death, as I have entirely given up all thoughts of settling in Carolina; and should I have a large family it will be necessary, in order to keep the younger ones from being carpenters and mantua-makers." In June, 1785, he announced the birth of a second son before the first was a year old; and he discoursed about a numerous progeny, and of his parent's decease, in terms that caused Mr. Iredell to say in communicating with a friend: "I am quite vexed (between ourselves) at the levity and indifference of Sir N. Duckinfield's letter, wrote in answer to mine giving a very particular, and to me very affecting, account of his mother's death. He bears it with all the cursed stoicism of a philosopher; and is still afraid that his wife will ruin him with a great number of children. He will deserve a Xantippe for his next wife, and a double set of children into the bargain. It is so intolerable to see a young man so insensible and so avaricious." The noticeable points of a letter dated in February, 1789, are the birth of a daughter, the allowance by the British Government of £3000 for his losses as a Loyalist, and the expression of joy that the Confiscation Act did not include "the negroes which he had lent to his mother."

The Baronet died in 1824. His wife was Katharine Warde, who deceased in 1823. His son Samuel, captain in the Dragoons, was drowned in 1810. His son John Lloyd succeeded him, but dying without issue in 1836, the title devolved on his third son, Henry Robert, the present Baronet. His fourth son, Charles Egerton, is (1855) in the military service of the East India Company. His daughter Katharine married R. P. Smith, M. D. His family is one of the most ancient in the county of Chester, and is said to be descended from the Norman house of De Massey.

DUDLEY, CHARLES. Last Royal Collector and Surveyor of the Customs at Newport, Rhode Island. He was son of Thomas and Mary (Leavitt) Dudley, of a highly respectable family of Staffordshire, England, and was born in that county in 1737. When Robinson was transferred to the Board of Commissioners of the Customs, Boston, and in 1768, he was appointed his successor at Newport. In November, 1775, he fled to the *Rose* ship-of-war. The Whig Committee seized his personal property soon after, sold a part, and stored the rest in Providence. The Committee voted, subsequently, "that one of his best beds, with the furniture, be presented to General Lee," who was in command in Rhode Island, and very busy with the Loyalists. In 1776 Mr. Dudley embarked at Boston for Halifax, with the British Army, and went to England the same year. He died at London in 1790.

His only child who lived to mature years, Charles E. Dudley, of Albany, New York, was a Senator in Congress from 1828 to 1833, and died in 1841. The Dudley Observatory is named in honor of this gentleman; and his widow, Blandina (Bleecker) Dudley, contributed, at various times, the sum of

$75,000 to erect and endow it. She died at Albany, March, 1863. In her will, in addition to her former gifts, she bequeathed the sum of $30,000 for the maintenance in the Dudley Observatory, which she established, of a scientific chair, to be known as the "Blandina Professorship." This puts the institution in an excellent financial position, giving it a permanent endowment of $80,000, which is safely invested, and yields an annual income of $5600.

DUFFIELD, JOHN. Of New Jersey. In 1774 the Whigs destroyed some tea owned by him, by Stacy Hepburn, and a Captain Allen, the value of which they attempted to recover by suit at law. Joseph Reed, of Philadelphia, was their counsel, but they failed.

DUFFUS, CHARLES. He died at St. John, New Brunswick, in 1818, at the age of seventy.

DULANY, DANIEL. Of Maryland. Early in the controversy, he and Charles Carroll engaged in a warm newspaper discussion, which attracted much interest. Dulany wrote over the signature of *Antilore*, and his Whig antagonist adopted that of the *First Citizen*. Dulany was an eminent lawyer, and was considered one of the most distinguished men of his time. Before the Revolution he held the offices of Secretary and Attorney-General of Maryland, and was a member of the Council. Few memorials remain of him, but he is ever mentioned in terms of the highest respect. Mr. Quincy, of Massachusetts, while on his journey to the South in 1773, spoke of spending "three hours with the celebrated Daniel Dulany."

Though a Loyalist at last, he stood up manfully against the Stamp Act. These words, uttered in 1765, are glorious: "A garment of linsey-wolsey," said he, "when made the distinction of patriotism, is more honorable than the plumes and the diadem of an emperor, without it. Let the manufacture of America be the symbol of dignity and the badge of virtue, and it will soon break the fetters of distress."

He survived the Revolution several years. " He was one of the most refined gentlemen and flourishing counsellors of his day, and dignified his profession by the liberality and grace with which he exercised it. Like Edward Rutledge, of South Carolina, he took no fee from the widow and orphan. We can barely remember his benevolent mien and silver locks, as, when superannuated, he walked the streets of Baltimore; his chief pleasure, after all his high aspirations, grave labors, and bright successes of life, being the distribution of gingerbread, with which he was constantly supplied, for the crowd of children who watched and followed their venerable provider."

DULANY, LLOYD. Of Annapolis, Maryland. On the 27th of May, 1774, the Whigs of that city passed the following Resolution: "That it is the opinion of this meeting that the gentlemen of the law of this Province bring no suit for the recovery of any debt due from any inhabitant of this Province to any inhabitant of Great Britain, until the said Act [Boston Port Bill] be repealed." Three days after, Mr. Dulany's name appeared at the head of the following Protest: "*Dissentient.* 1. Because we are impressed with a full conviction, that this resolution is founded in treachery and rashness, inasmuch as it is big with bankruptcy and ruin to those inhabitants of Great Britain, who, relying with unlimited security on our good faith and integrity, have made us masters of their fortunes; condemning them unheard, for not having interposed their influence with Parliament in favor of the town of Boston, without duly weighing the force with which that influence would probably have operated, or whether in their conduct they were actuated by wisdom and policy, or by corruption and avarice.

"2. Because, whilst the inhabitants of Great Britain are partially despoiled of every legal remedy to recover what is justly due to them, no provision is made to prevent us from being harrassed by the prosecution of internal suits, but our fortunes and persons are left at the mercy of domestic creditors, without a possibility of extricating ourselves, unless by a general convulsion; an event, in the contemplation of sober reason, replete with horror.

"3. Because our credit, as a commercial people, will expire under the wound; for what confidence can possibly be reposed in those who shall have exhibited the most avowed and most striking proof that they are not to be bound by obligations as sacred as human invention can suggest."

Dulany was killed in a duel with the *Reverend* Bennet Allen, Hyde Park, London, in 1782. The seconds were a Mr. De Lancey and a Mr. Robert Morris, both, I conclude, Loyalists. The cause of the fatal meeting was an article in a London newspaper, in 1779, touching the character of Dulany, (among other Americans) with whom Allen was not pleased. Walter Dulany, son of Walter Dulany of Maryland, married the widow of Lloyd Dulany, in 1785.

DULANY, DANIEL. Of Maryland. Son of Walter. At first, he enrolled himself in the militia, and seemed inclined to the popular cause; but refusing to sign the Test, he incurred the displeasure of the Whigs, and fled. Attainted, and estate confiscated.

DUMARESQUE, PHILIP. Merchant, of Boston. An Addresser of Hutchinson in 1774, and of Gage in 1775. In 1776, with his family of seven persons, he went to Halifax. Two years later he was proscribed and banished. He was appointed Collector of the Customs at New Providence, Nassau, and died there. His wife was Rebecca, daughter of Dr. Sylvester Gardiner. His children were — Philip, a captain in the Royal Navy; James, who married Sarah Farwell, of Vassalborough, Maine; Francis, a physician in Jamaica; and a daughter, Rebecca. Persons of his lineage are now living in Boston and vicinity. Perhaps the Lieutenant Dumaresque of the British Navy, attached to the *Hawke* sloop-of-war, drowned in 1812, was also of his family. The *Hawke* lay off Calspot Castle, where she was employed to attend the Duke of Clarence. Lieutenant D. went up to Southampton to dine with Admiral Ferguson; on his return, his boat upset.

DUNBAR, DANIEL. Of Halifax, Massachusetts. Was an officer in the militia, and in 1774 a mob demanded of him the surrender of the colors of his company. He refused, when the multitude broke into his house, took him out, forced him to get upon a rail, where he was held and tossed up and down until he was exhausted. He was then dragged and beaten, and gave up the standard to save his life. In 1776 he went to Halifax, Nova Scotia, with the Royal Army. In 1778 he was proscribed and banished.

DUNBAR, JESSE. Of Halifax, Massachusetts. Bought some fat cattle of a Mandamus Councillor in 1774, and drove them to Plymouth for sale. The Whigs soon learned with whom Dunbar had presumed to deal, and after he had slaughtered, skinned, and hung up one of the beasts, commenced punishing him for the offence. His tormentors, it appears, put the dead ox in a cart, and fixing Dunbar in his belly, carted him four miles, and required him to pay one dollar for the ride. He then was delivered over to a Kingston mob, who carted him four other miles, and exacted another dollar. A Duxbury mob then took him, and after beating him in the face with the creature's tripe, and endeavoring to cover his person with it, carried him to Councillor Thomas's house, and compelled him to pay a further sum of money. Flinging his beef into the road, they now left him to recover and return as he could.

DUNBAR, MOSES. Of Bristol, Connecticut. He was born in Plymouth, Connecticut. He was convicted of holding a captain's commission under Sir William Howe, and of enlisting men for the Royal Army, by the Superior Court, January, 1777, and soon after, while under sentence of death, cleared himself of his irons, knocked down the sentries, and escaped from jail, but was apprehended. The " Connecticut Courant" announced that, " On Wednesday, March 19, Moses Dunbar will be executed. A sermon will be preached at the jail to the prisoner, by the Rev. Abraham Jarvis of Middleton; and a sermon in the North Meeting-house to the spectators, by the Rev. Nathan Perkins." There was still another homily by Rev. Nathan Stone, which was printed, and which closes thus: " Bloody and deceitful men shall not live out half their days." Dunbar was hung on the day designated, (March 19, 1777,) in the presence of a " prodigious concourse of people."

His son Moses came to an untimely end. His widow, whose maiden name was Esther Adams, retired to the British Army, and remained with it some time; but returned to Bristol, married Chauncey Jerome, a Loyalist, and with her husband, went to Nova Scotia. At the peace, they settled at their old home in Connecticut, and were the parents of several children. She died in 1825, aged sixty-six. Dunbar's house was standing in 1859.

DUNHAM. Captain Asher Dunham and Daniel Dunham were among the Loyalists who went to St. John, New Brunswick, in 1783, and both received grants of city lots. John Dunham, who emigrated the same year, and who was a captain in the militia of that Province, died at Carleton in 1829, aged eighty-one.

DUNMORE, EARL OF. Last Royal Governor of Virginia. He succeeded to the peerage in 1756; was appointed Governor of New York in 1770; assumed the Executive Chair of Virginia in 1772, and administered the government until the popular party compelled him to seek safety on board of a ship-of-war. He soon collected a number of vessels, and was joined by many Loyalists who had become obnoxious, and who, from necessity or fear, abandoned their homes. Washington said, December, 1775, "I do not think that forcing his Lordship on shipboard is sufficient. Nothing less than depriving him of life or liberty will secure peace to Virginia, as motives of resentment actuate his conduct to a degree equal to the total destruction of that colony."

Lord Dunmore, with his fleet of fugitives, continued on the coasts and rivers of Virginia for a part of the year 1776; and as every place was now strictly guarded, these unhappy people, who had put themselves under his protection, underwent great distresses. The heat of the weather, the badness and scarcity of water and provisions, with the closeness and filth of the small vessels in which they were crowded, by degrees produced that malignant distemper which is known by the name of the jail or pestilential fever. This dreadful disorder particularly affected the Negroes, most of whom it swept away. After various adventures, in which they were driven from place to place, and from island to island, by the Virginians, several of the vessels were driven on shore in a gale of wind, and the wretched fugitives became captives to their own countrymen. At length, every place being shut against the remainder, and neither water nor provisions to be obtained, even at the expense of blood, it was found necessary, towards the beginning of August, 1776, to burn the smaller vessels, and to send the remainder, amounting to between forty and fifty sail, with the exiles, to seek shelter in Florida, Bermudas, and the West Indies. In this manner ended the hopes entertained by the employment of the Negroes to suppress the rebellion in the Southern colonies. This measure tended infinitely to inflame the discontents in those colonies, without adding anything to the strength of the Royal arms.

He is represented as both needy and greedy. "To get money was the rule of action which included his whole administrative conduct." In 1779 his name appears in the Confiscation Act of New York. He was appointed Governor of the Bermudas in 1786. He died in England in 1809. His daughter Augusta married the Duke of Sussex, sixth son of King George Third. Lady Dunmore, who died at Southwood House, near Ramsgate, in 1818, was Elizabeth, daughter of the Earl of Galloway; to her daughter Virginia (thus named at the request of the Council and Assembly of Virginia) she bequeathed her villa at Twickenham and all her personal property. In 1848 a London paper announced the death of Sir Augustus Frederic d'Este, son of his late Royal Highness the Duke of Sussex, by Lady Augusta Murray, daughter of the Earl of Dunmore, to whom his Royal Highness was married at Rome, in 1793. Upon the death of the Duke, in 1843, Sir Augustus Frederic preferred his claim to succeed to the titles and honors of his father, and the claim was heard by the House of Lords in that year, when, after proof was given of the marriage of his father and mother, and of the birth of Sir Augustus Frederic in 1794, a question was submitted to the Judges upon the effect of the Royal Marriage

Act, 12 George III. The Judges pronounced their opinion to be that that statute had incapacitated the descendants of George II. from contracting a legal marriage without the consent of the Crown, either within the British dominions or elsewhere, whereupon the House of Lords resolved that Sir Augustus Frederic had not established his claim. The Hon. Charles Augustus Murray, who visited the United States in 1836, and again in 1851, is a lineal descendant of Lord Dunmore.

DUNN, JOHN. Of North Carolina. Major in the militia. In 1775, notoriously inimical to the Whigs, he was seized and sent to South Carolina. Frances, his wife, petitioned the Provincial Congress of North Carolina in his behalf, without success. He was, however, released; but apprehended again in 1776, he was allowed the liberty of living in Salisbury on parole, on condition that he should appear once every day at the house of Maxwell Chambers, and give security in £1000 for his good behavior.

DUNN, JOHN. Of New York. He left the United States at the termination of hostilities, and was one of the founders of St. Andrew, New Brunswick, and through life contributed to its improvement and prosperity. For many years he held the honorable and lucrative post of Comptroller of his Majesty's Customs at that port. He died at St. Andrew, April 14, 1829, aged seventy-six. His wife, Elizabeth, survived until January, 1835, and at her decease was seventy-three. He was a man proverbially kind, liberal, and hospitable.

DUYCKINGS, ———. Of New Jersey. Colonel in the militia. In 1777 Colonel Weedon wrote the Council of Pennsylvania that he was an "infamous character;" that he had been in the service of the Whigs; but, when the British entered New Jersey, he took the oath of allegiance to the Crown. Weedon sent him prisoner to the Council, by order of Washington.

EASTERBROOKS, JAMES. He was an early settler of New Brunswick, and was a magistrate and member of the House of Assembly for many years. He died at Sackville, in that Province, in 1842, at the age of eighty-five.

EDDY, CHARLES, and THOMAS. Of Philadelphia. Ironmongers. Attainted of treason and their estates confiscated. Charles was ordered to Virginia; went to England, and was in London, July, 1779.

EDEN, SIR ROBERT, Baronet, and last Royal Governor of Maryland. His wife was Caroline, sister and co-heir of the last Lord Baltimore.

He was appointed Governor in 1768, and continued in office until 1776, when the Royal authority ceased. But as he was accomplished, kind, and courteous, the Whigs allowed him to remain in Maryland without restraint. When, however, some despatches addressed to him by Lord George Germain were intercepted, his arrest was ordered by General Lee. The Whig Council of Safety declined compliance; and and Sir Robert was permitted to embark for England, in the sloop-of-war *Fowey*. He was created a Baronet, September, 1776. He returned to Maryland in 1784, " to look after his lady's estate;" and died near Annapolis in 1785. His son, Sir William Eden, (subsequently Lord Auckland) who deceased in 1814, was one of the Lords of Trade and Plantations in 1776, one of the Commissioners to America in 1778, and, later, Ambassador to Spain and to Holland.

EDGETT, JOEL. Of New York. He went to New Brunswick at the peace, and resided there until his death, February, 1841, at the house of his son John, at Hillsborough, aged eighty years.

EDMISTON, REV. WILLIAM. Of Maryland. Episcopal minister. In 1775 the Committee of Baltimore ordered him to appear and answer to the charges against him; he obeyed, and made a written explanation which was voted satisfactory. In November, 1776, he was at Albany, New York, and asked General Gates to allow him to go to General Howe on private business, and promised to return at any specified time. He was in England previous to July, 1779.

EDSON, JOSIAH. Of Bridgewater, Massachusetts. He

was a noted politician of the time, and was known by the two most odious appellations which prevailed; namely, as a *Rescinder* and a *Mandamus Councillor*. Hutchinson speaks of him in 1771, when he was a member of the House of Representatives, as one of the several gentlemen of that body, who, in common times, would have had great weight, but who, then, discouraged by the great superiority of the numbers against them, were inactive. In 1774 Mr. Edson was driven from his house by a mob, and was compelled to reside in Boston, under protection of the British troops; and at the evacuation, in 1776, he accompanied the army to Halifax. He went from Halifax to New York, and died in that city, or on Long Island, not long after his arrival. He was a graduate of Harvard University, a colonel in the militia, a deacon of the church, and a respectable, virtuous man. He is alluded to in "McFingal," as "that old simplicity of Edson."

EDWARDS, MORGAN. A Baptist clergyman. He was born in Wales in 1722, and came to America in 1761. He was at first pastor of a church in Philadelphia, and, subsequently, labored in various places, either as lecturer or preacher. Opposed to the Revolution, he gave up the ministry during the war. He was an eccentric man, and among his acts was the preaching of his own funeral sermon. He lived a quarter of a century after the solemn farce, dying in 1795, aged seventy-two. He published many sermons, and left numerous manuscripts.

EDWARDS, STEPHEN. Of New Jersey. An amiable young man, who joined the adherents to the Crown at New York, near the close of the war. Sent, by Colonel Taylor of a Loyalist corps, to Monmouth County to ascertain the Whig force there, he was arrested at midnight, in his father's house, in bed with his wife, disguised in a female's night-cap, by a party under Jonathan Forman, a Whig captain of horse, taken to Freehold, tried as a spy by a court-martial, and two days afterward, executed. His father and mother arrived in town the morning of his death, to inquire into his situation; and returned home with his corpse. The Forman and Edwards families had been on terms of intimate friendship.

ELLIOT, ANDREW. Of New York. He was Collector of the Customs for the port of New York, from about the year 1764 until the Revolution, and performed his official duties in a manner highly satisfactory. His first difficulty with the people of a serious nature occurred in 1774, when he seized some fire-arms, and was threatened with a visit from the " Mohawks and River Indians," or, in other words, with a coat of tar and feathers. After the Royal Army took possession of New York, he continued to perform his duties of Collector, and during the war held various important offices. In 1782 he was not only at the head of the Customs, but was Lieutenant-Governor, Receiver-General of Quit-rents, Superintendent-General of Police, and Chief of the Superintendent Department, established by Sir William Howe in 1777. And when, in 1780, Sir Henry Clinton made his last effort to save André, Mr. Elliot was one of the three eminent persons who were sent to confer with Washington. Mr. Elliot's estate in New York was confiscated; and the Executive Council of Pennsylvania, to reach property possessed by him in that State, ordered by proclamation, that on his failing to appear within a specified time, to take his trial on the charge of treason, he should stand attainted.

His family sailed for England in the *Nonesuch*, of 64 guns, June, 1783; and his furniture was sold at auction in September of that year, at his house in Bowery Lane. His daughter Elizabeth married the tenth Lord Cathcart, in 1779; and Sir George Cathcart, who fell at the battle of Inkerman, in the Crimean war, 1854, was the fourth son of this marriage. The present Earl (1857) is the second son. Mr. Elliot's daughter Eleanor married the Right Hon. Robert Digby, Admiral of the Fleet, and died in England in 1830; her first husband was a Jauncey, of New York.

ELLIOT, CAPTAIN ——. Noted for his revengeful disposition and infamous deeds. In the documents of the time, McKee, Elliot, and Simon Girty, are mentioned together, and as forming a sort of triumvirate. The three were imprisoned by the Whigs at Pittsburgh, but made their escape, and in

1778 traversed the country to enlist the savages against the Rebels. The effects of their councils were long felt and deplored. After the Revolution, and during the Indian troubles of Washington's administration, Elliot's hostile feelings towards the country which he had abandoned, were sufficiently manifest to deserve universal and lasting detestation. He was dismissed from the British Colonial service about the year 1801, without trial, but whether for misconduct, is unknown to the writer.

ELLWOOD, JOHN. Of the county of Bucks, Pennsylvania. In 1778 he was tried for acting as pilot to the Royal fleet and army, in the invasion of the State by Sir William Howe, and sentenced " to be hanged by the neck till he be dead." He was not executed. In 1783 Humphreys wrote Galloway, that Mr. Ellwood " was out of his head at the time of his trial, and, indeed, ever since the army left Philadelphia." The records of the Council showed that he was pardoned July 15, 1789.

EMES, JOHN. Of Pennsylvania. Deserted from the State galleys. Joined the British at Philadelphia. Captured at sea in 1779, tried by a court-martial, and, September 20th, in prison.

EMERSON, THOMAS. A physician. He died at Fredericton, New Brunswick, in 1843, aged eighty-one.

ENSOR, GEORGE. Of Southwark, Pennsylvania. Attainted of treason and property confiscated. At the peace, accompanied by his family of five persons, he went from New York to Shelburne, Nova Scotia, where the Crown granted him one town lot. His losses in consequence of his loyalty were estimated at £600. He died at Shelburne in 1805, leaving several children.

ERVING, JOHN. Of Boston. He was one of the most eminent merchants in America, and a member of the Council of Massachusetts for twenty years. The Hon. Robert C. Winthrop, his great-grandson, in a public address in 1845, thus refers to him : " A few dollars earned on a Commencement Day, by ferrying passengers over Charles River when there was no bridge — shipped to Lisbon in the shape of fish, and from thence to London in the shape of fruit, and from thence brought home to be reinvested in fish, and to be reëntered upon the same triangular circuit of trade — laid the foundations of the largest fortune of the day, a hundred years ago." Mr. Erving died in Boston in 1786, aged ninety-three.

ERVING, JOHN, JR. Of Boston. He graduated at Harvard University in 1747. In 1760 he signed the Boston Memorial, and was thus one of the fifty-eight who were the first men in America to array themselves against the officers of the Crown. But in 1774 he was an Addresser of Hutchinson, and the same year was appointed a mandamus councillor. In 1776 he fled to Halifax, and went thence to England. In 1778 he was proscribed and banished; and in 1779 his property was confiscated under the Conspiracy Act. He died at Bath, England, in 1816, aged eighty-nine years. His wife, Maria Catharina, (youngest daughter of Governor Shirley) with whom he lived quite sixty years, died a few months before him. His son, Dr. Shirley Erving, died at Boston in 1813, aged fifty-five.

ERVING, GEORGE. A merchant, of Boston. He was one of the fifty-eight memorialists who were the first men in America to array themselves against the officers of the Crown. He was an Addresser of Hutchinson in 1774; was proscribed under the Act of 1778; and his estate was confiscated under the Conspiracy Act of 1779. He went to Halifax at the evacuation, with his family of five persons, and thence to England. He died in London in 1806, at the age of seventy. His wife was a daughter of the Hon. Isaac Royall, of Medford. His son, George W. Ervine, was American Consul at London, Special Minister to Denmark, and Minister Plenipotentiary to Spain. A distinguished gentleman in Boston kindly furnishes me with the following passage in a letter received by him from the son just mentioned: "Many a time and oft" has my father "expressed to me his heart-bitter regrets, and that his only consolation was that his errors had not deprived me of my rights as an American. I have committed a great fault, but you are not responsible. I brought you away a child (of five years), but remember that when you are twenty-one, you are freed from my authority as father, and will then return to your native country — and so he sent me, and there commences my history. . . . . He remained to the day of his death an empassioned American."

EVANS, ABEL. In 1778, in a letter to Galloway, he said: "The number of horses, employed to transport flour from Maryland and Pennsylvania to Boston, were immense. These were principally taken from the farmers southward of New York, as those in the Continental Army were mostly rendered unfit for service through hard usage and bad feeding. Carrying so much provision so far, and over very bad roads, has destroyed many more of the horses belonging to the farmers. From these circumstances judge how badly the Continental Army must be prepared for another campaign." Evans was then in New York — " obliged to go into such business as he could get to do."

EVERSFIELD, REV. JOHN. Of Maryland. Episcopal minister. He was born in England, and belonged to a noble family. He came to America in 1727, and the following year was placed over the parish of St. Paul's, Prince George's County. He possessed a good library, and was a man of great learning. In 1776 he was arrested, and his case examined by the Maryland Convention; with the result that, in consideration of his age and infirmities, and his want of ability to exert any dangerous influence, he be discharged, on payment of the expenses of his confinement. He died in 1780, aged about eighty. His wife was Eleanor Claggett, — an aunt of the bishop of that surname, — by whom he received a large landed estate. Several children survived him; one of whom, John, was an Episcopal clergyman, and settled in England.

EVERITT, GEORGE. Was a quartermaster in the King's service. Went to New Brunswick in 1783, and died at Fredericton in 1829, aged seventy.

EVERITT, BENJAMIN, DANIEL, JAMES, and NICHOLAS. Of

Queen's County, New York. Acknowledged allegiance, October, 1776. James signed a Declaration of loyalty previously; settled in Nova Scotia subsequently, and died in Digby in 1799.

FAGAN, JAKE. Of Monmouth County, New Jersey. One of the "Pine Robbers." These miscreants plundered whenever they could, and changed sides as often as interest dictated. Jake, after a career of crime, was shot in 1778, by a party of Whigs who lay in ambush. After his body was buried, it was disinterred, enveloped in a tarred cloth, and suspended in chains with iron bands around it, until the birds of prey picked the flesh from its bones, and the skeleton fell to the ground in pieces. There is a tradition, also, that his skull was afterwards placed against the tree on which his body was hung, with a pipe in its mouth.

FAIRCHILD, JAMES M. He went to New Brunswick in 1783, and died at St. John in 1807.

FAIRFAX, LORD THOMAS. He was the son of Thomas, the fifth Lord Fairfax, and of Catharine, daughter of Lord Culpepper, and was born in England in 1691. He was educated at Oxford, and was a good scholar. Succeeding to the title and to the family estate in Virginia, he came over to that Colony about the year 1739. After residing there a year, he returned to England; but desirous of improving and inducing rapid settlements on his land, and pleased with America, he determined to make Virginia the place of his permanent abode. Another account is that he sought seclusion in consequence of disappointment in love. Whatever the cause, he closed his affairs in England, and came a second time to his estate in 1745. He lived several years with William Fairfax, at Belvoir, but at length fixed his residence a few miles from Winchester, on the western side of the Blue Ridge, where he laid out a farm, and put it under high cultivation. His mansion house was called Greenway Court, and he lived in a style of liberal hospitality. He was fond of hunting and indulged in the diversion nearly to excess. I find it said that Christ Church, Alexandria, and the Church at Falls Church

Corners, and the Hotel in Alexandria, which was the headquarters of General Washington, were built of bricks brought from England by Lord Fairfax. He was kind to the poor, and allowed them a large part of the surplus produce of the land under his immediate management, and afforded them the use of other parts of his estate on terms almost nominal. Indulgent to all who held lands under him and to all around him, faithful in the discharge of his private duties and in the performance of several honorable public trusts, he lived respected and beloved by men of all parties. Though a frank and open Loyalist, he was never insulted or molested by the Whigs. When he heard of the surrender of Cornwallis, it is related that he said to the servant, "*Come, Joe, carry me to bed, for it is high time for me to die.*" Nor did he long survive this event. He died at Greenway Court in 1782, in the ninety-second year of his age, much lamented. His literary attainments were highly respectable, and it is said that in his youth he was a contributor to the "Spectator." His remains were deposited under the communion-table of the Episcopal Church at Winchester, but were removed in 1833, to provide a place for the erection of a pile of buildings on the site of the church. He was a dark, swarthy man, more than six feet in height, of a large frame, and of extraordinary strength.

Lord Fairfax was the friend and patron of Washington's early life, and though he died before the mother country acknowledged the independence of the thirteen Colonies, he saw, in the most intense anguish, that the widow's son, who surveyed his lands, was destined under Providence to be the great instrument to dismember the British empire.

His barony and his immense domain in Virginia, between the rivers Potomac and Rappahannock, consisting, as appears by parliamentary papers, of five million two hundred and eighty-two thousand acres, descended to his only surviving brother, Robert Fairfax, who was the seventh Lord Fairfax, and who died at Leeds Castle, England, in 1791. But as this domain was in possession of Lord Thomas during the Revolutionary controversy, it was confiscated. Lord Robert, however, (claiming in behalf of himself; of Frances Martin, his widowed sister; of Denny Fairfax, a clergyman; of Philip and Thomas Martin, his nephews; and three Misses Martin, his nieces), applied to the British Government for compensation, under the provision made to Loyalist sufferers, and stated the value of the estate at £98,000. The commissioners made a special report upon this claim, but do not appear to have come to a final decision with regard to it; and after their labors were closed, it was among the few cases which were referred to Parliament for settlement. It was considered by a committee of that body, who, as the commissioners had done, reduced it to £60,000. Lord Robert's life interest therein, they find, by the established rules of computation, at £13,758. The value of the life interest Mr. Pitt recommended to be paid, but at this time (1792) advised no compensation to those who possessed the reversionary interest. But it is believed that, at a subsequent period, an allowance was made to nearly or quite the sum originally claimed.

His estate was one of the largest and most valuable in America at the Revolution. It was granted May 8, 1681, by Charles the Second to Thomas Lord Culpepper, the grandfather of Lord Thomas and Lord Robert Fairfax, on a "rent of £6 13s. 4d., payable as therein mentioned." At Lord Culpepper's death it became the property of his daughter, the Right Honorable Catharine, Lady Fairfax, who, by her will of April 21, 1719, devised the whole in trust thus: "Upon trust in the first place by mortgage, a sale of sufficient part of the estates thereby devised, to raise a sufficient sum for discharging all her debts, legacies, and funeral expenses; and after such mortgage sale and disposition," as follows, namely: —

"To the use of her eldest son, Thomas Lord Fairfax, and his assigns for life. Remainder to the first and other sons of said Thomas Fairfax, in tail male. Remainder to her second son, Henry Culpepper Fairfax, and his assigns, for life. Remainder to the first and other sons of said Henry Culpepper

Fairfax, in tail male. Remainder to her third son, Robert Fairfax, and his assigns, for life. Remainder to trustees to preserve contingent remainders. Remainder to the first and other sons of said Robert Fairfax, in tail male. Remainder to the daughters of the said testatrix, as tenants in common, in tail. Remainder to the right heirs of the said testatrix, in fee."

Such was the tenure of the Fairfax estate in Virginia. The magnitude of the property, and the circumstances of the case, caused an unusual degree of investigation in Parliament, and Lord Robert's memorial for relief was the subject of a separate and elaborate report. His individual loss, if computed at the value of his life interest, was less than that of several of the Loyalists whose property was confiscated; though we have seen that the Government gave him, without hesitation, nearly seventy thousand dollars, after reducing his valuation more than a quarter part. A considerable portion of this estate had been granted prior to the Revolution, upon the quit-rent system, and thus a part of its value had been transferred to others. Still the reversionary interest on the decease of Lord Robert, which the committee of Parliament fixed at a sum equal to a quarter of a million of dollars, was by no means extravagant, even if the worth of lands at that period be alone considered.

Perhaps the reader has journeyed through the present counties of Lancaster, Northumberland, Richmond, Westmoreland, Stafford, King George, Prince William, Fairfax, Loudoun, Fauquier, Culpepper, Clarke, Madison, Page, Shenandoah, Hardy, Hampshire, Morgan, Berkely, Jefferson and Frederick — twenty-one in all — and embracing nearly one quarter of Virginia; — perhaps the eye that glances at this page has surveyed everything between the Potomac and the Rappahannock; — did the thought occur that this whole territory once belonged to a single family; that though the Fairfax of the Revolutionary era was the friend of Washington, every acre was confiscated simply because of loyalty to the British Crown? Such a grant, after the lapse of generations, and in the progress of civilization, we deem entirely wrong; but, made in accordance with the spirit of the age, it was valid. The many battles on the Fairfax domain, in the present unhallowed Rebellion, will render the country between the Potomac and the Rappahannock memorable in all coming time.

FAIRFAX, GEORGE WILLIAM. Of Virginia. He was the great-grandson of Thomas, the fourth Lord Fairfax. His father was the Hon. Colonel William Fairfax, who was Lieutenant of the county of Fairfax, Collector of the Customs of South Potomac, member and President of the Council in Virginia. He was educated in England, but was the early companion of Washington, and his associate as surveyor of lands. On the death of his father in 1757, he succeeded to his estate. He married a daughter of Colonel Carey, of Hampton, became a member of the Council, and lived at Belvoir. Some property in Yorkshire descended to him in 1773, and he went to England; and in consequence of the political difficulties which followed, did not return to America. He fixed his residence at Bath, where he died in 1787, aged sixty-three. During the war he evinced much kindness to American prisoners who were carried to England. A part of his Virginia estate was confiscated, by which his income was much reduced. Washington esteemed him highly, and they were ever friends. The illustrious Commander-in-Chief was named an executor of his will, but declined fulfilling the trust in consequence of his public engagements. Mr. Fairfax left no children. He bequeathed his American property to Ferdinando, the second son of his only surviving brother.

FAIRFAX, LORD BRYAN. Of Virginia. He was the third son of the Hon. Colonel William Fairfax. His wife was a daughter of Wilson Carey, of Virginia, and his residence was at Towlston Hall in Fairfax County, though for some years, during the latter part of his life, he was an Episcopal clergyman at Alexandria. An affectionate intercourse existed between him and Washington throughout life; both were of too elevated a cast to allow political differences of opinion to alienate and separate them. In 1774 Washington expressed an earnest wish that he should stand as a candidate for the House of Burgesses, but he declined. He was opposed to strong measures, and in favor of redress by remonstrances and petitions. "There are scarce any at Alexandria," he wrote, "of my opinion; and though the few I have elsewhere conversed with on the subject are so, yet from them I could learn that many thought otherwise; so that I believe I should at this time give general dissatisfaction, and therefore it would be more proper to decline, even upon this account, as well as because it would necessarily lead me into great expenses, which my circumstances will not allow." Washington, in reply, remarked that he would heartily join in his political sentiments "so far as relates to a humble and dutiful petition to the throne, provided there was the most distant hope of success. But," said he, "have we not tried this already? Have we not addressed the Lords, and remonstrated to the Commons? And to what end? Did they deign to look at our petitions?" &c.

Prior to July 18, 1774, Mr. Fairfax attended several meetings of the Whigs of Fairfax County, but at that time withdrew from them. The immediate cause of withdrawal seems to have been his disapprobation of some of the resolutions prepared by a committee, and submitted to a general meeting of the inhabitants of the county. Washington was chairman of both the committee and the meeting, and Fairfax addressed to him a communication, expressing his views and objections, which he desired might be publicly read. Yet the two friends did not relinquish their correspondence upon the great questions which agitated the country; and the letters of Washington to this gentleman contain the fullest and most satisfactory exposition of his sentiments that Mr. Sparks has preserved. On the death of Robert Fairfax (in 1791), who was the seventh Lord Fairfax, Bryan Fairfax succeeded to the title, and was the eighth Baron of the name. Benevolence and kindness were marked traits in his character, and he was universally respected and beloved. Washington bequeathed to him an elegant Bible in three volumes folio. Lord Bryan died at Mount Eagle, near Cameron, in 1802, aged seventy-five, after a long illness, which he bore with resignation.

Two of his sons were Ferdinando and Thomas. The latter, as we shall see, inherited the empty title of Lord Fairfax. His grandson Henry, a graduate at West Point, raised a company in the late war with Mexico, much against the wishes of his relatives and friends, and died a victim to the climate, soon after arriving at the scene of strife. Lord Thomas Fairfax, after his succession to the barony, chose to live much in retirement, to superintend "his paternal estates on the Potomac, and to exercise a genuine old English hospitality, combined with the simplicity of the land in which he dwelt." "He uniformly declined, from Americans, any deference to his rank, preferring to be regarded as simply a gentleman of the county which bears his family name." He died at his seat in Virginia, in 1846, in his eighty-fourth year. Margaret, his widow, died in 1858, at the age of seventy-five. The present Baron is Lord Charles Snowden Fairfax, grandson of Lord Thomas.

FAIRWEATHER, BENJAMIN, JEDEDIAH, and THOMAS. Settled in New Brunswick in 1783, and received grants of lands. Thomas died at Norton in that Colony in 1825, at the age of seventy-seven, and Elizabeth, his widow, at the same place, in 1846, aged seventy-nine. Jedediah died at Norton in 1831, at the age of ninety-six.

FALES, DAVID. Of Dedham, Massachusetts. In 1763 he removed to Maine, upon the Waldo Patent, and within the limits of the present town of Thomaston; where he practised as a physician, taught school, and surveyed lands. He was also employed by Mr. Flucker, the Secretary of Massachusetts, and son-in-law of General Waldo, as agent of lands embraced in the Patent. He wrote a remarkable fair hand, was methodical in business, but slow, and very tardy in coming to the relief of a patient. In 1775 the Whigs, in the vicinity of his home, offered him the alternative of signing a Test of fidelity to the popular cause, or of riding on the "wooden horse."

He refused to side with the "Rebels," and escaped the rail; for his wife prepared a pailful of flip, and his sons became sureties for his good conduct. I find him in Maine in 1790, when, at Thomaston, his name appears as one of a committee to select the site for a meeting-house in Warren.

FANNING, EDMUND. Of North Carolina. General in the British Army. Son of Colonel Phineas Fanning. Born on Long Island, New York. Graduated at Yale College; studied law; removed to North Carolina, and commenced practice. Appointed colonel in the militia in 1763, and two years later, clerk of the Superior Court. Subsequently, he was a man of considerable note in the Colony, and respectable men aver that he was remarkable "for all the vices that degrade the most abandoned and profligate minion." Among the public offices which he held, was that of Recorder of Deeds for the county of Orange; and it is alleged, that to his abuses in this capacity, the war or rebellion of the Regulators in Governor Tryon's administration, is, in a good measure, to be attributed. The averment is, that, by his vicious character, "nearly all the estates in Orange were loaded with doubts as to their titles, with exorbitant fees for recording new and unnecessary deeds, and high taxes to support a government which supported his wickedness." This charge rests on very high authority; and during the war of the Regulators against the Royal Government, neither the person nor property of Fanning were respected. His losses were presented to the Assembly by Governor Martin, the successor of Tryon, but that body not only peremptorily refused to consider the subject, but administered a rebuke to the Governor, for thus trifling "with the dignity of the House." It is not impossible that his unpopularity was greater than his offences deserved; since neither the members of the Assembly, nor the people at large, were, at this juncture, in a frame of mind to do exact justice to opponents. Fanning followed Governor Tryon to New York, and became his secretary. In 1777 he raised a corps of four hundred and sixty Loyalists, which bore the name of the Associated Refugees, or King's American Regiment, and of which he had command. To aid in the organization of this body, £500 were subscribed at Staten Island, £310 in King's County, £219 in the town of Jamaica, and £2000 in the city of New York. While stationed in Rhode Island, August, 1778, he had "a smart engagement with the enemy," said General Pigot, "and obliged them to retreat to their main body." In March of the following year, a part of his regiment, and other Loyalists, embarked in seven vessels, protected by three privateers, on an expedition, "to get stock," or cattle, at the eastward. The chronicle has it that they landed on Nantucket and brought off a number of hogs, a quantity of oil, and three vessels. On the 16th of June, the whole corps sailed for New York. While his regiment was on Long Island, some of his men entered a house, tied the owner of it to a bedpost, and then held a candle under the ends of his fingers, to torture him to disclose the hiding-place of his money. The general charge that "Fanning's corps were rude and ill behaved," is supported by evidence. In 1779 the property of Colonel Fanning in North Carolina was confiscated. In 1782 he was in office as Surveyor-General of New York. He went to Nova Scotia near the close of the war, and September 23d, 1783, was sworn in as Councillor and Lieutenant-Governor of that Colony. About the year 1786 he was appointed Lieutenant-Governor of Prince Edward Island; and having served nearly nineteen years, was succeeded in 1805 by Des Barres, who is celebrated for his charts of parts of the American coast.

Fanning was appointed Major-General in 1793, Lieutenant-General in 1799, and General in 1808. He died in Upper Seymour Street, London, in 1818. Whigs, as we have seen, said that his character was bad. At the time of his decease, a friendly pen wrote: "The world did not contain a better man in all the various relations of life: as a husband, a parent, and a friend — as a landlord and master, he was kind and indulgent. He was much distinguished in the American war, and raised a regiment there, by which he lost a very large property." His only son, A. F. Fanning, a captain in the 22d Foot, died in 1812. "Neither the General nor any of his family ever recovered from that blow." Mrs. Fanning and three daughters survived.

FANNING, DAVID. Of North Carolina. He was born in Virginia in 1755, and was bred to a trade. In 1775, to use his own words, he was a planter "in the back part of the Southern Provinces." His first military service was performed under Colonel Thomas Fletchell, in the affair with Major Andrew Williamson. In a memorial to the Commissioners on Loyalists' Claims, he states, that during the Revolution he had command of bodies of men from one hundred to nine hundred and fifty in number; that he was engaged against "the Rebels" thirty-six times in North Carolina, and four times in South Carolina, — all of which skirmishes and battles he planned; that he was wounded twice, and made prisoner no less than on fourteen occasions; that, at the peace, he went to Florida, where he settled two hundred and fifty souls; that his property in North Carolina had been confiscated; and that he and his family were in great distress. This paper is dated at St. John, New Brunswick, in March, 1786. Of his course in the Revolution, another remarks: "Always well mounted and accompanied by a band of kindred spirits, he swept over the country like a Camanche chief, surprising parties of Whigs when off their guard; he often gave no quarter. In lying in ambush or pouncing upon them at their homes, he seized and murdered or tortured the obnoxious patriots, and then plundered and burnt their dwellings. By a series of bold adventures he took the town of Cross Creek, now Fayetteville, captured the Whig militia officers of the county of Chatham, when sitting in court-martial at Hillsborough, and by a sudden descent on Hillsborough, at dawn of day, about the middle of September, seized and carried off the Governor of the State."

In 1799 Fanning removed from New Brunswick to Nova Scotia. In February, 1801, as appears by papers in his own handwriting, which are in my possession, he was under sentence of death. He was a Freemason, and Oliver Arnold, Master of Lodge No. 21, King's County, petitioned Governor

Carleton to pardon him. By this document it seems that Fanning was convicted on the testimony of a single witness; and this fact is stated as a reason why mercy should be extended to him. The *crime* is not mentioned by Arnold, or in any of the other papers which I have examined; but, from several expressions which occur, and from the manner of Fanning's reference to Sarah London, or, as he calls her, "Sall London," she must have accused him of violating her person, and have procured his conviction. He was pardoned. In 1804, his correspondence shows that he abused — much abused — a gentleman of St. John, who "contributed greatly in saving his life;" while, subsequently, it affords ample evidence that he was often involved in quarrels with his neighbors, and in lawsuits with others. In truth, he was in trouble everywhere. In North Carolina he was declared an outlaw, and was one of the three who are excepted by name in the Act of General Pardon and Oblivion; and not a Whig there or elsewhere, as far as I know, ever spoke or wrote of him in kindness; while his fellow-Loyalists in New Brunswick and Nova Scotia often expressed their indignation at his words and deeds. In 1812, Fanning solicited military employment in the war with the United States, without success. Officers, however, who served with him in the Revolution, be it said in justice, testified to "his services and character as a brave soldier." He died at Digby, in 1825, at the age of seventy.

FANNING, THOMAS. Of Suffolk County, New York. Addresser of Governor Tryon, November, 1776; and deputed to present the submission of the committees of that county the month previous. In June, 1778, a party of Whigs from Connecticut seized him and carried him off. He was a kinsman, perhaps a brother, of Edmund.

FANUEIL, BENJAMIN. Of Boston. An eminent merchant. He was one of the consignees of the tea which was destroyed in that town in December, 1773. He died at Cambridge, Massachusetts, in 1785, aged eighty-four.

FANUEIL, BENJAMIN, JR. Of Boston. He went to England, and was in London, March, 1777.

FARLEY, JOSEPH. Of Georgia. In the effort to reëstablish the Royal Government in 1779, he was appointed provost marshal.

FARRINGTON, THOMAS. Of Groton, Massachusetts. Lieutenant-Colonel in the Continental Army. In May, 1777, by order of General Heath, he was tried by a court-martial for "passing counterfeit money, knowing it to be such," found guilty, unanimously sentenced to be dismissed from the army, and rendered incapable of holding any military office under Congress. This done, he was committed to jail, to be dealt with by the civil authorities.

FARNHAM, JOHN. Of Monmouth County, New Jersey. A Tory marauder. In an affray in New Jersey, he attempted to shoot a young Whig into whose father's house he and a band of Tories and negroes had broken; but was prevented by Lippincott, the murderer of Huddy.

FARNSWORTH, DAVID. In 1778 he was tried as a spy, convicted of the offence, and executed at Hartford, Connecticut, on the 10th of November. A large amount of counterfeit Continental money was found in his possession.

FAULKNER, THOMAS. Of North Carolina. Secretary of the Colony. Went to England, and died there in 1782.

FAYERWEATHER, REV. SAMUEL. Of Rhode Island. Episcopal minister. He was son of Thomas Fayerweather of Boston, and graduated at Harvard University in 1743. Ordained a Congregationalist, he was settled at Newport, Rhode Island. His first service as an Episcopalian, after his return from England, was in South Carolina; but the climate injured his health, and he applied to the Society for the Propagation of the Gospel for a mission at the North. He was accordingly transferred to the parish of St. Paul's, Rhode Island, in 1760. In 1774 the Whigs of his flock objected to the reading of prayers for the King and Royal family; and, as he could not dispense with them, as he thought, without the violation of his ordination vows, his church was closed. He preached occasionally, however, in private houses, without molestation. It is said, indeed, that personally he favored the popular cause.

He died in 1781, and was buried under the communion-table of his church. The University of Oxford conferred the degree of A. M. in 1756.

FEMALES. [See *Women*.]

FENTON, JOHN. Of New Hampshire. He was a captain in the British Army, but disposing of his commission, settled in New Hampshire, where he became a colonel in the militia, clerk in the Court of Common Pleas, and Judge of Probate for the county of Grafton. In 1775 he was also a member of the House of Assembly for the town of Plymouth, and was expelled. Enraged at the indignity, and at the measures of the Whigs generally, he gave vent to his passions, and fell into the hands of the people, who pursued him to the residence of Governor Wentworth with a field-piece, which they threatened to discharge unless he was delivered up. Fenton surrendered, and was sent to the Committee of Safety at Exeter for trial. "Upon a full hearing of sundry complaints against" him in Provincial Congress, it was voted, that he was "an enemy to the liberties of America," and that he should "be confined in the jail at Exeter," and " be supported like a gentleman, at the expense of the Colony, until further orders." By a subsequent vote it was ordered, that his place of confinement should be at the Whig camp. September 19, 1775, the Continental Congress instructed Washington to discharge him on his parole of honor, to proceed to New York and thence to Great Britain, and not to bear arms against the American people. Property confiscated, and banished, 1778.

FENTON, LEWIS. A Tory robber and outlaw, who infested the pine barrens of New Jersey. He was originally a blacksmith, and learned his trade at Freehold, New Jersey. His first crime appears to have been the robbing of a tailor's shop; when word was sent to him that, unless he returned his plunder, he should be hunted down and shot. He was killed in Monmouth County, New Jersey, in 1779, by a party who went in pursuit of him.

FENWICKE, EDWARD. Of South Carolina. He was opposed to the measures of the Ministry in 1774, since he was in London that year, and joined Franklin, Lee, and other patriots then in England, in a remonstrance against the passage of the bill for the Government of Massachusetts Bay. He married a daughter of John Stuart, Superintendent of Indian Affairs; and, in 1776, petitioned the House of Assembly to allow him to hold as property thirty negroes who, as he averred, Stuart designed to give him as a part of the marriage portion of his wife. Stuart had then fled, and his effects had been seized. Fenwicke was a Congratulator of Cornwallis on his success at Camden in 1780. In 1782 his estate was confiscated, and he was banished. In 1785, by Act of the General Assembly, his property was restored, and he was allowed to remain in the State one year.

FERGUSON, HENRY HUGH. Of Pennsylvania. During the war he was made a commissary of prisoners. His wife was Elizabeth, a daughter of Doctor Graeme, the Collector of Philadelphia, and granddaughter of Sir William Keith, one of the proprietary Governors of Pennsylvania. In 1778, soon after he was attainted and proscribed, Mrs. Ferguson made a long statement to the Council, in which she gave a narrative of his conduct from September, 1775, (when, as appears, he embarked for Bristol, England,) until her appeal in his behalf. "As to my little estate," she remarked, "it is patrimonial, and left me in fee simple by my father." In 1779 she appealed to the Council not to allow the sale of her property "in consequence of her husband's right by marriage," setting forth, as she thought, "good and cogent reasons" for her prayer. The estate was, however, confiscated; but a part of it was restored to her by the Legislature in 1781. She separated from her husband, and died in 1801.

FERRIS, JOSEPH. Of Stamford, Connecticut. He raised a company, joined Colonel Butler, and was a captain in the Rangers. During the war he was taken prisoner by a brother-in-law who was a Whig, but escaped from captivity. After the peace he went to Newfoundland, but removed to New Brunswick, where he settled. He was fond of visits to the States and to the scenes of his youth; and sometimes met those whom he had opposed in skirmishes and battles. He lived in Eastport, Maine, after it was captured by the British forces in the war of 1812, but returned to New Brunswick on its being surrendered to the United States. He died at Indian Island, New Brunswick, in 1836, aged ninety-two. He enjoyed half-pay from the close of the Revolution until his decease, a period of fifty-three years.

FERRIS, JOSHUA. Of New York. "An old offender," said Colonel Thomas, to the New York Convention, August, 1776, when sending him to that body; "and has been sought for long since by the Committee of this county to answer for his repeated offences, particularly for being in arms against his country," &c.

FEWTRELL, JOHN. Of South Carolina. He was a Judge of the Superior Court; and was permitted to depart from the State.

FINDLEY, HUGH. He and John Foxcroft were the two Postmasters-General of the thirteen Colonies, and were continued at the head of that Department until 1782, certainly, and probably until the peace.

FINLEY, JAMES. Sergeant in Price's company of Riflemen. Tried by a general court-martial, at Cambridge, Mass., Sept. 1775, "for expressing himself disrespectfully of the Continental Association, and drinking General Gage's health"; and sentenced to be deprived of his arms and accoutrements, to be put in a horse-cart with a rope around his neck, to be drummed out of the army, and rendered forever incapable of military service.

FISHER, REV. NATHANIEL. Of Salem, Massachusetts. Episcopal minister. He was born at Dedham, Massachusetts, in 1742, and graduated at Harvard University in 1763. In the early part of the Revolution he was imprisoned for his loyalty. He was employed by the Society for the Propagation of the Gospel in Foreign Parts, as a schoolmaster at Granville, Nova Scotia, soon after his release; and in 1778, — having been to England for ordination, — he was stationed at Annapolis in that Province, as Assistant Rector. He returned to the

United States late in 1781, and was soon after admitted to citizenship in Massachusetts, on taking the oath of allegiance to that Commonwealth. In February, 1782, he entered upon his duties as Rector of St. Peter's Church, Salem. After a ministry of more than thirty years, he died in that city in December, 1812, on Sunday, a few minutes after returning to his house from performing divine service, at the age of seventy. His wife was Silence Baker, of Dedham, by whom he was the father of two sons and a daughter. "Two of his children were cut off in the bloom of youth and beauty," towards the close of his life, and " for a moment he seemed desolate and dismayed." It is written, that, " as a father and husband, he was affectionate and kind; as a friend, faithful and sincere; . . . and as a Christian, firm in his belief, and benevolent in his life." In person, he was strongly built, and of a large frame. One of his sisters was the mother of the statesman and orator, Fisher Ames.

FISHER, MIERS. Of Philadelphia. Said John Adams, in 1774: "Dined with Mr. Miers Fisher, a young Quaker, and a lawyer. We saw his library, which is clever. But this plain Friend and his plain though pretty wife, with her *Thees* and *Thous*, had provided us the most costly entertainment: ducks, ham, chickens, pig, tarts, creams, custards, jellies, fools, trifles, floating islands, beer, porter, punch, wine, and a long &c. We had a large collection of lawyers at table," &c. In the rapidity of events, Mr. Fisher was left behind; and in 1777 he was apprehended and confined at Philadelphia; and finally ordered, with other Loyalists of that city, to Virginia. He was distinguished in his profession, an eloquent advocate, and a lover of science. He died at Philadelphia in 1819, aged seventy-one.

FISHER, SAMUEL R. Of Philadelphia. Brother of Miers Fisher. In 1779, a letter, addressed by him to his brother, Jabez M., was intercepted, and submitted by the Council to the Chief Justice, with the remark that it contained information which appeared to call for legal reprehension and punishment. He was accordingly committed, and ordered to recognize with a surety in £500. Hours were spent by the Chief Justice himself in the endeavor to prevail upon him to execute the required bond, but he absolutely refused. He was not, however, deprived of his liberty by the sheriff, until the Council issued a positive order to that officer to confine him.

FISHER, JABEZ MAUD. Of Philadelphia. Brother of Samuel R. Fisher. He departed the State. In 1779 he was a merchant in New York; went to England, was a Loyal Addresser of the King, and died there the same year. In 1782, Messrs. Joshua Fisher & Sons, of Philadelphia, petitioned the Council of Pennsylvania to grant Samuel R. Fisher, of that house, leave to go to England by way of New York, to assist in adjusting his concerns. The petition was rejected.

FISHER, TURNER. Of Boston. Son of Wilfred Fisher. He accompanied the British troops from Boston to Halifax, and, entering the Royal Navy, became a sailing-master. After the Revolution, he married Esther, the daughter of Ezekiel Foster, of Machias, Maine, and settled in New Brunswick. He was in Boston about the time of the war of 1812, but his subsequent fate is unknown to his family. His son, Wilfred Fisher, Esq., is a merchant and magistrate of the island of Grand Menan, New Brunswick. His wife died in November, 1844, at the age of eighty-eight years, at the residence of her son.

FISHER, WILFRED. Of Boston. At the evacuation of that town, he accompanied the British troops to Halifax, where he received an appointment which attached him to a corps of light-horse. He died at Halifax before the close of the war. He was proscribed and banished under the Act of 1778, and his estate in Boston was confiscated. His son Wilfred was a Whig, and a ship-master. Captured by the British, he was carried to New York, and died there a prisoner, during the Revolution.

FISHER, JOHN. Naval-officer, at Portsmouth, New Hampshire. Salary, derivable from fees, £200 per annum. Was proscribed by the Act of New Hampshire of 1778. He went to England, and was secretary to Lord George Germain. His wife, Anna, sister of John Wentworth, the last Royal Governor of New Hampshire, died at Bath, England, in 1811, aged sixty-six.

FITCH, THOMAS. Of Connecticut. He graduated at Yale College in 1721, and devoted himself to the profession of the law. He held the offices of Councillor, Judge of the Superior Court, and Lieutenant-Governor; and in 1754 was elected Governor. These various stations he filled with unsurpassed integrity and wisdom. His legal knowledge is said to have equalled, and perhaps exceeded, that of any other lawyer of Connecticut during the period of her Colonial history. In 1765 he took the oath of office prescribed in the Stamp Act, and was driven into retirement in consequence the next year; having occupied the Executive Chair for the whole period between 1754 and 1766. His successor was the Honorable William Pitkin.

Copy of inscription on the monument of Governor Fitch, at Norwalk, Connecticut: "The Hon'ble Thomas Fitch, Esq., Gov. of the Colony of Connecticut. Eminent and distinguished among mortals for great abilities, large acquirements, and a virtuous character: a clear, strong, sedate mind: an accurate, extensive acquaintance with law, and civil government: a happy talent of presiding: close application, and strict fidelity in the discharge of important truths: no less than for his employments, by the voice of the people, in the chief offices of state, and at the head of the colony. Having served his generation, by the will of God, fell asleep, July 18, Ann. Domini, 1774, in the 75th year of his age."

FITCH, SAMUEL. Of Boston. An Addresser of Hutchinson in 1774. In 1776 he went to Halifax with his family of six persons. In 1778 he was proscribed and banished. He held the office of Solicitor to the Board of Commissioners; and, like most of his official associates, was included in the Conspiracy Act of 1779. He went to England, was a Loyalist Addresser of the King in 1779, and was abroad in 1783.

I conclude that the Samuel Fitch who graduated at Yale College in 1742, and died in 1784, was the subject of this notice.

FITCH, ELEAZER, JR. Of Windham, Connecticut. Sheriff of Windham County. More than one hundred citizens of that county petitioned the House of Assembly, September, 1776, for his removal from office, on account of many words and acts, which they designate, in opposition to the popular cause. Among them are the singular surnames of Devotion, Doughset, Greenslitt, Bibens.

FITCH, BENJAMIN. Of Maine. Went to the Kennebec River in 1760, and was employed there by Dr. Sylvester Gardiner, as a millwright. Violent in his opposition to the Whigs, he was compelled to leave the country. He enlisted, "and was killed fighting for the king." His wife was Ann McCausland.

FITZPATRICK, JAMES. Of Pennsylvania. A Tory marauder, known as "Captain Fitz." At first, a Whig, and in the Continental Army. He roamed the county of Chester, was a terror to the Whigs, and seemingly delighted in perils and escapes. His exploits were the theme of every tongue. At last, in 1778, when a reward of one thousand dollars had been offered for his apprehension, he entered a house to "levy his dues on the cursed Rebels," and was seized and overpowered by Robert McPher and a girl named Rachel Walker. Conveyed to prison in Philadelphia, he broke his handcuffs twice in one night; and, sent to another jail, he filed off his irons, and got out of his dungeon. He was hanged at last at Chester, Pennsylvania.

FITZ-RANDOLPH, ———. Of New Jersey. Lieutenant in the Loyal Militia. Killed near Elizabethtown, while acting with the Queen's Rangers.

FITZSIMMONS, PETER. A merchant. At Newtown, New York, at some time in the war. In 1782 he opened a tavern there, which was much frequented by soldiers and Loyalists. He also kept a ferry. At the peace, he went to St. John, New Brunswick.

FLEMING, JOHN. Printer, of Boston. Was proscribed and banished by the Act of 1778. He was copartner with Mien. Some of the books which they printed had a false imprint, and were palmed off as London editions, because Mien said, that books thus published met with a better sale. In 1767 they commenced the " Boston Chronicle," a paper which, in the second year of its publication, espoused the Royal cause, and became extremely abusive of numbers of the most respectable Whigs of Boston. To avoid the effects of popular resentment, Mien thought fit to leave the country. The "Chronicle" was the first paper published twice a week in New England; and was suspended in 1770. Fleming found it prudent to retire from Boston in 1773, and embarked for England in that year with his family. He came to the United States more than once, subsequent to 1790, as the agent of a commercial house in Europe. His residence was in France for some years, and he died there.

FLETCHALL, THOMAS. Of South Carolina. He was a colonel, and at the head of a considerable force of Loyalists in that State, during the difficulties with the Cunninghams in 1775; and signed the truce or treaty which was agreed upon between the Whigs and their opponents. In 1776 he was committed to prison in Charleston, by order of the Provincial Congress. After the surrender of Charleston, he was in commission under the Crown. In 1782 his estate was confiscated. He appears to have been a person of much consideration in South Carolina, previous to the Revolution; and to have been regarded as of rather doubtful, or undecided politics, though the Whigs made him a member of an important standing committee, raised with the design of carrying out the views of the Continental Congress.

FLEWELLING, ABEL, and MORRIS. Of New York. Settled in New Brunswick at the peace, and were grantees of lands in St. John. Abel became a magistrate, and died at Maugerville in 1814, aged sixty-eight.

FLOYD, RICHARD. Of New York. He was the eldest son of Hon. Richard Floyd, a colonel of New York militia, a

Judge of the Common Pleas, and a gentleman of wealth and reputation. His wife was Arrabella, a daughter of Judge David Jones, of Queen's County, New York. His children were Elizabeth, who married John Peter De Lancey, and was the mother of the wife of Cooper, the great American novelist; Anne, a younger daughter; and one son, David Richard. The latter, in pursuance of the will of Judge Jones, and by legal authority, adopted the name of Jones; he died in 1826, leaving two sons, to wit: Brigadier-General Thomas Floyd Jones, and Major-General Henry Floyd Jones. Mr. Floyd's estate was confiscated; and abandoning the country, he died at St. John, New Brunswick. His family was one of the most ancient in New York, and is distinguished in its annals. Descended from the same ancestor was the Whig General William Floyd, who signed the Declaration of Independence. The Floyds were of Welsh origin, and the first of the name emigrated in 1654, and settled at Brookhaven, Long Island, where many of his descendants continued until the Revolution.

FLOYD, BENJAMIN. Of Brookhaven, Suffolk County, New York. In 1775 he circulated a paper for signatures, to support the Royal authority, in opposition to the proceedings of the Whigs, and obtained the names of about one hundred persons. A party of "Rebels," in 1778, entered his house at night, compelled a servant to show them in which room he was in bed, seized him, and carried him to Norwalk, Connecticut. The next year, another party of about twenty, in whale-boats, robbed his dwelling of £600, and the most valuable part of his household goods. He was a major in the New York Militia.

FLUCKER, THOMAS. Last Secretary of the Province of Massachusetts Bay. In 1765 he was member of a committee of the Council to consider and report what could be done to prevent difficulties in the proceedings of the courts of justice; and, three years later, his name occurs in the State Papers, as appointed by the same body to assist in drafting an Address to the King. March 2d, 1774, when Lieutenant-Governor

Oliver was senseless and dying, John Adams records: "Flucker has laid in to be Lieutenant-Governor, and has persuaded Hutchinson to write in his favor. This will make a difficulty." Though unsuccessful, he was appointed a Mandamus Councillor. Whig mechanics of Boston met at the Green Dragon tavern, and were so careful of their secrets that Colonel Paul Revere (who was one of them) says they swore on the Bible, every time they met, to discover nothing except to Hancock, Samuel Adams, Warren, and Church. The latter, proved a traitor, and Secretary Flucker was the first to acquaint a person of Loyalist connections, who (a Whig at heart) told Revere, that all their transactions were communicated to General Gage. In 1776 Flucker was in London, and a member of the "Brompton Row Tory Club," or Association of Loyalists, who met weekly for conversation and a dinner. He died in England suddenly, in 1783. He married Hannah, daughter of General Waldo, proprietor of the Waldo Patent, Maine, to whose heirs the domain descended. The parts which belonged to Mrs. Flucker and her two brothers, were confiscated. Henry Knox, Chief of Artillery in the Revolution and Secretary of War in Washington's administration, who married Flucker's daughter, acquired a very large share of it on easy terms, settled at Thomaston and built an elegant mansion, in which he himself died in 1806, and his wife in 1824. Mrs. Flucker remained in England, but survived her husband only three years.

FLUCKER, THOMAS, JR. Of Massachusetts. Son of Thomas Flucker. He graduated at Harvard University in 1773, and in the Revolution was an officer in the British service. By the University Catalogue, it appears that he and his father died the same year, 1783.

FOLLIOT, GEORGE. Of New York. He was elected a member of the Provincial Congress for the city and county of New York, in 1775, but declined serving, and the vacancy was filled in June of that year. In 1776 he was an Addresser of Lord and Sir William Howe. He was also appointed a member of the Committee of One Hundred, but refused to act. His estate of twenty-one acres was sold by the Commissioners of Confiscation, in 1784.

FORBES, REV. ELI. Of Massachusetts. Congregational minister. He graduated at Harvard University in 1751, and was ordained at Brookfield the next year. He was dismissed in 1776, "on suspicion of entertaining Tory principles;" and was soon after installed over the First Parish in Gloucester: He died in 1804, aged seventy-seven. His first wife was a daughter of the Rev. Ebenezer Parkman of Westborough, by whom he was the father of two children, Eli and Polly: His second wife, who died in 1780, was Lucy, daughter of the Rev. Thomas Smith, of Falmouth, (now Portland,) Maine, and widow of Thomas Sanders, of Gloucester.

FORBES, GILBERT. Gunsmith, of Broadway, New York. In 1776 he was arrested and put in irons, on the charge of being concerned in the plot of certain adherents of the Crown to murder a number of Whig officers, to blow up the magazine, &c. When told that he had but a short time to live, he asked to be carried before Congress, and said he would confess all he knew. He is described as "a short, thick man, with a white coat."

FORD, WILLIAM. Captain of Loyalist refugees. In 1781, with thirty-eight men, "when the good people of Middlesex were assembled, and devoutly praying for their great and good ally," he surrounded their church, and took from thence "fifty notorious Rebels, their Reverend teacher, and their horses, forty in number." Though harrassed in returning to his boats, he carried off "every Rebel and every horse." Three of his men were slightly wounded. This exploit was thought extremely meritorious in Loyalists circles; and Ford's "bravery, coolness and alertness," were duly praised in an official report.

FORD, ELISHA. Of Marshfield, Massachusetts. He was seized, carted to the liberty-pole in Duxbury, and compelled to sign a Recantation. He was afterwards in jail at Plymouth, Massachusetts, and ordered by Resolve, June, 1776, to remain there at his own expense.

FORD, SAMUEL. Second Lieutenant of the *Effingham* galley. In 1778 he was tried for desertion to the Royal side during the siege of Fort Mifflin; convicted, and sentenced to death.

FORD, JOHN. Of New Jersey. Compelled to leave his residence to avoid the Whigs who molested him, he fled to the Royal forces on Staten Island, where he remained some years. In 1783 Sir Guy Carleton commissioned him to take charge of a company of Loyalists, who were emigrating from New York to Nova Scotia. He settled at St. John, New Brunswick, and received the grant of a city lot; but removed to Hampton, and became one of the best farmers in that Colony. He died at Hampton in 1823, aged seventy-seven.

FORREST, JAMES. Merchant, of Boston. An Addresser of Hutchinson in 1774. In 1775 he commanded, in Boston, the Loyal Irish Volunteers, a company raised to mount guard every evening, armed, and distinguished by a white cockade. Went to Halifax in 1776, with his family of six persons. Served as a volunteer in the battle of Germantown, 1777, and was wounded. Proscribed and banished, 1778.

FORRESTER, GEORGE PEABODY. Died at Hampton, King's County, New Brunswick, in 1840, aged eighty-three years.

FORRESTER, JOSEPH. At the peace, was one of the grantees of St. John, New Brunswick. In 1795 he was a member of the Loyal Artillery of that city. He died while at Boston in 1804, aged forty-six.

FORSTER, MOSES. In September, 1779, he was at Halifax, Nova Scotia, a stranger and in distress. As a Loyalist, he had been imprisoned on shore a year; harrassed by a Whig committee; driven from his family; taken out of bed and conveyed one hundred and twenty miles to a guardship, and then transported. He had a wife and eight children; and, at the above date, was about embarking for New York.

FOSTER, THOMAS. Of Plymouth, Massachusetts. He represented that town in the General Court several years; and in 1765 instructions were furnished him to govern his course on the exciting questions of the time. He accompanied the British Army to Halifax in 1776. Aside from his political preferences, he was esteemed by his townsmen for his attention and fidelity to the municipal and civil concerns intrusted to his care. His father, Deacon John Foster, was also a representative from Plymouth, and pursued an independent line of conduct in that relation, never accepting of Executive favors. His son Thomas was a graduate of Harvard University, and instructed a school at Plymouth. His grandson Thomas was an officer of a bank at Charleston, South Carolina, and died there in 1808, aged fifty-eight. Branches of this family settled in Middleborough and Kingston, Massachusetts, and in Norfolk, Virginia.

FOSTER, EDWARD. Of Boston. Addresser of Hutchinson, 1774; went to Halifax, 1776; was proscribed and banished in 1778. He settled at Dartmouth, Nova Scotia, and managed large iron-works there. He died in 1786, leaving thirteen children.

FOSTER, EDWARD, JR. Of Boston. Son of Edward. Went to Halifax in 1776; was proscribed and banished in 1778. About the year 1814 he settled in Union, Maine, and died there in 1822, aged seventy-two.

FOWLE, ROBERT. Served an apprenticeship with his uncle, Daniel Fowle, of Portsmouth, and became his partner in the publication of the "New Hampshire Gazette," the only newspaper in New Hampshire at the beginning of the Revolution. As the nephew was a Loyalist, and the uncle a Whig, their connection terminated in 1774; when Robert established himself as a printer at Exeter. The new paper currency, which he printed, having been counterfeited soon after, suspicion rested on him as a participant in the crime; and his flight to the British lines in New York, and thence abroad, served to confirm the impression. Some years after the peace he returned to the United States, married the widow of his younger brother, and lived in New Hampshire until his decease. His father was John Fowle, first a silent partner of Rogers & Fowle, of Boston, and subsequently an Episcopal clergyman at Norwalk, Connecticut. The firm of Rogers

& Fowle printed the first edition of the New Testament in the English language which was published in this country. Robert, the subject of this notice, received a pension from the British Government.

FOWLER, JONATHAN. Of West Chester County, New York. Judge of the Superior Court. He was seized by a party of Whigs, who carried him to New Haven, where he signed an apology for protesting against Congress. At the peace, he went to Digby, Nova Scotia, and was a merchant and ship-owner. He soon died, and his family returned to the United States.

FOWLER, CALEB. Of New York. In 1782 he was an ensign in the Loyal American Regiment. He settled in New Brunswick; received half-pay, and died on the river St. John.

FOWLER, CALEB. Of West Chester County, New York. He was one of the Loyalist Protesters at White Plains, April, 1775, who denounced Whig Congresses and Committees, and who pledged themselves "at the hazard of their lives and properties, to support the King and Constitution." He entered the Royal service, and was a captain in the Loyal American Regiment. At the peace he retired to New Brunswick on half-pay. He died near Fredericton.

FOWLER. Of New York. Samuel was permitted to return to the State in 1784, on petition of Whigs. — Of Massachusetts. John, who, accompanied by his wife and two children, arrived at St. John, New Brunswick, in the ship *Union*, in the spring of 1783. Of those whose places of residence are unknown, were William, who was a captain, and Gilbert, who was an ensign in the Loyal American Regiment; Gabriel, who settled in New Brunswick in 1783, and died in that Colony in 1832, at the age of seventy-five; Daniel, who boasted of being a firm Loyalist, who settled in the same, and died in King's County in 1813, aged sixty-five; Henry, who died in the same county in 1843, at the age of eighty-seven; and another, who, a captain in De Lancey's Brigade, was killed on an incursion to Horseneck in 1780. Still again, Amos, Aaron, Andrew,

Josiah, and Jeremiah Fowler, in 1783, were petitioners for lands in Nova Scotia.

FOUGHT, GEORGE. Of New York. He went to New Brunswick in 1783, and died at St. John in 1823, aged eighty-three.

FOULIS, JAMES. Of South Carolina. Episcopal minister. Entered upon his duties in 1770; went to England in 1779.

FOUNTAIN, STEPHEN. Of Stamford, Connecticut. He wrote a letter, addressed to "Darias Olmstead, at Norwalk, This with care," September, 1776; but the letter was really to his mother, brothers, and sister. He had a wife, and sent his love to her. He was an ignorant man; and his letter is full of errors and exaggerations. Convicted the same year, by three Whig committees, of taking up arms, of corresponding with the British ships, and seducing many to espouse the Royal side, he was made prisoner, carried to Congress, and committed. He arrived at St. John, New Brunswick, with his wife, in 1783, in the ship *Union*.

FOUNTAIN, JOHN. Went to Shelburne, Nova Scotia, in 1783, where he had a fine vegetable and flower garden. The story is that he used to let the boys eat currants at a penny each. He removed to Deer Island, New Brunswick, and died there in 1829, aged eighty-five.

FOXCROFT, JOHN. One of the two Postmasters-General of the Crown in the thirteen Colonies. He discharged the post-rider between New York and Boston, April, 1775, as he informed the Whig Committee of the former city, because the mails had been stopped, the bags broken open, and many of the letters taken out and publicly read. "A Constitutional Post-office rose on the ruins of the Parliamentary one," in May of the same year. "The post, from New York for the eastward, sets out about nine o'clock on Monday, about noon on Thursday, and returns on Wednesdays and Saturdays." In 1776, we have three incidents; thus, in February, the following letter to Tuthil Hulbart, Boston: —

"DEAR SIR, — You will excuse my troubling you with the enclosed bill, which I beg you will receive in a sterling bill of exchange, if to be had, and remit it to Mr. *Benson Fearon*, Merchant, in *London*, advising me of it by the first opportunity. I must not omit mentioning to you, that the first bill was remitted to Mr. *Harry Lloyd*, who never acknowledged the receipt of it; and therefore it probably miscarried. Your negotiating this matter will lay me under a great obligation; but in return, you know, if I can render you any service this way, you have only to command me. I have not had one line from you since the affair at *Lexington;* nor from *Sukey* since she left us. Mrs. *Foxcroft* and my little girls are well. She joins me in sincere regards to you and family.

"I am yours, as ever,

"JOHN FOXCROFT."

Next, in March, when the Provincial Congress allowed him to go on board the ships in New York harbor, to sort and count, for delivery, letters from abroad. Last, in November, when he was a prisoner in Philadelphia. In 1789 he was at liberty on parole, and in New York. After the war he was agent for the British packets in the last-named city, and died there in 1790.

FOXCROFT, THOMAS. Joint Postmaster-General with John. Went to England, and died there suddenly in 1785. Elizabeth, their sister, and wife of Benson Fearon, died in England, 1801.

FOY, EDWARD. Of Virginia. He entered the British Army in 1757, and was a captain in 1764. He accompanied Lord Dunmore to New York, as his private secretary, in 1770; and served in the same capacity when his Lordship was transferred to the government of Virginia. He returned to England in 1775; but probably came back to America a year or two afterward.

FRANCIS, THOMAS. A negro slave, purchased by Philip Lott of Elihu Spencer, of New Jersey. He ran away to New York on 2d November, 1782, and was enlisted by Captain Thelwal into the Jamaica Rangers. He was reclaimed by the American Commissioners, in June, 1783; but Sir Guy Carleton refused to give him up, since he had joined him under the sanction of the Negro Proclamation.

FRANKLAND, LADY AGNES. Of Massachusetts. Wife of Sir Charles Henry Frankland, Baronet. According to "Burke's Peerage," her maiden name was Agnes Brown; others call her Agnes Surrage. The story told of her is romantic enough. Sir Charles, who was a grandson of Frances, daughter of Oliver Cromwell, was appointed Collector of the Customs for the port of Boston, in 1741; and first saw Agnes at Marblehead, when she was about sixteen years of age, and a servant-girl at a tavern. She was of "matchless beauty," and, the Baronet becoming enamored with her, obtained the consent of her parents to take her to Boston, where he placed her at school, "clothed her in the best, and in every way sought to develop her body and mind." The end was, that he won her affections, and, as her humble rank presented obstacles to marriage, she consented to live with him as his mistress. This arrangement caused great commotion; and Sir Charles bought an estate in Hopkinton, built a house upon it, and removed thither, with "his Agnes and some of his boon companions." Some years afterwards he was appointed Consul-General to Portugal, and took Agnes with him. At the moment of the great earthquake at Lisbon, 1755, he was riding out; "his horses were swallowed in the opening earth, and his carriage was covered with the ruins of falling buildings;" and he himself expected to be crushed to death. While he lay buried, "the evils of his past career came forcibly to mind; and, if saved, he resolved to live a better life." Meantime his mistress was in search of him, found the spot, heard his voice, and offered a large reward for his rescue. The day after this fearful event, he led Agnes to the altar; and the marriage ceremony was repeated in the Episcopal form, after his return to England. He came again to Boston, and purchased an estate in Garden Court, North Square, near or adjoining the house of Governor Hutchinson, where he is said to have lived in much style. While Collector, he was often absent; and, finally, in 1759, was suspended for inattention to duty; and William Sheaffe, who had often had charge of the business of the office, was appointed in his stead. The Baronet's mansion at Hopkinton (burned in 1858) attracted many visitors; on going over it myself, I could hardly imagine — altered as it was — that while he occupied it, he "maintained the splendor of an English nobleman;" and the terms "elegant, very large and fine," often applied to it, seemed quite extravagant. He died at Bath, England, in 1765, and was succeeded by his brother Thomas, who, an Admiral of the White, married Susan, granddaughter of Chief Justice Rhett, of South Carolina.

Lady Frankland, accompanied by her natural son, arrived in America from Bristol in 1768; and designed, probably, to remain. At Hopkinton, May, 1775; and, alarmed at the movements of the people, her Ladyship asked leave to remove to Boston. The Committee of Safety gave her liberty to pass to the capital with six trunks, one chest, three beds and bedding for the same, six sheep, two pigs, one small keg of pickled tongues, some hay, three bags of corn, and such other goods as she should think proper to carry thither; and gave her a written permit accordingly, signed by "Benjamin Church, Jr., Chairman." Thus protected, she set out on her journey with her attendants; but was arrested by a party of armed men, who detained her person and her effects, until an order for the release of both was obtained." To prevent further annoyance, the Provincial Congress furnished her with an escort; and, by two resolves subsequently, allowed her to take seven trunks, all her beds and bedding, all her boxes and crates, a basket of chickens, two barrels and a hamper, two horses and chaises, one phaeton, some ham and veal, and sundry small bundles; and required all persons who had any of her property in possession to place the same, essentially, at her disposal. The "arms and ammunition," deposited in a chaise, a committee retained. These details are not trivial, because they show the spirit of the time. Lady Frankland was in Boston on the 17th of June, and gazed from her own house upon the conflict on Bunker's Hill. She returned to England. In 1782 she married John Drew, a banker of Chichester; and died at that place the year after, at about the age of fifty-five.

FRANKLIN, WILLIAM. Last Royal Governor of New Jersey. Natural son of Benjamin Franklin. Born about the year 1731.

His father said of him: "Will. is now nineteen years of age, a tall, proper youth, and much of a beau. He acquired a habit of idleness, ... but begins of late to apply himself to business, and I hope will become an industrious man. He imagined his father had got enough for him, but I have assured him that I intend to spend what little I have myself, if it please God that I live long enough; and, as he by no means wants acuteness, he can see by my going on, that I mean to be as good as my word." He served as postmaster of Philadelphia, and as clerk of the House of Assembly of Pennsylvania. In the French war he was a captain, and gained praise for his conduct at Ticonderoga. Before the peace he went to England with his father. While there, Mr. Strahan wrote Mrs. Franklin: "Your son I really think one of the prettiest young gentlemen I ever knew from America. He seems to me to have a solidity of judgment, not very often to be met with in one of his years." On the other hand, Rev. Jacob Bailey records (March 5, 1760): "This morning waited upon the famous Mr. Benjamin Franklin, and received an invitation to dine..... His son dined with us, a barrister-at-law. He is a gentleman of good education, but has passed away the flower of his youth in too many extravagancies."

While abroad, young Franklin visited Scotland, and became acquainted with the celebrated Earl of Bute, who recommended him to Lord Fairfax, who secured for him, as is said, the appointment of Governor of New Jersey, in 1763, without the solicitation of himself or his father. Whatever the truth, John Penn, who was in England, said in a letter to Lord Stirling, that the business was managed so privately that "there was no opportunity of counteracting, or, indeed, doing one single thing that might put a stop to this shameful affair. I make no doubt but the people of New Jersey will make some remonstrance upon this indignity put upon them. .... What a dishonor and disgrace it must be to a country to have such a man at the head of it, and to sit down contented ! .... If any *gentleman* had been appointed, it would have been a different case," &c.

The biographer of his Lordship remarks that the disgust at Franklin's appointment, " arose in part, probably, from the illegitimacy of his birth," but principally from his "timeserving conduct and courtier-like propensities ; " and he adds that the Governor " was originally a Whig, but became, *ex virtute officii*, a Tory."

Governor Franklin's first serious dispute with the Assembly appears to have been caused by his course in relation to the removal of the Treasurer of the Colony, who was a defaulter. On the 11th of June, 1774, the Whigs of Essex County met in Convention, and adopted various resolutions expressive of their sentiments on the alarming state of affairs, which gave Governor Franklin much uneasiness. In January, 1775, he met the Assembly. A considerable part of his speech is devoted to the controversy between the Colonies and the mother country, and to warnings to the members against imitating the example of those whose course of conduct was likely to involve the country in afflictive calamities.

The Governor and the Assembly parted in bad temper. An attempt was made to reduce his Excellency's salary from £1200 to £1000, and in appropriating £60 for the payment of the rent of his house, the condition that he should reside either at Perth Amboy or Burlington was annexed to the grant. His situation was unhappy. All intercourse between himself and his father had now been suspended for more than a year; and he was involved in a helpless quarrel with the delegates and the people of New Jersey. On the 13th of February, 1775, he prorogued the Assembly. In March, a letter alleged to have been written by him to Lord Dartmouth, was laid before the House of Commons by Lord North, which in America caused much excitement; and when the Assembly of New Jersey met in the following month of May, a message was sent to the Governor, requesting him to inform that body whether it was genuine, or whether it contained the substance of any letter which he had written relative to the measures adopted at the last session of the Assembly. In his answer, he explicitly denies its authenticity, and that no similar sentiments had been uttered by him in any communication to the King's ministers. But his message of reply is bitter and uncompromising throughout. "It has been my unhappiness almost every session during the existence of the present Assembly," — is the opening remark, — "that a majority of the members of the House have suffered themselves to be persuaded to seize on every opportunity of arraigning my conduct, or fomenting some dispute, let the occasion be ever so trifling, or let me be ever so careful to avoid giving any just cause of offence. This, too, has been done with such an eagerness in the promoters of it, as can only be accounted for on a supposition that they are either actuated by unmanly private resentment, or by a conviction that their whole political consequence depends upon a contention with their Governor." He concludes this ill-natured document with saying, that those who knew him best would do him the justice "to allow that no office of honor in the power of the Crown to bestow would ever influence him to forget or neglect the duty he owed his country, nor the most furious rage of the most intemperate zealots induce him to swerve from the duty he owed his Majesty." The Assembly was prorogued on the 20th of May, (and on the day of transmitting this answer), to meet on the 20th of June following; but affairs had now reached a crisis, and Governor Franklin never communicated with that body again. Three days after the prorogation, the first Provincial Congress of New Jersey commenced their session at Trenton, and the Royal Government soon ceased to be respected, and to exist. A constitution was adopted in July, 1776; and William Livingston, a member of the first Continental Congress, became Franklin's successor.

The deposed representative of Royalty was declared to be an enemy to his country, and ordered to be sent a prisoner to Connecticut. He was accordingly placed in the custody of a guard commanded by a captain, who had orders to deliver him to Governor Trumbull. The officer in charge halted at Hackensack, and was rebuked by Washington for his delay. The Commander-in-Chief was of the opinion, from circumstances communicated to him, that the fallen Governor designed to effect his escape; that his refusal to sign the parole proposed by the Whig Convention of New Jersey, and a letter to Mrs. Franklin which had been intercepted, afforded sufficient reasons for the exercise of great watchfulness and care. It appears that he was indulged in selecting the place of his confinement, and that he made choice of Connecticut. He was conveyed to East Windsor, and quartered in the house of Captain Ebenezer Grant.[1] In 1777 he requested liberty to visit his wife, who was a few miles distant and sick. In reply, he received the following letter: —

"Head-Quarters, July 25th, 1777.

"Sir, — I have this moment received yours of the 22d inst. by express. I heartily sympathize with you in your distressing situation; but, however strong my inclination to comply with your request, it is by no means in my power to supersede a positive Resolution of Congress, under which your present confinement took place. I have enclosed your letter to them; and shall be happy, if it may be found consistent with propriety, to concur with your wishes in a matter of so delicate and interesting a nature. I sincerely hope a speedy restoration of Mrs. Franklin's health may relieve you from the anxiety her present declining condition must naturally give you.

"I am, with due respect,
"Sir, your most obedient servant,
"G. Washington."

Congress declined to allow the Governor to visit his wife, and he continued at East Windsor. This lady was born in the West Indies; it is said that she was much affected by the severity of Doctor Franklin to her husband while he was a prisoner. She died in 1778, in her forty-ninth year, and it is

[1] This building is still (1844) standing, it is near the Theological Seminary.

inscribed on the monumental tablet erected to her memory in St. Paul's Church, New York, that, "Compelled to part from the husband she loved, and at length despairing of the soothing hope of his speedy return, she sunk under accumulated distresses," &c.

In 1778, after the arrival in America of Sir Henry Clinton, an exchange was effected, and Governor Franklin was released. Little seems to be known of his proceeding during the remainder of the war. He served for a short period as President of the Board of Loyalists which was organized in New York; but soon went to England. The adherents of the Crown were greatly alarmed at the distinction made between themselves and other subjects, in the articles of capitulation of Cornwallis at Yorktown, and Franklin wrote to Lord George Germain, who was then Secretary for the American Department, on the subject. His Lordship, in answer, stated that "the alarm taken by the Loyal Refugees is not to be wondered at," and that, by command of his Majesty, he had directed Sir Henry Clinton to make the strongest assurances for their "welfare and safety."

In West's picture of the "Reception of the American Loyalists by Great Britain, in the year 1783," Governor Franklin and Sir William Pepperell are the prominent personages represented, and are placed at the head of the group of figures; the first (in the words of the description or explanation) is a "son of Doctor Benjamin Franklin, who having his Majesty's commission of Governor of New Jersey, preserved his fidelity and loyalty to his Sovereign from the commencement to the conclusion of the contest, notwithstanding powerful incitements to the contrary." [1]

In 1784, the father and son, after an estrangement of ten years, became reconciled to one another. The son appears to have made the first overture. Doctor Franklin, in acknowledging the receipt of his letter, says in reply, on the 16th of August of that year: "I am glad to find that you desire to

[1] For the remainder of the description of this picture, see notice of Sir William Pepperell.

revive the affectionate intercourse that formerly existed between us. It will be very agreeable to me; indeed nothing has ever hurt me so much, and affected me with such keen sensations, as to find myself deserted in my old age by my only son; and not only deserted, but to find him taking up arms against me in a cause wherein my good fame, fortune, and life, were all at stake. You conceived, you say, that your duty to your king and regard for your country required this. I ought not to blame you for differing in sentiment with me in public affairs. We are all men, subject to errors. Our opinions are not in our power; they are formed and governed much by circumstances, that are often as inexplicable as they are irresistible. Your situation was such, that few would have censured your remaining neuter, though there are natural duties which precede political ones, and cannot be extinguished by them. This is a disagreeable subject; I drop it. And we will endeavor, as you propose, mutually to forget what has happened relating to it, as well as we can."

The Doctor, I conclude, was never able to forget, entirely, the alienation which had happened between them. In a letter to the Rev. Dr. Byles (1788), he said: "I, too, have a daughter, who lives with me, and is the comfort of my declining years, while my son is estranged from me by the part he took in the late war, and keeps aloof, residing in England, whose cause he *espoused;* whereby the old proverb is exemplified: —

"My son is my son till he gets him a wife,
But my daughter's my daughter all the days of her life."

In his will, dated June 23, 1789, a few months before his own decease, he thus remembers his son William, late Governor of the Jerseys: —

"I give and devise all the lands I hold, or have a right to in the Province of Nova Scotia, to hold to him, his heirs and assigns forever. I also give to him all my books and papers which he has in his possession, and all debts standing against him on my account-books, willing that no payment for, nor restitution of, the same be required of him by my executors.

The part he acted against me in the late war, which is of public notoriety, will account for my leaving him no more of an estate he endeavored to deprive me of."

Though the part he acted against his father was of public notoriety, rumors reached the ears of the Commissioners of Loyalist Claims, that the disagreement between the Doctor and his son had been collusive, and was more politic than sincere; and the Governor was accordingly required to exhibit proofs of his loyalty and uniform attachment to the Royal cause. The commissioners themselves, probably, entertained no doubts on the subject, but examined the charge to satisfy the public, and to relieve the accused from what they believed to be an unfounded imputation. Among the witnesses who testified in his favor was Sir Henry Clinton. He made a schedule of his losses, which were by no means considerable. Indeed, Governor Franklin must have been poor. His personal estate was valued at only £1800, which sum the commissioners allowed him. He had several shares in back lands and grants, but as he was indebted to his father, and had conveyed to him all his real property in New York and New Jersey, the loss of his office and its emoluments, and the £1800 above mentioned, comprised the principal items in his account, and for which he claimed compensation. Governor Franklin continued in England during the remainder of his life. He enjoyed a pension, it is believed, of the amount of £800 per annum. He died in November, 1813, at the age of about eighty-two. Some years after the death of his first wife, he married a lady who was born in Ireland. His son, William Temple Franklin, who edited the works of Doctor Franklin, died at Paris, in May, 1823.

FRANKS, DAVID. Of Pennsylvania. Commissary of British prisoners. In 1778, detected in endeavoring to transmit within the enemy's lines a letter which was deemed to contain sentiments inimical to the Whig cause, General Arnold, who was then in command at Philadelphia, was directed by Congress to cause his immediate arrest and confinement in jail. It was resolved, also, that he should no longer perform the duties of Commissary; and that Washington give information of these proceedings to Sir Henry Clinton, with a view to the appointment of a successor. In January, 1779, he applied for leave to send his clerk, Patrick Rice, to New York, to settle his public accounts, which was granted. In 1780 he was ordered to depart the State; but, as he delayed, on the 18th of November a pass for himself and daughter to New York was sent from the Council, with the suggestion that compulsory measures would be adopted, on further disobedience to the mandate of banishment. He replied on the 21st, giving his reasons for remaining in Philadelphia so long; and asked that his pass might be amended to include a servant-woman and his necessary baggage. He wrote again on the 22d, stating an excuse; and on the 23d President Reed informed him that he was expected to set out on his journey the next day; that his excuse, in the opinion of the Council, was a very frivolous one; and that no further indulgence would be allowed him by that body.

FRAZER, CHARLES. Of South Carolina. After the fall of Charleston, in 1780, he was "town-major." Upon the application of an individual for rations, he issued an order, from which I extract sufficient to show its nature. Thus: "All difficulties with regard to provisions ought to have been considered before people entered into rebellion, or, in the course of these twelve months, while they have been allowed to walk about on parole. All militia prisoners and others on parole, are to keep their paroles and to remain in their houses. . . . . It is ordered that no person, now a prisoner on parole, in Charleston, shall have the liberty of exercising any profession, trade, mechanic art, business, or occupation; and his his Majesty's subjects are hereby strictly enjoined and required not to employ such person or persons on any pretence." In 1781 (July 26) he addressed the following note to the ill-fated Colonel Isaac Hayne: "Sir, I am charged by the commandant to inform you, that a council of general officers will assemble to-morrow, at ten o'clock, in the hall of the Province, to try you." He wrote the next day to announce, that, instead of "a council," his case would be submitted to "a court of inquiry, composed of four general officers and five captains"; and that he would be allowed materials for writing, and to select counsel. On the 29th of July, he addressed a third note, in which he said: "The Adjutant of the town will be so good as to go to Colonel Hayne, in the Provost's prison, and inform him, that . . . .Lord Rawdon and Lieutenant-Colonel Nesbit Balfour have resolved upon his execution, on Tuesday, the 31st instant, at six o'clock," in consequence of the decision of the court of inquiry, "for having been found under arms, and employed in raising a regiment to oppose the British Government, though he had become a subject, and had accepted the protection of that government after the reduction of Charleston."

FRAZER, JAMES. Of South Carolina. Physician. In 1781 he was Acting Barrack-master of Charleston, and in July of that year promulgated an order forbidding persons "living under the Rebel Government" to let or lease any house without special license; as it was intended to take all dwellings as might be wanted for the public service, "paying to the owners of those secured by the capitulation, a reasonable rent for the same"; by which course the Loyalists would be "in possession of their own houses within a short space of time." He was also a British Deputy Commissary of Prisoners. It is stated on the best authority, that, having harangued the unfortunate Whigs under his care, to induce them to enlist in the Royal service, without the anticipated success, he pronounced this terrible sentence: "You shall be put on board of the prison-ships, where you cannot expect anything more but to perish miserably; the rations hitherto allowed for the support of your wives and children, from this day, shall be withheld; the consequence of which will be, they must starve in the streets." He lost his estate under the Confiscation Act of 1782. A Doctor James Frazer died at Charleston in 1803, — possibly the same.

FRAZER, JOHN. Of New York. Was born in Scotland, emigrated to New York some years prior to the Revolution, went to Nova Scotia at the peace, and died at Shelburne in 1840, aged eighty-eight.

FRAZER, LEWIS. Settled in New Brunswick in 1783, and died in King's County in 1835, aged seventy-two; Mary Harkley Frazer, his widow, who was born in Charleston, South Carolina, died at St. John, New Brunswick, 1836, at the age of seventy-three.

FRENCH, THOMAS. Of New York, and probably of Long Island. Captain in De Lancey's First Battalion.

The following marvellous incident seems to rest on good authority: — In 1779, when Colonel Cruger was ordered to evacuate Sunbury, French was directed to convey the invalids to Savannah by inland navigation, in small vessels. On the passage, circumstances compelled him to land, and to fortify his camp, in front of which he placed four vessels, manned by forty seamen. His soldiers were one hundred and eleven in number; and he had one hundred and thirty stand of arms. Colonel White, of Georgia, determined to capture him by stratagem; and, to effect his purpose, kindled fires on shore in the manner of a camp, rode about giving orders in a tone of voice to be heard by French, and then went to him with a flag, and demanded him to surrender. White's party consisted of six persons; but French, believing that he led a large force, submitted himself prisoner of war, with his whole detachment, one hundred and thirty stand of arms, the vessels, and their crews. Four of the vessels were armed, and the largest mounted fourteen guns. After the articles of capitulation were signed, White pretended that it was difficult to restrain his men; and, to continue the deception, ordered his captives to go on shore unarmed, and to follow the guides, whom he would send to them, and by whom they would be conducted to Lincoln's army; while he, with his troops, would follow in their rear. Most of French's men were Loyalists, and, dreading to fall into the hands of the Whig militia, this plan was gladly adopted. The prisoners arrived safely in camp.

FRENCH, JOSEPH. Of Jamaica, New York. He was

elected to the Provincial Congress in 1775, but declined to take his seat on the ground that the majority of the freeholders of that town were opposed to being represented in that body. In February, 1776, he was a close prisoner; and in a communication to the Provincial Congress, stating his case and praying to be released, he remarked that he had been in confinement thirty-four days, — three days in his own house, with twelve men and an officer to guard him when sick in bed. In 1777 Jamaica contributed £219 to a corps of Loyalists raised in New York at the instance of Governor Tryon, which sum passed through the hands of Mr. French. In 1780 he was an Addresser of Governor Robertson.

FRENCH, JAMES. Of New York. He accepted a commission in De Lancey's First Battalion, and in 1782 was a captain. He went to St. John, New Brunswick, in 1783, was the grantee of a city lot, and received half-pay. He settled in the county of York, and was a magistrate for several years. He died in that county in 1820, aged seventy-five.

FRENCH, ———. A Loyalist in arms, and of some note. He was killed in the battle of Bennington.

FREY, HENDRICK. Of New York. He served the Crown during the war, and was a major. After the peace he returned to his native State. In 1797 he and Brant met at Canajoharie, where, at a tavern, "they had a merry time of it during the livelong night. Many of their adventures were recounted, among which was a duel that had been fought by Frey, to whom Brant acted as second." The meeting of the Chief and the Major is described as "like that of two brothers."

FREY, PHILIP R. Of Tryon (now Montgomery) County, New York. He entered the military service of the King, and was an ensign in the Eighth Regiment. He was engaged in the battle of Wyoming. He died at Palestine, Montgomery (formerly Tryon) County, in 1823. His son, Samuel C. Frey, settled in Upper Canada, and communicated particulars of the sanguinary scenes at Wyoming, for Colonel Stone's use, in writing his "Life of Brant." The testimony of the Freys is, that Brant was not present with Butler at Wyoming, and this, according to the son, the father steadily maintained through life.

FRINK, NATHAN. He was born at Pomfret, Connecticut. He entered the British military service, and was a captain of cavalry in the American Legion, and aide-de-camp to Arnold after his treason, and was engaged in the burning of New London. At the peace he went to St. John, New Brunswick, where he remained several years, but removed to St. Andrew, and finally to St. Stephen in the same Colony. He died at the latter place, December 4, 1817, aged sixty years. His wife, Hester, died at St. Stephen, February 22, 1824, at the age of sixty-five. His sister Alida married Schuyler, the oldest son of General Israel Putnam. Seven children survived him. His son James was a magistrate and ship-owner of St. Stephen, and married Martha G. Prescott, a niece of Roger Sherman. Captain Frink was educated for the bar. In New Brunswick he was a merchant and ship-owner; and a magistrate of Charlotte County for about thirty years. He received half-pay as an officer. His family connections in the United States are highly respectable. It is believed that his political sympathies were originally adverse to the Royal cause, and that less intolerance, on the part of his Whig neighbors and friends, would have produced a different line of conduct on his part.

FRYE, PETER. Of Salem, Massachusetts. Graduated at Harvard University in 1744. He was representative to the General Court, and being a member in 1768, was a Rescinder. He was also a Judge of the Court of Common Pleas, Register of Probate, and Colonel of Militia in the County of Essex. His name appears among the Salem Addressers of Gage, June, 1774. He died in England, February, 1820, aged ninety-seven years. The first husband of his daughter Love was Doctor Peter Oliver, a Massachusetts Loyalist; and her second was Admiral Sir John Knight of the British Navy. Lady Knight died at her seat near London, in 1839.

FRYE, PETER PICKMAN. A soldier in the Continental Army. In May, 1777, he was sentenced to be shot at New York, for desertion, with the design of joining the Royal Army.

FULTON, JAMES. Of New Hampshire. In 1778 he was proscribed and banished. In 1782 he was a captain in the King's American Dragoons. James Fulton, Esq., a magistrate in the county of Halifax, died in Nova Scotia in 1826.

FUSTNER, ANDREW GEORGE. In November, 1788, Washington wrote the President of the Council of Pennsylvania, that Fustner was a brother-in-law of Rankin of York County; that he went out of New York frequently as a spy, by way of Stark River, through New Jersey, and thence to Lancaster; from which facts, means might be devised, perhaps, to apprehend him.

GABEL, JOHN. Was one of the first of the Loyalists who settled in New Brunswick, and died at St. John in 1816, aged eighty-four.

GAGE, THOMAS. The first military and the last Royal Governor of Massachusetts. His father was the first Viscount Gage. He came to America with Braddock, in command of the 44th Regiment, and was wounded in the fatal engagement of the 9th of July. It is said that his indecision was the cause of the defeat. He was with Amherst in the expedition against Ticonderoga, and with Wolfe at Quebec. In 1761 he was promoted to the rank of Major-General; and, two years later, was made Commander-in-Chief of the British forces in North America. In 1770 he was a Lieutenant-General. His home was in New York, and he lived in a large double house, surrounded with elegant gardens, on the site now occupied by the stores 67 and 69 Broad Street. In 1774 he removed to Boston, and assumed the administration of civil and military affairs in Massachusetts. Sir William Howe was his successor in command of the army. His wife was Margaret, daughter of Peter Kemble, President of the Council of New Jersey. He died in England, in 1787; his widow survived until 1824, and at her decease was ninety years of age. His son was the third Viscount Gage.

In 1848, General William H. Sumner, who died at Jamaica Plain, Massachusetts, October, 1861, married Mary Dickinson Kemble, of New York, daughter of Peter Kemble, granddaughter of General Cadwallader, and niece of the subject of this notice. This lady survives, but has no child. A Resolve of the Legislature of Massachusetts in 1862, requested the Governor to receive the portrait of Governor Gage, bequeathed by General Sumner, and cause the same to be placed in the State Library.

GAINE, HUGH. Printer and bookseller, of New York; and publisher of the "New York Mercury." Died April 25, 1807, aged eighty-one years. His political creed seems to have consisted of but one article, and that — *to keep with the strongest party.* At first he was a Whig, and when, in 1776, the British troops were about to take possession of New York, he retreated with his press to Newark; but, in the belief that the Whigs would be subdued and the Revolution suppressed, he soon after privately withdrew from Newark, and returned to New York, where he printed under the protection of the King's Army, and devoted the "Mercury" to the support of the Royal cause. At the conclusion of the war, he petitioned the Legislature of the State for liberty to remain in the city, which was granted; but he discontinued the publication of his paper, and turned his attention to the printing and selling of books. He occupied a stand in Hanover Square more than forty years, and by close application to business, regularity and punctuality, he acquired a handsome estate. As a citizen, he was moral and highly respectable. As a politician, his unstable course excited several poetical essays from a wit of the time; among them is a versification of his petition to the new Government, already alluded to, of some three hundred and fifty lines. The writer's manner may be judged of by the following extract. After relating the evils of his sojourn at Newark, Gaine is made to speak thus of his return to New York, and taking part with the Loyalists: —

"As matters have gone, it was plainly a blunder,
But *then* I expected the Whigs must knock under;

And I always adhere to the sword that is longest,
And stick to the party that's like to be strongest;
That you have succeeded is merely a chance ;
I never once dreamt of the conduct of France ! —
If alliance with her you were promised — at least
You ought to have showed me your *star in the East*,
Not let me go off uninformed as a beast.
When your army I saw without stockings or shoes,
Or victuals or *money* — to pay them their dues,
Excepting your wretched Congressional paper,
That stunk in my nose like the snuff of a taper," &c.

GALE, SAMUEL. Of Cumberland County, New Hampshire Grants. He was born in England, in 1747, and was well educated. He came to America about the year 1770, as a paymaster in the British Army; but, quitting the service, settled in the county above mentioned. In 1774 the infamous Crean Brush resigned as clerk of the Court, and he was appointed to the place. During the difficulties between the Whigs and Loyalists of Cumberland in 1775, — as particularly related in the notice of W. Patterson, — he does not appear to have conducted with wisdom or decorum. According to the account of the affair drawn up by the Whig Committee, he drew a pistol upon the multitude, who asked for a parley, and exclaimed, "d—n the parley with such d——d rascals as you are;" and holding up his weapon, added, "I will hold no parley with such d——d rascals, but this." Collision soon followed, and human life was taken. An investigation followed. He was imprisoned first in his own town, and next in Northampton, Massachusetts. Released at last, he repaired to New York, where he was joined by his family. In 1776 he was again seized and sent to jail in Fairfield, Connecticut, and while there wrote a long letter to John McKisson, in which he complains of the manner of his arrest and of his subsequent treatment. I extract a single passage. "In this intolerable place," he said, "the wind, when cold, fairly chills every vein in my body. The smoke, when there is a fire, not only blinds, but nearly suffocates me; and the continued smell of the room has, I fear, tended to rot my very vitals. In the morning I have perpetually a sickness at the stomach; about noon comes on a fever, which, in about three hours, is succeeded by an ague." Again, he said he wished for liberty on parole, that " I may finish my intended publication on Surveying, which, you will know, is allowed by all parties to be a matter of great actual service to America." He went to Canada before the peace, and became Provincial Secretary. He accompanied Governor Prescott to England, to assist in adjusting some difficulties that had occurred during his administration; and while abroad, he wrote and published an " Essay on Public Credit," which Mr. Pitt is said to have approved. Mr. Gale returned to Canada after several years' absence; lived in retirement, and died in Farnham, in 1826. His wife was Rebecca, daughter of Colonel Samuel Wells, of Brattleborough.

GALLOWAY, JOSEPH. He was a son of Peter Galloway, and was born in Maryland about the year 1730. His family was respectable, and of good estate, and his education was probably the best that could be obtained in the Middle Colonies. He went early in life to Philadelphia, commenced the practice of the law, became eminent in his profession, and held many important trusts. He married the daughter of the Hon. Lawrence Growdon, who was for a long period Speaker of the Assembly of Pennsylvania, by which connection he enjoyed a considerable fortune. In 1764 Mr. Galloway was a member of the Assembly, and on the question of a change of the government from the Proprietary to the Royal form, as in some other Colonies, made an able speech in answer to the celebrated Dickinson, who opposed the petition. Both speeches were published. Galloway continued in the Assembly for some years, and attained the Speaker's chair of that body. In 1774 he was elected a member of the Whig Congress of the Continent, and took his seat, and was an active participant in its leading recommendations and measures. On the 20th of October, Congress adopted the celebrated measure of " Non-Importation, Non-Consumption, and Non-Exportation," and ordered that the several members subscribe their names to it. The signature of Mr. Galloway is among them; and his name is to be found, also, to the "Address to the Inhabitants of the Province of Quebec." Near the close of the session he was appointed, with Mr. Adams and others, to revise the minutes of Congress.

No man in Pennsylvania, at this time, was more in favor with the popular party. In the attack upon the proprietary rights, he had been regarded the leader; and with Franklin,[1] he was on terms of intimacy and confidence. His disaffection or disinclination to continue in the public councils soon became manifest. By the proceedings of the House of Assembly of Pennsylvania, on the 12th of May, 1775, it appears, that "Joseph Galloway, Esq., having repeatedly moved in Assembly to be excused from serving as a Deputy in the Continental Congress, the House this day took his motion in consideration, and do hereby agree to excuse him from that service." In 1776 he abandoned the Whigs, and became one of the most virulent and proscriptive Loyalists of the time. His former friends often felt the force of his powers, and the evil effects of his influence with the agents of the Crown, both in America and England. He joined the Royal Army in New York soon after his defection, and continued there until June of 1778. As he prepared to embark for England, with his only daughter, he wrote his "ever dear and only sister," a parting letter, which is very affectionate in its tone, and in which he said: "I call this country ungrateful, because I have attempted to save it from the distress it at present feels, and because it has not only rejected my endeavors, but returned me evil for good. I feel for its misery; but I feel it is not finished — its cup is not yet full — still deeper distress will attend it."

He was examined before Parliament, in 1779, on the inquiry into the conduct of Sir William Howe and General Burgoyne, and gave some very singular opinions. Thus, he said that four fifths of the whole American people, at the be-

[1] A will, executed by Franklin, some years prior to 1784, was left in his care.

ginning of hostilities, were loyal or well affected to the Crown; that if proper use had been made of men and means, the rebellion might have been speedily and happily terminated; that in a military sense, America was not particularly strong; that the British troops were superior to their opponents, not in the open field, but in bush fighting; and that such was the nature of the country, soldiers could carry provisions for nineteen days, on their backs. To all this, it was well replied, that though bred a lawyer, and used to business, he could be hardly made to recollect anything which related to himself when a Whig and a member of the Continental Congress; yet, that merely with the British Army for protection, and utterly ignorant of the profession of arms, he presumed to possess an accurate knowledge of the complicated business of the camp; and to decide, in a manner which old and experienced commanders hesitated to do, upon all the great operations of war. Between this time and the peace, his pen was almost constantly employed on subjects connected with the war, and its management on the part of officers of the Crown. In addition to an extensive correspondence with Loyalists who continued in America, he published "Observations on the Conduct of Sir William Howe"; a "Letter to Howe on his Naval Conduct"; "Letters to a Nobleman on the Conduct of the War in the Middle Colonies"; "Reply to the Observations of General Howe"; "Cool Thoughts on the Consequences of American Independence"; "Candid Examination of the Claims of Great Britain and her Colonies"; and "Reflections on the American Rebellion."

His estate, which he valued at £40,000, was confiscated by Pennsylvania, in pursuance of his proscription and attainder. A large part of his property was derived from his wife, and a considerable proportion of it was restored finally to his daughter. When the agency for prosecuting the claims of the Loyalists to compensation was formed, Mr. Galloway was appointed a member of the Board for Pennsylvania and Delaware. But his own pretensions to consideration were disputed. The circumstance, that he had been a Whig and a member of the first Continental Congress, occasioned a jealousy among the adherents of the Crown, who had never changed sides, and the Commissioners made a minute investigation into his conduct. They examined numerous witnesses, among whom were General Gage, Lord Cornwallis, and Sir William Howe; and they found and reported him to be "an active though not an early Loyalist," and of course entitled to compensation. A tract attributed to him, on the subject of "The Loyalist Claims for Losses," was published in 1788; from which, as the reader will remember, some extracts appear in the preliminary remarks of this volume. He died in England, September, 1803, at the age of seventy-three years.

His path was filled with vexations and troubles. He was a politician by nature; and he had many qualities indispensable to success in political life. For some years prior to the Revolution, he was the secret or open mover of many of the public issues that arose. In the alienation of friends he was unfortunate. In 1766 he connected himself with Goddard and Wharton, in publishing a newspaper called the "Pennsylvania Chronicle." By the terms of the arrangement, he and Wharton were to furnish a share of the necessary capital, and Goddard was to print and manage the concern. And it is a singular fact connected with this matter, that the articles of copartnership provided for the admission of Franklin as a partner, should he choose to join them on his coming home from England, where he was then absent. But the philosopher never availed himself of the opportunity; the three partners quarrelled, separated on the worst possible terms, and Goddard and Galloway filled the public prints with the vilest mutual abuse. The difficulty reached the ears of Franklin, and he thus wrote to his son William from London: "I cast my eye over Goddard's piece against our friend, Mr. Galloway, and then lit my fire with it. I think such feeble, malicious attacks cannot hurt him." The events of a few years produced strange changes in the relations of the several parties here spoken of, and show the effects of civil war in a most striking manner. Galloway, as has been said, turned Loyalist, and Franklin renounced him; while Goddard, who made the "feeble and malicious attacks," was appointed to the second office in the Continental Post-office Department, when Franklin was placed at its head. While, again, Goddard, soured and disaffected, on the retirement of Franklin from that service, because he was not named to succeed him, incurred the displeasure of the Whigs, and was the object of hate, and the victim of mobs. And yet again; Franklin's only son, the Royal Governor of New Jersey, also became a Loyalist; which entirely alienated his father, so that there was no intercourse between them for ten years.

Galloway, after deserting the Whigs, was the mark at which many writers levelled their wit and their anger. Trumbull says of him, that "he began by being a flaming patriot, but being disgusted at his own want of influence and the greater popularity of others, he turned Tory, wrote against the measures of Congress, and absconded;" and, that "just before his escape, a trunk was put on board a vessel in the Delaware, to be delivered to" him, which, on opening, "he found contained only, as Shakspeare says,

'A halter gratis, and leave to hang himself.'"

Trumbull, in his "McFingal," still further discourses thus:

"Did you not, in as vile and shallow way,
Fright our poor Philadelphian, Galloway,
Your Congress when the loyal ribald
Belied, berated, and bescribbled?
What ropes and halters did you send,
Terrific emblems of his end,
Till, lest he 'd hang in more than effigy,
Fled in a fog the trembling refugee?"

The unhappy Loyalist deserved all that was said of him; since it seems improbable that he changed sides from conviction and from justifiable motives. A man of so great aptitude for the administration of affairs, of so mature judgment, of so much political experience, of so penetrating sagacity, of powers of mind that led his fellows in masses, can hardly stand excused, upon the most charitable view of his conduct that is possible.

GALLOWAY, ———. Serjeant in the Queen's Rangers. Unhorsed and wounded in battle. He lamented the loss of the heel of his boot, which was shot away, says his commander, more than his wound.

GALLOPP, WILLIAM. He settled in Charlotte County, New Brunswick, and was a magistrate. He died in that county about the year 1806.

GAMBLE, JAMES. Of North Carolina. Estate confiscated. Residence unknown.

GAMBLE, DAVID. Belonged to the Eighth Pennsylvania Regiment, but deserted. In 1778 he was tried for this offence, and for having in his possession counterfeit Continental money; and was sentenced to suffer death.

GANEY, MICAJAH. Of South Carolina. He lived on the Little Pedee; and at the head of some Loyalists of that region, sallied out of swamps to distress the Whigs. Marion had required that he should obey his orders as brigadier of the district, but he refused. Yet, in 1781, when the Royal Army met with reverses, Ganey entered into a treaty of neutrality, which was renewed the year following. By the terms of the last arrangement, the Tory band were forgiven treason, secured in the possession of their property, and placed under the protection of the laws, on the condition of delivering up their plunder, and demeaning themselves as peaceable citizens of South Carolina; while those who preferred to leave the country, were permitted to go within the British lines, and to carry off or sell their effects. He was considered an excellent partisan officer, and, in the judgment of some, able to cope with Marion himself.

GARDEN, ALEXANDER. Of South Carolina. A Congratulator of Cornwallis on his success at Camden in 1780. In 1782 his estate was confiscated, and he was banished. Doctor Garden fitted himself for professional pursuits at Edinburgh. He acquired a fortune. He was much devoted to the study of natural history, and was a valuable writer in that branch of science, especially in botany. He went to England in 1783, and died in London in 1791, at the age of sixty-three years. He was doctor of medicine and of divinity, and a Fellow of the Royal Society.

GARDEN, WILLIAM. He received employment under the Crown, after the Revolution; and at the time of his decease was Assistant Deputy Commissary-General of the garrison at Fredericton, New Brunswick. He sank under the pressure of sickness and trouble; and closed his life in the county of York, New Brunswick, in 1812, aged sixty-three. His daughter Jane, wife of William Thompson, of Toronto, Upper Canada, died at Woodstock, New Brunswick, in 1848, in her sixty-second year.

GARDINER, SYLVESTER. Of Boston. Physician. Descended from the first emigrant of the name to the Narragansett country; and born at South Kingston, Rhode Island, in 1707. He fitted himself for the practice of medicine in England and France; entered upon and pursued a successful professional career in Boston. He acquired great wealth, and became proprietor of one twelfth part of the "Plymouth Purchase," so called, on the Kennebec River, Maine. His efforts to settle this large domain were unceasing from the year 1753 to the Revolution. He was made perpetual moderator of the proprietors at all their meetings; he executed their plans; built mills, houses, stores, and wharves; cleared lands; made generous offers to emigrants; established an Episcopal mission; and furnished the people of that region with their first religious instruction. And most of all this was accomplished with his own money. The evidence uniformly is, that he was a man of broad and liberal views, of great zeal, energy, and public spirit. In Boston he was held in much respect by all classes. Of the "Government Party," he entertained as guests, Sir William Pepperell, Governor Hutchinson, Earl Percy, Admiral Graves, Major Pitcairn, General Gage, Major Small, and others. An Addresser of the Royal Governors in 1774 and the year following, he became identified with the Royal cause. But, hard upon threescore and ten, he did not mean to quit his native country. He yielded to the counsels, to the "impetuosity" of a young wife, and was ruined. In 1776, at the evacuation, he abandoned all, and found temporary shelter at Halifax. The vessel in which he embarked was destitute of common comforts, poorly supplied with provisions, and the cabin, which he and several members of his family occupied, was small and crowded with passengers. In 1778 his name appeared in the Proscription and Banishment Act. He settled at Poole, England.

In addition to his lands in Maine, he had a large property in Boston, both real and personal, most of which was confiscated.

In 1785 he returned to the United States. For a part of his losses, he petitioned Massachusetts for compensation. He had never borne arms, he said, nor entered into any association, combination, or subscription, against the Whigs. When he quitted Boston, he stated, too, that he had in possession a valuable stock of drugs, medicines, paints, groceries, and dye stuffs, which,. having a vessel fully equipped and entirely under his control, he could easily have carried off, but which he left, of choice, for the benefit of the country, which he knew was in need. The claim was acknowledged to the extent of giving his heirs tickets in the State Land Lottery, by which they obtained nearly six thousand acres in the county of Washington, Maine.

From the confiscation, Massachusetts derived, indeed, but little benefit. As relates to the property just mentioned, Washington, on taking possession of Boston, ordered the medicines, &c., in Doctor Gardiner's store to be transferred to the hospital department for the use of the Continental Army; but the State authorities interfered, and required delivery to the Sheriff of Suffolk County. The result, however, was a vote of the Council complying with the requisition of the Commander-in-Chief. The Commonwealth received nothing from the lands on the Kennebec, because the Attorney-General found his suit illegally prosecuted, and because peace was concluded while his second action was pending. As concerns the remaining part of Dr. Gardiner's estate, there is a strange story, namely: that it was nearly all absorbed in the payment of fictitious claims against him, which there was no one here to dispute. A gentleman of the highest respectability informs me that he was once walking with the Doctor's executor, when they were met by a man who had been allowed payment of an unjust demand, and who was asked by the executor, "How could you bring such a charge?" "La, Mr. Hallowell," was the reply, "I would not injure you for the world. The account was correct: *I only omitted to say it was paid; it was doing you no harm; everybody was doing the same; and I was in want of the money.*" The subject of this notice died at Newport, Rhode Island, suddenly, August 8, 1786, in his eightieth year, and his remains were interred under Trinity Church. In the Episcopal Church, Gardiner, Maine, there is a marble cenotaph to his memory. His first wife was Anne, daughter of Doctor John Gibbons of Boston; his second, Abigail Eppes of Virginia; his third, Catharine Goldthwaite. His children were six. First, John, born in Boston in 1731; bred to the law in England; practised in the Courts of Westminster Hall; Attorney-General of St. Christopher's; denied promotion by the British Government, because of his sympathy for the Whigs; returned to Massachusetts at the peace; one of the leaders in the movement which transferred King's Chapel to the Unitarians; settled in Pownalborough, Maine, and was member of the General Court; embarked at home for Boston, in 1793; wrecked on the passage and perished. Second, William, of whom presently. Third, Anne, who married the second son of the Earl of Altamont. Next, Hannah, the wife of Robert Hallowell. Fifth, Rebecca, wife of Philip Dumarisque. Last, Abigail, who married Oliver Whipple, counsellor-at-law, Cumberland, Rhode Island, and subsequently of Portsmouth, New Hampshire. The husbands of Hannah and Rebecca are mentioned in these volumes.

Under the provisions of Doctor Gardiner's will, nearly the whole of his estate in Maine passed to Hannah's only son, Robert Hallowell, who, as one of the conditions of that instrument, added the name of Gardiner. John, as is stated, failed to become the principal heir, in consequence of his political and religious opinions; and William "was not an efficient man." [See *Robert Hallowell.*]

GARDINER, WILLIAM. Of Maine. Son of Doctor Sylvester Gardiner. Settled on his father's lands on the Kennebec, prior to the Revolution. He gave offence to the Whigs because he "would drink tea"; because he refused to swear allegiance to their cause; and because he called them "Rebels." Arrangements were made to take him from his bed at night, and tar and feather him; but a Whig, friendly to him, carried him to a place of safety. He was, however, made prisoner, tried, and sent to jail in Boston. In March, 1778, he petitioned for release, and was soon after allowed to return home, where "he was regarded as a harmless man, and was suffered for the most part to remain unmolested, except by petty annoyances." He died unmarried at Gardiner, and his remains were interred "beneath the Episcopal vestry."

GARDINER, NATHANIEL. Of Pownalborough, Maine. Kinsman of Doctor Sylvester Gardiner. A steady Loyalist, and distinguished for the use of both influence and fortune in behalf of distressed adherents to the Crown. For a year or two, the account of him is contradictory. By one of his own letters it appears that, in 1780, he was in command of an armed schooner called the *Golden Pippin;* was captured by "a detachment of General Wadsworth's Rebels," near the Penobscot; and conveyed to jail in Falmouth (now Portland). On the way, "he was taken to a gallows, and told that that was his place." He says he was allowed neither bed nor blanket; that he laid down on a plank floor full of spike-heads an inch high; that neither food nor drink was ordered for him; that had not his son brought him some money, he should have died of cruel treatment. Kept in prison four months, and robbed, he relates, of his clothes and pocket-book, he escaped, and went to New York. At the peace he removed to Shelburne, Nova Scotia. Before living in Maine, he was a magistrate in Rhode Island.

GARDINER, ABRAM. Of Long Island, New York. Colonel in the militia. In 1776 he tendered the oath of allegiance to the inhabitants of South and Easthampton. The same year he was taken prisoner by Colonel Livingston, and his case reported to Governor Trumbull of Connecticut.

GARDNER, HENRY. Of Salem, Massachusetts. An Addresser of Gage on his arrival in 1774. He died at Malden in 1817, aged seventy-one.

GARNETT, SAMUEL. Of Massachusetts. Was in London in 1779, and addressed the King. Of the Massachusetts family, I conclude, were Patrick, who was an ensign in the Prince of Wales American Volunteers; and Joseph, who settled in New Brunswick, was Master in Chancery, and Deputy Surrogate, and died in St. Andrew in 1801.

GARRETTSON, REV. FREEBORN. Minister of the Methodist Episcopal Church. He was born in Maryland in 1752, and was admitted to the ministry, "on trial," in 1776. The next year, while stationed in Virginia, he refused to take the oath of fidelity to the Whigs, and was told that he must leave the State or go to jail. But he was not then molested. In 1778, however, when preaching in Maryland, he was met by a man who seized his horse's bridle, and who beat him over the head and shoulders with a large stick. In the affray, Mr. Garrettson's horse started off at full speed, but his assailant, who was also mounted, pursued, and, in passing him, struck a blow which, with the injury in falling to the ground, rendered him senseless. Again, in 1778, an officer waited upon him with a process, and threatened to confine him in prison. A year later, he was stationed in Delaware, "where he found himself an object of suspicion and molestation"; and at Salisbury "he was informed that a mob had already collected, consisting of some of the first people in the county, with a determination to effect his imprisonment." He escaped a second time; but in Maryland, in 1780, while engaged in a religious service, he was seized by a party of about twenty persons, and hurried off to jail; "where he had a dirty floor for a bed, and his saddle-bags for a pillow." His friends soon interposed, and the Governor released him.

In 1785 he went to Nova Scotia as a missionary; and while there, founded a Methodist society at Halifax. He returned in 1787, preached several times in private houses in Boston, and then visited Rhode Island. From this period until 1817, he was actively employed in various parts of New England and the Middle States, and became distinguished. For the ten years preceding his decease, he was on the list of "supernumaries," but yet he continued his labors as "a minister at large." He died at New York in 1827, aged seventy-five. His widow, Catharine, daughter of Chancellor Robert R. Livingston, died in 1849, in her ninety-seventh year. He left one child, a daughter.

GARRISON, JOSEPH. Of Massachusetts. He was born in 1734. Notes from the family record, furnished me by two of his grandsons, show that he was in Nova Scotia as early, certainly, as 1773. Of his course during the Revolution little is known. Descendants admit his loyalty. He was in New Brunswick, probably, before the peace; and is still remembered in that Province as a skilful miner, and as the discoverer of the "Grand Lake Coal Mines," which of late years have been extensively worked. He died on the river St. John. Mary Palmer, who was born in Byfield, Massachusetts, in 1741, and to whom he was married in 1764, bore him five children previous to the war, and four between 1776 and 1783, as follows: "Hannah (the eldest), who married John Lunt, lived at Eastport, Maine, some years, removed to the Penobscot, and died there about the year 1843; Elizabeth, or Betsey, who married William Simpson, and died at Kingston, New Brunswick, in 1845; Joseph, who died on Deer Island, New Brunswick, in 1819, aged fifty-two; Daniel, who was drowned in the river St. John, about the year 1798; Abijah, of whom presently; Sarah,[1] who married Joseph Clark; Nathaniel, who died at the city of St. John

[1] Lived on the river St. John in 1848.

in 1817; Silas;[1] and William, who died on the river St. John in 1843.

Abijah, the third son, was born in Nova Scotia, within the limits of the present Province of New Brunswick, in 1773. He lived awhile at St. John, but removed to Newburyport, Massachusetts, where he resided some years. He returned to his native Province, finally, and probably died there; of his fate, however, persons of his lineage know nothing. Fanny Lloyd, his wife, was born on Deer Island, Passamaquoddy Bay, New Brunswick, in 1776, and had issue — Mary Ann, Caroline, James Hotley, William Lloyd, and Elizabeth. The youngest son, William Lloyd Garrison, of Boston, who was born at Newburyport, December 10, 1805, and who, — universally known for his labors to abolish slavery, — is the sole survivor.

GARRISON, JOHN. He became an inhabitant of New Brunswick, at the peace, and was a member of the House of Assembly for several years. His end was sad. He died on the river St. John in 1810.

GATCHEUS, JACOB. Of Philadelphia. Joined the British in that city, and went with the Royal Army to New York, in 1778. The next year he was captain of the privateer *Impertinent*, was captured, and committed to prison.

GATCHELL, DENNIS. Of Maine. Whig at first, committee man, and captain in the militia. Repented, in 1779, of having been "a furious and revengeful Rebel," and acknowledged that he deserved no mercy from a sovereign he had so greatly abused, but still flattered himself with hopes of forgiveness. Possibly the Gatchells of the island of Grand Menan, Bay of Fundy, are of his lineage. His home, I conjecture, was near the mouth of the Kennebec.

GAY, REV. EBENEZER, D. D. Minister, of Hingham, Massachusetts. In doubt as to his course in the Revolution, his name was omitted in the first edition of this work. He was born in 1696, graduated at Harvard University in 1714, and was ordained in 1718. He died in 1787, at the age of

[1] Lived on the river St. John in 1848.

ninety, and in the sixty-ninth year of his ministry. The Rev. Doctor Chauncey "pronounces him to have been one of the greatest and most valuable men in the country."

GAY, MARTIN. Founder, of Boston. Son of the preceding. An Addresser of Hutchinson in 1774, and of Gage in 1775; was proscribed and banished in 1778. He went to Halifax in 1776, with his family. I suppose he returned; a gentleman of this name died at Boston in 1809, aged eighty-two.

GAY, SAMUEL. Of Massachusetts. Son of Martin Gay. He was born in Boston, and graduated at Harvard University in 1775. Soon after the beginning of the Revolution, he abandoned his native country. He settled in New Brunswick, and was a member of the first House of Assembly organized in the Colony, and represented the county of Westmoreland several years. He was also a magistrate of that county, and Chief Justice of the Court of Common Pleas. He died at Fort Cumberland, New Brunswick, (where his father had a grant of land from the Crown,) January 21, 1847, in the ninety-third year of his age. The late Hon. Ebenezer Gay, of Hingham, Massachusetts, was his brother.

GAYNOR, JAMES, and PETER. Were grantees of St. John, New Brunswick, in 1783. James was a member of the Loyal Artillery in 1795, and died at St. John in 1823, at the age of seventy-two.

GEAKE, SAMUEL. A Whig, who was taken prisoner by the British, corrupted, and induced to act as a spy. After entering the service of the enemy, he enlisted among his former friends, the better to accomplish his purpose of betraying them. His designs were ascertained, and he was arrested in 1778, tried, and condemned to die. He confessed his crime, but Washington spared his life, because the court-martial that tried him was irregularly constituted, and because his testimony was deemed important against Hammell, formerly brigade-major to General James Clinton, who had also entered into treasonable designs with the British. Geake, according to his confession, was to receive a commission of lieutenant in a corps that Hammell was to command, as soon as it could be raised from deserters from the American Army.

GEDDES, CHARLES. Died at Halifax, Nova Scotia, in 1807, aged fifty-six.

GELSTON, SAMUEL. Of Massachusetts. Physician. In January, 1776, he was held to answer before a joint committee of the Council and House. During the proceedings against him, it appears that he escaped from the custody of the messenger, fled to Rhode Island, where he was apprehended and brought back. Early in February, the committee reported, that, by his own confession, he had contravened the Resolves of Congress, had supplied the enemy with various articles of provision; and that, "by other evidence, it appeared he was unfriendly to the rights and liberties of the country." Thereupon ordered, that "the said Samuel Gelston be forthwith confined in some jail in this Colony," &c. In July of the same year he was at the Elizabeth Islands, in the custody of Berachiah Basset, who was directed, by a Resolve of the Legislature, to send him under a proper guard to the five justices in the county of Suffolk, appointed specially to inquire into the conduct of persons accused of enmity to the Whigs.

GERRISH, MOSES. Of Massachusetts. He graduated at Harvard University in 1762. In the Revolution, he was attached to the commissary department of the Royal Army. After the peace, he, Thomas Ross, and one Jones, obtained license of occupation of the island of Grand Menan, New Brunswick, and its dependencies, and on condition of procuring forty settlers, a schoolmaster, and a minister, within seven years from the date of the license, were to receive a grant of the whole from the British Crown. They commenced the settlement of the island, and sold several lots in anticipation of their own title, but failed to fulfil the conditions, and did not obtain the expected grant. Jones returned to the United States, but Gerrish and Ross continued at Grand Menan. Gerrish was an able man. A gentleman who knew him long and intimately, remarks, that "he would spread more good sense on a sheet of paper than any person of my acquaintance." His powers were not, however, devoted to any regular pursuit. He never acquired any considerable property, "yet always seemed to have enough." He "did nothing, yet was always about something." He was a magistrate at Grand Menan for many years, and until his decease, in 1830, at the age of eighty years.

GEYER, FREDERICK WILLIAM. Merchant. Of Boston. Proscribed and banished in 1778; citizenship restored in 1789, by Act of the Legislature. In business with his son, No. 13 Union Street, Boston, in 1794. Died at Walpole, New Hampshire, in 1803. A daughter, who died near London in 1854, at the age of about eighty-eight, married Mr. Marryatt, and was the mother of the late Captain Marryatt of the British Navy, and author of numerous popular works of fiction.

GIDNEY, JOSHUA. Of a place near Poughkeepsie, New York. He was imprisoned for his agency in spiking cannon in the vicinity of King's Bridge, but was released finally, and allowed to return to his family. Subsequently, he raised and commanded a company of Loyalists. At the peace, accompanied by his family of six persons, he went from New York to Shelburne, Nova Scotia, where the Crown granted him one town lot. His losses in consequence of his loyalty were estimated at £670. He soon abandoned Shelburne and settled in New Brunswick, where he was a Judge of the Court of Common Pleas. He died about the year 1830, aged eighty-eight.

GIDNEY, JOSEPH. Of White Plains, New York. He was the owner of the land on which the battle of White Plains was fought, and conducted the British Army thither. At the peace, accompanied by his family, he went from New York to Shelburne, Nova Scotia, where the Crown granted him one water lot. His losses in consequences of his loyalty were estimated at £1800. He removed to Digby Neck in the same Province, and died at Bridgetown in 1811, aged seventy-three. Joshua was a half-brother.

GILBERT, THOMAS. Of Freetown, Massachusetts. His ancestor, John Gilbert, as is supposed, came from Devonshire,

England, at an age somewhat advanced, and lived first, with his family, at Dorchester. He died previous to 1654, but Winnifred, his widow, was then living. He, with Henry Andrews, were the two first representatives from Taunton to the General Court at Plymouth, in 1639. His sons, Thomas and John, removed with him to Taunton, and were among the first proprietors of that town. Of Thomas, Governor Winthrop gravely records, that, —

"8th mo. August 18, 1636: Thomas Gilbert brought before us; he was drunk at Serjeant Baulson's, and the constable being sent for he struck him. He was kept in prison all night, and the next day his father, John Gilbert, and his brother, John Gilbert of Dorchester, undertook in £40 that John Gilbert the younger would appear at Court to answer for him, and perform the order of the Court, &c. The reason was, that he was to go to England presently, and not known to have been in any way disordered, and was his father's oldest son, who was a grave, honest gentleman, &c. They did undertake, also, that he should acknowledge his fault openly to the constable," &c.

Thomas went to England, as he intended, and never returned, but died there in 1676. His wife, Jane, who was a daughter of Hugh Rossiter, and his children, remained at Taunton. His marriage is supposed to have been the first that occurred in that town. The name of his oldest son was Thomas, who was the immediate ancestor of Thomas Gilbert, the Loyalist, who is the subject of this notice, and who, on his mother's side, was descended from Governor William Bradford, the second chief magistrate of Plymouth Colony. In 1745, the Thomas, of whom we are now to speak, was a captain at the memorable siege and reduction of Louisburg, under Sir William Pepperell. In the French war of 1755, he was a lieutenant-colonel in the Massachusetts forces under Brigadier-General Ruggles. He was engaged in the attempt against Crown Point; and after the fall of Colonel Ephraim Williams, in the battle with the French, under Baron Dieskau, at Lake George, he succeeded to the command of the regiment.

In the Revolutionary controversy he took an early and decided stand in behalf of the Crown. At this time he was a member of the House of Representatives, a justice of the quorum, and a colonel in the militia. In 1774 a large body of the people proceeded to Freetown, to desire him not to accept of the office of sheriff under the new laws, and to inform him that if he acted under the commission which, it was reported he had received, he "must abide by the consequences." Soon after he was at Dartmouth; and a party of about a hundred assaulted the house in which he was a lodger; but with the help of the family he prevented their entrance. In the autumn of 1774 the commotions in Bristol County had become so great that an armed force was deemed requisite, by General Gage, to keep the people in subjection to the king's authority; and, at his request, Colonel Gilbert raised and commanded a body of three hundred Loyalists. In March, 1775, he wrote the following letter to the Hon. James Wallace, Esquire, commander of his Majesty's ship *Rose*, Newport, which was intercepted, and which appears to have been the second addressed by him to that officer.

"Honorable Sir:—Since writing the lines on the 21st by Mr. Phillips, many insults and threats are, and have been made against those soldiers which have taken our arms and train, and exercise in the King's name; and on Monday next the Captains muster at the south part of the town, when we have great reason to fear thousands of the Rebels will attack them, and take our lives, or the King's arms, or perhaps both. I, Sir, ask the favor of one of His Majesty's Tenders, or some other vessel of force, might be at or near Bowers', in order, if any of our people should be obliged to retreat, they may be taken on board. Nothing but the last extremity will oblige them to quit the ground."

These proceedings attracted immediate attention, and produced great indignation. In April, 1775, the Congress of Massachusetts unanimously declared that "Colonel Thomas Gilbert is an inveterate enemy to his country, to reason, to justice, and the common rights of mankind;" and, that "whoever had knowingly espoused his cause, or taken up arms for its support, does, in common with himself, deserve to be instantly cut off from the benefit of commerce with, or countenance of, any friend of virtue, America, or the human race." These words are explicit enough; and contain as full and as comprehensive denunciation as can be found in the records of any deliberative body during the controversy. And Congress, in further speaking of him, use the term, — "Gilbert and his banditti."

A few days after the passage of these resolutions of bitter censure, Colonel Gilbert fled to the *Rose*, which vessel was still at Newport, Rhode Island, and thence to Boston. On the 4th of May, 1775, he wrote to his sons, from Boston, thus: —

"On the 27th of April, I left the ship, took passage on board a packet sloop on the first instant, in health arrived here, where I expect to stay till the Rebels are subdued, which I believe will not be long first, as the ships and troops are daily expected. My greatest fears are, you will be seduced or compelled to take arms with the deluded people. Dear sons, if these wicked sinners, the Rebels, entice you, believe them not, but die by the sword rather than be hanged as Rebels, which will certainly be your fate sooner or later if you join them, or be killed in battle, and will be no more than you deserve. I wish you in Boston, and all the friends to government. The Rebels have proclaimed that those friends may have liberty, and come in; but as all their declarations have hitherto proved, I fear, false, this may be so. Let Ruggles know his father wants him here. You may come by water from Newport. If here, the King will give you provisions and pay you wages; but by experience you know neither your persons nor estates are safe in the country, for as soon as you have raised anything, they [the Rebels] will rob you of it, as they are more savage and cruel than heathens, or any other creatures, and, it is generally thought, than devils. You will put yourselves out of their power as soon as possible. This is from your affectionate father."

In 1776 Colonel Gilbert accompanied the Royal Army to Halifax; and in 1778 he was proscribed and banished. He continued with the King's troops during the war, "often employed, and constantly rendering every service in his power, for the suppression of the Rebellion." In 1783 he went to Nova Scotia, and on the 16th of November of that year he was at Conway, in the county of Annapolis, and a petitioner to Governor Parr for a grant of lands. At a subsequent period, he settled in New Brunswick, and died on the river St. John, near the year 1796, aged about eighty-two. On retiring from service, at the close of the French war, Colonel Gilbert declined to receive half-pay. He held no commission in the Revolution, and was consequently entitled to no allowance as a disbanded officer; but he received compensation as a Loyalist for his losses.

GILBERT, THOMAS, JR. Of Berkley, Massachusetts. Son of Francis. He fled to Boston in 1775, and joined his father; but it is believed did not accompany him to Halifax. In 1778 he was proscribed and banished. During the war he continued with the Royal troops, and was active in his endeavors to suppress the popular movement. He settled in New Brunswick after the war, and died on the river St. John.

GILBERT, BRADFORD. Of Freetown, Massachusetts. Brother of Thomas, Jr. In 1778 he was proscribed and banished. He settled in New Brunswick in 1783, and received the grant of a lot in the city of St. John. In 1795 he was a member of the St. John Loyal Artillery, and in 1803 an alderman of the city. He died at St. John in 1814, aged sixty-eight. Ann, his widow, died in 1853, in her ninetieth year.

GILBERT, PEREZ. Of Freetown, Massachusetts. Brother of Bradford. He was proscribed and banished. He settled in New Brunswick with his father and brothers, and died in that Colony.

GILBERT, FRANCIS. He was Naval Officer of New Brunswick, and died at St. John in 1821, aged eighty-two.

GILBERT, SAMUEL. Of Berkley, Massachusetts. He was

a brother of Colonel Thomas, and went with him to Halifax in 1776. In 1778 he was proscribed and banished. He lived in New Brunswick for a time after the Revolution, but finally returned to the United States.

GILFROY, JOHN. Boatswain of the *Montgomery*, armed ship of the State of Pennsylvania. Tried for mutiny, (in 1778,) and for joining the side of the Crown, in Philadelphia; found guilty, and sentenced to death.

GILIAN, WILLIAM. Of Monmouth County, New Jersey. A Tory marauder. When about to stab an aged Whig of the name of Russell, into whose house he had broken, he was shot by Russell's son, who lay wounded on the floor.

GILL, THOMAS. Of Delaware. Died in York County, New Brunswick, in 1833, aged seventy-seven. Mary, his widow, a native of Newport, Rhode Island, died in the same county, 1837, at the age of eighty-one.

GILLIES, ARCHIBALD. Died at Carleton, New Brunswick, in 1821, aged sixty-six.

GILMAN, PETER. Of Gilmanton, New Hampshire. He was son of Major John Gilman, and was born in 1704. He commanded a regiment in the French war; was Speaker of the Assembly; and member of the Council of New Hampshire. Ordered, November, 1775, by the Provincial Congress, that he confine himself to the town of Exeter, and not depart thence without leave of that body or the Committee of Safety. He died in 1788, aged eighty-four.

GILMOUR, ROBERT. He was banished and attainted, and his estate was confiscated. In 1794 he represented to the British Government, that, at the time of his banishment, debts were due to him in America, which he had been unable to recover. I suppose this person to have belonged to New Hampshire, and the same who was proscribed by Act of that State in 1778.

GILPIN, THOMAS. Of Philadelphia. In 1777 he was confined in that city for being inimical to the Whig cause, and ordered to Virginia a prisoner. He died in exile at Winchester, March, 1778.

GIRTY, SIMON. Of Pennsylvania. Indian Interpreter. Was born out of wedlock. His father was a sot; his mother a bawd. He figures in the difficulties of Doctor Conolly and his party, with the authorities of Pennsylvania, in 1774. Girty's career was entirely infamous. He was an early prisoner of the Whigs at Pittsburg, but escaped. In 1778 he went through the Indian country to Detroit, with McKee and Elliot, proclaiming to the savages that the Rebels were determined to destroy them, and that " their only chance of safety was to espouse the cause of the Crown and fight." In 1782 Colonel Crawford was captured by the Indians and perished at the stake, after suffering the most horrible and excruciating tortures, which Girty saw with much satisfaction. This is the statement of his enemies; and it is but fair to say here that he denied the charge and averred that he exerted himself to save the Colonel until his own life was in peril. The same year his instigations caused the removal of the Moravian missionaries, who were quietly and usefully laboring among the Wyandots. He personally engaged in driving away these self-denying ministers, treated them with great harshness on the march, and subsequently procured their arrest. At the defeat of St. Clair, in 1791, Girty was present on the British side; and saw and knew General Butler, who lay upon the field writhing from the agony of his wounds. The traitor told a savage warrior that the wounded man was a high officer; whereupon the Indian buried his tomahawk in Butler's head, whose scalp was immediately torn off, and whose heart was taken out and divided into as many pieces as there were tribes engaged in the battle.

In 1793 Commissioners on the part of the United States attempted to negotiate with the Confederated Nations for an adjustment of our difficulties with the Indians, when Girty acted as interpreter. His conduct was exceedingly insolent; and it is related that he was not only false in his duty as an interpreter, but that he run a quill or long feather through the cartilege of his nose cross-wise, to show his contempt for the American gentlemen present. The failure of the negotiation, it is supposed, was in a good measure owing to the evil influence of Girty and other Loyalists. He adhered to the British to the last, and was killed under Proctor in 1813, in the battle of the Thames.

GLEN, WILLIAM. Of South Carolina. An Addresser of Sir Henry Clinton in 1780, and also a Petitioner to be armed on the side of the Crown. He was banished, and in 1782 his property was confiscated. He went to England.

GLOVER, SAMUEL. Ensign in De Lancey's Brigade. In 1776 he was captured on Long Island, and committed to jail in New London. He is called "a notorious offender." Among the papers found upon his person, was one from the captain of his company authorizing him to enlist men "for the defence of the liberty of America." Thus did Loyalists sometimes use the words of the Whigs.

GLOVER, ——. Of Newtown, Connecticut. In 1779, under the direction of Sir Henry Clinton, he and eight other Loyalists crossed Long Island Sound in a boat, for the purpose of capturing Major-General Silliman, who had been appointed to command on the opposite shore of Connecticut. Glover had been employed by the General, and was familiar with his house. The party approached his dwelling at night, and awoke himself and family by a violent assault upon the door. Silliman attempted to fire, but his musket only flashed; when the assailants broke through a window and seized him, and bore him off. On approaching the Long Island shore, Colonel Simcoe, of the Loyalist corps of Queen's Rangers, was in waiting, and exclaimed, "Have you got him?" He was answered, "Yes." "Have you lost any men?" "No." "That is well," said Simcoe; "your Sillimans are not worth a man, nor your Washingtons."

GODDARD, WILLIAM. Son of Giles Goddard, Postmaster of New London, Connecticut, had a checkered career. He was bred a printer, and established the first printing-press at Providence, Rhode Island, in 1762; and soon after began the publication of a newspaper. Not meeting with sufficient encouragement, he went to New York, and connected himself with John Holt in publishing the "New York Gazette and Post-Boy." After the repeal of the Stamp Act, in 1766, he removed to Philadelphia, and became the partner of Galloway and Wharton, in a paper called the "Pennsylvania Chronicle." These gentlemen were, in the end, both Loyalists. It would seem that the firm expected that Franklin, who was then in England, would take an interest in the concern; and provision was made in the articles of copartnership accordingly. The "Chronicle" was ably conducted. Galloway was an eminent lawyer, a writer of great vigor, and, as was supposed, a friend of the popular cause. In 1770, after many disputes, the partners — who, in the meantime, had admitted Benjamin Towne as a member of their establishment — came to an open rupture; and, having dissolved their connection, filled the public prints, handbills, and pamphlets, with the ebullitions of their animosity. Unable to meet the demands against the firm, Goddard, in great embarrassment, left Philadelphia, in 1773, and went to Baltimore, in quest of more lucrative business and greater tranquillity of life. Here he started another newspaper; but the plan of setting up a line of post-riders from New Hampshire to Georgia, in opposition to the Post-office establishment of the Crown, soon engaged the attention of leading minds; and Goddard, intrusting his printing affairs to the care of his sister, journeyed throughout the Colonies, to promote the adoption of the measure. He was eminently successful, as the Whigs entered into the scheme with great readiness, and cheerfully subscribed the necessary funds. Goddard was appointed Surveyor of the Roads and Comptroller of the Offices, on the organization of the Department; and on the retirement of Franklin, who was placed at its head, expected to succeed him as Postmaster-General. To his great disappointment, Bache, son-in-law to Franklin, received the place; and Goddard resigned his situation in disgust. It was supposed that now he not only suffered his ardor in the Whig cause to abate, but that he actually abandoned his political principles. He resumed his residence in Baltimore, where his paper, the

"Maryland Journal," had been and was still continued by and in the name of his sister; but in which it was known that he had an interest, and over which, it was believed, that he maintained the entire control. Early in 1777, two articles, one of which was signed " Tom Tell Truth," and the other, " Caveto," appeared in the " Journal," and excited the indignation of the Baltimore Whig Club, who, on the 4th of March, resolved, —

"That William Goddard do leave this town by twelve o'clock to-morrow morning, and the County in three days," &c. He immediately claimed the protection of the Assembly, then in session at Annapolis; and though that body formally and severely rebuked the Club, there was no resisting the popular impulse against him, and before the quarrel was ended, he was mobbed on several occasions, and otherwise insulted and ill-treated. This was especially the case in 1779, when the publication in the " Journal " of certain Queries, excited the ire of the Whig Club anew, and caused a great ferment. He was variously employed until 1784, when he appeared as the proper proprietor of the "Journal." In 1787 he became involved in a bitter controversy with the publisher of a rival print, in which he displayed eminent ability. In 1792 he sold his press, and bidding adieu to the cares and turmoils of party and political strifes, retired to a farm in Johnston, Rhode Island. He subsequently changed his abode to Providence, where he continued to reside until his decease in 1817, aged seventy-seven years.

Goddard was a man of fine talents, and, as the manager of a press, had, it is said, few or no superiors. General Charles Lee continued his friend, and bequeathed him a portion of his extensive landed estate in Virginia. Lee, it will be remembered, failed in the execution of his orders at the battle of Monmouth, was disgraced, and spent the remainder of his days in retirement. He was the writer of the Queries which caused Goddard's trouble with the Whig Club in 1779.

William Goddard, late Professor in Brown University, a gentleman of rare literary attainments, and of great social and moral worth, was son of the subject of this notice.

Godden, ———. Of North Carolina. Colonel of a Loyalist corps. Killed at Elizabethtown, North Carolina, in 1781, in the attack of the Whigs under Colonel Brown. [See *Slingsby*.]

Golding, Stephen. Residence unknown. Settled in New Brunswick in 1783; and died at Long Island, in that Province, in June, 1845, at the age of eighty-three years. For the thirty years previous to his decease, he held a commission of the peace for Queen's County. For fifty-five years he was an officer in the Provincial Militia, and retired with the rank of major. He was a consistent member of the Church of England. His descendants are numerous,— namely, eleven children, seventy-one grandchildren, and seventy-four great-grandchildren.

Golding, Palmer. Of Worcester, Massachusetts. A true friend to Government, and a captain in the militia. Early in 1775, he was returning from a visit to a friend, who was suspected of desertion from the Whigs, and of being a Tory, and whose political course he was supposed to influence, when he was knocked down, and much bruised and wounded.

Golding, Zenus. Died at French Village, New Brunswick, in 1814, aged fifty-six.

Goldsmith, Henry. He settled in New Brunswick, and was Collector of the Customs for the port of St. Andrew.

Goldthwaite, Thomas. Of Maine. Born in Chelsea, Massachusetts. Grantee, with Francis Bernard, son of the Governor, of a large tract of land in Prospect, on the Penobscot, on condition of settling thereon thirty families, of building an Episcopal church, and employing a minister. The enterprise was interrupted by the Revolution. Both adhered to the Crown, and forfeited their property. In 1763 he was appointed to the command of Fort Pownall; was superseded in 1770; but restored by Governor Hutchinson. In 1775 he allowed Mowat, who burned Falmouth (now Portland), to carry off the cannon; and the same year his petition to the General Court to be paid for his services while in garrison, was read, referred, but final action deferred. The Provincial Congress, in an Address to the Indians of Maine, remarked : " Captain Goldthwaite has given up Fort Pownal into the hands of our enemies; we are angry at it, and we hear you are angry with him, and we do not wonder at it." He solemnized the first marriage on the Penobscot; was a Judge of the Court of Common Pleas, and a colonel in the militia. The account of him is, that he was an extortioner, arbitrary and cruel. Early in the war he embarked for Nova Scotia, was shipwrecked on the passage, and perished.

GOLDTHWAITE, PHILIP. Of Maine. He was one of the two persons of Saco and Biddeford, Maine, who was dealt with by the Whigs of that section for their loyal principles. He was an officer of the Customs, and lived at Winter Harbor. As soon as the war commenced, he placed himself under British protection at Boston.

GOLDTHWAITE, JOSEPH. Of Massachusetts. Major, and Barrack-master of the King's troops in Boston. Brother of Philip. An Addresser of Hutchinson. In August, 1775, Hannah, his wife, crossed Winnisimmet Ferry, was arrested, and taken under guard to the General Court at Watertown. It appeared on her examination that her health was impaired, and an order was passed to allow her to visit Stafford for the benefit of the waters there, but to be under the care of the Selectmen; and afterwards to retire to the house of her brother, Joseph Brigham, at Rehoboth, and to be under the supervision of the Committee of Correspondence. In 1778, Mr. Goldthwaite was proscribed and banished. Administration on the estate of Joseph Goldthwaite, of Weston, was advertised by Joseph Gower, of Boston, August 23, 1782.

GOLDTHWAITE, EZEKIEL. Of Boston. Was an Addresser of Hutchinson in 1774, and a Protester against the Whigs the same year. He was Register of Deeds for the county of Suffolk. The Rev. John Bacon, who was minister of the Old South, and whose son, Ezekiel, was a member of Congress before the war of 1812, married his daughter. Though Mr. Goldthwaite became an Addresser, he was one of the fifty-eight Boston memorialists, who, in 1760, arrayed themselves against the Crown officers, and set the ball of the Revolution in motion. Elizabeth, his widow, died at Boston, in 1794, aged eighty.

GOOD, DAVID. Went to New Brunswick in 1783, and died at King's-clear, county of York, 1842, aged ninety-five. His widow, with whom he lived sixty years, survives (1845), as do one hundred and eleven descendants.

GOODALE, NATHAN. Of Salem, Massachusetts. Graduated at Harvard University in 1759. An Addresser of Hutchinson in 1774, but signed a recantation. The same year, however, he was an Addresser of Gage. Early in 1775 he secured a retreat at Nantucket. After the organization of the Federal Government, he was Clerk of the United States Courts in Massachusetts. In 1794, the title of a book was entered in his office, to secure copyright, in the following words: "*These are the Predictions of John Nobles, Astrologer and Doctor.*" He died at Newton in 1806, aged sixty-five. Mary, his wife, died in Boston, in 1794, aged fifty-seven.

GOODRICH, JOHN. Of Virginia. He seems to have enjoyed the confidence of the Whigs in 1775, since it appears that he was employed to import gunpowder, to the value of £5000, and was entrusted with that sum in advance; since, too, he incurred the displeasure of Lord Dunmore, who caused him to be seized and confined. In January, 1776, he petitioned the Virginia Convention for an adjustment of his accounts, which caused much debate in that body, and led to developments presently to be related in the notices of his sons. In March, 1776, the father and five sons had abandoned their houses, plantations, negroes, and stock, and were serving the Crown under Lord Dunmore. At the same time, his Lordship had five of their vessels in his fleet, under orders to constantly run up the rivers of Virginia, and seize, burn, or destroy, everything that was water-borne. In a despatch to the Secretary of State, his Lordship remarks that the members of this family were natives of the Colony; that they were spirited, active, and industrious; and that it had cost him much pains and trouble to secure them to the Royal cause. Harassed by both parties, Mr. Goodrich declared at last that "he did not value life." In June, 1776, he was in prison, in chains, and sick. His wife petitioned in his behalf; and, after inquiry into his condition, he was relieved of his fetters, and taken under guard to a place suitable for the recovery of health. In prison a second time, the Convention of Virginia ordered provision out of his estate for the support of his wife and young children. He was released finally, and went to England. He returned, and was engaged in fitting out privateers. In 1785, he was at Newport, Rhode Island, and asked leave to settle there with his family, offering, if permission was given, to bring twenty sail of vessels, and to establish himself in mercantile business; but he had taken so active a part in the war, that, upon a vote of the town, his request was refused by a large majority. I lose sight of him here. Margaret, his widow, died at Grove House, Topsham, England, in 1810, aged eighty. His daughter, Agatha Wells, married Robert Shedden, a Loyalist who is noticed in these pages, and whose descendants in England are persons of consideration.

GOODRICH, JOHN, JR. Of Virginia. Son of John. He was implicated with his brother Bartlett in the case of the British goods, inasmuch as he received them, and offered them for sale. It appears, too, in the notice of William, that, as relates to a quantity of powder purchased for the Colony under the arrangement with his father, he was a party to the fraud of charging much more than the cost. The result was that the Convention held him up to public odium, by publishing a full account of his conduct.

GOODRICH, WILLIAM. Of Virginia. Son of John. In the matter of the gunpowder his conduct was inexcusable. He was implicated in two purchases of that article. First, he was sent to the West Indies by his father, in 1775, where he procured about four thousand pounds, which arrived safely in North Carolina. The importation was however discovered by Lord Dunmore, who seized and detained him until intimidated; when he disclosed the whole affair, and went in an armed vessel, despatched by his Lordship, to demand the value, and the money remaining in the agent's hands. This done, he was discharged; but when the Royal Governor was advised that he intended to be present at Williamsburg, he was again made prisoner, and kept from making any explanations during the investigation mentioned in the notices of his father and brothers. The second case was far worse: He rendered his account at the Treasury Office, and made oath that the cost was four shillings and sixpence the pound; whereas the evidence was that a part was bought at three shillings, and the remainder at two shillings and ninepence. In the dilemma, his brother John stated that Bartlett made the purchase for his own benefit, and afterward sold to William at the price William charged the Colony. At a later time, he fled from home, and commanded a King's tender in the waters of the Chesapeake. In 1776 he was a prisoner in Philadelphia jail, and was transferred thence to prison in Baltimore.

GOODRICH, BARTLETT. Of Virginia. Son of John. During the investigation referred to in the notice of his father, there was evidence that when at Antigua, October, 1775, he purchased goods of British manufacture, and sent them to Virginia packed in rum puncheons, where they were exposed for sale. The transaction was in violation of the Continental Association; and the Convention voted to expose it in the "Virginia Gazette," in order to warn all persons to forbear further dealings with him. He went to England.

GOODRICH, BRIDGER or BRIDGEN. Of Virginia. Son of John. Commanded an armed vessel under Lord Dunmore. In 1776, in prison at Philadelphia, with his brother William, and transferred to Baltimore. In 1778 he was at Bermuda, in command of a ship of twenty guns; and was still there in the Naval service, two years later.

GORDON, THOMAS KNOX. Of South Carolina. Born in 1728, and appointed Chief Justice of the Province in 1771. He went to England, and died there in 1796. His son John was lieutenant-colonel of the 50th Regiment, in the

British Army. The family seat is in the County of Down, Ireland.

GORDON, HARRY. Of Pennsylvania. Was summoned by proclamation to appear before November 1, 1781, else he would be attainted; and failing to do so, his estate was seized by the commissioners of forfeitures, and most of it sold. These proceedings were against Henry Gordon; and, by an Act of January, 1783, the misnomer was corrected, and the Executive Council of that State, under that law, sold the remainder of his estate in 1790. In the Revolution he held a military commission under the Crown.

GORDON, CHARLES. Attorney-at-law, of Cecil County, Maryland. In 1775, the Whig Committee of that county, at a meeting at Elk Ferry, "Resolved, That he lies under the imputation of being an enemy to this country, and as such we will have no dealings or communication with him, nor permit him to transact any business with us, or for us, either in a public or private capacity, which shall be commenced after the date hereof," &c. Mr. Gordon "had treated with great disrespect, and maliciously aspersed the Continental Congress, the Provincial Congress, and the Committee of this County; and had, at various times, and by sundry ways, vilified their proceedings." A newspaper controvery ensued, in which the delinquent admitted that his politics were not quite agreeable to his accusers, &c.

GORDON, ALEXANDER. A physician, of Norfolk, Virginia. In February, 1775, the Whig Committee of Observation held him up for public censure, for the importation of medicines, contrary to the Continental Association. This Committee was composed of thirteen persons, and they were unanimous in their opinion of the Doctor's delinquency. He went to England, and was a Loyalist Addresser of the King, July, 1779.

GORE, JOHN. Of Boston. An Addresser of Gage. At the evacuation in 1776, went to Halifax with the Royal Army, and thence to England. Proscribed and banished in 1778; citizenship restored by Act of the Legislature in 1787.

He died in Boston, in 1796, aged seventy-seven. His son, Hon. Christopher Gore, was long one of the most conspicuous public characters of Massachusetts, and a gentleman of eminent worth and talents.

Gorham, David. Of Massachusetts. Graduated at Harvard University in 1738. In 1774 he was one of the barristers and attorneys of Massachusetts who addressed Hutchinson. He died in 1786.

Gornell, ———. Sergeant in the Whig Army. Under Greene, in South Carolina, he plotted to betray that officer to the British, with his entire force. When his plans were nearly matured he was arrested, and, upon sentence of a court-martial, executed.

Gort, William. Of New York. In 1780 he and James Plateau, another Loyalist, hired the house of Garret Putnam, a Whig, who, receiving orders to repair to Fort Hunter, took his family with him. Two days after Putnam's departure, a party of Sir John Johnson's Royal Greens came to the settlement (now embraced in the town of Mohawk), and, supposing the house was still occupied by Whigs, entered it at night, and murdered and scalped two men. In the morning, the dead bodies of Gort and Plateau revealed to them that they had murdered two friends.

Gorum, Nathaniel. Went to New Brunswick in 1783. He died at Kingston, in that Province, February 9, 1846, aged ninety-four years. Numerous offspring of children, grandchildren, and great-grandchildren, survive.

Goss, Rev. Thomas. Of Bolton, Massachusetts. Congregational minister. Graduated at Harvard University in 1737, and was settled about the year 1741. During the Revolutionary controversy he became much involved with his people; but it was finally agreed that he should read a declaration from his pulpit, and send a copy to the eldest deacon. This he did, but his enemies said that, instead of reading the paper distinctly, as was expected, "he intermixed it with his sermon, so that many of the congregation did not understand that he had read it at all; and inquired why he had not done as he promised." To this Mr. Goss replied, that, "According to the best of his remembrance, the said declaration was *distinctly* read before the text itself; but most *certainly* before the sermon, and not intermixed with it; and it was done with this design, that the sermon might be attended to without prejudice." The quarrel was renewed. At last, it was proposed that if he would take a dismission, the question of salary, under the contract of settlement, should be referred to the "general session of the peace." No arrangement was made, however; and the disaffected party, without applying to him to call a meeting of the church, got together and voted to dismiss him "as pastor, teacher, and brother." The town in public meeting concurred, and "on the succeeding Lord's day, by violence did prevent him from entering the desk." The next movement was the denial of further support, and the hiring of another preacher. He died in 1780, aged sixty-three. His friends erected a monument to his memory.

GOUCHER, JOSEPH. Went to St. John, New Brunswick, at the peace, and was a grantee of that city.

GOULD, JOHN. Of Massachusetts. Went to England, and was a Loyalist Addresser of the King in 1779.

GRAHAM, JOHN. Of Ulster County, New York. In 1775 a number of his Majesty's loyal subjects met at his house and erected a Royal Standard, on a mast seventy-five feet high, with the following inscription: —

"In testimony of our unshaken loyalty and incorruptible fidelity to the best of Kings; of our inviolable affection and attachment to our parent State and the British Constitution; of our abhorrence of and aversion to a Republican Government; of our detestation of all treasonable associations, unlawful combinations, seditious meetings, tumultuous assemblies, and execrable mobs; and of all measures that have a tendency to alienate the affections of the people from their rightful Sovereign, or lessen their regard for our most excellent Constitution; and to make known to all men that we are ready, when properly called upon, at the hazard of our lives and of everything dear to us, to defend the King, support the magistrates in the execution of the laws, and maintain the just rights and constitutional liberties of free-born Englishmen, this Standard, by the name of the King's Standard, was erected, by a number of his Majesty's loyal and faithful subjects in Ulster County, on the 10th day of February, in the 15th year of the reign of our most excellent sovereign, George the Third, whom God long preserve."

GRAHAM, JOHN. Of Georgia. Lieutenant-Governor of that Colony. He went to England. After the death of Sir James Wright, he and William Knox were appointed joint agents of the Georgia Loyalists for prosecuting their claims for losses. Attainted and estate confiscated. He was in London in 1788.

GRANT, JAMES. Of Salem, Massachusetts. Was an Addresser of Gage in 1774. Went to Halifax, but returned, and was at Boston in January, 1776; at which time he had been promised a commission in the Royal Army. Mary, his widow, died at Salem, in 1792, aged fifty-nine.

GRANT, ALEXANDER. Major in the New York Volunteers. Killed, 1777, in the storming of Forts Montgomery and Clinton. His widow perished in 1787, of cold and exposure when wrecked near St. John, New Brunswick, in crossing the Bay of Fundy.

GRANT, DANIEL. Was a native of Gillespie, Sutherland, Scotland, and emigrated to the United States. At the peace he removed with other Loyalists to St. Andrew, New Brunswick, where he continued to reside, and where he reared a numerous family. He died January, 1834, aged eighty-two years.

GRANT, WILLIAM. Of Virginia. In 1776 he taught a school, and was "zealous for Government." A Whig force was raised to repel the Cherokees, and "to screen himself from being deemed a Tory," he joined a company of riflemen to be stationed at the mouth of one of the tributaries of the Ohio. He wrote a "Narrative," dated November 24, 1777, on board the "*Queen* Indiaman at Gravesend," England, and styles himself, "late a Sergeant in the Rebel Army."

GRAVES, JOHN. Of Providence, Rhode Island. He was the vicar of Clapham, Yorkshire, England, and in 1754 came to Providence, to succeed the Rev. John Checkley, an Episcopal clergyman, who died the previous year, and as the Missionary of the Society for the Propagation of the Gospel in Foreign Parts. In 1770 Mr. Graves wrote to the Society, that "the face of public affairs here is melancholy. Altar against altar in the Church, and such open, bold attacks upon the State, as, I believe, the English annals do not furnish us with the like since the reign of King Charles I." These were signs of the coming storm. In September, 1776, he wrote: "Since independency has been proclaimed here, my two churches have been shut up; still I go on to baptize their children, visit their sick, bury their dead, and frequent their respective houses with the same freedom as usual;" and adds, with gratitude, that "their benefactions to me since the above period have been great, and far beyond what I have ever experienced from them before; founded upon their commiserating sense that the necessary means of supporting my large family — a wife and seven children — were now entirely cut off." In 1782 Mr. Graves was expelled from the parsonage and glebe, because he refused to open his church in conformity with the principles of independency. He soon after resigned his ministry, after a labor of twenty-six years. He died at Providence, in 1785.

GRAVES, JOHN. Of Pittsfield, Massachusetts. In 1775 he was sent to the jail at Northampton, on the charge of holding improper intercourse with General Gage at Boston. Accused, May, 1776, of assisting Captain McKay, a prisoner, to escape, in direct violation of his parole, he was sent to Hartford jail, and put in close confinement. In a letter to James Warren, it is said that Graves appeared to be "a low-spirited, insidious fellow." In 1778 proscribed and banished.

GRAVES, REV. MATTHEW. An Episcopal minister at New London, Connecticut. He was sent there by the Society for the Propagation of the Gospel, in 1745, and continued his labors for the period of thirty-three years. Refusing, in 1778, to omit the usual prayer for the King, he was driven from his church, on Sunday, before he had time to divest himself of his surplice. He fled to the house of a Whig, who, one of his flock, protected him. But though displaced, he remained in New London for some time; and was compelled "to sell almost all his property, and to take up money on very disadvantageous terms," in order to support himself. Finally, he went to New York, and died there, in 1780, unmarried. "In person he was ungainly; of low stature, rather corpulent, with particularly short legs." A maiden sister who lived with, and who accompanied him in his exile, returned to New London, lonely and disconsolate, and was allowed to occupy two rooms in the parsonage; she subsequently removed to Providence.

GRAY, HARRISON. Receiver-General of Massachusetts. He was an Addresser of Hutchinson, was a Mandamus Councillor, was proscribed and banished, and was among those whose estates were confiscated by statute. In the House of Representatives, August 8, 1775, "Ordered, that Mr. Hopkins be directed to inquire how the Committee of Supplies have disposed of the horse and chaise formerly Harrison Gray's, which was used by the late Dr. Warren, and came to the hands of the said Committee after Dr. Warren's death." The next day, "Ordered, that Dr. William Eustis be, and hereby is directed, immediately to deliver to the Committee of Supplies the horse and chaise which were in the possession of the late Doctor Warren, and which formerly belonged to Harrison Gray, of Boston." In 1776, at the evacuation, he went to Halifax with his family of four persons. He was passenger in one of the six vessels that arrived at London from Halifax, prior to June 10, 1776, laden with Loyalists and their families.

At his house in London, in 1789, or the year after, Arthur Savage gave the Rev. Mr. Montague a bullet taken from the body of General Warren the day after his death. [See *Arthur Savage.*] Mr. Gray was a timid man; and was accused of being on both sides in politics, according as he met Whig or Tory. In private life he was remarkably exemplary.

In "McFingal" it is said, —

> "What Puritan could ever pray
> In godlier tones than Treasurer Gray;
> Or at town-meetings speechifying,
> Could utter more melodious whine,
> And shut his eyes, and vent his moan,
> Like owl afflicted in the sun?"

Mr. Gray died in England. His only daughter, Elizabeth, was the first wife of Samuel Allyne Otis, and mother of Harrison Gray Otis, who, a distinguished statesman while the Federalists were in the ascendency, died at Boston, in 1849, aged eighty-four.

GRAY, JOHN. Of Boston. Son of Harrison Gray. He went to Ireland soon after the battle of Lexington. Hearing that the difficulties would probably be adjusted, he embarked for Massachusetts, and was made prisoner off Newburyport. He was in Newbury jail, February, 1776, when, at the solicitation of his sister, the wife of Samuel Allyne Otis, as communicated to the Council by James Otis, an order was passed to allow his removal to Barnstable, on condition of giving bond with security in £1000, not to pass without the limits of that town, or deal or correspond with the enemy. Mr. Gray was in London, January, 1781. Possibly, the John Gray who died at Boston in 1805, aged sixty-five, was the same.

GRAY, JOSEPH. Of Boston. A native of Massachusetts, and born in 1729. The Christian name of his father does not appear, but his mother was Rebecca, daughter of John West, a rich farmer of Bradford, or Haverhill, Massachusetts. The "old people" were displeased with the match, and cut off Rebecca with one pine-tree, or a piece of silver valued at one shilling." The family papers show that the grand-uncle of the subject of this notice (Benjamin Gray, of Boston, who died in 1741, or the year following) received a letter from an uncle in England, informing him that he was "next heir to a title and an estate" there; and that, being of the religious sect called "New Lights," he replied he would not abandon his faith "to be made King of England."

Of Mr. Gray's course in the Revolution, I find nothing. He settled at Halifax, Nova Scotia, and was a member of the firm of Proctor & Gray, merchants. He died in 1808, at that city, or at Windsor, at the age of seventy-four. His wife was Mary, daughter of the Hon. Joseph Gerrish. His third son, the Rev. Benjamin Gerrish Gray, D. D., who was born in 1768, married Mary, daughter of Nathaniel Ray Thomas, a Loyalist, [see notice,] and was many years Rector of St. George's Parish, Halifax, and afterwards of an Episcopal Church in St. John, New Brunswick, died at the latter city in 1854. His fourth son, William, was born in 1777; was British Consul for Virginia for a long time, and died in England, in 1845, or a year later. His other children were Mary, Rebecca, Elizabeth Breynton, Joseph Gerrish, Mary Gerrish, Amelia Ann, William Spry, Lydia Hancock, Ann Susanna, Susanna, Sarah, and Alexander. A grandson (son of Benjamin Gerrish), the Rev. John William Deming Gray, D. D., has been Rector of Trinity Church, St. John, New Brunswick, now (1861) quite twenty years. In December, 1857, he preached a sermon "designed to recommend the principles of the Loyalists of 1783," which was published. The main points of this discourse are: — First, the Loyalists " believed in the Bible as a Revelation from God;" second, they entertained "a respect for the ordinances of religion;" third, "they were just in their dealings with their fellowmen;" and fourth, "they were loyal to their earthly sovereign." His son, Benjamin Gerrish Gray, (the third of this name,) is a counsellor-at-law, in Boston.

GRAY, JOHN. Of Boston. Brother of Joseph Gray. He was bred to business in that town by Caleb Blanchard. About the year 1768 he went to England, but returned previous to hostilities, and was appointed Deputy-Collector of the Customs, in which office he was popular. In 1776 he embarked for Halifax with the Royal Army, and before the close of that year was at Charleston, South Carolina, and in prison. He was still in that city as late as 1780, when he was an Addresser of Sir Henry Clinton. Before the last mentioned date, however, he had engaged in business as a commission merchant, and had purchased a plantation on account of himself and of John Simpson, a fellow Loyalist, of Boston. But, involved, politically, beyond the hope of extrication, he sold his interest in the plantation, and invested the proceeds in indigo and in a ship, with the intention of sailing for London. The Whig authorities not only defeated this plan, but seized his vessel and her cargo; and the result was, that of both he saved barely one hundred guineas. With this sum, he fled to his brother Joseph at Halifax, who procured for him a passage to England in a ship-of-war. Without any accession to his fortune, yet, with letters to the agents of the East India Company, he soon embarked for India, and, on his arrival there, was well received. The family account is, that he wrote a treatise on the Cultivation of Indigo, which the Governor and Council considered so valuable as to grant him £4000 sterling, and, jointly with a Mr. Powell, an extensive tract of land. The two grantees, assisted by the Company, established a factory, and began the culture of indigo, which — as is stated in the papers before me — was the first attempt to cultivate this beautiful dye in India.

Both died suddenly, in 1782, on the same day. Gray was at the plantation, and Powell was two hundred miles distant, at the factory; and the supposition was that they had incurred the jealousy of the natives, who caused their death by poison. Powell's brother told Joseph Gray, prior to 1799, that the estate of our Loyalist and his associate had become "the greatest indigo plantation in the known world."

GRAY, SAMUEL. Of Boston. Brother of Joseph Gray. He died in that town about the year 1776, leaving issue, male and female. His wife was a daughter of Captain Henry Atkins, of Boston.

GRAY, THOMAS. Of Boston. Merchant. A Protester against the Whigs, and one of the Addressers of Hutchinson. He died at Boston in 1783.

GRAY, JESSE. "Of a Southern State." Went to Shelburne, Nova Scotia, at the peace. Removed to an island near Yarmouth, in the same Province, where he had a large grant of land for his military services. Died about the year 1840.

GRAY, BENJAMIN DINGLEY. Of Virginia. Was one of the Non-Associators, or a person who refused to join the Continental Association, and was posted by the Whig Committee in March, 1775, accordingly. On seeing his name in the list, he said " that he looked upon this Committee as a pack of damned rascals, for advertising him as they had done," &c. Subsequently, the Committee denounced his conduct by a resolution, in which they declare that he should "be looked upon as inimical to the liberties of America," and that "no person ought to have commercial intercourse with him."

GRAY, WILLIAM. Of Westchester County, New York. Was a Protester in 1775; settled in New Brunswick at the peace; was a magistrate of King's County; and died in 1824, aged ninety-six. A Loyalist of this name was a captain in the New York Volunteers.

GRAY, JUSTUS. Settled in New Brunswick at the peace, and died in that Province in 1843.

GREEN, FRANCIS. Of Boston. Merchant. Second son of Hon. Benjamin Green, President of the Council and Commander-in-Chief of Nova Scotia, whose ancestor was John Green, who settled in Cambridge, Massachusetts, about the year 1639. Born in Boston in 1742, and graduated at Harvard University in 1760. While yet a student, his father accepted for him an ensign's commission in the 40th Regiment, under a promise of leave of absence until he should have completed his studies. But the war with France interrupted this arrangement; and, in 1757, he joined his corps at Halifax. He was present at the siege of Louisburg in 1758, and remained in the garrison there until June, 1760, when he accompanied his regiment to Quebec. He relates that, while at the capitol of Cape Breton, the tedium of military life in that lone, desolate region, was relieved by shooting, hunting, fishing, assemblies, and plays; that the officers fitted up quite a pretty theatre, in which they were the actors; that he " was urged to take an active part, and performed several characters in tragedy and comedy, not without commendation." In June, 1761, the 40th crossed the St. Lawrence; and by marches, and in batteaux, passed through the wilderness to Crown Point; thence proceeded by the usual route of the time, to New York, and embarked for the West Indies. He records, that he assisted in the siege of Martinique; that he went to Antigua and St. Christophers with his Lieutenant-Colonel, where, in six days, they purchased and hired four hundred negroes, and joined the fleet in time to participate in the reduction of Havana. At the peace, having served four campaigns, "with credit, but very little promotion," he determined to quit the army. In 1765, he went to England, and, the year after, sold his commission of lieutenant, returned to Boston, and settled in mercantile business.

At the beginning of the Revolutionary controversy, he "adhered to the old Constitution," he relates, though always a firm friend to civil liberty, "and an avowed enemy to the pretended unlimited power of Parliamentary taxation, in the hope of an honorable compromise, without recourse to arms." In 1774 he went to Connecticut on business, and stopped at Windham. The "Sons of Liberty" assumed that his designs were political, and surrounding the tavern, uttered insulting shouts and words, and threatened him with a ride on "the Tory cart," unless he instantly departed. He journeyed to Norwich, where he was greeted with the ringing of the bell, and other manifestations of the popular excitement; and "the cart," or departure within fifteen minutes, were the terms offered. He attempted to address the throng, but was seized by a very stout man, who called him "a rascal." The fearful "cart," with a high scaffolding for a seat, was driven up, and preparations were made to compel him to mount it, when he entered his own carriage, and, mid scoffs and hissings, the beating of drums, and blowing of horns, drove away. On his return to Boston, he offered a reward for the apprehension of "the ruffians"; but they were merry over his advertisement, and, reprinting it in handbills, circulated it, with their comments. An Addresser of Hutchinson and of Gage, he embarked with the British at the evacuation of Boston, in 1776, (accompanied by his three young children,) and went to Halifax, where he was appointed a magistrate. In 1777 he repaired to New York. In 1778 he was proscribed and banished. In 1780 he arrived in England. In June, 1784, he returned to Nova Scotia; and while in that Colony, was elected Sheriff of the county of Halifax for three successive years, and appointed Senior Judge of the Court of Common Pleas.

In 1796, six hundred Maroons were transferred from Jamaica, by order of the Government, and the Commissioners for their settlement purchased his lands and buildings at Preston, Cole Harbor, and Dartmouth. This sale, the inadequacy of his official income, his "predilection for the land of his ancestors," and, to use his own words, the fact that "at that period his country was respectably Federal, and appeared to open its eyes to discern the folly of an alliance with France," are enumerated as the principal reasons for removing to the United States. He fixed his residence at Medford, Massachusetts, in 1797, and died there in 1809, at the age of sixty-seven, the last of the male branch of his family, of the fourth American generation.

The document placed at my disposal by one of his relatives — from which I have quoted — shows that Mr. Green was benevolent and humane, and a gentleman of elevated sentiments. It affords evidence, too, that he was vain of himself and of his lineage. His account of the honors and offices conferred upon his father, is tediously minute, and gives a clue to his political character. Plainly enough, he was a sturdy monarchist when a British subject, and a bitter foe to democracy after he became an American citizen.

His afflictions and misfortunes were many and severe; yet he seems to have borne all his domestic, and a part of his pecuniary losses, in a proper spirit. His first wife died, and two children perished under distressing circumstances; and he suffered by accusations of "false, envious, and malicious brethren." As a Loyalist, he abandoned a considerable amount of property in Boston; as a merchant, at New York, subsequently, in a single month, he was the loser, without insurance, of one half of an armed brig of sixteen guns and seventy men, and of four valuable vessels, of which he was sole owner; and later, after he came to Medford, as an underwriter he paid away twenty-five thousand dollars in the course of two years.

The great error of his life was, a willingness to live and to die — as John Adams has it — "a Colonist"; and I have been amazed, from the outset of my researches, that, of the Americans who were engaged in commerce, a single one should have adhered to the power that branded them with an epithet, and visited them with the pains and penalties of *smuggling*, whenever detected in prosecuting voyages to countries not included in the British dominions.

Bare justice to his memory demands that this brief outline should conclude with a respectful notice of his efforts to ameliorate the condition of mutes. His son Charles was discovered to be deaf when a child; and, at the age of eight, was sent to a private institution in Edinburgh, where he remained nearly six years, and became a proficient in language both oral and written, in arithmetic, geography, and painting. In the hope of doing good to others as unfortunate as his son, Mr. Green published a pamphlet in London, in 1783, entitled, "Vox Oculis Subjecta; or, A Dissertation on the Curious and Important Art of imparting Speech, and the Knowledge of Language, to the Deaf and Dumb; with a proposal for extending and perpetuating the benefits thereof." This was followed, after his return to Massachusetts, by various essays in the "Boston Palladium," and other newspapers, in 1803, and two succeeding years, in which he endeavored to convince his countrymen of the practicability of educating mutes; and finally, by the translation of the whole of the Abbé de l'Epee's work, showing *his* manner of instructing the deaf and dumb, called, "Institutions des Sounds et Muets."

His first wife, Susanna, daughter of Joseph Green, died during the siege of Boston, and in November, 1775. Of their five children, one was burned to death at the age of four; two others died young; Charles, the mute, was drowned, when seventeen; and Susanna, who deceased in 1802, married Stephen H. Binney, of Halifax. In 1785 he was united to Harriet, daughter of David Matthews, and was the father of Harriet Matthews, Henry Francis, Anna Winslow, and Eliza Atkinson, born in Nova Scotia; of Mary Hall and Matthews W., born in Medford. The oldest son by the second marriage, Henry Francis, now lives (1860) at Bellows Falls.

GREEN, JOSEPH. Of Boston. Born in 1706, and graduated at Harvard University, 1726. A wit, a poet, and a merchant. He was appointed Mandamus Councillor, but, it is believed, did not take the oath of office. His name is found among the Addressers of Hutchinson. He went to England, and died there, in 1780, aged seventy-four. He published several of his performances, which were mostly humorous: of these may be mentioned, the burlesque on a psalm of his fellow wit, Doctor Byles; ridicule of free-masons, and lamentation on Mr. Old Tenor — paper money. He was proscribed and banished. Though this gentleman was found, finally, among the adherents of the Crown, and became an exile, he. was one of the fifty-eight Boston memorialists in 1760; and in 1764 was a member of a committee with Samuel Adams, to report instructions to the Boston representatives. This report is very — Whiggish.

In 1776, he was member of the Loyalist Club formed in London by the exiles from Massachusetts, for social intercourse. They met once a week; discussed the news of the time, their own condition, and dined. The number present was from twelve to twenty-five. We may be sure that, with his reputation, he was always welcome. I give the following as a specimen of his humor. A farmer who had just lost his hired man, went to Boston to get Joe to write an epitaph: Green, on being told of all the good qualities of the deceased, and especially that he could rake faster than anybody, present company, of course, excepted, — immediately wrote, —

"Here lies the body of John Cole,
His master loved him like his soul;
He could rake hay, none could rake faster,
Except that raking dog, his master."

An epitaph composed for him in early life was in these words: —

"*Siste viator*, here lies one,
Whose life was whim, whose soul was pun;
And if you go too near his hearse,
He'll join you in both prose and verse."

GREEN, THOMAS. Of Pennsylvania. Was ordered by proclamation to appear and be tried, or to stand attainted. A Loyalist of the name of Thomas Green died in New Brunswick previous to the year 1805; his widow married Clayton Tilton, of Musquash, New Brunswick.

GREEN, WILLIAM. Drummer in Washington's Guard. Concerned in the Hickey plot against the life of the Commander-in-Chief, in 1776. He was the leading witness at the trial of Hickey before the court-martial, and the recipient of "one dollar per man from Forbes for every man he shall enlist." Green, in his testimony, said that "all Forbes proposed to me was, that, when the King's forces arrived, we should cut away King's Bridge, and then go on board a ship of war, which would be in East River to receive us."

GREENE, RICHARD. Of Rhode Island. He was born in that Colony, in 1725. He owned and lived on a large estate. "His furniture and wines were imported from England. Servants, both white and colored, were numerous. . . . . . Always employing an overseer . . . . . accounts for his having leisure to entertain more company, perhaps, than any other private gentleman in Rhode Island, and he was remarkable for very great hospitality. A large proportion of his visitors were some of the most distinguished personages of the day."

He regarded the Revolution, at the beginning, as a rebellion against lawful authority; and suffered in consequence of his *avowed* opinion, as well as for his *supposed* acts, subsequently, in aid of the British. It is averred that "he remained strictly neutral." He died in 1779. The common people called him "King Richard," to distinguish him from others of the same name, and for his charity to the poor, and his magnificent manner of living. It is said of him, too, that he neither purchased soldier's certificates, nor paid a debt in Continental money. His wife was Sarah, daughter of Thomas Fry, of East Greenwich. Of his fourteen children, eleven survived him.

GREENE, RICHARD. Of Boston. Addresser of Gage in 1775; the Council of Massachusetts ordered his arrest, April, 1776. He died at Boston, in 1817, aged eighty-seven.

GREENE, DAVID. Of Boston. At the Latin School in 1757; an Addresser of Hutchinson in 1774; proscribed and banished in 1778. Went to England. Returned, and citizenship restored by Act of the Legislature in 1789. Died at Ballstown Springs, in 1812, aged sixty-three. At the time of his decease, a friendly pen wrote: — "Very few persons have passed through life so much beloved and esteemed as Mr. Greene, by a numerous circle of friends and acquaintance. His singular sweetness of temper, his undeviating politeness, his uncommon attention to strangers, and his extensive connexions in business, made him known and admired in every part of the Union; and he was justly considered, both at home and abroad, as one of the most accomplished gentlemen of New England. He was for many years a distinguished merchant, and was alike esteemed for his integrity and his attention to business. During the latter years of his life he was President of the Union Insurance Company."

GREENE, BENJAMIN. Of Boston. Protester in 1774; an Addresser of Hutchinson the same year. In 1776 the Council of Massachusetts ordered his arrest. Died in Boston in 1807, aged sixty.

GREENLAW, JONATHAN. Of Castine, Maine. Brother of Charles Greenlaw. At the evacuation of Castine by the Royal forces, in 1783, he removed to St. Andrew, New Brunswick, where he died, in 1818, aged eighty. His sons, six in number, were Whigs. His son William, the only one who entered the service, was a soldier under Washington, and at the peace settled at Deer Isle, Maine, where he died, in 1838, aged eighty-seven. His son, the late Jonathan Babbage Greenlaw, was a ship-master, and lived at Eastport, Maine.

GREENLAW, WILLIAM. Of St. George's River, Maine. Brother of Charles. He remained on his farm during the war, and continuing in the country after the close of the strife, died at St. George in 1828.

GREENLAW, CHARLES. Of Castine, Maine. Brother of Ebenezer. He accompanied Jonathan and Ebenezer to St. Andrew, where he settled, and died in 1811, aged about sixty-eight.

GREENLAW, EBENEZER. Of Castine, Maine. Brother of Charles. He removed to St. Andrew, New Brunswick, at the peace, where he died about the year 1810, aged seventy.

GREENLEAF, STEPHEN. Of Boston. Was Sheriff of Suffolk County. He was a Protester against the Whigs in 1774, and one of the ninety-seven gentlemen and principal inhabitants of the capital who addressed Gage on his departure in 1775. His arrest ordered by the Council of Massachusetts, April, 1776. He died at Boston, in 1795, aged ninety-one.

GREENWOOD, SAMUEL. Of Boston. A Sandemanian. Was a Protester in 1774; accompanied the Royal Army to Halifax in 1776; remained in Nova Scotia, and died at Halifax. His son, Samuel, died at the same place, in 1832, aged fifty-seven.

GREGORY, WILLIAM. Of Maine. Kept a sort of tavern in a log-house, at George's River. Was often plundered by both parties. "Reckoned a Tory." Was a jolly, light-minded fellow; much fonder of a merry story than of political discussions, and loved money better than England or America.

GREGORY, WILLIAM. Of South Carolina. An Assistant Judge of the Superior Court under the Royal Government; was allowed to depart the country. The only native American on the bench, at the beginning of the Revolution, was

William Henry Drayton, who was a Whig; he made the last circuit with Gregory and his other associates, in the spring of 1775.

GREGORY, RICHARD P. Settled in New Brunswick at the peace, and died at Kingston in that Province, in 1847, in his ninety-sixth year.

GRIDLEY, BENJAMIN. A lawyer, of Boston. Graduated at Harvard University in 1751. John Adams said of him, in 1769, that he possessed capacity, real sentiment, fancy, wit, humor, judgment, and observation; yet, that he had no business of any kind, was in bed till ten in the morning, laughed, drank, and frolicked, and neither studied nor practised his profession. He was among the barristers and attorneys who addressed Hutchinson in 1774, and one of the Addressers of Gage in 1775. He went to Halifax in 1776. In 1778 he was proscribed and banished. He was in England at the close of the Revolution.

GRIERSON, ——. Colonel in the Loyal Militia. A man of unshaken loyalty in every change of fortune, and, before the alienations of civil war, universally respected. In 1781, at the siege of Augusta, Georgia, he occupied an outwork which bore his own name, and which, after some resistance, he evacuated with the design of joining Browne in Fort Cornwallis. He was made prisoner, however, and murdered. One account is, that, confined in a house with his three children, "an unknown marksman," disguised and on horseback, rode rapidly up to the building, dashed into the room in which Grierson was kept, and, without dismounting, shot him dead, then wheeled about, and escaped. Another version is, that he was killed by a well-known Whig, who said that in 1780 Grierson chained his father — seventy-eight years of age — to a cart, and dragged him forty miles in two days; and that he ordered the driver to apply the whip whenever the old man attempted to rest himself by leaning on the cart. One hundred guineas were offered for the discovery of the assassin, without success. The Loyalists averred that this reward was a mere pretence; and that Grierson's body was stripped, mangled by the soldiers, and thrown into a ditch.

GRIERSON, JAMES. Was a native of the Highlands of Scotland, and emigrated to America before the Revolution. He served in the Royal Army, and at the peace settled in New Brunswick, where he died, in 1846, at the great age of one hundred and five years. He was a pensioner of the British Government more than sixty years.

GRISWOLD, SETH. Settled in New Brunswick in 1783, and died at Queensbury, York County, in 1838, aged eighty-one years.

GRISWOLD, DANIEL. Of Litchfield, Connecticut. Advertised in 1776, by the Committee of that town, " as an enemy to the natural rights of mankind." The next year he was tried by a court-martial as a traitor and spy, and executed.

GROUNDWATER, ———. Of South Carolina. Early in the war in command of a small vessel, and of service to the Whigs in supplying them with articles of necessity. In 1779 he was taken going over to the enemy, tried, and executed. Some interest was made to save his life; but, suspected of assisting to set fire to a part of Charleston, " the inhabitants were so incensed against him that he suffered to appease them."

GROUT, JOHN. Of Cumberland County, New Hampshire Grants. Born in Lunenburg, Massachusetts, in 1731. When he removed to the " Grants," he had a wife and several children; and the authorities, on the ground that his family would become chargeable as paupers, held him to answer. He prevented forcible ejectment by a promise " on honor, and as a lawyer," that he would voluntarily depart. Restless in his disposition, and, as it seems, meddlesome withal, he was often in trouble in the place to which he next went; and was at last put in prison for debt. In the controversy which preceded the appeal to arms, he was violent and denunciatory in his acts and words against the Whigs, and met harsh treatment in return. His own account is that he was threatened with death. In 1777 he abandoned the country; and in 1779 was forbidden, by Act of the General Assembly of Vermont, to return. He settled in Canada. " His end was as tragic as his life had been turbulent and unhappy." He set out for the purpose of paying a large sum of money which he had collected for another, but never reached the end of his journey. It was supposed that he was drowned; but, in the lapse of years, a convict under sentence of death confessed that he murdered John Grout, and described the place of his burial, which, when examined, revealed human bones.

GRYMES, JOHN RANDOLPH. Of Virginia. Major in the Queen's Rangers. In 1776 he joined Lord Dunmore, and raised and commanded a troop of horse. His Lordship, in a letter to Lord George Germain, remarks that Mr. Grymes was a great acquisition to the Royal cause; that he was of the first family in Virginia, a gentleman of fortune, of amiable character, of strict honor, and brave, active, able. The same year Mr. Grymes was expelled from his estate, and thirty-five negroes, horses, cattle, and furniture, fell into Whig hands.

Subsequently, he was attached to the Rangers, and won the confidence of Simcoe, and of the corps. Near the close of the year 1778 he resigned; and soon after went to England. While there, an invasion from France was apprehended; and the Loyalists in London offered to form themselves into a company, which met the approval of the King, and in the choice of officers, Major Grymes was elected ensign. In 1788 he was agent for prosecuting the claims of adherents of the Crown in his native State. He returned to Virginia. In England he married a daughter of John Randolph, the last Royal Attorney-General of the "Old Dominion," and brother of Peyton Randolph, President of Congress. Mrs. Grymes died in London in 1791.

GRYMES, HENRY. Of Virginia. Went to England, and died there in 1804. Delirious, in consequence, as was supposed, of a disappointment in marriage, he broke his skull with a stone, and took out a piece of the bone three inches by two; and, concluding that this would put an end to his existence, he tore out a part of his brains. But he lived until the evening of the following day, and his reason was so far restored before his death that he told his friends the cause of his mangled condition. "Through the whole of his life, he supported an unsullied character."

GUEST, WILLIAM. Of South Carolina. In 1776, committed to jail in Charleston, by the Provincial Congress, for alleged offences "inimical to, and destructive of," the peace of that Colony. In commission of the Crown after the surrender of Charleston. Estate confiscated; but the General Assembly gave his wife Sarah and her children, subsequently, five hundred acres of any of his lands which had not been sold by the commissioners.

GUTHREY, THOMAS. Of Pennsylvania. Deserted from the State galleys. Joined the British in Philadelphia. Captured at sea. In prison in 1779, and to be tried for treason.

GUYON, PETER. Of Staten Island, New York. At the peace, accompanied by his family of five persons, and by one servant, he went from New York to Shelburne, Nova Scotia. His losses, in consequence of his loyalty, were estimated at £1900. He was among the few who remained at Shelburne, and died there about the year 1825.

HABERSHAM, JAMES. Of Georgia. He was born in England in 1712; and, against the wishes of his friends, accompanied the celebrated Whitefield to Savannah, in 1738. He engaged as teacher of a school for orphan and destitute children, soon after his arrival; and, subsequently, became interested in similar works of benevolence. Of the Orphan House he was President. He formed a commercial partnership in 1744, which was the first in Georgia. Ten years later, he was appointed Secretary of the Colony, and a member of the Council. He was the acting Governor of Georgia in 1771, during the temporary absence of Sir James Wright. In April, 1775, he wrote to a friend in London thus: — "The fiery patriots in Charleston have stopped all dealings with us, and will not suffer any goods to be landed there from Great Britain; and I suppose the Northern Provinces will follow their example. The people on this Continent are generally almost in a state of madness and desperation; and should not conciliatory measures take place on your side, I know not what may be the consequences. I fear an open rebellion against the parent State, and consequently amongst ourselves. Some of the inflammatory resolutions and measures taken and published in the Northern Colonies, I think, too plainly portend this. However, I must and do, upon every occasion, declare that I would not choose to live here any longer than we are in a state of proper subordination to, and under the protection of, Great Britain, although I cannot altogether approve of the steps she has lately taken, and do most cordially wish that a permanent line of government was drawn and pursued by the mother and her children; and may God give your Senators wisdom to do it, and heal the breach; otherwise, I cannot think of the event but with horror and grief. Father against son, and son against father, and the nearest relations and friends combating with each other! I may perhaps say the truth, cutting each other's throats. Dreadful to think of, much worse to experience. But I will have done with this disagreeable subject," &c.

He went to New Jersey soon after writing the above letter, and died at New Brunswick, August, 1775. The three sons who survived him were Whigs.

HADDEN, ISAAC. In 1782 he was a lieutenant in the First Battalion of New Jersey Volunteers. He retired on half-pay, and settled in New Brunswick, where he was Clerk of the House of Assembly. He died in that Colony.

HADDEN, ———. Major-General in the Royal Artillery. He entered the army during the war, and served under Burgoyne and Cornwallis. At the peace he went to England. In 1793, when a captain in the Artillery, he was selected by the Duke of Richmond for his secretary. Subsequently, he received a staff appointment; and, in Portugal, acted in the capacity of Adjutant-General under Sir Charles Stuart. Later, he was Surveyor-General of the Ordnance Department, and Major-General. He died in England in 1817.

HAGGERTY, PATRICK. In 1782 he was a lieutenant in the First Battalion of New Jersey Volunteers. At the peace he went to Digby, Nova Scotia, where he soon died; leaving no family.

HAINS, BARTHOLOMEW. Of New York. Lost his property by confiscation. Settled at Westport, Nova Scotia, where he was an officer of the Customs and a magistrate, and where he died, leaving a large family, of whom John is now (1861) the only survivor.

HAIT, JAMES. Of Connecticut. At the peace he went to St. John, New Brunswick, and was a grantee of that city. In 1784 he was one of the two vendue masters of the district of the river St. John. He removed from that Province about the year 1799, and died at Newfield, Connecticut, in 1804.

HAKE, ———. He was in England in 1784, when his name was freely used in Loyalist tracts published at London. I cite two instances: — There were "fifty-five signers to Mr. Hake's Memorial"; *he* was "loyal to get rid of his debts." The charge of dishonesty was repelled by "*Viator*"; who said that "Mr. Hake owed in England, and not in America, and if he had a design against his creditors, he should have joined the rebellion," &c.

HALIBURTON, JOHN. Of Rhode Island. Physician. Went to Halifax, Nova Scotia. During the Revolution, a surgeon in the British Navy. At the peace, resumed practice and acquired a high professional reputation; held public offices, and was a member of the Council. He died at Halifax in 1808, aged sixty-nine. His wife, Susanna, who deceased in 1804, was a sister of Admiral Brenton. His son, John, was an officer in the British Navy; his daughter, Elizabeth, married Lord Stewart. In 1859, his son, Brenton Haliburton, who was born in Rhode Island, — Chief Justice of Nova Scotia, — received the honor of knighthood. The gentlemen of the legal profession at Halifax waited upon the venerable jurist, then in his eighty-sixth year, in a body, and addressed him in terms of deep affection. His reply was so proper that I preserve it.

"*My Brethren of the Bench and of the Bar:* — Accept my heartfelt thanks for the kind and affectionate address which you have given to me upon her Most Gracious Majesty's conferring upon me the dignity of a Knight of the United Kingdom of Great Britain and Ireland.

"Although at my age I ought to be, and I humbly trust I am, more solicitous to obtain the blessed promises which our gracious Saviour has made to all believers in his Holy Gospel, than any earthly honors, yet I value highly the approbation of a Sovereign esteemed and beloved by her subjects for her public and private virtues.

"To our respected Governor, His Excellency the Earl of Mulgrave, I feel great gratitude for having, totally unsolicited by me, brought my services under Her Royal consideration, to which I attribute the honor that has been conferred upon me.

"I consider this honor as paid to the profession to which I belong, and it greatly increases my gratification so to consider it.

"I am much indebted to my brethern of the Bench for the satisfaction which I learn my judgments have given; for, generally speaking, it is with their concurrence and approval that those judgments have been pronounced; and I am sure they will join with me in declaring that the labors of the Bench have frequently been greatly diminished by the industry and talent of the Bar.

"And now, gentlemen, accept of an old man's affectionate prayer for your welfare. May you at the close of life feel the great comfort of having made your peace with God through the merits of your Saviour.

"God bless you all."

Sir Brenton died at Halifax in 1860. As a jurist he was able, painstaking and conscientious; as a man, of cheerful disposition and great liberality of opinion.

HALL, REV. WILLARD. Minister of Westford, Massachusetts. Graduated at Harvard University in 1722. Date of ordination not ascertained. Complaints against him in May, 1775; final hearing June 4, 1776, before the Committees of the towns of Dunstable, Littleton, Westford, and Acton, and the decision, that, "in divers instances, he hath shown himself unfriendly to the cause of the United American Colonies." The affair seems to have caused much trouble; but my materials are too fragmentary for a narrative. He died in 1779.

HALL, ———. Of South Carolina. Lieutenant in the King's Rangers. A Whig at first, and in command of a small fort on the frontier of his native State, which he treacherously surrendered to the Cherokees, who killed the garrison, men, women, and children, without discrimination. In 1779 Hall was taken prisoner, tried, and condemned to death. "At the gallows he confessed his crime, and acknowledged the justice of his sentence."

HALL, JAMES. Of Boston. His name is connected with one of the memorable incidents of the Revolutionary controversy. In 1773 he was in command of the ship *Dartmouth*, owned by Francis Rotch, and arrived at Boston on the 28th of November, with one hundred and twelve chests of the celebrated Tea, which was thrown overboard in the following month of December. The next year he was an Addresser of Hutchinson, and in 1778 was proscribed and banished. The morning after Hall's arrival in 1773, the following notice appeared:—

"FRIENDS, BRETHERN, COUNTRYMEN.

"That worst of all plagues, the detested TEA, shipped for this port by the East India Company, is now arrived in this harbor. The hour of destruction, or manly opposition to the machinations of Tyranny, stares you in the face. Every friend to his country, to himself, and to posterity, is now called upon to meet at Faneuil Hall at nine o'olock this day, (at which time the bells will ring,) to make a united and successful resistance to this last, worst, and most destructive measure of administration.

"Boston, November 29, 1773."

Bruce, in the *Eleanor*, and Coffin, in the *Beaver*, came into port soon after; and the mob, disguised as Indians, threw the cargoes of the three vessels, consisting of two hundred and forty whole, and one hundred half chests, into the harbor.

HALLET, DANIEL. In 1782 he was a lieutenant in De Lancey's Second Battalion. At the peace he went to St. John,

New Brunswick, and was a grantee of that city. He received half-pay. He died in the county of York, in that Province, 1827, aged seventy-six.

HALLET, SAMUEL. Of Long Island, New York. In 1776, arrested, and sent to the Continental Congress. Ordered back, and placed under guard by the Convention of New York. Petitioned for release, and finally discharged on parole, on payment of expenses, and on recognizing in £500. In 1782 he was a captain in De Lancey's Second Battalion. He settled at St. John, New Brunswick, and in 1784 received the grant of a city lot. In 1792 he was a member of the Vestry of the Episcopal Church. Elizabeth, his widow, died at St. John in 1804, aged sixty-nine.

HALLOWELL, ROBERT. Of Boston. Comptroller of the Customs. In office early in life; and Collector of the Customs at Portsmouth, New Hampshire, before the age of twenty-five. He arrived at Boston, from London, in 1764, and entered upon his duties as Comptroller. The next year, a mob surrounded his elegant house in Hanover Street, tore down his fences, broke his windows, and, forcing the doors at last, destroyed furniture, stole money, scattered books and papers, and drank of the wines in the cellar to drunkenness. In 1768, he ordered Hancock's vessel, the *Liberty*, seized for smuggling wine, to be removed from the wharf to a place covered by the guns of the *Romney* frigate; and, in the affray which occurred, received wounds and bruises that at the moment seemed mortal. When the port of Boston was shut, June 1, 1774, he removed his office to Plymouth. In 1775, he was an Addresser of Gage; and, the year following, with his family of five persons, he accompanied the British Army to Halifax. In 1778 he was proscribed and banished. He went to England, and settled at Bristol. The executor of his own father, and of his wife's father, he came to the United States in 1788 and in 1790, on business. In 1792 he removed to Boston with his family; and lived in the homestead, Batterymarch Street, which, because of his mother's life interest, had not been confiscated. He was kindly received by former friends, and became intimate with some distinguished Whigs. In 1816, infirm and in failing health, he went to Gardiner, Maine, to reside with his son; and died there, April, 1818, in his seventy-ninth year. His wife was Hannah, daughter of Doctor Sylvester Gardiner. His children were Hannah and Anne, who died unmarried; and Robert, who, in 1802, added the name of his maternal grandfather, — the Hon. Robert Hallowell Gardiner, late President of the Maine Historical Society, — who is now living (1864) and a gentleman of great wealth and respectability. Two of Mr. Hallowell's sisters died in England; Sarah, wife of Samuel Vaughan, in 1809; and Anne, widow of General Gould, in 1812.

HALLOWELL, BENJAMIN. Of Boston. Brother of the preceding. Commissioner of the Customs. In early life he commanded a small armed vessel. The Commissioners were extremely obnoxious; and when Mr. Hallowell accepted, in addition, the office of Mandamus Councillor, he became a special object of public indignation. To mention that, in 1774, while passing through Cambridge in his chaise, he was pursued toward Boston by about one hundred and sixty men on horseback, at full gallop, is sufficient to show the popular feeling. In August, 1775, there was a "street fight between Commissioner Hallowell and Admiral Graves;" of which the newspapers contain the details. In January, 1776, he wrote to his son, Ward, in London, — " Your mother has sent Nickey's little spoon, your can, and a pair of tea-tongs, by Sir William Pepperell, who is a passenger in the *Trident* transport." On the 10th of March following, Mr. Hallowell and his family of six persons embarked for Halifax in the *Hellespont*, a mere victualler to the British fleet. The passage was only six days; but the vessel was detained in Nantasket Roads just three weeks. In the cabin, by his own account, there were thirty-seven persons, "men, women, and children; parents, masters and mistresses, obliged to pig together on the floor, there being no berths," until they departed the harbor. In July, 1776, he sailed for England in the ship *Aston Hall.* While at Halifax, he said, in a letter before me: "If I can be of the least service to either army or navy, I will stay in America until this Rebellion is subdued." It appears from another letter that he frequently tendered himself to the Commander-in-Chief, without success.

In 1784, Mrs. Adams was in England; and she relates that both Mr. Hallowell and his wife treated her with respect and kindness, and urged her to take lodgings with them, which she declined. She records, too, that they lived in handsome style, but not as splendidly as when in Boston. She accepted an invitation to "an unceremonious family dinner," as Mrs. Hallowell called it, and met the Rev. Dr. Walter, Rector of Trinity Church, and two other gentlemen, who belonged to Massachusetts. In the autumn of 1796, Mr. Hallowell came to Boston. He was accompanied by his daughter, Mrs. Elmsley, and by her husband, who had just been appointed Chief Justice[1] of Upper Canada. The party were the guests of his brother Robert until early in the next summer. During his stay, the odium which attached to his official relations to the Crown seemed to have been forgotten, since he was received by his former associates with the greatest kindness and hospitality. He died at York, Upper Canada, in 1799, aged seventy-five, and was the last survivor of the Board of Commissioners. The British Government granted him lands in Manchester, and two other towns in Nova Scotia, and a township in Upper Canada, which bears his name. He was a large proprietor of lands on the Kennebec, Maine, prior to the Revolution; but proscribed and banished in 1778, and included in the Conspiracy Act a year later, his entire estate was confiscated. His country residence at Jamaica Plain was used as a hospital by the Whig Army during the siege of Boston; and his pleasure-grounds were converted into a place of burial for soldiers who died. This property was seized and sold by the Com-

---

[1] John Elmsley, Chief Justice of Lower Canada, died at Montreal, in 1805, in his forty-third year. The Duke of Portland was his friend and patron.

monwealth; but as the fee was in Mrs. Hallowell, her heirs sued to recover of the person who held under the deed of the Commissioners of Confiscation, and obtained judgment in 1803, in the United States Circuit Court.

For Mr. Hallowell's two sons, see, in these pages, Sir Benjamin Hallowell Carew, and Ward Nicholas Boylston.

HAMILTON, JOHN. Lieutenant-Colonel Commandant of the North Carolina Volunteers. By one account, he was a merchant of Halifax, North Carolina; by another, he lived at Norfolk, Virginia, where his hospitality and other estimable qualities won universal respect. Business led him often from home, and, at the beginning of the Revolution, his acquaintance at the South was extensive, and the confidence in his integrity almost unlimited. A distinguished Whig, who met him in battle, remarks that Colonel Hamilton was a Loyalist, because he believed England in the right; that the native goodness of his heart, as well as motives of policy, led him to discountenance the war of extermination which was waged in the Carolinas; and that his influence was ever exerted on the side of mercy. The biographer of Judge Iredell says that "He so deported himself to such Whigs of North Carolina, as by the fortune of war became objects of charity, as to secure the cordial regard of the best men in the ranks of his enemies;" and adds, that "He was the very crest of Tory organization in the South." Such is the testimony of his foes; and I delight to record it. Stedman, who served under Sir William Howe, Sir Henry Clinton, and the Marquis of Cornwallis, and who wrote "The History of the Origin, Progress and Termination of the American War," uses these emphatic words: "The British nation owed more, perhaps, to Colonel Hamilton, of the North Carolina Regiment, than to any other individual Loyalist in the British service." He was engaged in nearly every action in the three Southern Colonies; was wounded and taken prisoner; and finally placed in command of the garrison at St. Augustine.

North Carolina and Virginia attainted him of treason, and

confiscated his estates. After the peace he was British Consul for the last named State, and lived at Norfolk. I find him in communication with his Government for the last time in 1794, when some French ships-of-war in Hampton Roads had captured the *Scorpion*, and he was endeavoring to obtain the release of several gentlemen who were prisoners. In the same year, his agent at London, in behalf of the firm of which he was a member, presented a memorial to the British Government on the subject of debts due in America at the time of his banishment, which had not been recovered, and prayed for relief. He died in England, in 1817, at a very advanced age. He is described as "a short, stout, red-faced man; well bred, and well fed," and " of high tone and spirit."

HAMILTON, JAMES. Of Pennsylvania. In 1777, a prisoner on parole. In a communication to the Council, he represented his advanced age; a disorder which was the source of much discomfort; his extensive concerns, which required his constant care, &c., as reasons why he should be permitted to remain in his own house; and he asked, that, in case of his removal, he might be allowed, among other things, to appoint his nephew, William Hamilton, to manage his affairs during his absence. The Council, in reply, suggested Easton, Bethlehem, or Reading, for his retreat; and said that there were unanswerable objections to his proposition as related to his nephew. In March, 1778, he was under restraint at Northampton; and in a long communication, in which he spoke of his losses, the absence from his nearest friends, his age, and the alarming condition of his health, he solicited leave to return to his family. The boon was soon granted. On the 23d of April, an order passed the Council for his discharge; and he was informed that he was at full liberty to act as he pleased. In May, he applied for a pass not only for himself and four servants, but for a baggage-wagon and driver to go to Philadelphia, which was refused; because he had not taken an oath or affirmation to support the Whig Government; and because he had asked to take property within the British lines. But, as related to his own person and his ailments, he was furnished with a protection to visit Philadelphia to consult a physician; and allowed to remain there two weeks.

HAMILTON, WILLIAM. Of Pennsylvania. He was proprietor of the principal part of the site of the city of Lancaster, in that State. This land escaped confiscation, and ground-rents, to a considerable extent, are yet (1849) claimed and collected under his title. The Courts have acknowledged the validity of the call upon occupants for the rents, but there exists much unwillingness to pay them, and efforts have been made to avoid, or to commute them. The original proprietor of Lancaster was, I suppose, James Hamilton. Witham Marshe was there in 1744, with the commissioners of various Colonies, who were sent to form a treaty with the Six Nations, and recorded in his journal that this gentleman " made a ball and opened it, by dancing two minuets with two of the ladies here, which last danced wilder time than any Indians." Mr. Hamilton raised a regiment in the neighborhood of his residence on the Schuylkill; but resigned at the Declaration of Independence. He was a gentleman of wealth, and the family to which he belonged possessed more influence than any other in the Colony, except the " Allens." His beautiful country seat was called the " Woodlands." Isaac Ogden wrote Galloway, in 1778, — " Billy Hamilton had a narrow escape; his trial for treason against the States lasted twelve hours. I have seen a gentleman who attended his trial; he informed me that his acquittal was owing to a defect of proof of a paper from Lord Cornwallis, his direction being torn off." He was in jail in Philadelphia, October 22d, 1780; at which date he addressed a letter to the President of the Council praying to be released.

HAMILTON, ARCHIBALD. Of Queen's County, New York. In June, 1776, he declared upon his honor that he would not " directly or indirectly oppose or contravene the measures of the Continental Congress, or of the Congress of" New York. He, however, became an active friend of the Crown, and aide-de-camp to General Robertson, and commandant of the militia of Queen's County, with the pay of the army. In December, 1780, his house, at Flushing, New York, was burned to the ground, together with the "elegant furniture, stock of provisions, various sorts of wines, spirits intended for the regale of his numerous friends, the military and other gentlemen of the neighborhood." His command consisted of seventeen companies. His name heads the Address to General Robertson, when he succeeded Tryon, as Governor of New York. Colonel Hamilton had the care of the two daughters of the Hon. Captain Napier, of the 80th Grenadiers, on the death of their mother, in 1780; his own wife, Alice, granddaughter of Lieutenant-Governor Colden, died the same year. The Colonel sailed for England, December 31, 1783; and the Miss Hamiltons embarked for London, October, 1783. He died at Edinburgh in 1795. A son entered the British Army in the West Indies.

HAMILTON, PAUL, SEN. Of Charleston, South Carolina. An Addresser of Sir Henry Clinton in 1780. Was banished in 1782, and his property confiscated. He went to England before the peace, and died at Pentonville in 1797, in his seventy-second year. The simple record is: "He lost a very considerable fortune, and endured many hardships for his loyalty."

HAMILTON, WILLIAM. Of North Carolina. Captain in the corps of Volunteers. Went to England at the peace. Died in Scotland in 1834.

HAMILTON, ANDREW. Taken up at Kennebec, Maine, on suspicion of affording supplies to the enemy. In August, 1775, his case was examined by the General Court of Massachusetts; and an order passed, that — as he appeared to be a crafty, designing fellow, had formerly held a commission under the Crown, and had been very officious in prying into the management of public affairs — he be "sent to Springfield jail, to have the liberty of the yard during good behavior, otherwise to be put under close confinement," &c.

HAMILTON, THOMAS. Of Virginia. Planter. Died in England in 1781.

HAMM, ANDREW. Died in Westfield, New Brunswick, 1816, aged sixty-two.

HAMMELL, ———. An officer of the American service, and brigade-major to General James Clinton. He was taken prisoner by Sir Henry Clinton, and entered into treasonable designs against his former friends. By the confession of Geake, a confederate, who was arrested, he was promised, for his defection to the Whigs, the office of Colonel of a new Irish regiment, to be raised from deserters from the American Army, and such others as could be enlisted.

HANCOCK, THOMAS. Bookseller, and subsequently a merchant of Boston. Was the son of the Rev. John Hancock, of Lexington, Massachusetts. Relinquishing his business of binding and selling books, he turned his attention to merchandise, generally, and became one of the principal commercial characters of New England. He acquired a large fortune, and, having no children, bequeathed the greater part of his estate to his nephew, John Hancock, who occupies a conspicuous rank among the Whigs of the Revolution. Among his other bequests was that of £1000, for the purpose of founding a professorship of Hebrew and other Oriental languages at Harvard University. He was a member of the House of Representatives, and of the Council of Massachusetts. While going into the Council-chamber, on the 1st of August, 1764, he was seized with apoplexy, and died the same day, aged sixty-two years. He had the character of benevolence, and of liberal religious and political sentiments. He was always on the side of Government; and though his death occurred early in the controversy, party lines were as well defined in Massachusetts in his time as afterwards. Hutchinson sets the sum which he left his nephew at more than £50,000 sterling; besides the reversion of £20,000 after the decease of his widow. From the same authority, it would seem that a considerable proportion of his property was acquired in the Dutch tea trade, which, under the British navigation laws, was illicit; and from supplying the officers of the army, ordnance, and navy.

HANFORD, THOMAS. Of Connecticut. At the peace he went to St. John, New Brunswick, and was a grantee of that city. He became an eminent merchant. In 1795 he was a member of the Loyal Artillery. He died at St. John in 1826, aged seventy-three. Ann, his widow, survived several years, and died at the age of seventy-eight.

HANKS, JOHN. Of New Jersey. A man of whom it is said: "He was worse than Satan himself." He was brought up by a Whig of the name of Beesley, who was his benefactor, and who, in the Revolution, had a son in the militia. This son, Hanks saw engaged with a person of his own political sympathies, and rushed towards him to slay him. The young Whig, in piteous tones, reminded the Tory of their former relations, and begged him to spare his life. Hanks, deaf to the appeal, sternly replied that because of that very intimacy he meant to kill him, and immediately stabbed him. The youth lived long enough to tell his tale to friends who soon came to the spot.

HAPPIE, GEORGE. Of Duchess County, New York. He arrived at St. John, New Brunswick, with his wife, in the spring of 1783, in the ship *Union*.

HARDENBROOK, THEOPHILUS. Of New York. "We had some grand toory rides in this city this week," wrote Peter Elting, June 13, 1776. "Yesterday, several of them ware handled verry roughly being caried trugh the streets on rails, there cloaths tore from there becks and there bodies pritty well mingled the dust." Hardenbrook was one of the victims. "There is hardly a toory face to be seen this morning," said Elting, in continuation.

HARDENBROOK, JOHN. Of New York. An assistant alderman of the city. In 1776, an Addresser of Lord and Sir William Howe.

HARDING, WILLIAM. Went to St. John, New Brunswick, in 1783, and was a grantee of that city. He died there, in 1818, aged seventy-three.

HARDY, ELIAS. He settled at St. John, New Brunswick, and devoted himself to the profession of the law. While at the bar, General Arnold sued Hoyt, his former partner, for slander, and for saying that the traitor burned his warehouse, in order to defraud the company that had underwritten upon the property; and Mr. Hardy was retained as Hoyt's counsel. Arnold's side of the case was managed by the first Ward Chipman, and Jonathan Bliss, both of whom were subsequently on the Bench of New Brunswick. The jury returned a verdict of two shillings and sixpence damages. A gentleman who heard the trial assures me that the public at the time, and that Arnold's own counsel, entertained no doubt of his guilt. In 1792 Mr. Hardy was a member of the House of Assembly. He died at St. John soon after, as papers which relate to the administration of his estate bear the date of 1799.

HARE, LIEUTENANT ———. Of New York. Entered the service of the Crown, and was engaged in the bloody border affrays with Brant and the Johnsons. In 1779 he was seized by the Whigs, tried by a court-martial, convicted and hanged. General Schuyler said, "In executing Hare, we have rid the State of the greatest villain in it." General Clinton remarked that his death gave entire satisfaction to all the inhabitants in the region where his infamous deeds were committed.

HARPER, JAMES. Of Newtown, Queen's County, New York. He was born in Ipswich, England, and emigrated to America ten or fifteen years before the Revolution. Well educated, he was at first a teacher, but finally settled as a farmer. During the war he was not active; yet, it is known that his sympathies were on the side of the Crown. He remained in the country, and died, I conclude, at or near Newtown. His character commanded universal esteem. His wife was of one of the most respectable families of Long Island. His son James, (father of Messrs. Harper & Brothers,) who was a mere lad at the beginning of hostilities, married a daughter of Jacobus Kollyer, who, a Whig, "was wounded in fighting for his country."

The four brothers — grandsons of the subject of this notice — who compose the great American publishing-house, were born at Newtown, and were bred printers. James and John served their time in different offices in New York. Joseph Wesley and Fletcher were apprentices to their elder brothers, and, on coming of age, were admitted partners. In 1853, the establishment of Harper & Brothers was burned, with a loss of $1,000,000, of which the sum of $250,000 only was reimbursed by insurance. Their present (1864) business edifice, which is fire-proof, covers about half an acre of ground, and, including the cellars, is seven stories high. They have in use forty-five presses, of which three are cylinder; and employ six hundred persons, of whom three hundred and fifty are males. They have published nearly if not quite two thousand different works. Their "Harpers' New Monthly Magazine" was first issued in 1850, and in a few years obtained a circulation of one hundred and seventy-five thousand copies. Seven sons of the four brothers have been trained to, and are engaged in the business of the house.

HARPER, THOMAS. He was banished and attainted, and his estate was confiscated. In a memorial dated at London, in 1794, he represented to the British Government that debts due to him in America, at the time of his banishment, were still unpaid, and he desired relief. That proscribed Loyalists could recover sums of money owing to them, appears to have been conceded both in England and America, and several decisions of Courts in the United States affirmed the opinion.

HARPER, ISAAC. Of Boston. At the evacuation, in 1776, he remained in town. Imprisoned, he petitioned the Council, in October of that year, to be released. He could not tell, he said, why he was confined, except that some malicious person or persons had procured his committal. He said further that he was languishing, and in want of many of the necessaries of life; that his wife, daughter, and indeed his whole family, were sickly, without means of support, and would soon become objects of great distress.

HARRINGTON, REV. TIMOTHY. Of Lancaster, Massachusetts. Congregational minister. Graduated at Harvard University in 1737, and after a brief ministry in Swansey, New Hampshire, was settled at Lancaster in 1748. It is related that before the Revolution, he used to pray for the health of "our excellent King George," like other good subjects; that after the war began, he so far forgot himself one Sunday in his pulpit devotions as to fall into his old form, and that recollecting himself, he immediately added — "*O Lord, I mean George Washington.*" It is related, too, that in 1777 a list of "Tories," or proscribed persons, was posted up in town-meeting; that his name was added, on motion of some one who disliked him; and that he rose up, "his hairs touched with silver, and his benignant features kindling into a glow of honest indignation, and, baring his bosom before his people, he exclaimed, — "Strike, strike here with your daggers! I am a true friend to my country." That, however, he was opposed to the Whigs is not disputed. He thought separation would ruin the Colonies. He is represented as one of the most pure and gentle-hearted among New England pastors; as a scholar of remarkable attainments, for the last century; as possessed of warm and Catholic affections; as a man extremely prudent and cautious; and as sometimes yielding too much for the sake of peace. He died in 1795, after a ministry of forty-seven years.

HARRIS, JOSEPH. A runaway mulatto slave, belonging to Mr. Henry King, of Hampton, Virginia. In 1775 he gave information against a smuggling schooner, which was seized in Cherry-stone Creek, and on being threatened with death, was recommended to Captain Squew, of his Majesty's ship *Otter*, and Captain Montague, of the *Fowey*, as a pilot. Montague said he had always appeared very sober and prudent, and that he was a freeman. Harris, it seems, had been a pilot in the waters of Virginia, but was driven from the employment after giving intelligence against the illicit trader.

HARRISON ———. Major, and in command of "a large body of Tories." Marion was often in pursuit, and finally attacked him. In the battle, Harrison received a mortal wound at the hands of Captain Conyers.

HARRISON, THOMAS. "A finished villain," who passed by as many as six different names. While under sentence of death at Boston, and the day before the time appointed for his execution, May 21, 1778, he escaped. He had been "branded" on the forehead, and had lost both ears by "cropping," and wore his hair in a manner to conceal these marks of infamy. He was soon apprehended, and in July shot on Boston Common. On his way from prison, he confessed that his life had been atrociously wicked, but refused to give his real name, because he wished to conceal his fate from his friends. He said, however, that his initials were R. I., and these letters, at his request, were placed on his coffin. His last crime was desertion.

HARRISON, CHARLES. He was a captain in the Second Battalion of New Jersey Volunteers. At the peace he went to St. John, New Brunswick, and was a grantee of that city. He received half-pay. He was lieutenant-colonel in the militia of New Brunswick. His fate is unknown. The late General William Henry Harrison, President of the United States, was a relative.

HARRISON, RICHARD ACKLOM. Of Boston. Son of the Collector of the Customs. In 1768, in the affray that followed the seizure of Hancock's vessel for smuggling wine, he was thrown down, dragged by the hair of his head, and very seriously injured. One account is that he barely escaped death.

HARRISON, JOSEPH. Collector of the Customs at Boston in 1768, and after the seizure of Hancock's sloop in that year, was roughly treated by the mob, and pelted with stones. The windows of his house, which was adjacent to the Common, were also broken; and a large pleasure-boat belonging to him was dragged through the streets and burned near his residence, amidst loud shouts and huzzas. Peter Harrison was Collector of the port of New Haven, Connecticut, and died before June, 1775. The subject of this notice was in England, in 1777, with his wife and daughter.

HART, ———. Of Duke's County, New York. He was apprehended at Providence, Rhode Island, May, 1777, tried for holding a commission under Sir William Howe, and for recruiting for the Royal Army, and executed the second day after his arrest.

HARTSHORN, LAWRENCE. Of Shrewsbury, New Jersey. Fled to New York, where he was a merchant, and where he assisted the Royal cause by communicating important information. At the peace he went to Halifax, Nova Scotia, where he resumed business, and was a member of the House of Assembly and of the Executive Council. He died in 1822, aged sixty-five. His son Lawrence is now (1861) Treasurer of the city of Halifax.

HARTWELL, EDWARD. He was a member of the General Court of Massachusetts in 1771; and Hutchinson speaks of him as one of those on the ministerial side, who, in common times, would have had great weight.

HASELL, JAMES. A member of his Majesty's Council of North Carolina. In March of 1775 he was present in Council, and advised Governor Martin to issue his Proclamation against the Whig Convention to assemble at Newbern on the following 3d of April. "The Board," says the record, "conceiving the highest detestation of such proceedings, were unanimous in advising his Excellency to inhibit such illegal meetings." While Governor Martin was absent at New York, for the benefit of his health, Mr. Hasell, as President of the Council, administered the government; but with less energy and popularity than the Governor. He was also appointed to act as Chief Justice during the absence of Judge Howard.

HASTINGS, JOSEPH STACY. Of New Hampshire. He graduated at Harvard University in 1762, and was ordained at North Hampton in 1767. After a few years he embraced Sandemanianism, and resigned his ministerial office in 1774. He went to Halifax, but returned to Boston, where he kept a grocery store. He died in 1807, while on a journey to Vermont.

HATCH, NATHANIEL. Of Dorchester, Massachusetts. He graduated at Harvard University in 1742; and, subsequently, held the office of Clerk of the Courts. In 1776 he accompanied the British troops to Halifax, at the evacuation of Boston. In 1778 he was proscribed and banished, and in 1779 was included in the Conspiracy Act, by which his estate was confiscated. He died in 1780.

HATCH, HAWES. Of Boston. Brother of Christopher Hatch. He went to Halifax with the Royal Army in 1776. In 1778 he was proscribed and banished. He entered the service, and in 1782 was a captain in De Lancey's Second Battalion. He retired on half-pay at the close of the war, and was a grantee of the city of St. John. For some years after the Revolution he lived at and in the vicinity of Eastport, Maine. He died at Lebanon, New Hampshire, in 1797.

HATCH, CHRISTOPHER. Of Boston. When the Royal Army evacuated that town, March, 1776, cannon, shot, and shells were left on his wharf, and in the dock. In 1778 he was proscribed and banished. He accepted a commission under the Crown, and was a captain in the Loyal American Regiment. He was wounded, and commended for his gallantry. At the peace he retired on half-pay, (about £80 per annum.) He was a grantee of the city of St. John, New Brunswick, but soon after going there established himself as a merchant near the frontier, and, finally, at St. Andrew, Charlotte County. He was a magistrate, and colonel in the militia. He died at St. Andrew, 1819, aged seventy. Elizabeth, his widow, died at the same place, 1830, at the age of seventy-five. His son, the late Harris Hatch, of St. Andrew, was a gentleman of consideration, and held the offices of member of her Majesty's Council, Commissioner of Bankruptcies, Surrogate, Registrar of Deeds, member of the Board of Education, Lieutenant-Colonel in the militia, and Judge of the Court of Common Pleas.

HATFIELD, ISAAC. Of New York. He was Lieutenant-Colonel and Commandant of the Loyal Westchester Volunteers. In January, 1780, at about one o'clock in the morning, a party of Whigs attacked him, and drove him and his men into his quarters, when, from the chambers and other rooms, they kept up a fire upon their assailants, until a straw bed was set in flames. As the building burned, the inmates escaped at the windows. The Colonel, three of his officers, and eleven privates, were taken prisoners. At the peace he went to St. John, New Brunswick, and was a grantee of that city. He subsequently settled in Digby, Nova Scotia, and lived there thirty-six years, until his decease. He died in 1822, aged seventy-four.

HATFIELD, DANIEL. In 1783 was a grantee of St. John, New Brunswick. Mary, his widow, died at Springfield, in that Province, in 1848, aged ninety-one.

HATFIELD, ABRAHAM. Of Westchester County, New York. The Loyalists who adopted the Protest against Whig Congresses and Committees, and pledged their lives and properties to support the King and Constitution, April, 1775, met at his house. A correspondent remarks that he probably died on his farm, at White Plains, early in the war. Gilbert, his oldest son, died at the same place about the year 1828.

HATFIELD, DAVID. Of New York. He went to St. John, New Brunswick, in 1783, and was one of the founders of the city. He used to relate that in 1784 he sold a city lot and a log-house for four dollars; that some lots the same year sold for only one dollar; others for a jug of rum; and that the highest sum paid for choice money in King Street was but twenty dollars. Mr. Hatfield established himself in business, and for half a century was a principal merchant. He died at St. John, in 1843, aged eighty. Ann, his widow, died in 1845, at the age of seventy-seven. Recounting, on one occasion, to a gentleman of Maine, the sufferings and difficulties of himself and his companions in exile on their first arrival in St. John, he was asked by his American friend why he went there. He straightened himself up, and with emotion that brought tears to his eyes, replied, "For my loyalty, sir!" and in a moment added: "Sir, my principles are as dear to me as yours can be to you."

HATFIELD, ———. Of New Jersey. Joined the British; and in 1782 was tried, convicted of treason, and sentenced to death. His case caused an earnest letter from Sir Henry Clinton to Washington.

HATFIELD, JOHN SMITH. Of Elizabethtown, New Jersey. He joined the Royal forces at or in the vicinity of New York in 1778, and by his course of conduct subsequently involved himself in much misery. One infamous act is well authenticated. A Tory, sent out as a spy by the British, was taken within the American lines, regularly tried by a court-martial, found guilty, and executed. This act Hatfield and some other Tories determined to revenge, by retaliating upon one Ball, who, contrary to law, was in the habit of secretly supplying the British camp at Staten island with provisions. The first time that Ball went over to that island, after the execution of the spy, (of which it does not appear that he had any knowledge,) he was seized by Hatfield, against the express orders of the British commanding officer, and carried beyond the British lines, where Hatfield hung him with his own hands. The British officer sent a message to the Whig commander in the vicinity, disavowing the deed, and declaring that those alone who had perpetrated the act ought to suffer for it.

Some time after the war, about the year 1788, Hatfield returned to New Jersey, where the murder of Ball was committed, and was arrested and imprisoned. A witness at the examination testified that he heard Hatfield say that "he had hanged Ball, and wished he had many more Rebels, as he would repeat the deed with pleasure;" and he testified, also, that Hatfield had showed him the tree on which he suspended Ball, and the place where he buried his victim. While Hatfield was in jail at Newark, his debaucheries were excessive, and nearly cost him his life. He was put upon his trial at the regular term of the Court of Bergen County, New Jersey, but no witnesses appeared against him, and he was released from prison on bail, when he immediately fled, and never returned to the State. This case formed a subject of inquiry and comment, in the correspondence between Mr. Jefferson, Secretary of State, and Mr. Hammond, the British Minister, in 1792; the latter adducing the proceedings against Hatfield as one of the alleged infractions of the treaty of peace.

HATFIELD, CORNELIUS. Of New Jersey. Was a captain in the Royal service, and engaged in predatory excursions. Implicated in the murder of Ball. Fled to Nova Scotia. Returned to New Jersey in 1807, and was arrested.

HATHAWAY, EBENEZER, JR. Of Freetown, Massachusetts. He was proscribed and banished. Entering the Royal service, he was a captain; but disagreeing with his colonel, resigned his commission on the promise of a majority in a new corps, but in this he was disappointed. After ascertaining that he was not likely to receive employment on the land, he fitted out and commanded a privateer. While thus engaged he was captured, and with his officers and crew confined in Simsbury Mines. He had been extremely active in annoying the Whigs, and having excited their deepest enmity, was tried for his life, but escaped conviction. His most celebrated feats consisted in carrying off Committee-men, and he frequently went thirty miles in boisterous weather to capture one; and he used to say that "he would willingly run any risk, and incur any fatigue, to make these busy and troublesome creatures his prisoners." He endured much for the cause of the Crown, but was unable to obtain pecuniary recompense, and in consequence of his resignation did not receive a pension. His hardships and wounds during the war ruined his health. He died on the river St. John, New Brunswick, about the year 1811, aged sixty-three. Seven sons survived him, namely: Ebenezer, Warren, Calvin Luther, Charles Reed, James Gilbert, Cushi, and Thomas Gilbert. His wife was of Whig principles, and remained true to them throughout her life, though compelled by the course of events to follow him into hopeless and interminable exile. One of her sons, a gentleman of wealth, who resides (1847) in New Brunswick, has related to me the following interesting incident: "My father," said he, "was the son of a Tory captain; my mother, the daughter of a Whig major; and the two families were thus divided, even to some of the collateral branches. The political discussions were, of consequence, frequent and warm. On the birth of one of my brothers, it was insisted, on the one side, that he should receive a Whig, and on the other, a Tory name. Neither party would yield, and after many disputes, my father proposed to take the Bible, and give the child the first proper name he should see on opening it. This was assented to; the name happened to be Cushi, and Cushi was my brother called during his life."

HATHAWAY, SHADRACH, and CALVIN. Of Freetown, Massachusetts. Were proscribed and banished in 1778. They both died in exile; the former during the war, on Long Island, New York.

HATHAWAY, LUTHER. Of Freetown, Massachusetts. Brother of Ebenezer Hathaway. In 1778 he was proscribed and banished. He was in the Royal service as lieutenant of a corps called the Loyal New Englanders. He settled in Nova Scotia, and died at Cornwallis in 1833.

HAWXHURST, WILLIAM. Of New York. Merchant, "dealing in pig-iron, anchors, potash, kettles, negro wenches and children, horses," &c. In 1776 he was an Addresser of Lord and Sir William Howe.

HAY, JOHN. Of Massachusetts. Died at St. John, New Brunswick, in 1812, at the age of forty-three.

HAYES, JOHN, and WILLIAM. Of New York. John was seized at Long Island, in 1775, sent to Massachusetts, and confined within the limits of the town of Lunenburg. At the peace, accompanied by his family of three persons, he went from New York to Shelburne, Nova Scotia, where he was living about the year 1805. William, with a family of six, went to the same place at the same time.

HAYTER, WILLIAM. At the peace he went to St. John, New Brunswick, and was a grantee of that city. He died there in 1817, aged eighty-eight years.

HAZARD, THOMAS. Of Rhode Island. A merchant of wealth. He abandoned home, fled to the British, and in 1782 was in New York. His wife Eunice, with seven young children, were reduced to great distress; and, on petition for relief, the General Assembly directed that the rents of a part of his property should be paid to her. His estate was confiscated; but, had he not "indignantly refused to make a satisfactory submission," it might have been restored. He went to England in 1785; and the British Government, in consideration of his loyalty and sacrifices, granted him five thousand acres of land in New Brunswick. He died aged, at St. John, New Brunswick, in 1804.

The name of Thomas was so common in the Hazard family, that each one who bore it had a particular appellation, of necessity; and Updike has a pleasant story on the subject. Thus, — *College* Tom was a student; *Bedford* Tom lived in New Bedford; *Barley* Tom boasted of the barley he raised on an acre; *Virginia* Tom married in Virginia; *Little Neck* Tom lived on a Neck so called; *Nailer* Tom was a blacksmith, and made excellent nails; *Rock* Tom occupied the Rocky farm; *Fiddle-head* Tom, had a head which resembled a Dutch fiddle reversed; *Pistol* Tom, was wounded by the explosion of a pistol; *Derrick* Tom, used the word derrick as a by-word, &c., &c. The subject of the above notice was *Virginia Tom*. Thirty-two "Tom Hazards" were living at one time.

HAZEN, JOHN. Removed from Massachusetts to New Brunswick in 1775. He became a magistrate, and died in the county of Sunbury in 1828, aged seventy-three.

HEAD, SIR EDMUND, Baronet. He was banished, and his estate was confiscated. In 1794 he applied to the British Government, in a petition dated at London, to interpose for the recovery of some large debts due to him in America at the time of his banishment. His father was a merchant of London. He died in 1796; and was succeeded by his son John, Rector of Raleigh in Sussex, and Curate of Egerton, Kent, who married Jane, only child and heiress of Thomas Walker, and died in 1838. Sir Edmund Walker Head, third Baronet, who was born in 1805, married a daughter of the Rev. Philip Yorke, followed Sir William Colebrook (1848) as Lieutenant-Governor of New Brunswick, and is now (1860) Governor-General of British America, is the son of Sir John and Lady Jane. The first wife of the first

Baronet was Mary, only daughter of Daniel Raineaux, of Dublin; the second, Dorothy, daughter of Maximilian Western, of Coke Thorpe, County of Oxford.

HEAD, FREDERICK. Of Long Island, New York. A prisoner prior to August, 1779. While deprived of his liberty, his house was plundered four times; the last marauders took clothing and provisions to the value of £200.

HEATH, ANDREW. Of Germantown, Pennsylvania. Dressed in a green uniform, and thus intending probably to escape detection, he acted as a guide to the Royal Army, previous to the battle there; and absented himself until the peace.

HECHT, FREDERICK WILLIAM. Of New York. Lived on Queen (now Pearl) Street. In 1776, an Addresser of Lord and Sir William Howe; and commissioned the same year a captain in the Royal service. By birth a German.

HEDGE, REV. LEMUEL. Of Warwick, Massachusetts. Congregational minister. He graduated at Harvard University in 1759, and was ordained the following year. In 1775 he was disarmed, and ordered to confine himself to Warwick. He died at Hardwick, in 1777, in the forty-fourth year of his age, of a fever, which, as is said, was caused by the excitement and fatigue endured by him when in the hands of a lawless band of thirty or forty persons, who seized him, and carried him to Northampton. Joseph Warren was his classmate and friend; and Holland relates that the Whig had in his pocket, when he fell on Bunker's Hill, a letter " from Mr. Hedge, in which he professed a sincere interest in the liberty of his country, although he admitted his doubts in regard to the issue of the Revolutionary struggle."

HELME, JAMES. Of Rhode Island. Chief Justice of the Supreme Court. He was elected by the General Assembly in 1767, or the year preceding. Rome, in his celebrated letter, affects to believe that he was the only upright man on that Bench; and predicted, that, " For his honesty and candor, I am persuaded he will be deposed at the next election, unless they [the Whigs, I suppose] should be still in hopes of making a convert of him." He remained in office until the Royal Government was at an end. He died at South Kingston, Rhode Island, in 1777. His wife was a daughter of Adam Powell.

HELMER, ———. Of Tryon (now Montgomery) County, New York. He accompanied Sir John Johnson to Canada, when the Baronet violated his parole and fled; and was one of the party who, in 1778, returned to Johnstown for the purpose of securing some of Sir John's valuable effects. While bearing off the iron-chest, he injured his ankle, and was compelled to go to his father's house, where he remained concealed. But in the spring of 1779 he was arrested as a spy, tried, and sentenced to death, chiefly on his own admissions to the Court.

HEMEON. Of New Jersey. Four went from New York in 1783 to Shelburne, Nova Scotia: namely, Adam, who lost £600 by his loyalty, and who had a family of ten; George, of whom I glean nothing; Henry, whose family consisted of five; and Philip, who died in 1837, aged eighty-nine. A descendant of one of these has been Mayor of Halifax.

HENDERSON, THOMAS. In 1782 he was a lieutenant in the Loyal American Regiment. He went to New Brunswick at the peace, and in 1803 lived at the island of Campo-Bello, where he was an officer of the Customs. He removed to St. Andrew, in the same Province, and died there, 1828, aged seventy-seven.

HENEY, JOSIAH. Was born near Portland, Maine, in 1754, and died at Deer Island, New Brunswick, in 1836, aged eighty-two years. He went to Halifax in the Revolution, and married at Windsor; but returned to Maine, and resided for some time at Castine. Changing his abode again, he lived at the place where he deceased about forty years. His son Archibald, who was long a packet-master between Eastport and St. John, died at Deer Island in 1848, aged sixty-two, leaving a wife and large family. Two other sons, Josiah and Henry, are now (1850) residents of that island.

HENLEY, JAMES. Of Maryland. In 1782 he was an

ensign in the Maryland Loyalists, and adjutant of the corps. He retired at the peace, when he was a lieutenant, on half-pay. In 1783 he embarked at New York for Nova Scotia; with a part of his own regiment and a part of the second battalion of De Lancey's brigade, in the transport ship *Martha*, and was wrecked, near the end of the passage, off Tusket River. Of about one hundred and seventy men, women, and children, sixty-five were saved. Lieutenant Henley, Lieutenant Stirling, and Doctor Stafford, got upon a piece of the wreck, and floated at sea two days and two nights, nearly to the waist in water, during which time Stirling perished. On the third day, the survivors drifted to an island, where they remained seven days, poorly clad, and without fire and food. The sixty-two others who escaped, were taken from rafts by four fishing vessels which belonged to Massachusetts, and landed at Yarmouth, Nova Scotia.

HENNIGAN. Of New York. Three went to St. John, New Brunswick, at the peace, and were grantees of the city; namely: Adam, a native of Germany, and his two sons, Christopher and Michael. The last abandoned property in New York estimated to be worth £5000.

HENNY, ———. Captain in the South Carolina Royalists. Killed in 1779, during the siege of Savannah.

HEPBURN, JAMES. Of North Carolina. He was attached to a corps of Loyalists as secretary, and in 1776 was taken prisoner and confined. He was in New York in 1782, and a notary-public.

HERKIMER, COLONEL HANJOST, or JOHN JOOST. Of New York. He was a son of Johan Jost Herkimer, one of the Palatines of the German Flats, New York; and a brother of the Whig General, Nicholas Herkimer. He served in various county offices until the Revolution. His property was confiscated. He went to Canada, and died there before 1787.

HERON, ———. Of Reading, Connecticut. He was a member of the Legislature, and of the County Correspondence, as late as April, 1780. On the 4th of September of that year, he went to New York with a flag of truce, and while there, gave "information" to the Royal officers. At the moment of his treachery he was employed in the office of Public Accounts, and possessed the confidence of the Whigs. His own declarations, as stated in the paper before me, were, that "He was ever an enemy to the declaration of independency; but he said little, except to the most trusty Loyalists. He stands well with the officers of the Continental Army; with General Parsons he is intimate, and is not suspected. He was at an interview between General Parsons and Mr. Izard, who arrived in Terney's Fleet, and went on to Philadelphia," &c., &c. The "information" occupies several printed pages.

HERSEY, ABNER. Of Barnstable, Massachusetts. Physician. Of some distinction in his profession; just in his dealings; and of rigid morality. But, eccentric, whimsical, and capricious, domestic happiness and social intercourse were strangers in his family. He lived principally on milk and vegetables, and wore a coat made of seven tanned calf-skins. He railed at the fashions of the time, and he railed at the people with whom he mingled. Of his *sincerity*, we have the following instance. The widow of his brother and a female friend proposed to visit him, and so informed him by letter. He answered:—"Madam, I can't have you here: I am sick, and my wife is sick; I have no hay nor corn for your horses; I have no servants, and I had rather be chained to a galley-oar than wait on you myself." He died in 1787, aged sixty-five. His will is one of the strangest documents on record; and the Legislature interferred, finally, to put an end to his absurd scheme to perpetuate his estate. He was the founder of the professorship of the theory and practice of medicine in Harvard University. Hannah, his widow, died at Barnstable in 1794, aged sixty-four.

HEWES, SHUBAEL. Of Boston. The Council of Massachusetts ordered his arrest, April, 1776. Prior to the evacuation, he was chief butcher to the British Army. He died at Boston in 1813, aged eighty-one.

HEWLETT, RICHARD. Of Hempstead, New York. He was a captain in the French war, and assisted in the capture of Fort Frontenac. In the Revolutionary strife, he took an early and active part on the side of the King. In 1775 he told a distinguished Whig that he had mustered his command a few days previously, when, "had your battalion appeared, we should have warmed their sides." Before the close of that year he received from the *Asia* ship-of-war a great quantity of ammunition, some small-arms, and a cannon. In March, 1776, his course had rendered him very obnoxious to the Whigs; and General Lee directed that "Richard Hewlett is to have no conditions offered to him, but is to be secured without ceremony." He accepted a commission when De Lancey's corps was raised, and was lieutenant-colonel of the third of De Lancey's Battalions.

In command of the garrison of two hundred and sixty men at Setauket, Long Island, New York, in 1777, immediate surrender was demanded by General Parsons. The Colonel asked his soldiers if he should submit. "No!" was the response. "Then," said he, "I'll stick to you as long as there's a man left." After a cannonade of two or three hours, the Whigs retreated; and the Colonel was complimented for his good conduct in general orders. Some months after, the post was abandoned. January 2, 1778, "one hundred and thirty Tories from the west end of Long Island, commanded" by him, "came down to Southold, Oyster Pond," and robbed the inhabitants of clothing, money, grain, cattle, &c. At the close of the war he retired on half-pay, and settled in New Brunswick. He was a grantee of the city of St. John, and its mayor. He died on the river St. John, near Gagetown, in 1789. His widow, whose maiden name was Mary Townsend, died on Long Island, New York, in 1819, aged eighty-five.

HEWLETT, THOMAS. Of New York. Son of Colonel Richard. He was a captain in the New York Volunteers, and in 1780 was killed at Hanging Rock, while looking out of the loophole of a block-house, to see what the "Rebels" were doing.

HEYDEN, S. A captain in the King's Rangers. In 1777, made prisoner, violated his parole, and sent to the Council of Pennsylvania. In November, 1782, he had retired to the Island of St. John, Gulf of St. Lawrence, where he invited other Loyalists to follow him.

HICKEY, EDWARD. Went to Cape Breton; returned to the United States, and died at Boston in 1793.

HICKEY, THOMAS. In 1776 a plot of the disaffected to the Whig cause extended to Washington's own camp, and part of his guard were engaged in it. Hickey was one of the number. He was tried, and having been convicted by the unanimous opinion of a court-martial, was executed on the 28th of June of that year, in a field between McDougall's and Huntington's camps, near the *Bowery Lane*, New York, in the presence of nearly twenty thousand spectators.

HICKS, JONATHAN. Of Massachusetts. He graduated at Harvard University in 1770, and fitted himself for the practice of medicine. In 1773 or 1774 he was at Gardinerston, (now Gardiner, Maine,) where he " expressed himself highly against Whig Committees, calling them Rebels, and using other opprobious language against the people who appeared for liberty." He was afterwards at Plymouth, Massachusetts, and continued the same course of conduct, and " at certain times appeared very high, and once drew his sword, or spear upon certain persons." The evening after the battle of Lexington, he left Plymouth, and took shelter with a detachment of the Royal troops at Marshfield, and finally retired to Boston. Soon after, General Gage despatched the sloop *Polly* to Nova Scotia for supplies, and he embarked; designing, as he said, to remain at Halifax, " if he could find business, in order to be out of the noise." On the passage, the *Polly* was captured, and Hicks was sent prisoner to the Provincial Congress. That body ordered a Committee to investigate his case in June, 1775; and as Hicks himself owned that his conduct had, on the whole, been that of a person " whom the people for liberty call a Tory," he was sent under guard to Concord, and committed to jail. He entered the Royal service, subsequently, and was a surgeon. He died at Demarara, in 1826.

HICKS, CHARLES. Of Long Island, New York. Arrested by order of the Provincial Congress, and sent to Connecticut; but released on parole, and under recognizance of £500 to be of good behavior. In 1780 an Addresser of Governor Robertson. The same year he was in command of a party of Loyal militia; and some Whigs having captured a schooner in Jamaica Bay, in August, he assembled his company, and with a few volunteers, in two boats, went in quest of them. He offered the "Rebels" good quarters, provided they would surrender; this they refused, and a smart action ensued, in which the Whigs were overcome. They accordingly accepted the terms at first rejected, and became prisoners. Twenty-eight thus fell into Hicks's hands, of whom one was a clergyman.

HICKS, JOHN. Printer, of Boston. Was born in Cambridge, Massachusetts, and was proscribed and banished in 1778. His father was a Whig, and lost his life in the affair of Lexington. John, it was supposed, was a Whig also; but in 1773, he and Nathaniel Mills bought the "Massachusetts Gazette and Post-Boy" of Green and Russell, and devoted it to the support of the measures of the Ministry. His paper was conducted with much ability, spirit, and vigor. Among the writers for it were persons of great political knowledge and judgment. It was believed at the time that officers of the British Army were likewise contributors to its columns. Hicks went to Halifax in 1776, and continued with the Royal troops at different posts throughout the war, supporting, professionally, the side which he last espoused; and on the evacuation of New York, went again to Halifax, Nova Scotia, where he remained a few years, and then returned to Boston. Having acquired considerable property by his business during the Revolution, he purchased an estate at Newton, Massachusetts, on which he resided until his death.

HICKS, GILBERT. Sheriff of Bucks, Pennsylvania. In 1776, and in the fall of that year, by calling court in the King's name, gave great offence to the Whigs. A mob assembled to hang him, but he escaped their hands; and after concealing himself in the woods for several weeks, effected his escape. Attainted of treason and estate confiscated. He "went to Nova Scotia, where he received some land, and an annual pension. Some few years after he was assassinated on his way home, after receiving his pay."

HILL, REV. ABRAHAM. Of Shutesbury, Massachusetts. Congregational minister. He graduated at Harvard University in 1737, and was ordained in 1742. After a ministry of about thirty-four years, and in 1776, his flock refused to hear him preach. "His Toryism was most offensive." He was put in the pound, and herrings were thrown over to him to eat. In 1778 he was dismissed. Subsequently, he sued for arrears of salary, and recovered judgment. He was the only Loyalist in town of any note. Until compelled, he refused to pay the taxes imposed by the Whigs; and brought an action in the Court of Common Pleas to regain the amount paid against his will. He died in 1788.

HILL, WILLIAM. Of Massachusetts. Embarked with his family of sixteen persons at Boston for Halifax, with the Royal Army. At the peace, accompanied by his family of eighteen persons, and by five servants, he went from New York to Shelburne, Nova Scotia, where the Crown granted him fifty acres of land, one town and one water lot. His losses in consequence of his loyalty were estimated at £330.

HILL, ERSKINE. Of Connecticut. Member of the Reading Loyalist Association.

HILL, JOHN. Of Long Island, New York. In 1782 he was an Inspector in the Superintendent Department established at New York, and was stationed at Brooklyn. He settled at Digby, Nova Scotia, at the peace, and died there without family.

HILL, RICHARD. Brother of John; also settled at Digby, was a magistrate, and Acting Collector of the Customs. Administration on his estate advertised, June, 1808.

HILL, HENRY. Of Bucks County, Pennsylvania; and Patrick, of Wyoming; attainted of treason and property confiscated; John, also attainted, but surrendered himself and was discharged.

HILL, THOMAS. Of Wyoming. It is stated that he was engaged in the Massacre in 1778, and that with his own hands he killed his mother and several other relatives; but, like the story of similar deeds by the Terrys, the relation is of doubtful truth.

HILL, JOSHUA. Of Delaware. Attainted of treason and estate confiscated. At the peace, accompanied by his family of three persons, and by one servant, he went from New York to Shelburne, Nova Scotia, where the Crown granted him fifty acres of land, one town and one water lot. His losses in consequence of his loyalty were estimated at £10,000.

HILL, RICHARD. Of South Carolina. The Act of 1782 confiscates estate in the possession of his heirs or devisees.

HILT, WILLIAM. Died at St. John, New Brunswick, in 1822, aged seventy.

HILTON, BENJAMIN, JR. Of Schenectady, New York. Attorney-at-law. In December, 1775, he wrote a letter to Alexander White, Sheriff of the county of Tryon, which, in the opinion of the Committee of the city and county of Albany, contained expressions of "unwarrantable exultation in the distress and defeat which he supposed a part of the Continental Army had sustained" in Canada; and which caused various proceedings against him. At last, the Committee voted their "disdain of his impotent attempts" to traduce the Whig troops in question; and "to dismiss him from further prosecution."

HOGG, JOHN. Of North Carolina. One of the last official acts of Governor Martin was to commission this gentleman as a magistrate for the county of Orange. The Whigs at this time (1775) had so far obtained the ascendency in the public councils, as to cause his Excellency to dissolve the Assembly; and no new House was elected during the remaining period of his administration.

HOLLAND, SAMUEL. Surveyor-General of the Colonies north of Virginia. A major in the French war, and engaged in the expeditions against Louisburg and Quebec. When Wolfe fell, he was near. In 1773 he announced his intention to make Perth Amboy, New Jersey, his head-quarters, and wrote to a gentleman there to inquire for houses to accommodate himself and his assistants. He had then completed the surveys as far west as Boston. Proposed in 1774 to get round Cape Cod and to New London; and said it would be at least six years before he should be able to finish his labors. In 1775, he wrote Lord Dartmouth that he was ready to run the line between Massachusetts and New York. By a communication laid before the Provincial Congress of Massachusetts in July, 1775, it appears that he had loaned to Alexder Shepard, junior, (who also was a surveyor,) a plan or survey of Maine, which Shephard disliked to return, fearing that it might be used in a manner prejudicial to the Whig cause, as Holland was an adherent of the Crown, and then in New Jersey. Congress considered the matter, and by resolve, recommended to Shephard to retain Holland's plan, and another which he himself had made, until leave should be granted for other disposition of them. Major Holland went to Lower Canada, where he resumed his duties of Surveyor-General, in which capacity he served nearly fifty years. He died in that Province in 1801, and, at the time of his decease, was a member of the Executive and Legislative Councils.

HOLLAND, STEPHEN. Of Londonderry, New Hampshire. He was a colonel in the militia, a member of the House of Assembly, and a man of note. In 1775 he appeared at a town-meeting, and made a written declaration that the charges against him, as being an enemy to his country, were false; and concluded with saying that "he was ready to assist his countrymen in the glorious cause of liberty, at the risk of his life and fortune." But in 1778 his estate was confiscated, and he was proscribed and banished. He was a gentleman of culture, easy address, and influence. He went to England, thence to Ireland, and died soon after the peace.

HOLLAND, JOHN. Of New Hampshire. Proscribed and

banished. A Loyalist of this name was sheriff of the county of St. John, New Brunswick, in 1792, and died in that Province in 1806.

HOLLAND, RICHARD. Of Massachusetts. He was proscribed and banished. In 1782 he was an ensign of infantry in the Queen's Rangers. At the peace he went to St. John, New Brunswick, and was a grantee of that city. He settled subsequently on the coast, at Dipper Harbor, where he now (1843) lives, and receives half-pay.

HOLLIDAY, WILLIAM. Of Charleston, South Carolina. In 1780, Judge Pendleton, of South Carolina, as was alleged, violated his parole to Sir Henry Clinton, and fled from Charleston, and Lord Cornwallis threatened to retaliate upon his Whig prisoners. The case was submitted to Congress, and the act of escape justified, on the ground that Holliday, at the head of a band of Tories, had determined to seize the Judge in his quarters in the night, and hang him at the town-gate.

HOLLINGSWORTH, ———. Of Georgia. Captain in the corps of the infamous McGirth. In 1780, while on an expedition to South Carolina, his party murdered seventeen men on their farms, in one or two days; and, for miles, the country was a scene of ruin. Disappointed at not finding a particular Whig of whom they were in quest, they took the flint out of the lock of a musket, and put his wife's thumb in its place, and applied the screw, in order to compel her to disclose the place of his concealment. Two Loyalists of this surname, Timothy and Valentine, were attainted of treason in Georgia, and lost their estates by confiscation. The above was probably one of them.

HOLT, MOSES. Captain in the Pennsylvania Loyalists. After the war he settled in William Henry (now Sorel) district of Montreal, Canada, where he acquired valuable real estate, and was a magistrate. He received half-pay. He died at William Henry in 1799. His first wife bore him William Johnson, and two daughters, Beeda and Melinda. His second wife, Esther Solomon, was the mother of Guy Solomon and George Garth.

HOLT, WILLIAM JOHNSON. Son of the preceding, ensign in Ferguson's Rangers. This corps formed a part of the army of Burgoyne at the time of his surrender, and, with other Provincial prisoners, retired to Canada, by permission of Gates. The subject of this notice settled in Montreal, where he held the lucrative office of Inspector of Pot and Pearl Ashes, and where he accumulated considerable property. He received half-pay for nearly fifty years. He died at Montreal in 1826. By his first wife, (Ruah Stevens, of Pittsfield, Massachusetts,) he was the father of a large family of sons and daughters; by his second wife, (Elizabeth Cuyler,) he left no issue. His sixth son, Charles Adolphus, alone has surviving male children, of whom the eldest, Charles Gates Holt is (1864) a distinguished counsellor-at-law, and a gentleman of the highest respectability, at Quebec. In February, 1864, he was appointed one of her " Majesty's Counsel learned in the Law," and thus is entitled to wear the " silk robe."

HOLYOKE, EDWARD AUGUSTUS. Of Salem, Massachusetts. Son of President Holyoke, of Harvard University; was born August 13, 1728, and graduated in 1746. His first wife was a daughter of Colonel Benjamin Pickman, of Salem; his second, of Nathaniel Viall, of Boston. He was an Addresser of Hutchinson, on his departure, and of Gage, on his arrival, and for addressing the first became a Recanter. He committed himself no more, and was allowed to remain in the country without molestation. He died at Salem, March 31, 1829, aged one hundred years, having practised medicine for seventy-nine years. On the day he was a century old, his professional brethren of Boston and Salem, to the number of about fifty, gave him a public dinner.

HOMER, JOSEPH. In 1776 he accompanied the Royal Army from Boston to Halifax; and immediately fixing his abode in Barrington, Nova Scotia, lived there ever after. He held the offices of Collector of his Majesty's Customs, and of Collector of Colonial Duties, and was a magistrate. He died in 1837, at the age of eighty-one.

HONEYMAN, JAMES. Of Rhode Island. Last Royal Advocate-General of the Court of Vice-Admiralty in that Colony. His father was Rector of Trinity Church, Newport. He was born in 1710. Educated to the bar, he acquired distinction early; and, while yet young, was elected Attorney-General, and held the office until it was abolished, in 1741. Subsequently, he was much employed in public business; and finally appointed Advocate-General. He "was a sound and able lawyer, and enjoyed an extensive practice through the Colony." His wife was Elizabeth Golding. He died in 1788, at the age of sixty-seven. The husbands of his daughters adhered to the Royal side, and much that he bequeathed them was confiscated; but on petition, the Legislature made restoration.

HOOD, ZACHARIAH. Stamp-Master for Maryland. In 1765 a mob of several hundred pulled down his house in Annapolis, which he was repairing, as was supposed, for a stamp-office. Unwilling to relinquish the post, because he wanted its emoluments, yet terrified, he fled to New York, and, for entire safety, lived in the Fort. Assailed even there by the "Sons of Liberty," he consented to resign, and to swear that he was sincere in renouncing his odious office.

HOOGHTELING, WILLIAM. He deserted from a Whig regiment raised in New York, at the instance, as he averred, of his stepfather and of others of his family, and became a marauder, or Tory robber. In May, 1779, he was executed at Albany.

HOOK, JOHN. A wealthy Scot, living in Campbell County, Virginia. When Cornwallis had invaded the State in 1781, an American Commissary, one Venables, seized two of Hook's cattle for the use of the Whigs. After the peace, Hook, who was generally believed to be unfriendly to the cause, sued Venables for trespass on the case, the act of taking the oxen having been, it would seem, high-handed and not in due form of law. Patrick Henry was for the defence, William Cowan for the plaintiff. Mr. Henry, by exciting the passions of the jury against the alleged Tory predilections of the plaintiff, gained the case. After dwelling on the shouts of triumph which hailed the final success of Washington's arms, he continued: "but hark! what notes of discord are these which disturb the general joy, and silence the acclamations of victory?—they are the notes of *John Hook*, bawling hoarsely through the American camp, *beef! beef! beef!*"

HOOPER, WILLIAM. Of Boston. He was settled first as a Congregational minister of the West Church; but succeeded Mr. Davenport as Rector of Trinity Church in 1747. A number of Congregational clergymen became Episcopalians about the same time. He was a man of eloquence and talents. He died in 1767. The Rev. Doctor Walter was his successor. His son, William, graduated at Harvard University in 1760, studied law with James Otis, emigrated to North Carolina after the Stamp Act troubles, and became a member of Congress, and a signer of the Declaration of Independence. Mr. Jefferson has left behind him the recorded opinion, distinctly and pointedly expressed, that in the Congress of 1776 he was a rank Tory. Possibly it was so; but most men — very likely — will regard William Hooper the younger, as of a very different political school. The fact that he was a signer, affords very *questionable* proof of his attachment to the British Crown, at the least. And some persons — not improbably — will be ready to ask, "If the signers of the Declaration of Independence were Tories, where shall we look for the Whigs?"

HOOPER, GEORGE. Of North Carolina. Brother of William Hooper, a signer of the Declaration of Independence. He took refuge in South Carolina. In the winter of 1782 he was at Charleston, "in suspense what to do;" and in the summer of that year, at Wilmington, with his family, in a flag of truce. In 1783 he visited North Carolina again, and was suffered to live unmolested several weeks; but a warrant for his arrest was issued, finally, and he departed. Accompanied by his wife, he went to Wilmington still again, in 1785, and saw his brother William, who said: "Our meeting was awkward, distant, and distressing to me." It was remarked of Mrs. Hooper, that she had grown "more easy and affable."

A lawyer of note in North Carolina, who wrote many sneering and querulous letters, said in 1787 : " In this quarter, where we are not famed for any intimacy with Scripture, we were for some time at a loss to know who Gallio was; but a New England man, one George Hooper, found in the eighteenth chapter of the Acts of the Apostles, that Gallio, before whom the Jews brought Paul, was deputy of Achaia. The application would have better suited his purpose, had the Judge substituted the Assembly in the place of Judge Gallio, himself for the Apostle, and the lawyers for the Jews; but the fool had not understanding sufficient to apply the text, so as to prove from Scripture his own righteousness. Having taken the name of Judge Gallio upon himself, it may very properly be applied to him for the future." The Loyalist, at this period, seems to have had a home in or near Wilmington, and to have been in the toils of the law. At the close of the year 1787, his Whig brother, William, remarked: "George, after court, called Spencer, with due spirit and decency, to account for expressions which he had made use of respecting himself and Maclaine in Burgynn's business. Spencer degraded himself." Our Loyalist, later in life, was a distinguished merchant at Wilmington, and the first President of the Bank of Cape Fear.

HOOPER, THOMAS. Of North Carolina. Brother of William Hooper, a signer of the Declaration of Independence. An Addresser of Sir Henry Clinton, at Charleston, in 1780. In February, 1782, he was still in that city, transacting a large business, and rapidly accumulating a fortune; but the expectation was, that his wife would soon embark for England, and that he would follow her. In July, 1785, they had been abroad, and had returned to Wilmington, North Carolina. Both were in consumption, "both were going to Rhode Island, — flying from death, which was at no great distance from them!" "Mrs. Hooper," wrote one who then saw her, "is a very fine woman, much polished by her tour through Britain ; alas! yet but a little while, and how useless all her accomplishments." Possibly, they recovered ; for on the last day of the year 1787, I find that husband and wife were guests of their brother William, at Point Repose, North Carolina, without a word about their health.

HOOPER, JOSEPH. Of Marblehead, Massachusetts. Was a graduate of Harvard University, of the class of 1763. In 1774 he was an Addresser of Hutchinson, and in 1775 abandoned home for England, where he was a manufacturer of paper, and where he died in 1812. Several persons of Marblehead of the name of Hooper were Addressers of Hutchinson. To wit: Robert; Robert, Jr.; Robert the third, and Sweet. One of the Robert's died in that town in 1790; and another in 1814, aged seventy-two.

HOPKINS, ———. Of Georgia. In 1775 he ridiculed the Whig Committee of Safety personally, and spoke in contempt of their objects. In consequence of which, he was tarred and feathered by a mob, who, to complete his disgrace, placed him in a cart, which was illuminated for the occasion, and carried through the streets of Savannah, attended by a crowd, for several hours. In 1778, John Hopkins, of Georgia, was attainted and lost his estate by confiscation; probably the same.

HOPTON, JOHN. Of Charleston, South Carolina. An Addresser of Sir Henry Clinton in 1780. He was also a Petitioner to be armed on the side of the Crown. He was banished, and in 1782 his property was confiscated. Prior to the Revolution he was a merchant. At the evacuation of Charleston he left the country. The British Government made him a partial allowance for his losses. He died in 1831.

HORRY, DANIEL. Of South Carolina. In 1774, after the port of Boston was shut by Act of Parliament, he was a member of the committee of the city of Charleston to receive donations for the sufferers in that town. In 1782 his estate was amerced twelve per cent.

HORSEMANDEN, DANIEL. Of New York. He was recorder of the city; and, subsequently, President of the Council, and Chief Justice of the Colony. In 1773, at which time he held the last-named office, he was appointed a commissioner under the great seal of England, to inquire into the affair of burning the King's ship *Gaspee*, by a party of Whigs of Rhode Island, the previous year. In 1776, he, with Oliver De·Lancey, and nine hundred and forty-six others of the city and county of New York, were Addressers of Lord Howe; and on the same day (October 16,) he addressed Governor Tryon. The same year, the latter said that the Chief Justice was very old and feeble, and his infirmities would probably prevent his attendance at the meetings of the Council.

In 1777 Judge Horsemanden wrote Tryon, that when he went to Newport about the *Gaspee*, he was ill of rheumatism, was unable to walk without help, and at a time of life drawing near fourscore; that he was obliged to take his wife, carriage, and two horses with him, &c.; that the Commissioners adjourned to the next year, when he went again "under the like circumstances;" that he had expended upwards of £200 of his own money on these occasions, "which remains out of pocket this day, and hitherto my trouble for nothing;" while his regular salary as Chief Justice was much in arrears, &c., and he solicited the Governor's good offices with Lord George Germain. The Judge died in 1778, and was buried in Trinity church-yard. His "History of the Negro Plot, or New York Conspiracy," was republished in 1810. Of the conspirators of whom this publication treats, fourteen were burnt and eighteen were hanged. He was engaged in the public affairs of New York for a period of thirty years.

HORSFIELD, THOMAS. Of New York. In July, 1783, he was at New York, and one of the fifty-five petitioners. [See *Abijah Willard*.] He went to St. John, New Brunswick, soon after, and was one of the grantees of that city. In that Province he was a magistrate. He died at St. John, 1819, aged seventy-nine. Ann, his wife, died in 1815, at the age of seventy-two. Mr. Horsfield left a large and valuable estate. His son James, also a Loyalist, accompanied him to New Brunswick, and received a grant of land.

HOUGH, BENJAMIN. A magistrate of the New Hampshire Grants, now Vermont. He was seized, beaten, stripped of his property, driven from his family, and compelled to take refuge in New York. Furnished with a document of which the following is a copy, he began his sad journey: —

"Sunderland, 30 January, 1775.

"This may certify the inhabitants of New Hampshire Grants, that Benjamin Hough has this day received a full punishment for his crimes committed heretofore against this country, and our inhabitants are ordered to give him, the said Hough, a free and unmolested passage toward the city of New York, or to the westward of our Grants, he behaving as becometh. Given under hands the day and date aforesaid.

"ETHAN ALLEN.
"SETH WARNER."

When Ethan Allen was both judge and executive officer, there can be no doubt of the sufficiency of punishment. Hough, it seems, was tied to a tree and received two hundred lashes, and he was told that if he returned from his banishment he should receive five hundred lashes more. Among the grave offences charged against him was, that he had informed the Governor of New York of the mobbing and injury of Benjamin Spencer, Esquire, a gentleman of his own political sentiments.

HOUSECKER, NICHOLAS. Of Lancaster County, Pennsylvania. Attainted of treason and property confiscated. He was originally a Whig, and was commissioned a major in Wayne's command; but went over to the enemy. It is said of him, that he was "a soldier of fortune, and a true mercenary."

HOUSTON, SIR PATRICK. Of Georgia. In 1777 the Committee of Safety for the parish of St. John, gave permission to him and two others to ship rice to Surinam, under bond and security that it should not be landed in a British port; but, by the agency of William Panton, a Loyalist mentioned in this work, the destination of the vessels was changed, and the bond was forfeited. The result was that Houston was included in the Banishment and Confiscation Act. He had an estate in South Carolina, which, in 1782, was amerced twelve per cent. I find the death of Sir *George* Houston, Baronet, in Georgia, in 1795.

HOUSTON, JOHN. Of Bedford, New Hampshire. Minister. An early and zealous Loyalist. In 1775 the town voted to shut his church. He replied in writing, in a manner discreditable. Insisting upon occupying his pulpit, the doors and windows were fastened against him. Finally, "the people" elected a committee to inflict the disgraceful punishment of the "wooden horse." Compelled to mount the rail, a pair of kitchen-tongs were placed astride his neck, and, mid jeers and shouts, he rode about six miles. A year later, he refused to sign the Test. He preached in Vermont subsequently, but was not again settled. In 1782 there was a Loyalist Associator of this name at New York, with a family of five persons, to settle at Shelburne, Nova Scotia.

HOUSTON, JAMES. Of North Carolina. On the passage of the Stamp Act, he was appointed Stamp-Master of that Colony. On the arrival of the ship with the Stamped Paper, he was an inmate of Governor Tryon's house. A large mob repaired to the palace — as it was called — and demanded that Houston should come to the door; but Tryon "refused to allow the claims of such a body to an audience," and persisted in his course, until the threat of the multitude to fire his dwelling was on the point of being executed. Houston was led out finally, and conducted to the market-place, where he took an oath never to perform the duties of his office.

HOVENDON, RICHARD. Of Pennsylvania. Was a captain of cavalry in the British Legion. He acted for a time with the Queen's Rangers in the neighborhood of Philadelphia, and in his excursions made prize of quantities of clothing. His company was finally incorporated into Tarleton's Legion. Attainted of treason and estate confiscated.

HOWARD, MARTIN. Of North Carolina. He removed to that Colony from Rhode Island. During the Stamp Act excitement, in 1765, his effigy was drawn through the streets, and hung on a gallows; his house at Newport was destroyed, and his person injured. He fled to North Carolina, where, after the suicide of Judge Berry, he was appointed a member of the Council, and Chief Justice. His reputation does not appear to have been good; nor does it seem that the calm and moderate respected him; while from others he sometimes received abuse, and even bodily harm. Careful pens speak of his profligate character, and of his corrupt and wicked designs, and aver that the members of the Assembly hated him.

In the great riot at Hillsborough in 1770, Judge Howard was driven from the Bench, but the mob respected his associate, Judge Moore. In 1774 Howard's judicial functions ceased, in consequence of the tumults and disorders of the times; and the suspension from office of one who " was notoriously destitute not only of the common virtues of humanity, but of all sympathy whatever with the community in which he lived," was a matter of much joy. In 1775 he was present in Council, and expressed the highest detestation of unlawful meetings, and advised Governor Martin to inhibit and forbid the assembling of the Whig Convention appointed at Newbern. In July, 1777, he embarked with his family for a Northern port, and visited Rhode Island. In conversation with Secretary Wood, he observed: " Henry, you may rely upon it, I shall have no quarrel with the Sons of Liberty of Newport; it was they who made me Chief Justice of North Carolina, with a thousand pounds sterling a year."

He went to England in 1778, and reported to fellow-Loyalists that a number of gentlemen of influence and property, who had been neutral, to see which way the contest would finally end, had lately joined the Royal side. He died in England, December, 1781. James Center married one of his daughters, and after her decease, became the husband of another.

HOWARD, JOHN. In 1782 he was a captain in the King's Orange Rangers. For some part of the contest, he was under command of Tarleton, and had much difficulty with that officer. He and Colonel Beverley Robinson were intimate.

He settled in New Brunswick, and was a magistrate many years. He died at Hampton, 1824, aged eighty-two.

HOWARD, SHEFFIELD. Of New York. Lost a large amount of property during the war. His daughter Anne married Major Bingham; and, a widow, became the wife of Sir Thomas Hay, Baronet. Sir James Douglas Hamilton Hay, the present (1857) baronet, is the oldest son of the second marriage.

HOWE, JOHN. Of Boston. He was proscribed and banished. He was a native of that town, and at the Revolutionary era conducted, in connection with Mrs. Draper, the "Massachusetts Gazette and Boston News Letter."

His son Joseph, of whom presently, in a speech in Faneuil Hall, July 4, 1858, thus spoke: "Mr. Mayor, I never come to Boston without feeling that I am at home, for I find friends everywhere and relatives not a few. I have partaken, on former occasions, of its unbounded hospitality. We have not forgotten, in the Provinces, — who that was present will ever forget? — the noble celebration with which you inaugurated your great public works. I told you, on that occasion, that my father was a Boston boy. He, like Franklin and like the Governor of your State (who has just done himself honor by referring to the fact), learnt the printing business in this city. He had just completed his apprenticeship, and was engaged to a very pretty girl, when the Revolution broke out. He saw the battle of Bunker's Hill from one of the old houses here — he nursed the wounded when it was over. Adhering to the British side, he was driven out at the evacuation, and retired to Newport, where his betrothed followed him. They were married there, and afterwards settled at Halifax. He left all his household goods and gods behind him, carrying away nothing but his principles and the pretty girl. (Great laughter and applause.)

"The Loyalists who left these States, were not, it must be confessed, as good Republicans as you are; but they loved liberty under their old forms, and their descendants love it too. My father, though a true Briton to the day of his death, loved

New England, and old Boston especially, with filial regard. He never lost an opportunity of serving a Boston man, if in his power. At the close of your railway banquet, one gentleman told me that my father had, during the last war, taken his father from the Military Prison at Melville Island, and sent him back to Boston. Another, on the same evening, showed me a gold watch sent by an uncle, who died in the West Indies, to his family. It was pawned by a sailor in Halifax, but redeemed by my father, and sent to the dead man's relatives. And so it was, all his life. He loved his sovereign, but he loved Boston too, and whenever he got sick in his latter days, we used to send him up here to recruit. A sight of the old scenes and a walk upon Boston Common were sure to do him good, and he generally came back uncommonly well." (Laughter.)

Elsewhere, the same son remarked: "For thirty years he was my instructor, my playfellow, almost my daily companion. To him I owe my fondness for reading, my familiarity with the Bible, my knowledge of old Colonial and American incidents and characteristics. He left me nothing but his example and the memory of his many virtues, for all that he ever earned was given to the poor. He was too good for this world; but the remembrance of his high principle, his cheerfulness, his childlike simplicity, and truly Christian character, is never absent from my mind."

The subject of this notice established a newspaper at Halifax, and was King's Printer. He died in that city, greatly lamented, in 1835, in his eighty-second year. Mary, his widow, deceased in 1837, aged seventy-four. His son, William Howe, Assistant Commissary-General, who died at Halifax, January, 1843, aged fifty-seven; John Howe, Queen's Printer, and Deputy Postmaster-General, who died at the same place the same year, and David Howe, who published a paper at St. Andrew, New Brunswick, some twenty years ago, were his sons. Of the same relation is the Hon. Joseph Howe, late of the Council, and Collector of Excise at Halifax, and the present leader of the Liberal party of Nova

Scotia, and (1860) Secretary of the Province. His "Speeches and Public Letters," published in Boston, 2 vols. 8vo., in 1858, contain demands upon the Home Government for the extension of Colonial rights and privileges, which have no parallel in the documentary history of the Revolution. In a word, this son of a Loyalist speaks in bolder tones than any Whig of '76 dared to do in his loftiest mood.

HOYT, JAMES. Of Fairfield County, Connecticut. Was a member of the Association in 1775; went to St. John, New Brunswick, in 1783, and became a merchant. He was a member of the Loyal Artillery in 1795, and died in King's County, in that Province, in 1803.

HOYT, MONSON. In 1782 he was a lieutenant in the Prince of Wales's American Volunteers, and quartermaster of the corps. He retired on half-pay; settled in New Brunswick; engaged in commercial business, and was a partner with General Arnold at St. John. He publicly accused Arnold of burning his warehouse; and was sued by the traitor for defamation. The jury gave damages of two shillings and sixpence currency, (just fifty cents.) In 1792 he married Lucretia Hammond, of Long Island, New York, and was probably a resident of that State.

HOYT, ISRAEL. Of Fairfield County, Connecticut. Died in Kingston, New Brunswick, in 1803, aged sixty-one.

HUBBARD, REV. BELA, D. D. Of Connecticut. Episcopal minister. He was born at Guilford, Connecticut, in 1739, and was bred a Congregationalist. He graduated at Yale College in 1758, and, five years afterwards, went to England for ordination. After his return, he officiated first in his native town and in Killingworth. In 1767 he was transferred to the mission of New and West Haven, and continued his ministry there until the Revolution. His loyalty was well known; but, more fortunate than most clergymen of his communion, he escaped personal indignity, and was allowed to perform his official duties without serious molestation. In the latter years of his life his services were confined principally to Trinity Church, New Haven. It is said that,

"Wherever there was human wretchedness to be relieved, he was on the alert to act the part of an angel of mercy"; that, "the sick and afflicted among his own people looked up to him as the kindest of friends, as well as the most attentive of pastors; and there was no sacrifice that he was not ready to make to dispel the night-clouds of sorrow from the humblest dwelling."

He died December, 1812, in his seventy-fourth year. He married Grace Dunbar Hill, who survived until 1820. Two sons graduated at Yale, namely: Bela, who became a Judge in Louisiana, and died in 1841; and Thomas Hill, who was a member of Congress from New York, and died at Utica in 1857, at the age of seventy-six. A daughter married Timothy Pitkin, a well-remembered statesman, who published "A Statistical View of the Commerce of the United States," and "A Political and Civil History of the United States, from 1763 to the close of Washington's Administration"; and who died at New Haven in 1847. Mrs. Pitkin was living in 1855.

HUBBARD, REV. JOHN. Of Northfield, Massachusetts. Congregational minister. He graduated at Yale College in 1747, and settled at Northfield in 1750. He "fell under suspicion, particularly because he prayed for the King and not for Congress"; and in 1779 a council was called to deal with him. He agreed to maintain entire silence as to royalty, and "not to say or do anything against the cause of the country, the Continental Congress, or the army, but pray for the prosperity, success, and happiness of the same"; and the difficulty ended. After a ministry of upwards of forty-four years, he died at Northfield in 1794, at the age of sixty-eight.

HUBBARD, WILLIAM. At the peace he went to St. John, New Brunswick, and was a grantee of that city. He settled in the county of Sunbury, and was Register of Deeds and Wills; Deputy Surrogate; member of the House of Assembly; and Chief Justice of the Court of Common Pleas. He died in that county in 1813.

HUBBARD, ADAM. Of Schoharie, New York. Was repeatedly made prisoner in his own house. For a time, keeper of the light-house on Sandy Hook. Removed to Shelburne, Nova Scotia, and was drowned there in 1784. His widow removed to Yarmouth. His daughter Margaret, widow of Ethel Davis, died in 1859, aged ninety-five.

HUBBARD, ISAAC. He settled in New Brunswick, and, at his decease, was the senior magistrate of the county of Sunbury. He died at Burton, 1834, aged eighty-six.

HUBBARD, NATHANIEL. Went to St. John, New Brunswick, in 1783, and was a grantee of that city. He removed to the parish of Burton, county of Sunbury, where he was a magistrate, and where he died in 1824, aged seventy-eight.

HUBBEL, ———. A captain under the Board of Associated Loyalists at New York. In the spring of 1781 he was stationed at Lloyd's Neck; but was in the habit, it would seem, of putting his command in whale-boats and making incursions by water. The Board, in reporting the proceedings of this "spirited Loyalist," state in detail the incidents of burning guard-houses, of destroying mills, flour, and salt-works; of carrying off sheep and cattle, and of the courage he displayed when in conflict with the "Rebels."

HUBBEL, AMMON. Served on the Royal side under Colonel Ludlow. Settled in New Brunswick, 1783; died at Burton in that Province in 1848, aged ninety, leaving numerous descendants.

HUBBEL, NATHAN. Of Fairfield County, Connecticut. At the peace, a large part of the town of Guysborough, Nova Scotia, was granted to him and two hundred and seventy-eight others, who, during the war, had been connected with the civil department of the Royal Army and Navy. He was twice married, and, as is said, the father of nineteen children.

HUCK, CHRISTIAN. A lawyer, of Philadelphia. He abandoned that city and went within the British lines at New York. In the course of the war, he joined Tarleton at the South, and was a captain of dragoons. He was killed in an affray with a party he was sent to disperse, in 1780. At the very moment of the attack in which he was slain, several women were on their knees, imploring him to spare their families and their property. During his command, he had distressed the people by every kind of insult and injury. He was so profane as to say that, "God Almighty was turned Rebel; but if there were twenty Gods on their side, they should all be conquered." Attainted of treason and property confiscated. "A miscreant who excited universal abhorrence for his cruelty and profanity." Known as the "Swearing Captain."

HUDKINS, ———. Corporal in the Queen's Rangers. Fell, covered with wounds, and died on the field.

HUGHES, JOHN. Of Philadelphia. In 1765 he was appointed Stamp-Master of Pennsylvania, but seemingly declined. The Whigs thought he was insincere; and when his commission arrived, the bells were muffled, the colors set at half-mast, and, fearing harm to his person, some friends who were armed guarded his house. The multitude waited upon him and compelled him to resign. It was insinuated that Franklin was too indifferent as to the operation of the Stamp Act; and that the family of Hughes, offended at the Doctor's course, subsequently preserved letters for the purpose of accusation. On the death of James Nevin, Collector of the Customs at Portsmouth, New Hampshire, in 1769, Mr. Hughes succeeded to that office. In common with officers of the Customs of other ports, he encountered difficulties in executing his duties; and property which he seized was rescued by disguised men, armed with clubs. In 1772 he returned to Philadelphia.

HUGHES, SAMUEL. Of Boston. He was one of the fifty-eight Boston memorialists in 1760, but followed the Royal Army to Halifax in 1776. In 1778 he was proscribed and banished. In 1784 administration was granted John Hazen on the estate of a Loyalist of this name, who died on the river St. John, New Brunswick. Elizabeth, widow of Samuel, of Boston, died at that town in 1795, aged seventy-six.

HUGHES, JOSEPH. Of North Carolina. Allowed by the

of Chandos. His wife was Mary, daughter of Stephen Shewell, merchant of Philadelphia, whose sister was the wife of Benjamin West. Mr. Hunt was the father of Leigh Hunt, one of the most eminent of the literary men of England at the present time, who died in London, in 1859, aged seventy-four. J. Thornton Hunt, son of Leigh, formerly editor of the "Spectator and Morning Chronicle," is now (1860) in the United States.

Speaking of Leigh Hunt and his American blood, Hawthorne says, "his person was thoroughly American, and of the best type, as were likewise his manners; for we are the best — as well as the worst — mannered people in the world!"

HUNT, JOHN. Of Philadelphia. In 1777 he was ordered to be sent prisoner to Virginia, for disaffection to the Whig cause. During the proceedings against him, he demanded a hearing before the President and Council, because, he said, imprisonment without trial was unlawful. A Loyalist of this name was a lieutenant in the Guides and Pioneers.

HUNT, COSBY. Of New York. In 1782 he was a lieutenant in the New York Volunteers, and adjutant of the corps. He settled in New Brunswick, and received half-pay. He was drowned in the river St. John previous to the year 1805.

HUNT, WILLIAM. Of North Castle, West Chester County, New York. He took shelter with De Lancey's corps; and at the peace returned to his estate, protected, as he averred, by the 6th article of the treaty. But he was arrested and tried on eleven suits for trespasses committed by him, as was alleged while in service and belonging to the "Cow Boys." The plaintiffs all recovered judgment, and he was cast into prison. In January, 1786, he claimed the interposition of the British Consul of New York, at whose instance the facts were examined by Mr. Jay, who expressed the opinion that Congress need not interfere in the matter, or even give an answer.

HUNTER, JOHN. Of Norfolk, Virginia. "An active

man;" and in December, 1775, aide-de-camp to Lord Dunmore. In July, 1776, a refugee with his family, on board the brigantine *Hammond*, one of the vessels of his Lordship's fleet on the waters of the Chesapeake. Mr. Hunter went to England previous to July, 1779.

HUNTER, WILLIAM. Of Virginia. His father, whose name was William, was a native of Virginia, and was a printer, at Williamsburg, to the House of Burgesses; and having a relative who was paymaster to the King's troops in America, obtained the appointment of Deputy Postmaster-General for the Colonies under Franklin, which office he held until his death, in 1761. The subject of this notice attained to his majority about the time the Revolution began, and being a Loyalist, attached himself to the British standard, and eventually left the country.

HUNTINGTON, MINOR. Of Connecticut. Went to Nova Scotia at the peace, settled at Yarmouth, where he was a surveyor, prothonotary, and an officer in the militia. He died about the year 1845. Herbert Huntington, his son, is a leading Liberal politician in that Province.

HUSTON, JOSHUA. The leader of a party of "New York horse-thieves." In 1778, in an adventure to West Chester County, he and three others attempted to break into the house of a Whig, who, acquainted with the design, resolved to defend himself. Huston, while entering a window, was stabbed and carried to a fellow Tory's, where he died and was buried in a field. Those who had suffered at his hands threatened to search for his body, and if they found it, to hang it upon a gallows.

HUSTON, ROBERT. Of Pennsylvania. He was born in Ireland, and came to America while young. He settled near Philadelphia, as a farmer. In the Revolution he belonged to a troop of heavy dragoons, and was often engaged in skirmishes in New Jersey and West Chester County, New York. At the peace, accompanied by his family, he went from New York to Shelburne, Nova Scotia, where the Crown granted him one farm, one town and one water lot. He

settled at Yarmouth in the same Province, subsequently, and engaged in navigation and trade. He died in 1842, aged eighty-eight, leaving two children, one of whom is (1861) the wife of Edward K. Timpany, Esq., of Digby.

HUTCHINSON, THOMAS. Governor of Massachusetts. His father was Honorable Thomas Hutchinson, a merchant, and member of the Council, who died in 1739. The subject of this notice was born in 1711, and graduated at Harvard University in 1727, and applied himself to commerce. Unsuccessful as a merchant, he devoted himself to politics, and rose to the highest distinction, having been a member of the House of Representatives, and Speaker of that body; Judge of Probate; member of the Council; Lieutenant-Governor; Judge of the Supreme Court; and Governor. The regularity of his life, his sympathy for the distressed, his affability, his integrity, his industry, his talents for business and the administration of affairs, his fluency and grace as a public speaker, his command of temper and courteousness under provocation; united to form a rare man, and to give him a rare influence. A Judge of the highest Judicial Court, a member of the Council, and Lieutenant-Governor at the same time, — he seems to have performed the duties of these incompatible offices to the satisfaction of the community. And the fact that, unlike most of the Crown officers, he was a native of Massachusetts, and not of the Episcopal communion, added to his popularity.

The Revolution produced a fearful change of sentiment, and he became an exile; was attainted, and lost his property by confiscation. His political ruin gave him inconceivable anguish, and prematurely closed his life. There were tales, indeed, that his death was produced by his own act; but this is not probable. After his retirement to England, a baronetcy was offered him, but he declined it. He died in 1780, aged sixty-nine, and was buried at Croydon, England. It may not be possible to form a correct opinion of the character and motives of action of Governor Hutchinson. But I cannot think that his contemporaries among the

Whigs did him exact justice. The spontaneous and universal respect in which he was held by all parties, previous to the Revolutionary controversy, — the long, faithful, and highly valuable services which he rendered his native Colony, — surely entitled him to honorable mention then, and to our regard now. Had he lived at any other period, his claim to be included among the worthies of Massachusetts would not, probably, be doubted. It is to be deeply lamented, that, being the son of a merchant, himself bred a merchant, and his own sons merchants, he did not see, or would not see, that if the navigation acts and laws of trade were enforced, the commerce of the Colonies would be ruined at a blow. His position enabled him to have prevented the enforcement of the hated measures of commercial restriction, and he is hardly to be held excused for using his influence on the adverse side. As a historian, no man was more familiar with the opposition to these laws when Randolph and Andros, a century before, attempted to fasten them upon New England; and he knew, that all that a single Colony could do, to shake off the Royal authority, was done by Massachusetts, in the time of these hated emissaries of the British Crown. Could he have thought that the opposition of his countrymen would be less, in his own time, when they were required to sacrifice an extensive and rich commerce, — a commerce unlawful by the statute book, but yet permitted, for a long course of years, by the officers of the customs? It does not appear probable. And yet, how is his pertinacious adherence to the measures of the ministry to be accounted for? Did he think the measures just? The Whigs of his generation almost unanimously believed that he knew that the servants of the King were in the wrong, but that his ambition, and full confidence that he espoused the winning side, caused his assent to, and support of, their acts. It may be so. His private virtues, his historical labors, his high station, his commanding influence, his sorrows, have an interest which none who are acquainted with his life can fail to feel. The third volume of his "History of Massachusetts," which embraces his own career, is, if the circumstances under which it was written are considered, a work of singular moderation and fairness; and its statements are to be received, probably, with quite as much respect as the records of any gentleman who writes of his own times, his own deeds, and his own enemies. I can never cease to regret that Governor Hutchinson countenanced the revival of the long-obsolete statutory provisions, affecting the navigation and maritime interests of his country; I forget, in his melancholy end, all else.

HUTCHINSON, THOMAS, JR. Of Massachusetts. Son of Governor Hutchinson. He was a merchant of Boston, and a third part of the tea destroyed there was consigned to him and his brother Elisha. He was a Mandamus Councillor, and an Addresser of Gage; and was proscribed and banished. He went to England, and died there in 1811, aged seventy-one.

HUTCHINSON, ELISHA. Of Massachusetts. Brother and commercial partner of Thomas Hutchinson, Jr. He graduated at Harvard University in 1762. He was proscribed and banished. He died in England in 1824, aged eighty. His wife Mary, who was the eldest daughter of Colonel George Watson, of Plymouth, Massachusetts, died at Birmingham, England, in 1803.

HUTCHINSON, FOSTER. Of Massachusetts. Brother of Governor Hutchinson. He graduated at Harvard University in 1748. Raised to the bench of the Supreme Court, he was one of the last of the Royal Judges of that Colony. His name appears among the Mandamus Councillors, among those who were proscribed and banished, and among those whose estates were confiscated. He went to Halifax in 1776, with his family of twelve persons. He died in Nova Scotia in 1799. His son Foster, an Assistant Judge of the Supreme Court of that Colony, died in 1815; and his daughter Abigail deceased at Halifax, July, 1843, aged seventy-four.

HUTCHINSON, ELIAKIM. Of Boston. He graduated at Harvard University in 1730; and became a member of the Council, and the Judge of a Court. He died in 1775. His widow, the eldest daughter of Governor Shirley, died at

London in 1790. Mr. Hutchison was owner of the mansion in Roxbury built by his father-in-law, which became the property of Governor Eustis, and which is now (1864) occupied by his relict.

HUTCHINSON, WILLIAM. Of Massachusetts. He graduated at Harvard University in 1762. In 1775 he went to England, and subsequently held an office in the Bahamas. He died in 1791, in Europe. A son, it is believed, of Hon. Foster Hutchinson.

HUTCHINSON, WILLIAM. In 1782 he was captain lieutenant of the First Battalion of New Jersey Volunteers. He retired on half-pay, and lived in New Brunswick; but removed to Upper Canada, where he died.

HUTCHINSON, MATTHEW. Went to Shelburne, Nova Scotia, in 1783, and died soon after.

HUTTON, WILLIAM. Died at St. John, New Brunswick, in 1799, aged forty-two. The surname may be Hulton.

HYSON, MICHAEL. Of Pennsylvania. He went to Nova Scotia during hostilities. He married when upwards of a hundred years old. He died at Ship Harbor, Nova Scotia, in 1833, aged one hundred and three. His third wife survived him, as also numerous descendants of the second, third, and fourth generations from him.

ILIFF, ———. Taken prisoner in New Jersey, tried, and hanged.

INGERSOLL, JARED. Of Connecticut. He was born in Milford, Connecticut, in 1722. In 1742 he graduated at Yale College. He settled in New Haven, and engaged in the practice of the law. In 1757 he was agent of the Colony in England. In 1765 he received the appointment of Stamp-distributor, and arrived at Boston on his way to enter upon the duties of the office. While at Boston, many attentions were paid to him; and on his departure, Mr. Oliver, who had received the same appointment for Massachusetts, accompanied him out of town. This act occasioned murmuring among the people; an inflammatory article appeared in the next "Boston Gazette;" labels were posted on the Liberty Tree; and, finally, a mob destroyed Oliver's building, designed for his stamp-office.

In Connecticut, matters reached the same extremity; and it was threatened before his arrival there, that he should be hung on the first tree after he entered the Colony. Though this threat was not executed, effigies of his person were made in several places, tried in form, and condemned to be burned. Mr. Ingersoll formally resigned his office at New Haven, in August, 1765; but his resignation was not deemed satisfactory to the people of another section; and a large body set out for that town with a determination to compel a more explicit declaration of his intentions. They met him at Weathersfield, where they obtained the required satisfaction; and extorted from him the cry, three times, " Liberty and Property." Hundreds then escorted him to Hartford. About the year 1770 he was commissioned Judge of Vice-Admiralty for the Colonies of New York, New Jersey, Pennsylvania, Maryland, and Virginia, and removed to Philadelphia.

In 1777, he, John Adams, and several others, boarded with a widow in Philadelphia, who had buried four husbands, and was ready for a fifth. The lion-hearted Whig said: " Between the fun of Thornton, the gravity of Sherman, and the formal toryism of Ingersoll, Adams will have a curious life of it."

The Revolution put an end to Mr. Ingersoll's duties, and he returned to Connecticut. He died at New Haven, 1781, at the age of fifty-nine. His son Jared, a gentleman of distinguished worth and talents, held various public stations, and was a candidate for the Vice-Presidency of the United States in 1812.

INGERSOLL, DAVID. Of Great Barrington, Massachusetts. He graduated at Yale College in 1761. His name appears among the barristers and attorneys who addressed Hutchinson in 1774. He was proscribed and banished in 1778. During the troubles which preceded the shedding of blood, he was seized by a mob, carried to Connecticut, and imprisoned; while, on a second outbreak of the popular displeasure against him, his house was assailed, he was driven from it, and his enclosures were laid waste. He went to England, and died there in 1796, aged fifty-seven. He married, in 1783, Frances Rebecca Ryley, who survived him less than three months. He left two sons, Philip Ryley, who died in 1808, leaving issue; and Frederick Horton, who was living in 1853.

INGLEBY, THOMAS. Died at St. John, New Brunswick, in 1813, aged fifty-four. Eliza, his wife, died at the same place, 1811, at the age of fifty-seven.

INGLIS, REV. CHARLES, D. D. Of New York. Episcopal Bishop of Nova Scotia. He became an Assistant Rector of Trinity Church, New York, in 1764, and continued to officiate until Washington took possession of that city, in 1776, when he went up the Hudson River. On the decease of Rev. Dr. Auchmuty, in 1777, he succeeded as Rector. The church had been burned, and he was inducted into office by placing his hands on the ruins, in presence of the wardens, and taking the usual obligations. He resigned in 1783. It is here stated, on his authority, that, with a single exception, all the Episcopal missionaries were faithful to the Crown. He published an answer (1776) to Paine's "Common Sense," which the Whigs seized and burned; but two editions were printed subsequently at Philadelphia.

Washington, designing to attend his church, soon after assuming command in New York sent word by one of his Generals that he would be glad to have the prayers for the King and Royal family omitted.[1] To this message Mr. Inglis paid no attention; and, on seeing the Whig Chief not long after, remonstrated with him on the unreasonableness of the request, saying that he must know the clergy could not comply with it; that he could shut up the churches, but was without the power to make the ministers depart from their duty. Afterwards, Mr. Inglis, as he passed the streets, was called a Tory, a traitor to his country, and threatened with violence

[1] This fact is stated on the authority of letters sent by Episcopal missionaries in America to the Society for Propagating the Gospel; and must have been communicated by Mr. Inglis himself.

if he continued to pray for the King. At last, to silence him, about one hundred and fifty armed men entered his church on Sunday, with bayonets fixed, drums beating, and fifes playing, and stood in the aisle a few minutes; when, on invitation of the sexton, they took seats in the pews. The congregation were in consternation, and several women fainted; but Mr. Inglis continued the service, and read the offensive prayers as usual, though some of his flock expected that he would be shot. In August, 1776, he retired to Long Island, where he was met by the Whig Committee, who entered into a discussion about seizing him. To avoid this, he kept concealed as much as possible until Washington's defeat, when he was at liberty, and without apprehensions. He followed the Royal Army to New York, and found that his house had been plundered of everything of value. In September, 1776, as already mentioned, Trinity Church was burned, with nearly one thousand other buildings. The Tories accused that the fire was the work of Rebels, who secreted themselves for the purpose, and who applied the torch in different parts of the city at the same moment, by concert.

November 28, 1776, Mrs. Inglis was at New Windsor, and asked Mr. Duane, by letter, to procure leave for her to join her husband in New York, with her family and effects. She had been absent, she said, nearly fourteen months, had three helpless babes, was greatly distressed, and had need of every friend to comfort her. Besides his wife and these children, his family consisted at this time of Mrs. Crooke, (his mother-in-law,) two white servant-women, a nurse, and a white servant-boy. All, finally, joined him, under a flag of truce.

After Galloway, the great Pennsylvania Loyalist, went to England, Doctor Inglis was a correspondent, and his letters evince no little harshness. I give one of his predictions. In a letter, dated at New York, December, 1778, he said: "The rebellion, be assured, is on the decline; its vigor and its resources are nearly spent, and nothing but a little perseverance, and a moderate share of prudence and exertion on the part of Britain, is necessary to suppress it totally."

In a published controversy between "A Consistent Loyalist" and "Viator," at London, in 1784, he himself is treated with severity.

In 1787 he was appointed Bishop of Nova Scotia; and was the first-Colonial Bishop in the British dominions in any part of the world. He was consecrated at Lambeth. In 1809 he became a member of the Council. He died in 1816, aged eighty-two. His wife was Margaret Crooke, "a lady of a very ample fortune," and daughter of John Crooke, of Ulster County, New York. Mrs. Inglis died in 1783, aged thirty-five, after a long and painful illness.

Dr. Inglis and his wife are included in the Confiscation Act of New York. His eldest daughter married Brenton Halliburton, Chief Justice of Nova Scotia. Anne married the Rev. George Pidgeon, and died at Halifax in 1827, at the age of fifty-one. John, a son, who was consecrated Bishop of Nova Scotia, and appointed a member of the Council in 1825, died at London in 1850. His grandson — son of the second Bishop — Major-General Sir John Eardley Wilmot Inglis, who was knighted for his gallant defence of the garrison of Lucknow, in the late Sepoy rebellion, died in Germany in 1862, at the age of fifty.

INGRAHAM, DUNCAN. Of South Carolina. The only Loyalist of his family. He went to England in 1774, and remained in Europe until after the peace. John Adams met him several times in Paris, and mentions him in his diary. On Mr. Ingraham's return, he gave his adherence to the new Government; and allowed his son William, who was killed at the age of twenty, to enter the Navy. His nephew, Duncan N. Ingraham, also of the United States Navy, was widely and justly applauded for demanding and obtaining the release of Koszta, as an American citizen. This nephew was promoted to a captaincy in 1855, and, when the present Rebellion broke out, was Chief of the Bureau of Ordnance. Like many others, he forsook the flag under which he had received many honors, to join the Rebels. January 31, 1863, with Beauregard he issued an "official proclamation," declaring the blockade of Charleston to be raised by a superior force of the States in rebellion. Captain Ingraham married Harriet Rutledge Laurens, of South Carolina, a granddaughter, on the paternal side, of Henry Laurens, the President of the first Continental Congress.

INGRAM, JAMES. Of Virginia. Removed to Maryland in 1777; went to England, and was in London, July, 1779.

INMAN, GEORGE. Of Cambridge, Massachusetts. He graduated at Harvard University in 1772, and became an officer in the British Army. He died in 1789.

INMAN, RALPH. Of Massachusetts, and, I suppose, of Cambridge. He was an Addresser of Gage in 1775, and, early the next year, a refugee in Boston. In April, 1776, his arrest was ordered by the Council. In 1784, he was named in the Act to incorporate the Boston Episcopal Charitable Society. He died at Cambridge in 1788, aged seventy-five. Captain Linzee, of the British Navy, married a daughter.

INNIS, ALEXANDER. Colonel of the South Carolina Royalists. In 1780 he was in command of a large party of British and Tories, and was defeated at Musgrove's Mills on the Enoree River; and was himself wounded. In 1782 he was Inspector-General of Loyalist forces.

INSLEE, ———. Of New Jersey. Lieutenant under the Board of Associated Loyalists at New York. Killed, in 1781, in the attack on the Whig post at Tom's River, New Jersey.

IREDELL, ———. Lieutenant of "the armed boatmen" under the Board of Associated Loyalists at New York. Killed, 1781, in the attack on the Whigs at Tom's River, New Jersey.

IRELAND, JOHN. Of Long Island, New York. In 1777 he was taken in arms at Lloyd's Neck, and retained a prisoner; but in the spring of 1778 he was allowed to return home to procure clothing and other necessaries, on condition that he should deliver himself to his captors in thirty days.

IRVING, ALEXANDER. Of South Carolina. At one time Inspector of Imports and Exports at Boston. In October, 1775, Receiver-General of Quit Rents, Charleston. Taken prisoner at sea, April, 1776, and carried to New London, Connecticut. Went to England previous to July, 1779.

IRVINE, ———. Of South Carolina. Lieutenant-Governor. Estate confiscated in 1782.

IVES, DAVID. Of Rhode Island. I suppose he was a captain in a corps called the Associated Loyalists. At the peace he went to St. John, New Brunswick, and was a grantee of that city.

IVES, JOHN. Of Rhode Island. Went to New Brunswick, and was appointed master-carpenter of ordnance. He died at St. John in 1804, aged fifty-six.

JACKSON, RICHARD. Of Berkshire County, Massachusetts. Of this man there is a singular but well-authenticated story. Having adhered to the Crown from a conviction of duty, he felt bound to aid his Sovereign in suppressing the Rebellion, by all means in his power. When, therefore, the news reached him, in 1777, that Colonel Baum was advancing with a body of troops towards Bennington, he prepared to join him. In the battle of Hoosac — erroneously called the battle of Bennington — he was taken prisoner, and sent to Great Barrington, then the shire town of Berkshire; and by General Fellows, the sheriff, committed to prison. The county jail was in so ruinous a condition that Jackson could easily escape; but of this he had no intention. He felt that he had acted right, and determined to abide the consequences. After quietly remaining in jail a few days, he told General Fellows that he was losing his time, earned nothing, and wished permission to go out to work in the daytime, and promised to return at evening and be confined for the night. His great simplicity and honesty of character led the sheriff to confide in his word. Jackson accordingly went out to labor almost every week-day, for some months. In May of 1778, he was to be tried at Springfield for high treason, and General Fellows made the necessary preparations to conduct him to that town in person. But Jackson said, "he could go alone quite as well," and thus save the sheriff both inconvenience and expense. Again, General Fellows confided in his integrity; and he commenced his journey. In the woods of Tyringham, he met the Hon. T. Edwards, who asked him the object of his travel. Jackson answered, that he "was going to Springfield, to be tried for his life." To Springfield he did go, was tried for his life, found guilty, and condemned to die. Application was, however, made to the executive authority of the State to pardon him. But it was reasoned by the members of the Board, that the facts against Jackson were clear and incontestable, that his crime was unquestionably high treason, and that, if he were pardoned, all others who might commit the same crime ought to meet with the same clemency. But Mr. Edwards, who was a member of the Board, told the story of meeting Jackson, with great particularity, yet without embellishment. The simple truth moved the hearts of his associates, and their feelings as men prevailed against reasons of State policy. Jackson was pardoned, and returned to his family.

JACKSON, WILLIAM. Merchant, of Boston. An Addresser of Hutchinson in 1774, and of Gage in 1775; was proscribed and banished in 1778. He went to England, where he died in 1810, at the age of seventy-nine.

JACKSON, ———. Marauder and murderer. Executed at St. John, New Brunswick, in 1785. At the scaffold he was contrite for his sins, and said, "there is only one thing he dared not hope pardon for — that was the murder of Benjamin Mitchell." [See *John Mitchell*.] Possibly Jackson may not have belonged to the Royal side, but was "a refugee" at the peace, for his crimes.

JACKSON, WILLIAM. Of Charleston, South Carolina. Merchant. In 1782, a Loyalist Associator at New York, to remove to Shelburne, Nova Scotia, the following year. Settled at Woodstock, New Brunswick, as did a son. His grandson, Charles Andrew Jackson, now (1860) lives at Eastport, Maine.

JACOBS, JOHN. Executed at Charleston, South Carolina, in February, 1777, for issuing counterfeit money.

JAFFREY, GEORGE. Of Portsmouth, New Hampshire. Graduated at Harvard University in 1736. He became a merchant. In 1744 he was appointed Clerk of the Superior Court of New Hampshire, and held that office twenty-two years. In 1766 he was admitted one of his Majesty's Council, and soon after received the post of Treasurer of the Province. He possessed a large estate, and was one of the original purchasers of Mason's Patent. He was molested on account of his political opinions several times. When removed by the Whigs from the office of Treasurer, he paid over to his successor £1516 4s. 8d., being the exact balance of public moneys in his hands. He was ordered, November, 1775, by the Provincial Congress, to remove ten miles at least from Portsmouth, and not to leave the place selected without leave of that body, or the Committee of Safety. General Sullivan interposed and wrote the Committee that Mr. Jaffrey had assisted in the construction of military works, and "ought not in justice to be deemed an enemy to his country, or be treated as such." Though opposed for his attachment to the Crown, he left behind him an unsullied reputation for strict integrity, punctuality in his dealings, and correctness of manners. He died at Portsmouth in 1802, aged eighty-six years.

JAMES, JACOB. Of Pennsylvania. Captain in the British Legion. He was distinguished as a partisan in the winter of 1777, and was particularly active in kidnapping Whigs of note in the vicinity of Philadelphia. He was also extremely troublesome to the country as a horse-thief, to supply the British Army. Subsequently, his troop of horse joined Tarleton's corps. In April, 1780, James was a prisoner in North Carolina; and the President of Pennsylvania wrote Governor Caswell, asking that he might not be exchanged as a common prisoner of war, but be retained in close custody until opportunity occurred to send him home for trial, where, "it may be presumed, he will suffer the punishment his many villanies and offences so justly deserve." He was attainted of treason and his estate confiscated.

JAMES, FRANK. Pilot to the Royal fleet in New York harbor. Received half-pay. In March, 1776, Lord Stirling sent a secret party with express orders to take or destroy him. Died at Shelburne, Nova Scotia, in 1809.

JAMES, JOHN. Of Pennsylvania. An emissary of Sir William Howe. In 1777 the Council of Pennsylvania transmitted to Colonel Smith a warrant for his apprehension, " in order to his condign punishment."

JAMES, BENJAMIN, and ABEL. Attainted of treason; property of the latter confiscated; the former surrendered himself and was discharged.

There was also in the city of New York a Major James, whose house was attacked and plundered by a mob.

JAMES, EDWARD. A lieutenant in the King's Orange Rangers. Residence unknown.

JARVIS, REV. ABRAHAM. Of Connecticut. Bishop in the Episcopal Church. He was born at Norwalk, Connecticut, in 1739, and graduated at Yale College in 1761. While prosecuting his theological studies, he accepted an invitation to officiate as lay-reader at Middletown; and, on his return from England, (where he was ordained in 1764) he was settled there, as Rector of Christ Church. His parish was united and flourishing until the beginning of the Revolution, when he was "subjected to great inconveniences and sore trials." In July, 1776, he presided at a Convention of the Episcopal Clergy of Connecticut, "at which it was resolved to suspend all public worship in their churches, as it would be unsafe to continue the reading of the entire Liturgy." In 1796 he was appointed successor of Bishop Seabury, but declined. Unanimously elected a second time, however, a year later, he accepted the office, but continued Rector at Middletown until 1799, when he removed to Cheshire. In 1803 he transferred his residence to New Haven. He died in 1813, in his seventy-fourth year. His first wife, who died in 1801, was Ann, daughter of Samuel Farmar, of New York. In 1806 he married the widow of Nathaniel Lewis, of Philadelphia. His son, the late Samuel Farmar Jarvis, D. D., LL. D., graduated at Yale in 1805, and was the first Rector of St. Paul's Church, Boston.

JARVIS, STEPHEN. In 1782 he was a lieutenant of cavalry in the South Carolina Royalists. He was in New Brunswick after the Revolution, but went to Upper Canada, and died at Toronto, at the residence of Rev. Doctor Phillips, 1840, aged eighty-four. During his service in the Revolution he was in several actions.

JARVIS, MUNSON. Of Connecticut. He was born in Norwalk, in 1742. In April, 1776, the Committee of Inspection advertised him as an enemy to his country. December, 1783, a warrant was issued on petition of the Selectmen of Stamford, ordering him and his family to depart that town without delay, and never return. He went to St. John, New Brunswick, and was a grantee of that city. In 1792 he was a member of the vestry of the Episcopal Church. At a later time, he was a member of the House of Assembly. He died at St. John, 1825, at the age of eighty-three. His son, the Hon. Edward James Jarvis, was formerly a member of the Council of New Brunswick, and Chief Justice of Prince Edward Island; died at Spring Park, in that Colony, in 1852, aged sixty-three; universally respected for his upright character as a jurist, and for the urbanity of his manners. The Judge's wife, who deceased in 1847, was Elizabeth, daughter of Robert Gray, Treasurer of the same Colony.

JARVIS, SAMUEL. Of Stamford, Connecticut. Seized in his house at night, and with his family put into a boat and conveyed to Long Island. In landing, he waded waist-deep to the shore. From the effects of this affair he did not recover, though he survived about a year. He died September, 1780, aged sixty.

JARVIS, WILLIAM. An officer of cavalry in the Queen's Rangers. Wounded at the siege of Yorktown. At the peace he settled in Upper Canada, and became Secretary of that Province. He died at York in 1817. His widow, Hannah, a daughter of Rev. Doctor Peters, of Hebron, Connecticut, died at Queenston, Upper Canada, 1845, aged eighty-three.

JARVIS, ———. Of Danbury, Connecticut. Guide to the British Army across the country to that town. Went to Nova Scotia. After many years, in the hope that his offence had been forgotten, he returned; but a multitude surrounded his father's house, prepared to tar and feather him. Search was made by a party that entered. Concealed in an ash-oven by his sister, he escaped, and never again set foot in his native place.

JARVIS, SAMUEL. Of Connecticut. Warrant issued December, 1783, on petition of the Selectmen of Stamford, ordering him to depart that town and never return, he went, to St. John, New Brunswick, and was a grantee of that city.

JARVIS, NATHANIEL. Also a grantee of the same city.

JARVIS, ROBERT. Of Massachusetts. An Addresser of Hutchinson in 1774, and of Gage in 1775. He went to Halifax in 1776, and was proscribed and banished in 1778. He was in London, July, 1779, a Loyalist Addresser.

JARVIS, JOHN. A Protester against the Whigs in 1774. A Loyalist of the same Christian name settled in New Brunswick, and died at Portland, in that Province, in 1845, aged ninety-three.

JAUNCEY, JAMES. Of New York. He, like Low and Sherbrook, was an associate with Jay on the Committee of Correspondence of Fifty, and probably, at the outset, was inclined to take the side of the Whigs. His property was confiscated. In 1775 he was a member of the House of Assembly, and one of the fourteen of that body who, in the recess, addressed General Gage, at Boston, on the subject of "the unhappy contest." He went to England, and died at London in 1790. "As he was entering the door of Providence Chapel . . . . he dropped down and expired immediately. He was an American Loyalist; was well known for his constant practice of relieving the poor at chapel doors, and in the street. He is said to have died worth £100,000." His house in New York was "near Bethune Street of our day."

JAUNCEY, JAMES, JR. Of New York. Son of James. In 1773 he married Miss Elliot, niece of Sir Gilbert Elliot, Treasurer of the British Navy, and was soon after appointed Master of the Rolls. In 1775 he was sworn in as a member of the Council, in place of Sir William Johnson, deceased. In 1776, he, his father, and mother, were prisoners at Middletown, Connecticut. He applied to Washington to be released, and was referred to the Provincial Congress. In 1777 he died, and was buried in Trinity church-yard. How eventful these four years!

JAUNCEY, WILLIAM. Of New York. He was arrested and sent prisoner to Middletown, Connecticut, but was released on parole.

JEFFRIES, JOHN. Of Boston. Proscribed and banished. He was born at Boston in 1744, and graduated at Harvard University in 1763; and having pursued his medical studies with Doctor Lloyd, of that town, and attended the medical schools of England, commenced practice. From 1771 to 1774 he was surgeon of a British ship-of-the-line, in Boston harbor. After the battle of Bunker's Hill, he assisted in dressing the wounded of the Royal Army, and, it is said, identified the body of Warren, in the presence of Sir William Howe. At the evacuation he embarked with the troops and went to Halifax, and was appointed chief of the surgical staff of Nova Scotia. In 1779 he went to England; and, returning to America, held a high professional employment to the British forces at Charleston and New York. In 1780 he resigned; and going to England again, commenced practice in London. In 1785 he crossed the British Channel in a balloon. He returned to Boston in the ship *Lucretia*, in 1790. He was eminent as a surgeon, midwife, and physician. He attended the poor as cheerfully and as faithfully as the rich, and was never known to refuse a professional call. He died in his native town in 1819, aged seventy-five.

JEFFREY, PATRICK. Of Boston. Went to England. Mary, his wife, died in Bath, England, in 1808. He returned to Massachusetts, and died at Milton in 1812. His house and lot on Tremont Street, sold, in 1803, for $41,000.

JENKINS, EDWARD. Of Georgia. Episcopal minister. In the effort to reëstablish the Royal Government in 1779, he was appointed Rector of Christ Church, Savannah.

JENKINS, JOHN. Of South Carolina. An Episcopal minister. In 1782 he was Chaplain of the South Carolina

Royalists, and was banished. Ten years afterward, he was preaching in Charleston, but without a regular parish.

JENKINSON, DANIEL. Died at Kingston, New Brunswick, in 1827, aged seventy-three.

JENNINGS, JOHN. Of Sandwich, Massachusetts. In 1778 arrested and imprisoned for his disaffection to the popular cause. A Loyalist of this name died at Grand Lake, New Brunswick, in 1839, at the great age of one hundred and three years.

JENNINGS, WILLIAM. Of South Carolina. An Addresser of Sir Henry Clinton; banished, and estate confiscated.

JENNINGS, EZEKIEL. Of Fairfield, Connecticut. Fled to Long Island in 1776. The fact was communicated to Washington.

JENNINGS, THOMAS. Went to St John, New Brunswick, at the peace, and was grantee of a city lot. He died there in the year 1805.

JEROME, CHAUNCEY. Of Bristol, Connecticut. He married the widow of Moses Dunbar, who was executed in 1777, and went with her to Nova Scotia. At the peace he returned, and passed the rest of his days in Bristol. He was the father of several children.

JOHNSON, SIR WILLIAM, Baronet. A Major-General of the militia of New York, Superintendent-General of Indian Affairs, &c. Was born in Ireland, about the year 1714. His uncle, Sir Peter Warren, a naval officer of distinguished merit, married a lady of New York, and purchased a considerable tract of country in the interior of that Colony, and induced him to come to America to take charge of his affairs, when at about the age of twenty. Johnson established his residence on the Mohawk, and applying himself to the study of the Indian character and language, soon acquired an ascendency over the native tribes, that has never, probably, been surpassed. His rise in affairs was rapid. In 1755 he was placed in command of the Colonial forces of New York, destined to operate against the French, and for his services was created a Baronet, and received a grant of £5000 in money.

But his right to rewards so munificent has been severely, and perhaps not improperly, disputed, since his success at the battle of Lake George—which was his principal claim to the Royal regard—was mainly due to the exertions and good conduct of the brave General Lyman, of Connecticut, after he was wounded. In 1759, and in 1760, Sir William's military operations were highly beneficial to the Crown, and he retired at the close of the French war, in much favor. He had been able to organize an Indian force of one thousand men,—a greater number than had ever before been seen in arms at one time in the cause of England. Sir William possessed talents as an orator, and deeply impressed the Indians with his powers; and his shrewdness in treating and dealing with them is said to have been remarkable. Allen relates, that on his receiving from England some finely laced clothes, the Mohawk chief, Hendrick, became possessed with the desire of equalling the Baronet in the splendor of his apparel, and with a demure face pretended to have dreamed that Sir William had presented him with a suit of the decorated garments. As the solemn hint could not be mistaken or avoided, the Indian monarch was gratified, and went away highly pleased with the success of his device. But, alas for Hendrick's shortsighted sagacity, in a few days Sir William, in turn, had a dream, to the effect that the Chief had given him several thousand acres of land. "The land is yours," said Hendrick, "but now, Sir William, I never dream with you again; you dream too hard for me."

The Baronet's seat was Johnson Hall, Johnstown, Tryon County, New York, about twenty-four miles from Schenectady, on the Mohawk River. He died there suddenly, July 11, 1774, aged sixty years. Owing to his influence, and that of his family and connections, there were more Loyalists, probably, in the valley of the Mohawk, the population considered, than in any other section of the northern Colonies.

As the Revolutionary troubles progressed, the unhappiness of Sir William is represented to have been very great. And it is said, that no inconsiderable part of his sorrow arose from the contest within his own bosom, between his love of liberty and sympathy with the oppressions of the people, on the one hand, and the duty which he owed the Sovereign whom he had long served, and whose rewards had been princely, on the other. It has been asserted, even, that his distress of mind became insupportable, and that he died by his own hand. The tradition is, that on the day of his decease he received despatches which showed that civil war was inevitable and near; while another version is, that these despatches required of him the use of his influence with the Indian tribes to secure their services to the Crown in the event of blows. That the employments and news of the last day of his life deeply excited him, there is sufficient proof; but, as his system was predisposed to apoplexy, and as he was seized with a fit and lingered some hours, it is very uncertain whether he committed suicide. Some weight, however, appears to have been given to his declaration in the spring of 1774, and soon after his return from England, in substance, that he "*should never live to see the Colonies and the mother country in a state of open war.*" That this declaration was made with a view to self-destruction, is possible; yet a man, who had so much at stake, was far more likely to have spoken it as expressive of his strong hope of the final accommodation of the difficulties which existed.

Sir William was uncommonly tall and well-made. His countenance was fine, but melancholy; and he possessed a remarkable command of it, under the most exciting circumstances. Johnson Hall is still (1842) standing, and is occupied by Mr. Wells. In Sir William's time it was surrounded by a stone breastwork. The hall itself is of wood, but the wings are of stone. The two daughters of Sir William Johnson were educated almost in solitude, and in the following singular manner: Their mother died when they were young, and bequeathed them to the care of a friend, who was the widow of an officer killed in battle. She retired from the world, and devoted herself to her fair pupils; to whom she taught the nicest and most ingenious kinds of needlework, and reading and writing. In the morning, the two girls rose early, read their Bible, fed their birds, tended their flowers, and breakfasted. Later in the day, they employed themselves with their needles, and in reading. After dinner, in summer, they regularly took a long walk, and in the winter they rode a distance upon a sledge. Thus uniformly passed their lives, year after year; and at the age of sixteen, they had read no books except the Scriptures, their prayer-book, some romances, and "Rollin's Ancient History"; nor had they ever seen a lady, except their mother and her friend. Their dress was quite as uniform as their habits of life. And though they continually made articles of ornament, according to the fashion of the day, they wore none of them, but summer and winter, and without the least change, appeared in wrappers of the finest chintz, and green silk petticoats. Their hair, which was long and beautiful, they tied behind with a simple ribbon. In summer, they covered their heads with a large calash; in winter, long scarlet mantles completely enveloped their persons. Sir William did not live with them, but visited their apartment daily. One married Colonel Guy Johnson, the other Colonel Daniel Claus. Their manners soon became polished, they soon acquired the habits of society, and made excellent wives.

JOHNSON, SIR JOHN. Of New York. Knight and Baronet, was the son of Sir William Johnson, to whose estates and title he succeeded, and to whose office of Major-General in the militia of New York he was appointed in November of 1774. The father, we have seen, was removed from the difficulties which attended an elevated position in society at the Revolutionary era, before the commencement of hostilities; and a brief notice of the career of the son will show that these difficulties were neither few nor easily surmounted. The office of General Superintendent of Indian Affairs, on the death of Sir William, passed into the hands of Colonel Guy Johnson, (who married a daughter of Sir William Johnson,) but in other respects the new Baronet was the heir, not only of his parent's fortune and honors, but of his cares, perplexities and perils. Of the early life of Sir John, not much appears to be known; he, however, served under his father, and acquired considerable military experience. He was not as popular as Sir William, being less social and less acquainted with human nature; and failed to secure in so preëminent a degree the affections of the retainers of Johnson Hall, and of the Indian tribes. Yet he took means to secure the favor of the latter.

His official relations and supposed political sympathies caused a strict watch to be kept upon his movements, and early in 1776 a Whig force of some hundreds, under command of General Schuyler, was despatched to Tryon County, to counteract his reported designs, to disarm the Loyalists said to be embodied there, and to obtain satisfactory assurances for the future good conduct of the Baronet and his friends and dependents. The General executed these delicate and responsible duties in a manner highly satisfactory to Congress, and received a vote of thanks. Reluctant to proceed to extremities, he opened a correspondence with Sir John, and proposed an arrangement by which the shedding of blood would be spared and the objects of his mission be accomplished. After some modification of the original terms, an accommodation was effected, by which Sir John stipulated to a pacific line of conduct, and to remain within certain prescribed limits, on his parole of honor. For some unexplained reason, this agreement was soon violated, and the Whigs attempted to secure the Baronet's person. Sir John, learning of this intention, hastily secured his most valuable effects, and fled to the woods, with about seven hundred followers, determined to proceed to Canada. After enduring almost every imaginable hardship and deprivation, he and the principal part of his associates arrived at Montreal.

He was soon commissioned a Colonel, and raised two battalions of Loyalists, who bore the designation of the Royal Greens. From the time of organizing this corps, he became one of the most active, and one of the bitterest foes that the Whigs encountered during the contest; so true is it, as was said by the wise man of Israel, that "A brother offended is harder to be won than a strong city; and their contentions are like the bars of a castle." Sir John was in several regular and fairly conducted battles. He invested Fort Stanwix in 1777, and defeated the brave General Herkimer, and in 1780 was defeated himself by General Van Rensselaer, at Fox's Mills. In predatory enterprises, the Royal Greens enjoy an infamous celebrity. They committed quite every enormity known in savage warfare. Their own former neighbors and friends on the Mohawk were objects of their sweetest revenge, and suffered even more at their hands than strangers; and the chieftain Brant, though he be compelled to bear the worst, and all of the charges which have been made against him and his warriors, will not answer to posterity for any darker or more damning deeds than those which the Royal Greens perpetrated. Upon one occasion, their Colonel was thus addressed by Mr. Sammons, an aged and respectable Whig: "See what you have done, Sir John. You have taken myself and my sons prisoners, burnt my dwelling to ashes, and left the helpless members of my family with no covering but the heavens above, and no prospect but desolation around them. Did we treat you in this manner when you were in the power of the Tryon County Committee? Do you remember when we were consulted by General Schuyler, and you agreed to surrender your arms? Do you not remember that you then agreed to remain neutral, and that upon that condition General Schuyler left you at liberty on your parole? These conditions you violated. You went off to Canada; enrolled yourself in the service of the King; raised a regiment of the disaffected, who abandoned their country with you; and you have now returned to wage a cruel war against us, by burning our dwellings, and robbing us of our property. I was your friend in the Committee of Safety," continued the bold Whig, "and exerted myself to save your person from injury. And how am I requited? Your Indians have murdered and scalped old Mr. Fonda, at the age of eighty years; a man who, I have heard your father say, was like a father to him when he settled in Johnstown and Kingsborough. You cannot be successful, Sir John, in such a warfare, and you will never enjoy your property more."

In the flight of the Baronet from the Hall, in 1776, Lady Johnson and the family papers, plate, and Bible, were left behind. An incident with regard to each will show the state and necessities of the times. Her Ladyship — who was Mary Watts, of the city of New York, daughter of Honorable John Watts, a member of the Council of the Colony, and sister of the late venerable John Watts, who died in September, 1836 — was removed to Albany, where it was designed by the local Whig authorities that she should be detained as a kind of hostage for the good conduct of her husband. She solicited the Commander-in-Chief to release her, but Washington declined to interfere. Lady Johnson possessed much beauty, understanding, and vivacity. Her playful humor exhilarated the whole household. The papers were buried in an iron chest, and in 1778 General Haldimand, at the request of Sir John, sent a party of men to carry them away. On taking them up, they were found to be mouldy, rotten, and illegible, in consequence of the dampness which had been admitted through the open joints of the chest. To recover the silver, the Baronet, in 1780, went to Johnstown himself. It was found where a faithful slave had buried it, and was transferred to the knapsacks of about forty soldiers, who took it to Montreal. The devotion of the slave is worthy of remembrance. He had long lived with Sir John's father, who was so much attached to him that he caused him to be baptized by his own name of William. When the estate was confiscated by the Provincial Congress of New York, William formed a part of it, and was sold, but finally, by a repurchase or otherwise, returned to the Baronet's family. While he remained with his purchaser, who was a Whig, he never gave the least hint as to the valuables of Sir John, though he had secreted them all. The family Bible was sold with the furniture, by auction, at Fort Hunter. John Taylor, late Lieutenant-Governor of New York, was the purchaser of the sacred volume, and on discovering that it contained the family record, he wrote a civil note to Sir John offering to restore it. Some time afterward, a messenger from the Baronet called for the Bible, but did his errand in a manner rude and offensive. "I have come," said he, "for Sir William's Bible, and there are the four guineas which it cost." On being asked what word Sir John had sent, he replied, "to pay four guineas, and take the book."

Soon after the close of the contest, Sir John went to England, but returned, in 1785, and established his residence in Canada. He was appointed Superintendent-General and Inspector-General of Indian Affairs in British North America, and for several years he was also a member of the Legislative Council of Canada. To compensate him for his losses, the British Government made him several grants of lands.

It is thought that he was a conscientious Loyalist; and this may be allowed. He lived in a style of luxury and splendor, which few country gentlemen in America possessed the means to support. His domains were as large and as fair as those of any Colonist of his time, the estate of Lord Fairfax only excepted; and no American hazarded more, probably, in the cause of the Crown. Faithfulness to duty is never a crime; and if he sacrificed his home, his fortune, and his country, for his principles, he deserves admiration. But all approbation of his course during the Revolutionary struggle must end here. The conduct of the Whigs towards him may have been harsh, and, in the beginning, too harsh for his offences. There may be room to doubt, whether, prior to the arrangement with General Schuyler, he did more than any zealous loyal gentleman would consider he was bound to do, to put down the disloyal proceedings in his neighborhood, and at his very door. The charges found against him in the documents of the day, may, in some particulars, be false, or highly colored. But there still remains unanswered the very grave question, whether, as a civilized man, he was not bound to observe the rules of civilized warfare.

Sir John died at Montreal, in 1830, aged eighty-eight, and was succeeded by his oldest surviving son, Sir Adam Gordon Johnson. Lady Johnson, who, as already said, was Mary, daughter of John Watts, of New York, died in 1815. By one account, the issue of this marriage was ten sons and four daughters. But the following notice of his children is believed to be accurate: William, a Lieutenant-Colonel in the British Army, married Susan, daughter of Governor Stephen De Lancey, and died in 1811, — his widow became the wife of Sir Hudson Lowe, Napoleon's keeper at St. Helena; Warren, Major of the 60th Foot, died in 1802; Adam Gordon, born in 1781, succeeded to the Baronetcy, as above; John, born in 1782; James Stephen, killed at Barbadoes; Robert Thomas, Captain in the Army, drowned in Canada, in 1811; Charles Christopher, a Field Officer in the Army; Archibald Kennedy, born in 1792; Anne, married Colonel Edward McDonnell, Quartermaster-General to the Forces in Canada, survived her husband, and died near London in 1848; Catharine Maria, married Major-General Bowes, who fell at Salamanca in 1812, who herself died at Anglesey, near Gosport, in 1850; and last, Marianna. "The title is now (1862) held by Sir William Johnson, of Twickenham, near London, an officer in the Royal Artillery of England. He was born in 1830, and succeeded, as fourth Baronet, on the demise of his uncle, Sir Adam Gordon, in 1843."

JOHNSON, GUY. Of New York. He married a daughter of Sir William Johnson, and at the death of the Baronet succeeded him as Superintendent of the Indian Department. He was well versed in the business of that office, having long held the place of deputy under his father-in-law. His own assistant or deputy was Colonel Daniel Claus, who also married a daughter of Sir William. His residence was in Tryon County, near the Baronial Hall. Colonel Johnson's intemperate zeal for his Royal master caused the first affray in that county. In the early part of 1775, about three hundred Whigs assembled at the house of John Veeder, in Caughnawaga, for the purpose of deliberating upon the public concerns, and the setting up of a Liberty-pole. Their proceedings were interrupted by the arrival of Sir John Johnson, Colonel Claus, Colonel John Butler, and Colonel Johnson, with a large number of their retainers, well armed. Colonel Johnson mounted a high stoop and addressed the people. In the course of his remarks, he became so abusive that Jacob Sammons interrupted him, and pronounced him a liar and a villain. Johnson thereupon seized Sammons by the throat, and called him a d——d villain in return. A scuffle ensued, in which Sammons was severely injured. The Whigs present, the members of three families excepted, fled, and left Sammons to fight with the enraged Loyalists as he best could.

The following extracts from a correspondence in 1775, will throw light on the proceedings of the time, and on the course of the subject of this notice. I have received " repeated accounts," he said, " that either the New Englanders, or some persons in or about the city of Albany, or town of Schenectady, are coming up, to a considerable number, to seize and imprison me, on a ridiculous and malicious report that I intend to make the Indians destroy the inhabitants, or to that effect. The absurdity of this apprehension may easily be seen by men of sense ; but as many credulous and ignorant persons may be led astray and inclined to believe it, and as they have already sent down accounts, examinations, &c., from busy people here, that I can fully prove to be totally devoid of all foundation, it is become the duty of all those who have authority or influence to disabuse the public, and prevent consequences which I foresee with very great concern, and most cordially wish may be timely prevented. Any differences in political ideas can never justify such extravagant opinions; and I little imagined that they should have gained belief amongst any order of people who know my character, station, and the large property I have in the country, and the duties of my office, which are to preserve tranquillity amongst the Indians, hear their grievances, &c., and prevent them from falling upon the trade and frontiers. . . . . In the discharge of this duty I likewise essentially serve the public. But should I neglect myself, and be tamely made prisoner, it is clear to all who know anything of Indians, they will not sit still and see their Council fire extinguished, and Superintendent driven from his duty, but will come upon the frontiers, in revenge, with a power sufficient to commit horrid devastation. It is therefore become as necessary to the public, as to myself, that my person should be defended. But as the measures I am necessitated to make for that purpose may occasion the propagation of additional falsehoods, and may at last appear to the Indians in a light that is not for the benefit of the public, I should heartily wish, gentlemen, that you could take such measures for removing these apprehensions, as may enable me to discharge my duties (which do not interfere with the public) without the protection of armed men and the apprehension of insult. And as the public are much interested in this, I must beg to have your answer as soon as possible."

Again in May, 1775, Colonel Johnson said, in a communication to the Whig Committee of Schenectady, that he had "taken precaution to give a very hot and disagreeable reception to any persons that shall attempt to invade his retreat"; yet that, "at the same time, he had no intention to disturb those who chose to permit him the honest exercise of his reason and the duties of his office." Meantime, the Tryon County Committee and the Colonel became involved in difficulty, and the former, in denouncing his proceedings, used the following among other equally severe expressions: "Colonel Johnson's conduct in raising fortifications round his house, keeping a number of Indians and armed men constantly about him, and stopping and searching travellers upon the King's highway, and stopping our communication with Albany, is very alarming to this county, and is highly arbitrary, illegal, oppressive, and unwarrantable; and confirms us in our fears, that his design is to keep us in awe, and oblige us to submit to a state of slavery"; and abhorring that state, they resolved "to defend their freedom with their lives and fortunes." On the 2d of June, 1775, the Committee of Tryon County, in a long letter, begged him to use his "endeavors to dissuade the Indians from interfering in the dispute with the Mother Country and the Colonies."

"We cannot think," they continue, "that, as you and your family possess very large estates in this county, you are unfavorable to American freedom, although you may differ with us in the mode of obtaining redress." His course was watched with much anxiety. It was well known that the Johnsons could induce the Six Nations to remain neutral, or to take part with the Crown, at their pleasure. The Rev. Doctor Wheelock wrote to the New Hampshire Provincial Congress, from Dartmouth College, June 28th, that he had "seen a man direct from Albany, and late from Mount Johnson," who informed him that Colonel Johnson had "received presents to the amount of three thousand pounds from the King, to be disposed of to engage the Indians within his jurisdiction against the Colonies; and that all his endeavors for that purpose had been fruitless. Not one of the Indians would receive the presents."

We next find the subject of this notice in collision with the Provincial Congress of New York. In his reply to a letter from that body, dated July 8th, he says:— "As to the endeavors you speak of, to reconcile the unhappy differences between the Parent State and these Colonies, be assured I ardently wish to see them. As yet, I am sorry to say, I have not been able to discover any attempt of that kind, but that of the Assembly's, the only true legal representatives of the people; and as to the individuals who you say officiously interrupt, in my quarter, the mode and measures you think necessary for these salutary purposes, I am really a stranger to them. If you mean myself, you must have been grossly imposed on. I once, indeed, went with reluctance, at the request of several of the principal inhabitants, to one of the people's meetings, which I found had been called by an itinerant New England leather-dresser, and conducted by others, if possible, more contemptible. I had, therefore, little inclination to revisit such men, or attend to their absurdities." In conclusion, and in allusion to the fears that his influence would be used to excite the Indians to hostilities, he remarks: " I trust I shall always manifest more humanity than to promote the destruction of the innocent inhabitants of a Colony to which I have been always warmly attached, — a declaration that must appear perfectly suitable to the character of a man of honor and principle, who can on no account neglect those duties that are consistent therewith, however they may differ from sentiments now adopted in so many parts of America."

Notwithstanding the many and the explicit assurances of Colonel Johnson, Brant, the acknowledged chief of the Six Nations, joined the royal standard; and whatever were the Colonel's own purposes and intentions, the force of circumstances or his own inclination induced him to retire to Canada, and thence to repair to scenes of savage warfare; and his name appears in the bloody exploits of the Mohawk chieftain, and the miscreant Butler. That, at the time he was in communication with the Committees of Albany, Schenectady, and Tryon County, and with the Provincial Congress of New York, he was also in communication with Brant, seems certain. The chief, who signed himself " secretary to Guy Johnson," wrote the Oneidas, in the Mohawk tongue, thus : " Written at Guy Johnson's, May, 1775. This is your letter, you great ones or sachems. Guy Johnson says he will be glad if you get this intelligence, you Oneidas, how it goes with him now, and he is now more certain of the intention of the Boston people. Guy Johnson is in great fear of being taken prisoner by the Bostonians. We Mohawks are obliged to watch him constantly," &c. This letter was found in an Indian path, and was lost, as was supposed, by the person to whom it had been entrusted. It is certain, too, that Johnson, Brant, and the Butlers, — father and son, — fled to Canada together. Colonel Johnson, in 1780, was about forty years of age; and is described " as being a short, pursy man, of stern countenance and haughty demeanor, — dressed in a British uniform, powdered locks, and a cocked hat." His mansion — Guy Park — is still (1840) standing. It is of stone, and situated about a mile from the village of Amsterdam, on the north bank of the Mohawk. His estate was confiscated.

He went to England at the peace; was a petitioner for relief in 1784, and died there in 1788. His daughter Mary was the wife of Lieut.-General Colin Campbell, and mother of Major-General Sir Guy Campbell, Baronet, and C. B.

JOHNSON, AUGUSTUS. Of Rhode Island. Judge of the Court of Vice-Admiralty for the Southern District of North America. He was born in Amboy, New Jersey, about the year 1730. He went to Rhode Island very young, and studied law with Matthew Robinson, who married his mother. "He had an unlimited confidence in his own ability, and would acknowledge no superior." In 1757 he was appointed Attorney-General, and held the office nine years. One of the three Stamp-Masters, in 1765, he was constantly hissed and insulted in the streets, and in the autumn of that year, his house was surrounded by an infuriated multitude. Still later, he was seized, treated with indignity, and a promise exacted that he would resign. When the news of the repeal of the Stamp Act was received at Newport, a gallows was erected near the State House, and the effigies of Mr. Johnson and his associates were conveyed through the streets in a cart, with halters about their necks, and hanged and burned, amid shouts and tumult. Such was the hostile feeling, that he fled to an armed ship in the harbor. At the evacuation of Rhode Island, in 1779, he went to New York with the Royal Army. His property was confiscated. He was a pensioner of the British Government. His son, Matthew Robinson Johnson, was a major in the army, but disposed of his commission, and returned to his native State, in the year 1800, where he died, leaving a widow, who was alive in 1842.

JOHNSON, REV. THOMAS. Of Virginia. Episcopal minister. Denounced by the Charlotte County Committee, as an enemy to his country. Among the charges against him was, that at the "Ordinary of Mr. John Tankersly, with a bowl of grog in his hand, he drank success to the British arms."

JOHNSON, THOMAS. He went to England with Lord

Cornwallis, and was appointed a messenger to the Lords Commissioners of the Treasury. He died in King Street, Westminster, 1799.

JOHNSON, WILLIAM. Of Connecticut, or New York. At the peace he went from New York to Shelburne, Nova Scotia, where the Crown granted him one town lot. He was twenty years of age, and unmarried. Removed to Digby, in the same Province, and died there in 1850, leaving a large family.

JOHNSON, ICHABOD. Of New Jersey. A Tory plunderer. His deeds of guilt caused the Whig authorities to offer a reward for his apprehension, and he was finally killed, in 1783, in an affray with a party of light-horse and militia.

JOHNSON, ———. Captain in the Loyalist force under Colonel Thomas Browne. Killed in the siege of Augusta, Georgia, in 1780.

JOHNSON, NATHANIEL. Died at Sussex, King's County, New Brunswick, in 1830, aged eighty-eight years.

JOHNSON, WILLIAM. Of Delaware. In 1778, a party of Whigs attempted to take him from his house, but were beaten off. They returned the next day, in greater force, when he fled. After his flight his house was burned, and Samens, one of his party, was hanged on the spot.

JOHNSON. Four went to Shelburne, Nova Scotia, at the peace, namely: John, of Philadelphia, unmarried; John, of New York; George and Harmon, of New Jersey, with their families. John, of New York, was a merchant, and lost £3000 by his loyalty; George lost £1000, and Harmon £700. George was living at Shelburne about the year 1805.

JOHNSTON, GEORGE MILLIGEN. Of South Carolina. Surgeon-General of all the British Garrisons in South Carolina and Georgia. "In public life he was conspicious for his loyalty, having, at the beginning of the American Rebellion, not only risked his life, but sacrificed considerable property, in consequence of his unalterable attachment to the British Government." He went to Great Britain, and died in Scotland, in 1799, his seventy-second year. Mary, his wife, a native of Charleston, died at College-Green, Bristol, England, in 1797, aged sixty-six.

JOHNSTON, LEWIS. Residence unknown. Was banished and attainted, and his estate confiscated. In 1794 he represented to the British Government, by his attorney, John Irvine, that, at the time of his banishment, several large debts were due to him in America, which he had not been able to recover. It appears to have been conceded that the Confiscation Acts did not embrace sums of money owing to proscribed Loyalists, though many of them found great difficulty in enforcing payment.

JOHNSTON, ANDREW. Captain in the Florida Rangers. Killed in 1780, in the attack on Augusta, Georgia.

JOHNSTON, LAURENCE. Of Pennsylvania. In 1777, Governor Livingston sent him prisoner to the President of Pennsylvania, and said, that he appeared "to be an impudent, determined villain, undoubtedly in the service of the enemy;" and that, if he examined him apart from his companion, he would "find Johnston one of the greatest liars he ever met with."

JOHONNET, PETER. Distiller, of Boston. An Addresser of Gage in 1775; was proscribed and banished in 1778. He went to Halifax in 1776, thence to England, and was a Loyalist Addresser of the King in 1779. He died at London, in 1809, aged seventy-nine.

JOHONNET, FRANCIS. Of Boston. Went to England, and was in London, July, 1776. He died previous to March, 1777. Mary, his widow, who died at Boston, in 1797, administered upon his estate in Massachusetts.

JOLLIE, MARTIN. Of Georgia. In the effort, 1779, to re-establish the Royal Government, he was appointed a member of the Council, a Commissioner of Claims, a Judge of the Superior Court, and of Admiralty; and to take possession of the negroes and property of active Whigs.

JONES, THOMAS. Of New York. By his marriage to a daughter of Lieutenant-Governor James De Lancey, and a sister of the wife of the celebrated Sir William Draper, he became connected also with the families of Sir Peter Warren, of the British Navy, and of Sir William Johnson, of New York. At the Revolutionary era, he was a Judge of the Supreme Court, and, in consequence of his adherence to the Royal cause, lost his estate under the Confiscation Act. In 1779, in retaliation for the capture of General Silliman by Glover and others, a party of Whigs determined to seize upon Judge Jones, at his seat on Long Island. Twenty-five volunteered for the purpose, under command of Captain Daniel Hawley, of Newfield, (now Bridgeport,) Connecticut. Hawley and his associates crossed the Sound on the night of November 4th, and reached Judge Jones's house,—a distance of fifty-two miles—on the evening of the 6th. There was a ball, and the music and dancing prevented an alarm. The Judge was standing in his entry when the assailants opened the door, and was taken prisoner and borne off. A party of Royal soldiers was near, and Jones, in passing, *hemmed* very loud to attract their attention. Hawley told him not to repeat the sound, but he disobeyed, and was threatened with death unless he desisted from further endeavors to induce the soldiers to come to his rescue. Though six of the Whigs were captured by a troop of horse, the remainder of the party carried their prisoner safely to Connecticut. The lady of General Silliman invited the Judge to breakfast, and he not only accepted of her hospitality for the morning, but continued her guest for several days. But he remained gloomy, distant, and reserved. In May, 1780, the object of his seizure was accomplished; the British commander having, at that time, consented to give up General Silliman and his son, in exchange for the Judge and a Mr. Hewlett,—the Whigs, however, throwing in as a sort of make-weight one Washburn, a Tory of infamous character. Judge Jones retired to England, and there passed the remainder of his life, and, as it is believed, in retirement.

JONES, JOHN. Of Maine. Captain in Rogers's Rangers. Of a dark complexion, he was called "Mahogany Jones." Prior to the war, he lived at or near Pownalborough, and was surveyor of the Plymouth Company. As the troubles increased, the Whigs accused him of secreting tea, and broke open his store. Next, they fastened him to a long rope, and dragged him through the water until he was nearly drowned. Finally, to put an end to his exertions against the popular cause, he was committed to jail in Boston. He escaped, went to Quebec in 1780, and received a commission in the Rangers. In Maine again before the peace, he annoyed his personal foes there repeatedly. Among his feats was the capture of his "old enemy," General Charles Cushing, of Pownalborough. Jones's own story is, in substance, that, pretending to be a Whig and a friend, Cushing rose from his bed, put on his breeches, came down stairs, obtained a candle, and opened the door; that Mrs. Cushing soon followed her husband, but returned, put her head out of the chamber window, and screamed "Murder!" and that he told her, if she did not hold her tongue, his Indians would scalp her. Further, that he gave the General shoes and stockings, and marched him off through the woods four days to the British post, (now Castine,) at the mouth of the Penobscot.

Jones, immediately after the peace, was at Grand Menan, Bay of Fundy, and interested in lands granted on that island to Loyalists. In 1784, he resumed his business as surveyor, on the river St. Croix. At length, "his Toryism forgotten," he removed to the Kennebec. In 1793, he made a map of the country on the last named river. Of great courage, he surveyed the Company's lands "at a time when *squatters*, disguised as Indians, threatened the lives of all who should attempt" that service. He died at Augusta, Maine.

At *Jones's Eddy*, below Bath, Mr. Charles Vaughan, a wealthy merchant of Boston, designed to found a great seaport, and erected wharves and buildings to accommodate the business which he expected would be transacted there; hence the map above mentioned. The project was an utter failure.

JONES, OWEN, JR. Of Pennsylvania. In 1777, ordered by the Board of War to be removed from Winchester to Staunton, there to be kept in close jail, and to be deprived of the free use of writing materials, because he had kept up a correspondence with persons in Pennsylvania, and had exchanged gold at extravagant premiums for paper money. He appealed to Mr. Duane, on the ground of former friendship, and as his only acquaintance in Congress, to use his influence to "alleviate this cruel sentence"; and averred that his only offence consisted in sending sixteen half-joes to be converted into Continental money, in order to supply himself with the necessaries of life.

JONES, DAVID. Of Connecticut. Suffered much at the hands of the Sons of Liberty, in 1775; and the Rev. Dr. Peters, of Hebron, in a letter to his mother, recommended that he "should draught a narrative of his woes," to be sent to him at Boston. This, as I suppose, was the David Jones who entered the Royal service, and was a captain. If so, he was to have married the beautiful Jane McCrea, whose cruel death, in 1777, by the Indians, is universally known and lamented. The fate of Captain Jones is uncertain. One account is, that, desperate and careless of life, he was slain in the battle of Bemis's Heights; another, that he died about three years afterward, broken-hearted and insane; while Lossing says, that he lived in Canada to old age, and died within a few years. He never married. After Jane's death he was sad and silent, and avoided society as much as circumstances would permit.

JONES, ELISHA. Of Weston, Massachusetts. Colonel in the militia. Died in 1775, aged sixty-six. He was the father of fourteen sons and of one daughter.

JONES, ELISHA. Of Weston, Massachusetts. Son of Colonel Elisha. Went to Weymouth, Nova Scotia, but died in the United States, in 1784, leaving seven children.

JONES, JOSIAH. Physician, of Weston, Massachusetts. Son of Colonel Elisha. He joined the British Army at Boston, soon after the battle of Lexington, in 1775, and was sent by General Gage, in the sloop *Polly*, to Nova Scotia, to procure hay and other articles for the use of the troops. On the passage he was made prisoner, and sent by the Committee of Arundel,

Maine, to the Provincial Congress; and after due investigation of his case by a committee of that body, he was committed to jail at Concord. Obtaining release, after some months' imprisonment, he again joined the Royal forces, and received an appointment in the Commissary Department. In 1782 he went to Annapolis, Nova Scotia, where he settled. He made a voyage to England to obtain half-pay, and was successful. He was senior Judge of the Court of Common Pleas for the county of Annapolis many years. He died in 1825, at Annapolis, aged eighty; and Margaret Jude, his widow, died at Digby, Nova Scotia, in 1828, at the age of eighty-four. Four children survived him, namely: Stephen; Charlotte, the wife of Dr. Thomas White, of Westport, Nova Scotia; Charles, a merchant of Halifax; and Edward, a merchant of Westport. His property in Massachusetts was confiscated. Dr. Jones was a man of good powers, and of a cultivated mind. His family retain the impression that he was educated at Harvard University, but his name does not appear on the catalogue of graduates.

JONES, SIMEON. Of Weston, Massachusetts. Son of Colonel Elisha. In 1782 he was a lieutenant in the King's American Dragoons. He went to St. John, New Brunswick, at the peace, and received the grant of a city lot in 1784. He removed to Nova Scotia, and died at Weymouth, in 1823, at the age of seventy-two.

JONES, STEPHEN. Of Weston, Massachusetts. Son of Colonel Elisha. Graduated at Harvard University in 1775. He accepted a commission under the Crown, and was an officer in the King's American Dragoons. He settled in Nova Scotia at the close of the contest, and, at his decease, was the oldest magistrate of the county of Annapolis. He was the last survivor of fourteen sons. He died at Weymouth, Nova Scotia, in 1830, aged seventy-six. He married Sarah Goldsbury, who (1861) survives, at the age of ninety. His son, Guy Carleton Jones, holds a public office at Digby, Nova Scotia.

JONES, ISAAC. Of Weston, Massachusetts. Innholder

and trader. In January, 1775, the Whig Convention of Worcester County denounced him in the following terms: "Resolved, That it be earnestly recommended to all the inhabitants of this county, not to have any commercial connections with Isaac Jones, but to shun his house and person, and to treat him with the contempt he deserves; and should any persons in this county be so lost to a sense of their duty, after this recommendation, as to have any commercial connections with the said Tory, we do advise the inhabitants of this county to treat such persons with the utmost neglect." He died at Weston, in 1813, at the age of eighty-five.

JONES, EDWARD. Settled in New Brunswick at the peace, and died at Spoon Island, in that Province, in 1831, aged eighty-eight.

JONES, CALEB. Of Maryland. Sheriff of Somerset County. In 1776, ordered in the Council of Safety, after hearing depositions in his favor, that he recognize in £200, with good security, for due obedience to the Whig authorities. Some months after, he escaped from Baltimore, and arrived at New York in the frigate *Brune*. He entered the Maryland Loyalists subsequently, and was a captain. At the peace he went to St. John, New Brunswick, and was a grantee of that city. Elizabeth, his wife, died at St. John, in 1812, aged sixty-eight.

JONES, ———. Cornet in the Queen's Rangers. Killed in the siege of Yorktown, and buried at Williamsburg with military honors.

JONES, EDWARD. Of Ridgefield, Connecticut. Was executed by General Putnam, in 1779, at a place called Gallows' Hill. The scene is described as shocking. "The man on whom the duty of hangman devolved left the camp, and on the day of execution could not be found. A couple of boys, about the age of twelve years, were ordered by General Putnam to perform the duties of the absconding hangman. The gallows was about twenty feet from the ground. Jones was compelled to ascend the ladder, and the rope around his neck was attached to the cross-beam. General

Putnam then ordered Jones to jump from the ladder. 'No, General Putnam,' said Jones, 'I am innocent of the crime laid to my charge; I shall not do it.' Putnam then ordered the boys before mentioned to turn the ladder over. These boys were deeply affected with the trying scene; they cried and sobbed loudly, and earnestly entreated to be excused from doing anything on this distressing occasion. Putnam, drawing his sword, ordered them forward, and compelled them at the sword's point to obey his orders."

JONES, ———. Captain in Ganey's Tory banditti. An infamous fellow. One of his murders was singularly atrocious. He promised Colonel Kobb, who surrendered a prisoner of war, personal safety, but immediately killed him in the presence of his wife and children, and burned his house.

JONES, ICHABOD. Of Maine. He removed from Boston about 1765, and was a land and mill-owner. In the House of Representatives, August, 1775, it was resolved: "Whereas Ichabod Jones, late of Machias, a known enemy to the rights and liberties of America, has fled, leaving at Machias a considerable estate, real and personal: It is therefore recommended to the Committee of Safety of that place to take effectual care of said estate, agreeable to the resolves and recommendations of the late Provincial Congress." In August, 1776, Mr. Jones, as appears in his petition to the Council and House of Representatives, was confined to the town of Northampton, under large bonds, and with scanty means of subsistence. Again, that, when seized at Machias, the people there owed him and his associates nearly £4000; that he had been informed of the possession of his property by the new authorities, and that he desired to be heard touching his conduct and his pecuniary affairs.

JONES, JOHN. A corporal in the First Regiment of Pennsylvania Artillery. He deserted to the Royal side, and gave "intelligence," dated February 15, 1780. In this paper he says that he "listed August, 1776, for three years, but because he had no certificate to show, was obliged to take the one hundred dollars, and serve for the war."

JONES, JOHN. Of Bristol, Connecticut. Son of Captain Nathaniel Jones. He graduated at Yale College in 1776, and went immediately to Long Island, as Captain of Marines. He was killed at sea, in the first fight in which the vessel was engaged, and, probably, before the close of the year 1776.

JONES, ———. Of North Carolina. Notorious marauder. Taken and hung.

JONES, JONATHAN. Of New York. Brother of Jane McCrea's lover. Late in 1776, he assisted in raising a company in Canada, and joined the British in garrison at Crown Point. Later in the war he was a captain, and served under General Frazer.

JORDAN, JOHN, FRANCIS, and JAMES. Removed to New Brunswick in 1783. John and Francis were grantees of St. John. James died in that city, in 1846, aged eighty-five years.

JOUETTE or JEWETT, ZENOPHON. Of New Jersey. In 1782 he was an ensign in the First Battalion of New Jersey Volunteers. He settled in New Brunswick, and received half-pay. In 1792 he held the office of Sheriff of York County. He relinquished the post during the war of 1812, and was attached to a regiment raised in that Colony. He was Gentleman Usher of the Black Rod to the Council many years. He died at St. John in 1843.

JOY, JOHN. Housewright, of Boston. An Addresser of Hutchinson in 1774, and of Gage in 1775. In 1776 he went to Halifax, with his family of seven persons, and was proscribed and banished in 1778. In 1779 he was in England.

JUDSON, CHAPMAN. Went to St. John, New Brunswick, at the peace, and was grantee of a city lot. He received an appointment in the Ordnance Department. He died at St. John, in 1817, at the age of sixty-six.

KEAN, WILLIAM. Of Pennsylvania. He was Adjutant of the Pennsylvania Loyalists, and settled in New Brunswick after the corps was disbanded. Ann, his widow, died at St. John, in 1820, aged sixty-four.

KEARSLEY, JOHN. Of Philadelphia. Physician. A man of ardent feelings; his zealous attachment to the Royal cause, and his impetuous temper, made him obnoxious to those whose acts he opposed. He was seized at his own house, in the summer or autumn of 1775, and carted through the streets to the tune of the "Rogue's March." In the affray, he was wounded in the hand by a bayonet. When mounted, the mob gave a loud huzza; and the Doctor, to show his contempt of " the people," took his wig in his injured hand, and swinging it around his head, huzzaed louder and longer than his persecutors. The ride over, it was determined to tar and feather him; but this was abandoned, to the disappointment of many. The doors and windows of his house were, however, broken by stones and brickbats. The same year he was put in prison, for writing letters abusive of the Whigs; and, while there, Stephen Bayard was allowed to attend to the settlement of his affairs. His sufferings caused insanity, which continued until his decease. He died in prison about fifteen months after his ride in the "Tory cart." He was attainted of treason, and his estate confiscated. His uncle, of the same Christian name, and a physician of Philadelphia, died there in 1772.

KEATING, ———. Captain in the New Jersey Volunteers, in 1777, and sent to Trenton.

KEECH, ROBERT. Of New York. Died in Dorchester, New Brunswick, in 1842, at the age of eighty-three.

KEEN, REYNOLD. Of Pennsylvania. Attainted of treason. Pardoned by Act of the Assembly, and such part of his estate as had not been sold by the Commissioners of Confiscation, restored to him.

KELLOCK, ALEXANDER. Surgeon in the Queen's Rangers. Very capable and attentive to his duties, records the commander of that corps. When, in 1779, Simcoe was wounded and taken prisoner, Kellock went to Brunswick, New Jersey, with a flag to attend him, and Governor Livingston ordered that he should not be molested.

KELLY, ———. Deserted from the Whig Army, and joined the Queen's Rangers as a sergeant. Taken prisoner, and put in jail to await execution. Released on the threat of Simcoe, that, if Kelly suffered death, he would leave to the mercy of his soldiers the first six Rebels who should fall into his hands.

KELLY, WALDRON. Residence unknown. A captain in the Royal Garrison Battalion.

KELLY, JOHN. Died at St. John, New Brunswick, in 1827, at the age of eighty-one. He was blind sixteen years.

KELLY, WILLIAM. Died at the same place, in 1826, aged seventy-four.

KELSALL, ROGER. Of Georgia. In the effort to reëstablish the Royal Government, in 1779, he was appointed a member of the Council, a Commissioner of Claims, and a Commissioner to take possession of the negroes and other property of active Whigs. Attainted of treason and estate confiscated.

KEMBLE, STEPHEN. Deputy Adjutant-General of the British Army in 1777. I suppose of the New Jersey family, and a relative of the wife of General Gage.

KEMP, ———. Of Georgia. Lieutenant in the King's Rangers. Stripped and killed, with nine of his men, for refusing to join the Whigs, on becoming prisoners. Eleven of the perpetrators fell into the hands of the Loyalists and were hung.

KEMPE, JOHN TABOR. Of New York. Last Royal Attorney-General. While absent in England, in 1767, the duties of his office were entrusted to James Duane. Governor Tryon wrote Lord Dartmouth, November, 1775, that "the sword is drawn," and that the Attorney-General was with him on board the ship *Duchess of Gordon*, in the harbor of New York. In February, 1776, Mr. Kempe had been transferred to the *Asia* ship of war, in the waters of Raritan Bay; and, while there, he wrote the following lines to greet Cortlandt Skinner, Attorney-General of New Jersey: —

> Welcome, welcome, brother Tory,
> To this merry floating place!
> I came here a while before ye; —
> Coming here is no disgrace.

Freedom finds a safe retreat here,
On the bosom of the wave;
You she invites to meet here.
Welcome, then, thou Tory brave!

As you serve, like us, the King, sir,
In a hammock you must lay;
Better far 't is so to swing, sir,
Than to swing another way.

Though we 've not dry land to walk on,
The quarter-deck is smooth to tread;
Hear how fast, while we are talking,
Barrow [1] trips it overhead.

Should vile Whigs come here to plunder,
Quick we send them whence they came;
They should hear the *Asia* thunder,
And see the *Phœnix* in a flame.

Neptune's gallant sons befriend us,
While at anchor here we ride;
Britain's wooden walls defend us,—
Britain's glory, and her pride.

His property was confiscated. The wife of Francis Lewis, a signer of the Declaration of Independence, having fallen into the hands of the enemy, and the wife of Mr. Kempe having become a prisoner of the Whigs, an exchange was effected towards the close of 1776.

The Whigs established a government in 1777; but as the British Army held the city of New York, Long and Staten Islands, &c., there was also a Royal government, and Mr. Kempe was considered in office during the war. Yet his name seldom appears. I find it last, July 30, 1782, in a correspondence between Sir Guy Carleton and Washington, in connection with the Huddy murder. [See *Richard Lippincott.*] The Attorney-General's furniture was sold at auction in New York, June, 1783. He went to England and died there. His widow deceased at Clifton, in 1831, and his daughter, Anne, at the same place, in 1838.

[1] The deputy paymaster of the Royal Army, who was also a refugee on board the *Asia*, and continually walked the deck.

KENAN, FELIX. Of North Carolina. He was Sheriff of the County of Duplin, and was dismissed by the Provincial Congress, May, 1776. A man of whom it was pithily said, " he had not the independence to be a Tory, or the honesty to be a Whig." Thousands, in different parts of the country, were as like him as possible. He bore arms under General McDonald, at Moore's Creek Bridge.

KENDRICK, THOMAS. He died on the Island of Campo Bello, New Brunswick, in 1821, aged seventy-two.

*KENNEDY, PATRICK. Of Baltimore. Physician. Escaped to New York in 1777, and subsequently was a captain in the Maryland Loyalists. In 1783 he embarked for Nova Scotia, in the transport ship *Martha*, and was wrecked on the passage. [See *James Henley*.] He and several others were saved by some fishing vessels. He was a grantee of the city of St. John, New Brunswick.

KENT, BENJAMIN. Of Massachusetts. Graduated at Harvard University in 1727. He was minister at Marlborough for a short time, but entered upon the profession of the law, and established himself at Boston. He was a Whig, it appears, for awhile, and his name is to be found among those of Samuel Adams, Cushing, Warren, Hancock, and other prominent leaders of the patriot band. A Refugee; he died at Halifax, Nova Scotia, in 1788, aged eighty-one. Elizabeth, his widow, survived until 1802. He was eccentric, and a wit. His conduct as a clergyman is said to have been unclerical and humorous. John Adams, in 1759, said: "Kent is for fun, drollery, humor, flouts, jeers, contempt. He has an irregular, immethodical head, but his thoughts are often good, and his expressions happy." From a letter written by Kent, in 1771, I extract a single line: " Saint Paul, though sometimes a little inclined to Toryism, was a very sensible gentleman, and he expressly damns the fearful as well as the unbelieving."

To the gentlemen who have suggested that the subject of this notice was not a Loyalist, I return my warm thanks for the endeavor to correct an inaccuracy in this work; but the name was not inserted in the first edition without thought, and is retained now, after due consideration of the circumstances to which my attention has since been kindly directed.

KENT, STEPHEN. Went to St. John, New Brunswick, at the peace, was a grantee of that city, and died there in 1828, aged eighty.

KERR, JAMES. He accepted a commission under the Crown, and was a captain in the Queen's Rangers. The corps was disbanded at the close of the war, when he retired on half-pay. He went to St. John, New Brunswick, and was a grantee of that city; but removed to King's County, Nova Scotia, where he settled, and was a colonel in the militia. He died at Amherst, Nova Scotia, in 1830, at the age of seventy-six. Eliza, his widow, died at Cornwallis, Nova Scotia, 1840, aged seventy-four. Three sons and a daughter preceded him, but twelve children survived him.

KETCHAM, ISAAC. Of New York. Died in King's County, New Brunswick, in 1820, aged sixty-four. His widow died in 1821, at the age of fifty-four.

KEY, PHILIP BARTON. Of Maryland. He joined the British Army after the Declaration of Independence; and in 1778 held a commission in the Maryland Loyalists. Four years later, he was a captain in that corps. He served in Florida, was made prisoner there, but, released on parole, he went to England. At the peace he retired on half-pay. In 1785 he returned to Maryland, and five years afterward settled in Annapolis. He was elected to the General Assembly in 1794, and was a member of that body for some time. Previous to his first election, he sold his half-pay to General Forrest, his brother-in-law. The General became bankrupt in 1802, when, greatly indebted to Mr. Key, transfer was made back in satisfaction *pro tanto* of the debt; but as the General's family were in a destitute condition, they received the benefit of the half-pay for three years. In 1806, Mr. Key directed his agent in London to resign, at the proper office, all further claims on the British Government; and he himself made a formal resignation of the same, in 1807, in a letter addressed to his Majesty's minister at Washington.

Mr. Key was elected to the Tenth Congress, and his right to a seat in that body was contested. The facts above stated, assented to by Mr. Key, appear in the report of the Committee on Elections. The vote in the House was close; on the 18th of March, 1808, his right was affirmed, 57 to 52. It should be added, that, though he was a military officer of the Crown, he never took the oath of allegiance. From the debate, it is to be inferred that much of the opposition to him was on the ground that he was not a citizen of Maryland.

I make a single extract from Mr. Key's own speech: — "His constituents knew the very circumstances of the follies of his early life, and his enemies had represented to them, that, having been once, twenty years ago, in the British Army, he was not a proper person to represent them. The people scouted the idea; . . . they knew me from my infancy; . . . but I had returned to my country, like the prodigal son to his father; had felt as an American should feel; was received, forgiven, . . . of which the most convincing proof is . . . my election" to this House. He served in Congress until the year 1813. As a lawyer he was distinguished. He died at Georgetown, District of Columbia, in 1815.

KEY, ROBERT. A soldier in the Continental Army; in April, 1777, executed at Coventry, Rhode Island, for attempting to desert to the Royal Army.

KIDDER, REUBEN. Of New Ipswich, New Hampshire. He was the richest man in that town, and at the Revolutionary era had done more than any other person to promote its growth and prosperity. He was agent of lands owned by the Wentworths, and other gentlemen of note in Portsmouth; and, appointed a magistrate and a colonel in the militia by the last Governor Wentworth, felt honestly bound to adhere to the Crown. He was superseded in his civil and military offices, and was inactive during the war. He refused to acknowledge the Whig Government of the State, but remained upon his estate without molestation. Though opposed to the Revolution, he still paid the taxes levied upon his property, and thus lost nothing but his influence and popularity. He died at New Ipswich, in 1793, aged seventy.

KILBORN, BENJAMIN. Of Litchfield, Connecticut. Lieutenant in a company of militia; cashiered by the House of Assembly (December, 1775,) for his "toryism."

KING, COLONEL RICHARD. Of South Carolina. He commanded the "South Carolina Loyal Militia," under Cruger, at Ninety-Six, when besieged by General Greene, in 1781, and had permission to leave; and as his two hundred men were mounted, he might have retired to Charleston or Georgia, but he turned his horses loose in the woods, and resolved to remain and assist in the defence. He died before the peace. His estate, in the possession of his heirs, was confiscated.

KING, EDWARD. A Sandemanian, of Boston. An Addresser of Hutchinson in 1774, and a Protester against the Whigs. Embarked for Halifax with the King's Army in 1776. Samuel, also of Boston, accompanied him, and died at Halifax, in 1822, at the age of seventy-one.

KING, WILLIAM. Settled in New Brunswick; was clerk in the Royal Engineer Department; died at Fredericton, the capital of that Province, in 1804.

KIP, SAMUEL. Of West Chester County, New York. His family relations to the British Government, and his intimacy with Colonel De Lancey, are assigned as reasons for predisposing him to espouse the Royal cause. He raised a company of cavalry, and "embarked all his interests in the contest." He was a landholder, and his soldiers were principally his own tenants. In charging a body of Whig troops, in West Chester County, in 1781, his horse was killed, and he was himself severely wounded. He survived the close of the war several years. His reputation was that of "an active and daring partisan officer."

KIP, JACOBUS. Of Kipsburgh, New York. Captain in the British Infantry. Died before the peace, which saved his estate from confiscation.

KIRKLAND, MOSES. Of South Carolina. A man "whose

vanity and ambition had not been sufficiently gratified by his countrymen." He owned a plantation in the back part of the State, with several negroes. At the outset, he took part with the Whigs, and his disaffection is said to have arisen from his being " overlooked by the Provincial Congress in the military appointments." He changed sides in the affair with the Cunninghams, July, 1775. At the time of his desertion, he commanded a troop of Rangers, who followed him to a man, and, by his influence, others in the Whig service joined the Royal party. A short time before his defection, Kirkland was placed upon an important standing committee raised by the Provincial Congress to act throughout the Colony.

He arrived at St. Augustine, Florida, September, 1775. The account of his flight, as, I suppose, given by himself, is, that William Henry Drayton endeavored to win him to the Whig cause, but failed; that then a reward of two thousand pounds sterling was offered for his apprehension; that, after a journey of two hundred miles, he arrived at Lord William Campbell's house, and thence fled to a man-of-war; and that his son, a lad of twelve or thirteen, escaped in the disguise of a girl. Further, that after his departure, his plantation was robbed of five thousand pounds of indigo, and his sixty negroes were stolen or dispersed. Early in the contest, he was employed by Stuart, the Indian Agent of the British authorities with the Cherokees and Creeks, to concert measures with General Gage for an attack on the Southern States. The plan appears to have been, for the Royal forces to operate by sea, and the savages by land. Kirkland was captured on his voyage to Boston, his papers were seized, and the plot fully discovered. He escaped from the Philadelphia jail, May, 1776, and was advertised thus: — "He is a stout corpulent man, between fifty and sixty years of age, about five feet ten inches high, of a swarthy complexion, fresh colored, and wears his own gray hair tied behind. He had on a green coat faced with blue velvet, a blue velvet waistcoat, and brown velvet breeches," &c. After the surrender of Charleston, in 1780, he held a commission under the Crown. His estate was confiscated.

KIRK, THOMAS. Of Boston. Officer of the Customs. When Hancock's vessel, laden with wines from Madeira, arrived at Boston, he went on board in the common course of duty. In the evening, several proposals were made to him to allow the cargo to be smuggled, which he rejected; and, in consequence, was confined below, until the wines were taken on shore. The master made entry of a part the next day, but seizure followed for a *false* entry. [See *Hallowell*, and *Harrison, Collectors of the Customs.*]

KIRK, RICHARD. Of New York. In 1776 he was an Addresser of Lord Howe. He owned the place now called Cedarmere, from a little lake on it, quite encircled with red-cedars, and now the residence of William Cullen Bryant. "Kirk, in his time," Mr. Bryant kindly wrote me, (March 4, 1861,) "gathered the water from several springs, breaking out at the foot of the hills close to the harbor, into a pond with an irregular embankment, and used it to turn the machinery of a paper-mill; one of the first erected in this country. The mill was burned down a few years since, and afterwards the place came into my possession."

KISSAM, DANIEL. Of Long Island, New York. A magistrate, and known as "Justice Kissam." In 1774 he was a member of the Committee of Correspondence, and the next year, of the House of Assembly, and also one of the fourteen who addressed General Gage at Boston, on the subject of the "unhappy contest." In 1776 he was confined, but released by the Provincial Congress, under recognizance of £500. Property confiscated in 1779. He fell from his horse, in 1782, and died. An estate of three hundred and thirty acres, which he owned, was sold by the Commissioners of Confiscation, in 1784.

KISSAM, BENJAMIN T. Of Long Island, New York. Brother of Major Kissam. Made prisoner at Justice Kissam's house, North Hempstead, in 1781. Died in 1847, aged eighty-six.

KISSAM, ———. Of Long Island, New York. Major. An Addresser of Governor Robertson in 1780. The next year he was seized at the house of Justice Kissam, by a party of Whigs. He died at the age of eighty-three.

KISSAM, BENJAMIN. "A leading lawyer in the city of New York, under whom Lindley Murray, the grammarian, and John Jay, Chief Justice of the United States, read law." In 1776, an Addresser of Lord and Sir William Howe.

KISSICK, PHILIP. Of New York. Vintner and distiller. Offered for sale "Home-spun brandy and gin, very little inferior to French brandy and Holland gin." In 1776, an Addresser of Lord and Sir William Howe. He is to be remembered for his benefactions to Whigs, who, carried to the "sugar-house," needed food and money. One of the prisoners fed by him was James Schureman, who in after years was a member of the House, and of the Senate of the United States.

KITCHEN, THOMAS. Settled in New Brunswick in 1788. In 1799 he was murdered.

KITCHING, JAMES. Of Georgia. Collector and Commissioner of the Customs, and Naval Officer for the port of Sunbury. Subscribed oath of office, March, 1770. He was in England in 1779. Attainted, and estate confiscated.

KNAPP, JOHN COGGHILL. Of New York. "A notorious pettifogger, — a convict who had fled from England for his own benefit." In 1776, an Addresser of Lord and Sir William Howe.

KNEELAND, WILLIAM. Of Cambridge, Mass. Physician. He graduated at Harvard University in 1751; and was elected Steward of that Institution by the Corporation, in 1778; "but, as he had been deemed unfriendly to the cause of American Independence," the Overseers objected to the choice, and refused to concur. The former body accordingly requested his predecessor to resume his duties, until another Steward should be chosen. The discussions that arose in this case do not belong to this place, further than to say, that the Corporation asserted, and have since exercised the right, of electing that officer without action on the part of the Overseers. Dr. Kneeland was Register of Probate, and for several years President of the Massachusetts Medical Society. He died in 1788.

KNEELAND, REV. EBENEZER. Episcopal minister. He graduated at Yale College in 1761, and four years after went to England for ordination. He served for a time as Chaplain in the British Army, but in January, 1768, he was appointed an Assistant to Dr. Samuel Johnson, of Stratford, Connecticut. Dr. J. had conceived the idea of making Stratford a resort for young students in divinity, to prepare them for Holy Orders, and using Mr. Kneeland to aid him in the work. He speaks of him in one of his letters as "very well qualified to continue it when he was gone." On the death of Rev. Dr. Johnson, in 1772, Mr. Kneeland succeeded to the Rectorship, and probably continued the missionary of the Society for the Propagation of the Gospel, &c., until his death, April 17, 1777. His body was buried in the church-yard at Stratford. He married Charity, the eldest daughter of Dr. Johnson, but left no children.

KNIGHT, JOSHUA. Of Pennsylvania. Attainted of treason, and property confiscated. He lived near Philadelphia, and owned an estate of value. Early in the Revolution he abandoned everything, went to the island of Campo Bello, New Brunswick, where, for a winter, he occupied a fisherman's salthouse, or hut. Joined finally by other Loyalists from his native Province, he settled on the mainland of the Bay of Fundy, at a place called Pennfield, in honor of William Penn. Mr. Knight died at about the age of seventy-five, leaving four sons. The original agreement between the founders of Pennfield, made at Philadelphia, in 1782, placed at my disposal by gentlemen of his lineage, has been of service to me.

KNOX, THOMAS. Of New York. A petitioner for lands in Nova Scotia, in 1783, and one of the two agents of the fifty-four other petitioners. In a Loyalist pamphlet, published in London, in 1784, his conduct is severely criticized. Thus, he is accused of "chicanery," and of having the audacity to insult the Governor of Nova Scotia with impertinent letters.

KNOX, WILLIAM. Of Georgia. Previous to the Revolution, he appears to have been the Agent of that Colony and of Florida; and to have been much in England. At some period of the struggle, he was appointed Under Secretary of State in the American Department. In 1780, he formed a plan to divide Maine, and to give the name of *New Ireland* to the territory between the Penobscot and the St. Croix, with Thomas Oliver for Governor, and Daniel Leonard for Chief Justice. This project was countenanced by the King, and by the Ministry; but was abandoned in consequence of the opposition of Wedderburne, the Attorney-General, who said the whole of Maine was included in the charter of Massachusetts. After the death of Sir James Wright, Mr. Knox was employed by the Loyalists of Georgia to present their claims for losses. He was at London in 1788.

KNOWLES, ISRAEL. Of Sandwich, Massachusetts. Imprisoned for his offences, real or alleged, in February, 1778.

KNOWLES, S. Of Rhode Island. Estate was confiscated previous to the peace, and by the Act of October, 1783, he was banished from the State, on pain of death if he returned.

KNUTTON, JOHN. Of Boston. Proscribed and banished in 1778. He died at St. John, New Brunswick, in 1827, aged eighty-five; and his widow, Margaret, who, at her marriage, in 1802, was the widow of David Blair, at the same place, in 1829, at the age of seventy-two. They settled there in 1783, and he was a grantee of the city.

KOLLOCK, SIMON. Of Delaware. In 1777, Henry Fisher wrote the Navy Board of Pennsylvania that he had been on shore from the *Roebuck*, with a large sum of counterfeit thirty dollar bills; that he had enlisted nearly one hundred men, and had gone to New York in a schooner " to join the rascally crew." He entered the King's service, and in 1782 was a captain in the Loyal American Regiment. He settled in Nova Scotia. His wife, Ann Catharine, died in 1845, at the advanced age of ninety-seven. Simon Kollock, Jr., of Sussex County, Delaware, was proscribed under the Act of 1778; perhaps the same.